R. Gupta's®

Popular Master Guide

BPSC

Bihar Public Service Commission

Primary Teacher

Recruitment Exam

Paper-1: Language
Paper-2: General Studies

by

RPH Editorial Board

2026
EDITION

RAMESH PUBLISHING HOUSE, NEW DELHI

Published by
O.P. Gupta *for* Ramesh Publishing House

Admin. Office
12-H, New Daryaganj Road, Opp. Officers' Mess,
New Delhi-110002 ✆ 23275224, 23245124

E-mail: info@rameshpublishinghouse.com
For Online Shopping: www.rameshpublishinghouse.com

Showroom
• Balaji Market, Nai Sarak, Delhi-6 ✆ 23253720, 23282525
• 4457, Nai Sarak, Delhi-6, ✆ 23918938

Book Code: R-2515

ISBN: 978-93-5477-558-1

Price: ₹ 360

Printed at: B.K. Offset, Delhi

WRITTEN EXAMINATION

For Primary School Teacher (Class 1-5)

Paper	Subjects	No. of Questions	Duration	Total Marks	
1.	Language (Qualifying)	100 Part-I : 25 & Part-II : 75	02 hours	100 Part-I : 25 & Part-II : 75	• It Consists of 02 parts, Part-I and Part-II. • Part-I — English Language which is compulsory for all. • Part-II — Hindi Language / Urdu Language / Begali Language. Candidate has to opt any one of the three languages. • The qualifying marks in this paper is at least 30% in both the parts, but there will be no negative marking.
2.	General Studies	120	02 hours	120	• It consists of Elementary Mathematics, Mental ability test, General Awareness, General Science, Social Science, Indian National Movements, Geography and Environment. • The Questions of General Studies will be related to the syllabus of the Primary School but its standard according to the prescribed minimum qualification of the candidate.

CONTENTS

Previous Years' Paper

Bihar Public Service Commission (BPSC)

Primary School Teacher

Recruitment Exam, 2024

(Exam held on 20-07-2024)

PAPER-1: LANGUAGE

Part-I : English Language

Directions (Qs. No. 1 to 5): *Read the passage given below and on the basis of the passage, answer the questions that follow.*

People are always communicating, verbally and non-verbally. Research shows that only seven per cent of communication is through words. The rest of the communication process takes place through body language, eye contact and the various signals words cannot convey. A person should be sensitive enough to understand as to how the communication is being received and processed. All communication should be sensitive to eye movement, posture and gesture, skin colour, breathing rate and facial expression to be understood completely.

1. Words communicate just _____ per cent.

A. seventy
B. seven
C. hundred
D. More than one of the above
E. None of the above

2. These are some nouns from the passage.

A. body, person
B. should, through
C. being, how
D. More than one of the above
E. None of the above

3. Communication must include.

A. eye movement
B. breathing rate
C. body language
D. More than one of the above
E. None of the above

4. Which are the two kinds of communication?

A. Verbal and non-verbal
B. Posture and gesture
C. Spoken and written
D. More than one of the above
E. None of the above

5. The passage is about:

A. Disadvantages of words
B. Nature of communication
C. Communication failure
D. More than one of the above
E. None of the above

Directions (Qs. No. 6 to 8): *Fill in the blanks.*

6. Had we _____ punctual, we would have _____ the train.

A. been, caught
B. were, boarded
C. are, got
D. More than one of the above
E. None of the above

7. You can't _____ with other people.

A. arguing
B. shouted
C. quarreling
D. More than one of the above
E. None of the above

8. Since she is a _____, she has to talk a lot.

A. jockey
B. cook
C. radio jockey
D. More than one of the above
E. None of the above

1. B	2. A	3. D	4. A	5. B	6. A	7. E	8. C

Part-II : हिन्दी भाषा

निर्देशः (प्र.सं. 9 से 14 तक)ः इस खंड में नीचे दिए गए गद्यांश से संबंधित प्रश्न दिए गए हैं। सही विकल्प चुनकर उत्तर पत्रक में अंकित कीजिये।

राष्ट्र के सर्वांगीण विकास के लिए चरित्र निर्माण परम आवश्यक है। जिस प्रकार वर्तमान में भौतिक निर्माण का कार्य अनके योजनाओं के माध्यम से तीव्र गति के साथ संपन्न हो रहा है, वैसे ही वर्तमान की सबसे बड़ी आवश्यकता यह है कि देशवासियों के चरित्र निर्माण के लिए भी प्रयत्न किया जाए। उत्तम चरित्रवान व्यक्ति ही राष्ट्र की सर्वोच्च संपदा है। जनतंत्र के लिए जो यह एक महान कल्याणकारी योजना है। जन-समाज में राष्ट्र, संस्कृति, समाज एवं परिवार के प्रति हमारा क्या कर्तव्य है इसका पूर्ण रूप से बोध कराना एवं राष्ट्र में व्याप्त समग्र भ्रष्टाचार के प्रति निषेधात्मक वातावरण का निर्माण करना ही चरित्र निर्माण का प्रथम सोपान है।

पाश्चात्य शिक्षा और संस्कृति के प्रभाव से आज हमारे मस्तिष्क में भारतीयता के प्रति हीन भावना उत्पन्न हो गई है। चरित्र निर्माण, जो कि बाल्यावस्था व्यवस्था से ही ऋषिकुल, गुरुकुल, आचार्यकुल की शिक्षा के द्वारा प्राचीन समय से किया जाता था, आज की लार्ड मैकाले की शिक्षा पद्धति से संचालित स्कूलों एवं कॉलेजों के लिए एक हास्यास्पद विषय बन गया है। आज यदि कोई पुरातन संस्कारी विद्यार्थी संध्यावंदन या शिखा-सूत्र रखकर भारतीय संस्कृतिमय में जीवन बिताता है, तो अन्य छात्र उसे 'बुद्ध' या अप्रगतिशील कहकर उसका मजाक उड़ाते हैं। आज हम अपने भारतीय आदर्शों को परित्याग करके पश्चिम के अंधानुकरण को प्रगति मान बैठे हैं। इसका घातक परिणाम चरित्र दोष के रूप में आज देश में सर्वत्र दृष्टिगोचर हो रहा है।

9. जनतंत्र के लिए लाभकारी हो सकते हैं।

A. निष्ठावान श्रमिक
B. शक्तिशाली सिपाही
C. उत्तम चरित्रवान व्यक्ति
D. धनवान व्यक्ति
E. उपर्युक्त में से कोई नहीं

10. राष्ट्र की सर्वोच्च संपदा हैः

A. स्वार्थी व्यक्ति
B. लार्ड मैकाले की शिक्षा पद्धति
C. पाश्चात्य संस्कृति
D. चरित्रवान व्यक्ति
E. उपर्युक्त में से कोई नहीं

11. अप्रगतिशील रूप में मजाक उड़ाया जाता है, जोः

A. पाश्चात्य संस्कृति को हृदय से अपनाता है
B. भारतीय संस्कृतिमय जीवन बिताता है
C. धार्मिक वातावरण में जीवन बिताता है
D. सत्संग में अधिक समय नहीं बिताता है
E. उपर्युक्त में से कोई नहीं

12. चरित्र निर्माण की परम आवश्यकता हैः

A. समाजोपयोगी कार्यों के लिए
B. मानवमात्र के कल्याण के लिए
C. राष्ट्र की योजनाओं के संचालन के लिए
D. राष्ट्र के सर्वांगीण विकास के लिए
E. उपर्युक्त में से कोई नहीं

13. उन्नत राष्ट्र के लिए विकास का प्रथम सोपान हैः

A. भ्रष्टाचार के प्रति निषेधात्मक वातावरण
B. चरित्र निर्माण के शैक्षणिक वातावरण
C. राजनीति के कुशल दाँव-पेंच
D. जनता में साम्प्रदायिक सद्भाव
E. उपर्युक्त में से कोई नहीं

14. भारतीयता के प्रति हीन भावना का कारण हैः

A. पुरातन संस्कारी संस्कृतिमय जीवन
B. वर्तमान वैज्ञानिक शिक्षा पद्धति
C. प्राचीन गुरुकुल की शिक्षा पद्धति
D. लार्ड मैकाले की शिक्षा पद्धति
E. उपर्युक्त में से कोई नहीं

निर्देशः (प्र.सं. 15 से 20 तक)ः इस खंड में नीचे दिए गए गद्यांश से संबंधित प्रश्न दिए गए हैं। सही विकल्प चुनकर उत्तर पत्रक में अंकित कीजिये।

विकास क्रम में पशुता हमारा जन्मसिद्ध अधिकार है और मनुष्यता हमारे युग-युगांतर के अनवरत अध्यवसाय से अर्जित अमूल्य निधि। इसी से हम अपने पूर्व स्वप्न के लिए, सामंजस्यपूर्ण आदर्श के लिए और उदात्त भावनाओं के लिए प्राण की बाजी लगाते रहे हैं। जब हम से ऐसा करने की शक्ति शेष नहीं रह जाती तब हम एक मिथ्या दम्भ के साथ पशुता की ओर लौट चलते हैं क्योंकि वहाँ पहुँचने के लिए न किसी पराक्रम की आवश्यकता है और न साधन की। हम अपने शरीर को निश्चेष्ट छोड़कर हिमालय के शिखर से पाताल की गहराई तक सहज ही लुढ़कते चले आ सकते हैं। परंतु उसे ऊंचाई के सहस्त्र अंशों तक पहुँचने में हमारे पाँव काँपने लगेंगे, साँस फूलने लगेगी और आँखों के सामने अंधेरा छा जाएगा।

15. मनुष्य पशुता की ओर कब लौटता है?

A. जब वह मनुष्यता का आदर्श भूल जाता है
B. जब वह स्वप्न देखना बंद कर देता है
C. जब वह जीवन के सामंजस्य की स्थापना के लिए प्रयास छोड़ देता है
D. जब वह मिथ्या दम्भ से भर जाता है
E. उपर्युक्त में से कोई नहीं

9. C	10. D	11. B	12. D	13. A	14. D	15. D

16. मनुष्य मिथ्या दम्भ के साथ पशुता की ओर लौट चलते हैं:
A. जब सृजनात्मक कार्य करने की शक्ति नहीं रहती
B. जब ऊर्जा सक्रिय हो
C. जब कोई पराक्रमी हो
D. जब स्वार्थ वृति हो
E. उपर्युक्त में से कोई नहीं

17. पूरे अवतरण का सारांश है कि:
A. मनुष्य, पशुता से बढ़कर है
B. मनुष्य को चाहिए कि वह पशुता को पीछे छोड़कर मनुष्यता के लिए प्रयास करें
C. अवनति की ओर जाना उन्नति की ओर जाने से आसान है
D. मनुष्यता, मनुष्य की सतत साधना का प्रतीक है
E. उपर्युक्त में से कोई नहीं

18. प्रारम्भ में मुद्रित अंश का आशय है कि:
A. मनुष्यता मनुष्य की अमूल्य निधि है
B. विकास क्रम का नतीजा है कि हम पशु से मनुष्य बन गए
C. जन्म से पशु और मनुष्य में कोई अंतर नहीं है
D. युगांतर की साधना से मनुष्य पशुता से ऊपर उठकर मनुष्यता के गुण प्राप्त कर सकता है
E. उपर्युक्त में से कोई नहीं

19. अंतिम वाक्य में जो मुद्रित है, लेखक कहना चाहता है कि:
A. मनुष्यता का अर्जुन हिमालय पर चढ़ने जैसा कठिन है
B. मनुष्यता से पतित होना पाताल में गिरने जैसा आसान है
C. मनुष्यता प्राप्त करने में मनुष्य के पैर काँपने लगते हैं
D. मनुष्य की आँखों के आगे अंधेरा छा जाता है
E. उपर्युक्त में से कोई नहीं

20. अवतरण का उपर्युक्त शीर्षक होगा:
A. मनुष्यता की प्राप्ति
B. मानव जीवन का लक्ष्य
C. मनुष्य का जन्मसिद्ध अधिकार
D. पशुता बनाम मनुष्यता
E. उपर्युक्त में से कोई नहीं

21. ''गंगा गए गंगादास, जमुना गए जमुनादास''
लोकोक्ति का सही अर्थ है:
A. आदर्शवादी
B. चरित्रहीन
C. यथार्थवादी
D. सिद्धांतहीन
E. उपर्युक्त में से कोई नहीं

22. 'अपनाना' क्रिया किस सर्वनाम से बनी है?
A. संज्ञा से | B. विशेषण से
C. क्रिया से | D. सर्वनाम से
E. उपर्युक्त में से कोई नहीं

23. 'र' का विवरण है:
A. वर्त्स्य, लुंठित, सघोष, अल्पप्राण व्यंजन
B. पार्श्विक, सघोष, स्पर्श, अल्पप्राण व्यंजन
C. वर्त्स्य, लुंठित, अघोष, महाप्राण व्यंजन
D. वर्त्स्य, संघर्षी, अघोष, महाप्राण व्यंजन
E. उपर्युक्त में से कोई नहीं

24. साधारण वाक्य को मिश्रित वाक्य में बदलिए।
''सीता को देखते ही मुझे रीता की याद आ जाती है।''
A. जब मैं सीता की ओर देखता हूँ तब मुझे रीता की याद आ जाती है।
B. जब सीता की ओर देखता हूँ तब मुझे रीता क्यों याद आती है?
C. जब मैं सीता की ओर देखता हूँ तब मुझे रीता दिखाई देती है।
D. मैं सीता की ओर देखता हूँ और मुझे रीता की याद आ जाती है।
E. उपर्युक्त में से कोई नहीं

25. प्रयत्न के आधार पर 'ल' किस प्रकार की ध्वनि है?
A. पार्श्विक | B. संघर्षशील
C. उत्क्षिप्त | D. प्रकंपित
E. उपर्युक्त में से कोई नहीं

26. 'निराकार' में उपसर्ग है:
A. निर् | B. नि
C. निरा | D. उपर्युक्त में से एक से अधिक
E. उपर्युक्त में से कोई नहीं

27. ''कबीर वाणी के डिक्टेटर थे'' इस वाक्य में किस विराम चिह्न का प्रयोग हुआ है?
A. अल्प विराम | B. पुनरुक्ति सूचक
C. उद्धरण चिह्न | D. लाघव चिह्न
E. उपर्युक्त में से कोई नहीं

28. ''मैंने आम ले लिया है।'' का बहुवचन क्या होगा?
A. हमने आम ले लिये हैं। | B. मैंने आम लिए है।
C. मैंने आम ले लिये है। | D. हमने आम ले लिये।
E. उपर्युक्त में से कोई नहीं

16. A	**17.** A	**18.** D	**19.** E	**20.** D	**21.** D	**22.** D
23. A	**24.** A	**25.** A	**26.** A	**27.** C	**28.** A	

29. छंद पढ़ते समय आने वाले विराम को क्या कहते हैं?

A. गति
B. लय
C. गण
D. यति
E. उपर्युक्त में से कोई नहीं

30. जिस समास में दोनों पद प्रधान होता है, उसे क्या कहते हैं?

A. द्वंद्व समास
B. बहुव्रीहि समास
C. अव्ययी समास
D. द्विगु समास
E. उपर्युक्त में से कोई नहीं

PAPER-2: GENERAL STUDIES

31. What are the last signs of the activities of a volcano?

A. Geysers
B. Craters
C. Fumaroles
D. More than one of the above
E. None of the above

32. The electric fuse works on the:

A. Chemical effect of current
B. Magnetic effect of current
C. Heating effect of current
D. More than one of the above
E. None of the above

33. Who was the militant peasant leader of Bihar?

A. Raj Kumar Shukla
B. Swami Sahajanand Saraswati
C. Rajendra Prasad
D. More than one of the above
E. None of the above

34. By selling 39 dozens of mangoes, a vendor earns a profit equal to the sale proceeds of 13 dozens of mangoes. What is the percentage of his profit?

A. 33%
B. 50%
C. 26%
D. More than one of the above
E. None of the above

35. Who resisted the new system of taxation against the exploitative forces?

A. Tribes of Khandesh in 1856
B. Santhals of Bihar in 1855-56
C. Tribes of Chotanagpur in 1850
D. More than one of the above
E. None of the above

36. Which of the following is warm blooded animal?

A. Toad
B. Crocodile
C. Fish
D. More than one of the above
E. None of the above

37. Bankim Chandra Chatterjee's novel, 'Anandmath' was published in:

A. 1881
B. 1882
C. 1880
D. More than one of the above
E. None of the above

38. Dry ice is:

A. Solid nitrogen
B. Solid oxygen
C. Solid carbon dioxide
D. More than one of the above
E. None of the above

39. In National Park protection is given to:

A. Only Fauna
B. The whole ecosystem
C. Only Flora
D. More than one of the above
E. None of the above

40. Which film received the most awards in the Golden Globes 2024 held in Los Angeles?

A. The Flower Moon
B. The Holdovers
C. Oppenheimer
D. More than one of the above
E. None of the above

41. Some facts about Ozone (O_3) are:

A. It absorbs high wavelength radiation
B. It is most stable gas of the atmosphere
C. It is found in mesosphere
D. More than one of the above
E. None of the above

42. Which is the major component of biogas?

A. Hydrogen sulphide
B. Methane
C. Hydrogen
D. More than one of the above
E. None of the above

29. D	**30.** A	**31.** C	**32.** C	**33.** B	**34.** B	**35.** B
36. E	**37.** B	**38.** C	**39.** B	**40.** C	**41.** E	**42.** B

43. The Indian Standard Time (IST) remains how much ahead from Greenwich Mean Time (GMT)?

A. 05½ hours
B. 06 hours
C. 05 hours
D. More than one of the above
E. None of the above

44. In which forest do the majority of species of birds inhabit the mountainous areas?

A. Pine forest
B. Bush forest
C. Oak forest
D. More than one of the above
E. None of the above

45. Earth day is celebrated on every 22nd April related with:

A. End of the Second World War day
B. Declaration of no use of nuclear weapons on earth planet
C. Public awareness about environment issues
D. More than one of the above
E. None of the above

46. Which one of the following earthquakes is very severe and disastrous?

A. Volcanic earthquake
B. Tectonic earthquake
C. Plutonic earthquake
D. More than one of the above
E. None of the above

47. At the time of the First Round Table Conference, the Governor-General of India was:

A. Lord Reading
B. Lord Linlithgow
C. Lord Irwin
D. More than one of the above
E. None of the above

48. Find the smallest number of five digits which when divided by 15, 30, 38, 40 respectively always leaves 2 as remainder.

A. 11398
B. 11402
C. 2282
D. More than one of the above
E. None of the above

49. The Silent Valley is located in the State of:

A. Kerala
B. Madhya Pradesh
C. Chhattisgarh
D. More than one of the above
E. None of the above

50. Pollutants responsible for acid rains are:

A. CO_2
B. Water vapours
C. SO_2
D. More than one of the above
E. None of the above

51. What is true for phylum echinodermata?

A. They are triploblastic and have coelomic cavity.
B. They have a peculiar water driven tube system.
C. They are exclusively free living marine animals.
D. More than one of the above
E. None of the above

52. Which of the following is the source of renewable energy?

A. Coal
B. Nuclear fuel
C. Petroleum
D. More than one of the above
E. None of the above

53. Who among the following was the Members of the State Re-organisation Commission (SRC) in 1953?

A. K.M. Panikkar
B. Hriday Nath Kunzru
C. Fazal Ali
D. More than one of the above
E. None of the above

54. Which of the following is *not* an endocrine gland?

A. Thyroid
B. Pituitary
C. Lacrimal
D. More than one of the above
E. None of the above

55. Choose the odd one from the following.

A. Mumbai
B. Saharanpur
C. Kolkata
D. More than one of the above
E. None of the above

56. N is the brother of M. K is sister of M. P is the brother of O and O is daughter of N. Who is the uncle of P?

A. M
B. K
C. N
D. More than one of the above
E. None of the above

43. A	**44.** A	**45.** C	**46.** B	**47.** C	**48.** B	**49.** A
50. D	**51.** D	**52.** E	**53.** D	**54.** C	**55.** B	**56.** A

57. Which of the following facts are mentioned in the decision of the Supreme Court regarding Bilkis Bano?

1. Bilkis Bano challenges premature release of convicts in Supreme Court on 30 November 2022.
2. On 23 April 2019, the Supreme Court granted compensation of Rs. 50 lakh to Bilkis Bano from the Gujarat Government.
3. On 8 January 2024, the Supreme Court canceled the order regarding premature release of 11 convicts.
4. Justice B.V. Nagarathna and Justice Ujjal Bhuiyan gave the decision.

A. Only 2
B. Only 3
C. Only 1
D. More than one of the above
E. None of the above

58. INSAT-3DS launched from Sriharikota on 18 February 2024 will be used:

A. For telecommunication
B. For information about military activities of neighbouring countries
C. In the field of meteorology
D. More than one of the above
E. None of the above

59. The polling of by-elections in some Constituencies was cancelled in 2016, in which of the following States of India?

A. Telangana
B. Kerala
C. Tamil Nadu
D. More than one of the above
E. None of the above

60. The distance between the Earth and the Sun is greater during:

A. Aphelion
B. Perihelion
C. Summer solstice
D. More than one of the above
E. None of the above

61. The major and top source of oxygen in the atmosphere is:

A. Photosynthesis by forest plants
B. Photosynthesis by oceanic plants
C. Photosynthesis by grassland ecosystem
D. More than one of the above
E. None of the above

62. The value of

$$\frac{18}{\left(5+\sqrt{7}\right)}+\frac{4}{\left(\sqrt{7}+\sqrt{3}\right)}+\frac{1}{\left(\sqrt{3}+\sqrt{2}\right)}+\frac{1}{\left(\sqrt{2}+1\right)}$$ is:

A. 4
B. 3
C. 5
D. More than one of the above
E. None of the above

63. Who assassinated Sir Curzon Wylie in London?

A. V.D. Savarkar
B. Udham Singh
C. Madan Lal Dhingra
D. More than one of the above
E. None of the above

64. The 'Operation Barga' gained sustainable support to which of the following State Government of India, in the country?

A. The State Government in West Bengal
B. The State Government in Kerala
C. The State Government in Assam
D. More than one of the above
E. None of the above

65. Which one of the following is a plant hormone?

A. Cytokinin
B. Insulin
C. Oestrogen
D. More than one of the above
E. None of the above

66. How many rectangles are there in the figure given below?

A. 9
B. 12
C. 8
D. More than one of the above
E. None of the above

67. Atmosphere receives most of its energy from:

A. Long wave terrestrial radiation
B. Short wave terrestrial radiation
C. Sun
D. More than one of the above
E. None of the above

57. D	58. C	59. C	60. A	61. B	62. A
63. C	64. A	65. A	66. A	67. A	

68. Which one among the following represents the meaningful sequence of the words given below?

1. Interview 2. Appointment
3. Selection 4. Advertisement
5. Application

A. 4, 5, 1, 2, 3
B. 4, 5, 2, 1, 3
C. 4, 5, 1, 3, 2
D. More than one of the above
E. None of the above

69. Which of the following is known as the longest canal in India?

A. Setu Samudram Shipping Canal
B. Sharda Canal
C. Indira Gandhi Canal
D. More than one of the above
E. None of the above

70. A clock is started at 12:00 noon. By 10 minutes past 05:00, the hour hand has turned through:

A. 145°
B. 155°
C. 135°
D. More than one of the above
E. None of the above

71. Mohan walked 20 meter towards North, then turned left and walked 10 meter. Again he turned right and walked 20 meter. From here he turned again right and walked 10 meter. How far is he now from his starting point ?

A. 30 meter
B. 40 meter
C. 20 meter
D. More than one of the above
E. None of the above

72. Which one of the following National Parks is ***not*** correctly matched ?

A. Guindy – Tamil Nadu
B. Bhagwan Mahavir – Bihar
C. Balpakram – Meghalaya
D. More than one of the above
E. None of the above

73. Which number will come at missing value (X) from the numbers given in options on a logical way in the figure given below?

4	3	9	12
6	5	15	50
2	3	75	X

A. 48
B. 32
C. 50
D. More than one of the above
E. None of the above

74. The reversal of partition of Bengal was carried out during the time of:

A. Lord Minto
B. Lord Hardinge
C. Lord Curzon
D. More than one of the above
E. None of the above

75. The sonar technique is used to determine:

A. To locate under water hills
B. To locate ice-bergs
C. The depth of the sea
D. More than one of the above
E. None of the above

76. In a food chain, insectivorous plants trophic level is:

A. Primary consumer
B. Secondary consumer
C. Producer
D. More than one of the above
E. None of the above

77. As 'Accident' is related to 'Precaution', in the same way 'Illness' is related to which one of the following?

A. Doctor
B. Cleanliness
C. Pollution
D. More than one of the above
E. None of the above

78. A number is decreased by 5% and then increased by 10%. What is the per cent increase or decrease of the number thus obtained from the original number?

A. 4% increase
B. 4.5% decrease
C. 4.5% increase
D. More than one of the above
E. None of the above

79. The Congress Socialist Party was formed in:

A. June 1934
B. July 1934
C. May 1934
D. More than one of the above
E. None of the above

68. C	**69.** C	**70.** B	**71.** B	**72.** B	**73.** C
74. B	**75.** D	**76.** C	**77.** B	**78.** C	**79.** C

80. In a class of 50 students serial number of Avirat is 25th. What will be his serial number from the last?

A. 26th
B. 27th
C. 25th
D. More than one of the above
E. None of the above

81. Which of the following is the record of suspension of MPs in the new Parliament House of India?

A. 16 MPs of DMK were suspended
B. 13 MPs of TMC were suspended
C. 41 MPs of Congress were suspended
D. More than one of the above
E. None of the above

82. Who was the 'political guru' of Mahatma Gandhi?

A. Dadabhai Naoroji
B. Pherozeshah Mehta
C. Gopal Krishna Gokhale
D. More than one of the above
E. None of the above

83. Mulching of the soil is associated with:

A. Reducing weed growth
B. Improving fertility and health of soil
C. Conservation of soil moisture
D. More than one of the above
E. None of the above

84. It is given that $\sqrt{4489} = 67$, what is the value of $\sqrt{44.89} + \sqrt{0.4489} + \sqrt{0.004489} + \sqrt{0.00004489}$?

A. 74.437
B. 744.37
C. 7.4437
D. More than one of the above
E. None of the above

85. The Voter Verified Paper Audit Trial (VVPAT) came into existence in which of the following years in the country?

A. 2013
B. 2014
C. 2012
D. More than one of the above
E. None of the above

86. Who among the following had been the first unopposed and unanimously elected President in India?

A. Neelam Sanjeeva Reddy
B. Dr. Radha Krishnan
C. Dr. Rajendra Prasad
D. More than one of the above
E. None of the above

87. The change in focal length of human eye is caused due to:

A. Pupil
B. Cornea
C. Ciliary muscles
D. More than one of the above
E. None of the above

88. Which one word among the following words can ***not*** be formed with the letters of the word 'CARPENTER' ?

A. PAINTER
B. CARPET
C. REPENT
D. More than one of the above
E. None of the above

89. The banks of which river is planned to be developed as West Bengal Government Tea Park?

A. Hooghly
B. Brahmaputra
C. Ganga
D. More than one of the above
E. None of the above

90. Follow that rule to choose the set in options which has been followed in the set (6, 18, 54).

A. (15, 45, 135)
B. (20, 30, 40)
C. (12, 24, 72)
D. More than one of the above
E. None of the above

91. At what rate of simple interest, a certain sum of money becomes its seven times in 24 years?

A. 24% per annum
B. 25% per annum
C. 22% per annum
D. More than one of the above
E. None of the above

92. If day before yesterday it was Monday, then which will be the day on day after tomorrow?

A. Friday
B. Saturday
C. Wednesday
D. More than one of the above
E. None of the above

80. A	**81.** E	**82.** C	**83.** D	**84.** C	**85.** A	**86.** A
87. C	**88.** A	**89.** A	**90.** A	**91.** B	**92.** A	

93. Which one of the following sequences of the Himalayan ranges from south to north is correct?
A. Ladakh – Zaskar – Pir Panjal – Karakoram
B. Pir Panjal – Zaskar – Ladakh – Karakoram
C. Karakoram – Ladakh – Zaskar – Pir Panjal
D. More than one of the above
E. None of the above

94. Tungsten is used in which of the following?
A. Metal extraction
B. Electric bulb
C. Insulator
D. More than one of the above
E. None of the above

95. 1. Aditya L1 Lagrange Point – 1 accessed 6 January 2024.
2. It have seven payload.
3. Aditya L1 has a magnetometer mounted on the deck of the vehicle.
4. Visible Emission Line Coronograph in Aditya L1 will send 1440 photos to Earth every day.

Which of the above is/are true?
A. Only 2
B. Only 3
C. Only 1
D. More than one of the above
E. None of the above

96. If 6 * 7 = 2, 3 * 5 = 5, 5 * 8 = 0, then what will be the value of 6 * 8?
A. 4
B. 8
C. 2
D. More than one of the above
E. None of the above

97. The number of daily visitors of a zoo on Sunday is 680 and on other days is 332. If the first day of a 30 days month is Sunday, what will be the average number of daily visitors of the zoo in that month?
A. 390
B. 396
C. 385
D. More than one of the above
E. None of the above

98. Tamil Nadu Coast receives rainfall during winter season due to:
A. Retreating of South-west Monsoon
B. South-west Monsoon
C. Western Disturbance
D. More than one of the above
E. None of the above

99. Which one number among the numbers given in options will come in the place of question mark (?) in the series given below?
17, 27, 38, 50, 63, ?
A. 81
B. 83
C. 77
D. More than one of the above
E. None of the above

100. The best method to prevent flood is:
A. Grazing
B. Afforestation
C. Deforestation
D. More than one of the above
E. None of the above

101. How many of the total number of people have been the Chief Ministers in Bihar since 26th Jan. 1950 to the beginning of 2024?
A. Only 23 people
B. Only 25 people
C. Only 21 people
D. More than one of the above
E. None of the above

102. What is the length of diameter of a circular ground whose area is equal to the sum of the area of a circle of radius 8 m and a triangle of area 36 πm^2?
A. 15 m
B. 20 m
C. 10 m
D. More than one of the above
E. None of the above

103. The animals found in desert are called:
A. Deserticolous
B. Desertimalia
C. Desertimals
D. More than one of the above
E. None of the above

104. In Bihar, which of the following facts have been revealed by Bihar Caste Survey, 2023?
A. Upper Caste 15.52%
B. Scheduled Caste and Scheduled Tribe 21.33%
C. Backward Caste 63.14%
D. More than one of the above
E. None of the above

93. B	**94.** B	**95.** D	**96.** B	**97.** A	**98.** A
99. C	**100.** B	**101.** A	**102.** B	**103.** A	**104.** D

105. The famous Indian National Army trials took place at the Red Fort, Delhi in:

A. 1945
B. 1946
C. 1944
D. More than one of the above
E. None of the above

106. On dividing $a^3 + b^3 + c^3 - 3abc$ by $a + b + c$, the quotient obtained is:

A. $a^2 + b^2 + c^2 - bc - ca + ab$
B. $a^2 + b^2 + c^2 + bc + ca + ab$
C. $a^2 + b^2 + c^2 - bc - ca - ab$
D. More than one of the above
E. None of the above

107. Five boys are sitting in a line having their faces at the North. P is at the right of Q. T is on the left of Q but on the right of R. If P is on the left of S, who is sitting at the middle of all of them?

A. R
B. Q
C. S
D. More than one of the above
E. None of the above

108. Joint military exercise by India and Japan was conducted in Mahajan area of Rajasthan on 25 February 2024. The name of the joint military exercise was:

A. Atal Guardian 2024
B. Nagasaki Guardian 2024
C. Dharma Guardian 2024
D. More than one of the above
E. None of the above

109. Which of the following crops can ***not*** be cultivated in river?

A. Water chestnut
B. Lotus
C. Fox nut
D. More than one of the above
E. None of the above

110. In an examination of Hindi, English and Mathematics subjects, the total marks are 120, 140 and 100 respectively. A student gets 40%, 55% and 45% marks in these subjects respectively. How many marks should he get in Science subject out of the total 180 marks in it so that his combined percentage of marks obtained in all the four subjects becomes 60%?

A. 156
B. 160
C. 154
D. More than one of the above
E. None of the above

111. Padmashree Ushakiran Khan had the following achievements:

1. Sahitya Akademi Award 2010
2. Bharat Bharati 2019
3. Maithili - Kachahi Bans
4. Hindi-Anuttarit Prashna

A. Only 2
B. Only 1
C. Only 3
D. More than one of the above
E. None of the above

112. Who among the following was the Prime Minister of India, when 73rd and 74th Amendments of the Constitution came into existence?

A. P.V. Narasimha Rao
B. H.D. Deve Gowda
C. Chandra Shekhar
D. More than one of the above
E. None of the above

113. Chemically rust is:

A. Hydrated ferric oxide
B. Hydrated ferrous oxide
C. Only ferric oxide
D. More than one of the above
E. None of the above

114. In English alphabet which letter is opposite to letter P?

A. K
B. N
C. L
D. More than one of the above
E. None of the above

115. In which of the following States of India, the maximum teak forest is found?

A. Bihar
B. Karnataka
C. Madhya Pradesh
D. More than one of the above
E. None of the above

116. The relationship between algae and fungi in Lichens is called as:

A. Commensalism
B. Protocooperation
C. Mutualism
D. More than one of the above
E. None of the above

105. A	**106.** C	**107.** B	**108.** C	**109.** D	**110.** C
111. D	**112.** A	**113.** A	**114.** A	**115.** C	**116.** C

117. A rectangle has an area 30 cm^2 and perimeter 26 cm. Its length (in cm) is:

A. 8
B. 10
C. 6
D. More than one of the above
E. None of the above

118. What are the characters that make a plant a hydrophyte?

A. Absence of mechanical tissue
B. Presence of aerenchyma
C. Presence of well developed vascular system
D. More than one of the above
E. None of the above

119. Indira Gandhi National Center for the Arts has created a language atlas by conducting speech surveys all over India. It is an autonomous body under the Union Ministry of Culture. What is meant by the language atlas of India?

A. Ethnic map of India
B. It is language mapping project of India
C. Natural map of India
D. More than one of the above
E. None of the above

120. The type of mirror used in vehicles to see the traffic on the rear side is:

A. Concave
B. Plane
C. Convex
D. More than one of the above
E. None of the above

121. With reference to India and its relations with neighbours, which of the following statements is/are correct?

A. The foreign policy of India is based on peace and non-violence.
B. Panchsheel principles are the result of India's determination to peace.
C. India is one of the founders of Non-alignment Movement.
D. More than one of the above
E. None of the above

122. Kargil is located on the bank of:

A. Suru river
B. Jhelum river
C. Indus river
D. More than one of the above
E. None of the above

123. A completes a work in 15 days, B completes the same work in 8 days while B and C jointly complete the same work in 4 days. If A and C jointly complete the same work in x days while A and B jointly complete it in y days, what is the value of x/y ?

A. 1
B. 1½
C. ½
D. More than one of the above
E. None of the above

124. The Prime Minister Lal Bahadur Shastri faced which of the following issues challenging the basic values and goals of Indian Nation?

A. The shortage of food for social and economic transformation
B. The war with Pakistan in 1965
C. The Anti Hindi Agitation in South
D. More than one of the above
E. None of the above

125. Which country's Space Agencies have allowed Private Companies to conduct tours of the International Space Station?

A. Bhutan, Nepal, Singapur
B. Guyana, Burundi, Paraguay
C. Turkey, Sweden, Italy
D. More than one of the above
E. None of the above

126. SPMs are used for tracking air quality and for regulating air pollution. Here SPM stands for:

A. Solidified Particulate Matter
B. Suspended Particulate Matter
C. Soluble Particulate Matter
D. More than one of the above
E. None of the above

127. Which of the following constitute a food chain?

A. Grass, deer and tiger
B. Grass, fish and cow
C. Grass, rabbit and elephant
D. More than one of the above
E. None of the above

128. Which was the main centre of activities of Wahabis in Bihar?

A. Jagdishpur
B. Champaran
C. Patna
D. More than one of the above
E. None of the above

117. B	**118.** D	**119.** B	**120.** C	**121.** D	**122.** A
123. A	**124.** D	**125.** C	**126.** B	**127.** A	**128.** C

129. The iron pillar wonder of ancient Indian metallurgy is situated in:

A. Pune
B. Delhi
C. Lucknow
D. More than one of the above
E. None of the above

130. The thorough economic liberalisation in India initiated from which of the following years?

A. After 1991
B. After 2001
C. After 1981
D. More than one of the above
E. None of the above

131. Brahmo Samaj's influence was confined mostly to the:

A. Rural Bengal
B. Both rural and urban educated groups
C. Urban educated groups
D. More than one of the above
E. None of the above

132. In a coded language 'PROBLEM' is written as 'MPERLOB'. In the same coded language how will you write 'NUMBERS'?

A. SNRUEBM
B. SRUNEMB
C. SNRUEMB
D. More than one of the above
E. None of the above

133. Which of the following is the important reason for ethnic violence in Manipur from 3 May, 2023?

A. Meitei Community should be given share in jobs reserved for Kuki Community
B. Lack of resources to Meitei Community
C. Meitei Community should be given the status of tribe
D. More than one of the above
E. None of the above

134. The political tendency to build our Nation mainly on Nationalism is led by which of the following Political Party in India?

A. Indian National Congress
B. Bharatiya Janata Party
C. Socialist Party
D. More than one of the above
E. None of the above

135. The lengths of the diagonals of a rhombus are $2a$ and $2b$. Its perimeter is:

A. $2\sqrt{a^2 + b^2}$
B. $4ab$
C. $4\sqrt{a^2 + b^2}$
D. More than one of the above
E. None of the above

136. Which bridge was inaugurated by Prime Minister Narendra Modi on 24 February 2024 to connect Dwarka in the Gulf of Kutch region?

A. Kutch Bridge
B. Sudarshan Bridge
C. Dwarka Bridge
D. More than one of the above
E. None of the above

137. In a food chain, which trophic level has highest energy level?

A. Consumers of first trophic level
B. Consumers of top trophic level
C. Producers
D. More than one of the above
E. None of the above

138. Which of the following will turn blue litmus red?

A. Washing soda solution
B. Vinegar
C. Baking soda solution
D. More than one of the above
E. None of the above

139. The country India shares longest international boundary with:

A. Pakistan
B. Nepal
C. Bangladesh
D. More than one of the above
E. None of the above

140. Which of the following is the oldest river valley project in Bihar?

A. Damodar River Valley Project
B. Sone River Valley Project
C. Kosi River Valley Project
D. More than one of the above
E. None of the above

141. The values of x and y satisfying the equations $2x + 3y = 77$ and $3x + 2y = 73$ are respectively;

A. 12 and 18
B. 11 and 19
C. 13 and 17
D. More than one of the above
E. None of the above

129. B	**130.** A	**131.** C	**132.** C	**133.** D	**134.** B	**135.** C
136. B	**137.** C	**138.** B	**139.** C	**140.** A	**141.** C	

142. Which of the following Constitutional Amendment in India made judiciary subservient of Parliament?
A. 42nd Constitutional Amendment
B. 43rd Constitutional Amendment
C. 40th Constitutional Amendment
D. More than one of the above
E. None of the above

143. Which area does China claim as its "Sacred territory"?
A. Tibet
B. Taiwan
C. Macau
D. More than one of the above
E. None of the above

144. The grassland with scattered trees is called as:
A. Savanna
B. Agroforest
C. Rain forest
D. More than one of the above
E. None of the above

145. Who founded the Indian National Congress in 1885?
A. Surendranath Banerjee
B. Gopal Krishna Gokhale
C. Dadabhai Naoroji
D. More than one of the above
E. None of the above

146. The value of $\frac{2\{(467+359)^2 - 2\times 467\times 359\}}{(467)^2+(359)^2}$ is:
A. 2
B. 3
C. 1
D. More than one of the above
E. None of the above

147. The Preamble of the Constitution of India guarantees justice. It means India allows its people:
A. To elect their representatives
B. To have certain basic rights
C. To participate in the decision making
D. More than one of the above
E. None of the above

148. Which one of the North-eastern States of India has the highest concentration of tribal population?
A. Nagaland
B. Mizoram
C. Meghalaya
D. More than one of the above
E. None of the above

149. Which of the ecological pyramids show both upright and inverted types?
A. Pyramid of number
B. Pyramid of biomass
C. Pyramid of energy
D. More than one of the above
E. None of the above

150. How many kilometers is the total length of Atal Setu connecting Mumbai and New Mumbai?
A. 21.5 kilometers
B. 21.8 kilometers
C. 21.3 kilometers
D. More than one of the above
E. None of the above

EXPLANATORY ANSWERS

1. (B): Research in the passage clearly states that only seven per cent of communication is done through words. This highlights the minimal role verbal language plays in the total communication process compared to non-verbal elements like body language and facial expressions.

2. (A): "Body" and "person" are both nouns because they represent things—"body" refers to the physical form and "person" refers to an individual human being. These words name objects or entities, fulfilling the role of a noun in grammar.

3. (D): The passage mentions that complete communication must be sensitive to "eye movement", "posture and gesture", "breathing rate", and "facial expression". Therefore, options (A) eye movement, (B) breathing rate, and (C) body language are all part of effective communication, making (D) the correct answer.

4. (A): The passage opens by stating that "People are always communicating, verbally and non-verbally". This directly identifies the two kinds of communication, verbal (spoken words) and non-verbal (body language, facial expressions, etc.), making A the accurate answer.

5. (B): The passage explains the components of communication, especially emphasizing non-verbal aspects such as gestures and expressions. It seeks to inform the reader about how communication truly functions beyond just words, thereby discussing the nature of communication.

6. (A): The correct sentence is: "Had we been punctual, we would have caught the train". This is an example of

142. A	143. D	144. A	145. E	146. A	147. B	148. B	149. D	150. B

a third conditional sentence, which is used to talk about hypothetical situations in the past. The correct structure is "Had + subject + past participle", followed by "would have + past participle". "Been" (past participle of 'be') and "caught" (past participle of 'catch') fit grammatically and logically.

7. (E): The sentence is: "You can't____with other people". None of the given options fit grammatically. "Arguing"and "quarreling" are gerunds and require restructuring the sentence. "Shouted" is a past tense verb and doesn't fit here. The correct verb should be "argue"—"You can't argue with other people". Since this isn't one of the choices, (E) is the correct option.

8. (C): The correct sentence is: "Since she is a radio jockey, she has to talk a lot". A radio jockey's main job involves speaking extensively over the radio, making this choice contextually appropriate. While "jockey" alone typically refers to a horse rider and "cook" doesn't imply frequent speaking, only "radio jockey" fits the context of someone needing to talk a lot.

9. (C): गद्यांश में स्पष्ट रूप से कहा गया है कि "उत्तम चरित्रवान व्यक्ति ही राष्ट्र की सर्वोच्च संपदा है" और यह जनतंत्र के लिए एक महान कल्याणकारी योजना है। इसका अर्थ है कि जनतंत्र की सफलता के लिए चरित्रवान नागरिक आवश्यक हैं, क्योंकि वे नीतियों के प्रति सजग रहते हैं और समाज को सही दिशा में ले जाते हैं।

10. (D): गद्यांश में यह बात स्पष्ट रूप से कही गई है कि "उत्तम चरित्रवान व्यक्ति ही राष्ट्र की सर्वोच्च संपदा है।" इसका तात्पर्य है कि आर्थिक, भौतिक या सैन्य संसाधनों की तुलना में एक उत्तम चरित्र वाला नागरिक राष्ट्र के लिए अधिक महत्त्वपूर्ण है क्योंकि वह अपने कर्तव्यों को निष्ठा और ईमानदारी से निभाता है।

11. (B): गद्यांश में बताया गया है कि आज यदि कोई विद्यार्थी संध्यावंदन करता है या शिखा-सूत्र धारण करता है, तो अन्य छात्र उसे 'बुद्ध' या 'अप्रगतिशील' कहकर उसका मजाक उड़ाते हैं। इसका सीधा संकेत है कि भारतीय परंपरा एवं संस्कृति के अनुसार जीवन जीने वाले को अप्रगतिशील समझा जाता है।

12. (D): गद्यांश का आरंभ ही इस बात से होता है कि "राष्ट्र के सर्वांगीण विकास के लिए चरित्र निर्माण परम आवश्यक है।" लेखक यह बताना चाहता है कि केवल भौतिक योजनाएं पर्याप्त नहीं हैं, बल्कि चरित्र निर्माण द्वारा नागरिकों को नैतिक रूप से सशक्त बनाना भी विकास की अनिवार्य शर्त है।

13. (A): गद्यांश में कहा गया है कि "राष्ट्र में व्याप्त समग्र भ्रष्टाचार के प्रति निषेधात्मक वातावरण का निर्माण करना ही चरित्र निर्माण का प्रथम सोपान है।" यानी देश में चरित्र निर्माण की शुरुआत भ्रष्टाचार के विरुद्ध जन-जागरूकता और नैतिक विरोध के माहौल से होती है।

14. (D): गद्यांश में उल्लेख है कि "लॉर्ड मैकाले की शिक्षा पद्धति से संचालित स्कूलों एवं कॉलेजों" ने चरित्र निर्माण को हास्यास्पद विषय बना दिया है। साथ ही, इसी पद्धति ने भारतीयता के प्रति हीन भावना उत्पन्न की है, क्योंकि यह पाश्चात्य संस्कृति को प्राथमिकता देती है और भारतीय मूल्यों को कमतर दिखाती है।

15. (D): गद्यांश में स्पष्ट रूप से कहा गया है कि जब मनुष्य में ऐसा करने की शक्ति शेष नहीं रहती, तब वह "मिथ्या दम्भ" के साथ पशुता की ओर लौट जाता है। अर्थात् जब व्यक्ति में मनुष्यता की साधना का सामर्थ्य नहीं रह जाता, तब वह झूठे अहंकार या आत्मछल के साथ अधोगति स्वीकार कर लेता है, क्योंकि उसमें कोई परिश्रम नहीं लगता।

16. (A): गद्यांश में बताया गया है कि जब हममें ऐसा करने की शक्ति नहीं रह जाती–अर्थात् मनुष्यता, सामंजस्य, और आदर्शों के लिए प्रयत्न करने की सृजनात्मक शक्ति समाप्त हो जाती है–तब हम मिथ्या दम्भ के साथ पशुता की ओर लौटते हैं। यह बताता है कि गिरावट में प्रयास की आवश्यकता नहीं होती, लेकिन सृजनात्मक प्रयास हेतु शक्ति चाहिए।

17. (A): पूरे अवतरण में यह प्रतिपादित किया गया है कि पशुता तो सहज प्राप्त है, लेकिन मनुष्यता एक दीर्घकालीन साधना का फल है। मनुष्य अपनी चेतना, परिश्रम और उदात्त भावनाओं के कारण पशुता से ऊपर उठता है। यही भाव इस विकल्प को सारांश के रूप में सही बनाता है।

18. (D): अवतरण के आरंभ में ही कहा गया है कि "पशुता जन्मसिद्ध अधिकार है" जबकि "मनुष्यता युग-युगांतर के अनवरत अध्यवसाय से अर्जित अमूल्य निधि है।" इसका अर्थ यह है कि मनुष्यता सहज नहीं बल्कि दीर्घकालीन साधना से प्राप्त होती है, जो इस विकल्प में ठीक से प्रतिबिंबित होता है।

19. (E): अंतिम वाक्य में लेखक कहता है कि "हम अपने शरीर को निश्चेष्ट छोड़कर हिमालय के शिखर से पाताल की गहराई तक सहज ही लुढ़कते चले आ सकते हैं। परंतु उसे ऊँचाई के सहस्त्र अंशों तक पहुँचने में हमारे पाँव काँपने लगेंगे..."। इसका आशय यह है कि पतन सहज है, लेकिहन उन्नति अत्यंत कठिन–परंतु दिए गए विकल्पों में कोई एक विकल्प इस समग्र अर्थ को पूरी तरह नहीं दर्शाता, इसलिए सही उत्तर E है।

20. (D): पूरा अवतरण पशुता और मनुष्यता के बीच के अंतर, संघर्ष और प्रयास को केन्द्र में रखकर लिखा गया है। इसमें मनुष्य की सहज पशु प्रवृत्ति और अर्जित मनुष्यत्व के बीच का द्वंद्व दर्शाया गया है। अतः "पशुता बनाम मनुष्यता" शीर्षक इस विचार की सटीक अभिव्यक्ति है।

21. (D): "गंगा गए गंगादास, जमुना गए जमुनादास" लोकोक्ति का अर्थ है–जो व्यक्ति जहां जाता है, वहीं का रंग-ढंग और व्यवहार अपना लेता है, बिना किसी स्थायी सिद्धांत या मूल्यों के। यह कहावत ऐसे लोगों पर लागू होती है जो परिस्थिति के अनुसार अपना आचरण बदलते हैं। इसीलिए इसका सही अर्थ 'सिद्धांतहीन' है।

22. (D): 'अपनाना' क्रिया 'अपना' सर्वनाम से बनी है, जो स्वत्व या अधिकार को दर्शाता है। 'अपना' सर्वनाम है और इसमें '–ना' प्रत्यय जोड़कर यह क्रिया बनी है। उदाहरणस्वरूपः "उसने उस विचार को अपना लिया" में अपनाना क्रिया सर्वनाम 'अपना' से व्युत्पन्न है।

23. (A): 'र' वर्ण का स्वरूप वर्त्स्य (जिह्वा के अग्रभाग से उत्पन्न), लुंठित (जिह्वा की एक हल्की लपक से), सघोष (ध्वनि युक्त), और अल्पप्राण (बिना विशेष प्राणवायु के उच्चरित) होता है। यह वर्ण 'र' के उच्चारण की ध्वन्यात्मक प्रकृति को सही ढंग से परिभाषित करता है।

24. (A): दिए गए वाक्य में 'सीता को देखते ही' एक अव्ययी भाव है, जो समय का बोध कराता है। इसे मिश्र वाक्य में बदलने के लिए उपवाक्य "जब मैं सीता की ओर देखता हूँ" का प्रयोग उपयुक्त है। यह समय-सम्बंधी उपवाक्य के माध्यम से मूल वाक्य की भावना को यथार्थ रूप से मिश्र वाक्य में प्रस्तुत करता है।

25. (A): प्रयत्न के आधार पर 'ल' वर्ण को पाश्विक ध्वनि कहा जाता है क्योंकि यह जिह्वा के एक पार्श्व भाग के उपयोग से उच्चरित होता है। पाश्विक ध्वनियाँ वे होती हैं जिनमें जिह्वा का किनारा (पार्श्व) प्रयुक्त होता है। 'ल' वर्ण इसी प्रयत्न की श्रेणी में आता है।

26. (A): 'निराकार' शब्द में 'निर्' उपसर्ग है, जिसका अर्थ होता है "बिना" या "रहित"। 'आकार' का अर्थ होता है "रूप" और 'निर्' उपसर्ग जोड़ने पर इसका अर्थ होता है "जिसका कोई आकार नहीं हो", अर्थात् 'रूपहीन'। संस्कृत और हिंदी व्याकरण में 'निर्' उपसर्ग कई शब्दों में इस अर्थ में प्रयुक्त होता है, जैसे 'निर्दोष', 'निर्जीव' आदि।

27. (C): वाक्य "कबीर वाणी के डिक्टेटर थे" में यह वाक्य उद्धरण चिह्न (" ") के भीतर लिखा गया है। उद्धरण चिह्न का प्रयोग किसी के कथन, विचार या विशेष शब्द को स्पष्ट रूप से प्रस्तुत करने के लिए किया जाता है। यह आमतौर पर प्रत्यक्ष उद्धरण या विशेष रूप से उल्लेखनीय वाक्यांशों को दिखाने के लिए उपयोग में लाया जाता है।

28. (A): वाक्य "मैंने आम ले लिया है।" का बहुवचन बनाने पर कर्ता 'मैंने' का बहुवचन 'हमने' होगा और क्रिया 'ले लिया है' का बहुवचन रूप 'ले लिये हैं' होगा। इसलिए सही वाक्य होगा—"हमने आम ले लिये हैं।" यह व्याकरण के अनुसार कर्ता और क्रिया दोनों के बहुवचन रूप में सही है।

29. (D): छंद पढ़ते समय जो विराम आता है, उसे 'यति' कहते हैं। यति का अर्थ है—छंद के भीतर निर्धारित स्थान पर रुकना या ठहराव। यह काव्य में भाव की स्पष्टता, संगीतात्मकता और सौंदर्य को बनाए रखने में सहायक होता है। यति छंद के भीतर संगीतात्मक सामंजस्य बनाने का कार्य करता है।

30. (A): द्वंद्व समास वह होता है जिसमें दोनों पद प्रधान होते हैं और दोनों का समुचित महत्व रहता है। उदाहरणः 'राम-लक्ष्मण', 'सूर्य-चंद्र', आदि। इसमें दोनों पदों को अलग-अलग महत्व देकर एक साथ जोड़ा जाता है और समुच्चय बोध होता है, जिससे यह समास अन्य समासों से भिन्न होता है।

31. (C): Fumaroles are openings near volcanoes that emit steam and volcanic gases such as sulfur dioxide. They are considered one of the final signs of volcanic activity, occurring even after lava flows and eruptions have ceased. The presence of fumaroles indicates that the volcano is still geothermally active, although not erupting.

32. (C): An electric fuse works on the principle of the heating effect of current. When excessive current flows through the circuit, the fuse wire, which has low melting point, heats up and melts, thereby breaking the circuit and preventing damage to electrical appliances. This safety mechanism relies entirely on the heat generated due to resistance.

33. (B): Swami Sahajanand Saraswati was a prominent militant peasant leader of Bihar who fought vigorously for farmers' rights and against the zamindari system. He founded the All India Kisan Sabha and was known for mobilizing peasants against exploitation, making him a central figure in the agrarian movement.

34. (B): Let the selling price of 1 dozen mangoes be ₹ 1 (for simplicity).

Total sale proceeds for 39 dozens = ₹ 39

Profit = sale proceeds of 13 dozens
= 13

Cost price = Selling price − Profit
= ₹ 39 − ₹ 13 = ₹ 26

Profit % = (Profit/Cost Price) × 100
= (13/26) × 100 = 50%

Hence, the vendor earns a profit of 50%.

35. (B): The Santhal rebellion of 1855–56 was a major uprising led by the Santhal tribes in present-day Jharkhand and Bihar. They revolted against exploitative moneylenders, landlords, and the British colonial tax system. This movement was a clear resistance to the oppressive taxation and economic exploitation imposed on them.

36. (E): Warm-blooded animals maintain a constant internal body temperature regardless of external conditions. Among the options, toad (an amphibian), crocodile (a reptile), and fish (aquatic vertebrate) are all cold-blooded animals. They rely on the environment to regulate their body temperature. Hence, none of the given options are warm-blooded.

37. (B): Anandmath, the famous nationalist novel written by Bankim Chandra Chatterjee, was published in 1882. This novel played a key role in inspiring patriotism during the Indian freedom movement and contains the national song Vande Mataram. Its publication year is historically recorded as 1882.

38. (C): Dry ice is the solid form of carbon dioxide (CO_2). It is called "dry" because it sublimates directly from a solid to gas at atmospheric pressure, without passing through the liquid phase. It is commonly used for refrigeration and special effects due to its extremely low temperature and fog-like vapour.

39. (B): In a National Park, protection is granted not only to individual species of plants (flora) or animals (fauna), but to the entire ecosystem — including landscapes, water bodies, and all organisms. The primary objective is conservation of biodiversity in its natural habitat, making the protection comprehensive.

40. (C): At the Golden Globes 2024 held in Los Angeles, Oppenheimer, directed by Christopher Nolan, received the most awards including Best Motion Picture – Drama, Best Director, and Best Actor. The film was critically acclaimed and dominated the ceremony, making this the correct answer.

41. (E): Ozone (O_3) primarily absorbs ultraviolet (UV) radiation, particularly in the shorter wavelength range (not high wavelength), and is located in the stratosphere, not the mesosphere. Also, it is not the most stable gas of the atmosphere — in fact, it is relatively reactive. Thus, none of the options A, B, or C are fully correct, making option E the right answer.

42. (B): Methane (CH_4) is the major component of biogas, making up approximately 50–75% of its content. Biogas is produced by the anaerobic digestion of organic matter, and methane is the primary energy-yielding component, used for cooking and electricity. Hydrogen sulphide and hydrogen are present only in trace amounts.

43. (A): Indian Standard Time (IST) is 5 hours and 30 minutes ahead of Greenwich Mean Time (GMT). IST is calculated from the 82.5° E longitude, which passes near Mirzapur in Uttar Pradesh, India. Therefore, when it is 12:00 noon GMT, it is 5:30 PM IST.

44. (A): Pine forests, especially those found in Himalayan and subalpine regions, are known to host a wide range of bird species due to their unique ecosystem structure, canopy cover, and availability of food sources. Many migratory and resident birds inhabit these forest types, particularly in mountainous zones.

45. (C): Earth Day, celebrated every year on 22nd April, is dedicated to raising public awareness about environmental protection, climate change, pollution, and conservation. It was first celebrated in 1970 and is now observed globally to promote sustainable living and eco-consciousness.

46. (B): Tectonic earthquakes are the most severe and disastrous as they are caused by sudden movements along faults or fractures in the Earth's crust due to tectonic plate motion. These quakes release massive energy and often result in widespread destruction. Most of the world's major earthquakes, including those in Japan, California, and Turkey, are tectonic in origin.

47. (C): The First Round Table Conference was held in London from November 1930 to January 1931. At that time, Lord Irwin was the Governor-General and Viceroy of India (serving from 1926 to 1931). He played a critical role during this period, including handling the civil disobedience movement and initiating dialogues with Indian leaders.

48. (B): The question asks for the smallest five-digit number which when divided by 15, 30, 38, and 40 leaves a remainder of 2 in each case.

To solve this, follow these steps:

First, subtract the remainder 2 to convert the condition into a multiple situation:

Let the required number be N.

Then, N - 2 must be divisible by 15, 30, 38, and 40.

Compute LCM of 15, 30, 38, and 40:

Prime factors:

$$15 = 3 \times 5$$
$$30 = 2 \times 3 \times 5$$
$$38 = 2 \times 19$$
$$40 = 2^3 \times 5$$
$$\text{LCM} = 2^3 \times 3 \times 5 \times 19 = 11400$$

So, N - 2 = 11400, and therefore:

$$N = 11400 + 2 = 11402$$

Now, verify if 11402 is a five-digit number (yes) and satisfies the condition.

Hence, the correct answer is B: 11402.

49. (A): Silent Valley is a national park located in the Nilgiri Hills of Kerala. It is one of the last undisturbed tracts of South Western Ghats rainforest and is known for its rich biodiversity, especially rare and endangered species. It became a national park in 1984 after public outcry prevented a hydroelectric project in the area.

50. (D): Acid rain is caused by sulfur dioxide (SO_2) and nitrogen oxides (NO_x), which react with water vapor in the atmosphere to form sulfuric acid (H_2SO_4) and nitric acid (HNO_3). Hence, both SO_2 and NO_x are responsible pollutants. Since NO_x is implied in addition to SO_2, the correct answer is "More than one of the above".

51. (D): All of the given statements about phylum Echinodermata are true. Echinoderms are triploblastic and coelomate animals (A), they possess a water vascular system for movement and feeding (B), and they are exclusively free-living marine organisms (C). Thus, more than one of the above statements are correct.

52. (E): Coal, petroleum, and nuclear fuel are all non-renewable sources of energy. They are derived from finite natural reserves that cannot be replenished on a human timescale. Renewable energy sources would include solar, wind, hydro, and geothermal — none of which are listed here, so the correct answer is "None of the above".

53. (D): The States Reorganisation Commission (SRC) of 1953 had three members: Fazal Ali (Chairman), K.M. Panikkar, and Hriday Nath Kunzru. The commission was formed to recommend the reorganization of Indian states based on linguistic lines. Since all three options are correct members, "More than one of the above" is the correct answer.

54. (C): The lacrimal gland is responsible for producing tears but it is not an endocrine gland. Endocrine glands, such as the thyroid and pituitary, secrete hormones directly into the bloodstream. In contrast, the lacrimal gland is an exocrine gland, which secretes its product via ducts, making it the odd one out in this list.

55. (B): Mumbai and Kolkata are both metropolitan cities and state capitals located on the coastline with significant economic and urban development. Saharanpur, on the other hand, is an inland city with smaller urban scale and different demographic and economic characteristics. Thus, Saharanpur is the odd one out.

56. (A): Let's break it down step by step based on the relationships:

N is the brother of M → N and M are brothers.

K is the sister of M → K is also a sibling of M (and therefore of N as well).

O is the daughter of N → N has a daughter named O.

P is the brother of O → P is the son of N (because O is N's daughter, so P and O are siblings, children of N).

So, P is N's son, and we are asked: Who is the uncle of P?

N is P's father.
N's brother is M.
Therefore, M is the uncle of P.
Correct answer: A: M.

57. **(D):** On 30 November 2022, Bilkis Bano filed a plea in the Supreme Court challenging the premature release of the 11 convicts. On 23 April 2019, the Supreme Court directed the Gujarat Government to pay her Rs. 50 lakh compensation. On 8 January 2024, the Supreme Court, in a significant judgment by Justices B.V. Nagarathna and Ujjal Bhuiyan, cancelled the premature release of the 11 convicts. Thus, facts 1, 2, 3, and 4 are all mentioned in the Supreme Court's decision, validating that more than one of the listed facts is correct.

58. **(C):** INSAT-3DS, launched by ISRO from Sriharikota on 18 February 2024, is a meteorological satellite. It is designed to enhance weather forecasting, storm tracking, and monitoring of the Earth's surface. This satellite aids in disaster warning services and supports atmospheric and oceanic observations. It is not purposed for telecommunications or military surveillance, confirming its sole focus on meteorology.

59. **(C):** In 2016, by-elections in certain constituencies of Tamil Nadu were cancelled due to widespread allegations of electoral malpractices, such as vote-buying and illegal inducements to voters. The Election Commission intervened to uphold the integrity of the democratic process. There were no such widespread cancellations in Telangana or Kerala during that year, confirming Tamil Nadu as the correct answer.

60. **(A):** The Earth is farthest from the Sun during aphelion, which occurs around early July each year. During aphelion, the Earth-Sun distance is approximately 152.1 million kilometers. In contrast, during perihelion (early January), Earth is closest to the Sun at about 147.1 million kilometers. Summer solstice refers to the longest day in the Northern Hemisphere and does not relate directly to Earth's orbital distance from the Sun.

61. **(B):** The top source of atmospheric oxygen is photosynthesis by phytoplankton in the oceans. These microscopic marine plants, including algae and cyanobacteria, contribute to over 50% of the Earth's oxygen supply. Due to the vast surface area of oceans and their ability to support high phytoplankton productivity, they surpass terrestrial sources like forests and grasslands in oxygen generation.

62. **(A):** Given:

$$\frac{18}{5+\sqrt{7}}+\frac{4}{\sqrt{7}+\sqrt{3}}+\frac{1}{\sqrt{3}+\sqrt{2}}+\frac{1}{\sqrt{2}+1}$$

On solving the denominator of each term, we get

1. $\frac{18}{5+\sqrt{7}}=\frac{18(5-\sqrt{7})}{(5+\sqrt{7})(5-\sqrt{7})}=\frac{18(5-\sqrt{7})}{18}=5-\sqrt{7}$

2. $\frac{4}{\sqrt{7}+\sqrt{3}}=\frac{4(\sqrt{7}-\sqrt{3})}{(\sqrt{7})^2-(\sqrt{3})^2}=\frac{4(\sqrt{7}-\sqrt{3})}{4}=\sqrt{7}-\sqrt{3}$

3. $\frac{1}{\sqrt{3}+\sqrt{2}}=\frac{\sqrt{3}-\sqrt{2}}{1}=\sqrt{3}-\sqrt{2}$

4. $\frac{1}{\sqrt{2}+1}=\frac{\sqrt{2}-1}{1}=\sqrt{2}-1$

Now let's add up all the terms:

$$(5-\sqrt{7})+(\sqrt{7}-\sqrt{3})+(\sqrt{3}-\sqrt{2})+(\sqrt{2}-1)$$

All the square roots are crossed out, the remainder is:

$$5 - 1 = 4$$

So, the correct answer is: A: 4.

63. **(C):** Madan Lal Dhingra assassinated Sir William Hutt Curzon-Wyllie in London on 1 July 1909. He was an Indian revolutionary who sought to draw international attention to British colonial rule in India. The assassination was one of the earliest acts of political violence against a British official by an Indian abroad, and Dhingra was later executed for the act.

64. **(A):** Operation Barga was a land reform movement launched by the West Bengal government in the late 1970s to record the rights of sharecroppers (bargadars) and protect them from eviction. It successfully brought tenancy reforms by recognizing and registering sharecroppers, ensuring them a greater share of the produce and legal protection, and became a model of agrarian reform in India.

65. **(A):** Cytokinins are a class of plant hormones that promote cell division, or cytokinesis, in plant roots and shoots. They are essential in regulating plant growth, development, and differentiation. In contrast, insulin and oestrogen are animal hormones — insulin regulates blood sugar in animals, and oestrogen is a primary female sex hormone in mammals.

66. **(A):** Looking at the figure carefully, the figure is made up of a rectangular body with a triangular tip on the left and three segments on the right. Count the total number of rectangles:

1. Three small horizontal rectangles on the extreme right (in top row, middle row and bottom row) = 3 rectangles
2. Two small rectangles horizontally in two segments along with the triangle on the extreme left = 2 rectangles
3. Two long strips on the top and bottom = 2 large rectangles
4. On ling strip in the middle which runs through the middle of the whole figure = 1 rectangle
5. One largest rectangle forming the whole figure = 1 rectangle

Thus, the total number of rectangles is:

3 (right) + 2 (left) + 2 (top-bottom) + 1 (middle) + 1 (whole) = 9 rectangles

So, the correct answer is: A: 9

67. **(A):** The atmosphere receives most of its energy indirectly from the Earth's surface, which absorbs shortwave solar radiation and re-emits it as longwave terrestrial radiation.

This longwave infrared radiation is then absorbed by greenhouse gases like CO_2, H_2O vapour, and others, heating the atmosphere. While the Sun is the original energy source, the atmosphere gains most of its direct heat from the longwave radiation emitted by Earth's surface.

68. (C): The logical and meaningful sequence is: Advertisement (4) is issued first, inviting candidates. Application (5) is then submitted by interested individuals. Interview (1) is conducted for shortlisted candidates. Selection (3) is made from interviewees, and finally, Appointment (2) is given to the selected candidate. This sequence represents the real-world process of recruitment in the oorrect chronological order.

69. (C): The Indira Gandhi Canal is the longest canal in India, stretching over 650 kilometers. It originates from the Harike Barrage at the confluence of the Sutlej and Beas rivers in Punjab and irrigates the northwestern regions of Rajasthan. It was constructed to transform the arid Thar Desert into cultivable land, making it a significant irrigation infrastructure project in India.

71. (B): Analyse the motion of Mohan step by step:

- First he walked 20 m in the north direction. Let the initial position be (0, 0) the new position will be: (0, 20)
- Then he turned left and walked 10 m, i.e., in the west direction. New position: (–10, 20)
- Then he turned right and walked 20 m, i.e., in the north direction. New position: (–10, 40)
- Then again turning right he walked 10 m, i.e., in the east direction. New position: (0, 40)

Now the distance between Mohan's nitial position, (0, 0) and final position (0, 40):

Distance $= \sqrt{(0-0)^2+(40-0)^2} = \sqrt{0+1600} = \sqrt{1600}$

$= 40$ M

So the correct answer is: B : 40 m

72. (B): This match is incorrect. Bhagwan Mahavir National Park is located in Goa, not Bihar. It is known for its rich biodiversity and the famous Dudhsagar Falls. The other options are correctly matched: Guindy National Park is in Tamil Nadu, and Balpakram National Park is in Meghalaya. Hence, the correct answer is B.

73. (C): In the question, three lines are given, each line contains four numbers. Let us analyse the argument according to the third line:

Third line:

2 3 75 ×

Now, based on the first two numbers, the third number 75 is given. If we see:

$2 \times 3 = 6$

Now, $75 - 6 = 69$

No clear argument follows. Now let us try to get the fourth term × by multiplying the first two numbers:

First row:

$4 \times 3 = 12 \Rightarrow 12 \times 1 = 12$

(Here the last term is 12, fits correctly)

Second row:

$6 \times 5 = 30 \Rightarrow 30 \times 1.66 = 50$

(Here the last term is 50, fits correctly)

Third row:

$2 \times 3 = 6$

$\Rightarrow$ Now if we do 6×8.33, we get 50

This shows that the third row is also made in the same ratio.

So, × = 50 is the most appropriate and logical number.

So the correct answer is: C: 50

74. (B): The reversal of the Partition of Bengal was announced in 1911 during the tenure of Lord Hardinge (Hardinge II), who served as the Viceroy of India from 1910 to 1916. The partition, initially carried out in 1905 by Lord Curzon, had led to widespread protests, especially in Bengal. The British government, facing strong opposition and the Swadeshi movement, decided to annul the partition in 1911 during the Delhi Durbar under Lord Hardinge.

75. (D): The sonar technique (Sound Navigation and Ranging) is primarily used to measure the depth of the sea, but it is also effectively used to locate underwater hills, submerged objects, and even icebergs in some advanced applications. Sonar works by emitting sound pulses and measuring their echo time after hitting an object. Hence, options A and C are both correct, making option D the correct choice.

76. (C): Insectivorous plants, like the pitcher plant and Venus flytrap, are primarily autotrophic and conduct photosynthesis, which places them in the producer trophic level. While they do trap and digest insects to obtain nitrogen and other nutrients from poor soil environments, their energy source remains sunlight. Thus, trophically, they are considered producers, not consumers.

77. (B): Just as "precaution" helps in preventing "accidents", similarly, "cleanliness" helps in preventing "illness". The relationship is one of preventive action and outcome. While a doctor treats illness and pollution may cause it, cleanliness is directly related to its prevention, making it the most analogous pair in logic and structure.

78. (C): Let the original number be 100. Decreasing it by 5% gives $100 - 5 = 95$

Then increasing 95 by 10%:

10% of 95 = 9.5,

so, new number = 95 + 9.5 = 104.5.

Now, compare with the original:

104.5 – 100 = 4.5,

which is a 4.5% increase from the original value.

79. (C): The Congress Socialist Party (CSP) was formed in May 1934 within the Indian National Congress by socialist leaders like Acharya Narendra Deva and Jayaprakash Narayan. The objective was to promote socialist principles within the broader nationalist movement. It played an influential role in mobilizing youth and workers in the independence struggle.

80. (A): Avirat's position from the front is 25th in a class of 50 students. To find his position from the last, subtract his position from the total and add 1:

Position from the last = 50 − 25 + 1 = 26th.

Therefore, Avirat is 26th from the last, making option A the correct answer.

81. (E): In December 2023, a record number of MPs (over 140) were suspended from the Indian Parliament during the Winter Session, primarily from opposition parties, for disrupting proceedings. However, the specific figures mentioned in the options — 16 DMK MPs, 13 TMC MPs, and 41 Congress MPs — do not individually or collectively represent accurate official tallies, as the exact suspensions were not officially attributed in this breakdown by party. Therefore, none of the individual statements A, B, or C is verifiably correct, making E the correct answer.

82. (C): Gopal Krishna Gokhale was considered the political guru of Mahatma Gandhi. Gandhi himself acknowledged this in his writings, referring to Gokhale as his mentor who guided him during his early political career in India. Gokhale was a moderate nationalist, a senior leader of the Indian National Congress, and a founder of the Servants of India Society. His ideals deeply influenced Gandhi's philosophy of nonviolent resistance.

83. (D): Mulching is a method of covering the soil with organic (e.g., straw, leaves) or inorganic (e.g., plastic) material. It has multiple benefits: it helps reduce weed growth by blocking sunlight, improves soil fertility by adding nutrients when organic mulch decomposes, and conserves soil moisture by reducing evaporation. Since all options A, B, and C are correct, the correct answer is D: More than one of the above.

84. (C): We are given

$\sqrt{4489} = 67$

Now we have to find:

$\sqrt{44.89} + \sqrt{0.4489} + \sqrt{0.004489} + \sqrt{0.00004489}$

Now note that all the numbers are decimals forms of 4489. So we can write then as follows:

1. $\sqrt{44.89} = \sqrt{\dfrac{4489}{100}} = \dfrac{67}{10} = 6.7$
2. $\sqrt{0.4489} = \sqrt{\dfrac{4489}{10000}} = \dfrac{67}{100} = 0.67$
3. $\sqrt{0.004489} = \sqrt{\dfrac{4489}{1000000}} = \dfrac{67}{1000} = 0.067$
4. $\sqrt{0.00004489} = \sqrt{\dfrac{4489}{100000000}} = \dfrac{67}{10000} = 0.0067$

Now add:

6.7 + 0.67 + 0.067 + 0.0067 = 7.4437

So the correct answer is C: 7.4437.

85. (A): The Voter Verified Paper Audit Trail (VVPAT) system was first introduced in India in 2013 during a by-election in the Noksen Assembly constituency of Nagaland. It was implemented by the Election Commission of India as an additional layer of verifiability to Electronic Voting Machines (EVMs), allowing voters to verify that their votes are cast as intended. Its successful trial paved the way for broader adoption in future elections.

86. (A): Neelam Sanjeeva Reddy was the first and only President of India elected unopposed in 1977. No other candidate filed nominations against him, making it a unanimous election by default. He had earlier served as the Speaker of the Lok Sabha and was a prominent leader of the Janata Party. His unopposed election was a historic event in Indian presidential history.

87. (C): The ciliary muscles in the human eye are responsible for changing the shape of the eye's lens, thereby adjusting its focal length. This process, known as accommodation, allows the eye to focus on objects at varying distances. Neither the pupil nor the cornea changes the focal length; the pupil regulates light entry, and the cornea provides initial light refraction but is fixed in shape.

88. (A): The word PAINTER cannot be formed from the letters of CARPENTER. Although many letters are common, PAINTER requires the letter "I", which does not appear in the word "CARPENTER". On the other hand, the words CARPET, REPENT can be formed using available letters. Therefore, A is the correct choice.

89. (A): The West Bengal Government has planned to develop a Tea Park along the banks of the Hooghly River. The initiative is aimed at enhancing tea processing, packaging, storage, and export facilities in the region. The location was strategically chosen for its connectivity and proximity to ports, which facilitates trade logistics for tea producers.

90. (A): The given set is (6, 18, 54).

Check the pattern:

18 ÷ 6 = 3, and 54 ÷ 18 = 3 → Each term is multiplied by 3 to get the next.

Apply this rule to the options:

A. (15, 45, 135) → 45 ÷ 15 = 3, 135 ÷ 45 = 3 → follows the same pattern.

B. (20, 30, 40) → 30 ÷ 20 = 1.5, 40 ÷ 30 ≈ 1.33 → does not follow the pattern.

C. (12, 24, 72) → 24 ÷ 12 = 2, 72 ÷ 24 = 3 → inconsistent multiplier, so not valid.

Thus, only A follows the rule, making option A the correct answer.

91. (B): If a sum of money becomes seven times in 24 years, it means that:

Simple interest = 6 times the principal (because total amount = principal + interest = 7P ⇒ interest = 6P)

Now,

Formula of simple interest:

$$SI = \frac{P \times R \times T}{100} \Rightarrow 6P = \frac{P \times R \times 24}{100} \Rightarrow 6 = \frac{24R}{100}$$

$$\Rightarrow R = \frac{600}{24} = 25\%$$

So the annual rate is 25%.

92. **(A):** If day before yesterday was Monday, then: Yesterday was Tuesday, today is Wednesday, tomorrow is Thursday, and day after tomorrow is Friday.
Hence, the correct answer is Friday.

93. **(B):** Pir Panjal - Zaskar - Ladakh - Karakoram: The correct south to north sequence of the Himalayan ranges is:
Pir Panjal (southernmost) → Zaskar → Ladakh → Karakoram (northernmost and along the India-China border).
This order follows their geographical positions in the Trans-Himalayan region and Greater Himalayas, making option B correct.

94. **(B):** Tungsten is used in electric bulbs because of its very high melting point (about 3422°C) and good electrical conductivity. This makes it ideal for use in the filament of incandescent bulbs, where it glows without melting. Tungsten is not used as an insulator or directly for metal extraction, making B the correct option.

95. **(D):** More than one of the above:
Statement 1 is true – Aditya L1 reached Lagrange Point 1 (L1) on 6 January 2024, marking India's first solar observatory mission successfully entering its operational orbit.
Statement 2 is false – The sentence is grammatically incorrect ("It have" should be "It has"), and while Aditya L1 does carry seven payloads, the phrasing invalidates it in formal assessments.
Statement 3 is true – Aditya L1 carries a magnetometer mounted on its deck to measure magnetic field fluctuations in the solar wind.
Statement 4 is true – The Visible Emission Line Coronograph (VELC) aboard Aditya L1 is designed to send around 1440 images daily to monitor solar corona activity.
Since statements 1, 3, and 4 are correct, the right answer is D: More than one of the above.

96. **(B):** The special symbol × given in the question does not mean ordinary multiplication but the unit digit of the product of the numbers is taken.
Check:
$6 \times 7 = 42 \rightarrow$ Last digit $= 2$
$3 \times 5 = 15 \rightarrow$ Last digit $= 5$
$5 \times 8 = 40 \rightarrow$ Last digit $= 0$
Now, apply the same rule:
$6 \times 8 = 48 \rightarrow$ Last digit $= 8$
So the correct answer is: B: 8.

97. **(A):** Given:
Visitors on Sundays = 680
Visitors on other days = 332
Month has 30 days, and the 1st is Sunday
So there are 5 Sundays (days 1, 8, 15, 22, 29)
Remaining 25 days are weekdays

$$\text{Total visitors} = (5 \times 680) + (25 \times 332) = 3400 + 8300 = 11{,}700$$

Average daily visitors = 11,700 ÷ 30 = 390.

98. **(A):** The Tamil Nadu Coast receives most of its rainfall during the winter season due to the retreating (or northeast) monsoon, which is the return flow of the South-west Monsoon winds. As these winds pass over the Bay of Bengal and reach Tamil Nadu, they pick up moisture and cause rainfall. Western Disturbances affect North and Northwest India during winter and do not significantly impact Tamil Nadu. Thus, the correct answer is A.

99. **(C):** Series: 17, 27, 38, 50, 63, ?
Let's find the pattern by calculating the differences:
$27 - 17 = 10$
$38 - 27 = 11$
$50 - 38 = 12$
$63 - 50 = 13$
The differences are increasing by 1:
10, 11, 12, 13...
So the next difference should be 14
$63 + 14 = 77$
So the next term is 77
Correct answer: C: 77

100. **(B):** Afforestation, or planting of trees, is one of the most effective methods to prevent flooding. Tree roots hold soil in place, increase water absorption, reduce runoff, and stabilize the water cycle. In contrast, deforestation increases flood risk, and grazing contributes to land degradation. Therefore, the best preventive method for floods among the options is B: Afforestation.

101. **(A):** Since 26 January 1950, a total of 23 individuals have served as Chief Ministers of Bihar. This count includes leaders who have held the position multiple times, such as Nitish Kumar, but each person is counted only once regardless of the number of terms served. The first Chief Minister after India's transition to a republic was Shri Krishna Sinha, who served from 26 January 1950 until 31 January 1961. As of early 2024, Nitish Kumar is the incumbent Chief Minister, having held the office multiple times since 2000. Therefore, the correct answer is A: Only 23 people.

102. **(B):** According to the question,
Area of a circle with radius 8 m

$$= \pi r^2 = \pi \times 64 = 64\pi$$

The area of the triangle is $= 36\pi$

$$\text{Sum} = 64\pi + 36\pi = 100\pi$$

Now this area is equal to a new cycle, whose area

$$A = \pi R^2 = 100\pi$$

$$\Rightarrow \quad R^2 = 100 \Rightarrow R = 10$$

So the diameter $= 2R = 20$ m.

103. (A): The correct term for animals that live in desert environments is "Deserticolous". It comes from the Latin root "colous", meaning dwelling or inhabiting. These animals have specific adaptations like water retention, nocturnal habits, and heat resistance to survive arid climates. The other terms like "Desertimals" and "Desertimalia" are not scientifically recognized or standard biological classifications.

104. (D): The Bihar Caste Survey 2023 revealed the following major caste-wise population data: Upper Castes account for 15.52%, Scheduled Castes and Scheduled Tribes together make up 21.33%, and Backward Castes (including EBCs and OBCs) form the majority with 63.14%. Since all three statements (A, B, and C) are accurate as per the official caste survey report, the correct answer is D: More than one of the above.

105. (A): The Indian National Army (INA) trials began in November 1945 at the Red Fort, Delhi, where three officers — Shah Nawaz Khan, Prem Kumar Sehgal, and Gurbaksh Singh Dhillon — were tried for treason against the British Crown. These trials were highly publicized and evoked strong nationalist sentiments across India, intensifying the demand for independence. Hence, 1945 is the correct year, making A the right choice.

106. (C): $a^2 + b^2 + c^2 - bc - ca - ab$

To solve this question, we have to use an important algebraic identity:

$$a^3 + b^3 + c^3 - 3abc = (a + b + c)(a^2 + b^2 + c^2 - ab - bc - ca)$$

Now, if we divide this polynomial by $a + b + c$, there will be no remainder and the quotient will be:

$$\frac{a^3 + b^3 + c^3 - 3abc}{a+b+c} = a^2 + b^2 + c^2 - ab - bc - ca$$

This is exactly in the same form as given in option C (though the order of terms is changed, the mathematical value remains the same)

So, the correct answer is C: $a^2 + b^2 + c^2 - bc - ca - ab$.

107. (B): According to the given order:

P is to the right of Q ⇒ Q...P

T is to the left of Q but to the right of R ⇒ R...T...Q

P is to the left of S ⇒ P...S

Now add all;

R–T–Q–P–S (all facing north(

Third in the middle is : Q

So, correct answe is B: Q.

108. (C): On 25 February 2024, India and Japan commenced the fifth edition of their joint military exercise named Dharma Guardian at the Mahajan Field Firing Range in Rajasthan. This annual exercise aims to enhance military cooperation and interoperability between the Indian Army and the Japan Ground Self-Defense Force (JGSDF). The 2024 edition focused on joint operations in semi-urban environments, including tactical drills, intelligence sharing, and heliborne operations, under the framework of the United Nations Charter.

109. (D): More than one of the above: Crops like Water Chestnut (Trapa natans), Lotus (Nelumbo nucifera), and Fox Nut (Euryale ferox) are typically cultivated in still or slow-moving water bodies such as ponds and lakes. These aquatic plants require stable water conditions for optimal growth. Fast-moving river waters are unsuitable for their cultivation due to factors like strong currents and fluctuating water levels, which can disrupt their growth and anchorage.

110. (C): Total marks:

Hindi = 120, English = 140,

Mathematics = 100, Science = 180

Total marks = 120 + 140 + 100 + 180 = 540

Marks obtained:

Hindi: 120 × 0.4 = 48

English: 140 × 0.55 = 77

Mathematics: 100 × 0.45 = 45

Total in all three = 48 + 77 + 45 = 170

Total required to get 60%: 540 × 0.6 = 324

In Science required = 324 – 170 = 154

So, correct answer C: 154.

111. (D): Padmashree Ushakiran Khan is a renowned writer who has contributed significantly to both Hindi and Maithili literature. She received the Sahitya Akademi Award in 2011 (for her Maithili novel Sirjanhaar), and was also honored with Bharat Bharati Award in 2019, a top literary award from the Bihar government. Her known works include "Maithili – Kachahi Bans" and "Anuttarit Prashna" in Hindi. Therefore, more than one of the listed achievements are correct, making D the right answer.

112. (A): The 73rd and 74th Amendments to the Indian Constitution, which gave constitutional status to Panchayati Raj and Municipalities respectively, came into effect in 1993. These landmark reforms were enacted under the leadership of Prime Minister P.V. Narasimha Rao, who served from 1991 to 1996. These amendments significantly empowered local governance through decentralization.

113. (A): Rust is the reddish-brown substance formed on iron or steel by oxidation in the presence of moisture. Chemically, it is hydrated ferric oxide, typically written as $Fe_2O_3.xH_2O$. It forms through a redox reaction where iron reacts with oxygen and water. Ferrous oxide (FeO) or dry ferric oxide (Fe_2O_3) without water does not qualify as rust, confirming that A is correct.

114. (A): In the English alphabet, to find the opposite letter to 'P', count its position:

P is the 16th letter from the start. The alphabet has 26 letters, so the opposite position is:

27 – 16 = 11, which is the 11th letter, i.e., K.

So, K is opposite to P in terms of symmetrical position from the start and end of the alphabet.

115. (C): Madhya Pradesh has the largest teak forest cover in India. The climatic and soil conditions in this central Indian state are highly suitable for teak (Tectona grandis) growth. The forests of Jabalpur, Balaghat, Mandla, and Chhindwara districts are particularly rich in natural teak. Other states like Maharashtra and Chhattisgarh also grow teak, but MP has the maximum area under its cover.

116. (C): In lichens, algae (or cyanobacteria) and fungi live together in a mutualistic relationship. The algae perform photosynthesis and provide nutrients (carbohydrates) to the fungi, while the fungi offer protection, moisture, and minerals to the algae. Both partners benefit from this association, which is the defining feature of mutualism. Hence, the correct answer is C: Mutualism.

117. (B): The area of the rectangle $= l \times b = 30$

Perimeter $= 2(l + b) = 26 \Rightarrow l + b = 13$

Now $l + b = 13$ and $lb = 30$

This is the equation of two unknowns:

Let, $l = x$, Then, $b = 13 - x$

Therefore,

$x(13 - x) = 30 \Rightarrow 13x - x^2 = 30$

$\Rightarrow x^2 - 13x + 30 = 0$

Quadratic equation

$x^2 - 13x + 30 = 0 \Rightarrow x = 10$ or $x = 3$

So the length = 10 cm (since the length is greater)

Therefore, the correct answer is:B

118. (D): More than one of the above: Hydrophytes are plants adapted to grow in water or very moist environments. They often lack mechanical tissue because water provides natural support. They also possess aerenchyma, a spongy tissue that contains large air spaces to facilitate buoyancy and gas exchange. However, they generally do not have a well-developed vascular system since water is readily available and does not need to be transported over long distances. Therefore, both A and B are correct, making D the correct option.

119. (B): The Language Atlas of India, created by the Indira Gandhi National Centre for the Arts, is a language mapping project based on comprehensive speech surveys across the country. It visually represents the distribution, diversity, and geographical spread of languages and dialects spoken in India. It is not an ethnic or natural map but focuses specifically on linguistic information, so B is the accurate choice.

120. (C): Convex mirrors are used in the rearview mirrors of vehicles because they diverge light rays, providing a wider field of view. This allows drivers to see more of the traffic behind them than flat or concave mirrors would. They also produce erect, diminished images, which are useful for observing multiple objects at a glance. Therefore, C is the correct answer.

121. (D): India's foreign policy is fundamentally grounded in the principles of peace and non-violence, inspired by Mahatma Gandhi's ideology. The Panchsheel principles, signed with China in 1954, reflect this vision of peaceful coexistence. Additionally, India was one of the founding members of the Non-Aligned Movement (NAM) during the Cold War, promoting independence from superpower influence. Hence, all statements A, B, and C are correct, and the right answer is D.

122. (A): Kargil, located in the Union Territory of Ladakh, lies on the banks of the Suru River, a tributary of the Indus. The river originates from the Panzella glacier and flows through the Zanskar range. It is an important river for the region's agriculture and settlements. Kargil is not situated on the Jhelum or main Indus rivers, so A is the correct choice.

123. (A): A does the work in 15 days

$\Rightarrow$ Per day capacity of A = 1/15

B does the work in 8 days $\Rightarrow$ Per day capacity of B = 1/8

B + C together in 4 days $\Rightarrow$ B + C = 1/4

Now, C = 1/4 − 1/8 = 1/8

$\Rightarrow$ C also does the work alone in 8 days

Now:

$$A + C = 1/15 + 1/8 = \frac{8+15}{120} = \frac{23}{120}$$

$$\Rightarrow \quad x = 120/23$$

$$A + B = 1/15 + 1/8 = \frac{8+15}{120} = \frac{23}{120}$$

$$\Rightarrow \quad y = 120/23$$

Then $$x/y = \frac{120/23}{120/23} = 1$$

Hence correct answer: A.

124. (D): More than one of the above: Prime Minister Lal Bahadur Shastri faced several major national challenges during his short tenure. He dealt with severe food shortages, promoting the "Jai Jawan Jai Kisan" slogan to boost both agriculture and defense. He also led India during the 1965 war with Pakistan, a crucial event testing India's sovereignty. Additionally, there was the Anti-Hindi agitation in South India, especially in Tamil Nadu, opposing the imposition of Hindi. Since all these challenged India's unity and development goals, the correct option is D: More than one of the above.

125. (C): The National Aeronautics and Space Administration (NASA) and other partners like the European Space Agency (ESA) have begun allowing private companies to send tourists to the International Space Station (ISS). Companies from countries such as Italy, Turkey, and Sweden have collaborated or sent astronauts on private missions through agencies like Axiom Space. Countries listed in other options do not have operational capabilities or agreements for such missions. Hence, C is the correct answer.

126. (B): SPM stands for Suspended Particulate Matter, which includes microscopic solid or liquid particles suspended in air. These particles, such as dust, soot, and smoke, are major pollutants and are tracked to assess air quality and manage air pollution control measures. They pose serious health risks when inhaled, especially for respiratory and cardiovascular systems. Thus, B is the correct option.

127. (A): A food chain is a linear sequence showing how energy and nutrients flow from producers to consumers. In this chain:

Grass is the producer,

Deer is the primary consumer (herbivore), and

Tiger is the secondary consumer (carnivore).

This is a valid and complete food chain. Other options contain mismatched or non-linear links, so A is correct.

128. (C): The Wahabi movement, an Islamic revivalist movement in India during the 19th century, found its main center in Bihar at Patna. Under the leadership of Syed Ahmed Barelvi and Vilayat Ali, the movement gained momentum in Patna, which became the key hub for its organizational and ideological activities. Champaran and Jagdishpur had other historical importance, but not specifically for Wahabi activities. Therefore, C is correct.

129. (B): The Iron Pillar of Delhi, located in the Qutub Minar complex, is an ancient metallurgical marvel dating back to the 4th century CE, during the reign of Chandragupta II. It stands about 7.2 meters tall and is notable for its high resistance to corrosion despite being over 1600 years old. This enduring quality showcases the advanced scientific knowledge in metallurgy possessed by ancient Indian craftsmen.

130. (A): India's economic liberalization began in 1991, under the leadership of Prime Minister P.V. Narasimha Rao and Finance Minister Dr. Manmohan Singh. Faced with a balance of payments crisis, the Indian government introduced major reforms such as deregulation, reduction in import tariffs, and promotion of foreign investment. These steps marked the beginning of a market-oriented economy, making 1991 the turning point for India's economic policy.

131. (C): The Brahmo Samaj, founded by Raja Ram Mohan Roy in 1828, aimed to reform religious practices and promote monotheism. Its teachings appealed primarily to the urban educated middle class, particularly in Calcutta and other urban centers of Bengal. Its influence was minimal in rural areas due to the traditionalism and illiteracy prevalent in those regions, making C the most accurate description.

133. (D): The ethnic violence in Manipur starting from 3 May 2023 stemmed from multiple intertwined reasons, primarily surrounding the demand by the Meitei community for Scheduled Tribe status, which many Kuki and Naga groups opposed, fearing dilution of their existing rights in education, jobs, and land. The issue also touches upon resource competition and long-standing ethnic distrust, making D: More than one of the above the appropriate answer.

134. (B): The Bharatiya Janata Party (BJP) is known for its strong ideological emphasis on Hindu nationalism (Hindutva) and building the national identity primarily on the basis of cultural and historical unity. This nationalist approach is central to its political messaging and policies. While other parties emphasize secularism, socialism, or pluralism, it is BJP that most directly aligns with nationalism as the foundational political ideology.

135. (C): Rhombus is characterized by the fact that all its four sides are equal tand the two diagonals bisect each other at right angles. Here the lengths of the diagonals are given:

$$\text{One diagonal} = 2a$$

$$\text{The other diagonal} = 2b$$

Each side is joined by half of the diagonals to form a right-angled triangle,

Then, $\text{Side} = \sqrt{a^2+b^2}$

Hence, $\text{Perimeter} = 4 \times \sqrt{a^2+b^2}$

Hence the correct answer is: C: $4\sqrt{a^2+b^2}$

136. (B): Prime Minister Narendra Modi inaugurated the Sudarshan Setu on February 25, 2024. This 2.32 km-long cable-stayed bridge connects Okha mainland to Beyt Dwarka island in Gujarat's Devbhumi Dwarka district. Constructed at a cost of approximately ₹ 980 crore, it is India's longest cable-stayed bridge. The bridge features a unique design with footpaths adorned with verses from the Bhagavad Gita and images of Lord Krishna, along with solar panels generating one megawatt of electricity.

137. (C): In a food chain, producers, such as green plants and algae, occupy the first trophic level and have the highest energy content. They convert solar energy into chemical energy through photosynthesis, forming the base of the energy pyramid. As energy is transferred to higher trophic levels (herbivores, carnivores), approximately 90% is lost at each level due to metabolic processes, leaving producers with the most energy.

138. (B): Vinegar is an acidic solution containing acetic acid. Acids have the property of turning blue litmus paper red. Therefore, when blue litmus paper is introduced to vinegar, it changes color to red, indicating the presence of an acid. In contrast, substances like washing soda and baking soda are basic and would turn red litmus paper blue.

139. (C): India shares its longest international boundary with Bangladesh, stretching approximately 4,096 kilometers. This extensive border spans several Indian states, including West Bengal, Assam, Meghalaya, Tripura, and Mizoram. In comparison, India's border with Pakistan is about 3,323 kilometers, and with Nepal, it's around 1,751 kilometers.

140. (A): Son River Valley Project is one of the oldest canal project of India.

- It was started during the British rule and the Son Canal system was started in 1878.
- This scheme is mainly spread in Rohtas, Aurangabad and Bhojpur districts.
- It is considered to be the oldest river valley project of Bihar.

Damodar Valley Project was established on 7 July, 1948 by the Government of India and the then Government of Bihar and Bengal.

- This scheme was inspired by the US and its objective was flood control, power generation and irrigation.

- The initial dams like Tilaiya (1953), Konar (1955), Maithan (1957) were built in Jharkhand (then part of Bihar)
- Therefore, its operation and benefits have also been related to Bihar.

Thus both the schemes come under the major and old river valley projects of Bihar.

The correct anwer is D: more than one of the above

141. (C): The given equations are:

1. $2x + 3y = 77$
2. $3x + 2y = 73$

To solve them, solve both the equations:

Step 1: Multiply equation (1) by 3 and equation (2) by 2 so that the coefficients are equal:

1. $6x + 9y = 231$
2. $6x + 4y = 146$

Now subtract:

$(6x + 9y) - (6x + 4y) = 231 - 146 \Rightarrow 5y = 85 \Rightarrow y = 17$

Now substitute $y = 17$ in any of the original equations:

$2x + 3 \times 17 = 77 \Rightarrow 2x + 51 = 77 \Rightarrow 2x = 26 \Rightarrow x = 13$

So Answer: $x = 13$, $y = 17$

So correct answer: C.

142. (A): The 42nd Amendment Act of 1976, enacted during the Emergency period under Prime Minister Indira Gandhi, is often referred to as the "Mini-Constitution" due to its sweeping changes. It curtailed the powers of the judiciary by making the Parliament's laws virtually beyond judicial review in certain areas, particularly concerning the Directive Principles. This amendment attempted to make the judiciary subservient to the Parliament, leading to a significant shift in the balance of power, hence A is the correct answer.

143. (D): China claims multiple regions as part of its "sacred territory". These include Tibet, which it annexed in 1951; Taiwan, which it considers a breakaway province despite its independent government; and Macau, which is now a Special Administrative Region under Chinese sovereignty but was once a Portuguese colony. Among these, both Tibet and Taiwan are particularly emphasized in China's nationalistic narrative and territorial integrity claims, so D: More than one of the above is correct.

144. (A): A savanna is a type of grassland ecosystem characterized by grasses interspersed with scattered trees or shrubs. It typically occurs in regions with a distinct dry and wet season, such as in parts of Africa, South America, and Australia. The tree density is low enough not to form a closed canopy, allowing sunlight to reach the ground and support grass growth. Therefore, A is the correct answer.

145. (E): The Indian National Congress (INC) was founded in 1885 by Allan Octavian Hume, a retired British civil servant, with the support of Indian leaders like Dadabhai Naoroji and Dinshaw Wacha. Though the listed individuals were prominent nationalists, none of them actually founded the Congress. Hence, the correct answer is E: None of the above.

146. (A): Simplify the expression given in the question first:

$$\frac{2\left((467+359)^2 - 2\times 467\times 359\right)}{467^2+359^2}$$

Let us recognize the part above:

$(467 + 359)^2 = 467^2 + 359^2 + 2.\ 467.\ 359$

So the whole part above will become:

$2\ (467^2 + 359^2 + 2.\ 467.\ 359 - 2.\ 467.\ 359)$

$= 2(467^2 + 359^2)$

Now complete fraction

$$\frac{2(467^2+359^2)}{467^2+359^2} = 2$$

Therefore, the correct answer is: A: 2.

147. (B): The Preamble to the Constitution of India guarantees Justice - social, economic, and political to all citizens. This concept of justice ensures that individuals are not discriminated against on social or economic grounds and are protected by the legal system. It also includes access to basic rights like equality, liberty, and fair legal treatment. Hence, the correct interpretation aligning with the Preamble is B: To have certain basic rights.

148. (B): Among the northeastern states of India, Mizoram has the highest concentration of tribal population, with over 94% of its residents belonging to Scheduled Tribes, as per Census data. Although states like Nagaland and Meghalaya also have high tribal percentages, Mizoram ranks the highest in terms of proportion of tribal population to total population, making B the correct answer.

149. (D): Both the Pyramid of Number and Pyramid of Biomass can be either upright or inverted, depending on the ecosystem. For example, in a grassland ecosystem, both pyramids are usually upright. But in a forest (where one tree supports many herbivores) or aquatic ecosystem (where biomass of producers is less than primary consumers), these pyramids can become inverted. Pyramid of Energy, however, is always upright due to the unidirectional flow of energy. Therefore, the correct answer is D: More than one of the above.

150. (B): The Atal Setu, also known as the Mumbai Trans Harbour Link (MTHL), is India's longest sea bridge, connecting Mumbai with Navi Mumbai. It was inaugurated in January 2024 and spans a total length of 21.8 kilometers, including approach roads. This bridge is a major infrastructure project aimed at reducing travel time and easing congestion. Thus, the correct answer is B: 21.8 kilometers.

English Language

1

Comprehension Passages

ENGLISH LANGUAGE COMPREHENSION

The objective of language comprehension test is to ascertain the ability of the candidates to understand the passage properly.

Therefore candidates are required to take notice of the following points:

1. Read the full passage very attentively and intelligently.
2. Try to comprehend the gist of it.
3. Make a mental note of all the important details and points given in the passage.
4. Read the passage for the second time in case you have not been able to understand it satisfactorily.
5. Divide the time proportionately for all the passages.
6. Answer the questions on the basis of facts, as given in the paragraph.
7. Don't waste much time in answering the questions of any one passage.
8. Check all the answers once again, very carefully, to see whether any question is left unanswered by mistake.

MODEL QUESTIONS (FOR PRACTICE)

Directions: *Each of the following passages is followed by five questions. Read the passage carefully and then answer the questions that follow each. For each question, four probable answers A, B, C and D are given. Only one out of these is correct. Choose the correct answer.*

PASSAGE-1

The use of words like 'welcome', 'thank you', 'please', etc., at the right moment reflects a polite nature. The civic sense also lies within the scope of good manners. We should not shout or talk loudly in public places like hospitals and libraries and create disturbance. We should not cheat people or make fun of them. Cleanliness is also necessary. We must not throw the waste on roads and make use of dustbins. We should not harm the public property as it belongs to all of us. While in a queue, discipline should be maintained. We must give fair chance to others.

1. Expressions like 'welcome' 'thank you' and 'please' reflect
   A. happiness B. discipline
   C. civic sense D. polite nature
2. While in a library, we should
   A. respect others B. avoid arguments
   C. talk in low tone D. be courteous
3. A public property belongs to
   A. nobody B. all of us
   C. government D. one who maintains it
4. Discipline is
   A. the rule of proper conduct or action
   B. the rule of road sense
   C. making use of dustbins
   D. forming a queue
5. The most appropriate title for this passage would be
   A. Polite Nature B. Courtesy
   C. Good Manners D. Civic Sense

PASSAGE-2

There is an old proverb 'Early to bed and early to rise makes a man healthy and wise.' I am in the habit of getting up early in the morning and have formed the habit of taking long morning walks in the past two years. It is a light exercise and best for physical fitness. The morning air which is fresh and pure is beneficial for the lungs. The early rays of the rising sun are good for healthy skin. 'Health is wealth' and doctors also recommend morning walk to their patients for gaining sound health and freshness of energy.

1. What is good for lungs?
   A. Sunrays B. Fresh air
   C. Sound sleep D. Light exercise
2. What is a light exercise?
   A. Early to bed B. Early to rise
   C. Morning walk D. Gaining sound health
3. What is good for skin?
   A. Fresh air B. Morning air
   C. Morning walk D. Rising sun's rays
4. What is best for physical fitness?
   A. Light exercise B. Long morning walk
   C. Early to rise D. Fresh and pure air
5. Long morning walk
   A. bring sound sleep
   B. ensures physical fitness
   C. ensures healthy skin
   D. keeps healthy, wealthy and wise

PASSAGE-3

Mahatma Gandhi lived a splendid long life and has set great moral standards before us. He showed to the world the true way to peace. He wished to see India prosper but he became a martyr for the noble cause of Hindu-Muslim unity at the time of partition when a religious fanatic, Nathuram Godse, shot him dead on January 30, 1948. His last words were 'Hey Ram'. He lived and died for his country and countryman.

1. Mahatma Gandhi showed the world the true way to
   A. prosperity B. love
   C. truth D. peace
2. Mahatma Gandhi became a martyr for the noble cause of
   A. truth B. non-violence
   C. freedom of India D. Hindu-Muslim unity
3. Mahatma Gandhi was shot dead
   A. before India achieved independence
   B. by a mad man
   C. by an intolerant religious person
   D. by a non-religious person
4. Mahatma Gandhi set great moral standards. It means
   A. he was a great religious teacher
   B. he was a great moralist
   C. he made India morally stronger
   D. moral was everything to him
5. Gandhiji lived and died for his country and countryman. It means
   A. he was born in India and died in India
   B. he was a patriot
   C. he was a great moralist
   D. he sacrified his life for India and her people

PASSAGE-4

On one hot day a crow felt very thirsty. He flew from one place to another in search of water. After long hours of labour he found a pitcher. Eagerly, he perched on the mouth of the pitcher, He found that the water was at the bottom of the vessel. He tried his best to dip his beak but did not succeed. He did not know what to do. Suddenly some pebbles lying nearby gave him an idea. One by one he dropped the pebbles with his beak into the pitcher. The level of water slowly came up to the mouth of the pitcher. The crow then drank the water and quenched his thirst.

1. The crow found a pitcher
   A. as it flew
   B. after many hours of labour
   C. full of water
   D. which was empty
2. What is the moral of the passage?
   A. No pains, no gains
   B. God helps those who help themselves
   C. Necessity is the mother of invention
   D. Try and try again, you will succeed at last
3. The crow flew from place to place
   A. in search of pitcher B. in search of pebbles
   C. in search of water D. in search of a vessel
4. The pitcher, the crow found
   A. was full of water
   B. was dry
   C. had little water in the bottom
   D. had water up to its mouth
5. As the crow dropped pebbles into the pitcher, what happend?
   A. The pitcher broke down
   B. The water leaked one of the pitcher
   C. The level of water into the pitcher rose up slowly
   D. Water level immediately rose to the mouth of the pitcher

PASSAGE-5

Once upon a time a crane and a fox lived in a forest. They were good friend. One day the fox invited the crane to a feast. He made a tasty food and served it before the crane on a plate. The crane could not eat anything because of the long beak. But the fox licked all his food. The crane felt insulted. He decided to teach the fox a lesson. Next day he invited the fox. He prepared the same tasty food and placed it in front of the fox inside a narrow glass. The crane ate easily while the fox looked on. Now, it was the fox's turn to remain hungry.

1. What is the moral of the passage?
   A. Beware of the wicked
   B. One good turn deserves another
   C. Be contented with what you have
   D. Tit for tat
2. The crane could not eat tasty food because the
   A. food was served in a shallow plate
   B. food was very hot
   C. food was served in a long jar
   D. crane was not hungry
3. The fox had to remain hungry because
   A. the food served was not enough in quantity
   B. the food was served inside a narrow glass
   C. the food served was not tasty
   D. the food was all liquid
4. Why did the crane feel insulted?
   A. Because he was invited to feast but he could not eat anything
   B. Because the food was served in a shallow plate and he could not eat
   C. Because the food was too hot
   D. Because the fox gulped all the food quickly
5. The crane successfully taught a lesson to the fox when he invited the fox to a feast and served the food
   A. in a narrow glass B. in a large plate
   C. in a broken plate D. in a long jar

PASSAGE-6

The family set down at the table and began to talk about the summer holidays. They had to decide a place to visit during the vacation. Should they go to their village or to a hill station? The parents preferred the village while the children wished to go the hill station. After few moments of discussion the elders decided to visit both the places. First they shall go to the village for a week and then stay at the hill station for the remaining days. For the first time the family shall be together during the holidays. The children were happy with the holiday plan.

1. The purpose for which the family set down at the table was
A. to decide a place to visit during the vacation
B. to educate the children how to carry articles during a visit to a hill station
C. to decide the date when they should start their journey
D. to tell the children that they will visit a hill station during this vacation

2. The final plan was to visit
A. their village
B. a hill station
C. their village as well as a hill station
D. their home town

3. The final decision was made by
A. the boys B. the girls
C. the women D. the elders

4. They decided first to go to their village and stay there for
A. a day B. a week
C. ten days D. a fortnight

5. Why were children happy?
A. Because a hill station was included in their holiday plan
B. Because a visit to their village was excluded from their holiday pl...
C. Because their choice prevailed
D. Because they were going all alone to the hill station

PASSAGE-7

Once Govind intended to go on pilgrimage with his family. He asked Mirind to accompany. But for his trade's reason, he did not go with him. So Govind thought it safe to leave the box of his jewellery with him, as it was dangerous to leave it in a lone house or take it on the journey. So he went to him with the box. He took him to a lonely place under a tree and handed it over to him. He told Mirind, "Keep it safe with you. I shall return from the journey after six month then I shall take it back from you." Mirind said, "Don't worry, I shall keep it as safe as own."

1. Govind intended to go
A. for a business trip
B. to a hill station
C. on a long journey to a sacred place
D. to his home town for a long period

2. Why did Govind leave his box of jewellery with Mirind?
A. Because it was not safe to take the box with him on a long journey
B. Because Mirind was his fast friend
C. Because the box was very heavy
D. Because his house was unsafe

3. Why did Govind take Mirind to a lonely place?
A. To tell him that the box contained valuable jewellery
B. So that no third person could see box
C. To show him what was within the box
D. To tell him that the box will remain with him

4. Where did Govind hand over the box of jewellery to Mirind?
A. At Mirind's house
B. At his own house
C. In a lonely place
D. In a lonely place under a tree

5. It was not safe to leave the box in a lone house. Here the word 'lone house' means
A. a house in a deserted place
B. a house where none lives
C. a house without door and lock
D. a house near the forest

PASSAGE-8

Zahir-ud-din Babar was the first Mughal emperor of India. A descendent of Timur on father's side and Changez Khan on his mother's side, Babar was a brave warrior. After defeating Ibrahim Lodhi in the First Battle of Panipat in 1526 he entered Delhi and soon gained control over Agra. After many more battles with Rajputs he extended his empire over Punjab, Uttar Pradesh and north Bihar. He died at a young age of 48 years in 1530 at his capital Agra without getting much time to consolidate his victories.

1. Zahir-ud-din Babar was the first
A. Muslim ruler of India B. Mughal ruler of India
C. Afghan ruler of India D. Turk ruler of India

2. Babar was born in the years
A. 1480 B. 1482
C. 1492 D. 1962

3. Babar first occupied
A. Punjab B. Agra
C. Delhi D. Panipat

4. Babar was a brave warrior. Here brave warrior means
A. courageous soldier B. a kind hearted soldier
C. a clever fighter D. a victorious general

5. Babar extended his empire over Punjab and Uttar Pradesh after many more battles with the
A. Afghans B. Rajputs
C. Mughals D. Lodhies

PASSAGE-9

Our National Flag is tricolour. It has three equal horizontal strips. The strip at the top is saffron, in the middle is white and at the bottom is green. The ratio of width to length of the flag is 2 : 3. In the centre of the white strip is a wheel in navy blue. The wheel represents the *chakra*. Its design is similar to the wheel which appears on the abacus of the Sarnath Lion Capital of Ashoka. Its diameter approximates to the width of the white strip. The wheel has 24 spokes. It was adopted by Constituent Assembly on July 22, 1947. We love our national flag. We respect it. We are ready to sacrifice our life to protect its honour. It represents the nation. So it is a symbol of national honour.

1. In our national flag the wheel is located in the centre of

A. saffron strip B. white strip
C. green strip D. blue strip

2. In our national flag which of the strips is at the bottom in our national flag

A. blue C. saffron
B. white D. green

3. Why do we love our national flag?

A. Because it is tricolour
B. Because it has three strips
C. Because it has a wheel at the centre
D. Because it is a symbol of national honour

4. Our national flag was approved by

A. President
B. Lok Sabha
C. Parliament
D. Constituent Assembly

5. The diameter approximates to the width of the white strip. Here the word 'approximates' means

A. is more or less equal
B. is exactly equal
C. is not equal
D. is related

PASSAGE-10

Distance in large cities are long. All the people do not have their own means of transport. They have to depend upon the state or private buses. The number of bus users is very large. Every bus stop is, therefore, crowded. The number of buses is not adequate. Thus people suffer the torture of long wait at the bus stop. Some bus stops are quite orderly. People form queues and get into the buses turn by turn. However, often this order is forgotten and confusion spreads when the bus comes and the law of jungle prevails.

1. Why are the bus stops crowded?

A. Because they are small is size
B. Because the number of passengers is very large
C. Because they are situated at some busy centre
D. Because people do not form queues

2. Long wait at the bus stop is the result of

A. over-crowding in the buses
B. late running of buses
C. shortage of buses
D. slow speed of buses

3. Some bus stops are quite orderly where

A. there is no crowd
B. the number of buses is adequate
C. people do not have to wait for long
D. people form queues and enter the buses one by one

4. Most of the people who travel by buses are

A. non-working
B. do not have their own vehicles
C. have to go a long distance
D. live in large cities

5. What happens when people do not have their own transport?

A. They have to wait for a bus at a bus stop
B. They have to depend upon the state or private buses
C. They have to travel long distances
D. They form queues and get into buses one by one

ANSWERS

	1	2	3	4	5
Passage 1.	D	C	B	A	C
Passage 2.	B	C	D	B	B
Passage 3.	D	D	C	B	D
Passage 4.	B	C	C	C	C
Passage 5.	D	A	B	B	A
Passage 6.	A	C	D	B	A
Passage 7.	C	A	B	D	B
Passage 8.	B	B	C	A	B
Passage 9.	B	D	D	D	A
Passage 10.	B	C	D	B	B

●●●

2

English Grammar

PARTS OF SPEECH

Part of speech	Definition or Function	Examples
Noun	Name of a person, place, animal, quality or thing	Ram, boy, dog pen, sun, Delhi, truth, honesty
Pronoun	Used in place of a noun	I, you, he she, they
Articles & Determiners	Points out indefinite and definite nouns	a, an, the, few, some
Adjective	Describes a noun or pronoun	big, honest, wooden valuable, quiet, deep, soft, narrow
Adverb	Describes a verb, an adjective or another adverb	silently, widely, softly, quietly, very, carefully
Verb	Tells about action or state of something or someone	is, am, was, have, do, like, walk, work, make, throw, tell
Conjuction	Joins words, clauses or sentences	and, but, when, yet, while, else
Preposition	Links a noun or pronoun to another word	at, to, after, on for, under, over, with
Interjection	Expresses sudden feelings or emotions	Ah!, Alas!, oh!, ouch!, hi!, well!, Hurrah!

NOUNS

A word which denotes a person, a thing, an animal or a place is said to be a noun.

There are two noun numbers in English — the *Singular* and the *Plural*.

Singular Numbers : A noun that denotes one person or one thing, is said to be in the Singular number. For example — book, pencil, bird, dog, hen etc. are in singular number.

Plural Number : A noun that denotes more than one person or one thing is said to be in plural number. For example — boys, pens, lions, girls, men etc. are in plural number.

REMEMBER

Singular	*Plural*	*Singular*	*Plural*
Cat	Cats	Book	Books
Pen	Pens	Room	Rooms
Tree	Trees	Bus	Buses
Bush	Bushes	Box	Boxes
Glass	Glasses	Dish	Dishes
Judge	Judges	Tax	Taxes
Watch	Watches	Calf	Calves
Thief	Thieves	Knife	Knives
Scarf	Scarves	Wife	Wives
Leaf	Leaves	Wolf	Wolves
Half	Halves	Monarch	Monarchs
Roof	Roofs	Hoof	Hoofs
Gulf	Gulfs	Staff	Staffs
Radio	Radios	Bamboo	Bamboos
Folio	Folios	Hero	Heroes
Volcano	Volcanoes	Mango	Mangoes
Potato	Potatoes	Photo	Photos
Piano	Pianos	Baby	Babies
Fly	Flies	Country	Countries
Lady	Ladies	Boy	Boys
Monkey	Monkeys	Ox	Oxen
Child	Children	Man	Men
Woman	Women	Tooth	Teeth
Axis	Axes	Basis	Bases
Foot	Feet	Goose	Geese
Englishman	Englishmen	Radius	Radii
Vertex	Vertices	Stimulus	Stimuli

1. Note the plurals of the following nouns:

Singular	*Plural*	*Singular*	*Plural*
copy	copies	cry	cries
baby	babies	duty	duties
body	bodies	country	countries
family	families	diary	diaries
fly	flies	fairy	fairies
city	cities	spy	spies
army	armies	storey	storeys
bay	bays	monkey	monkeys

2. The following nouns do not undergo any change in plural form, in general.

Singular	*Plural*	*Singular*	*Plural*
deer	deer	sheep	sheep
thousand	thousand	pair	pair
hundred	hundred	score	score
dozen	dozen	gross	gross

Note: We can write—

(*a*) thousands of men; (*b*) two pairs of shoes; (*c*) dozens of mangoes; (*d*) scores of people etc. But—
(*a*) two thousand rupees; (*b*) three hundred men; (*c*) five dozen eggs, etc.

3. The following nouns are usually used in plural forms. They take a plural verb after them—

eatables	fetters	surroundings
riches	alms	spectacles
trousers	pants	scissors
premises	thanks	annals
congratulations	goods	shorts
tongs	pains	arms
breeches	(for troubles)	

4. The following are the nouns which are plural in appearance but are usually used in singular number. They are followed by a singular verb—

news	politics	physics
mathematics	economics	ethics
politics	classics	gallows
statistics	athletics	innings
mechanics	summons	mumps

5. Collective nouns often used as plurals—

public	police	cattle
audience	clergy	folk
people	poultry	nation
elite	gentry	glitterati

6. The nouns that are usually used in singular forms—

advice	hair	rice
fuel	alphabet	machinery
offspring	issue	furniture
mischief	stationery	luggage
bedding	information	abuse

7. Material nouns are always used in singular number—

gold	copper	milk
water	silk	wool

Note: They may be used in plural with a different meaning. copper coins (coppers), chains or fetters (irons), cans made of tin (tins).

GENDERS

The difference in sex is denoted by Gender in grammar. The various genders are as follows :

1. **Masculine Gender :** A noun that denotes a male is said to be of the masculine gender, as man, uncle, ox, boy etc.
2. **Feminine Gender :** A noun that denotes a female is said to be of feminine gender, as woman, aunt, princess, cow etc.
3. **Common Gender :** Nouns which denote both males and females are said to be of the common gender, as friend, cousin, person, parent, baby etc.
4. **Neuter Gender :** A noun that denotes the name of object without life is said to be of neuter gender, as file, table, pencil.

REMEMBER

Masculine	*Feminine*
Boy	Girl
Son	Daughter
Brother	Sister
Murderer	Murderess
Sorcerer	Sorceress
Son-in-law	Daughter-in-law
Father-in-law	Mother-in-law
Man-servant	Maid-servant
Land-lord	Land-lady
Bachelor	Maid
Gentleman	Lady
Monk	Nun
Earl	Countess
Lad	Lass
Sir	Madam
Duke	Dutchess
Emperor	Empress
Milk-man	Milk-maid
Pea-cock	Pea-hen
Step-father	Step-mother
Hero	Heroine
Viceroy	Vicerine
Mr.	Mrs.
Governor	Governess
Master	Mistress
Wizard	Witch
Heir	Heiress
Host	Hostess
Lion	Lioness
Mayor	Mayoress
Actor	Actress
Buck	Doe
Colt	Filly
Dog	Bitch
Horse	Mare
Count	Countess
Hunter	Huntress
Prince	Princess
Abbot	Abbess
God	Goddess
Author	Authoress
Ox	Cow
Widower	Widow
Grand-father	Grand-mother
He-goat	She-goat
Milk-man	Milk-woman
Bridegroom	Bride
Tiger	Tigress
Priest	Priestess
Poet	Poetess
Shepherd	Shepherdess
Nephew	Niece
Stag	Hind

PRONOUNS

The repetition of a noun in a sentence or a set of sentences is really boring. So, instead of repeating the noun, we can use a word (for that noun) called the pronoun.
"A pronoun is a word that we use instead of a noun".

Example:
This is *Sachin. He* plays cricket.
Note: *He* is the pronoun used in place of *Sachin.*

Kinds of Pronouns

1. **Personal pronouns :** A pronoun which is used instead of the name of a person is known as a 'Personal Pronoun'. A list of the 'Personal pronouns' is listed below :

   I, my, mine, me, we (First Person)
   You, your, yours (Second Person)
   He, his, him, she, her, hers, it,
   its, they, their, theirs, them (Third Person)

2. **Demonstrative, Indefinite and Distributive Pronouns :**

   (a) Demonstrative Pronouns : Pronouns used to point out the objects to which they refer are called Demonstrative Pronouns.

   Examples :
   (i) *This* is a present from my uncle.
   (ii) *These* are merely excuses.
   (iii) Bembay mangoes are better than *those* of Bangaluru.

   (b) Indefinite Pronouns : All pronouns which refer to persons or things in a general way and do not refer to any particular person or thing are called Indefinite Pronouns.

   Examples :
   (i) *Somebody* has stolen my watch.
   (ii) *Few* escaped unhurt.
   (iii) Did you ask *anybody* to come?

   (c) Distributive Pronouns : Each, either, neither are called distributive pronouns because they refer to persons or things one at a time. For this reason they are always singular and followed by the verb in singular.

   Examples :
   (i) *Each* of the men received a reward.
   (ii) *These* men received *each* a reward.
   (iii) *Either* of you can go.

3. **Relative Pronouns :** A relative pronoun refers or relates to some noun going before, which is called its Antecedent.

   Examples :
   (i) I met Hari *who* used to live here.
   (ii) I have found the pen *which* I had lost.
   (iii) Here is the book *that* you lent me.

4. **Interrogative Pronouns :** These pronouns, are used for asking questions.

   Examples :
   (i) *Whose* book is this?
   (ii) *What* will all the neighbours say?
   (iii) *Which* do you prefer, tea or coffee?

Note : Interrogative pronouns can also be used in asking indirect questions. Consider the following examples :
(i) I asked *who* was speaking.
(ii) Tell me *what* you have done.
(iii) Say *which* you would like best.

Behaviour of the Pronouns

1. If three pronouns are used together in the same sentence they are arranged in the following order :

2	+	3	+	1
↓		↓		↓
Second Person		Third Person		First Person

   Examples :
   I, you and he must help *that* poor man. (Incorrect)
   You, he and I must help *that* poor man. Correct)
2. When two or more singular nouns are joined by and, the pronoun used for them should be plural.

   Examples :
   Mohan and Sohan are friends. *They* play football. *They* live at Lajpat Nagar.
3. But if these nouns joined by and refer to the same person or thing, the pronoun used should be singular.

   Examples :
   (i) Delhi, the beautiful city and the capital of India, is famous for *its* historical monuments.
   (ii) The manager and owner of the firm expressed *his* views on the demands of the workers.
4. When two nouns are used with as well as, the pronoun agrees with the first subject.

   Examples :
   (a) Mohan as well as his friends is doing *his* work.
   (b) The students as well as their teachers are doing *their* work.
5. When two singular nouns joined by 'and' are preceded by *each* or *every,* the pronoun used must be singular and should agree in gender with the second noun.

   Examples :
   (a) Every man and every woman will do *her* best for the nation.
   (b) Each boy and each girl went to *her* house.
6. When two nouns are joined by using 'with', the pronoun agrees with the noun coming before 'with'.

   Examples :
   (a) The boy with *his* parents has gone to see a movie.
   (b) The children with *their* parents have gone to picnic.
7. When two different nouns are joined by either......... or; neither .... nor, the pronoun is used according to the number and gender of the second noun.

Examples :
(a) Either your sister or you have done *your* work.
(b) Neither the students nor the teacher was in *his* class.

8. The pronoun coming after '*than*' must be in the same case as that coming before '*than*'.

Examples :
(a) She plays better than *me*. (Incorrect)
She plays better than *I*. (Correct)
(b) His elder brother is more intelligent than *him*. (Incorrect)
His elder brother is more intelligent than *he*. (Correct)

9. 'Many a' always takes a singular pronoun and singular verb.

Example :
Many a soldier has met *his* death in the battle field.

10. 'Who', 'Whose', 'Whom' are used only for persons.

Examples :
(a) *Who* is knocking at the door?
(b) *Whose* pen is this?
(c) *What* do you want?

11. 'Which' is used for things.

Example : *Which* game do you like?

MULTIPLE CHOICE QUESTIONS

Directions: *In the following questions choose the correct options to fill the blanks.*

1. The place was so dirty that ..... wished to run away from there.
A. everybody B. anybody
C. few D. some

2. ..... was there to help me.
A. Somebody B. Anything
C. Anybody D. Nobody

3. Is there ...... to eat?
A. some B. something
C. any D. few

4. ..... of the students were making a great noise.
A. Anyone B. Somebody
C. Many D. Nobody

5. ..... of the students can solve this sum.
A. Someone B. Anybody
C. Somebody D. None

6. ...... of us should try our best to make India a heaven.
A. Any B. Somebody
C. Anybody D. All

7. ...... of us do not know the real meaning of our lives.
A. Any B. Something
C. Several D. Many

8. My .... black.
A. hairs are B. hair is
C. hairs shall D. hair will

9. She saw two .... on the last Sunday.
A. thiefs B. theifs
C. thieves D. theives

10. My sister is a ....
A. bacheloress B. bachelor
C. unmaried D. spinster

11. One is supposed to do ....
A. our duty B. their duty
C. one's duty D. his duty

12. Take anything .... you want.
A. that B. which
C. than D. then

13. I cannot tolerate ....
A. separated you B. your separation
C. separation from you D. you separated

14. He is .... faithful partner.
A. Yours B. You
C. Your D. Your's

15. Ajay is more smart than ....
A. her B. hers
C. herself D. she

16. Vivek works harder than ....
A. me B. I
C. her D. his

17. They should help ....
A. the poor people B. the poor
C. the poor persons D. the poor peoples

18. .... are mad.
A. All his sons B. His all sons
C. Sons all his D. All sons his

19. The poor fellow .... to fate.
A. resigned B. resigned himself
C. resigned itself D. resigned themselves

20. Nobody will help you but ....
A. I B. me
C. ours D. his

21. It is a good chance, You must avail .... this opportunity.
A. of B. yourself of
C. for D. from

22. The person who is elected .... my relative.
A. is B. he is
C. his D. him

23. He made ....
A. yours mention B. mention of you
C. mention for you D. mention about you

24. .... I know, he is quite faithful.
A. As far as B. So far as
C. So far this D. So far so

25. It is a duty of a person to take .... for his family.
A. pain B. pains
C. pain-killers D. pained

26. She does not love .... husband.
A. his B. her
C. its D. their

27. Let .... work together.
A. him and me B. he and I
C. he and him D. I and me

28. Copper, Silver and Gold ....
A. each will do B. either will do
C. any one will do D. any will do

29. Jessica and Roma are very irregular .... habits.
A. in her B. in their
C. in its D. in every

30. One likes to enjoy .... who was a great poet.
A. The sonnets of Shakespeare
B. Shakespeare's sonnets
C. Sonnets
D. Shakespeare

ANSWERS

1	2	3	4	5	6	7	8	9	10
A	D	B	C	D	D	D	B	C	D
11	12	13	14	15	16	17	18	19	20
C	A	C	C	D	B	B	A	B	B
21	22	23	24	25	26	27	28	29	30
B	A	B	A	B	B	A	C	B	A

ARTICLES

The family of the articles has only three members. They are : A, An and The. However, they fall under two groups :
(a) Definite Article *(b)* Indefinite Article

'The' is known as definite article whereas 'a' and 'an' are known as indefinite articles.

Use of the Definite Article 'The'

'The' is used before

1. The superlative degree :
He is the ablest man of the town.
(ablest is a superlative degree)
2. The name of states, countries etc. having a descriptive name :
(i) The J & K is a small state. (J & K is a descriptive name)
(ii) He lives in the U.S.A. (U.S.A. is a descriptive name)
(But the Delhi and the America are wrong because neither Delhi nor America is a descriptive name)
3. The names of the scriptures :
The Gita is a holy book. (Gita is a scripture)
4. Name of newspapers :
The Tribune is published from Chandigarh.
5. Name of rivers, canals, seas, oceans, bays, gulfs, groups of islands etc. :
(i) The Ganga is a holy river.
(ii) The Indian Ocean is the deepest ocean.
(iii) The Persian Gulf is a narrow gulf.
6. The name of famous buildings :
The Taj is one of the best buildings in India.
7. The names of nationals, sects and communities:
(i) The English defeated the Germans in the World War.
(ii) The rich should help the poor.
(iii) The Hindus believe in the caste system.
8. Proper nouns used as common nouns :
(i) Kalidas is the Shakespeare of India.
(ii) Delhi is the London of India.
9. Famous historical events :
The Industrial Revolution changed the face of England.
10. The directions and the celestial bodies:
The sun rises in the east.
11. Titles : Akbar, the Great was loved by his subjects.

Do not use 'the'

1. Before languages :
The English is an international language. (Incorrect)
English is an international language. (Correct)
2. Before the names of games :
The hockey is a popular game. (Incorrect)
Hockey is a popular game. (Correct)

Use of the Indefinite Articles 'A' and 'An'

'A' is used before :

1. All singular common nouns beginning with a consonant :
(i) A boy sings a song.
(ii) A black and a white cow were grazing in the field.
2. If a word begins with a vowel but gives the sound of a consonant, 'a' should be used before it :
(i) He was helped in his work by a European.
(ii) He is a one-eyed man.
(iii) It is a useful work.

'An' is used as follows :

1. All singular common nouns beginning with a vowel (*i.e.*, a, e, i, o, u) :
   (i) He is an artist. (ii) He is an old man. (iii) I intend to buy an umbrella.
2. If a word starts with a consonant but gives the sound of a vowel, "an" should be used before it :
   (i) Brutus is an honourable man.
   (ii) He is an honour to his profession.
   (iii) He is an L.L.B.

Demonstratives, that, these and those

1. The demonstrative adjectives and pronouns are for objects nearby the speaker:
   this (singular) those (plural)
   and for objects far away from the speaker.
   That (singular) those (plural)
2. Demonstratives are the only adjectives that agree in number with their nouns.
   That hat is nice.
   Those hats are nice.
3. When there is the idea of selection, the pronoun "one" (or "ones") often follows the demonstrative.
   I want a book. I'll get this (one).
   If the demonstrative is followed by an adjective, "one"(or "ones") must be used.
   I want a book. I'll get this big one.

MULTIPLE CHOICE QUESTIONS

Directions: *In the following questions choose the correct options to fill the blanks.*

1. .... will have to be paid for this material.
A. Half rupee B. Half a rupee
C. A half rupee D. An half rupee

2. .... is taking keen interest in India.
A. The USA B. USA
C. An USA D. A USA

3. Only .... can save our country.
A. the Hitler B. a Hitler
C. Hitler D. an Hitler

4. I can run for ....
A. hundred miles B. the hundred miles
C. a hundred miles D. an hundred miles.

5. .... man-eater has been killed.
A. The B. A
C. An D. Either A or B

6. What .... fine idea!
A. the B. an
C. a D. No article

7. .... earth is moving around the sun.
A. An B. A
C. The D. No article

8. This is .... first example while I got.
A. the B. a
C. an D. No article

9. This is .... house which was built during earthquake.
A. a B. an
C. the D. No article

10. .... America is a rich country.
A. The B. An
C. A D. No article

11. .... U.S.A. is a developed country.
A. A B. An
C. The D. No article

12. .... Bible is a holy book.
A. A B. The
C. An D. No article

13. .... rich should help the poor.
A. The B. A
C. An D. No article

14. .... Gold is a costly metal.
A. The B. A
C. An D. No article

15. Kalidas is .... Shakespeare of India.
A. a B. an
C. the D. No article

16. I cannot do .... difficult work.
A. a such B. the such
C. such the D. such a

17. How foolish .... plan it is!
A. a B. an
C. the D. No article

18. An ink is .... useful article.
A. an B. a
C. the D. No article

19. There are .... husband and wife.
A. a B. an
C. the D. No article

20. He is learning .... French
A. the B. a
C. an D. No article

ANSWERS

1	2	3	4	5	6	7	8	9	10
B	A	B	C	D	C	C	A	C	D
11	**12**	**13**	**14**	**15**	**16**	**17**	**18**	**19**	**20**
C	B	A	D	C	D	A	B	D	D

ADJECTIVES & ADVERBS

An Adjective is a word which adds something to the meaning of a noun or a pronoun.

Mridula is an *intelligent* girl. He has a *black* goat.
He is a *brilliant* student. She is a *clever* girl.
It is a *beautiful* picture.

In the sentences given above, the words in italics are adjectives.

An Adverb is a word which qualifies the meaning of a Verb, an Adjective or another Adverb.

(*i*) He talks *slowly*.
(*ii*) He is a *very* good student.
(*iii*) He talks *very* slowly.

In sentence (*i*), *slowly* qualifies the verb *talks*.
In sentence (*ii*), *very* qualifies the adjective *good*.
In sentence (*iii*), *very* qualifies the adverb *slowly*.

Adjectives have three degrees of comparison :

1. **Positive Degree :** It expresses the common form of an adjective.
   Example :
   Ram is a *tall* boy.
   In the above sentence *tall* is an adjective and expresses the common form.
2. **Comparative Degree :** It expresses the more of the same form.
   Example :
   Ram is *taller* than Mahesh.
   In the above sentence *taller* is an adjective that expresses the more of the common form of the adjective *tall*.

   "When and How to Use" Comparative Degree?

   (a) Comparative Degree is used when two persons or two groups of persons or things are compared.
   Examples :
   (a)He is *wiser* than his younger brother.
   (b)This glass is *cleaner* than the other.

   (b) When two different qualities in the same person are compared, more is used instead of 'er' to form the comparative. The formula used in this case should be :
   More + Positive Degree
   She is *fairer* than polite. (Incorrect)
   She is *more fair* than polite. (Correct)

   (c) When selection of one out of two persons or things is meant, the degree of comparison is followed by of and *the* is used before it.
   Example :
   Zia is abler of *the* two sisters.

   (d) If two comparatives are used in the same sentence to impress upon an idea, both should be preceded by the definite article.
   Examples :
   (i) The higher you go, the cooler it is.
   (ii) The more we get, the more we desire.

   (e) When one person or thing is compared with another of the same kind, other is used after the comparative degree. In such sentences other is normally preceded by any or all.
   Examples :
   (i) Kalidas is greater than any dramatist. (Incorrect)
   Kalidas is greater than any other dramatist. (Correct)
   (ii) Lead is heavier than all metals. (Incorrect)
   Lead is heavier than all other metals. (Correct)

   (f) Senior, junior, superior, inferior, prior, anterior (earlier than) and posterior (later than) are always followed by 'to'.
   Examples :
   (i) Ram is senior *to* Mohan by three years.
   (ii) That pen is inferior *to* that.
   (iii) He is junior *to* me in rank.
   (iv) This event was posterior *to* that.

   Note: Never use *than* after the above mentioned adjectives.

Important Information

(a) 'Preferable' is also used as an adjective of the comparative degree. As such, it is always followed by *to* and not *a*.
Death is preferable than dishonour. (Incorrect)
Death is preferable *to* dishonour. (Correct)

(b) To intensify the Degree of comparison, we use *far* or *much* before the comparative.
Examples :
(i) This book is *far* better than that.
(ii) His performance was *much* better than Mohan's.
Warning : Always avoid the use of double comparatives.
Don't say : Ram is more cleverer than his younger brother.
Say: Ram is cleverer than his younger brother.

3. **Superlative Degree :** It expresses the most of the common form of an adjective.
   Example :
   He is the ablest man of the town.

How and when to use the Superlative Degree?

(a) The Superlative Degree is used when more than two persons or things are compared.
(b) The Superlative Degree is generally preceded by 'the' and followed by 'of' in most of the cases or otherwise.
(c) When an adjective of the superlative degree is preceded by a Possessive Adjective or a Noun in the Possessive case, 'the' should not be used before it.
Example :
Which is Kalidas' best play?

It will be a blunder to use 'the' before the Superlative Degree in such cases.

Don't say : Which is Kalidas' the best play.

(d) To intensify the degree of comparison, *by far* is used before the superlative degree.

Example :

India is *by far* the most beautiful country of the world.

Note: Always avoid the use of double superlatives.

Don't say : He is the most strongest boy in the class.

Say : He is the strongest boy in the class.

Use of some Important Adjectives

1. (a) '**Some**' is used as follows :
   (i) With countable nouns where it means— a little, a small quantity.
   (ii) In a question which shows some request.

   Examples :
   (i) There is some water in the bottle.
   (ii) Some of the students were absent yesterday.
   (iii) Will you have some milk?
   (iv) Will you buy some fruit for me?

   (b) **'Any'** is used as follows :
   (i) In negative sentences.
   (ii) In interrogative sentences.
   (iii) After 'Hardly', 'Scarcely' and 'Barely'.
   (iv) After 'If'.

   Examples :
   (i) There is not any sugar in the pot.
   (ii) We haven't any rice in the house.
   (iii) I have hardly any money.
   (iv) There are scarcely any plants in this field.
   (v) If there is any danger, blow the whistle.

2. (a) **Older :** Older (and oldest) are used for persons animals and things. But 'Older' and 'Oldest' refer to the persons who do not belong to the same family.

   Examples :
   (i) Radha is older than Shyama.
   (ii) John is the oldest member of the staff.
   'Older' and 'Oldest' refer to the persons who do not belong to the same family.

   (b) **Elder** (and **eldest**) are used in respect of the members of the same family like sons, daughters, brothers, sisters.

   Examples :
   (i) My elder sister is a lecturer.
   (ii) Meenakshi is the eldest of the three sisters.

   Note :
   (i) 'Elder' is not followed by 'than'.
   (ii) 'Elder' and 'Eldest' cannot be used for things.

3. (a) **'Few'** is negative and is the opposite of 'Many'. It means 'not many'.
   (b) **'A few'** is positive and means 'some at least'. It is the opposite of 'None'.
   (c) **'The few'** means 'minority' and suggests 'whether there is'.

   Examples :
   (i) We have few holidays in school.
   (ii) Only a few boys will fail in the examination.
   (iii) The few poems that he wrote are very popular.

4. (a) **Further** means 'something additional'.
   (b) **Farther** means 'a greater distance'.

   Examples :
   (i) Further discussion will be held in the office of the principal.
   (ii) Amritsar is farther from Delhi than Ambala.

5. (a) **Little** is negative. It means, 'not much', or 'hardly any'.
   (b) **A little** is positive. It means 'some quantity'.
   (c) **The little** denotes quantity. It means, 'not much but all that is, or whatever quantity there is'.

   Examples :
   (i) There is little hope of his success.
   (ii) He knows a little of everything.
   (iii) I have spent the little money I had.
   (iv) The little knowledge of shoe-making proved very useful to me.

6. (a) '**Much**' expresses 'quantity'.
   (b) '**Many**' expresses 'number'.
   (c) **'Many a'**—'Singular noun' and 'Singular verb' are used with 'many a'.

   Examples :
   (i) There is not *much* water in the jug.
   (ii) *Many* boys are absent today.
   (iii) *Many* a battle has been fought on the soil of India.

7. (a) '**Less**' denotes 'in a small degree'.
   (b) '**Fewer**' denotes 'number'.

   Examples :
   (i) He devotes less time to his studies.
   (ii) There are no fewer than ten chairs in this room.

8. (a) '**Each**' is used for a single number of 'two persons' or 'things'.
   (b) '**Every**' is used for a single number of 'many persons' or 'things'.

   Examples :
   (i) Each boy must take part in games.
   (ii) There are only two poets. Each poet recited his poem.
   (iii) Every man dies in this world.
   (iv) Every man is expected to do his duty.

9. (a) '**Either**' means one of the two or both.
   (b) '**Neither**' is negative of the either.

   Examples :
   (i) You may buy either of these two chairs.
   (ii) Neither of them could speak on the stage.

10. (a) '**Later**' expresses 'late in time'.
    (b) '**Latter**' means 'second in position or order'.

    Examples :
    (i) My father reached later than I expected.
    (ii) The latter position was better than the former.

Use of some Important Adverbs

1. (a) Also, too, enough:
   (i) He taught English. Also, he edited the school magazine
   (ii) He is a writer and also he is a painter.
   (iii) He is too obstinate to listen to any reason.
   (iv) This is too difficult a piece for the junior students.
   (v) Sarla was kind enough to help the poor.
   (vi) He is brave enough to help the truth.
   Note: 'Too' is used in a negative sense, but enough is used in a positive sense.

   (b) Fairly and rather: Both suggest the meaning 'moderately'. But, mainly 'fairly' is used with the words that denote a positive meaning and rather is used with the words that denote a negative meaning:
   (i) Rita did fairly well in that competition, but her performance was rather poor in sports.
   (ii) Mona is fairly rich, but she is rather stingy.
   Note: 'Rather' can also be used in a positive sense.
   (i) This is a rather interesting job.
   (ii) That boy is rather smart.

   (c) Hardly, barely, scarcely: These words mostly convey the negative suggestions and are almost similar.
   (i) I have hardly any strength now.
   (ii) There was barely any supply to the township,
   (iii) There were scarcely a hundred guests present.
   Note: With slight variance in the meaning, the words given above convey the idea of 'very little', 'not enough', 'lack of quantity and number'.

   (d) Yet, Still: These adverbs can often be used to connect the sentence units:
   (i) He has been defeated many times in the contest; still he wants to be a competitor.
   (ii) Mona was sick; yet she went on doing her work.

   (e) Alone:
   (i) He alone (none else) is capable of handling that fire,
   (ii) He hunted all alone in the forest. (not in any company)

Special Note:

(a) Apart from their conventional positions the adverbs might be used in different positions with different meanings and angles.
   (i) He had only four books.
   (ii) John only contacted his friend in need.
   (iii) He greeted me only.
   (iv) Only he greeted me there.

(b) Inversion: Some adverbs can be inverted *i.e.* placed in the beginning of the sentence and then be followed by an interrogative form. The most common of these adverb are: so, seldom, never, nowhere, under no circumstances, hardly, scarcely etc.
   (i) So big was the bus that it could not enter the narrow lane.
   (ii) Hardly had he reached the station when he received the message.

MULTIPLE CHOICE QUESTIONS

Directions: *In the following questions choose the correct options to fill the blanks.*

1. The girl whom you met is the .... sister of Ravi.
A. eldest B. elder
C. older D. oldest

2. The historical place is ....
A. seeing worth B. worthy of seeing
C. worth seeing D. worthy seeing

3. These flowers smell ....
A. sweet B. sweetly
C. more sweetly D. sweetest

4. .... aspirant cannot pass the entrance examination.
A. Each B. Every
C. All D. No

5. Harivansh Rai .... second Shakespeare.
A. is a B. is
C. is the D. is an

6. .... student in the class got prizes.
A. Each and every B. Every and each
C. Every D. Never

7. It is .... picture than the one we saw last Monday.
A. interesting B. much interesting
C. more interesting D. most interesting

8. She is clever ....
A. that her mother is B. as her mother is
C. to her mother is D. than her mother is

9. They will get ....
A. Red, green and black paper
B. Red, green black paper
C. Red and green and black paper
D. Red green black paper

10. Health is .... wealth.
A. preferable to B. more preferable than
C. more preferable to D. most preferable then

11. .... water that was in the jug evaporated.
A. Little B. The little
C. Small D. A small

12. He has not sung .... songs.
A. much B. most
C. more D. many

13. Srishti has searched .... office.
A. whole the B. the whole
C. a whole D. some whole

14. Premchand was .... best and .... famous writer.
A. a, the most B. the, a most
C. the, more D. the, the most

15. William Shakespeare is famous as ....
A. a poet and a dramatist
B. a poet and dramatist
C. the poet and the dramatist
D. a poet and the dramatist

16. What does .... leader suggest?
A. other B. another
C. others D. anothers

17. He .... money.
A. has few B. have few
C. has little D. have little

18. The .... boys are rewarded.
A. first two B. two first
C. firsts two D. two's first

19. He is .... brave.
A. stronger than
B. stronger then
C. more strong then
D. more strong than

20. No sooner said ....
A. so done B. and done
C. then done D. but done

21. She returned .... than I had thought.
A. quickly B. more quicker
C. more quickly D. quicker

22. He is .... foolish person.
A. rather the B. a rather
C. rather a D. rather

23. This pen .... rupees.
A. costs twenty B. twenty costs only
C. costs only twenty D. only costs twenty

24. It is .... pride.
A. nothing else but B. nothing else than
C. else nothing than D. but

25. This tea is .... to drink.
A. too hot B. very hot
C. enough hot D. much hot

ANSWERS

1	2	3	4	5	6	7	8	9	10
A	C	A	B	A	C	C	C	A	A
11	**12**	**13**	**14**	**15**	**16**	**17**	**18**	**19**	**20**
B	D	B	D	B	B	C	A	D	C
21	**22**	**23**	**24**	**25**					
C	C	C	A	A					

DETERMINERS

Determiners are actually Adjectives. They are always followed by nouns.

Determiners are of the following kinds:

1. **Demonstrative Determiners :** this, that, these, those
2. **Possessive Determiners :** my, our, your, his, her, its, their
3. **Quantitative Determiners :** some, any, much, enough, sufficient, whole, a little, the little, little, all, both
4. **Numerical Determiners:** a few, some, few, the few, any, several, many, no, etc.
   One, two, three ... (Cardinals)
   First, second, third ... (Ordinals)
5. **Distributive Determiners:** either, neither
6. **Articles: Indefinite:** a, an, **Definite:** the

MULTIPLE CHOICE QUESTIONS

Directions: *In the following questions choose the correct options to fill the blanks.*

1. Give me .... rice.
A. some B. few
C. a few D. any

2. ...... sheep grazing on the slope of the hill had gone away.
A. Any B. The few
C. This D. Much

3. Have you got .... magazines to read?
A. all B. much
C. some D. little

4. I have .... money that I want to spend on shares.
A. any B. much
C. less D. some

5. There is .... owl on the branch of the tree.
A. a B. the
C. an D. some

6. My brother is .... MBA.
A. a B. an
C. the D. any

7. Have you got .... cheese?
A. some B. many
C. a few D. few

8. No, I have not got .... cheese.
A. many B. few
C. any D. some

9. There is only .... milk left in the bottle.
A. enough B. few
C. much D. a little

10. There is .... hope of his recovery.
A. any B. little
C. many D. few

11. .... dogs were barking at the strangers.
A. Some B. Any
C. Much D. Less

12. The girl bought her father .... juice.
A. few B. some
C. any D. many

13. You should take .... honey everyday.
A. any B. many
C. a little D. a few

14. .... boy was punished by the teacher.
A. Either B. All
C. Any D. Many

15. .... girl was asked to join the army.
A. None B. Neither
C. All D. Any

16. .... water in the jug has been drunk by Mohan.
A. The little B. The few
C. A few D. Few

17. I shall play .... piano at the party.
A. some B. any
C. the D. few

18. .... labourers were found dead in the mine.
A. Any B. Fewer
C. Many D. Less

19. Could I borrow .... umbrella?
A. our B. your
C. yours D. my

20. My brother is standing in the .... row.
A. any B. many
C. some D. first

ANSWERS

1	2	3	4	5	6	7	8	9	10
A	B	C	D	C	B	A	C	D	B
11	**12**	**13**	**14**	**15**	**16**	**17**	**18**	**19**	**20**
A	B	C	A	B	A	C	C	B	D

THE VERB

A Verb is a word that tells something about the action or state of or happenning to a person or thing.

A Verb tells the following:

1. What a person or thing does.
Sachin goes to school daily.
The bell *rang* loudly.
Many birds fly in the sky.
She *sang* a song.

2. What a person or thing is.
India *is* the biggest democracy in the world.
Ram Mehar *is* very rich.
They *are* happy.

3. What is done to a person or thing.
You *are liked* by all.
Two thieves *were arrested.*
Four students *were punished* by the teacher.

4. What happens to a person or thing.
His maternal uncle *died* last week.
Two ships *sank* yesterday.
Leaves *turn* yellow in autumn.

5. What a person or thing has, had, and so on.
I *have* a new car.
He *had* a scooter last year.
He *has* several cows and goats.

It goes without saying that a verb is the most important part of a sentence. No sentence is complete without a Verb.

Important Information

1. If two or more singular nouns are joined by 'and' the verb used will be plural.
Example:
(i) He and I were going to the market.
(ii) Ram and Mohan are friends.

2. If two singular nouns joined by 'and' points out to the same thing or person, the verb used must be singular.
Example:
(i) Rice and curry is the favourite food of the Punjabis.
(ii) The Collector and District Magistrate is away.

3. In case two subjects are joined by 'as well as' the verb agrees with the first subject.
Example :
(i) Kanta as well as her children is playing.
(ii) Children as well as their mother are playing.
In the case of first sentence the verb (is) agrees with Kanta and in the case of second sentence the verb (are) agrees with the children.

4. 'Neither', 'Either', 'Every', 'Each', 'Everyone', and 'Many a' are followed by a singular verb.
Example :
(i) Either of the plans is to be adopted.
(ii) Neither of the two brothers is sure to pass.
(iii) Every student is expected to be obedient.
(iv) Everyone of them desires this.
(v) Many a person is drowned in the sea.

5. If two subjects are joined by 'Either .... or' / 'Neither .... nor', the verb agrees with the subject near to it.
   Example :
   (i) Either my brother or I am to do this work.
   (ii) Neither he nor they are prepared to do this work.
6. 'A great many' is always followed by a 'plural noun' and a 'plural verb'. For example :
   A great many students have been declared successful.
7. Similarly if two subjects are joined by 'with', 'together with', 'no less than', in addition to 'and not', etc. the verb agrees with the first subject.
   Example :
   (i) The boy with his parents has arrived.
   (ii) He, no less than I, is to blame.
8. Nouns, plural in form, but singular in meaning, take a singular verb.
   Example :
   This news was broadcast from television yesterday.

MULTIPLE CHOICE QUESTIONS

Directions: *In the following questions choose the correct options to fill the blanks.*

1. The bus with all its passengers .... lost.
A. were B. was
C. are D. would

2. You as well as I .... responsible for this work.
A. am B. are
C. was D. is

3. Raghava like all his companions .... a spoiled child.
A. are B. were
C. is D. will be

4. Pen and ink .... required for me.
A. are B. were
C. is D. has required

5. Every girl and every boy .... attended the seminar.
A. have B. has
C. is D. are

6. Not only she but all her sisters ...... been married.
A. has B. have
C. is D. are

7. There .... nothing but miseries in life.
A. is B. are
C. were D. will be

8. Neither prose nor poem .... given.
A. were B. was
C. has D. have

9. Either he or I ...., wrong.
A. is B. are
C. am D. were

10. Either Sulekha or Rekha .... coming here.
A. are B. is
C. were D. have

11. .... the child or his parents to blame?
A. Is B. Are
C. Were D. Has

12. You and I .... neighbours.
A. am B. are
C. was D. has

13. The house with all its belongings ..... sold away.
A. were B. are
C. was D. must

14. Either water or juice .... required.
A. is B. are
C. were D. has

15. There were not as many tables as .... required.
A. was B. were
C. is D. are

16. They each .... a book.
A. have B. are
C. has D. is

17. He and I .... class friends.
A. is B. am
C. was D. are

18. She as well as I .... guilty.
A. is B. are
C. am D. must be

19. Purushottam .... not read more on this chapter.
A. needs
B. has been need
C. need
D. had been need

20. He came .... to his aunt.
A. run B. running
C. to run D. in run

ANSWERS

1	2	3	4	5	6	7	8	9	10
B	B	C	C	B	B	A	B	C	B
11	12	13	14	15	16	17	18	19	20
A	B	C	A	B	A	D	A	C	B

CONJUNCTIONS

A conjunction is a word which connects words, clauses or sentences.

Look at the following sentences.

(i) He bought apples *and* mangoes.

(ii) God made the country *and* man made the town.

(iii) The door was open *but* there was no one in the house.

(iv) He knows that I am here *and* that I want to see him.

In the sentence (i), *and* connects two words—*apples* and *mangoes.*

In the sentence (ii), *and* connects two sentences—*God made the country* and *man made the town.*

In the sentence (iii), *but* connects two sentences— *The door was open* and *there was no one in the house.*

In the sentence (iv), *and* connects two clauses—*that I am here* and *that I want to see him.*

The main coordinating conjunctions are:

and, but, for, or, nor, also, either ..... or, neither ..... nor.

There are some conjunctions which are used in pairs. They are:

either .... or, ... neither .... nor, both .... and, though .... yet, whether .... or, not only .... but also.

Example: *Either* take it *or* leave it.

It is *neither* useful *nor* ornamental.

They *both* like *and* respect me.

Though he is suffering from high fever, *yet* he does not cry.

He does not care *whether* you go *or* stay.

He is *not only* doltish, *but also* obstinate.

The conjunctions which are used in pairs in this way, are called correlative conjunctions, or merely correlatives.

Use of Important Conjunctions

1. **As soon as :** As soon as denotes simultaneous time.
   Example : As soon as he saw his enemy, he took to his heels.
2. **No sooner .... than :**
   (a) 'No sooner' is always followed by 'than'.
   (b) Please remember that 'No sooner' is always followed by do/does/did. As such only first form of the verb should be used after the subject.
   Example :
   No sooner did he see his enemy than he took to his heels.
3. **Hardly :** Hardly is followed by when.
   Examples :
   (i) Hardly had I left the house when it started raining.
   (ii) We had hardly come into the room when his father began chastising him.
   Note :
   A. Hardly is never followed by than.
   B. 'Scarcely' can also be used in the sense and manner of 'Hardly'.
4. **Lest :** Lest is used in the sense of so that .... not. It is always followed by should. Lest is negative in sense. Hence 'not' should never be used with it.
   Example :
   Work hard lest you should fail.
   Note : 'Lest' is always followed by 'should' and not 'may'.
5. **Unless :** Unless expresses condition. It is also used in the negative sense. Use of 'not' is not allowed with unless because unless is already in the negative sense.
   Example :
   Unless you labour hard you will not pass.
6. **Until :** 'Until' expresses time. It means 'till not'.
   Example : Wait here until I return.
   Note : Until is in the negative sense. So 'not' should not be used with it. Example :
   Wait here until I do not return. (Incorrect)
   Wait here until I return. (Correct)
7. **As well as :** When two subjects are joined by 'as well as', the verb always agrees with the first subject.
   Examples :
   (i) The teacher as well as students is playing.
   (ii) Students as well as the teacher are playing.
   Note : 'Both' and 'as well as' cannot be used together in the same sentence.
   Examples :
   Both Sita as well as Kanta are beautiful. (Incorrect)
   Sita as well as Kanta is beautiful. (Correct)
   Both Sita and Kanta are beautiful. (Correct)
8. **As if :** 'As if' is used in the sense of pretension. While using 'as if' in a sentence, we should see that even the third person singular subject gets 'were'.
   Example : He talks as if he were mad.
9. **Till :** Till expresses time. Till is always used in the affirmative.
   Example :
   We did not come back till sunset.
10. **Rather than :** 'Rather than' is used in the sense of 'preference'. 'Rather' is always followed by 'than'.
    Example :
    I would rather die than submit.
11. **As long as/so long as :** Both express time during which an action or event takes place.
    Example :
    As long as there is life, there is hope.
12. **However :** It is both a subordinate and co-ordinate clause.
    Examples :
    (a) Mala worked hard, she however, failed.
    (b) However hard he may work, he cannot pass.
13. **Such as :** 'Such as' gives us the sense of 'like'. Such is always followed by 'as'.
    Example :
    Life is such a puzzle as cannot be solved.

MULTIPLE CHOICE QUESTIONS

Directions: *In the following questions choose the correct options to fill the blanks.*

1. Neither he .... his friend is good.
A. or B. and
C. but D. nor

2. The officer asked the peon .... why he was late.
A. that B. if
C. but D. No word needed

3. Both Ajay .... Vijay are intelligent.
A. or B. nor
C. and D. No word needed

4. No Sooner did the thief see the public .... he ran away.
A. then B. and
C. but D. than

5. Abhinav .... his brothers was going to Mumbai.
A. but
B. yet
C. No word needed
D. together with

6. He behaves .... he were the captain of the team.
A. as if B. as
C. No word needed D. that

7. Either Rupali .... Sonali is going to attend the meeting.
A. and B. but
C. nor D. or

8. Neither Nirmal .... Ashwinee is going to listen the speech.
A. and B. but
C. nor D. or

9. Ravi .... Prakash are going to Kolkata.
A. or B. nor
C. but D. and

10. Rice .... curry is my usual breakfast.
A. and B. but
C. then D. than

11. Hardly had he left .... his brother came.
A. then B. than
C. when D. that

12. I would rather have a copy .... a book.
A. then B. than
C. when D. that

13. He is no other .... my friend.
A. then B. than
C. when D. but

14. He saw a snake ....he awoke.
A. then B. when
C. than D. No word needed

15. Ten years have passed .... my grandmother died.
A. since B. when
C. then D. than

16. She is .... good .... bad.
A. either, not B. neither, or
C. neither, nor D. neither, than

17. The cellphone is both cheap .... best.
A. than B. and
C. then D. or

18. No sooner did the rogue see the police .... he disappeared.
A. then B. than
C. so D. because

19. Srishti will go .... Sanju goes.
A. if B. than
C. then D. although

20. She is wise .... timid.
A. and B. yet
C. but D. however

21. Make hay .... the sun shines.
A. though B. while
C. after D. before

22. He is so weak .... he cannot walk.
A. but B. that
C. then D. so

23. Although he is rich, ... he is unhappy.
A. but B. yet
C. so D. still

24. Wait here .... I come back.
A. till B. until
C. before D. after

25. He is my friend .... I shall help him.
A. so B. hence
C. that is why D. therefore

26. He must go away .... he will be beaten.
A. otherwise B. and
C. or D. else

27. God loves good men .... good men love God.
A. and B. or
C. that D. those

28. He was late .... he was not punished.
A. but B. yet
C. still D. therefore

29. Walk slowly ...., you may fall.
A. and B. or
C. so D. otherwise

30. Work hard, ... you will fail.
A. and B. or
C. otherwise D. else

ANSWERS

1	2	3	4	5	6	7	8	9	10
D	D	C	D	D	A	D	C	D	A
11	**12**	**13**	**14**	**15**	**16**	**17**	**18**	**19**	**20**
C	B	B	B	A	C	B	B	A	C
21	**22**	**23**	**24**	**25**	**26**	**27**	**28**	**29**	**30**
B	B	B	A	B	C	A	C	D	D

PREPOSITIONS

A *Preposition* is a word which is placed before a noun or a pronoun to show its relation to some other word in the sentence.

1. I saw a goat *in* the field.
2. I am fond *of* hot coffee.

In sentence 1, the word *in* shows the relation between two things—*goat* and *field.*

In sentence 2, the word *of* shows the relation between the attribute expressed by the adjective *found* and *tea.*

The words *in* and *of* are here used as prepositions.

The noun or pronoun which is used with a preposition is called its object. The noun or pronoun is in the objective case. It is governed by the preposition. Now it is absolutely clear that in sentence 1, the noun *field* is in the objective case. The word *field* is governed by the preposition *in.*

A preposition may have two or more objects.

The road runs over *hill* and *plain.*

Here, the words *hill* and *plain* are used as objects.

Use of Important Prepositions

1. Among, Between

'**Among**' is used for more than two persons or things; '**Between**' is used only for two.

Examples :

(i) Distribute these sweets *among* the poor students of the class.

(ii) Distribute these books *between* Ram and Shyam.

2. Among, In

'**Among**' is used before collective plural nouns. '**In**' is used before collective singular nouns.

Examples :

(i) I found him standing *among* the crowd.

(ii) I saw him in the crowd.

3. Beside, Besides

'**Beside**' means 'by the side of'. '**Besides**' means 'in addition to'.

Examples :

(i) The daughter was sitting *beside* her mother.

(ii) *Besides* his relatives, he invited his friends also.

4. In, Within

'**In**' means at the expiry of a period of time in future, '**Within**' means before the expiry of a period of time in any tense.

Examples :

(i) She will return *in* a week.

(ii) I shall finish my work *within* a weak.

5. On, Upon

'**On**' is used for things at rest; '**Upon**' is used for things in motion.

Examples :

(i) He is sitting *on* the floor.

(ii) The dog sprang *upon* the table.

6. By, With

'**By**' denotes the agent or doer, '**With**' denotes the instrument with which anything is done.

Examples :

(i) The bird was killed *by* the hunter with an arrow.

(ii) He beat the dog *with* a stick.

(iii) I shall reach here *by* five o'clock.

7. After, In

'**After**' means at the end of a period of time in the past. '**In**' means at the end of a period of time in future.

Examples :

(i) I shall return your book *in* a week.

(ii) He returned the book *after* a week.

8. For, From, Since

'**For**' is used before a noun denoting a period of time with all the tenses. '**From**' is used before a noun or phrase denoting a point of time, it is used in all the tenses. '**Since**' is used before a noun or phrase denoting some point of time and is always produced by a verb in the perfect continuous tense or third form of a verb.

Examples :

(i) We have been playing cards *for* two hours.

(ii) She stayed with her uncle *from* the 15th of March to the 15th of May.

(iii) I have been reading this book *since* morning.

9. Above, Over

'**Above**' means 'higher from', **Over** is used in the following four senses :

(i) In the sense of 'above' :
At noon, the sun is *over* our heads.

(ii) In the sense of 'beyond' :
I cannot get *over* my disappointment.

(iii) In the sense of 'Superiority' :
God *over* all blesses for ever more.

(iv) In the sense of 'Conclusion' :
It is all *over* with me.

10. At, Towards

'**At**' denotes the idea of aim, '**Towards**' denotes the idea of destination.

Examples :

(i) He threw the stone *at* the cat.
(ii) He went *towards* the house.

11. At, In, On

'At' is used as follows :

(i) **'At'** is used with small towns and villages. **Examples:**
(a) He was born *at* Sonepat.
(b) He lives *at* village Bangra. (Bangra is a village)

(ii) **'At'** is used before a noun denoting a definite point of time.

Example :

He called on me *at* 9 p.m. yesterday.

'In' is used as follows :

(iii) **'In'** is used with the names of big cities, provinces and countries.

Examples :

(a) His father lives *in* England.
(b) His younger brother lives *in* Calcutta.

(iv) **'In'** is used before the names of months and years.

Example :

His elder sister was born *in* 1972 *in* the month of May.

'On' is used with dates and names of days. **Examples:**
(a) I joined college *on* the 26th April.
(b) He will leave for Kolkata *on* Wednesday next.

Important Information

1. **'In'** is also used in the following phrases :
In the morning; In the evening, In winter, In summer.
2. **'In'** also denotes a place inside anything.
He travelled *in* a crowded bus.
3. **'At'** is used in the following phrases :
At home, *At* the station, *At* work, *At* play.

12. Below, Beneath

Below means 'of lower level in position, dignity and expectation' etc. *Beneath* means 'under'.

Examples :

(i) It is *below* my dignity to talk to her.
(ii) They rested *beneath* the shade of a tree.

13. In, Into, To

'**In**' expresses Rest or Motion inside anything. '**Into**' expresses Motion towards the inside of anything or change from one medium to another. '**To**' denotes motion from one place to another.

Examples :

(i) The boys are *in* the room.
(ii) Translate this passage from English *into* Hindi.
(iii) Every morning he goes *to* the temple.

14. Till, By, Of, Off

- 'Till' means upto or not earlier than.
- 'By' means not later than.
- 'Of' shows cause, source, separation, quality, contents, possession, apposition, point of reference, space in time etc.
- 'Off' shows separation at a near distance, and detached condition.

Consider the following examples:

(i) I shall work *till* 5 a.m.
(ii) Madhu died *of* cancer.
(iii) The nib *of* the pen is made *of* gold.
(iv) He presented me a bottle *of* perfume.
(v) Our principal is a man *of* principle.
(vi) He lived in the house *of* his friend.
(vii) *By* this time tomorrow, I'll have finished my job.
(viii) My house is *off* the road.
(ix) The book fell *off* the table.

MULTIPLE CHOICE QUESTIONS

Directions: *Tick the correct preposition for the blank in each of the following sentences.*

1. He applied ...... the manager.
A. for B. to
C. with D. by

2. Trust ...... God and do the right.
A. in B. for
C. to D. with

3. She is worthy ...... a prize.
A. with B. for
C. to D. of

4. Mr. Gomes has no taste ...... music.
A. of B. for
C. with D. to

5. You are hard ...... hearing.
A. at B. of
C. with D. for

6. He is sure ...... his success
A. for B. with
C. on D. of

7. Preeti was warned ...... the danger ahead.
A. for B. at
C. of D. about

8. I am thankful ...... you for a good advice.
A. for B. with
C. to D. of

9. Deepak would not surrender ...... the police.
A. with B. to
C. for D. on

10. The small plant in your lawn is very sensitive ...... touch.
A. on B. with
C. to D. about

11. Divya was sure to succeed ..... the examination.
A. for B. in
C. to D. with

12. Geeta was jealous ...... Ravina's beauty.
A. to B. with
C. for D. of

13. He was ignorant ..... what was happening there.
A. for B. of
C. to D. with

14. Your pen is inferior ...... mine.
A. than B. with
C. from D. to

15. Reenu is no match ...... Meenu.
A. to B. for
C. with D. upon

16. It is necessary ...... you to apply for this job.
A. on B. with
C. for D. to

17. Be loyal ...... your country.
A. for B. to
C. on D. with

18. Mukesh is junior ...... me.
A. than B. to
C. from D. of

19. Deepika was innocent ...... the crime.
A. of B. with
C. from D. to

20. I am desirous.... joining the Indian cricket team.
A. for B. of
C. to D. on

ANSWERS

1	2	3	4	5	6	7	8	9	10
B	A	D	B	B	D	D	D	B	D
11	**12**	**13**	**14**	**15**	**16**	**17**	**18**	**19**	**20**
B	D	B	D	B	D	B	B	A	B

SYNONYMS

A synonym is a word which conveys a meaning similar to the given word.

REMEMBER

Words	*Synonyms*
Add	Increase
Adequate	Enough
Adjust	Adapt
All	Aggregate
Allow	Permit
Abode	Dwelling
Apt	Proper
Assess	Appraise
Accuse	Calumniate
Abashed	Timid
Annoy	Displease
Ample	Enough, Sufficient
Amplify	Increase
Apathetic	Unenthusiastic
Accost	Address
Authentic	True
Adjust	Fit
Approve	Assent, Allow, Accept
Adapt	Conform
Adversary	Opponent, Rival, Competitor
Beat	Whack
Benign	Kind
Breeze	Zephyr
Baffle	Puzzle
Booty	Spoil

Words	*Synonyms*
Beauty	Charm
Beast	Animal
Bandit	Robber
Blaze	Shine
Bond	Tie
Bend	Twist
Bate	Diminish
Beg	Plead
Barbaric	Wild, Savage
Bashful	Shy, Reserved
Begin	Start
Blend	Mix, Mingle
Bizarre	Funny
Below	Under
Bedevil	Confuse
Bemoan	Lament
Babble	Nonsense
Blame	Fault
Behaviour	Demeanour
Call	Accost
Copy	Imitate
Close	Shut
Caress	Love
Camp	Stay
Connect	Attach
Cut	Injure, Curtail
Cling	Stick
Conical	Funny
Convey	Carry
Conspicuous	Prominent
Cheerful	Happy, Pleasant

Words	Synonyms
Curtail	Decrease
Cheerless	Sad, Dejected
Curious	Strange
Circumstance	Factor, Situation, Condition
Competent	Capable
Congruent	Overlapping
Cope	Deal, Endure
Confident	Sure
Complex	Intricate
Cajole	Coax, Flatter
Cunning	Crafty
Delectable	Joyful, Delightful
Devilish	Diabolical
Delicate	Soft
Devil	Fiend
Delay	Postpone
Dislike	Repugnance
Destroy	Ruin
Dwell	Live, Dilate
Declare	Pronounce
Drunk	Flushed
Deficient	Lacking
Damn	Condemn, Curse
Decrease	Diminish
Destruction	Devastation
Efficient	Competent
Ethnic	Racial
Enthral	Enslave
Earnest	Serious
Envious	Jealous
Ending	Final
Egg	Incite
Extempore	At once
Extensive	Far-ranging
Extra	Surplus
Existence	Life
Exceed	Overstep
Enormous	Vast
Excessive	Superfluous
Free	Unhindered
Frigid	Cold
Feed	Cater
Fame	Reputation
Frame	Make
First	Initial
Frighten	Terrorise, Intimidate
Fervent	Fervid
Fall	Decline
Feeble	Frail
Fickle	Changeable
Finish	Conclude
Fraud	Deception
Forgiving	Placable

Words	Synonyms
Grow	Develop
Greed	Avidity
Greet	Welcome
Grave	Serious
Group	Constellation
Given	Bestowed
Gratitude	Thankfulness
Have	Possess
Hire	Rent
Hit	Strike
Handsome	Beautiful
Hinder	Prevent
Heap	Pile
Hope	Expect
Hard	Harsh
Help	Aid
Hymn	Song
Henpecked	Enslaved
Hoodwink	Mystify, Cheat
Humble	Polite, Urbane, Modest
Harass	Vex, Trouble
Impart	Instil
Intact	Untouched
Instal	Establish
Indict	Impeach
Imitate	Ape
Instigate	Incite
Initiate	Start, Introduce
Inimical	Unfriendly
Insufferable	Intolerable
Impartiality	Justice
Jolly	Merry
Joyful	Delectable
Join	Conjoin
Kind	Benign
Kill	Murder
Kindred	Similar
Kinship	Relationship
Keen	Sharp
Knowledge	Scholarship
Lazy	Slothful
Large	Substantial, Gargantuan
Listless	Careless, Lackadaisical
Lax	Loose
Little	Small
Lifelike	Realistic
Lofty	High
Lenient	Soft, Gentle
Lacking	Deficient, Wanting
Lessen	Decrease
Middleclass	Bourgeois
Mitigate	Lessen, Abate
Modesty	Humility, Lowliness

Words	Synonyms
Mix	Mingle, Blend
Mixture	Mingling
Mixed	Assorted
Modify	Decrease
Mean	Imply
Multifarious	Varied
Miscarry	Abort
Note	Notice
Noble	Stately
Native	Indigenous
Needful	Necessary
Notify	Declare
Nervous	Shaky, Tremulous, Timid
Natural	Spontaneous
Near	Close
Normal	Natural
Offend	Displease
Oppress	Persecute, Tyrannize
Opponent	Adversary
Obstruct	Hinder, Check
Offence	Fault
Offender	Villain
Overstep	Exceed
Overlapping	Congruent
Occult	Mystic
Profane	Unholy
Patience	Forbearance
Pornographic	Obscene
Plenitude	Abundance
Prominent	Important
Prodigal	Spender
Procrastinate	Postpone
Promote	Develop, Honour
Persecute	Tyrannise
Profess	Claim
Pliant	Flexible
Plebian	Common
Polished	Sophisticated
Quake	Shake
Quit	Leave
Queer	Eccentric
Quell	Suppress
Quantify	Allot
Reply	Answer
Relinquish	Retire
Read	Peruse
Relation	Reference
Render	Do
Remainder	Residuals
Repeat	Reiterate
Repentant	Contrite
Retaliative	Retaliatory
Rumour	Hearsay
Reveal	Divulge

Words	Synonyms
Ritualistic	Ceremonious
Soft	Delicate
Sort	Kind, Choose, Select
Selfish	Egoistic
Sensual	Earthly
Suppress	Quell, Check
Stimulate	Provoke
Tasteless	Insipid
Travel	Journey
True	Authentic, Faithful, Truthful
Turbulence	Turmoil
Tragedy	Calamity
Tasteful	Tasty, Delicious
Touching	Painful
Thankful	Grateful
Tremendous	Great, Huge
Tough	Strong
Terminate	Conclude, End
Theory	Doctrine
Tell	Relate
Tremble	Shake, Shiver
Urge	Spur
Unbeaten	Unsubdued
Use	Utilize, Practise
Underhand	Unfair, Undue
Unfair	Unjust
Unravel	Reveal, Divulge
Unimportant	Common
Unconcerned	Apathetic
Unimitated	Inimitable
Unfortunate	Unlucky
Understand	Perceive, Comprehend
Vain	Proud, Haughty, Conceited, Shameless
Vale	Valley, Dale, Dell
Vice	Fault
Virtue	Quality
Veracity	Reality
Value	Price, Prize
Vex	Tease
Vibrate	Quiver, Shake
Violent	Excessive
Vivid	Clear, Lucid
Victory	Triumph
Vulgar	Indecent
Virtuous	Honest
Variegated	Varied, Multifarious
Well	Good
Yell	Cry, Shout
Yonder	There
Yearn	Wish, Desire
Yoke	Slavery
Zest	Earnestness, Enthusiasm
Zealous	Earnest

ANTONYMS

A antonym is a word which conveys a meaning opposite to the given word.

REMEMBER

Words	*Antonyms*
Abhor	Love
Abnormal	Normal
Able	Unable
Acceptable	Unacceptable
Adequate	Inadequate
Amusing	Boring
Angry	Calm
Apex	Bottom
Attract	Repel
Bad	Good
Barren	Fertile
Beautiful	Ugly
Bitter	Sweet
Brave	Cowardly
Brief	Lengthy
Bright	Dull
Calm	Violent
Careful	Careless
Clear	Vague, Cloudy
Cold	Hot
Cruel	Kind
Dear	Cheap
Deep	Shallow
Difficult	Easy
Direct	Indirect
Dishonest	Honest
Disobey	Obey
Encourage	Discourage
Enormous	Tiny
Excellent	Bad
Expensive	Cheap
Eat	Fast
Fair	Unfair
Fake	Authentic
False	True
Famous	Notorious
Fool	Genius
Generous	Miserly
Genius	Fool
Genuine	Unauthentic
Gigantic	Tiny
Glad	Depressed
Good	Bad
Great	Little
Happy	Sad
Hard	Soft
Hate	Love
Honest	Dishonest
Idle	Busy

Words	*Antonyms*
Immoral	Moral
Include	Exclude
Incorrect	Correct
Intelligent	Unintelligent
Kind	Cruel
Like	Dislike
Long	Short
Lucid	Vague
Major	Minor
Naive	Experienced
Nadir	Apex
Neat	Clumsy
Obedient	Disobedient
Obscure	Clear
Oppose	Support
Optimistic	Pessimistic
Out	In
Patience	Impatience
Peaceful	Belligerent
Pious	Impious
Polite	Impolite
Potent	Impotent
Prominent	Unimportant
Proper	Improper
Pure	Impure
Quick	Slow
Quiet	Disturbance
Real	False, Unreal
Reject	Select, Choose
Reliable	Unreliable
Respect	Disrespect
Right	Wrong
Robust	Feeble, Weak
Sad	Happy
Secret	Open
Sensible	Insensible
Severe	Mild
Sharp	Blunt
Simple	Complex
Sociable	Unsociable
Tall	Short
Tidy	Untidy
Uncanny	Canny
Violent	Calm
Vivid	Vague
Strong	Weak
Big	Small
Easy	Difficult
Fast	Slow
High	Low
Catchy	Unattractive
Ugly	Handsome, Beautiful, Tidy
Tasty	Insipid
Sonorous	Harsh

MULTIPLE CHOICE QUESTIONS

Directions (Qs. 1 to 20): *In the following questions choose the word which best expresses the meaning of the given word.*

1. ABSURD
A. Foolish B. Simple
C. Courageous D. Silly

2. ABANDON
A. Lose B. Profit
C. Vacate D. Foil

3. CAJOLE
A. Pause B. Lenient
C. Blast D. Lure

4. COMBAT
A. Fight B. Conflict
C. Shoot D. Quarrel

5. LAMENT
A. Condone B. Console
C. Complain D. Contribution

6. DEBACLE
A. Disgrace B. Defeat
C. Collapse D. Decline

7. SHIVER
A. Fear B. Tremble
C. Shake D. Ache

8. TORTURE
A. Terror B. Harassment
C. Torment D. Tranquility

9. LAUDABLE
A. Lovable B. Commendable
C. Profitable D. Oblivious

10. FIXED
A. Sterile B. Static
C. Stubborn D. Parennial

11. QUEER
A. Unfamiliar B. Cute
C. Curious D. Strange

12. SUFFICIENT
A. Fit B. Proper
C. Adequate D. Vast

13. GLOSS
A. Brightness B. Soothing
C. Rubbing D. Miracle

14. LONGING
A. Prune B. Apathy
C. Curtail D. Craving

15. JEER
A. Applaud B. Magnanimity
C. Avoid D. Scoff

16. ZENITH
A. Minimum B. Nadir
C. Plant D. Peak

17. GARB
A. Distort B. Dress
C. Trivial D. Rage

18. ABHOR
A. Rude B. Reconcile
C. Crave D. Detest

19. YIELD
A. Shum B. Incisive
C. Retain D. Surrender

20. YOKE
A. Twist B. Release
C. Link D. Extra

Directions (Qs. 21 to 26): *In the following questions choose the word which best expresses the opposite of the given word.*

21. TRAGIC
A. Dramatic B. Strong
C. Gentle D. Comic

22. ORAL
A. Verbal B. Sane
C. Minor D. Written

23. ADMIRE
A. Hate B. Unlike
C. Dislike D. Enough

24. VIOLENT
A. Gentle B. Savage
C. Haughty D. Decline

25. ADVERSITY
A. Windfall B. Inprosperity
C. Prosperity D. Slave

26. GENUINE
A. Spurious B. Obscure
C. Countless D. Apathetic

ANSWERS

1	2	3	4	5	6	7	8	9	10
D	C	D	A	C	C	B	C	B	B
11	**12**	**13**	**14**	**15**	**16**	**17**	**18**	**19**	**20**
D	C	A	D	D	D	B	D	D	C
21	**22**	**23**	**24**	**25**	**26**				
D	D	C	A	C	A				

●●●

3

Sentence Completion

It is such an exercise which starts with the primary schools and continues in the highest level of competitive examinations. One must practise it regularly to score well.

Directions (Qs. 1 to 15): *Pick out the most effective word(s) from the given words to fill in the blanks to make the sentence meaningfully complete.*

1. The student ...... that book from the library to study at home.

A. issued B. borrowed
C. hired D. lent

2. I wish I ...... a king.

A. was B. am
C. should be D. were

3. He ...... to listen to my arguments and walked away.

A. denied B. disliked
C. objected D. refused

4. The flow of blood was so ...... that the patient died.

A. intense B. adequate
C. profuse D. extensive

5. When I met her yesterday, it was the first time I ...... her since Christmas.

A. saw B. have seen
C. had seen D. have been seing

6. Can you pay ...... all these articles?

A. for B. of
C. off D. out

7. I ...... you to be at the party this evening.

A. expect B. hope
C. look forward to D. desire

8. ...... being a handicapped person, he is very cooperative and self-reliant.

A. Because B. Although
C. Since D. Despite

9. The child broke ...... from his mother and ran towards the painting.

A. away B. after
C. down D. with

10. With his ...... income, he finds it difficult to live a comfortable life.

A. brief
B. sufficient
C. meagre
D. huge

11. He could ...... a lot of money in such a short time by using his intelligence and working hard.

A. spend
B. spoil
C. exchange
D. accumulate

12. Though the brothers are twins, they look ......

A. alike B. handsome
C. indifferent D. different

13. Unfavourable weather conditions can ..... illness.

A. cure B. detect
C. treat D. enhance

14. No sooner did the bell ring, ... the actor started singing.

A. when B. than
C. after D. before

15. If I ...... realised it, I would not have acted on his advice.

A. was B. had
C. were D. have

Directions (Qs. 16 to 25): *In each question, an incomplete statement (Stem) followed by four fillers is given. Pick out the best one which can complete the incomplete stem correctly and meaningfully.*

16. Unless you work harder you will fail, means .....

A. if you fail you will work harder.
B. you must at least plan well than you will not fail.
C. hardly you will fail if you do not desire so.
D. if you do not put more efforts, then you will fail.

17. Even if it rains I shall come, means .....

A. if I come it will not rain.
B. if it rains I shall not come.
C. I will certainly come whether it rains or not.
D. whenever there is rain I shall come.

18. Dinesh is as stupid as he is lazy means .....

A. Dinesh is stupid because he is lazy.
B. Dinesh is lazy because he is stupid.
C. Dinesh is either stupid or lazy.
D. Dinesh is equally stupid and lazy.

19. He is so lazy that he .....

A. cannot depend on others for getting his work done.
B. cannot delay the schedule of completing the work.
C. can seldom complete his work on time.
D. dislike to postpone the work that he undertakes to do.

20. He always stammers in public meetings, but his today's speech .....
A. was fairly audible to everyone present in the hall.
B. was not received satisfactorily.
C. could not be understood properly.
D. was free from that defect.

21. In order to raise the company's profit, the employees.....
A. demanded two additional increments.
B. decided to go on paid holidays.
C. requested the management to implement new welfare schemes.
D. offered to work overtime without any compensation.

22. Although, he is reputed for making very candid statements, ...
A. his today's speech was not fairly audible.
B. his promises had always been realistic.
C. his speech was very interesting.
D. his today's statements were very ambiguous.

23. I felt somewhat more relaxed .....
A. but tense as compared to earlier.
B. and tense as compared to earlier.
C. as there was already no tension at all.
D. and tension-free as compared to earlier.

24. With great efforts his son succeeded in convincing him not to donate his entire wealth to an orphanage ....
A. and lead the life of a wealthy merchant.
B. but to a home for the forsaken children.
C. and make an orphan of himself.
D. as the orphanage needed a lot of donations.

25. Even though it is a very large house, ...
A. there is a lot of space available in it for children.
B. there is hardly any space available for children.
C. there is no dearth of space for children.
D. the servants take a long time to clean it.

ANSWERS

1	2	3	4	5	6	7	8	9	10
B	D	D	C	C	A	A	D	A	C
11	**12**	**13**	**14**	**15**	**16**	**17**	**18**	**19**	**20**
D	D	D	B	B	D	C	D	C	D
21	**22**	**23**	**24**	**25**					
D	D	D	C	B					

●●●

4

Spotting Errors

The most common errors in English are of spellings, grammar and usage of words. By regular practice, the errors can be easily spotted and minimised.

MULTIPLE CHOICE QUESTIONS

Directions: *In the following questions some of the sentences have errors and some are correct. Find out which part of a sentence has an error, the number of that part is your answer. If a sentence is free from errors, then your answer is D i.e., No error.*

1. (A) Either Ram or/(B) you is responsible/(C) for this action./(D) No error.
2. (A) The student flatly denied/(B) that he had copied/(C) in the examination hall./(D) No error.
3. (A) By the time you arrive tomorrow/(B) I have finished/(C) my work./(D) No error.
4. (A) The captain with the members of his team/(B) are returning/(C) after a fortnight./(D) No error.
5. (A) After returning from/(B) an all-India tour/(C) I had to describe about it./(D) No error.
6. (A) The teacher asked his students/(B) if they had gone through/(C) either of the three chapters included in the prescribed text./(D) No error.
7. (A) Do you know/(B) how old were you/(C) when you came here?/(D) No error.
8. (A) Beware of/(B) a fair-weather friend/(C) who is neither a friend in need nor a friend indeed./(D) No error.
9. (A) Copernicus proved/(B) that Earth/(C) moves round the Sun./(D) No error.
10. (A) The property/(B) was divided/(C) among the two brothers./(D) No error.
11. (A) I am quite certain/(B) that the lady is not only greedy/(C) but miserly./(D) No error.
12. (A) The brilliant success in the examination/(B) as well as his record in sports/(C) deserves high praise./(D) No error.
13. (A) I cannot find/(B) where has he gone/(C) though I have tried may best./(D) No error.
14. (A) If I was/(B) the Prime Minister of India/(C) I would work wonders/(D) No error.
15. (A) If it weren't/(B) for you,/(C) I wouldn't be alive today./(D) No error.
16. (A) He looked like a lion/(B) baulked from/(C) its prey./(D) No error.
17. (A) Widespread flooding/(B) is affecting/(C) large areas of the villages./(D) No error.
18. (A) If we really set to/(B) we can get the whole house/(C) cleaned in an afternoon./(D) No error.

ANSWERS

1	2	3	4	5	6	7	8	9	10
B	D	B	B	C	C	D	D	B	C
11	**12**	**13**	**14**	**15**	**16**	**17**	**18**	**19**	**20**
C	D	B	A	C	C	C	A	A	C

EXPLANATORY ANSWERS

1. Replace 'is' by 'are'.
2. No error.
3. Replace 'have' by 'would have'.
4. Replace 'are' by 'is'.
5. Replace 'had to describe' by 'described'.
6. Replace 'either' by 'any'.
7. No error.
8. No error.
9. Omit 'that'.
10. Replace 'among' by 'between'.
11. Add 'also'.
12. No error.
13. Replace 'has he' by 'he has'.
14. Replace 'was' by 'were'.
15. Replace 'wouldn't be' by 'would not have been'.
16. Replace 'its' by 'his'.
17. Replace 'areas' by 'area'.
18. Replace 'set to' by 'set on'.

er written by hand
andicraft B. Manuscript
andiwork D. Thesis

ally silent or talking little
rville B. Unequivocal
citurn D. Synoptic

p with a flat object
op B. Hew
aw D. Swat

on who speaks many languages
nguist B. Monolingual
lyglot D. Bilingual

sailing-boat built specially for racing
noe B. Yacht
gate D. Dinghy

orbit in space in relation to earth
ological B. Geo-synchronous
o-centric D. Geo-stationary

n which a writer makes a display of his knowledge
antic B. Verbose
npous D. Ornate

ous discourse
ich B. Stanza
ctorum D. Sermon

that provides refuge
lum B. Sanatorium
ter D. Orphanage

plan of a journey
elogue B. Travelkit
dule D. Itinerary

who insists on something
iplinarian B. Stickler
ntaneous D. Boaster

ng on transparent paper
print B. Blue print
tive D. Transparency

believes that all things and events in life are
nined is a
ist B. Puritan
st D. Tyrant

29. A school boy who cuts classes frequently is a
A. Defeatist B. Sycophant
C. Truant D. Martinet

30. The act of violating the sanctity of the church is
A. Blasphemy B. Heresy
C. Sacrilege D. Desecration

31. A place where monks live as a secluded community
A. Cathedral B. Diocese
C. Convent D. Monastery

32. One who is fond of fighting
A. Bellicose B. Aggressive
C. Belligerent D. Militant

33. Tending to move away from the centre or axis
A. Centrifugal B. Centripetal
C. Axiomatic D. Awry

34. Words inscribed on tomb
A. Epitome B. Epistle
C. Epilogue D. Epitaph

35. Leave or remove from a place considered dangerous
A. Evade B. Evacuate
C. Avoid D. Exterminate

36. Original inhabitants of a country
A. Abroge B. Aborger
C. Aborgory D. Aborigins

37. Government by the officials
A. Theocracy B. Plutocracy
C. Bureaucracy D. Democracy

38. Incapable of being exhausted
A. Inexhaustible B. Inaexhaustible
C. Exhaustable D. Non-tired

39. A person of good understanding, knowledge and reasoning power
A. Expert B. Intellectual
C. Snob D. Literate

40. One absorbed in his own thoughts and feelings rather than in things outside
A. Scholar B. Recluse
C. Introvert D. Intellectual

ANSWERS

2	3	4	5	6	7	8	9	10
D	D	D	C	C	D	A	B	A
12	**13**	**14**	**15**	**16**	**17**	**18**	**19**	**20**
B	A	B	A	B	C	D	A	B
22	**23**	**24**	**25**	**26**	**27**	**28**	**29**	**30**
A	D	A	D	B	D	A	C	C
32	**33**	**34**	**35**	**36**	**37**	**38**	**39**	**40**
A	A	D	B	B	C	A	B	C

●●●

5 One Word Substitution

There are many single words in English language which can be perfectly used for a number of words. These words help in expressing ideas in a short and correct manner for the right occasion. Such words not only increase the vocabulary but also enable you to economise in the use of words to a great extent.

Multiple Word Expression	*Substitution*
One who always looks towards the bright side of things	Optimist
One who always looks towards the dark side of things	Pessimist
The time when one develops from a child into an adult	Adolescence
The process of growing more plants in order to form a forest.	Afforestation
The science which deals with farming	Agriculture
From some other country or place etc.	Alien
A term, etc. giving more than one meaning	Ambiguous
A vehicle which is used to carry sick persons	Ambulance
An animal which can live both in water and on land	Amphibian
A lawless situation when there is no government	Anarchy
Belonging to the history of thousands of years old	Ancient
Once a year	Annual
A very old object but still valuable	Antique
Words of opposite meanings	Antonyms
Words of similar meanings	Synonyms
Signatures of a famous person	Autograph
A government led by one person with absolute authority	Autocracy
A written work of one's own life history	Autobiography
A person who has never been married	Bachelor
A person usually having no hair on his head	Bald
A place where one can deposit money and get interest	Bank
A person who cuts our hair	Barber
A building/group of buildings where soldiers live	Barracks
A person who makes buns and biscuits	Baker
A person who lives by asking people for food and money without doing any useful job	Beggar
The crime of having married to two persons at the same time	Bigamy
The branch of science which deals with the study of plants	Botany
Able to speak two languages	Bilingual
Able to speak more than two languages	Polyglot
The branch of science which deals with the living organisms	Biology
A powerful snow storm	Blizzard
A great successful book or movie	Blockbuster
A short news on the radio or TV	Bulletin
A system in which the most important works are organised by the government officials	Bureaucracy
A person who has no vision in his eyes	Blind
A page or a series of pages on which the information of days, weeks, months, etc. is given	Calendar
A person who eats human flesh	Cannibal
A complete list of items often arranged alphabetically	Catalogue
A sudden disaster	Catastrophe
A period of 100 years	Century

Multiple Word Expression	Substitution
A branch of science which deals with chemicals	Chemistry
A printed leaf usually issued by banks that we sign to carry certain financial deal	Cheque
A person who makes or mends shoes	Cobbler
A group of people who has been chosen by others to make decisions on their own	Committee
A building in which nuns live	Convent
An animal which feeds on other animals	Carnivorous
A person who does criticism	Critic
A person who cannot hear	Deaf
A condition in which one loses a lot of water from one's body because of vomiting, etc.	Dehydration
A system of government in which the people cast their votes to elect their leaders	Democracy
The study of skin problems	Dermatology
A long piece of land covered with sand	Desert
The art of managing relationships between countries	Diplomacy
A piece of information about the words in a book form	Dictionary
A piece of information about the telephone numbers of the people in a book from	Directory
A person in charge of a newspapers, magazine etc.	Editor
A person who thinks he is better than the others	Egoist
To leave your country and settle in some other country	Emigrate
A book or series of books giving almost all knowledge about an area or some persons etc.	Encyclopaedia
Study of insects	Entomology
Time when day and night are of the same duration	Equinox
To sell things out of the country	Export
To purchase things from some other country	Import
A plant or animal no longer in existence	Extinct
A situation when there is a shortage of food for a long period of time	Famine
An amount of money that we pay for some action or services	Fee
Related to women	Feminine
An animal strong and aggressive	Ferocious
A piece of land where plants grow easily from the soil that is favourable to them	Fertile
A work of literature having some imaginary events	Fiction
A large amount of water covering certain area	Flood
A person who sells flowers	Florist
A religious ceremony for burying or cremating a dead person	Funeral
A substance which kills fungus	Fungicide
A person studying or having studied the diseases and the related things of female reproductory system	Gynaecologist
The murder of the person of the same group race or country	Genocide
A substance which kills germs	Germicide
A situation in which many people die because of fire during war	Holocaust
The act of killing a person deliberately	Homicide
A word having the pronunciation as the other one does but it differs in meaning	Homophone
A word having the same spelling as the other one does but it is pronounced in some other way	Homonym
A person who is attracted towards the person of the same sex	Homosexual
Go across and parallel to the ground	Horizontal
A substance which kills the insects	Insecticide
That cannot be corrected	Incorrigible
That cannot be defeated	Invincible
That cannot be eaten	Inedible
That cannot be seen	Invisible
A place in a school or college where books are kept for the benefit of students, teachers etc.	Library
A place in a school or college where scientific experiments are performed	Laboratory

Multiple Word Expression
An official who is a judge in the lowest court
A piece of music or a book before it is printed
Related to men
One who believes in the existence of God
One who does not believe in the existence of good
That can be believed
That cannot be believed
That which dissolves in a solvent
That which does not dissolves in a solvent
Hard writing that can be read
Hard writing that cannot be read
A person who does jobs beneficial to mankind
A person who goes on foot
A person who fights for his own country
An act of killing oneself
A woman whose husband is dead
A man whose wife is dead
A person who eats vegetarian and non-vegetarian diets
Something which is everywhere at the same time
One who knows everything
A child who does not have parents
An award etc. given after the death of the person
The place where animals are kept for amusement and to increase the knowledge of t
The science which deals with the study of animals

MULTIPLE CHOICE QUESTIONS

Directions: *In questions given below, out of the four alternatives, choose the one which can be substituted for the given words/sentences.*

1. Something that relates to everyone in the world
A. General B. Common
C. Usual D. Universal

2. An expression of mild disapproval
A. Warning B. Denigration
C. Impertinence D. Reproof

3. One who is not easily pleased by anything
A. Maiden B. Medieval
C. Precarious D. Fastidious

4. Murder of a king
A. Infanticide B. Matricide
C. Genocide D. Regicide

5. A remedy for all diseases
A. Stoic B. Marvel
C. Panacea D. Recompense

6. A dramatic performance
A. Mask B. Mosque
C. Masque D. Mascot

7. Study of birds
A. Orology B. Optology
C. Ophthalmology D. Ornithology

8. Ready to believ
A. Credulous
C. Creditable

9. Incapable of be
A. Ductile
C. Obsolete

10. One who eats
A. Omnivoro
C. Irresistible

11. A place wher
A. An apiary
C. A hive

12. One who can
A. Incurable
C. Hardenec

13. One who is
A. Curator
C. Caretake

14. Continuing
A. Enmity
C. Quarrel

15. A voice lou
A. Audible
C. Laudab

16. A pap
A. H
C. H

17. Habitu
A. Se
C. Ta

18. To sla
A. Cl
C. G

19. A pers
A. Li
C. Po

20. A ligh
A. Ca
C. Fri

21. A fixe
A. Ge
C. Ge

22. A style
A. Pe
C. Po

23. A religi
A. Pre
C. San

24. A place
A. Asy
C. She

25. Detailed
A. Tra
C. Sch

26. A perso
A. Disc
C. Insta

27. A drawi
A. Red
C. Nega

28. One who predeterm
A. Fatal
C. Egois

1 D
11 A
21 D
31 D

6

Spelling Errors

There are thousands of words in English language. It is difficult to remember the spellings and meanings of all at once. Try to learn as many as you can. Use a dictionary regularly.

Directions: *Find the correctly spelt words.*

1. A. Damage B. Dammage C. Damaige D. Dammege

2. A. Efficiant B. Effecient C. Efficient D. Eficient

3. A. Schedule B. Schdule C. Schedale D. Schedeule

4. A. Occurad B. Occurred C. Ocurred D. Occured

5. A. Grieff B. Grief C. Grieef D. Grrief

6. A. Guarantee B. Garuntee C. Guaruntee D. Gaurantee

7. A. Meddicine B. Medicine C. Medicene D. Medicinne

8. A. Benefeted B. Benefitted C. Benifited D. Benefited

9. A. Acommodation B. Acomodation C. Accomodation D. Accommodation

10. A. Querrelsome B. Quarrelsame C. Quarrelsome D. Querralsome

11. A. Sympathetic B. Smypathetic C. Sympothetic D. Sympethetic

12. A. Prograssive B. Progressive C. Progresive D. Prograsive

13. A. Uncivilized B. Uncevilized C. Uncivillized D. Uncevelized

14. A. Extravagant B. Extreragent C. Extreregant D. Extravegent

15. A. Missunderstood B. Miesunderstood C. Misunderstood D. Misunderstod

16. A. Belligerent B. Beligirent C. Belligarant D. Belligerrent

17. A. Astonished B. Astronished C. Astoneshed D. Asstonished

18. A. Sincerely B. Sencerely C. Sincerelly D. Sincerrely

19. A. Rigourous B. Rigerous C. Rigorous D. Regerous

20. A. Satellite B. Sattellite C. Satelite D. Sattelite

21. A. Pesanger B. Passenger C. Pessenger D. Pasanger

22. A. Humurous B. Humorous C. Humoreus D. Humorrous

23. A. Exeggerate B. Exaggerate C. Exadgerate D. Exagerate

24. A. Fariegn B. Forein C. Foriegn D. Foreign

25. A. Excesive B. Excessive C. Exccessive D. Exccesive

26. A. Forcaust B. Forcast C. Forecast D. Forecaste

27. A. Paralleted B. Paralelled C. Parralleled D. Parallelled

28. A. Ocasion B. Occassion C. Occasion D. Ocassion

29. A. Boquet B. Bouquet C. Bouquete D. Bouquette

30. A. Chettering B. Chaterring C. Chattering D. Chatering

31. A. Discourage B. Disscourage C. Discourege D. Discaurage

32. A. Curageous B. Courageous C. Courrageous D. Couregeous

33. A. Abandon B. Abanddon C. Abendon D. Abbandon

34. A. Embarassment B. Emberrassement C. Embarrassment D. Embbaresment

35. A. Eccintric B. Eccentrie C. Eccentric D. Eccintrie

36. A. Occasional B. Occassional C. Occesional D. Occessional

37. A. Querrel B. Querral C. Quarrel D. Quarel

38. A. Contrebution B. Contribution C. Contributtion D. Conterbution

39. A. Desgrace B. Disgrece
C. Disgrice D. Disgrace

40. A. Harassment B. Herassment
C. Harasment D. Harassmient

41. A. Imaginative B. Imeginative
C. Imagenative D. Imaginetive

42. A. Suficient B. Suficiant
C. Sufficient D. Sufficiant

43. A. Adequate B. Edequate
C. Adaquete D. Edaquete

44. A. Expariended B. Experianced
C. Experienced D. Experrienced

45. A. Flatering B. Fletering
C. Flattering D. Fletaring

46. A. Cuttiveted B. Culltrivated
C. Cultivated D. Caltivated

47. A. Praiceworthy B. Peiseworthy
C. Praiseworthy D. Praisaworthy

48. A. Profesional B. Professionel
C. Professional D. Profissional

49. A. Ameteur B. Amateur
C. Amataur D. Amateor

50. A. Unfevourable B. Unfevaurable
C. Unfavourable D. Unfivourable

ANSWERS

1	2	3	4	5	6	7	8	9	10
A	C	A	B	B	A	B	B	D	C
11	**12**	**13**	**14**	**15**	**16**	**17**	**18**	**19**	**20**
A	B	A	A	C	A	A	A	C	A
21	**22**	**23**	**24**	**25**	**26**	**27**	**28**	**29**	**30**
B	B	B	D	B	C	A	C	B	C
31	**32**	**33**	**34**	**35**	**36**	**37**	**38**	**39**	**40**
A	B	A	C	C	A	C	B	D	A
41	**42**	**43**	**44**	**45**	**46**	**47**	**48**	**49**	**50**
A	C	A	C	A	C	C	C	B	C

●●●

हिन्दी भाषा
(व्याकरण एवं साहित्य)

व्याकरण

'व्याकरण' शब्द का अर्थ है– 'वाक् पृथक्करण-प्रक्रिया'। इसका निर्माण वि+आकरण यानि 'आ' उपसर्ग को 'कृ' धातु में जोड़कर जो रूप निष्पन्न होता है उसमें पुनः लुयुट् प्रत्यय जोड़ने से होता है। व्याकरण से भाषा में अनुशासन बना रहता है। वस्तुतः व्याकरण एक शास्त्र है। व्याकरण का निर्माण भाषा-विशेष के लिए होता है। अर्थात् प्रत्येक भाषा का अपना निजी व्याकरण होता है। इसके द्वारा भाषा विशेष के वर्ण, शब्द, ध्वनि और वाक्य के शुद्ध रूप एवं प्रयोग के नियम का सम्यक् निरूपण किया जाता है। दूसरे शब्दों में, व्याकरण वह शास्त्र है जिसका निर्माण भाषा-विशेष के लिए होता है और जिससे भाषा-विशेष के शुद्ध रूप तथा प्रयोग की नियमावली का ज्ञान होता है।

लिंग

हिन्दी में दो लिंग होते हैं–स्त्रीलिंग और पुल्लिंग। जो शब्द स्त्री जाति का बोध कराते हैं, उन्हें स्त्रीलिंग कहा जाता है, जैसे–राधा, लड़की, पुत्री, पुस्तक, शेरनी, चिड़िया आदि। इसके विपरीत जो शब्द पुरुष जाति का बोध कराते हैं, उन्हें पुल्लिंग कहा जाता है, जैसे–कृष्ण, शेर, बैल, गीदड़, पुत्र, लड़का। ध्यान रहे कि नपुंसक लिंग का प्रयोग संस्कृत में होता है, हिन्दी में नहीं होता।

कुछ शब्द जो प्रायः स्त्रीलिंग ही होते हैं–

(1) ईकारान्त शब्द। जैसे–चिट्ठी, पत्री, लेखनी, बोली, गोली, चोली, डोली इत्यादि।
अपवाद–मोती, घी, जी, पानी आदि शब्द पुल्लिंग हैं।

(2) नदियों के नाम। जैसे–गंगा, यमुना, सरस्वती, रावी इत्यादि।
प्रायः सभी नदियों के साथ नदी शब्द का प्रयोग किया जा सकता है।

(3) संस्कृत के स्त्रीलिंग और नपुंसक लिंग जैसे–आशा, माता, दिशा इत्यादि।

(4) राशियों, तिथियों और नक्षत्रों के नाम। जैसे–मेष, वृष, मिथुन, कन्या, तीज, प्रतिपदा, आश्विन, रोहणी आदि।

(5) धातुओं के नाम जैसे–चांदी, मिट्टी, धातु आदि।

(6) कुछ समुदाय वाचक संज्ञाएं। जैसे–सेना, शाला, फौज, टोली, सभा, श्रेणी, कक्षा इत्यादि।

(7) अनाज, दालें इत्यादि। जैसे–अरहर, मकई आदि।

(8) कुछ प्राणीवाचक शब्द। जैसे–भगिनी, गाय, कोयल, चील, मैना, बिल्ली आदि।

कुछ शब्द जो प्रायः पुल्लिंग ही होते हैं–

(1) पर्वतों आदि के नाम। जैसे–हिमालय, शिवालिक, विंध्याचल आदि।

(2) भावनावाचक संज्ञाएं–जिनके अन्त में आव, पन, पा, त्व हों। जैसे–चढ़ाव, बहाव, बड़प्पन, बचपन, रंडापा, बुढ़ापा, महत्व, पुरुषत्व।

(3) महीने और दिनों के नाम। जैसे–ज्येष्ठ, बैसाख, चैत्र, मंगलवार, रविवार।

(4) ग्रहों के नाम। जैसे–मंगल, बुध, राहु, केतु आदि।

(5) वर्णमाला के सभी अक्षर–केवल इ, ई और ऋ को छोड़कर।

(6) संस्कृत के नपुंसक लिंग। जैसे–दही, मधु आदि।

(7) पेड़, अनाज सम्बन्धी शब्द। जैसे–बड़, पीपल, आम, चावल, गेहूँ, बाजरा, उड़द।

(8) द्रव्यवाचक शब्द। जैसे–सोना, तांबा, लोहा, मोती, माणिक आदि।

पुल्लिंग से स्त्रीलिंग बनाने के नियम–

(1) अकारान्त और आकारान्त शब्दों के अन्त में ई जोड़ देने से स्त्रीलिंग बन जाता है। जैसे–

नाना–नानी	लड़का–लड़की	दादा–दादी
चाचा–चाची	पुत्र–पुत्री	देव–देवी
गीदड़–गीदड़ी	कबूतर–कबूतरी	नट–नटी

(2) कुछ आकारान्त शब्दों के अन्त का 'आ' हटा कर 'इया' जोड़ दिया जाता है। जैसे–

चिड़ा–चिड़िया	चूहा–चुहिया	डिब्बा–डिबिया
कुत्ता–कुतिया	बेटा–बिटिया	बूढ़ा–बुढ़िया

(3) कुछ व्यापार-सूचक (अकारान्त, आकारान्त, इकारान्त) शब्दों के पीछे 'इन' प्रत्यय लगाकर स्त्रीलिंग बनाते हैं। जैसे–

जुलाहा–जुलाहिन	धोबी–धोबिन	कहार–कहारिन
चमार–चमारिन	ठठेरा–ठठेरिन	ग्वाला–ग्वालिन

(4) कुछ प्राणीवाचक शब्दों के पीछे 'नी' या 'इनी' प्रत्यय लगाया जाता है। जैसे–

हंस–हंसिनी	जाट–जाटिनी	हाथी–हथिनी
शेर–शेरनी		

(5) कुछ प्राणीवाचक शब्दों के पीछे 'आनी' प्रत्यय भी लगाया जाता है। जैसे–

नौकर–नौकरानी	जेठ–जेठानी	देवर–देवरानी
चौधरी–चौधरानी	सेठ–सेठानी	मेहतर–मेहतरानी

(6) कुछ अकारान्त शब्दों के अन्त में 'आ' प्रत्यय लगाने से, जैसे–

शिव–शिवा	शूद्र–शूद्रा	प्रिय–प्रिया
बाल–बाला	सुत–सुता	

(7) कुछ शब्दों के अन्त में 'वती' या 'मती' लगाने से, जैसे–

भगवान्–भगवती	गुणवान्–गुणवती	श्रीमान्–श्रीमती
रूपवान्–रूपवती	बुद्धिमान्–बुद्धिमती	धनवान्–धनवती

(8) कुछ उपनाम सम्बन्धी शब्दों के अन्त में 'आइन' प्रत्यय लगाने से, जैसे–

लाला–ललाइन	ठाकुर–ठकुराइन	बाबू–बबुआइन
दुबे–दुबाइन	पण्डित–पण्डिताइन	

(9) कुछ शब्दों के अन्त में 'अक' आता है। उनको स्त्रीलिंग बनाने के लिए 'अक' प्रत्यय का 'इका' कर लिया जाता है। जैसे–

अध्यापक–अध्यापिका	सेवक–सेविका	नायक–नायिका
बालक–बालिका	प्रेषक–प्रेषिका	लेखक–लेखिका

(10) कुछ शब्दों के अन्त में 'त्री' लगाने से स्त्रीलिंग बन जाता है। जैसे–

कवि–कवयित्री　　कर्ता–कर्त्री

(11) कुछ इकारान्त शब्दों के अन्त में 'ई' प्रत्यय को 'इ' करके 'णी' लगाकर स्त्रीलिंग बना लिया जाता है। जैसे–

परोपकारी–परोपकारिणी　　अधिकारी–अधिकारिणी
सहधर्मी–सहधर्मिणी　　कल्याणकारी–कल्याणकारिणी

(12) कुछ पुल्लिंग शब्दों के स्त्रीलिंग सर्वथा भिन्न होते हैं, जैसे–

पिता–माता　　वर–वधु
राजा–रानी　　विद्वान–विदुषी

वचन

वचन का शाब्दिक अर्थ है- बोली। परन्तु हिन्दी में व्याकरण की दृष्टि में वचन का अर्थ संख्या से लिया जाता है। इसलिए वचन को परिभाषित करते हुए कहा जा सकता है– संज्ञा, सर्वनाम, विशेषण और क्रिया के जिस रूप से संख्या का बोध होता है, उसे वचन कहते हैं।

वचन के भेद

हिन्दी में वचन के दो भेद माने गए हैं (1) एकवचन (2) बहुवचन

(1) एकवचन (Singular Number) : जैसा कि नाम से स्पष्ट है, एकवचन विकारी शब्द का वह रूप है जिससे एक ही व्यक्ति या वस्तु का बोध होता है। उदाहरण- घोड़ा दौड़ता है। गाय चरती है। इन वाक्यों में 'घोड़ा' और 'गाय' से एक जानवर का बोध होता है। अतः ये एकवचन हैं।

(2) बहुवचन (Plural Number) : बहुवचन वह विकारी शब्द है जिससे एक से अधिक वस्तुओं, व्यक्तियों आदि का बोध होता है। जैसे- घोड़े चरते हैं। गायें दौड़ती हैं। 'घोड़े' और 'गायें' कहने से एक से अधिक जानवरों का बोध होता है। अतः ये बहुवचन हैं।

वचन के रूपान्तर : यद्यपि वचन के कारण संज्ञा, सर्वनाम, विशेषण और क्रिया के रूप में परिवर्तन होता है तथापि सर्वनाम, विशेषण और क्रिया के रूप मूलतः इनसे जुड़ी संख्या पर ही आधारित होते हैं। अतएव एकवचन में संज्ञा शब्दों के रूपान्तर की ही प्रमुखता है।

वचन के अधीन संज्ञा के रूप दो तरह से परिवर्तित होते हैं– (1) विभक्ति रहित (2) विभक्ति सहित

विभक्ति रहित संज्ञाओं के बहुवचन बनाने के नियम :

विभक्ति रहित संज्ञाओं का बहुवचन साधारणतः निम्नलिखित नियमों के अन्तर्गत बनाया जाता है-

1. पुल्लिंग संज्ञा के आकारान्त को एकारान्त कर बहुवचन बनाया जाता है। यथा-

एकवचन	बहुवचन	एकवचन	बहुवचन
घोड़ा	घोड़े	गधा	गधे
लड़का	लड़के		

अपवाद- मामा, नाना, बाबा, पिता, योद्धा, आत्मा, देवता, जामाता आदि। इन शब्दों के रूप दोनों वचनों में समान होते हैं।

2. पुल्लिंग आकारान्त शब्दों के अतिरिक्त अन्य मात्राओं से अन्त होने वाले शब्दों के रूप दोनों वचनों में एक समान रहते हैं। जैसे–

एकवचन	बहुवचन	एकवचन	बहुवचन
एक बालक	चार बालक	एक डाकू	चार डाकू
एक भाई	चार भाई	एक जौ	चार जौ

3. आकारान्त स्त्रीलिंग शब्दों के अन्त में 'एँ' जोड़ने से बहुवचन बनता है। जैसे–

एकवचन	बहुवचन	एकवचन	बहुवचन
शाखा	शाखाएँ	लता	लताएँ
माता	माताएँ	महिला	महिलाएँ

4. अकारान्त स्त्रीलिंग संज्ञा के बहुवचन शब्द में आगत अंतिम अ को यें कर देने से बनता है। जैसे–

एकवचन	बहुवचन	एकवचन	बहुवचन
गाय	गायें	रात	रातें
बात	बातें	आँख	आँखें
याद	यादें		

5. दीर्घ या ह्रस्व इकारान्त संज्ञाओं को ह्रस्व इकारान्त कर उनके अन्त में याँ जोड़ देने से बहुवचन बनता है। जैसे–

एकवचन	बहुवचन	एकवचन	बहुवचन
नारी	नारियाँ	पहेली	पहेलियाँ
लड़की	लड़कियाँ	सहेली	सहेलियाँ
नीति	नीतियाँ	नदी	नदियाँ
घड़ी	घड़ियाँ	छड़ी	छड़ियाँ
धोती	धोतियाँ	साड़ी	साड़ियाँ

6. जिन स्त्रीलिंग शब्दों के अन्त में 'या' आता है, 'या' पर चन्द्रबिन्दु लगाकर बहुवचन बनाया जाता है जैसे–

एकवचन	बहुवचन	एकवचन	बहुवचन
बुढ़िया	बुढ़ियाँ	चिड़िया	चिड़ियाँ
गुड़िया	गुड़ियाँ	डिबिया	डिबियाँ
दुनिया	दुनियाँ		

7. ह्रस्व या दीर्घ ऊकारान्त स्त्रीलिंग संज्ञाओं को ह्रस्व उकारान्त बनाकर अन्त में 'एँ' लगाने से बहुवचन का निर्माण होता है। जैसे-

एकवचन	बहुवचन	एकवचन	बहुवचन
धेनु	धेनुएँ	वस्तु	वस्तुएँ
बहू	बहुएँ	ऋतु	ऋतुएँ

8. कुछ शब्द समष्टि मूलक होते हैं। जैसे– गण, कुल, वृन्द, समूह, वर्ग, लोग, जन, मण्डल, दल, ग्राम, मण्डली आदि। ये शब्द विशेषतः वहाँ जोड़े जाते हैं, जहाँ दोनों वचनों में पुल्लिंग अथवा स्त्रीलिंग में एक ही रूप होते हैं।

उदाहरण :

एकवचन	बहुवचन	एकवचन	बहुवचन
पाठक	पाठकगण	आप	आप लोग
तुम	तुम लोग	छात्र	छात्रगण
विद्यार्थी	विद्यार्थीगण		

विभक्ति सहित संज्ञाओं के बहुवचन बनाने के नियम :-

सविभक्ति संज्ञाओं के बहुवचन बनाने के सामान्य नियम निम्नलिखित हैं–

1. संस्कृत शब्दों को छोड़कर हिन्दी के अकारान्त, आकारान्त तथा एकारान्त संज्ञाओं के अन्तिम अ, आ, ए के बदले बहुवचन बनाने में इसे 'ओं' कर दिया जाता है। जैसे-

एकवचन	बहुवचन
नर	नरों (का)
चीता	चीतों (द्वारा)
चोर	चोरों (ने)
घोड़ा	घोड़ों (को)

विभक्ति चिह्नों के साथ प्रयोग :

(क) नरों की कहानी।

(ख) चीतों का भय।

(ग) चोरों की पकड़।

(घ) घोड़ों की हिनहिनाहट।

कारक

संज्ञा या सर्वनाम के उस रूप को कारक कहते हैं जिससे उसका सम्बन्ध वाक्य के अन्य शब्दों विशेषतः क्रिया के साथ प्रकट होता है। वास्तव में, विभक्ति चिह्नों से युक्त संज्ञा या सर्वनाम शब्द ही वाक्य में अन्य शब्दों से सम्बन्ध प्रकट करते हैं।

ने, को, से, द्वारा– आदि विभक्ति चिह्न हैं। कारक का एक उदाहरण इस प्रकार है-'मोहन ने बाग में डण्डे से आम तोड़ा।' इस वाक्य में मोहन ने, डण्डे से, और आम संज्ञाओं के रूपान्तरण हैं। जिस तत्त्व के द्वारा इन रूपान्तरित संज्ञाओं का सम्बन्ध तोड़ा, क्रिया से स्पष्ट होता है, वही कारक है।

कारक-चिह्न

हिन्दी में कारक के आठ भेद माने जाते है :

	कारक	विभक्ति या कारक चिह्न
1.	कर्त्ता	ने
2.	कर्म	को
3.	करण	से, द्वारा
4.	सम्प्रदान	को, के लिए
5.	अपादान	से
6.	सम्बन्ध	का, के, की, रा, रे, री, ना, ने, नी
7.	अधिकरण	में, पर
8.	सम्बोधन	हे, हो, अरे, अजी, अहो आदि।

कारक-चिह्न/विभक्ति/परसर्ग

हिन्दी में कारक का ज्ञान कराने के लिए संज्ञा या सर्वनाम के साथ जो प्रत्यय लगाये जाते हैं, उन्हें ही व्याकरण में विभक्ति कहते हैं। हिन्दी में चूँकि विभक्ति चिह्न पद से अलग प्रयुक्त होते हैं इसलिए इन्हें 'परसर्ग' भी कहा जाता है। परसर्ग का शब्दिक अर्थ है- पीछे जुड़ना। कारक चिह्न सदैव संज्ञा या सर्वनाम के पीछे जुड़ते हैं।

(i) **कर्त्ता कारक :** कर्त्ता का अभिप्राय है, करने वाला। वाक्य में जो क्रिया सम्पन्न करता है, उसे कर्त्ता कहा जाता है। जैसे- राम पढ़ता है। सुरेश पत्र लिखता है। इन वाक्यों में राम और सुरेश कर्त्ता कारक हैं क्योंकि ये ही क्रिया को सम्पादित करने वाले हैं।

(ii) **कर्म कारक :** कर्त्ता द्वारा सम्पादित क्रिया का फल जिस पर पड़ता है, उसे 'कर्म' कहते हैं। जैसे– शीला ने राजेश को पढ़ाया। इस वाक्य में कर्त्ता है- शीला, क्रिया है– पढ़ाना। पढ़ाना क्रिया का फल राजेश पर स्पष्ट पड़ रहा है। इसलिए यहाँ राजेश कर्म कारक की स्थिति में है।

(iii) **करण कारक :** वाक्य में कारण कारक उस शब्द को कहते हैं जो क्रिया को पूर्ण करने में साधन के रूप में कर्ता का सहायक होकर आता है। जैसे– मैं कलम से लिखता हूँ। इस वाक्य में 'कलम से' करण कारक है क्योंकि लेखन-क्रिया में कलम साधन है।

(iv) **सम्प्रदान कारक :** कर्त्ता क्रिया की सिद्धि जिसके लिए करता है अथवा जिसको कुछ देता है, उसे प्रकट करने वाले शब्द रूप को सम्प्रदान कारक कहते हैं। जैसे– श्याम मीरा के लिए खिलौने लाया। राकेश शीला के लिए रोता है। इन वाक्यों में लाना और रोना क्रियाएँ क्रमशः मीरा और शीला के लिए सम्पादित की जा रही हैं। इसलिए मीरा और शीला के लिए शब्द रूप सम्प्रदान कारक है।

संधि

सन्धि शब्द का सामान्य अर्थ है– मेल अथवा मिलन। जब दो निकटवर्ती शब्दों का परस्पर मेल होता है, तो उसे संधि कहते हैं। संधि पहले वाले शब्द के अंतिम वर्ण और दूसरे वाले शब्द के प्रथम वर्ण (दोनों वर्णों) के मिलन से होती है। जब संधि होती है, तो दोनों शब्दों के मेल से बना शब्द (नया वाला शब्द) दोनों शब्दों का सामान्य संयोग मात्र नहीं होता, बल्कि उनके मेल से बना नया शब्द कुछ भिन्न होता है। यह भिन्नता या परिवर्तन उन्हीं दोनों वर्णों में होता है, जिनका मेल होता है। उदाहरण के लिए यदि हम 'हिम' और 'आलय' दोनों शब्दों की संधि करें, तो संधि से बनने वाला शब्द 'हिमालय' होगा। इसी प्रकार 'विद्या' और 'अर्थी' शब्दों की संधि से 'विद्यार्थी' शब्द बनता है।

संधि के मुख्य रूप से तीन भेद हैं– स्वर संधि, व्यंजन संधि और विसर्ग संधि।

(क) **स्वर संधिः** जब स्वर के साथ स्वर का मेल हो और स्वर में परिवर्तन हो, तो उसे स्वर संधि कहते हैं। उदाहरण के लिए 'छात्र' और आवास में 'त्र' और 'आ' का मेल होकर 'त्रा' बनेगा और संधि के फलस्वरूप बना शब्द 'छात्रावास' होगा।

इसी प्रकार 'रमा' और 'ईश' के मेल से 'रमेश' बनता है। 'महा' और 'ऋषि' के मेल से 'महर्षि' बनता है। 'यदि' और 'अपि' के मेल से 'यद्यपि' बनता है।

(ख) **व्यंजन संधिः** जब दो व्यंजनों के मेल से नया शब्द बनता है, तो उसे व्यंजन संधि कहते हैं। जैसे 'जगत' और 'नाथ' के मेल से 'जगन्नाथ' शब्द बनता है। 'तन्' और 'मय' के मेल से 'तन्मय' शब्द बनता है। 'सत्' और 'चित' के मेल से 'सच्चित' शब्द बनता है। 'सम्' और 'राट' के मेल से 'सम्राट' शब्द बनता है।

(ग) **विसर्ग संधिः** जब विसर्ग के साथ व्यंजन का मेल हो तो विसर्ग संधि ा होती है। जैसे– 'निः' और 'जन' के मेल से 'निर्जन' तथा 'दुः' और 'चरित्र' के मेल से 'दुश्चरित्र' बनता है।

संधि के प्रकार

हिन्दी में संधि के तीन प्रकार हैं–(1) स्वर संधि (2) व्यंजन संधि (3) विसर्ग संधि।

(1) स्वर संधि

दो स्वरों के मेल से जो विकार या वर्ण के रूप में परिवर्तन होता है, वही स्वर संधि कहलाता है।

स्वर संधि के भेदः स्वर संधि के निम्नलिखित पाँच भेद हैं :–

(क) दीर्घ संधि (ख) गुण संधि (ग) वृद्धि संधि (घ) यण् संधि (ङ) अयादि संधि।

(क) **दीर्घ संधिः** जब दो सवर्ण स्वरों का मेल होता है तो एक दीर्घ स्वर बन जाता है। यह दीर्घ संधि है। अ और आ सवर्ण स्वर हैं। इसी प्रकार इ ई उ ऊ और ऋ सवर्ण स्वर हैं। ह्स्व या दीर्घ अ इ उ ऋ के बाद यदि पूर्ववत् ह्स्व या दीर्घ स्वर हो तो दोनों के स्थान पर एक सवर्ण दीर्घ स्वर होता है।

जैसे– अ + अ = आ (नर + अधय = नराधय)
अ + आ = आ (कार्य + आलय = कार्यालय)
आ + अ = आ (विद्या + अर्थी = विद्यार्थी)
आ + आ = आ (महा + आशय = महाशय)
इ + इ = ई (मुनि + इन्द्र = मुनीन्द्र)
इ + ई = ई (कपि + ईश = कपीश)
ई + इ = ई (मही + इन्द्र = महीन्द्र)
ई + ई = ई (नदी + ईश = नदीश)
उ + उ = ऊ (साधु + उवाच = साधूवाच)

(ख) **गुण संधिः** अ या आ के बाद यदि इ या ई, उ या ऊ और ऋ आवे तो दोनों के मेल से क्रमशः ए, ओ अर हो जाता है।

जैसे– अ + इ = ए (नर + इन्द्र = नरेन्द्र)
आ + इ = ए (महा + इन्द्र = महेन्द्र)

(ग) **वृद्धि संधिः** अ या आ के बाद यदि ए या ऐ और ओ या औ का आगमन होता है, तो दोनों मिलकर क्रमशः ऐ और औ उत्पन्न करते हैं।

जैसे– अ + ए = ऐ (एक + एक = एकैक)
आ + ए = ऐ (तथा + एव = तथैव)

(घ) **यण संधिः** ह्स्व या दीर्घ इ, उ, ऋ के अनन्तर यदि कोई असवर्ण स्वर आता है तो 'इ' का यू, उ का व् और ऋ का र् हो जाता है।

जैसे– इ + आ = या (अति + आनन्द = अत्यानन्द)
इ + ए = ये (प्रति + एक = प्रत्येक)

(ङ) **अयादि संधिः** ए ऐ ओ औ के अनन्तर यदि कोई असवर्ण स्वर आये तो ए का अय्, ऐ का आय्, ओ का अव् और औ का आव् हो जाता है।

जैसे– ए + अ = अय (ने + अन = नयन)
ऐ + अ = आय (नै + अक = नायक)

(2) व्यंजन संधि

व्यंजन संधि उसे कहते हैं जिसमें संधि होने वाले दो वर्णों में से प्रथम वर्ण व्यंजन हो और दूसरा स्वर या व्यंजन हो।

जैसे– दिक् + गज = दिग्गज।

व्यंजन संधि के प्रमुख नियम इस प्रकार हैं–

(क) यदि किसी वर्ण के पहले व्यंजन के अनन्तर किसी वर्ग का पंचम वर्ण आता है तो प्रथम व्यंजन वर्ग का परिवर्तन उसी वर्ग के पंचम वर्ण में होता है।

जैसे– जगत् + नाथ = जगन्नाथ।
वाक् + मय = वाङ्मय।

(ख) यदि म् के बाद किसी स्पर्श वर्ण का आगमन होता है तो म् अनुस्वार में बदल जाता है।

जैसे– किम + चित् = किंचित् या किञ्चित्।
अहम् + कार = अहंकार या अहङ्कार।

(ग) यदि म् के बाद य र ल व (अन्तस्थ) और श ष स ह (ऊष्म) वर्ण हों तो 'म्' अनुस्वार में बदल दिया जाता है।

जैसे– सम् + षय = संशय।
सम् + सार = संसार।

(घ) यदि वर्ग के प्रथम वर्ण के अनन्तर कोई स्वर हो या किसी वर्ग का तृतीय, चतुर्थ व्यंजन हो या य र ल व में से कोई वर्ण आए तो वर्ग के प्रथम वर्ण के स्थान पर तृतीय वर्ण हो जाता है।

जैसे– वाक् + दन्त = वाग्दन्त।
सत् + गति = सद्गति।

(ङ) यदि च अथवा ज के अनन्तर न का आगमन होता है तो दोनों का स्थान ञ ले लेता है।

जैसे– यज् + न = यज्ञ।

(3) विसर्ग संधि

विसर्ग के साथ स्वर अथवा व्यंजन के मेल से उत्पन्न विकार को विसर्ग संधि कहा जाता है।

जैसे– मनः + रथ = मनोरथ।

विसर्ग संधि के प्रमुख नियम

(क) विसर्ग के बाद च् या छ् ट् या ठ् तथा त् या थ् आवे तो क्रमशः श, ष हो जाता है।

जैसे– निः + चय = निश्चय
निः + तार = निस्तार

(ख) यदि विसर्ग के बाद श, ष या स आवे तो विसर्ग को उसी परवर्ती सकार में बदल दिया जाता है।
जैसे– दुः + शासन = दुश्शासन
निः + सन्देह = निस्संदेह

(ग) यदि विसर्ग के पूर्व अ आवे और उसके बाद किसी वर्ग का तीसरा चौथा पाँचवां या य र ल व ह में से कोई व्यंजन आवे तो विसर्ग का 'उ' होता है और उ अपने पूर्ववर्ती अ के साथ जुड़कर ओ में रूपान्तरित हो जाता है।
जैसे– सरः + वर = सरोवर।
पयः + धर = पयोधर।

(घ) यदि विसर्ग के बाद र् व्यंजन आवे तो विसर्ग का पूर्ववर्त्ती स्वर दीर्घ हो जाता है साथ ही विसर्ग का लोप हो जाता है।
जैसे– निः + रव = नीरव।
निः + रोग = नीरोग।

(ङ) यदि विसर्ग के पूर्व अकार के अतिरिक्त कोई दूसरा स्वर हो और उसके बाद कोई स्वर हो अथवा किसी वर्ग का तीसरा, चौथा, पाँचवां वर्ण हो तो विसर्ग 'र' में रूपान्तरित होता है।
जैसे– दुः + गन्ध = दुर्गन्ध।
निः + रोग = नीरोग।

समास

अनेक शब्द जब मिलकर एक पद बन जाते हैं तो समास कहलाता है। अर्थात् जब दो या दो से अधिक पद अपने प्रत्ययों या विभक्तियों को छोड़कर मिलते हैं तब उस संयोग को समास कहते हैं।

समास की उपयोगिताः भाषा में समास की उपयोगिता कई दृष्टियों से है–

(क) समास से भाषा में संक्षिप्तता आती है।
(ख) समास से उच्चारण-प्रक्रिया में सहजता का बोध होता है।
(ग) भाषा समास के प्रयोग से चुस्त होती है।
(घ) भाषा के सौंदर्य में वृद्धि समास के प्रयोग से संभव है।

समास के भेद

पदों की प्रधानता को आधार मानकर समास को मुख्यतः चार भागों में विभाजित किया जाता है तथापि छः भेद स्वीकार किये जाते हैं।

(1) अव्ययीभाव समास – पहला पद प्रधान होता है।
(2) तत्पुरुष समास – दूसरा पद प्रधान होता है।
(3) द्वन्द्व समास – दोनों पद प्रधान होते हैं।
(4) बहुव्रीहि समास – कोई भी पद प्रधान नहीं होता है।

नोटः 'कर्मधारय' को तत्पुरुष का एक भेद माना गया है और 'द्विगु' को कर्मधारय का एक भेद माना गया है।

(1) अव्ययीभाव समास

अव्ययीभाव समास का पहला पद क्रिया-विशेषण अव्यय होता है और प्रधानता प्रायः प्रथम पद की ही होती है। जैसे– यथा समय (समय के अनुसार) प्रति वर्ष (प्रत्येक वर्ष)।

अव्ययीभाव समास के अन्तर्गत निम्नलिखित कोटि के पद आते हैं–

(क) अव्यय शब्दों के योग से बनने वाले समास– आचरण, व्यर्थ, यावज्जीवन, प्रतिदिन, यथा-संभव, आदि।
(ख) शब्दों की द्विरुक्ति से भी अव्ययीभाव समास बनता है। जैसे– वन-वन, घर-घर, मन्दिर-मन्दिर आदि।
(ग) द्विरुक्ति शब्दों के बीच में कभी-कभी ही, आ, ओं भी प्रयुक्त होते हैं। जैसे–एका-एक, हाथों-हाथ, मन-ही-मन आदि।

(2) तत्पुरुष समास

जिस समस्त पद में द्वितीय या अंतिम पद की प्रधानता को स्वीकारा जाता है उनमें तत्पुरुष समास होता है। जैसे :– राज-भवन (राजा का **भवन**)। उत्तर पद भवन प्रधान है।

तत्पुरुष समास के भेद

(i) व्यधिकरण तत्पुरुष– यह वास्तव में तत्पुरुष समास होता है।

(ii) समानाधिकरण तत्पुरुष– इस समास को कर्मधारय समास कहते हैं।

समस्त पदों में जिस कारक या विभक्ति चिह्न का लोप होता है उसी के आधार पर उसका नामकरण किया जाता है। तत्पुरुष समास में प्रथम पद कारक की स्थिति में होता है। इसके निम्नलिखित भेद हैं–

(क) **कर्म तत्पुरुषः** प्रथम पद कर्मधारय की स्थिति में होता है तथा कर्म की विभक्ति 'को' का लोप हो जाता है।
जैसे– गगन चुम्बी (गगन को चूमने वाला)
माखन चोर (माखन को चुराने वाला)

(ख) **करण तत्पुरुषः** प्रथम पद करण कारक की स्थिति में होता है और करण की विभक्ति चिह्न 'से' द्वारा 'के साथ' का लोप होता है।
जैसे– ईश्वर दत्त (ईश्वर द्वारा दत्त)
विश्व बन्ध (विश्व द्वारा बन्ध)

(ग) **सम्प्रदान तत्पुरुषः** प्रथम पद सम्प्रदान कारक में रहता है तथा सम्प्रदान की विभक्ति 'को', 'के लिए', 'निमित्त', 'हेतु' आदि का लोप होता है।
जैसे– स्वाधीनता संग्राम (स्वाधीनता के लिए संग्राम)

(घ) **अपादान तत्पुरुषः** इसमें भी प्रथम पद अपादान कारक में होता है तथा अपादान कारक के विभक्ति चिह्न 'से' का लोप हो जाता है।
जैसे– धर्म विमुख (धर्म से विमुख)

(ङ) **सम्बन्ध तत्पुरुषः** इसका पूर्व पद सम्बन्ध कारक में होता है तथा सम्बन्ध के विभक्ति चिह्न का, के, की का लोप होता है।
जैसे– वन मानुप (वन का मानुप)

(च) **अधिकरण तत्पुरुषः** अधिकरण तत्पुरुष में पहला पद अधिकरण कारक में होता है तथा अधिकरण कारक का विभक्ति चिह्न 'में' या 'पर' आदि का बोध होता है।

जैसे– आपबीती (आप पर बीती)

(3) द्वन्द्व समास

द्वन्द्व समास में दोनों ही पद प्रधान होते हैं और समस्त पद में दोनों पद संज्ञा या उसका समूह होता है। स्मरणीय है कि इसमें 'और', 'वा' 'अथवा', समुच्चय बोधक का लोप रहता है। इस समुच्चय बोधक के द्वारा दोनों पद जुड़े रहते हैं। द्वन्द्व समास के सामान्यतः निम्नलिखित भेद होते हैं :–

(क) **इतरेतर द्वन्द्वः** इतरेतर द्वन्द्व में समस्त पदों के बीच 'और' समुच्चय बोधक का लोप होता रहता है।

जैसे– माता-पिता (माता और पिता)
सीता-राम (सीता और राम)
देवर-भाभी (देवर और भाभी)

(ख) **समाहार द्वन्द्वः** समाहार द्वन्द्व में समस्त पद अपने अर्थ के अलावा उसी रूप के अन्य अर्थ का भी आभास देता है।

जैसे– नमक-रोटी (नमक और रोटी के अतिरिक्त और भी उसी कोटि की खाद्य-सामग्री) रुपया-पैसा, धन-दौलत, सेठ-साहूकार, मान-मर्यादा।

(ग) **वैकल्पिक द्वन्द्वः** वैकल्पिक द्वन्द्व में दोनों पदों के मध्य 'थ' और 'अथवा' समुच्चय बोधक का लोप रहता है। इस समस्त पद में साधारणतः दो परस्पर विरोधी शब्दों का योग होता है।

जैसे– मान-अपमान, धर्म-अधर्म, ज्ञान-अज्ञान, पाप-पुण्य, चार-छः, दो-चार, जात-कुजात, भला-बुरा।

(4) बहुब्रीहि समास

बहुब्रीहि समास उस समास को कहते हैं जिसमें दोनों ही पद अप्रधान होते हैं। उसमें एक नये अर्थ का संकेत मिलता है।

जैसे– चन्द्रशेखर (चन्द्रमा है शिखर पर जिसके अर्थात् शिव)
चतुर्भुज (चार भुजाएँ हैं जिनकी अर्थात् विष्णु)
गजानन (गज के समान मुख है जिसका अर्थात् गणेश)

(5) कर्मधारय (समानाधिकरण तत्पुरुष)

कर्मधारय समास में दोनों पद प्रधान होते हैं। इसके पदों में विशेषज्ञ-विशेषण, विषेशज्ञ-विशेषण, उपमान-उपमेय का भाव होता है।

जैसे– शशिमुख (शशि सम मुख), नीलाम्बर, पीताम्बर।

कर्मधारय के प्रकार– कर्मधारय के मुख्यतः दो भेद हैं– (1) विशेषता वाचक (2) उपमान वाचक।

(1) **विशेषता वाचक**

विशेषण पूर्वपदः पहला पद विशेषण होता है। जैसे–पीताम्बर, नीलकण्ठ, सुन्दर लाल, सद्गुण, खुशबू, बदबू, काली मिर्च, नीलगाय, छुटभैया।

विशेषणोत्तर पदः इसमें उत्तरपद विशेषण होता है। जैसे– पुरुषोतम, प्रभुदयाल, रामदहिन, देशान्तर, मुनीश्वर, युगान्तर, नराधम, जन्मान्तर।

विशेषणोभय पदः दोनों ही पद विशेषण होते हैं। जैसे– नील-पीत, मोटा ताजा, लाल पीला, श्याम सुन्दर, श्वेत-श्याम, भला-बुरा, खट्टा-मिट्ठा।

विशेष्योभय पदः दोनों ही पद विशेष्य होते हैं। जैसे– प्राणप्रिय, वज्रदेह।

(2) **विशेषता वाचक**

उपमानोत्तर पदः उत्तर पद उपमान होता है। जैसे– मुखारविन्द, राजर्षि।

(6) द्विगु समास

द्विगु समास कर्मधारय समास का एक भेद है। इस समास में पहला पद संख्या बोधक होता है और द्वितीय पद प्रधान होता है। संख्यावाची शब्द समुदाय (समाहार) के अर्थ में प्रयुक्त होता है।

जैसे–नवरत्न (नवरत्नों का समूह), अष्टाध्यायी (आठ अध्यायों का समाहार), त्रिभुवन, तिमाही, पंसेरी, सप्तशती, त्रिकाल, चौमाल।

वर्तनी

हिन्दी शब्दों को लिखने में वर्तनी का बड़ा महत्व है। प्रायः विद्यार्थी लिखने में वर्तनी सम्बन्धी अशुद्धियां करते हैं। ये अशुद्धियाँ संयुक्त वर्ण, विभक्ति चिह्न, क्रिया पद में तो होती ही है साथ ही, व ब तथा श ष स में भी देखने को मिलती हैं। इन अशुद्धियों से बचने का सही उपाय है कि शुद्ध वर्तनी का ज्ञान हो। और यह निरन्तर अभ्यास से ही सम्भव है।

पर्यायवाची

एकार्थ बोधक शब्दों को पर्यायवाची शब्द कहा जाता है। पर्यायवाची शब्दों में से कुछ पूर्ण पर्याय तथा कुछ अपूर्ण पर्याय की श्रेणी में आते हैं। पूर्ण पर्याय—कपि, वानर, मर्कट, प्लवंग आदि बन्दर के पर्याय हैं। अपूर्ण पर्याय—कृपा, दया, करुणा को कहा जाता है, किन्तु इनके प्रयोग में बहुत अन्तर है। भाषा के सूक्ष्म अध्ययन की दृष्टि से अपूर्ण पर्यायों के मध्य सूक्ष्म अन्तर होता है। इस अन्तर को देखते हुए ही उनका प्रयोग किया जाता है। हिन्दी के शब्द–भंडार की पर्याप्त वृद्धि हुई है। इस दिशा में डॉ. रघुवीर जैसे भाषा–पंडितों ने बहुत काम किया है। भारत सरकार का केन्द्रीय हिन्दी निदेशालय, अनुवाद ब्यूरो तथा राजभाषा विधायी आयोग आदि संस्थाओं द्वारा किए जा रहे शब्द रचना के कार्य सराहनीय हैं। हमारे देश में संस्कृत समृद्ध भाषा है जिससे हिन्दी को बहुत–से शब्द प्राप्त हुए हैं, अतएव पर्यायवाची शब्दों की दृष्टि से हिन्दी समृद्ध है।

विलोमार्थी शब्द

ऐसे शब्दों को विपरीतार्थक, विलोमार्थी अथवा विरोधी शब्द कहा जाता है जो किसी शब्द के ठीक विपरीत अर्थ प्रकट करते हैं। अंग्रेजी में जिन

शब्दों को एण्टानिम्स (Antonyms) कहा जाता है हिन्दी में वही शब्द विलोमार्थी अथवा प्रतिकूल अर्थ के बोधक कहे जाते हैं। अतएव विलोमार्थी शब्दों को यदि हम परिभाषाबद्ध करना चाहें तो कह सकते हैं कि—'किसी एक शब्द के ठीक विपरीत अर्थ प्रकट करने वाले शब्द विलोम कहे जाते हैं। इन शब्दों को विपर्याय के रूप में भी जाना जाता है।'

विलोमार्थी शब्दों का महत्त्व

भाषा कोई भी क्यों न हो उसकी सम्पन्नता उसके शब्दों की संख्या से जानी जाती है। आज विश्व में सर्वाधिक सम्पन्न भाषा अंग्रेजी है जिसके शब्दों का निरंतर वार्धक्य होता जाता है। नये-नये विज्ञानों का प्रादुर्भाव होने से उससे सम्बन्धित शब्द भी गढ़े जाते हैं। और उन शब्दों के प्रतिकूल शब्दों की आवश्यकता भी अनुभव की जाती है। नतीजतन शब्दों का सृजन अनवरत गति से चलता रहा है। हिन्दी में भी यह काम काफी द्रुतगति से हो रहा है। कोई माने या न माने किन्तु जब से केन्द्र में हिन्दी को राजभाषा का गरिमामय पद मिला है तब से उसके विकास की गति भी बढ़ी है। विभिन्न क्षेत्रों में उसका प्रवेश हो रहा है। विज्ञान, इंजीनियरी, चिकित्साशास्त्र, आणविकी आदि सभी से सम्बन्धित शब्दों की रचना हिन्दी में अबाध गति से की जा रही है। ये सब प्रभावी लक्षण हैं। शब्दों के समानार्थी तथा विपरीतार्थी दोनों की जरूरत पड़ती रहती है और आज के युग में जबकि प्रतियोगिता का महत्त्व काफ़ी बढ़ गया है विपरीतार्थी शब्द भी किसी के भाषाई ज्ञान की माप करने में उपादेय सिद्ध होते हैं।

इसके अतिरिक्त विपरीतार्थक शब्द किन्हीं दो अच्छी या बुरी वस्तुओं की तुलना करने के लिए भी काफी उपादेय सिद्ध होते हैं। ऐसे शब्दों के प्रयोग से भाषा में निखार आता है, भाषण प्रभावशाली बन जाता है तथा लेखन गरिमावान दिखाई पड़ने लगता है।

श्रुति समभिन्नार्थक शब्द

युग्म शब्द को श्रुतिसम भिन्नार्थक या समोच्चरित शब्द भी कहा जाता है। इस प्रकार के दो शब्दों में मामूली-सा अन्तर होता है। वह अन्तर मात्रागत या वर्णगत होता है। फलतः ऐसे शब्द सुनने में एक समान तो लगते हैं लेकिन अर्थ भिन्न-भिन्न होते हैं। हिन्दी में ऐसे शब्दों की संख्या अत्यधिक है। नीचे वैसे प्रमुख शब्द युग्मों को अर्थ सहित प्रस्तुत किया जा रहा है :

1. अंश = भाग/हिस्सा
   अंस = कन्धा
2. अपेक्षा = आवश्यकता/उम्मीद
   उपेक्षा = अवहेलना
3. अभिराम = सुन्दर
   अविराम = लगातार
4. अनल = आग
   अनिल = हवा
5. अवलम्ब = आश्रय/सहारा
   अविलम्ब = शीघ्र
6. अन्त = समाप्त/खतम
   अन्त्य = अन्तिम
7. अभिहित = कथित
   अविहित = अनुचित
8. अम्बुज = कमल
   अम्बुद = बादल
9. अलि = भ्रमर
   अली = सखी
10. उपकार = भलाई
    अपकार = बुराई
11. अजिक = ललाट
    अलीक = झूठ
12. अभिनय = स्वांग
    अविनय = उद्दण्डता
13. अतल = तलहीन
    अतुल = जिसकी तुलना न हो सके
14. अकथ = जो कहा नहीं जाय
    अथक = बिना थके हुए
15. अन्न = अनाज
    अन्य = दूसरा
16. आदि = आरम्भ/शुरू
    आदी = अभ्यस्त, अदरक
17. अभय = निर्भय
    उभय = दोनों
18. अर्जन = संग्रह
    अर्चन = पूजा
19. अमित = अत्यधिक
    अमीत = शत्रु
20. अणु = सूक्ष्म कण
    अनु = पीछे
21. अशक्त = असमर्थ
    असक्त = विरक्त
22. अब्ज = कमल
    अब्द = बादल
23. अवधि = समय
    अवधी = अवध की भाषा
24. अभ्यास = अनुशीलन
    अभ्याश = पड़ोस
25. आभरण = आभूषण
    आमरण = मरण तक
26. आकर = खान
    आकार = आकृति
27. आयत = चतुर्भुज
    आयात = बाहर से लाना
28. आर्त = दुःखी
    आर्द्र = गीला

29. आवास = वास स्थान
आभास = झलक
30. आवृत्त = घिरा हुआ
आवृत्ति = दुहराना
31. इत्र = सुगन्धित पदार्थ
इतर = दूसरा
32. स्त्री = महिला
इस्तिरी = कपड़े पर कलप करना
33. अरि = दुश्मन
अरी = स्त्री के लिए सम्बोधन
34. उद्यत = तैयार, तत्पर
उद्धत = उद्‌दण्ड
35. ऋतु = मौसम
ऋत = सत्य
36. कश = चाबुक
कष = कसौटी
37. कुल = वंश
कूल = किनारा
38. कलि = कलियुग
कली = अधखिला फूल
39. कपिश = मटमैला
कपीश = वन्दरों का राजा
40. कर्म = कार्य
क्रम = सिलसिला
41. कंगाल = दरिद्र
कंकाल = ठठरी (मानव की)
42. कटिबद्ध = तैयार
कटिवन्ध = कमर बन्द
43. करोड़ = सौ लाख की संख्या
क्रोड़ = गोद
44. कृत = किया हुआ
क्रीत = खरीदा हुआ
45. कृपण = कंजूस
कृपाण = कटार
46. कृषाण = किसान
कृशानु = आग
47. क्रान्ति = उलटफेर, आन्दोलन
कांति = चमक
48. कुट = किला
कूट = पहाड़ की चोटी
49. कुजन = दुर्जन
कूजन = पक्षियों का कलरव
50. केशर = सिंह की गर्दन के बाल
केसर = कुमकुम
51. कोष = खजाना
कोश = शब्द-संग्रह
कोस = दो मील की दूरी
52. खाद = उर्वरक
खाद्य = खाने की सामग्री
53. खोया = भूल गया
खोआ = दूध से निर्मित खाद्य पदार्थ
54. गिरि = पर्वत
गिरी = बीज/गूदा
55. चषक = प्याला
चसक = आदत
56. चरण = पैर
चारण = भाट
57. चिर = पुराना
चीर = वस्त्र
58. चिता = शव जलाने के लिए लकड़ियों की शय्या
चीता = एक हिंसक पशु
59. गृह = घर
ग्रह = नक्षत्र
60. करण = इन्द्रियाँ, करण कारक
कर्ण = कान
61. कुच = स्तर
कूच = प्रस्थान
62. कौर = ग्रास
कोर = किनारा
63. चतुष्पद = चौपाया
चतुष्पथ = चौराहा
64. चक्रवात = बवंडर
चक्रवाक = चकवा पक्षी
65. छत्र = छाता
छात्र = विद्यार्थी
66. क्षति = हानि
क्षिति = पृथ्वी
67. जलज = कमल
जलद = बादल
68. नीरज = कमल
नीरद = बादल
69. जघन्य = गर्हित
जघन = जाँघ
70. जगत् = संसार
जगत = कुएँ का चबूतरा
71. जामन = दूध जमाने के लिए प्रयुक्त पदार्थ
जामुन = एक फल
72. जेठ = वर्ष का एक महीना
ज्येष्ठ = बड़ा (उम्र में)
73. टुक = थोड़ा
टूक = टुकड़ा
74. टोटा = घाटा
टोंटा = बन्दूक का कारतूस

75. तरणि = सूर्य
तरणी = नाव
76. दाई = धायी, नौकरानी
दायी = जवाबदेह
77. दारु = लकड़ी
दारू = शराब
78. दिवा = दिन
दीया = दीपक
79. दिन = दिवस
दीन = गरीब
80. द्विप = हाथी
द्वीप = टापू
81. दुर्ग = गढ़
दुर्गा = एक देवी
82. दमन = दबाना
दामन = आँचल
83. तक्र = मट्ठा
तर्क = बहस
84. द्रव्य = धन
द्रव = तरल पदार्थ
85. देव = देवता
दैव = भाग्य
86. नहर = कृत्रिम नदी
नाहर = सिंह
87. नग = पहाड़
नाग = सर्प
88. नगर = शहर
नागर = चतुर व्यक्ति
89. नाश = ध्वंश
नास = सुंघनी
90. नारी = स्त्री
नाड़ी = नब्ज
91. निसान = झण्डा
निशान = चिह्न, प्रतीक
92. निर्जर = देवता
निर्झर = झरना
93. निहित = छिपा हुआ
निहत = मरा हुआ
94. नियत = निश्चित
नीयत = इरादा
नियति = भाग्य
95. नमित = नत
निमित्त = कारण
96. नीर = जल
नीड़ = घोंसला
97. निर्माण = बनाना
निर्वाण = मोक्ष

98. नकल = अनुकरण
नकुल = नेवला, पाण्डवों में एक
99. निधन = मृत्यु
निर्धन = गरीब
100. नित = प्रतिदिन
नीत = लाया हुआ
101. नीम = एक पेड़
नींव = आधार
102. नेत्र = आँख
नेतृ = नेता
103. पुरुष = मर्द
परुष = कठोर
104. परिधान = वस्त्र
प्रधान = मुख्य
105. पवन = हवा
पावन = पवित्र
106. पाहन = पत्थर
पाहुन = अतिथि
107. परवाह = चिन्ता
प्रवाह = बहाव
108. प्रहर = समय
प्रहार = चोट
109. परिताप = दुःख
प्रताप = पराक्रम
110. पथ = मार्ग
पथ्य = रोगी का भोजन
111. पट्ट = तख्ता
पट = वस्त्र
112. प्रमाण = सबूत
प्रणाम = नमस्कार
113. परिणाम = फल
परिमाण = मात्रा
114. प्रणय = प्रेम
परिणय = विवाह
115. परदेश = दूसरा देश
प्रदेश = प्रान्त, राज्य
116. परीक्षा = इम्तहान
परिक्षा = कीचड़
117. प्रदीप = दीपक
प्रतीप = उल्टा
118. पानी = जल
पाणि = हाथ
119. पास = निकट
पाश = बन्धन
120. पिक = कोयल
पीक = पान का थूक

121. प्रेषित = भेजा हुआ
प्रोषित = प्रवासी
122. फन = कला
फण = साँप का फण
123. बलि = बलिदान
बली = वीर
124. बहन = भगिनी
वहन = ढोना
125. बहु = बहुत
बहू = पुत्रवधू
126. बार = दफा
वार = दिन
127. वाण = तीर
बान = आदत
128. बात = वचन
वात = हवा
129. भवन = घर
भुवन = संसार
130. भट = योद्धा
भट्ट = पण्डित
131. भाल = ललाट
भार = वजन
132. मल = गन्दगी
मल्ल = पहलवान
133. मणि = रत्न
मणी = सर्प
134. मद = अहंकार
मद्य = शराब
135. मनुज = मनुष्य
मनोज = कामदेव
136. मांस = गोश्त
मास = महीना
137. मात्र = केवल
मातृ = माता
138. मेध = यज्ञ
मेघ = बादल
139. मेदा = पेट
मैदा = बारीक आटा
140. रत = तल्लीन
रक्त = खून
141. रेचक = दस्तावर
रोचक = रूचिकर
142. लक्ष = लाख
लक्ष्य = उद्देश्य
143. लवण = नमक
लवन = खेत के फसल की कटाई
144. वस्तु = चीज
वास्तु = इमारत, भवन
145. अकुल = बिना कुल के
आकुल = व्याकुल
146. वरद = वर देने वाला
विरद = यश
147. वरण = चुनना
वरन् = बल्कि
148. वाद = विचार/सिद्धान्त
वाद्य = बाजा
149. वदन = मुख
बदन = शरीर
150. विस्मृत = भूला हुआ
विस्मित = आश्चर्य में पड़ा हुआ
151. विपिन = जंगल
विपन्न = दुःखी, निर्धन
152. वित्त = धन
वृत्त = गोलाकार
153. विष = जहर
विस = कमल का डण्ठल
बीस = उन्नीस से एक अधिक संख्या
154. सम = समान
शय = संचय
155. सहर = सबेरा
शहर = नगर
156. शव = लाश
शब = रात
157. सिता = चीनी
सीता = जानकी
158. शस्त्र = हथियार
शास्त्र = ग्रन्थ
159. सर = तालाब
शर = बाण
160. सुर = देवता
सूर = अंधा
शूर = वीर
161. सुत = बेटा
सूत = सारथी, धागा
162. सप्त = सात
शप्त = शाप ग्रस्त
163. शंकर = शिव
संकर = दोगला
164. सर्ग = काव्य का अध्याय
स्वर्ग = कल्पित लोक
165. स्वपच = स्वयंवाकी
श्वपच = चाण्डाल

166.	सत्व	=	सार
	स्वत्व	=	अधिकार
167.	समिति	=	सभा
	सम्मति	=	सलाह
168.	शय्या	=	बिछावन
	सज्जा	=	सजावट
169.	संग	=	साथ
	संघ	=	समिति, संगठन
170.	शाला	=	घर
	साला	=	पत्नी का भाई
171.	सबल	=	ताकतवर
	शवल	=	चितकबरा
172.	सर्व	=	सभी
	शर्व	=	शंकर
173.	सुगन्ध	=	खुशबू
	सौगन्ध	=	कसम
174.	शुक्ति	=	सीप
	सूक्ति	=	अच्छी उक्ति
175.	शीशा	=	काँच
	सीसा	=	एक धातु
176.	सती	=	पतिव्रता नारी
	शती	=	शताब्दी
177.	श्वेत	=	सफेद
	श्वेद	=	पसीना
178.	शुक	=	सुग्गा
	शूक	=	जौ
179.	शिखर	=	चोटी (पर्वत की)
	शेखर	=	सिर
180.	शक्ल	=	चेहरा
	सकल	=	सम्पूर्ण
181.	हरि	=	विष्णु
	हरी	=	हरे रंग की
182.	सुमन	=	फूल
	सुअन	=	पुत्र
183.	संदेह	=	शक
	सदेह	=	सशरीर
184.	स्व	=	अपना
	श्व	=	आने वाला दिन
185.	शुचि	=	पवित्र
	सूची	=	विषय क्रम
186.	सुधि	=	स्मरण
	सुधी	=	समझदार, विद्वान्
187.	हल	=	जोतने का यंत्र
	हल्	=	शुद्ध व्यंजन
188.	भंगि	=	लहर
	भंगी	=	मेहतर
189.	दूत	=	संवाददाता
	द्यूत	=	जुआ का खेल
190.	देश	=	राज्य
	द्वेष	=	शत्रुता
191.	तरंग	=	लहर
	तुरंग	=	घोड़ा
192.	चालक	=	ड्राइवर
	चालाक	=	चतुर
193.	लोम	=	रोवाँ
	लोभ	=	लालच
194.	बिना	=	रहित, अभाव
	वीणा	=	एक वाद्य यंत्र
195.	प्रसाद	=	कृपा
	प्रासाद	=	महल
196.	भित्ति	=	दीवार
	भीति	=	डर
197.	मूल	=	जड़
	मूल्य	=	दाम
198.	अक्ष	=	धुरी
	यक्ष	=	एक देव योनि
199.	अश्व	=	घोड़ा
	अश्म	=	पत्थर
200.	आसन	=	बैठने की वस्तु
	अशन	=	भोजन
201.	अह	=	दिन
	अहि	=	साँप
202.	अणि	=	सूई की नोक
	अनी	=	फौज
203.	दारा	=	पत्नी
	द्वार	=	दरवाजा
204.	पृथा	=	कुन्ती
	प्रथा	=	रीति
205.	श्रवण	=	कान
	स्रवन	=	बहना
206.	श्याम	=	श्री कृष्ण
	स्याम	=	एक देश
207.	वृन्द	=	समूह
	वृन्त	=	डण्ठल
208.	मित	=	थोड़ा
	मित्र	=	दोस्त
209.	दुरति	=	पाप
	दुरत	=	छिपा
210.	चार	=	चार की संख्या
	चारु	=	सुन्दर

वाक्यों की शुद्धता

वाक्य में शब्दों के प्रयोग पर हमें विशेष ध्यान रखना चाहिए। प्रत्येक शब्द का अपना एक विशेष अर्थ होता है। एक ही अर्थ देने वाले कई शब्द हो सकते हैं, किन्तु हमें ध्यान रखना चाहिए कि किस प्रसंग में कौन-सा शब्द प्रयुक्त होगा और कौन-सा शब्द वहां उपयुंक्त नहीं बैठेगा। अनुपयुक्त शब्द का प्रयोग करने से अर्थ-भ्रान्ति पैदा होती है। शब्दों का ठीक प्रयोग करने से अभीष्ट अर्थ निकलेगा।

अशुद्धियों के कारणों का विश्लेषण करने के बाद हम देख सकते हैं कि वर्तनी की गलतियाँ होती हैं। ह्रस्व और दीर्घ मात्राओं की गलतियां होती हैं, संयुक्ताक्षरों की गलतियां होती हैं और वाक्यों के निर्माण में भी गलतियाँ होती हैं। मोटे तौर पर हम कह सकते हैं कि वर्ण, शब्द और वाक्य तीनों प्रकार की अशुद्धियाँ देखने को मिलती हैं। इन अशुद्धियों के कारण भाषा दूषित हो जाती है। यदि हम थोड़ी सी सावधानी बरतें, तो हम ऐसी अशुद्धियों से बच सकते हैं।

वाक्यांश के लिए एक शब्द

कथन में लम्बे-लम्बे वाक्यों का प्रयोग करने तथा शब्दों को परिभाषित करने के बजाय यदि एक शब्द का प्रयोग किया जाए तो कथन स्वत: संक्षिप्त और स्पष्ट हो जाता है। कुशल साहित्यकार अपनी रचनाओं में शब्दों का अपव्यय नहीं करते। वाक्य या वाक्यांश के लिए एक शब्द का प्रयोग कथन में आकर्षण और सौन्दर्य भर देता है। हिन्दी भाषा की यह विशेषता है कि उसे संस्कृत शब्दों का प्रचुर भण्डार सुलभ है। इसलिए हिन्दी भाषा कोश में ऐसे अनेक तत्सम शब्द हैं जो वाक्य या वाक्यांश के लिए प्रयोग में लाए जाते हैं।

अपने आशय और मन्तव्य को संक्षेप में प्रकट करने के लिए ही ऐसे शब्दों को गढ़ा गया है जिन्हें गागर में सागर कहा जा सकता है।

इसीलिए अपनी भाषा को समर्थ, प्रभावी तथा आकर्षक बनाने के लिए ऐसे शब्दों की जानकारी रखना नितान्त आवश्यक होता है। भाषा में शक्ति के स्रोत उसके शब्द माने जाते हैं। यहाँ इसी उद्देश्य से अनेक ऐसे शब्द संजोए गए हैं जिनका अर्थ पूरे वाक्य या वाक्यांश द्वारा ही स्पष्ट होता है। इनसे न केवल पाठकों के शब्द भण्डार में वृद्धि होगी वरन् वे हिन्दी भाषा लिखने में भी कुशल बन सकेंगे।

मुहावरा एवं लोकोक्तियां

मुहावरे

मुहावरा ऐसा शब्द-समूह होता है, जो अपने शब्दों के निहित अर्थ न देकर उससे भिन्न, किन्तु एक रूढ़ अर्थ देता है। मुहावरा अभिधेय अर्थ का अनुसरण नहीं करता : वह अपना विलक्षण अर्थ प्रकट करता है। चूँकि मुहावरा लोक-मानस की स्वाभाविक अभिव्यक्ति होता है, अत: इसमें दुरूहता नहीं होती। मुहावरा अपने लोक-परम्परागत रूप में ही शोभायमान और सार्थक होता है। इसका रूप और अर्थ दोनों ही प्राय: रूढ़ होते हैं।

मुहावरे का सम्बन्ध साहित्य से कम और भाषा से अधिक होता है। यह भाषा के सामर्थ्य का प्रतीक होता है। इसका सटीक अर्थ और निर्दिष्ट अर्थ होता है। मुहावरों के माध्यम से भाषा ऊर्जस्वी बनती है और अर्थ का सटीक सम्प्रेषण होता है। मुहावरेदार भाषा असरदार होती है।

मुहावरे एक दृष्टि से 'गागर में सागर' होते हैं। गुल खिलना, रंग में भंग होना, नौ-दो ग्यारह होना, गप हाँकना, चिकना घड़ा होना, नानी मरना आदि मुहावरे व्यापक अर्थ में परिपूर्ण हैं। इनका प्रयोग सुनते ही मन में इनका अर्थ अपने आप उभरने लगता है।

लोकोक्तियाँ

जैसाकि शब्द से ही स्पष्ट है लोकोक्ति का अर्थ है लोक + उक्ति; अर्थात् लोक में प्रचलित उक्ति। जो उक्ति समाज में चिरकाल से प्रचलित होती है, उसे लोक प्रचलित उक्ति अर्थात् लोकोक्ति कहते हैं। लोकोक्तियाँ भूतकाल के अनुभव और प्रेक्षण का संचय होती हैं। लोकोक्तियों में लोक-बोध, लोक-मान्यता और लोक-स्वीकृति होती है। कुछ लोकोक्तियाँ किसी अन्तर्कथा को अभिव्यक्त करती हैं। लोकोक्तियों के उद्भव को किसी स्थान या काल से नहीं जोड़ा जा सकता।

लोकोक्तियाँ अपने आप में पूर्ण वाक्य होती हैं। इनका उद्देश्य उक्ति चमत्कार पैदा करना नहीं होता। इनका अभिधात्मक अर्थ ही लिया जाता है। अत: इनके शाब्दिक अर्थ और सांकेतिक अर्थ में समानता होती है। इनका प्रयोग प्राय: दृष्टांत के लिए अथवा किसी बात का समर्थन करने के लिए किया जाता है। ये अभिव्यक्ति का सशक्त साधन हैं।

मुहावरों और लोकोक्तियों में अन्तर

मुहावरों और लोकोक्तियों में रूप सम्बन्धी और अर्थ सम्बन्धी भी अन्तर होता है।

रूप सम्बन्धी पहला अन्तर यह है कि मुहावरों के अन्त में अधिकांशत: **ना** होता है, जैसे सिर धुन**ना**, आँख लग**ना**, टेढ़ी खीर हो**ना**, मक्खी मार**ना**, आसमान सिर पर उठा**ना** आदि जबकि लोकोक्तियों के अन्त में **ना** नहीं होता; जैसे—आ बैल मुझे मार, का वर्षा जब कृषि सुखानी, दीवार के भी कान होते हैं, और धोबी का कुत्ता, घर का न घाट का, आदि।

रूप सम्बन्धी दूसरा अन्तर यह होता है कि मुहावरे मात्र शब्द-समूह होते हैं, जैसे 'गुल खिलाना'; इसे स्वतन्त्र रूप से प्रयोग में नहीं लाया जा सकता, किसी वाक्य में इसे उपयुक्त ढंग से प्रयुक्त किया जाता है; जैसे—'उस बूढ़ी औरत ने क्या गुल खिलाया'; इसके विपरीत लोकोक्ति का प्रयोग स्वतंत्र वाक्य के रूप में किया जा सकता है; जैसे—'न रहेगा बाँस, न बजेगी बाँसुरी'।

वस्तुनिष्ठ प्रश्न

संधि

1. 'मृत्यु + उपरांत' में संधि करने से एक शब्द होगा–
A. मृत्यूपरांत B. मृत्योपरांत
C. मृत्युपर्यन्त D. मर्त्योपरांत

2. 'अनधिकृत' शब्द का संधि-विग्रह होगा–
A. अन + अधिकृत B. अन् + अधिकृत
C. अन्य + अधिकृत D. अन्नधि + कृत

3. 'कपि + ईश' का सही संधि-संयोजन कीजिए–
A. कपिश B. कपीश
C. कपेश D. कपिशि

4. विसर्ग के साथ स्वर अथवा व्यंज़न के संयोग से जो विकार उत्पन्न होता है, उसे किस संधि के नाम से जानते हैं?
A. स्वर संधि B. व्यंजन संधि
C. विसर्ग संधि D. इनमें से कोई नहीं

5. 'परोपकार' शब्द का संधि-विच्छेद होगा–
A. परा + उपकार B. परो + पकार
C. परोप + कार D. पर + उपकार

6. 'मनः + रमा' में संधि करने से जो शब्द बनेगा, उसका सम्बन्ध किस संधि से होगा?
A. विसर्ग संधि B. स्वर संधि
C. व्यंजन संधि D. भाव संधि

7. 'चन्द्रोदय' में कौन-सी संधि है?
A. यण संधि B. दीर्घ संधि
C. वृद्धि संधि D. गुण संधि

8. निम्नलिखित में से 'वृद्धि स्वर संधि' किस शब्द में है?
A. रजनीश B. महौषध
C. यतीन्द्र D. शोधार्थी

9. 'सदाशय' का सही संधि-विच्छेद होगा–
A. सद + आशय B. सतत + आशय
C. सत् + आशय D. सदा + आशय

10. 'सन्मार्ग' में कौन-सी संधि है?
A. स्वर संधि B. व्यंजन संधि
C. विसर्ग संधि D. इनमें से कोई नहीं

11. 'ज्ञानोदय' में कौन-सी संधि है?
A. स्वर संधि B. व्यंजन संधि
C. विसर्ग संधि D. इनमें से कोई नहीं

12. 'निराधार' में कौन-सी संधि है?
A. स्वर संधि B. व्यंजन संधि
C. विसर्ग संधि D. इनमें से कोई नहीं

13. निम्नलिखित शब्दों में से किसमें विसर्ग संधि है?
A. अतएव B. नरेन्द्र
C. सज्जन D. सदैव

14. निम्नलिखित शब्दों में से किसमें व्यंजन संधि है?
A. सप्तर्षि B. निराधार
C. सत्कार D. हिमालय

15. 'जगन्नाथ' किस संधि का उदाहरण है?
A. व्यंजन संधि B. विसर्ग संधि
C. दीर्घ स्वर संधि D. यण स्वर संधि

16. निम्नलिखित शब्द का संधि-विच्छेद क्या होगा?
भानूदय
A. भानु + उदय B. भानू + उदय
C. भानू + ऊदय D. भानु + ऊदय

17. 'निर्गुण' का संधि-विच्छेद होगा–
A. निर + गुण B. नि + गुण
C. निः + गुण D. निर् + गुण

18. 'महेन्द्र' का संधि विच्छेद है–
A. मही + इन्द्र B. महो + इन्द्र
C. महा + इन्द्र D. इनमें से कोई नहीं

19. 'यद्यपि' का संधि विच्छेद है–
A. यदि + अपि B. यद् + यपि
C. यद्यि + अपि D. यद + अपि

20. निम्नलिखित में 'भारतेंदु' का सही संधि-विच्छेद है–
A. भारत + तेन्दु B. भार + तेन्दु
C. भारत + एन्दु D. भारत + इन्दु

21. 'उद्घाटन' शब्द का सही संधि-विच्छेद होगा–
A. उत् + घाटन B. उद् + घाटन
C. उद्ध + आटन D. इनमें से कोई नहीं

22. 'सत्कर्म' का संधि-विच्छेद है–
A. सत + कर्म B. सतत् + कर्म
C. सत् + कर्म D. सम + कर्म

23. 'अत्यन्त' शब्द का सही संधि-विग्रह है–
A. अत् + यन्त B. अति + यन्त
C. अति + अन्त D. अत् + अन्त

24. निम्नलिखित शब्द का सही संधि-विच्छेद चुनिए–
ब्रह्माण्ड
A. ब्रह्मा + अंड B. ब्रह्मण + अंड
C. बृहत् + अंड D. बृह + माण्ड

25. 'निरपेक्ष' शब्द का संधि-विच्छेद होगा–
A. निर् + पेक्ष B. नि + पेक्ष
C. निर + पेक्ष D. निः + अपेक्ष

26. तत् + शंकर की संधि होगी–

A. तत्शंकर B. तच्छंकर

C. तक्षंकर D. उपर्युक्त में से कोई नहीं

27. 'कठोपनिषद्' का संधि-विच्छेद होगा–

A. कटु + उपनिषद् B. कठो + उपनिषद्

C. कठोप + निषद् D. कठ + उपनिषद्

28. 'भावुक' का संधि-विच्छेद होगा–

A. भाव + उक B. भो + ऊक

C. भव्य + उक D. भौ + उक

29. 'विद्यामंदिर' का विग्रह होगा–

A. विद्या का मंदिर B. विद्या के लिए मंदिर

C. विद्या और मंदिर D. विद्या के समान मंदिर

30. 'उत्कोच' का संधि विच्छेद होगा–

A. उद् + कोच B. उत् + कोच

C. उत + कोच D. उद + कोच

31. कौन-सा शब्द विसर्ग संधि का नहीं है?

A. यशोगान B. निष्कपट

C. मनोहर D. अभिषेक

32. 'मनीषा' का संधि-विच्छेद है–

A. मनि + ईषा B. मनी + ईषा

C. मनस् + ईषा D. मणि + ईशा

33. निम्नलिखित में से दीर्घ संधि का उदाहरण कौन-सा है?

A. नरेश B. नेति

C. मध्वाचार्य D. कामायनी

34. 'अति + उक्ति' शब्दों की संधि करने पर शब्द होगा–

A. अत्युक्ति B. अत्योक्ति

C. अतियुक्ति D. अतिउक्ति

35. 'निराधार' शब्द का संधि-विच्छेद है–

A. निः + आधार B. निरा + आधार

C. निरम् + आधार D. निर् + आधार

36. 'अन्वेषण' का संधि-विच्छेद होगा–

A. अन + वेषण B. अनु + एषण

C. अनु + ऐषण D. अन् + वेषण

37. 'सज्जन' का संधि-विच्छेद होगा–

A. सज् + जन B. सद् + जन

C. सत् + जन D. स + ज् + जन

38. 'इत्यादि' का सन्धि-विच्छेद होगा–

A. इत + आदि B. इति + यादि

C. इति + आदि D. इत्य + आदि

39. 'दुर्जन' का सन्धि-विच्छेद होगा–

A. दुर + जन B. दु + जन

C. दुः + जन D. दु + रजन

40. 'नमस्ते' शब्द का सन्धि-विच्छेद है–

A. नम + स्ते B. नमस् + ते

C. नमः + स्ते D. नमः + ते

41. 'महोत्सव' का संधि-विच्छेद है–

A. महा + उत्सव B. महो + उत्सव

C. मह + ओत्सव D. मही + उत्सव

42. 'पवन' का शुद्ध सन्धि-विच्छेद है–

A. पो + अन B. पव + अन

C. पः + अवन D. पव + न्

43. 'विष्णवे' का संधि-विच्छेद है–

A. विष्णु + ए B. विष्णो + ए

C. विष्णु + अए D. विष्णु + अवे

44. 'स्वागतम्' में कौन-सी संधि है?

A. गुण संधि B. यण् संधि

C. वृद्धि संधि D. दीर्घ संधि

45. 'उच्चारण' में कौन-सी संधि है?

A. व्यंजन संधि B. स्वर संधि

C. विसर्ग संधि D. विलोम संधि

46. 'उल्लेख' का संधि-विच्छेद है–

A. उल् + लेख B. उत् + लेख

C. उल्ल + लेख D. उ + आलेख

47. 'अत्याचार' का शुद्ध संधि-विच्छेद है–

A. अत्य + आचार B. अति + चार

C. अत्या + चार D. अति + आचार

48. 'दिगम्बर' का संधि-विच्छेद क्या होगा?

A. दिग् + अम्बर B. दिक् + अम्बर

C. दिग + अम्बर D. दिक + अम्बर

49. 'पावक' का शुद्ध संधि-विच्छेद होगा–

A. पौ + अक B. पा + अवक

C. पव + अक् D. पाव + अक

50. 'उपैति' का संधि-विच्छेद बताइए–

A. अप + इति B. उपै + इति

C. उप + ऐति D. उप + एति

51. 'नवोढ़ा' का सन्धि-विच्छेद है–

A. नव + उढ़ा B. नवो + ढ़ा

C. नव + ऊढ़ा D. न + ओढ़ा

52. 'उड्डयनम' का सन्धि-विच्छेद होगा–

A. उत + डयनम् B. उद् + डयनम्

C. उड + अयनम् D. उड् + डयनम्

53. 'दिगंत' शब्द का संधि-विच्छेद होगा–

A. दिक् + अंत B. दिग् + अंत

C. दि + गंत D. दिग + अंत

54. 'परिच्छेद' में कौन-सी सन्धि है?
A. व्यंजन संधि B. दीर्घ संधि
C. विसर्ग संधि D. वृद्धि संधि

55. 'अन्यान्य' शब्द का संधि-विच्छेद होगा–
A. अ + न्यान्य B. अन्य + अन्य
C. अन् + यान्य D. अन्या + आन्य

56. व्यंजन संधि का उदाहरण नहीं है–
A. उत् + चारणम् = उच्चारणम्
B. रामस् + टीकते = रामष्टीकते
C. गंगा + उदकम = गंगोदकम्
D. सत् + चित् = सच्चित्

57. स्वस्त्यस्तु का संधि-विच्छेद होगा–
A. स्वस्ति + अस्तु B. स्वः + अस्त्यस्तु
C. स्वस्त्य + अस्तु D. स्व + स्त्यस्तु

58. 'तेजोमय' का सही सन्धि-विच्छेद है–
A. तेज + ओमय B. तेजः + अमय
C. तेजः + मय D. तेजो + मय

59. 'तथेति' का सन्धि-विच्छेद होगा–
A. तथ + इति B. ता + थेति
C. तथा + इति D. तथा + इत

60. 'वृहस्पति' का संधि-विच्छेद है–
A. वृहस + पति B. वृहस् + पति
C. वृहः + पति D. वृहश् + पति

61. 'व्याप्त' में संधि है–
A. गुण संधि B. दीर्घ संधि
C. यण् संधि D. अयादि संधि

62. 'पित्राकृतिः' का शुद्ध संधि विच्छेद है–
A. पितृ + आकृतिः B. पित्र + आकृतिः
C. पित्रृ + आकृतिः D. पितु + आकृतिः

63. 'न्यून' का संधि विच्छेद होगा–
A. नि + ऊन B. न्यू + नन
C. नव + ऊन D. नवी + नन

64. 'षडानन' में कौन-सी संधि है?
A. दीर्घ संधि B. वृद्धि संधि
C. यण संधि D. गुण संधि

65. 'धर्मात्मा' में कौन-सी संधि है?
A. स्वर संधि B. व्यंजन संधि
C. विसर्ग संधि D. यण संधि

66. 'रेखांकित' में प्रयुक्त संधि है–
A. गुण संधि B. वृद्धि संधि
C. दीर्घ संधि D. स्वर संधि

67. 'निश्छल' में कौन-सी संधि है?
A. गुण संधि B. स्वर संधि
C. दीर्घ संधि D. वृद्धि संधि

68. 'दुरुपयोग' में प्रयुक्त संधि है–
A. स्वर संधि B. यण संधि
C. गुण संधि D. दीर्घ संधि

69. 'अत्यावश्यक' का संधि विच्छेद है–
A. अ + आवश्यक B. अति + आवश्यक
C. अत्य + आवश्यक D. अत्या + वश्यक

70. 'वाङ्मय' का संधि विच्छेद है–
A. वांग + मय B. वाक् + मय
C. वान् + मय D. इनमें से कोई नहीं

71. 'उपर्युक्त' का संधि विच्छेद क्या है?
A. उप + रूक्त B. उपरि + उक्त
C. उपर + युक्त D. उपः + युक्त

72. 'चन्द्रोदय' शब्द में है–
A. स्वर संधि B. व्यंजन संधि
C. विसर्ग संधि D. इनमें से कोई नहीं

73. 'निष्कपट' का संधि विच्छेद है–
A. निः + कपट B. निष + कपट
C. नि + कपट D. इनमें से कोई नहीं

74. 'प्रत्युपकार' का सही संधि विच्छेद है–
A. प्रत्युप + कार B. प्रति + उपकार
C. प्रत्यु + उपकार D. प्रत्य + उपकार

75. 'स्वागत' शब्द का संधि विच्छेद है–
A. स्वा + गत B. स्व + आगत
C. सू + वागत D. सु + आगत

समास

निर्देश (प्र.सं. 1 से 70 तक): *नीचे दिए गए शब्दों में प्रयुक्त समास के नाम का चयन कीजिए–*

1. पीताम्बर–
A. तत्पुरुष B. अव्ययीभाव
C. बहुब्रीहि D. द्विगु

2. चरणकमल–
A. तत्पुरुष B. कर्मधारय
C. बहुब्रीहि D. अव्ययीभाव

3. घुड़सवार–
A. द्विगु B. कर्मधारय
C. तत्पुरुष D. अव्ययीभाव

4. स्वर्गप्राप्त–
A. कर्म तत्पुरुष B. करण तत्पुरुष
C. सम्प्रदान तत्पुरुष D. अपादान तत्पुरुष

5. गर्वशून्य–
A. कर्म-तत्पुरुष B. संप्रदान-तत्पुरुष
C. करण-तत्पुरुष D. अपादान-तत्पुरुष

6. 'लम्बोदर' में कौन-सा समास है?
A. तत्पुरुष B. बहुव्रीहि
C. द्विगु D. कर्मधारय

7. 'देवालय' में कौन-सा समास है?
A. तत्पुरुष B. बहुव्रीहि
C. द्विगु D. इनमें से कोई नहीं

8. 'खरा खोटा' शब्द में कौन-सा समास है?
A. द्वंद्व B. द्विगु
C. कर्मधारय D. बहुव्रीहि

9. 'निर्विवाद' में कौन-सा समास है?
A. कर्मधारय B. अव्ययीभाव
C. तत्पुरुष D. बहुव्रीहि

10. 'दहीबड़ा' में कौन-सा समास है?
A. तत्पुरुष B. द्विगु
C. बहुव्रीहि D. द्वन्द्व

11. 'चौराहा' में समास है–
A. तत्पुरुष B. द्वन्द्व
C. कर्मधारय D. द्विगु

12. 'माता-पिता' शब्द में समास है–
A. द्वन्द्व B. द्विगु
C. तत्पुरुष D. कर्मधारय

13. 'वज्रपाणि' शब्द में कौन-सा समास है?
A. तत्पुरुष B. बहुव्रीहि
C. द्वन्द्व D. द्विगु

14. 'देशभक्ति' शब्द में समास होगा–
A. अपादान तत्पुरुष B. सम्बन्ध तत्पुरुष
C. अधिकरण तत्पुरुष D. सम्प्रदान तत्पुरुष

15. 'सुनीता के बच्चे घास-फूस की तरह बढ़ रहे हैं।'
उपर्युक्त वाक्य में प्रयुक्त 'घास-फूस' शब्द में समास होगा–
A. कर्मधारय B. द्वन्द्व
C. द्विगु D. अव्ययीभाव

16. निम्नलिखित शब्दों में कौन-सा शब्द बहुव्रीहि समास का उदाहरण है?
A. शूलपाणि B. यथाक्रम
C. हँसमुख D. हथकड़ी

17. इनमें से कौन-सा शब्द 'द्विगु' समास है?
A. भुजदण्ड B. माखनचोर
C. पंचशील D. लज्जाशील

18. 'प्रतिदिन' शब्द में समास होगा–
A. द्विगु B. कर्मधारय
C. तत्पुरुष D. अव्ययीभाव

19. जिन समस्त पदों में पहला शब्द संख्यावाची हो और उससे समुदाय का बोध होता हो, तो उसे कहते हैं–
A. द्विगु समास B. द्वन्द्व समास
C. कर्मधारय समास D. अव्ययीभाव समास

20. जिसमें पहला शब्द विशेषण हो और दूसरा शब्द विशेष्य, तो उसे कौन-सा समास कहेंगे?
A. द्विगु B. कर्मधारय
C. द्वन्द्व D. तत्पुरुष

21. 'पंचवटी' शब्द के लिए दिए गए विकल्प में से उपयुक्त समास कौन-सा है?
A. द्विगु B. तत्पुरुष
C. बहुव्रीहि D. कर्मधारय

22. 'बुरा-भला' शब्द में कौन-सा समास है?
A. द्वन्द्व B. द्विगु
C. कर्मधारय D. तत्पुरुष

23. 'चिड़ीमार' शब्द में कौन-सा समास है?
A. द्विगु B. कर्मधारय
C. तत्पुरुष D. अव्ययीभाव

24. 'यथोचित' शब्द में समास बताइए–
A. अव्ययीभाव B. कर्मधारय
C. बहुव्रीहि D. तत्पुरुष

25. समास कहते हैं–
A. शब्दों के मेल को
B. अक्षर के मेल को
C. स्वर-से-स्वर के मेल को
D. स्वर के साथ व्यंजन के मेल को

26. 'शिवार्पण' शब्द में कौन-सा समास है?
A. अधिकरण तत्पुरुष B. करण तत्पुरुष
C. सम्प्रदान तत्पुरुष D. अपादान तत्पुरुष

27. निम्नलिखित में किसमें तत्पुरुष समास है?
A. पदप्राप्त B. शताब्दी
C. चौमासा D. भाई-बहन

28. 'रसगुल्ला' में कौन-सा समास है?
A. तत्पुरुष B. बहुव्रीहि
C. द्वन्द्व D. अव्ययीभाव

29. 'भुखमरा' का समास विग्रह होगा–
A. भूख से जो मर गया B. भूख से मरा हुआ
C. भूखों मर गया जो D. भूख द्वारा मरा हुआ

30. 'दशरथ सुत' में कौन-सा समास है?
A. तत्पुरुष B. बहुव्रीहि
C. द्विगु D. द्वन्द्व

31. 'अष्टाध्यायी' में कौन-सा समास है?
A. द्वन्द्व B. द्विगु
C. तत्पुरुष D. कर्मधारय

32. 'यथाशीघ्र' में कौन-सा समास है?
A. अव्ययीभाव B. द्वंद्व
C. कर्मधारय D. तत्पुरुष

33. चौखंभा में कौन-सा समास है?
A. बहुब्रीहि B. द्वन्द्व
C. द्विगु D. तत्पुरुष

34. कौन-सा समास विशेषण के रूप में प्रयुक्त होता है?
A. अव्ययीभाव B. तत्पुरुष
C. कर्मधारय D. बहुब्रीहि

35. द्विगु समास का उदाहरण होगा–
A. षट्कोण B. कुपुत्र
C. प्रतिवर्ष D. सूरसागर

36. कौन-सा शब्द अव्ययीभाव समास का उदाहरण है?
A. नवग्रह B. गाँठकर
C. महात्मा D. आमरण

37. 'राजपुत्र' में कौन-सा समास है?
A. बहुब्रीहि B. तत्पुरुष
C. द्विगु D. कर्मधारय

38. निम्नलिखित में से तत्पुरुष समास किसमें है?
A. नील गाय B. राजकुमार
C. त्रिलोचन D. दशानन

39. निम्नलिखित में द्वन्द्व समास बताइए–
A. प्रतिदिन B. चौमासा
C. घी-शक्कर D. महादेव

40. 'आजीवन' में कौन-सा समास है?
A. अव्ययीभाव B. तत्पुरुष
C. कर्मधारय D. द्विगु

41. निम्नलिखित में 'यथाविधि' का सही समास कौन-सा है?
A. अव्ययीभाव B. तत्पुरुष
C. कर्मधारय D. बहुब्रीहि

42. 'पर्णकुटी' शब्द का समास है–
A. तत्पुरुष B. द्वन्द्व
C. कर्मधारय D. बहुब्रीहि

43. निम्नलिखित में 'द्वन्द्व समास' का शब्द है–
A. आज-कल B. रातों-रात
C. दिन-दिन D. वीर पुरुष

44. 'निशिदिन' शब्द में प्रयुक्त समास है–
A. द्वन्द्व B. अव्ययीभाव
C. कर्मधारय D. तत्पुरुष

45. जिस समास में पहला शब्द प्रधान होता है और समूचा शब्द क्रिया विशेषण अव्यय होता है, उसे कौन-सा समास कहते हैं?
A. अव्ययीभाव B. तत्पुरुष
C. बहुब्रीहि D. द्वन्द्व

46. 'जलपिपासु' में कौन-सा समास है?
A. तत्पुरुष B. अव्ययीभाव
C. द्वन्द्व D. बहुब्रीहि

47. 'वनवास' में कौन-सा समास है?
A. तत्पुरुष B. कर्मधारय
C. द्वन्द्व D. बहुब्रीहि

48. 'दिगम्बर' में कौन-सा समास है?
A. बहुब्रीहि B. द्वन्द्व
C. द्विगु D. कर्मधारय

49. 'नरोत्तम' में कौन-सा समास है?
A. द्वन्द्व B. तत्पुरुष
C. अव्ययीभाव D. कर्मधारय

50. 'आजन्म' में कौन-सा समास है?
A. द्विगु B. तत्पुरुष
C. कर्मधारय D. अव्ययीभाव

51. 'अकालपीड़ित' में समास होगा–
A. कर्मधारय B. द्वन्द्व
C. तत्पुरुष D. बहुब्रीहि

52. 'जय-पराजय' में कौन-सा समास है?
A. द्वन्द्व B. कर्मधारय
C. द्विगु D. तत्पुरुष

53. 'वियोग-विकल' शब्द में प्रयुक्त समास है–
A. तत्पुरुष B. कर्मधारय
C. द्वन्द्व D. द्विगु

54. इन युग्मों में से कौन-सा सही नहीं है?
A. नीलोत्पलम् – कर्मधारय समास
B. दशाननः – बहुब्रीहि समास
C. रामलक्ष्मणौ – अव्ययीभाव समास
D. दिवारात्रि – द्वन्द्व समास

55. 'तिरंगा' शब्द में समास है–
A. द्वन्द्व B. अव्ययीभाव
C. द्विगु D. कर्मधारय

56. 'लम्बोदर' उदाहरण है–
A. बहुब्रीहि समास का B. द्वन्द्व समास का
C. द्विगु समास का D. कर्मधारय समास का

57. निम्नलिखित में से कर्मधारय समास किसमें है?
A. चक्रपाणि B. चतुर्थुगम्
C. नीलोत्पलम् D. माता-पिता

58. 'चक्रपाणिदर्शनार्थ' पद में मान्य समास है–
A. कर्मधारय B. तत्पुरुष
C. अव्ययीभाव D. बहुब्रीहि

59. 'कठपुतली' में कौन-सा समास है?
A. सम्प्रदान तत्पुरुष B. सम्बन्ध तत्पुरुष
C. अधिकरण तत्पुरुष D. कर्म तत्पुरुष

60. 'कष्टापन्नः' शब्द में समास है–
A. अव्ययीभाव B. तत्पुरुष
C. बहुब्रीहि D. कर्मधारय

61. 'चन्द्रकान्तिः' में समास है–
A. बहुब्रीहि B. कर्मधारय
C. तत्पुरुष D. इनमें से कोई नहीं

62. 'चन्द्रशेखर' में प्रयुक्त समास है–
A. तत्पुरुष B. कर्मधारय
C. बहुब्रीहि D. द्विगु

63. 'रात-दिन' में कौन-सा समास होता है?
A. द्वन्द्व B. द्विगु
C. कर्मधारय D. अव्ययीभाव

64. 'बहन-भाई' में समास है–
A. बहुब्रीहि B. तत्पुरुष
C. द्वन्द्व D. द्विगु

65. 'दशमुख' में कौन-सा समास है?
A. तत्पुरुष B. बहुब्रीहि
C. द्वन्द्व D. कर्मधारय

66. 'यथाशक्ति' में समास है–
A. द्विगु B. तत्पुरुष
C. कर्मधारय D. अव्ययीभाव

67. 'देशभक्ति' में समास है–
A. तत्पुरुष B. बहुब्रीहि
C. द्विगु D. कर्मधारय

68. 'हस्तलिखित' में प्रयुक्त समास है–
A. कर्मधारय B. तत्पुरुष
C. बहुब्रीहि D. द्वन्द्व

69. 'त्रिनेत्र' में कौन-सा समास है?
A. तत्पुरुष B. बहुब्रीहि
C. द्विगु D. द्वन्द्व

70. 'भरपेट' में कौन-सा समास है?
A. अव्ययीभाव B. कर्मधारय
C. तत्पुरुष D. बहुब्रीहि

वर्तनी

निर्देश (प्र.सं. 1 से 80 तक): *नीचे के प्रश्नों में एक शब्द की चार अलग-अलग वर्तनियां दी हुई हैं। इनमें से सही वर्तनी छाँटकर उस पर निशान लगाइये:*

1. A. जयोत्स्ना B. ज्योत्स्ना
C. जोत्स्ना D. ज्योत्सना

2. A. कवयित्री B. कवियित्री
C. कवियत्री D. कवित्री

3. A. उत्ज्वल B. उज्जवल
C. ऊज्जवल D. उज्ज्वल

4. A. छः B. छह
C. छह् D. छै

5. A. जिजीविषा B. जिजीवषा
C. जजीवषा D. जिजिवीषा

6. A. दृश्य B. द्रश्य
C. दृष्य D. द्रिश्य

7. A. इतिहासिक B. ऐतिहासिक
C. ऐतिहासीक D. ऐतीहासिक

8. A. वाङ्मय B. वाँङ्मय
C. वांग्मय D. वांगमय

9. A. सौर्हाद्र B. सैहार्द
C. सैर्हाद D. सौहार्द

10. A. आर्शीवाद B. आशिर्वाद
C. आशीर्वाद D. आर्शिवाद

11. A. भूगोलिक B. भूगौलिक
C. भोगोलिक D. भौगोलिक

12. A. सन्कीर्णता B. सन्कीरणता
C. संकीणता D. संकीर्णता

13. A. परचन्ड B. प्रचण्ड
C. प्रचान्ड D. परचण्ड

14. A. तार्क्रिक B. तार्किक
C. ताकि्क D. ताक्रिक

15. A. इर्षा B. ईर्षा
C. इर्ष्या D. ईर्ष्या

16. A. पूज्यनीय B. पुजनीय
C. पूजनीय D. पुज्यनीय

17. A. अधम्र B. अध्रम
C. अधर्म D. अधृम

18. A. अधिकृत B. अधिक्रित
C. अधिक्रित्त D. अधिर्कित

19. A. अनुकृम B. अनुक्रम
C. अनुकर्म D. अनुकम्र

20. A. अनवेषण B. अन्वेषण
C. अन्वेछण D. अन्वेशण

21. A. अभिशेक B. अभिषेख
C. अभिषेक D. अभीषेक

22. A. इच्छुक B. इक्षुक
C. इक्छुक D. इछिक

23. A. इन्र्दिय B. इन्द्यि
C. इन्दिय D. इन्द्रिय

24. A. उतकण्ठा B. उत्कण्ठा
C. उत्क्णठा D. उत्तकन्ठा

25. A. उर्मिला B. उम्रिला
C. उमिर्ला D. उर्मिला

26. A. रिषि B. ऋषि
C. त्रिृषि D. ऋशि्

27. A. एकागृ B. एकाग्र
C. एकार्ग D. एक्राग्र

28. A. ओजश्वि B. ओजस्वी
C. ओजश्वी D. ओजष्वी

29. A. औशधी B. औषधी
C. औषधि D. औष्धि

30. A. करम B. क्राम
C. कम्र D. कर्म

31. A. ग्रिहीत B. ग्रहीत
C. गृहीत D. गर्हित

32. A. कृतज्ञ B. क्रतज्ञ
C. क्रितज्ञ D. क्रितग्य

33. A. चतुदर्श B. चर्तुदश
C. चतुर्दश D. चतुद्रश

34. A. जर्जर B. जरर्जर
C. जज्रर D. जरजर

35. A. जघ्नय B. जघ्रय
C. जघ्न्य D. जघन्य

36. A. जेष्ठ B. ज्येश्ठ
C. ज्येष्ठ D. ज्येस्ठ

37. A. तपस्वनी B. तपस्विनी
C. तपिस्वनी D. तपिस्विनी

38. A. तादातमय B. तदात्म्य
C. तादात्म्य D. तादात्यम

39. A. तृष्णा B. तिृष्णा
C. त्रिष्णा D. तृश्णा

40. A. त्रिमूर्ती B. त्रिमुर्ति
C. त्रिमूर्ति D. त्रृमूर्ति

41. A. दक्छ B. दक्च्छ
C. दक्ष D. दज्ञ

42. A. द्रर्पन B. दर्पन
C. दपर्ण D. दर्पण

43. A. दामपत्य B. दम्पत्य
C. दाम्पत्य D. दाम्पत

44. A. दीप्पित B. दीपति
C. दीप्ति D. दीप्ती

45. A. दीर्घायु B. दीरघायु
C. दीघार्यु D. दीर्घियु

46. A. दुर्निती B. दुनीर्ति
C. दुरनीति D. दुर्नीति

47. A. दुर्दषा B. दुह्शा
C. दुर्दशा D. दुद्रशा

48. A. दुर्योधन B. दुयोर्धन
C. दूरयोधन D. द्रुयोधन

49. A. दुरबुद्धि B. दुर्बुधि
C. दुबुद्धि D. दुर्बुद्धि

50. A. धनुष्विद्या B. धनुर्विद्या
C. धर्नुविद्या D. धनुर्वेद्या

51. A. धर्म B. धृर्म
C. ध्रर्म D. धम्र

52. A. ध्रुर्व B. धुव्र
C. ध्रुव D. धुर्व

53. A. नम्रदिश्वर B. नम्रदेश्वर
C. नमर्देश्वर D. नर्मदिश्वर

54. A. निरक्षेप B. निक्क्षेप
C. निक्षेप D. निक्छेप

55. A. निर्गह B. नृग्रह
C. निग्रह D. निगर्ह

56. A. निरजीव B. निर्जीव
C. निृजीव D. निज्रीव

57. A. निम्रूल B. निर्मूल
C. निरमूल D. नृर्मूल

58. A. निवृत्त B. निव्रत्त
C. निवृत D. निृवत्त

59. A. प्रिक्रमा B. परीक्रमा
C. परिकृमा D. परिक्रमा

60. A. प्रयटन B. पृयटन
C. पर्यटन D. प्रर्यटन

61. A. प्रक्रिति B. प्रकृति
C. प्रक्रति D. पृक्रति

62. A. बर्हिमुख B. बहिर्मुख
C. बहिम्रुख D. बहिमुर्ख

63. A. भरतस्ना B. भर्त्सना
C. भर्तसना D. भर्तृसना

64. A. मूर्ती B. मूर्ति
C. मूर्तृि D. मूरती

65. A. गिद्ध B. गीध
C. गिद्धा D. ग्रिद्ध

66. A. निकर्सन B. निर्कषन
C. निकर्षण D. निर्कषण

67. A. निकृष्ट B. निक्रस्ट
C. निकृस्ट D. निक्रिष्ट

68. A. पार्थिव B. पार्थ्रिव
C. पार्थीव D. पाथिर्व

69. A. विदूश्क B. विदूष्क
C. विदूशक D. विदूषक

70. A. फुर्तीला B. फुर्त्तीला
C. फुर्तिला D. फुर्तला

71. A. वर्ज B. वज्र
C. वजृ D. वज्रृ

72. A. ब्रम्हचर्य B. ब्रह्मचर्य
C. बृह्मचर्य D. ब्रह्मर्चय

73. A. मत्स्य B. मतस्य
C. मत्सत्य D. मत्श्य

74. A. भ्रित्य B. भर्त्य
C. भृत्य D. भ्रत्य

75. A. निग्रंध B. निर्गंध
C. र्निगंध D. नृगंध

76. A. प्रकर्श B. प्रकर्ष
C. पृकर्श D. पृकर्ष

77. A. भद्र B. भदृ
C. भर्द्र D. भर्द

78. A. मंजूशा B. मंजूषा
C. मंजुषा D. मंजुशा

79. A. मुर्मूषु B. मुमुर्षू
C. मुमुर्षु D. मुमूर्पु

80. A. ब्राह्मण B. बृाह्मण
C. ब्राम्हण D. बृाहम्ण

निर्देश (प्र.सं. 81 से 115 तक): *नीचे प्रत्येक प्रश्न में A, B, C और D अक्षरांक में चार शब्द दिए गए हैं। जिनमें से एक में वर्तनी सम्बन्धी त्रुटि हो सकती है। उस त्रुटियुक्त शब्द का अक्षरांक ही आपका उत्तर होगा। यदि चारों शब्दों की वर्तनी सही है तो उत्तर दीजिए E अर्थात् 'सभी सही हैं'।*

81. A. अप्रयुक्त B. अतीषयोक्ति
C. अशोध्य D. सम्मति
E. सभी सही हैं

82. A. अभ्युक्ति B. इष्टतम
C. अपुरित D. उपस्थित
E. सभी सही हैं

83. A. उत्तरजिवीता B. प्रारक्षित
C. क्षैतिज D. आयातित
E. सभी सही हैं

84. A. आस्थगित B. आतिथ्य
C. अंतरिम D. निर्धारित
E. सभी सही हैं

85. A. किफायत B. परिस्थिति
C. संतुलित D. असिंचीत
E. सभी सही हैं

86. A. तात्पर्य B. महोत्सव
C. दंभ D. कृशक
E. सभी सही हैं

87. A. लक्षण B. व्यंजन
C. पगडंडी D. पारंगत
E. सभी सही हैं

88. A. स्थानापन्न B. व्यावशयिक
C. कोशिका D. आर्थिक
E. सभी सही हैं

89. A. दांडधिकारी B. प्राधिकरण
C. आदित्य D. क्रियान्वयन
E. सभी सही हैं

90. A. गोपनीयता B. कार्यवाही
C. उत्रदायित्व D. वयस्क
E. सभी सही हैं

91. A. चूल्लु B. जीविका
C. ठिठोली D. तकली
E. सभी सही हैं

92. A. नजरिया B. पंडीताइ
C. फरियादी D. बधाई
E. सभी सही हैं

93. A. प्रकाशकीय B. फाल्गुन
C. बधिर D. भोतिक
E. सभी सही हैं

94. A. हौसला B. स्वीकृति
C. व्यवासायिक D. लिपाई
E. सभी सही हैं

95. A. फलित B. बटोही
C. भजनीक D. मंडली
E. सभी सही हैं

96. A. अनामिष B. अपरिहार्य
C. किफायती D. गिलाफ
E. सभी सही हैं

97. A. गोधुलि B. चांचल्य
C. जिजीविषु D. तमोली
E. सभी सही हैं

98. A. तितिक्षा B. दखलंदाजी
C. दिप्ति D. दैनिकी
E. सभी सही हैं

99. A. नजदिकी B. नियोक्ता
C. परिणीता D. पाणिग्रहण
E. सभी सही हैं

100. A. पुनीत B. प्रख्यापीत
C. फरोख्त D. बुजुर्गी
E. सभी सही हैं

101. A. अद्‌भुत B. व्यंग्य
C. अदृश्य D. समारंभ
E. सभी सही हैं

102. A. लक्षण B. महात्मन
C. सम्पर्क D. कर्तज्ञ
E. सभी सही हैं

103. A. गझिन B. आशय
C. निशपादन D. आकर्षण
E. सभी सही हैं

104. A. उत्तरीय B. स्थान्नापन
C. कुंभ D. असामान्य
E. सभी सही हैं

105. A. न्ययाधिश B. पुरस्कृत
C. वारिद D. अधिशासी
E. सभी सही हैं

106. A. चिनाई B. तंबूल
C. ठिठोली D. तन्मय
E. सभी सही हैं

107. A. अगड़ाइ B. गठीला
C. खिलाफ D. कल्पनातीत
E. सभी सही हैं

108. A. सूरत B. वैधव्य
C. लतीका D. रेगिस्तान
E. सभी सही हैं

109. A. इति B. अखिलेश
C. कबूतर D. खेरात
E. सभी सही हैं

110. A. चमत्कृत B. जिल्द
C. तमोली D. दमित
E. सभी सही हैं

111. A. प्रहसन B. तात्पर्य
C. महसूल D. पाणिगृहण
E. सभी सही हैं

112. A. मस्तिष्क B. प्रोत्साहन
C. सम्वत् D. क्रियाविधि
E. सभी सही हैं

113. A. विचारणीय B. क्रन्दन
C. पर्यावर्ण D. उपलब्धि
E. सभी सही हैं

114. A विसतृत B. वाग्विलास
C. तात्कालिक D. अलंकार
E. सभी सही हैं

115. A. दृष्टांत B. रूढ़ि
C. सूचि D. आचमन
E. सभी सही हैं

पर्यायवाची

1. 'कमल' शब्द का पर्यायवाची होगा–
A. कन्दर्प B. अनंग
C. घनेश D. इन्दीवर

2. 'क्रोध' के लिए इन दिए गए पर्यायवाची शब्दों में एक गलत शब्द है, उसे चयनित कीजिए–
A. रोष B. अमर्ष
C. स्वत्व D. कोप

3. निम्नलिखित पर्यायवाची शब्दों में से जो एक शब्द 'मोर' का पर्यायवाची नहीं है, उसे चिन्हित कीजिए–
A. केकी B. कीश
C. शिखी D. शिखण्डी

4. इनमें से कौन-सा शब्द 'कृष्णा' का पर्यायवाची है?
A. राधा B. रुक्मिणी
C. द्रोपदी D. यशोदा

5. इनमें से एक शब्द 'बैल' का पर्यायवाची नहीं है, उसे चयनित कीजिए–
A. अश्म B. वृषभ
C. बलीवर्द D. गो

6. निम्नलिखित में से जो शब्द 'सौन्दर्य' का पर्यायवाची नहीं है, उसे चयनित कीजिए–
A. सुषमा B. शोभा
C. सुन्दरता D. रमणी

7. निम्नलिखित विकल्पों में से एक शब्द 'नदी' का पर्यायवाची नहीं है, उसे चयनित कीजिए–
A. तरंगिणी B. तटिनी
C. तरिणी D. सरिता

8. नीचे दिए गए विकल्पों में से एक शब्द 'घर' का पर्यायवाची नहीं है, उसे चयनित कीजिए–
A. भवन B. भुवन
C. निकेतन D. सदन

9. इनमें से कौन-सा शब्द 'पार्थ' का पर्यायवाची है?
A. भीष्म B. श्रीकृष्ण
C. युधिष्ठिर D. अर्जुन

10. 'दु:ख' का पर्यायवाची शब्द निम्नलिखित में से कौन-सा है?

A. व्यथा B. पीड़ा
C. वेदना D. ये सभी पर्याय हैं

11. नीचे दिए गए शब्दों में से एक शब्द 'गीदड़' का पर्यायवाची नहीं है, उसका चयन कीजिए–

A. खगेश B. शृंगाल
C. सियार D. जम्बुक

12. निम्न में से कौन चन्द्रमा का पर्यायवाची नहीं है?

A. शशि B. हिमकर
C. शशांक D. रूपक

13. निम्न में से कौन गाय का पर्यायवाची नहीं है?

A. हेरम्ब B. गौरी
C. भद्रा D. धेनु

14. कुत्ता का पर्यायवाची शब्द निम्नलिखित में से कौन-सा है?

A. सारमेय B. क्रमेलक
C. कीर D. नागान्तक

15. आनंद का पर्यायवाची नहीं है–

A. हर्ष B. उल्लास
C. चाह D. आह्लाद

16. 'कृशानु' का पर्यायवाची शब्द है–

A. अनल B. पवन
C. दोहित्री D. अनिल

17. 'द्रौपदी' का पर्याय नहीं है–

A. द्रुपदसुता B. याज्ञसेनी
C. पांचाली D. रमणी

18. 'महादेव' का पर्यायवाची शब्द चुनिए–

A. गरुड़ध्वज B. नारायण
C. चन्द्रशेखर D. विश्वम्भर

19. 'चन्द्रमा' का पर्यायवाची शब्द चुनिए–

A. निशाकर B. निशाचर
C. तरणि D. कृशानु

20. 'धन' का पर्यायवाची जो शब्द नहीं है, उसे चुनिए–

A. द्रव्य B. द्रव
C. सम्पदा D. दौलत

21. 'पुत्री' का पर्यायवाची शब्द नहीं है–

A. तनय B. सुता
C. आत्मजा D. दुहिता

22. निम्नलिखित में से कौन-सा शब्द 'कमल' का पर्यायवाची शब्द नहीं है?

A. सरोज B. अरविन्द
C. सलिल D. पंकज

23. निम्नलिखित किस समूह में सभी शब्द 'कामदेव' के पर्यायवाची हैं?

A. कंदर्प, मदन, मनसिज, मारक
B. मदन, मन्मथ, अनंग, कंदर्प
C. मान, त्रिपुर, मन्मथ, अनंग
D. मन्मथ, मनसिज, त्रिपुर, अनंग

24. कौन-सा शब्द जंगल शब्द का पर्यायवाची नहीं है?

A. अटवी B. कान्ता
C. कान्तार D. कानन

25. कौन-सा शब्द 'अम्बर' का पर्यायवाची है?

A. आकाश B. अवनि
C. मेघ D. बादल

26. कौन-सा शब्द 'मित्र' का पर्याय नहीं है?

A. अलि B. सखा
C. सुहृद D. मीत

27. निम्नांकित में किस शब्द का अर्थ कमल होता है?

A. उत्पल B. उपल
C. जलद D. नीरद

28. निम्नलिखित में 'पुत्री' शब्द के पर्यायवाची शब्द-समूह कौन हैं?

A. भार्या, कान्ता, अबला, वनिता
B. लड़की, बेटी, अचला, वसुधा
C. सुता, धरा, वसुमती, अचला
D. तनया, आत्मजा, दुहिता, तनुजा

29. निम्नलिखित शब्द-समूह में 'बिजली' के पर्यायवाची कौन हैं?

A. ज्योति, रोशनी, चमक, प्रभा
B. विद्युत, तड़ित, चपला, दामिनी
C. उजाला, प्रभंजन, विहग, निशापति
D. मंदाकिनी, अश्म, प्रस्तर, प्रभा

30. 'जलधि' शब्द का पर्यायवाची क्या है?

A. नहर B. नाव
C. नदी D. समुद्र

31. 'पंकज' शब्द का पर्यायवाची क्या है?

A. सूर्य B. कमल
C. चन्द्रमा D. अमृत

32. 'तरकश' का पर्यायवाची शब्द है–

A. तीर B. धनुष
C. प्रत्यंचा D. निषंग

33. 'स्त्री' का पर्यायवाची शब्द नहीं है–

A. तरुणी B. प्रमदा
C. ललाम D. ललना

34. 'गणेश' का पर्यायवाची शब्द है–

A. सुधांशु B. कुबेर
C. एकदंत D. सुधाकर

35. निम्नलिखित में से कौन-सा शब्द 'तलवार' का पर्यायवाची नहीं है?
A. असि B. खड्ग
C. कृपण D. चंद्रहास

36. इनमें से कौन 'कौआ' का पर्यायवाची है?
A. वायस B. पाली
C. भद्रा D. उदक

37. निम्न में से कौन 'पत्ता' का पर्यायवाची नहीं है?
A. दल B. पर्ण
C. पल्लव D. प्रसून

38. निम्न में से कौन 'हंस' का पर्यायवाची है?
A. मराल B. सारंग
C. अनीक D. अरि

39. निम्न में से कौन 'रण' का पर्यायवाची नहीं है?
A. युद्ध B. संग्राम
C. समर D. सार

40. इनमें से कौन 'युवती' का पर्यायवाची नहीं है?
A. तरुणी B. किशोरी
C. श्यामा D. यामिनी

41. निम्न में से कौन 'इन्द्र' का पर्यायवाची नहीं है?
A. सुरपति B. मघवा
C. धनाधिप D. सुरेश

42. इनमें से कौन 'सरस्वती' का पर्यायवाची नहीं है?
A. वीणापाणि B. वाचा
C. धनद D. शारदा

43. निम्न में से कौन 'कन्या' का पर्यायवाची नहीं है?
A. तनुजा B. आत्मजा
C. नन्दिनी D. भार्या

44. इनमें से कौन 'मयूर' का पर्यायवाची नहीं है?
A. सारंग B. शिखी
C. विशिख D. केकी

45. इनमें से कौन 'शेर' का पर्यायवाची नहीं है?
A. तुरंग B. मृगेन्द्र
C. मृगराज D. व्याघ्र

46. निम्न में से कौन 'अग्नि' का पर्यायवाची है?
A. अनल B. धनद
C. सारंग D. जाह्नवी

47. 'अलंकेश' पर्यायवाची शब्द है–
A. बादल का B. कल्पवृक्ष का
C. कुबेर का D. चपला का

48. इनमें से किस शब्द के पर्यायवाची गलत हैं?
A. कमल – जलज, पंकज, सरोज
B. पुष्प – कुसुम, फूल, सुमन
C. सरस्वती – गिरा, भारती, वाणी
D. सूर्य – दिवस, याम, वासर

49. निम्नलिखित में कौन-सा शब्द 'पताका' का पर्यायवाची नहीं है?
A. झण्डा B. निशान
C. प्रस्तर D. ध्वज

50. निम्नलिखित शब्दों में से 'हनुमान' का पर्यायवाची शब्द नहीं है–
A. रामभक्त B. पवनपुत्र
C. बजरंगबली D. कपीश्वर

51. 'खेचर' का पर्याय होगा–
A. आकाश में चलने वाला B. पक्षी
C. ग्रह D. इनमें से सभी

52. 'बटोही' का पर्यायवाची निम्न में से कौन शब्द-समूह होगा?
A. वटमार, एकाकी B. असहाय, दुर्गम
C. पथिक, राहगीर D. पाथेय, मेघ

53. निम्न में से कौन-सा शब्द समूह 'विरद' का पर्यायवाची होगा?
A. यश, ख्याति B. बीज, मूल
C. वृक्ष, पौधा D. विरही, वियोगी

54. 'यातु' का पर्यायवाची निम्न में से कौन शब्द-समूह होगा?
A. पथिक, कष्ट B. काल, हवा
C. यातना, हिंसा D. राक्षस, निशाचर

55. 'विभु' का पर्यायवाची शब्द-समूह होगा–
A. सर्वव्यापक, नित्य B. ब्रह्म, आत्मा
C. महान, ईश्वर D. चिरस्थायी, दृढ़

56. 'क्षुद्र' का पर्यायवाची शब्द-समूह होगा–
A. कंजूस, कृपण B. निर्धन, दरिद्र
C. अल्प, मामूली D. नीच, अधम

57. 'कुबेर' शब्द का निम्नलिखित में से कौन- सा शब्द पर्यायवाची नहीं है?
A. श्वान B. कोषपाल
C. धनपति D. यक्षपति

58. 'सेवक' का पर्यायवाची है–
A. परिचर्या B. यायावर
C. शायक D. परिचारक

59. 'पार्वती' का पर्यायवाची है–
A. कमला B. इला
C. गौरा D. विभा

60. 'अग्र' शब्द का पर्यायवाची नहीं है–
A. शिखर B. अगला
C. ज्येष्ठ D. दावा

61. निम्नलिखित में से कौन-सा एक 'जानकी' का पर्यायवाची नहीं है?
A. जनकात्मजा B. वैदेही
C. जनकसूता D. वामा

62. 'पुष्प' का पर्यायवाची नहीं है–
A. सुमन B. प्रसून
C. कुसुम D. निलय

63. 'पत्थर' का पर्यायवाची है–
A. हिमगिरि B. पाषाण
C. गिरि D. शैल

64. 'पावक' का पर्यायवाची शब्द निम्नलिखित में से कौन-सा है?
A. पृथ्वी B. जल
C. अग्नि D. वायु

65. निम्नलिखित में से जो शब्द 'पत्नी' का पर्याय न हो, उसे चिन्हित कीजिए–
A. कलत्र B. दौहित्र
C. भार्या D. जाया

66. 'अर्वाचीन' शब्द का पर्यायवाची है–
A. आधुनिक B. विदेशी
C. चीनी D. प्राचीन

विलोमार्थी शब्द

निर्देश (प्र.सं. 1 से 75 तक): *सही-सही विलोम शब्द चुनिए–*

1. अनादर
A. मान B. सम्मान
C. आदर D. सत्कार

2. अभिज्ञ
A. अज्ञानी B. अनभिज्ञ
C. अनिपुण D. मूर्ख

3. अथ
A. इति B. समाप्त
C. खत्म D. संपूर्ण

4. करुण
A. कठोर B. निष्ठुर
C. निर्दय D. कोमल

5. ऋजु
A. सीधा B. सरल
C. तिर्यक् D. वक्र

6. मौन
A. मुखर B. मूक
C. वाचाल D. प्रगल्भ

7. निर्दय
A. निर्भय B. सहृय
C. सभय D. सदय

8. तिमिर
A. प्रकाश्य B. आलोक
C. ज्योतिर्मय D. आभास

9. तीक्ष्ण
A. मंद B. तीव्र
C. प्रखर D. क्षीण

10. कृत्रिम
A. प्राकृतिक B. स्वनिर्मित
C. स्वाभाविक D. स्वचालित

11. उदात्त
A. उद्धत B. दानशील
C. अनुदात्त D. क्षमावान्

12. उदार
A. कठोर B. निर्भय
C. अपव्यय D. अनुदार

13. शुक्ल
A. काला B. कृष्ण
C. असित D. श्यामल

14. प्रस्थान
A. आगमन B. गमनागमन
C. निगम D. निर्गम

15. शूल
A. मूल B. धूल
C. फूल D. तूल

16. अपेक्षा
A. कामना B. भावना
C. अभीप्सा D. उपेक्षा

17. निरक्षर
A. शिक्षित B. अशिक्षित
C. साक्षर D. अक्षर

18. प्रकट
A. गुप्त B. लुप्त
C. सुप्त D. विलुप्त

19. उर्वर
A. उपजाऊ B. बंजर
C. गत्वर D. शस्यश्यामल

20. संधि
A. अनुग्रह B. ग्रह
C. विच्छेद D. मैत्री

21. संयोग
A. प्रयोग B. सुयोग
C. नियोग D. वियोग

22. विकास
A. सीमा B. ह्रास
C. दुबला D. नीचा

23. उत्थान
A. नमन B. पतन
C. उदय D. ध्वंस

24. क्षुद्र
A. क्षुद्रतर B. महान्
C. तुच्छ D. अवमान

25. इहलोक
A. उपकार B. पाताल
C. आदि D. परलोक

26. ज्योति
A. पुंज B. दीपक
C. तम D. रोशनी

27. यथार्थ
A. मनोवांछित B. अनुमानित
C. कल्पित D. सत्य

28. अमर
A. देवता B. मरणशील
C. मर्त्य D. दानव

29. आघात
A. अनाघात B. विस्तीर्ण
C. स्निग्ध D. डरपोक

30. व्यष्टि
A. सृष्टि B. वृष्टि
C. समष्टि D. इनमें से कोई नहीं

31. सज्जन
A. चापलूस B. व्यभिचारी
C. सहयोगी D. दुर्जन

32. उत्कर्ष
A. अपकर्ष B. परामर्श
C. संघर्ष D. विमर्श

33. क्षुधा
A. तृषा B. तृष्ण
C. तृप्ति D. मृगतृष्णा

34. सुबह
A. प्रातः B. शाम
C. रात D. दिन

35. अनुकूल
A. प्रतिकूल B. अपकूल
C. अनुकूलन D. सानूकूल

36. आहूत
A. अनागत B. आगत
C. अनेक D. अनाहूत

37. श्रीगणेश
A. समापन B. इतिश्री
C. अंत D. अथ

38. निंदा
A. स्तुति B. संस्तुति
C. संवेदना D. स्तवन

39. आचार
A. आनाचार B. अनाचार
C. अत्याचार D. विचार

40. सहज
A. असहज B. असली
C. अप्राकृतिक D. निर्मित

41. प्राच्य
A. उदीच्य B. प्रतीच्य
C. पाश्चात्य D. अर्वाचीन

42. गुण
A. दोष B. पुण्य
C. अधिक D. विशाल

43. 'लाघव' शब्द का विपरीतार्थक शब्द है–
A. विस्तार B. संक्षेप
C. लम्बा D. दीर्घकालीन

44. आहार
A. प्रतिहार B. साहार
C. अनाहार D. विहार

45. 'ध्वंस' शब्द का विलोम बताइए–
A. विनाश B. निर्माण
C. विध्वंस D. उत्कर्ष

46. 'वादी' का विलोमार्थी शब्द बताएँ–
A. समवादी B. कुवादी
C. अनुवादी D. प्रतिवादी

47. अतिवृष्टि का विलोमार्थी शब्द है–
A. अन्तरवृष्टि B. अल्पवृष्टि
C. असमयवृष्टि D. अस्तवृष्टि

48. आदि
A. अंत B. प्रारम्भ
C. व्याधि D. बर्बादी

49. शाश्वत
A. मृत्यु B. मर्त्य
C. नश्वर D. क्षणिक

50. व्यस्त
A. विश्रांत B. अभ्यस्त
C. अव्यस्त D. अतिव्यस्त

51. गत्यात्मक
A. गतिभाव B. स्थिर
C. अस्थिर D. प्रत्यात्मक

52. अज्ञ
A. अनज्ञ B. सुमज्ञ
C. विज्ञ D. कुमज्ञ

53. कटु
A. मधुर B. पटु
C. मृदु D. मीठा

54. नीरस
A. रसीला B. सरस
C. विरस D. अरस

55. ओजस्वनी
A. तेजस्वनी B. निर्जस्वी
C. निस्तेज D. तपस्वी

56. अर्पण
A. ग्रहण B. तर्पण
C. समर्पण D. प्रत्यर्पण

57. अनभिज्ञ
A. भिज्ञ B. अज्ञ
C. अभिज्ञ D. अतिभिज्ञ

58. अन्यमनस्क
A. स्वस्थ B. प्रसन्न
C. सजग D. सतर्क

59. अपव्यय
A. अधिव्यय B. व्यय
C. मितव्यय D. इनमें से कोई नहीं

60. आवरण
A. अनावरण B. आचरण
C. सुवरण D. अवज्ञा

61. गमन
A. आना B. उतरना
C. रुकना D. आगमन

62. राजा
A. देवता B. साथी
C. विज्ञ D. प्रजा

63. विश्लेषण
A. संश्लेषण B. गवेषण
C. विशेषण D. अन्वेषण

64. दिवस
A. विभावरी B. अरविन्द
C. प्रवाहिणी D. विचक्षण

65. निर्मल
A. पवित्र B. शुद्ध
C. मलिन D. मृदु

66. उद्यम
A. प्रवीण B. आलस्य
C. नीरज D. नृप

67. द्युति
A. छवि B. प्रभा
C. ज्योति D. अन्धकार

68. रुक्ष
A. पिच्छल B. चिक्कण
C. स्निग्ध D. सरस

69. विघटन
A. सामूहिकता B. संगठन
C. एकीकरण D. समष्टि

70. गरिमा
A. कालिमा B. लघुमा
C. अरुणिमा D. लालिमा

71. सामिष
A. निरामिष B. वैष्णव
C. शाकाहारी D. मांसरहित

72. अंधेरा
A. सुबह B. उजाला
C. प्रकाश D. झुरमुट

73. उदय
A. अस्त B. अवसान
C. विनाश D. नाभ

74. कुटिल
A. संत B. उदार
C. साधु D. सरल

75. ग्राह्य
A. त्याज्य B. ग्रहण
C. तरल D. वाञ्छा

वाक्यों की शुद्धता

निर्देश (प्र.सं. 1 से 35 तक): *नीचे दिए गए प्रश्नों में चार वाक्यों में एक वाक्य शुद्ध है और तीन अशुद्ध हैं। शुद्ध वाक्य को चुनिए।*

1. A. मैंने एक रुपए का सामान खरीदा
B. मैं एक रुपए का सामान खरीदा
C. मुझने एक रुपया का सामान खरीदा
D. मैं एक रुपया का सामान खरीदी

2. A. उसे कॉफी बनाना नहीं आता
B. उसे कॉफी बनानी नहीं आता
C. उसे कॉफी बनाना नहीं आती
D. उसे कॉफी बनाने को नहीं आते

3. A. देश का सम्मान की रक्षा करो
B. देश के सम्मान की रक्षा करो
C. देश को सम्मान की रक्षा करो
D. देश के लिए सम्मान की रक्षा करो

4. A. अतिथि को चाकू से काटकर फल खिलाओ
B. चाकू से अतिथि को काटकर फल खिलाओ
C. चाकू से फल काटकर अतिथि को खिलाओ
D. फल को काटकर चाकू से अतिथि को खिलाओ

5. A. राम ने पेट भर मिठाई खाई
B. राम ने पेट भर के मिठाई खाई
C. राम ने भरपेट मिठाई खाई
D. इनमें से सभी शुद्ध हैं

6. A. मैं आपकी सौजन्यता पर मुग्ध हूँ
B. मैं आपके सौजन्य पर मुग्ध हूँ
C. मैं आपके सुजन्य पर मुग्ध हूँ
D. इनमें से तीनों वाक्य अशुद्ध हैं

7. A. लाओ एक पानी का गिलास
B. एक पानी का गिलास लाओ
C. गिलास एक पानी का लाओ
D. एक गिलास पानी लाओ

8. A. हमारी सौभाग्यवती कन्या का विवाह होने जा रहा है।
B. हमारी आयुष्मती कन्या का विवाह होने जा रहा है।
C. हमारी सौभाग्यवती कन्या का विवाह होने जा रही है
D. इनमें से सभी शुद्ध हैं

9. A. माँ बच्चे को दूध धाय से पिला रही है
B. माँ बच्चे को दूध धाय से पिलवा रही है
C. माँ बच्चे को दूध धाय से पी रही है
D. माँ बच्चे को दूध धाय से चखा रही है

10. A. ये हमारे पास रहते हैं और वे दूर
B. वे हमारे पास रहते हैं और ये दूर
C. वे हमारे पास रहते हैं और वह दूर
D. ये हमारे पास रहते हैं और वह दूर

11. A. वेदों के छः अंग माने जाते हैं
B. वेदों में छः अंग माने जाते हैं
C. वेदों से छः अंग माने जाते हैं
D. वेदों पर छः अंग माने जाते हैं

12. A. भक्तों की सेना जा रही थी
B. भक्तों की मंडली जा रही थी
C. भक्तों की टुकड़ी जा रही थी
D. भक्तों की भीड़ जा रही थी

13. A. आपकी शंका का परिहार हुआ कि नहीं
B. आपकी शंका का निदान हुआ कि नहीं
C. आपकी शंका का समाधान हुआ कि नहीं
D. आपकी शंका निर्मूल हुई कि नहीं

14. A. यह ग्रंथ विद्वतापूर्ण लिखा गया है
B. यह ग्रंथ विद्वतापूर्वक लिखा गया है
C. यह ग्रंथ विद्वानपूर्ण लिखा गया है
D. यह ग्रंथ विद्वानपूर्वक लिखा गया है

15. A. वह टका-सा उत्तर देता है
B. वह टका-सा प्रश्न करता है
C. वह टका-सा जवाब देता है
D. इनमें से कोई नहीं

16. A. जो मिठाई पसन्द हों आप खा लो
B. जो मिठाई पसन्द हों तुम खा लो
C. जो मिठाइयाँ पसन्द हों तुम खा लो
D. जो मिठाइयाँ पसन्द हों उन्हें आप खाइए

17. A. हम बचपन में वहाँ जायेंगे
B. हम बचपन में वहाँ जाते रहे हैं
C. मैं बचपन में वहाँ जाता रहा
D. मैं बचपन में वहाँ जाऊँगा

18. A. प्रत्येक व्यक्ति कविता कर सकते हैं
B. प्रत्येक व्यक्ति कविता नहीं कर सकते हैं
C. प्रत्येक व्यक्ति कविता नहीं कर सकता
D. हर व्यक्ति कविता कर सकते हैं

19. A. हेम नरेश की पुस्तक दी
B. हेम ने नरेश को पुस्तक दी
C. हेम नरेश का पुस्तक देगा
D. हेम ने नरेश का पुस्तक दिया

20. A. मन्त्री ड्राइवर से कार चलवाता है
B. मन्त्री ड्राइवर की कार चलवाता है
C. मन्त्री ड्राइवर के लिए कार चलवाता है
D. मन्त्री ड्राइवर पर कार चलवाता है

21. A. उसकी आयु तीस वर्ष है इस समय
B. इस समय उसकी अवस्था तीस वर्ष है
C. तीस वर्ष की अवस्था है इस समय उसकी
D. इस समय तीस वर्ष की अवस्था है उसकी

22. A. रागिनी अपने आप चली गई
B. रागिनी खुद से चली गई
C. रागिनी अपने से ही चली गई
D. रागिनी आपके आप चली गई

23. A. श्याम पौधे को जल से सींच रहा है
B. पौधे को जल से सींच रहा है श्याम
C. श्याम पौधे सींच रहा है
D. जल से सींच रहा है श्याम पौधे को

24. A. वह उदद्ंडनीय है
B. वह दण्ड भोगने के योग्य है
C. वह दण्डयोग्य है
D. वह दण्ड देने के योग्य है

25. A. हमारे यहाँ तरुण नवयुवकों की शिक्षा का अच्छा प्रबन्ध है
B. हमारे यहाँ तरुण नवयुवकों का शिक्षा का अच्छा प्रबन्ध है
C. हमारे नवयुवकों की शिक्षा का यहाँ अच्छा प्रबन्ध है
D. हमारे यहाँ नवयुवकों की शिक्षा का अच्छा प्रबन्ध है

26. A. मुरझाया हुआ फूल वर्षा की फुहार से अभिसिंचित होकर पुनः खिल उठा
B. मुरझाई हुई फूल वर्षा की फुहार से अभिसिंचित होकर पुनः खिल उठा
C. मुरझाया हुआ फूल वर्षा की फुहार से अभिसिंचित होकर पुनः खिल उठी
D. मुरझाया हुआ फूल वर्षा के फुहार द्वारा अभिसिंचित होकर पुनः खिल उठे

27. A. आपके दर्शन दुर्लभ हैं
B. वह विलाप करके रोने लगा
C. हम लोग कुशलपूर्वक से हैं
D. उसे मृत्युदण्ड की सजा मिली है

28. A. तीन महानगरों के नाम बताइए
B. इस समस्या की औषधि मेरे पास है
C. चरखा कातना चाहिए
D. यह एक इतिहासिक घटना है

29. A. मेरे को कल छुट्टी जाना होगा
B. आप ही तो मना किये थे
C. मुझको लौटने में विलम्ब हो गया
D. कपड़े डालकर तुमने मेरे साथ क्या करा?

30. A. राम का बहन गांधीजी पर कविता लिखी है
B. राम का बहन गांधीजी पर कविता लिखा है
C. राम की बहन ने गांधीजी पर कविता लिखी है
D. राम की बहन गांधीजी के ऊपर कविता लिखा है

31. A. कवि ने सम्पादक को एक कविता भेजा
B. अध्यापिका ने शिष्य से प्रश्न पूछी
C. बच्चे ने कहा था, पर आप ने नहीं सुनी
D. अमित ने जेब से दस रुपए का नोट निकाला

32. A. पेड़ की पत्ता गिरी
B. पेड़ में से पत्ता गिरा
C. पत्ता गिर पड़ा पेड़ों से
D. पेड़ से पत्ता गिरा

33. A. बैल और बकरी घास चरती हैं
B. बैल और बकरी घास चरते हैं
C. बैल और बकरी घास चरता है
D. बैल और बकरी घास चरती है

34. A. महात्मा गांधी का देश सदा आभारी रहेगा
B. देश महात्मा गांधी का सदा आभारी रहेगा
C. आभारी रहेगा देश सदा महात्मा गांधी का
D. देश आभारी रहेगा सदा महात्मा गांधी का

35. A. कश्मीर में अनेक दर्शनीय स्थल देखने योग्य हैं
B. अनेक दर्शनीय स्थल कश्मीर में देखने योग्य हैं
C. कश्मीर में अनेक दर्शनीय स्थल हैं
D. अनेक दर्शनीय स्थल देखने योग्य हैं कश्मीर में

निर्देश (प्र.सं. 36 से 80 तक): *नीचे दिया गया हर एक वाक्य चार भागों में बाँटा गया है जिन्हें (A), (B), (C) और (D) अक्षरांक दिए गए हैं। आपको यह देखना है कि वाक्य के किसी भाग में व्याकरण, भाषा, वर्तनी, शब्दों के गलत प्रयोग या इसी तरह की कोई त्रुटि तो नहीं है। त्रुटि अगर हो तो वाक्य के किसी एक भाग में ही होगी। उस भाग का अक्षरांक ही उत्तर है। अगर वाक्य त्रुटिरहित है तो उत्तर (E) दीजिए।*

36. कैक्टस के पौधे में कई चमत्कारी गुण (A)/ होते हैं लेकिन यह दुखदायी की बात (B)/ है कि हमारे देश में अभी तक इस पर (C)/ बहुत अधिक ध्यान नहीं दिया गया है। (D)/ त्रुटिरहित (E).

37. वाणिज्यिक वाहन निर्माताओं के (A)/ अनुसार, ईंधन की कीमतों में तेजी के (B)/ बावजूद बिक्री वाणिज्यिक वाहनों की (C)/ में तेजी दर्ज की गई है। (D)/ त्रुटिरहित (E).

38. जब तपती और धूल भरी (A)/ सड़कों पर मोटी-मोटी बूँदें गिरतीं तब (B)/ उमस के साथ मिट्टी की (C)/ भुनी भुनी गंध वातावरण में फैल जाती थी। (D)/ त्रुटिरहित (E).

39. औसत अगर मध्यवर्गीय (A)/ परिवार की बात करें तो उसमें (B)/ स्त्री मन को समझने की (C)/ गुंजाइश बहुत कम होती है। (D)/ त्रुटिरहित (E).

40. सुखद स्मृतियाँ चमकीले वर्तमान (A)/ से कहीं ज्यादा आनंददायक, (B)/ दुष्प्रेरणादायक और स्फूर्ति (C)/ प्रदान करने वाली होती हैं। (D)/ त्रुटिरहित (E).

41. किसी तंदरुस्त वृद्ध की देहयष्टि (A)/ देखकर लग पड़ता है (B)/ कि आयु ने उनके शरीर (C)/ पर अपना प्रभाव नहीं डाला है। (D)/ त्रुटिरहित (E).

42. कोशिश करने से मसले (A)/ समय रहते हल हो जाएं (B)/ तो ठीक वरना मन (C)/ में ग्रंथियाँ बन जाती हैं। (D)/ त्रुटिरहित (E).

43. यदि कोई विकलांग व्यक्ति (A)/ घर का मुखिया हो (B)/ तो वह गरीबी रेखा से (C)/ नीचे के दायरे में आएगा। (D)/ त्रुटिरहित (E).

44. एक मध्यवर्गीय भारतीय परिवार में पिता (A)/ काम के बोझ या दूसरे कारणों से अपने (B)/ बच्चों से कट जाता है, जिसका बच्चों (C)/ के मन पर प्रतिकूल प्रभावशाली पड़ता है। (D)/ त्रुटिरहित (E).

45. अर्थव्यवस्था विश्व के बदतर हो रहे (A)/ हालात से चिंतित वित्त मंत्री ने (B)/ कहा कि सरकार के पास नरमी (C)/ से निपटने के विकल्प सीमित हैं। (D)/ त्रुटिरहित (E).

46. बचत बैंक खातों (A)/ में बैंकों द्वारा (B)/ ब्याज की अदायगी (C)/ किया जाता है। (D)/ त्रुटिरहित (E).

47. वर्ष 2010 को आधार (A)/ बना कर राष्ट्रीय स्तर पर (B)/ नया उपभोक्ता तूल्य (C)/ सूचकांक जारी किया गया है। (D)/ त्रुटिरहित (E).

48. गुजरात की (A)/ राजरानी गांधीनगर (B)/ में एक बहुत बड़े समारोह का (C)/ आयोजन किया गया है। (D)/ त्रुटिरहित (E).

49. विमानन क्षेत्र का (A)/ नामी कम्पनी की (B)/ मुश्किलें दिनोंदिन (C)/ बढ़ती जा रही हैं। (D)/ त्रुटिरहित (E).

50. सरकार अपनी योजनाओं (A)/ का लाभ केवल कमजोर (B)/ वर्ग के लोगों तक सीमित (C)/ रखने के कक्ष में नहीं है। (D)/ त्रुटिरहित (E).

51. भारत सरकार द्वारा अर्जित (A)/ कुल राजस्व की (B)/ अधिकतम राशि आय कर (C)/ से प्राप्त होती है। (D)/ त्रुटिरहित (E).

52. दूरदर्शन के अधिकारियों (A)/ ने लोकप्रिय वाहिका (B)/ का प्रसारण बंद करने (C)/ का आदेश दिया है। (D)/ त्रुटिरहित (E).

53. राष्ट्रीय एकता तथा मानवीय (A)/ मूल्यों के मूलभूत सिद्धान्तों (B)/ को म्यान में रखकर (C)/ पाठ्य-सामग्री तैयार की गई है। (D)/ त्रुटिरहित (E).

54. दोनों देशों के वाणी (A)/ सचिवों की बैठक में (B)/ परस्पर व्यापार बढ़ाने (C)/ के लिए सहमति हो गयी। (D)/ त्रुटिरहित (E).

55. कोश के इस (A)/ नए संस्करण में बहुत (B)/ से नए शब्द (C)/ शामिल किए गए हैं। (D)/ त्रुटिरहित (E).

56. बैंक से जारी होने वाले (A)/ सभी परिपत्र, आदेश आदि (B)/ कागज के बजाय डिजिटल (C)/ माध्यमों से प्रेषित किया जाता है। (D)/ त्रुटिरहित (E).

57. नियंत्रण प्राधिकारियों से (A)/ भी अपेक्षा की गई है (B)/ कि वे प्रतिदिन प्रतिवेदन (C)/ का अध्ययन अवश्य करें। (D)/ त्रुटिरहित (E).

58. ग्लोबल वार्मिंग रूपी (A)/ शत्रु पर आक्रमण कर उसे (B)/ परस्त करने में सभी (C)/ का योगदान होना चाहिए। (D)/ त्रुटिरहित (E).

59. पेड़ नहीं सोंचते कि झोंका (A)/ आए तो झूमें या न (B)/ झूमें वे झूमते हैं और अपने (C)/ जड़ों पर यकीन रहते हैं। (D)/ त्रुटिरहित (E).

60. कितने वर्षों की अवधि (A)/ तक खाते में कोई भी लेन-देन न (B)/ होने पर खाते को (C)/ निष्कृत माना जाता है? (D)/ त्रुटिरहित (E).

61. सामाजिक कुरीतियों (A)/ का मुख्य कारण (B)/ अज्ञानता है (C)/ यह बात एकदम सही है। (D)/ त्रुटिरहित (E).

62. उसकी सौन्दर्यता (A)/ देखकर मन मयूर (B)/ नृत्य करने लगा (C)/ दिलीप ने श्याम को बताया। (D)/ त्रुटिरहित (E).

63. नगेन्द्र जी (A)/ हिन्दी के (B)/ लब्धप्रतिष्ठित (C)/ आलोचक एवं लेखक हैं। (D)/ त्रुटिरहित (E).

64. साहित्य (A)/ और जीवन का (B)/ घनघोर (C)/ सम्बन्ध है। (D)/ त्रुटिरहित (E).

65. दिल्ली से (A)/ अनेकों (B)/ पत्र-पत्रिकाओं का (C)/ प्रकाशन होता है। (D)/ त्रुटिरहित (E).

66. गाय को घास (A)/ खिलाने से और पंछी (B)/ को दाना डालने (C)/ से पूण्य मिलता है। (D)/ त्रुटिरहित (E).

67. एक संख्या का पाँच (A)/ बटा-नौ दूसरी संख्या (B)/ के पच्चीस प्रतिशत (C)/ के सम्मान है। (D)/ त्रुटिरहित (E).

68. दिनेश की मासिक (A)/ आय सुरेश की (B)/ मासिक आय से (C)/ चुगना है। (D)/ त्रुटिरहित (E).

69. इस कार की कीमत कम (A)/ होगी और कम्पनी इसमें ज्यादा से ज्यादा (B)/ भारतीय पूर्जे लगाने (C)/ की कोशिश कर रही है। (D)/ त्रुटिरहित (E).

70. कहते हैं कि (A)/ हर दस कोश (B)/ पर बोली (C)/ बदलती है। (D)/ त्रुटिरहित (E).

71. वैश्वीकरण के इस (A)/ युग में हिन्दी भाषा (B)/ नीत नवीन शब्दों से (C)/ समृद्ध हो रही है। (D)/ त्रुटिरहित (E).

72. आज भी कई किसान (A)/ और कमजोर वर्ग के (B)/ लोग साहूकारों के अंगुल (C)/ में फँसे हुए हैं। (D)/ त्रुटिरहित (E).

73. हमें शिक्षा ऋण (A)/ लेने वाले ऋणकर्ताओं (B)/ से इस आश्रय की (C)/ शिकायतें प्राप्त हो रही हैं। (D)/ त्रुटिरहित (E).

74. बचत बैंक खाते में (A)/ एक महीना में अन्य (B)/ बैंक के ATM से (C)/ निःशुल्क 5 आहरणों की छूट हैं। (D)/ त्रुटिरहित (E).

75. कृपया बोधित (A)/ अनुदेश सभी पदाधिकारियों (B)/ को सूचित करने (C)/ की व्यवस्था करें। (D)/ त्रुटिरहित (E).

76. एक मादा सूअर अपनी (A)/ छः बच्चों के साथ जो (B)/ अभी नौ-नौ इंच से बड़े नहीं हुए (C)/ थे, रेलगाड़ी की तरह चलती जा रही थी। (D)/ त्रुटिरहित (E).

77. एक इरावती ही थी जिससे वह टूटी-फूटी (A)/ हिन्दी में बातें कर लेती थी, हालाँकि उसकी (B)/ पंजाबी हिन्दी और इरावती की कोंकणी (C)/ हिन्दी में जमीन- आसमान का फर्क था। (D)/ त्रुटिरहित (E).

78. अपने बेटे की वजह से ही वह (A)/ यहाँ परदेस में पड़ा था, जहाँ (B)/ न कोई उसकी जबान समझता था, न वह (C)/ किसी को जबान समझता था। (D)/ त्रुटिरहित (E).

79. चेचक के दागों और झुर्रियों से भरा (A)/ उसका चेहरा दीमक खाई लकड़ी की (B)/ तरह जाना पड़ता था, जो बदसूरत तो था (C)/ ही जुगुप्सा भी जगा देता था। (D)/ त्रुटिरहित (E).

80. शालिनी नित नेम की भांति दीपक जलाई (A)/ और एक अज्ञात देवता के सामने (B)/ हाथ जोड़ने की प्रक्रिया पूरी करके (C)/ घुटनों पर बाँहें रखे वहीं बैठी रही। (D)/ त्रुटिरहित (E).

वाक्यांश के लिए एक शब्द

1. एक स्थान से दूसरे स्थान पर जाना या ले जाना–
A. खिसका हुआ B. उखड़ा हुआ
C. स्थानच्युत D. विस्थापित

2. इंद्रियों को जीतने वाला–
A. अजातशत्रु B. इन्द्रस्वामी
C. जितेंद्रिय D. मुमुक्षु

3. एक ही कोख से जन्म लेने वाला–
A. संतति B. जातक
C. आत्मज D. सहोदर

4. अपनी इच्छा से चलने वाला–
A. स्वेच्छाचारी B. स्वच्छंद
C. अराजक D. स्वेच्छक

5. जो हर हाल में हो ही जाए–
A. होनहार B. अवश्यंभावी
C. भाग D. तत्पर

6. जो कठिनाई से समझ में आए–
A. दुर्गम B. दुर्बोध
C. दुर्लभ D. दुर्धर्ष

7. एक पर ही श्रद्धा अथवा आस्था रखने वाला–
A. एकाकी B. अलौकिक
C. अधिकारिक D. एकनिष्ठ

8. बड़ा बनने की इच्छा रखने वाला–
A. पदलोलुप B. चाटुकार
C. विवेकवान D. महत्वाकांक्षी

9. मन का दुर्भाव–
A. दृष्टिवैषम्य B. भेदभाव
C. मनोमालिन्य D. कलुषित

10. पूर्णतः स्वच्छ करना–
A. परिष्कार B. सुधार
C. आविष्कार D. पुनरोद्धार

11. जिसका जन्म उच्च कुल में हुआ हो–
A. सेठ B. अभद्र
C. अमीर D. कुलीन

12. ईश्वर को नहीं मानने वाला–
A. आस्तिक B. अधर्मवान
C. बंदा D. नास्तिक

13. उपकार मानने वाला–
A. कृतघ्न B. परोपकारी
C. अनोपचारी D. कृतज्ञ

14. किसी के पास रखी हुई दूसरे की वस्तु–
A. गिरवी B. जमानत
C. धरोहर D. सामान

15. एक स्थान से दूसरे स्थान को हटाया हुआ–
A. आंतरित B. प्रवासी
C. मुसाफिर D. स्थानांतरित

16. जिसे कठिनाई से भेदा जा सके–
A. अभेद्य B. दुर्भेद्य
C. दुर्दम्य D. अगम्य

17. जो सबको समान भाव से देखे–
A. दूरदर्शी B. क्रांतदर्शी
C. सूक्ष्मदर्शी D. समदर्शी

18. परलोक से सम्बन्धित–
A. पारलौकिक B. अलौकिक
C. इहलौकिक D. लौकिक

19. पीछे-पीछे चलने वाला–
A. अनुगामी B. प्रतिगामी
C. पश्चगामी D. अग्रगामी

20. जिसके हृदय में ममता नहीं है–
A. निर्दय B. कठोर
C. क्रूर D. निर्मम

21 जो व्यर्थ की बातें करता हो–
A. बहुभाषी B. कुवक्ता
C. वाचाल D. वाक्पटु

22. जो देखने में प्रिय लगता हो–
A. समदर्शी B. प्रियदर्शी
C. प्रियपात्र D. दर्शनप्रिय

23. अहसान न मानने वाला–
A. कृतज्ञ B. कृतघ्न
C. विश्वासघाती D. परोपजीवी

24. जिसे कठिनाई से जीता जा सके–
A. विजित B. अज्ञेय
C. अजेय D. दुर्जेय

25. बचपन और जवानी के बीच की अवस्था–
A. नवयुवा B. नवोढ़ा
C. वयःसंधि D. वयस्कता

26. पशुओं के समान व्यवहार करने वाला–
A. पाशविक B. पशुसा
C. क्रूर D. दानव

27. वह अग्नि जो जंगल में लग जाती है–
A. वनाग्नि B. दावानल
C. अनल D. प्रचंडाग्नि

28. वह वस्तु जो नाशवान है–
A. नाशक B. नासन्य
C. नासांतिक D. नश्वर

29. परिश्रम के बदले प्राप्त धनराशि–
A. मुद्रा B. करेंसी
C. पारिश्रमिक D. सिक्का

30. अधिक पढ़ी-लिखी महिला–
A. विदूषक B. विज्ञानी
C. अफसर D. विदुषी

31. दोपहर का समय–
A. अपराह्न B. पूर्वाह्न
C. अधपहर D. मध्याह्न

32. जिसके समान कोई दूसरा न हो–
A. असामान्य B. अद्वितीय
C. असाधारण D. महान्

33. जो अधिक व्यय न करता हो–
A. धन्नासेठ B. खर्चीला
C. अव्यय D. मितव्ययी

34. जो पृथ्वी से सम्बन्धित हो–
A. पार्थिव B. पृथ्वी
C. अलौकिक D. जड़

35. जो काटा न जा सके–
A. दो टूक B. तर्कातीत
C. अकाट्य D. निश्चित

36. जिसके पास कुछ भी न हो–
A. अकिंचन B. किंचित्
C. आकुंचन D. अलभ्य

37. अनिश्चित जीविका–
A. आंशिक सेवा B. अस्थायी सेवा
C. अर्द्ध रोजगार D. आकाशवृत्ति

38. जिस पर हमला न किया गया हो–
A. आक्रान्ता B. आक्रामक
C. अयोध्या D. अनाक्रान्त

39. जो बहुत मंद गति से कार्य करता हो–
A. मंथर B. दीर्घसूत्री
C. सत्वर D. मंदाक्रान्ता

40. उचित-अनुचित का ज्ञान रखने वाला–
A. विवेकी B. ज्ञानी
C. चतुर D. दूरदर्शी

41. जो अपने कर्त्तव्य का निश्चय न कर सके–
A. द्वन्द्वग्रस्त B. भ्रमित
C. किंकर्त्तव्यविमूढ़ D. द्विविधाग्रस्त

42. अनेक युगों से चला आने वाला–
A. समीचीन B. प्राचीन
C. कालान्तर D. सनातन

43. ऐसा कवि जो तत्काल रचना करता हो–
A. कविराज B. आशुकवि
C. महाकवि D. कवीश

44. जिस स्त्री का पति जीवित होता है–
A. कामिनी B. सुभगा
C. सधवा D. मधवा

45. अनुचित व्यय करने वाला–
A. अतिव्ययी B. मितव्ययी
C. दुर्व्ययी D. अपव्ययी

46. मुकदमा चलाने वाला–
A. प्रतिवादी B. मुकदमेबाज
C. वादी D. इनमें से कोई नहीं

47. जिस पर अभियोग लगाया गया हो–
A. प्रतिवादी B. अभियोगी
C. अभियुक्त D. याची

48. मोक्ष प्राप्त करने की इच्छा रखने वाला–
A. मोक्षेसु B. ममुक्ष
C. मुमुक्ष D. मुमुक्षु

49. 'वह स्त्री जिसका पति परदेस से आने वाला हो' के लिए एक शब्द है–
A. आगतपतिका B. प्रव्रत्स्यतपतिका
C. प्रेषितपतिका D. आगमिस्यतपतिका

50. 'जिसमें धैर्य न हो' के लिए एक शब्द है–
A. अधर B. धरातल
C. अधीर D. धीरता

51. 'जो पहले कभी न हुआ हो' के लिए एक शब्द है–
A. अद्भुत B. अभूतपूर्व
C. अपूर्व D. अनुपम

52. 'जिसे किसी से लगाव न हो' के लिए उपयुक्त एक शब्द है–
A. नश्वर B. लिप्सु
C. निर्लिप्त D. अलगाववादी

53. 'जो कुछ जानने की इच्छा रखता हो' के लिए एक शब्द है–
A. जिज्ञासु B. जननी
C. जानकी D. नीतिज्ञ

54. 'जो बात लोगों से सुनी गई हो' के लिए एक शब्द है–
A. अश्रुति B. सर्वप्रिय
C. लोकोक्ति D. किंवदन्ती

55. 'सबके समानाधिकार पर विश्वास' के लिए एक शब्द है–
A. अधिकारी B. समाजवाद
C. प्रगतिवाद D. अधिकारवाद

56. 'जिस बीमारी का ठीक होना सम्भव न हो' के लिए एक शब्द है–
A. असाध्य B. विकट
C. भयानक D. घातक

57. जिस पर विजय प्राप्त कर ली गई हो–
A. आक्रान्त B. अजेय
C. विजित D. पराजित

58. सूर्य के उदय होने का स्थान–
A. उदयाचल B. सूर्योदय
C. प्रभात स्थान D. गंधमादन

59. जो कहा न जा सके–
A. अकथित B. अकथनीय
C. अकथ्य D. नामुमकिन

60. जिसे बहुत बातें करनी आती हों–
A. वाचाल B. गम्भीर
C. समालोचक D. मुनि

61. जो स्त्री के वशीभूत हो–
A. स्त्रीदास B. गुलाम
C. स्त्रैण D. प्रेमी

62. जो समान न हो–
A. बराबर B. जटिल
C. अविषम D. विषम

63. जिसे पढ़ना-लिखना आता हो–
A. अल्पज्ञानी B. शिक्षित
C. बुद्धिजीवी D. साक्षर

64. जो खाना मुफ्त में मिलता हो–
A. भण्डार B. लंगर
C. खुराक D. राशन

65. जो अपने कर्त्तव्य को न जानता हो–
A. अनजान B. अज्ञानी
C. किंकर्त्तव्यविमूढ़ D. कर्त्तव्यहीन

66. 'युद्ध में स्थिर रहने वाला' के लिए एक शब्द है–
A. योद्धा B. साहसी
C. युधिष्ठिर D. वीर

67. 'जो ईश्वर में विश्वास रखता है' के लिए एक शब्द है–
A. आस्थावान B. धार्मिक
C. आध्यात्मिक D. आस्तिक

68. आयु में बड़ा व्यक्ति–
A. कनिष्ठ B. पूजनीय
C. ज्येष्ठ D. वरिष्ठ

69. नया उदित होने वाला–
A. नवोदित B. नवजात
C. नवागन्तुक D. इनमें से कोई नहीं

70. बहुत-सी भाषाओं को जानने वाला–
A. तत्वचिन्तक B. बहुज्ञ
C. बहुभाषाविद् D. भाषा-वैज्ञानिक

71. जो किसी की ओर मुँह किए हो–
A. अभिमुख B. अनमुख
C. सुमुख D. इनमें से कोई नहीं

72. 'सात सौ वाली' के लिए निम्नलिखित में से कौन-सा शब्द उपयुक्त है?
A. सतखड़ा B. सतनजा
C. सतमासा D. सतसई

73. 'तेज चलने वाला' के लिए एक शब्द है–
A. गतिशील B. चुस्त
C. कर्मठ D. द्रुतगामी

74. 'बिना स्वार्थ के कार्य करने वाला' के लिए एक शब्द होगा–
A. सहायक B. निस्वार्थी
C. पुण्यात्मा D. हितैषी

75. 'किसी की सहायता करने वाला' के लिए एक शब्द है–
A. सहकार B. सहायक
C. सहृदय D. सहचर

मुहावरा एवं लोकोक्तियाँ

1. 'सब्जबाग दिखाना' मुहावरा का अर्थ है–
A. बाग में घूमने जाना B. साग-सब्जी पैदा करना
C. प्रलोभन देना D. भयभीत करना

2. 'खुदा गंजे को नाखून न दे' लोकोक्ति का अभिप्राय है–
A. छोटे आदमी का प्रेम अस्थिर होता है
B. लज्जित होकर दूसरे पर क्रोध न निकाले
C. एक दोष पहले से था, दूसरा और आ गया
D. अत्याचारी को शक्ति नहीं मिलनी चाहिए

3. 'कभी नाव गाड़ी पर कभी गाड़ी नाव पर' लोकोक्ति का सही आशय है–
A. संघर्ष होना B. जीवन में उतार-चढ़ाव का क्रम
C. भलाई करना D. एक-से स्वभाव वाले होना

4. 'एक हाथ से ताली नहीं बजती' लोकोक्ति का अभिप्राय है–
A. शत्रुता दोनों पक्षों की गलती से होती है
B. संघर्ष बराबरी वाले दो पक्षों में होना चाहिए
C. एक आदमी से काम नहीं चलता
D. सराहना हेतु दोनों हाथ से ताली बजाएँ

5. 'उड़ती चिड़ियों के पंख गिनना' मुहावरा का सही अर्थ होगा–
A. अनुभवी होना B. वाक्चतुर होना
C. प्रतिभाशाली होना D. असंभव कार्य करना

6. 'नक्कारखाने में तूती की आवाज' मुहावरा का अर्थ है–
A. तूती की आवाज सबसे ऊँची होती है
B. नक्कारखाने में तूती नहीं बोलती
C. नकारे लोगों की सर्वत्र तूती बोलती रहती है
D. समर्थ व्यक्ति के सामने असमर्थ व्यक्ति का प्रभाव नहीं पड़ता

7. 'आँख के अंधे नाम नयनसुख' का सही अर्थ है–
A. गुणों के विरुद्ध नाम का होना
B. बुद्धिहीन, किन्तु पर्याप्त धनवान
C. अंधा आदमी प्रायः गुणवान होता है
D. एक आँख के अंधे को भी सभी सुखद आ सकते हैं

8. 'चिकना घड़ा होना' मुहावरा का सही अर्थ है–
A. चिकना चुपड़ा होना B. समृद्ध होना
C. निर्लज्ज होना D. मधुरभाषी होना

9. 'बेटा समय रहते न पढ़े, तो भविष्य में बुरी तरह पछताओगे' – वाक्य में 'बुरी तरह पछताओगे' के स्थान पर यह मुहावरा आ सकता है–
A. अंगारों पर लोटोगे B. आठ-आठ आँसू रोओगे
C. अंचरा पसारोगे D. कुएँ में गिरोगे

10. "मुहावरे का प्रयोग वाक्य के अन्तर्गत होता है और लोकोक्ति पूर्ण वाक्य में होती है।" यह कथन–
A. सही है
B. गलत है
C. कथन का प्रथम अंश सही है
D. कथन का अंतिम अंश सही है

11. 'समय के अनुसार काम करना चाहिए' अर्थ की बोधक लोकोक्ति है–
A. झूठ के पैर नहीं होते
B. जाके पांव न फटी बिवाई, सो क्या जाने पीर पराई
C. उँगली पकड़ कर पहुँचा पकड़ना
D. का बरसा जब कृषि सुखाने

12. 'भारत के अतुलित धन वैभव पर अंग्रजों ने दाँत गड़ा दिए'–वाक्य में प्रयुक्त 'दाँत गड़ा दिए' का अर्थ है–
A. किसी वस्तु को गलत ढंग से पाने की गहरी चाह
B. दूसरे की वस्तु देखकर ललचा जाना
C. दूसरे की वस्तु चुराने की चेष्टा करना
D. धोखे से दूसरे की वस्तु लेना

13. 'चाँद पर थूकना' मुहावरे का आशय है–
A. असम्भव काम करना
B. निरर्थक काम करना
C. सौंदर्य का अनादर करना
D. सम्माननीय का अनादर करना

14. 'नियम विरुद्ध कार्य करना' अर्थ के अनुकूल सही मुहावरा है–
A. सूरज को दिया दिखाना
B. उल्टी गंगा बहाना
C. दाई से पेट छिपाना
D. नौ दो ग्यारह हो जाना

15. 'खाला जी का घर' मुहावरे का क्या अर्थ है?
A. आसान कार्य B. मौसी का घर
C. भाई-भतीजावाद D. रिश्तेदार को लाभ पहुँचाना

16. 'सिर चढ़ाना' मुहावरे का अर्थ है–
A. मनमानी करने की छूट देना
B. सिर पर बैठाना
C. सिरदर्द का बहाना करना
D. सिर पर उठा लेना

17. किस लोकोक्ति का अर्थ "वैभव क्षणिक होता है" होगा?
A. साँच को आँच नहीं
B. अधजल गगरी छलकत जाए
C. पाँचों उँगलियाँ बराबर नहीं होतीं
D. चार दिन की चाँदनी फिर अँधेरी रात

18. 'आँधी के आम होना' मुहावरे का अर्थ है–
A. मुफ्त उपलब्ध होना
B. संयोगवश बहुत सस्ता उपलब्ध होना
C. वैभवशाली बनना
D. अत्यन्त प्रिय होना

19. 'पाँच सात की लकड़ी, एक जने का बोझ' लोकोक्ति का अर्थ है–
A. बहुत कठिन कार्य होना
B. असम्भव बड़ी शर्त रखना
C. छोटे या कमजोर व्यक्ति की बात को कोई नहीं मानता
D. मिलकर काम करने से कठिन कार्य भी सरल हो जाता है

20. इनमें से कौन एक लोकोक्ति है?
A. अंगूठा दिखाना B. अंधा होना
C. ऊँट के मुँह में जीरा D. इधर-उधर की हाँकना

21. 'कलम तोड़ना' मुहावरे का क्या अर्थ है?
A. सही लिखना
B. अच्छा लिखना
C. ज्यादा लिखना
D. बेकार लिखकर प्रायश्चित करना

22. 'ढाँक के तीन पात' का अर्थ है–
A. अपने स्थान पर अडिग रहना
B. साफ इनकार कर देना
C. बेकार घूमना
D. कभी किसी विशेषता से सम्पन्न न होना

23. 'घड़ों पानी पड़ जाना' मुहावरे का अर्थ है–
A. चिन्ता में डूब जाना B. बर्बाद हो जाना
C. पसीने से भीग जाना D. लज्जा से दब जाना

24. किस लोकोक्ति का अर्थ 'बिना परिश्रम के सफलता नहीं मिलती' होगा?
A. नौ दिन चले अढ़ाई कोस
B. जिन खोजा तिन पाइयाँ गहरे पानी पैठ
C. बालू से तेल निकालना
D. डूबते को तिनके का सहारा

25. 'हाथ कंगन को आरसी क्या' कहावत का अर्थ है–
A. समझदार के लिए उपदेश व्यर्थ है
B. प्रत्यक्ष के लिए प्रमाण की क्या आवश्यकता है
C. मूल्यवान वस्तु के सामने तुच्छ वस्तु का कोई महत्व नहीं
D. हाथ में कंगन ही चाहिए आरसी नहीं

26. 'दाँतों तले अंगुली दबाना' का अर्थ होगा–
A. मुसीबत में पड़ना
B. बहुत हैरान होना
C. आश्चर्य करना
D. दीनता प्रकट करना

27. 'अनिश्चितता' के भाव को प्रकट करने के लिए उपयुक्त मुहावरे का चयन कीजिए–
A. बंद मुट्‌ठी में क्या है
B. पर्दे के पीछे कौन है
C. न जाने भाग्य में क्या है
D. न जाने ऊँट किस करवट बैठेगा

28. 'कुपात्र की सहायता करना व्यर्थ है' इस उक्ति को चरितार्थ करने वाली कहावत है–
A. अंधे को न्यौता, दो जने आये
B. कुत्ते को खिलाई खीर, पाप में न पुण्य में
C. गधे की खाई खेती, न पाप में न पुण्य में
D. बन्दर क्या जाने अदरक का स्वाद

29. मूर्ख व्यक्ति के सामने ज्ञान की बातें करने के लिए उपयुक्त मुहावरा क्या होगा?
A. रेत से तेल निकालना
B. अंधे के आगे रोना
C. भैंस के आगे बीन बजाना
D. आकाश से बातें करना

30. निम्नलिखित मुहावरे का अर्थ बताइए–
'सिर से पानी गुजर जाना'
A. अच्छी चीज का और अच्छा हो जाना
B. अपमान सहन कर लेना
C. सहनशीलता की सीमा टूट जाना
D. बाढ़ आ जाना

31. 'बहती गंगा में हाथ धोना' इस मुहावरे का क्या अर्थ है?
A. अधिकाधिक उन्नति होना
B. अवसर का फायदा उठाना
C. असम्भव काम को सम्भव करना
D. बहुत परिश्रम करना

32. निम्नलिखित वाक्यों में मुहावरे का सही प्रयोग क्या है?
A. धोनी अच्छे क्रिकेट का प्रदर्शन करके राँची वापस पहुँचा तो लोगों ने मैदान मार लिया
B. धोनी अच्छे क्रिकेट का प्रदर्शन करके राँची वापस पहुँचा, तो लोगों के हाथ के तोते उड़ गए
C. धोनी अच्छे क्रिकेट का प्रदर्शन करके राँची वापस पहुँचा, तो लोगों ने तिल का ताड़ बना लिया
D. धोनी अच्छे क्रिकेट का प्रदर्शन करके राँची वापस पहुँचा, तो लोगों ने उसे सिर आँखों पर बिठा लिया

33. निम्नलिखित के लिए उपयुक्त मुहावरा क्या है?
'मुसीबत देखकर घबरा जाना'
A. नाक पर धब्बा लगना
B. नौ दो ग्यारह होना
C. दाँतों तले अंगुली दबाना
D. नानी याद आना

34. 'काठ की हांडी बार-बार नहीं चढ़ती' लोकोक्ति का अर्थ है–
A. बुरे लोग लाख प्रयत्न के बाद भी अपनी बुराई नहीं छोड़ते
B. कठिन काम अकेले आदमी के वश की बात नहीं है
C. छल कपट का काम एक बार ही होता है
D. दुष्ट व्यक्ति बात से नहीं, बल्कि दण्ड से ही मानता है

35. 'रंगा सियार' मुहावरे का अर्थ क्या है?
A. डरपोक व्यक्ति
B. धोखेबाज व्यक्ति
C. झूठ बोलने वाला व्यक्ति
D. वीर व्यक्ति

36. 'बेपेंदी का लोटा' मुहावरे का अर्थ क्या है?
A. निर्धन व्यक्ति
B. स्थिर विचारों का न होने वाला व्यक्ति
C. मूर्ख व्यक्ति
D. दुष्ट व्यक्ति

37. 'घी के दिए जलाना' मुहावरा का सही अर्थ है–
A. दीपावली मनाना
B. खुशी मनाना
C. रईसी प्रकट करना
D. अपने को विशिष्ट समझना

38. 'सोने में सुगन्ध' मुहावरा का सही अर्थ है–
A. सुन्दर वस्तु में और गुण होना
B. सुगंध से युक्त आभूषण
C. सुन्दर आभूषण होना
D. सुगन्धित सोना

39. 'आँख का अंधा गाँठ का पूरा' लोकोक्ति का सही अर्थ है–
A. अंधा परन्तु विवेकशील होना
B. मूर्ख धनी
C. अंधे के पास धन होना
D. आँखों का रोग

40. 'गोद में लड़का, शहर भर में ढिंढोरा' मुहावरा का सही अर्थ है–
A. छोटे शिशु को तलाशना
B. अत्यधिक शरारती बालक
C. पास में वस्तु रहते हुए चारों ओर खोजना
D. छोटे बालक की प्रशंसा करना

41. 'पानी का बुलबुला' मुहावरे का क्या अर्थ है?
A. शीघ्र नष्ट हो जाने वाला
B. स्वच्छंद हो जाना
C. हार कर भागना
D. कष्ट उठाना

42. 'चाँदी का जूता मारना' मुहावरे का सही अर्थ है–
A. लुभाना
B. आदर करना
C. शोभा बढ़ाना
D. रुपए के बल पर दबाना

43. 'आगे नाथ न पीछे पगहा' लोकोक्ति का क्या अर्थ है?
A. पूर्ण स्वतन्त्र
B. अपने मन की करना
C. बन्धन रहित होना
D. इधर-उधर भागना

44. 'अन्धे पीसे कुत्ते खाएं' लोकोक्ति का सही अर्थ क्या है?
A. बेहिसाब काम करना
B. असावधानी से अयोग्य को लाभ
C. लाचारी का अनुचित लाभ
D. अपना माल लुटाना

45. 'अधजल गगरी छलकत जाए' का क्या अर्थ है?
A. गगरी में छेद होना
B. बेकायदे काम करना
C. व्यर्थ की बातें करना
D. कम ज्ञान का अधिक प्रदर्शन

46. 'जस दूल्हा तसि बनी बराता' लोकोक्ति का क्या अर्थ है?
A. अच्छा दूल्हा और अच्छे साथी
B. अच्छा दूल्हा और खराब बराती
C. सभी लोगों का अच्छा होना
D. जैसा व्यक्ति वैसे साथी

47. 'तीन लोक से मथुरा न्यारी' लोकोक्ति का अर्थ है–
A. बहुत सुन्दर होना
B. दूर की वस्तु सुन्दर लगना
C. जरूरत से ज्यादा बड़ाई करना
D. कृष्ण भक्त होना

48. 'थोथा चना बाजे घना' लोकोक्ति का क्या अर्थ है?
A. बहुत अधिक बोलना
B. ओछे व्यक्ति अधिक दिखावा करते हैं
C. बढ़ा-चढ़ाकर बात करना
D. बहुत शोर करना

49. 'खग जाने खग ही की भाषा' का क्या अर्थ है?
A. पक्षियों की भाषा जानना
B. समान प्रवृत्ति वाले ही एक-दूसरे को समझते हैं
C. पक्षी अपनी भाषा स्वयं समझते हैं
D. पक्षियों की तरह बोलना

50. 'अदृश्य शत्रु' अर्थ के अनुरूप उपयुक्त मुहावरा है–
A. मीठी छुरी
B. मुँह में राम बगल में छूरी
C. पेट में दाढ़ी
D. आस्तीन का साँप

51. 'पापड़ बेलना' मुहावरे का क्या अर्थ है?
A. पापड़ बनाना
B. मुसीबत उठाना
C. खाना बनाना
D. पतली रोटी बेलना

52. 'पानी-पानी होना' मुहावरे का क्या अर्थ है?
A. घबड़ा जाना
B. बहुत भीग जाना
C. बहुत लज्जित होना
D. बाढ़ आ जाना

53. 'गूलर का फूल होना' मुहावरे का क्या अर्थ है?
A. सुगंधित होना
B. फूल की तरह खिलना
C. दुर्लभ होना
D. अति प्रसन्न होना

54. 'कान का कच्चा होना' मुहावरे का क्या अर्थ है?
A. कम सुनना
B. सुनी बात पर विश्वास करना
C. दूसरे की बात न मानना
D. कान का कमजोर होना

55. 'उन्नीस-बीस होना' मुहावरे का क्या अर्थ है?
A. बहुत कम अन्तर होना
B. बहुत अन्तर होना
C. हिसाब जोड़ना
D. भाग जाना

56. 'खून का घूँट पीना' मुहावरे का क्या अर्थ है?
A. गुस्सा करना
B. खून की उल्टी करना
C. क्रोध दबाना
D. दाँत से होठ कट जाना

57. 'पौ बारह होना' मुहावरे का सही अर्थ है–
A. सब तरह की सुख-सुविधाओं का होना
B. उपद्रव करना
C. पलायन कर जाना
D. प्रयासरत होना

58. 'कागजी घोड़े दौड़ाना' मुहावरे का सही अर्थ है–
A. प्रयास करना
B. लिखा-पढ़ी करना
C. कागज काला करना
D. व्यर्थ का काम करना

59. 'कान भरना' मुहावरे का अर्थ है–
A. धोखा देना
B. चाणक होना
C. चुगली करना
D. असर न होना

60. 'सिर उठाना' मुहावरे का सही अर्थ है–
A. रंग उतर जाना
B. भेद प्रकट करना
C. बहुत पछताना
D. विद्रोह करना

61. 'आडम्बर' बहुत, किन्तु वास्तविकता कुछ नहीं' के लिए सही लोकोक्ति है–
A. आँख का अंधा नाम नयनसुख
B. ऊँची दुकान, फीका पकवान
C. ऊँट के मुँह में जीरा
D. खोदा पहाड़, निकली चुहिया

62. 'चैन की वंशी बजाना' का अर्थ है–
A. साइकिल की चैन की बांसुरी बनाकर बजाना
B. मौज करना
C. फुर्सत में वंशी बजाना
D. बेरोजगार होना

63. 'आँख की किरकिरी होना' का अर्थ है–
A. अप्रिय लगना
B. धोखा देना
C. कष्टदायक होना
D. बहुत प्रिय होना

64. 'कीचड़ उछालना' मुहावरा का सही अर्थ है–
A. मल फेंकना
B. दूसरे के कपड़े गन्दे करना
C. बदनाम करना
D. दलदल में फँसना

65. 'अवांछित संवाद' अर्थ के लिए उपयुक्त मुहावरा है–
A. सिर खपाना
B. सिर खाना
C. सिर नीचा होना
D. सिर पड़ना

गद्यांश (अपठित-बोध)

गद्यांश 1

यदि हम निरन्तर प्रयत्न करेंगे तो निश्चय ही अपने सभी लक्ष्यों को प्राप्त कर लेंगे, किन्तु प्रायः देखा जाता है कि अधिक आशावादी लोग थोड़ा सा प्रयत्न करके अधिक फल की कामना करने लगते हैं और मनोवांछित फल प्राप्त न होने पर निराश हो जाते हैं। अतः जीवन में सफलता प्राप्त करने के लिए परिस्थितियों के समक्ष घुटने न टेकें, बल्कि दृढ़ता से उनका मुकाबला करें। याद रखें, जितना कठोर हमारा परिश्रम होगा उसका फल भी उतना ही मीठा होगा।

उपर्युक्त गद्यांश को ध्यानपूर्वक पढ़ें और निम्न प्रश्नों के उत्तर के लिए सही विकल्प को चुनें:

1. फल न मिलने पर कौन निराश हो जाते हैं?
A. आशावादी लोग B. कम आशावादी लोग
C. अधिक आशावादी लोग D. निराशावादी लोग

2. लक्ष्य प्राप्ति के लिए क्या किया जाना चाहिए?
A. फल की कामना B. हिम्मत से मुकाबला
C. निरन्तर प्रयत्न D. परिस्थितियों से मुकाबला

3. आशावादी शब्द का विलोम शब्द है:
A. निराश B. निराशावादी
B. दुखी D. अप्रसन्न

4. मनोवांछित शब्द का क्या अर्थ है?
A. इच्छित B. परीक्षित
C. लाभदायक D. मन को खुश करने वाले

5. परिश्रम शब्द का अर्थ है:
A. साहस B. हिम्मत
C. काम D. कठिन मेहनत

गद्यांश 2

पन्द्रह अगस्त 1947 को हमारा देश स्वतंत्र हुआ। स्वतन्त्रता प्राप्ति के बाद विश्व के दूसरे देशों के साथ भारत के राजनयिक एवं सांस्कृतिक सम्बन्ध जुड़े। पर्यटकों के साथ-साथ राजनीतिज्ञों और साहित्यकारों को भी विदेश यात्रा के पर्याप्त अवसर मिले। विभिन्न प्रकार की छात्रवृत्तियों के माध्यम से बहुत से लोग विदेशों में पढ़ने गए। बहुत से लोगों ने विदेशों में उपलब्ध आजीविका के अवसरों का लाभ उठाया। इन सबके परिणामस्वरूप प्रचुर मात्रा में यात्रावृत्तांत लिखे गए। विदेश-विषयक यात्रावृतांतों में रूस और स्वदेश-विषयक यात्रावृतांतों में लेखकों की दृष्टि कश्मीर से कन्याकुमारी तक व्याप्त हुई।

उपर्युक्त गद्यांश को ध्यानपूर्वक पढ़ें और निम्नलिखित प्रश्नों के उत्तर के लिए सही विकल्प को चुनें:

1. भारत कब स्वतंत्र हुआ?
A. 15 अगस्त 1947 B. 15 अगस्त 1946
C. 15 अगस्त 1948 D. 15 अगस्त 1949

2. स्वतंत्र भारत के अन्य देशों के साथ किस प्रकार के संबंध जुड़े?
A. राजनीतिक B. राजनयिक
C. धार्मिक D. राजनयिक एवं सांस्कृतिक

3. आजीविका का क्या अर्थ है?
A. उपार्जन B. वेतन
C. मेहनत D. रोजगार

4. यात्रा-वृत्तांत का क्या अर्थ है?
A. भ्रमण B. पर्यटन
C. सफरनामा D. विदेशभ्रमण

5. स्वतंत्र का विलोम शब्द है:
A. परतंत्र B. आजाद
C. गुलामी D. मुक्ति

गद्यांश 3

युवा वर्ग का मस्तिष्क नई-नई बातों की ओर ज्यादा तेज दौड़ता है। उसमें अन्य वर्ग के व्यक्तियों से अधिक आवेश और शक्ति होती है। इस अवस्था में यदि सही शिक्षा और उचित मार्ग-दर्शन न मिले तो यही शक्ति प्रेरणा और निर्माण के स्थान पर विनाश की ओर ले जाती है। बिगड़ने और बनने की यही आयु होती है। दुर्भाग्य से हमारे देश में शिक्षा पद्धति केवल उपाधि बाँटने का काम ही करती है। एक सम्पूर्ण व्यक्तित्वपूर्ण मनुष्य बनाना आज की शिक्षा पद्धति के लिए मुश्किल है।

उपर्युक्त गद्यांश को ध्यानपूर्वक पढ़ें और निम्नलिखित प्रश्नों के उत्तर के लिए सही विकल्प को चुनें।

1. निर्माण का विलोम शब्द क्या हैं?
A. रचना B. बनावट
C. विनाश D. सृजन

2. मार्ग-दर्शन का क्या अर्थ है?
A. उपाधि B. रास्ता
C. उद्देश्य D. रास्ता दिखलाना

3. शक्ति विनाश की ओर कब अग्रसर होती है?
A. अधिक आवेश और शक्ति के अभाव में
B. सही शिक्षा और उचित मार्ग दर्शन के अभाव में
C. दुर्भाग्यपूर्ण शिक्षा पद्धति के कारण
D. इनमें से कोई नहीं

4. हमारे देश की शिक्षा पद्धति क्या कार्य करती है?
A. मार्ग-दर्शन B. शक्ति प्रेरणा
C. उपाधि देना D. उपर्युक्त सभी

5. दुर्भाग्य का विपरीत शब्द है:
A. भाग्य B. सौभाग्य
C. भाग्यशाली D. भाग्यवान

गद्यांश 4

भिखारी की भाँति गिड़गिड़ाना प्रेम की भाषा नहीं है। यहाँ तक कि मुक्ति के लिए भगवान् की उपासना करना भी अधम उपासना में गिना जाता है। प्रेम कोई पुरस्कार नहीं चाहता। प्रेम सर्वथा प्रेम के लिए ही होता है। भक्त इसलिए प्रेम करता है कि बिना प्रेम किए वह रह ही नहीं सकता। जब तुम किसी मनोहर प्राकृतिक दृश्य को देखकर उस पर मोहित हो जाते हो तो तुम किसी फल की याचना नहीं करते और न वह दृश्य ही तुमसे कुछ माँगता है। फिर भी उस दृश्य का दर्शन तुम्हारे मन को आनंद से भर देता है।

उपर्युक्त गद्यांश को ध्यानपूर्वक पढ़ें और निम्नलिखित प्रश्नों के उत्तर के लिए सही विकल्प का चयन करें:

1. प्रेम का उद्देश्य क्या होता है?
A. मुक्ति B. उपासना
C. भक्ति D. प्रेम

2. मुक्ति का अर्थ है:
A. आजादी B. स्वतंत्रता
C. परतंत्र D. निर्वाण

3. कैसी उपासना अधम मानी गई है?
A. प्रेम की उपासना
B. भगवान की उपासना
C. मुक्ति की उपासना
D. भक्ति की उपासना

4. मनोहर शब्द हैं:
A. विशेषण B. संज्ञा
C. सर्वनाम D. अव्यव

5. प्राकृतिक शब्द का अर्थ है:
A. ईश्वरीय B. मानव संबंधी
C. प्रकृति संबंधी D. प्रेम संबंधी

गद्यांश 5

कुछ लोग भाग्यवादी होते हैं और सब-कुछ भाग्य के सहारे छोड़कर कर्म से विरत हो जाते हैं। ऐसे लोग समाज के लिए बोझ हैं। वे कभी कोई बड़ा काम नहीं कर पाते। बड़ी-बड़ी खोज, बड़े-बड़े आविष्कार और बड़े-बड़े निर्माण कार्य कर्मशील लोगों के द्वारा ही संभव हो सके हैं। हम अपनी बुद्धि और प्रतिभा तथा कार्य-क्षमता के बल पर सही मार्ग पर चल सकते हैं, किन्तु बिना कठिन श्रम के अपने लक्ष्य तक नहीं पहुँच सकते। कठिन परिश्रम करने के बाद पाई गई सफलता हमारे मन को अलौकिक आनंद से भर देती है। यदि हम अपने कार्य में अपेक्षित श्रम नहीं करते तो हमारा मन ग्लानि का अनुभव करता है।

उपर्युक्त गद्यांश को ध्यानपूर्वक पढ़ें और निम्नलिखित प्रश्नों के उत्तर के लिए सही विकल्प चुनें:

1. "आविष्कार" शब्द का अर्थ है :
A. अनुसंधान B. खोज
C. निर्माण D. विनाश

2. **अलौकिक** शब्द का क्या अर्थ है?
A. संसारिक B. भौतिक
C. अमानुषी D. प्राकृतिक

3. सफलता का विलोम क्या है?
A. सफल B. असफल
C. सफलतापूर्वक D. असफलता

4. परिश्रम करने और न करने से हमारे जीवन पर क्या प्रभाव पड़ता है?
A. लोग भाग्यवादी बन जाते हैं
B. कर्म से विरत हो जाते हैं
C. मन में ग्लानि का अनुभव होता है
D. इनमें से कोई नहीं

5. किस प्रकार के लोग समाज के लिए बोझ हैं?
A. भाग्यवादी B. कर्मठ
C. परिश्रमी D. प्रतिभाशाली

गद्यांश 6

वैदिक काल से हिमालय के पहाड़ बहुत पवित्र माने जाते हैं। इसमें कोई सन्देह नहीं कि हिमालय के पहाड़ों का दृश्य अति सुन्दर है। उसकी विशालता को देखकर मन में आनन्द और कृतज्ञता की लहर उठती है। ऐसा लगता है कि यह विशाल सृष्टि प्रभु की अनुपम देन है। सारी सृष्टि के प्रति समभाव जाग्रत होता है। वस्तुतः यह दृष्टि कोरी कल्पनात्मक या आध्यात्मिक नहीं है। देखा जाए तो सारे भारत की ज़लवायु का समतोल करने वाले यह हिमालय के पहाड़ हैं, विशेषकर उत्तरी भारत को वर्षा और पानी देने वाले ये ही हैं। गंगोत्री, यमुनोत्री, बद्री, केदार को तीर्थ माना जाता है, जो व्यर्थ कल्पना नहीं है। उन स्थानों से निकलने वाली पवित्र नदियाँ ही वास्तव में हमारी प्राणदात्री रही हैं।

उपर्युक्त गद्यांश को ध्यानपूर्वक पढ़ें और निम्नलिखित प्रश्नों के उत्तर के लिए सही विकल्प चुनें :

1. हिमालय के पर्वत बहुत पवित्र कब से माने जाते हैं?
A. पाषाण काल से
B. वैदिक काल से
C. प्राचीन काल से
D. आधुनिक काल से

2. विशालता शब्द है :
A. जातिवाचक B. भाववाचक
C. विशेषण D. सर्वनाम

3. भारत की जलवायु को समतोल कौन करता है?

A. गंगोत्री B. यमुनोत्री

C. केदार D. हिमालय

4. सृष्टि का समानार्थक शब्द है :

A. सृजन B. रचना

C. प्रकृति D. संसार

5. प्राणदात्री का क्या अर्थ है?

A. गंगोत्री

B. यमुनोत्री

C. प्राणसंचार करने वाली

D. समभाव जाग्रत करने वाली

गद्यांश 7

सच्चा मित्र एक शिक्षक की भाँति होता है। जिस प्रकार शिक्षक अपने छात्र को सन्मार्ग की ही ओर अग्रसर करता है, उसी प्रकार एक सच्चा मित्र अपने मित्र को पाप के गर्त में गिरने से बचाता है। मानव-जीवन अधिक रहस्यपूर्ण है। कभी-कभी जीवन में ऐसे अवसर उपस्थित हो जाते हैं, जब मनुष्य की धर्मबुद्धि नष्ट हो जाती है और उसका मन द्रुत गति से पाप की ओर दौड़ता है। ऐसे समय में मित्र का ही उपदेश अधिक कल्याणकारी सिद्ध होता है। मित्र के उपदेश का जितना प्रभाव हृदय पर पड़ता है, उतना और किसी का नहीं पड़ता है।

उपर्युक्त गद्यांश को ध्यानपूर्वक पढ़ें और निम्नलिखित प्रश्नों के उत्तर के लिए सही विकल्प चुनें :

1. सच्चा मित्र किस प्रकार का होता है?

A. विपत्ति में सहायता देने वाला

B. गलत मार्ग पर चलने से रोकने वाला

C. शिक्षक के भाँति

D. धार्मिक गुरु की तरह

2. सन्मार्ग शब्द का विपरीत शब्द है :

A. अग्रसर B. कुमार्ग

C. सुमार्ग D. मार्गदर्शक

3. व्यक्ति को पाप के गर्त्त में गिरने से कौन बचाता है?

A. शिक्षक B. भाई

C. पिता D. सच्चा मित्र

4. मानव पाप की ओर कब दौड़ता है?

A. जब स्वार्थी बन जाता है

B. जब धर्म-बुद्धि नष्ट हो जाती है

C. जब सच्चामित्र साथ छोड़ देता है

D. जब धनवान बन जाता है

5. उपदेश में कौन-सा उपसर्ग है?

A. उ B. उप

C. दे D. देश

गद्यांश 8

सब तरह के भावों को प्रकट करने की योग्यता रखने वाली और निर्दोष होने पर भी यदि कोई भाषा अपना निज का साहित्य नहीं रखती, तो वह रूपवती भिखारिन की तरह कदापि आदरणीय नहीं हो सकती। उनकी शोभा, उसकी बड़ी सम्पन्नता, उसकी मान-मर्यादा उसके साहित्य पर ही अवलम्बित रहती है। उसके विचारों और राजनैतिक स्थितियों का प्रतिबिम्ब देखने को यदि कहीं मिल सकता है, तो उसके ग्रन्थ साहित्य में मिल सकता है। सामाजिक शक्ति या सजीवता, सामाजिक अशक्ति या निर्जीवता और सामाजिक सभ्यता तथा असभ्यता का निर्णायक एकमात्र साहित्य है।

उपर्युक्त गद्यांश को ध्यानपूर्वक पढ़ें और निम्नलिखित प्रश्नों के उत्तर के लिए सही विकल्प चुनें :

1. साहित्य विहीन भाषा किस प्रकार की होती है?

A. आदरणीय B. भिखारिन

C. रूपवती D. रूपवती भिखारिन

2. रूपवती का पुल्लिंग रूप है:

A. रूपवान B. सुन्दर

C. सुन्दरी D. रूपवत

3. भाषा की मान मर्यादा किस पर निर्भर करती है?

A. लिपि पर B. साहित्यकार पर

C. भक्ति पर D. साहित्य पर

4. "सम्पन्नता" शब्द का विपरीत शब्द है:

A. गरीबी B. विपन्न

C. अमीर D. विपन्नता

5. राजनैतिक, सामाजिक शक्ति का दर्शन हमें किसमें मिलता है?

A. समाज B. राज्य

C. नेता D. साहित्य

गद्यांश 9

स्वतंत्र भारत का सम्पूर्ण दायित्व आज विद्यार्थियों के ही ऊपर है, क्योंकि आज जो विद्यार्थी हैं, वे ही कल स्वतंत्र भारत के नागरिक होंगे। भारत की उन्नति, उसका उत्थान उन्हीं की उन्नति और उत्थान पर निर्भर करता है। अतः विद्यार्थियों को चाहिए कि वे अपने भावी जीवन का निर्माण बड़ी सतर्कता और सावधानी के साथ करें। उन्हें प्रत्येक क्षण अपने राष्ट्र, अपने समाज, अपने धर्म, अपनी संस्कृति को अपनी आँखों के सामने रखना चाहिए, जिससे उनके जीवन से राष्ट्र को कुछ बल प्राप्त हो सके। जो विद्यार्थी राष्ट्रीय दृष्टिकोण से अपने जीवन का निर्माण नहीं करते, वे राष्ट्र और समाज के लिए भार-स्वरूप हैं।

उपर्युक्त गद्यांश को ध्यानपूर्वक पढ़ें और निम्नलिखित प्रश्नों के उत्तर के लिए सही विकल्प चुनें :

1. भारत की उन्नति किस पर निर्भर करती है?

A. युवाओं पर

B. नेताओं पर

C. साहित्यकारों पर

D. विद्यार्थियों पर

2. उन्नति का समानार्थक शब्द है :

A. पतन B. उत्थान

C. विकास D. उदय

3. उत्थान का विपरीत शब्द है :

A. उदय B. पतन

C. पराजय D. हार

4. किसे अपने जीवन का निर्माण सतर्कता और सावधानी से करना चाहिए?

A. युवाओं को B. नेताओं को

C. बच्चों को D. विद्यार्थियों को

5. धर्म, संस्कृति तथा समाज का रक्षक कौन है?

A. नागरिक B. ग्रामीण

C. विद्यार्थी D. युवा

गद्यांश 10

हास्य एक ऐसा माध्यम है, जो नीरस-जीवन को भी सुखद बना देता है। हास्य का जादू इतना प्रभावशाली होता है कि वह छूत के रोग की तरह चारों ओर फैल जाता है। जिसने कभी हँसना नहीं सीखा, सचमुच उसने जीना नहीं सीखा। सामान्यतः मनुष्य को जीवन में इतनी मुसीबतें झेलनी पड़ती हैं कि वह अपने जीवन को पहाड़ समझने लगता है। ऐसे दूभर जीवन को यदि जीने योग्य बनाना हो तो उसके लिए आवश्यक है कि जीवन में हँसने की गुंजाइश हो। हँसी के सहारे मनुष्य अपने कष्टों को भुलाने का प्रयत्न करता है। संघर्ष, तनाव, व्यस्तता, घुटन यदि आज के जीवन की सहज देन हैं, तो इनसे बचने के लिए यह आवश्यक है कि हम हँसना सीखें।

उपर्युक्त गद्यांश को ध्यानपूर्वक पढ़ें और निम्नलिखित प्रश्नों के उत्तर के लिए सही विकल्प चुनें :

1. नीरस जीवन को कौन सुखद बना देता है?

A. संगीत B. गीत

C. आमोद प्रमोद D. हास्य

2. नीरस का संधि विच्छेद है :

A. नी + रस

B. नि + रस

C. निः + रस

D. नीः + रस

3. किसका जीवन व्यर्थ है?

A. जिसने रोना नहीं सीखा

B. जिसने हँसना नहीं सीखा

C. जिसने गाना नहीं सीखा

D. इनमें से कोई नहीं

4. हँसना शब्द है :

A. संज्ञा B. विशेषण

C. क्रिया विशेषण D. क्रिया

5. तनाव और घुटन से बचने के लिए क्या करना चाहिए?

A. रोना चाहिए B. गाना चाहिए

C. हँसना चाहिए D. काम करना चाहिए

गद्यांश 11

किसी पुस्तक को पढ़ने में जल्दी नहीं करनी चाहिए, जो कुछ लेखक कहता है, उसे समझने की चेष्टा करनी चाहिए। प्रत्येक शब्द का अर्थ समझने की चेष्टा करनी चाहिए। यदि लेखक योग्य है, तो दूसरी बार वह पुस्तक और अधिक आनन्द देगी और तीसरी बार और अधिक। प्रत्येक बार अध्ययन करने पर आपको नवीन सुन्दर और नए विचार मिलेंगे और उसे आप जितना ही पढ़ेंगे, उतना ही स्नेह करने लगेंगे। सहस्रों व्यक्तियों ने गीता और रामायण तथा कुरान और बाइबिल को बार-बार पढ़ा है। उनका अनुभव है कि प्रत्येक बार उन्हें नई सूझ और नए विचार मिलते गए। कुछ लोग तो इस बात पर गर्व करते हैं कि उन्होंने अमुक पुस्तक को अनेक बार पढ़ा है, उन्हें कंठस्थ हो गई है।

उपर्युक्त गद्यांश को ध्यानपूर्वक पढ़ें और निम्नलिखित प्रश्नों के उत्तर के लिए सही विकल्प चुनें :

1. किसे समझने की चेष्टा करनी चाहिए?

A. पुस्तक B. रामायण

C. महाभारत D. गीता

2. पुस्तक की सजीवता किस पर निर्भर करती है?

A. लेखक B. प्रकाशक

C. पाठक D. चिन्तक

3. आनन्द का विपरीत शब्द है :

A. शोक B. दुख

C. संताप D. खुशी

4. नवीन, सुन्दर और नए विचार हमें कहाँ से प्राप्त होता हैं?

A. पुस्तक को बार-बार पढ़कर

B. सुनकर

C. भाषण से

D. अच्छे व्यक्तियों से मिलने पर

5. कंठस्थ शब्द का शब्दार्थ है :

A. कंठ में स्थित B. सुंदर कंठ

C. जबानी याद D. पंडित जी

गद्यांश 12

अहिंसा परम धर्म है और हिंसा आपद् धर्म। मनुष्य बराबर अहिंसा की ओर चलना चाहता है, किन्तु परिस्थितियाँ उससे हिंसा कराती है, अर्थात् परमधर्म की रक्षा के लिए आदमी बराबर आपद्धर्म से काम लेता रहा है। भारत अपनी सेनाओं को विघटित कर दे, तब भी उसका अपमान उससे अधिक होने वाला नहीं, जितना नेफा में हुआ। किन्तु परमधर्म पर टिकने की सामर्थ्य अगर भारत में नहीं है, तो आपद्धर्म पर उसे आना चाहिए। व्यवहारतः आपद्धर्म परमधर्म का विरोधी नहीं, उसका रक्षक है।

उपर्युक्त गद्यांश को ध्यानपूर्वक पढ़ें और निम्नलिखित प्रश्नों के उत्तर के लिए सही विकल्प चुनें :

1. **परमधर्म** का विपरीत शब्द है :
A. महान धर्म B. आपद्धर्म
C. सच्चाधर्म D. इनमें से कोई नहीं

2. आपद्धर्म किसे कहा जाता है?
A. अहिंसा B. सत्याग्रह
C. विपत्ति D. हिंसा

3. मानव से हिंसा कौन करवाती है?
A. लोभ B. स्वार्थ
C. द्वेष D. परिस्थितियाँ

4. **सामर्थ्य** का शब्दार्थ है :
A. संघर्ष B. परिश्रम
C. शक्ति D. पराक्रम

5. **परमधर्म** की रक्षा कौन करता है?
A. अहिंसा B. हिंसा
C. आपदधर्म D. युद्ध

गद्यांश 13

वर्तमान काल विज्ञापन का युग माना जाता है। समाचार-पत्रों के अतिरिक्त रेडियो और टेलीविजन भी विज्ञापन के सफल साधन हैं। विज्ञापन का मूल उद्देश्य उत्पादक और भोक्ता में सीधा सम्पर्क स्थापित करना होता है। जितना अधिक विज्ञापन किसी पदार्थ का होगा, उतनी ही उसकी लोकप्रियता बढ़ेगी। इन विज्ञापनों पर धन तो अधिक व्यय होता है, पर इनसे बिक्री बढ़ जाती है। ग्राहक जब इन आकर्षक विज्ञापनों को देखता है तो वह उस वस्तु-विशेष के प्रति आकृष्ट होकर उसे खरीदने को बाध्य हो जाता है।

उपर्युक्त गद्यांश को ध्यानपूर्वक पढ़ें और निम्नलिखित प्रश्नों के उत्तर के लिए सही विकल्प चुनें :

1. वर्तमान को किसका युग माना जाता है?
A. फैशन B. विज्ञापन
C. संगीत D. धन

2. उत्पादक तथा भोक्ता के बीच कौन संबंध स्थापित करता है?
A. टेलीविजन B. समाचार-पत्र
C. रेडियो D. विज्ञापन

3. **वर्तमान** शब्द का विपरीत शब्द है :
A. अर्वाचीन B. आधुनिक
C. आजकल D. प्राचीन

4. **आकर्षक** का शब्दार्थ है :
A. विकर्षक B. सुन्दर
C. मनमोहक D. आश्चर्यजनक

5. भोक्ता किस कारण वस्तुओं को खरीदने के लिए बाध्य हो जाता है?
A. विज्ञापन
B. आकर्षक विज्ञापन
C. लोकप्रियता के कारण
D. आसानी से उपलब्ध होना

गद्यांश 14

लगभग दो सौ वर्ष की गुलामी ने भारत के राष्ट्रीय स्वाभिमान को पैरों से रौंद डाला, हमारी संस्कृति को समाप्त कर दिया, हमारे विश्वासों को हिला दिया और हमारे आत्मविश्वास को चकनाचूर कर दिया, किन्तु अपने इस बूढ़े देश से प्यार करने वाले, इसके एक सामान्य संकेत पर प्राण न्यौछावर करने वाले दीवानों का अभाव न था। एक आवाज उठी और देखते ही देखते राष्ट्र का दबा हुआ आत्माभिमान उन्मत्त हो उठा। इतिहास साक्षी है जाने और अनजाने सहस्त्रों देशभक्त स्वतंत्रता की अनमोल निधि को पाने के लिए शहीद हो गए।

उपर्युक्त गद्यांश को ध्यानपूर्वक पढ़ें और निम्नलिखित प्रश्नों के उत्तर के लिए सही विकल्प चुनें :

1. **स्वाभिमान** का संधि विच्छेद है:
A. स्वा + भिमान B. स्वः + अभिमान
C. स्व + अभिमान D. स्वा + अभिमान

2. भारत का राष्ट्रीय स्वाभिमान किस कारण समाप्त हो गया था?
A. लम्बे गुलामी से
B. निरंकुश शासक से
C. स्वार्थी मानव से
D. धर्म के विनाश से

3. **आत्मविश्वास** का शब्दार्थ है
A. घमण्ड B. गर्व
C. अपने पर विश्वास D. अभिमान

4. भारत की अनमोल निधि को पाने के लिए कौन शहीद हो गए?
A. देशभक्त B. नेता
C. युवा D. युवती

5. **अनमोल निधि** का शब्दार्थ है:
A. अंनन्त खजाना B. अमूल्य खजाना
C. बहुमूल्य D. स्वतंत्रता

गद्यांश 15

दुनिया के विभिन्न देशों के विकास पर विहंगम दृष्टि डालने से यह स्पष्ट हो जाता है कि आज जिस देश ने वैज्ञानिक उपलब्धियों के सहारे अपना औद्योगीकरण कर लिया, उसी को उन्नत देश कहा जाता है। जिस देश में औद्योगीकरण का स्तर नीचा है, वह पिछड़ा हुआ देश कहा जाता है। वैज्ञानिक आविष्कारों और औद्योगीकरण के आधार पर ही किसी देश की प्रगति को आँका जाता रहा है। विज्ञान ने मानव को पूरी तरह बदल दिया है।

उपर्युक्त गद्यांश को ध्यानपूर्वक पढ़ें और निम्नलिखित प्रश्नों के उत्तर के लिए सही विकल्प चुनें :

1. **विहंगम दृष्टि** का क्या अर्थ है?

A. एक झलक　　B. गहन दृष्टि
C. गहन चिन्तन　　D. इनमें से कोई नहीं

2. **विकास** का विपरीत शब्द है :

A. उत्थान　　B. उदय
C. पतन　　D. विनाश

3. **वैज्ञानिक** शब्द में कौन-सा प्रत्यय हैं?

A. निक　　B. वै
C. ईक　　D. इक

4. मानव जीवन को किसने बदल दिया है :

A. विकास　　B. वैज्ञानिक
C. विज्ञान　　D. उद्योग

5. किसी भी देश की स्तर को किससे नापा जाता है?

A. उपलब्धियों पर　　B. औद्योगीकरण से
C. वैज्ञानिकों से　　D. आविष्कारों से

गद्यांश 16

विश्व का वर्तमान उन्नत रूप मानव-श्रम की ही कहानी कह रहा है। गगन चुंबी अट्टालिकाएँ, लंबी-चौड़ी सड़कें, बड़े-बड़े विशाल नगर आकाश में उड़ते वायुयान तथा मानव-जीवन को सुखी और समृद्ध बनाने में योगदान करने वाले ज्ञान-विज्ञान के अनन्त रूप-ये सभी मनुष्य के श्रम का जयघोष करते हैं। स्पष्ट है कि मनुष्य और उसका शरीर विधाता की अनुपम रचना है जो निश्चय ही महान उद्देश्यों की संपूर्ति के लिए दिया गया है। इस दुर्लभ तन को यदि हम आलस्य, प्रसाद अथवा घटिया कामों में गँवा देते हैं तो उस विधाता के प्रति अन्याय करते हैं।

उपर्युक्त गद्यांश को ध्यानपूर्वक पढ़ें और निम्नलिखित प्रश्नों के उत्तर के लिए सही विकल्प चुनें :

1. विश्व का वर्तमान रूप किसका उद्योतक है?

A. चिन्तक का　　B. नेता का
C. वैज्ञानिक का　　D. मानव श्रम

2. **गगन चुंबी अट्टालिकाएँ** का अर्थ है :

A. आकाश में उड़ने वाला　　B. आकाश को छूने वाला
C. बहुमंजिली इमारत　　D. इनमें से कोई नहीं

3. आकाश का समानार्थक शब्द है :

A. वसुन्धरा　　B. धरा
C. पयोद　　D. गगन

4. **सुखी** का विपरीत शब्द है :

A. प्रसन्न　　B. अप्रसन्न
C. दुखी　　D. उदासी

5. विधाता की अनुपम रचना क्या है?

A. मानव शरीर　　B. समुद्र
C. वन　　D. पृथ्वी

गद्यांश 17

हमारे देश में एक ऐसा भी युग था जब नैतिक और आध्यात्मिक विकास ही जीवन का वास्तविक लक्ष्य माना जाता था। अहिंसा की भावना सर्वोपरि थी। आज पूरा जीवन दर्शन ही बदल गया है। सर्वत्र पैसे की हाय-हाय तथा धन का उपार्जन ही मुख्य ध्येय हो गया है, भले ही धन- उपार्जन के तरीके गलत ही क्यों न हों? इन सबका असर मनुष्य के प्रतिदिन के जीवन पर पड़ रहा है। समाज का वातावरण दूषित हो गया है—

बाह्य वातावरण तो दूषित है ही, आज सब जानते हैं पर्यावरण की समस्याएँ कितनी चिन्तनीय हो उठी है। इन सबके कारण मानसिक और शारीरिक तनाव-खिंचाव और व्याधियाँ पैदा हो रही हैं।

उपर्युक्त गद्यांश को ध्यानपूर्वक पढ़ें और निम्नलिखित प्रश्नों के उत्तर के लिए सही विकल्प चुनें :

1. भारत का प्राचीन आदर्श था :

A. सत्य और अहिंसा
B. नैतिक और आध्यात्मिक विकास
C. धन उपार्जन
D. इनमें से कोई नहीं

2. **अहिंसा** का विपरीत शब्द है :

A. हिंसा　　B. सत्याग्रह
C. विनम्रता　　D. नैतिकता

3. जीवन दर्शन क्यों बदल गया है?

A. हिंसा के कारण
B. अहिंसा के कारण
C. धन लिप्सा के कारण
D. आध्यात्मिक विकास के कारण

4. समाज का वातावरण दूषित क्यों हो गया है?

A. शारीरिक तनाव
B. मानसिक व्याधियाँ
C. पर्यावरण की समस्याएँ
D. धन उपार्जन के गलत तरीके

5. **पर्यावरण** का शब्दार्थ है:

A. जलमंडल　　B. स्थलमंडल
C. वायुमंडल　　D. वातावरण

उत्तरमाला

संधि

1	**2**	**3**	**4**	**5**	**6**	**7**	**8**	**9**	**10**
A	A	B	C	D	A	D	B	C	B
11	**12**	**13**	**14**	**15**	**16**	**17**	**18**	**19**	**20**
A	C	A	C	A	A	C	C	A	D
21	**22**	**23**	**24**	**25**	**26**	**27**	**28**	**29**	**30**
A	C	C	A	A	B	D	D	A	B
31	**32**	**33**	**34**	**35**	**36**	**37**	**38**	**39**	**40**
D	C	C	A	A	B	C	C	C	D
41	**42**	**43**	**44**	**45**	**46**	**47**	**48**	**49**	**50**
A	A	B	B	A	B	D	B	A	C
51	**52**	**53**	**54**	**55**	**56**	**57**	**58**	**59**	**60**
C	A	A	A	B	C	A	C	C	C
61	**62**	**63**	**64**	**65**	**66**	**67**	**68**	**69**	**70**
C	A	A	A	A	C	B	A	B	B
71	**72**	**73**	**74**	**75**					
B	A	A	B	D					

समास

1	**2**	**3**	**4**	**5**	**6**	**7**	**8**	**9**	**10**
C	B	C	A	C	B	A	A	B	A
11	**12**	**13**	**14**	**15**	**16**	**17**	**18**	**19**	**20**
D	A	B	D	B	C	C	D	A	B
21	**22**	**23**	**24**	**25**	**26**	**27**	**28**	**29**	**30**
A	A	C	A	A	C	A	A	A	A
31	**32**	**33**	**34**	**35**	**36**	**37**	**38**	**39**	**40**
B	A	C	C	A	D	B	B	C	A
41	**42**	**43**	**44**	**45**	**46**	**47**	**48**	**49**	**50**
A	A	A	C	A	A	A	D	B	D
51	**52**	**53**	**54**	**55**	**56**	**57**	**58**	**59**	**60**
C	A	A	C	C	A	C	C	B	B
61	**62**	**63**	**64**	**65**	**66**	**67**	**68**	**69**	**70**
B	C	A	C	B	D	A	B	C	A

वर्तनी

1	**2**	**3**	**4**	**5**	**6**	**7**	**8**	**9**	**10**
B	A	D	B	A	A	B	A	D	C
11	**12**	**13**	**14**	**15**	**16**	**17**	**18**	**19**	**20**
D	D	B	B	D	C	C	A	B	B
21	**22**	**23**	**24**	**25**	**26**	**27**	**28**	**29**	**30**
C	A	D	B	D	B	B	B	C	D
31	**32**	**33**	**34**	**35**	**36**	**37**	**38**	**39**	**40**
C	A	C	A	D	C	B	C	A	C
41	**42**	**43**	**44**	**45**	**46**	**47**	**48**	**49**	**50**
C	D	C	C	A	D	C	A	D	B

51	52	53	54	55	56	57	58	59	60
A	C	D	C	C	B	B	A	D	C
61	62	63	64	65	66	67	68	69	70
B	B	B	B	A	C	A	A	D	B
71	72	73	74	75	76	77	78	79	80
B	B	A	C	B	B	A	B	D	A
81	82	83	84	85	86	87	88	89	90
B	C	A	A	D	D	E	B	A	C
91	92	93	94	95	96	97	98	99	100
A	B	D	C	C	A	A	C	A	B
101	102	103	104	105	106	107	108	109	110
E	D	C	B	A	B	A	C	D	E
111	112	113	114	115					
D	E	C	A	C					

पर्यायवाची

1	2	3	4	5	6	7	8	9	10
D	C	D	D	A	D	C	B	D	D
11	12	13	14	15	16	17	18	19	20
A	D	A	A	C	A	D	C	A	B
21	22	23	24	25	26	27	28	29	30
A	C	B	B	A	A	A	D	B	D
31	32	33	34	35	36	37	38	39	40
B	D	C	C	C	A	D	A	D	D
41	42	43	44	45	46	47	48	49	50
C	C	D	C	A	A	C	D	C	A
51	52	53	54	55	56	57	58	59	60
D	C	A	D	A	D	A	D	C	D
61	62	63	64	65	66				
D	D	B	C	B	A				

विलोमार्थी शब्द

1	2	3	4	5	6	7	8	9	10
C	B	A	B	D	A	D	A	A	A
11	12	13	14	15	16	17	18	19	20
C	D	B	A	C	D	C	A	B	C
21	22	23	24	25	26	27	28	29	30
D	B	B	B	D	C	C	C	A	C
31	32	33	34	35	36	37	38	39	40
D	A	C	B	A	D	B	A	B	A
41	42	43	44	45	46	47	48	49	50
C	A	A	C	B	D	B	A	D	C
51	52	53	54	55	56	57	58	59	60
B	C	A	B	D	A	C	C	C	A
61	62	63	64	65	66	67	68	69	70
D	D	A	A	C	B	D	C	B	B
71	72	73	74	75					
A	B	A	D	A					

वाक्यों की शुद्धता

1	2	3	4	5	6	7	8	9	10
A	A	B	C	C	B	D	A	B	A
11	12	13	14	15	16	17	18	19	20
A	B	C	B	C	D	C	C	B	A
21	22	23	24	25	26	27	28	29	30
B	A	C	C	D	A	A	A	C	C
31	32	33	34	35	36	37	38	39	40
D	D	B	B	C	B	C	D	A	C
41	42	43	44	45	46	47	48	49	50
A	E	A	D	A	D	C	B	A	D
51	52	53	54	55	56	57	58	59	60
C	B	C	A	B	D	A	C	C	D
61	62	63	64	65	66	67	68	69	70
C	A	C	C	B	D	D	D	C	B
71	72	73	74	75	76	77	78	79	80
C	C	C	B	A	A	B	D	C	A

वाक्यांश के लिए एक शब्द

1	2	3	4	5	6	7	8	9	10
D	C	D	A	B	B	D	D	C	A
11	12	13	14	15	16	17	18	19	20
D	D	D	C	D	B	D	A	A	D
21	22	23	24	25	26	27	28	29	30
C	B	B	D	C	A	B	D	C	D
31	32	33	34	35	36	37	38	39	40
D	B	D	A	C	A	D	D	A	A
41	42	43	44	45	46	47	48	49	50
C	D	B	C	D	C	C	D	D	C
51	52	53	54	55	56	57	58	59	60
B	C	A	D	B	A	C	A	B	A
61	62	63	64	65	66	67	68	69	70
C	D	D	B	C	C	D	C	A	C
71	72	73	74	75					
A	D	D	B	B					

मुहावरा एवं लोकोक्तियाँ

1	2	3	4	5	6	7	8	9	10
C	D	B	A	A	D	A	C	B	A
11	12	13	14	15	16	17	18	19	20
D	A	D	B	A	A	D	B	D	C
21	22	23	24	25	26	27	28	29	30
B	D	D	B	B	C	D	B	C	C

31	32	33	34	35	36	37	38	39	40
B	D	D	C	B	B	B	A	B	C
41	**42**	**43**	**44**	**45**	**46**	**47**	**48**	**49**	**50**
A	D	C	C	D	D	C	B	B	D
51	**52**	**53**	**54**	**55**	**56**	**57**	**58**	**59**	**60**
B	C	C	B	A	C	A	D	C	D
61	**62**	**63**	**64**	**65**					
B	B	A	C	B					

गद्यांश (अपठित-बोध)

गद्यांश 1

1. C **2.** D **3.** B **4.** A **5.** D

गद्यांश 2

1. A **2.** D **3.** D **4.** C **5.** A

गद्यांश 3

1. C **2.** D **3.** B **4.** C **5.** B

गद्यांश 4

1. D **2.** D **3.** C **4.** A **5.** C

गद्यांश 5

1. B **2.** D **3.** D **4.** C **5.** A

गद्यांश 6

1. B **2.** B **3.** D **4.** A **5.** C

गद्यांश 7

1. C **2.** B **3.** D **4.** B **5.** B

गद्यांश 8

1. D **2.** A **3.** D **4.** D **5.** D

गद्यांश 9

1. D **2.** B **3.** B **4.** D **5.** C

गद्यांश 10

1. D **2.** C **3.** B **4.** D **5.** C

गद्यांश 11

1. A **2.** A **3.** A **4.** A **5.** C

गद्यांश 12

1. B **2.** D **3.** D **4.** C **5.** C

गद्यांश 13

1. B **2.** D **3.** D **4.** C **5.** B

गद्यांश 14

1. C **2.** A **3.** C **4.** A **5.** B

गद्यांश 15

1. A **2.** D **3.** C **4.** C **5.** B

गद्यांश 16

1. D **2.** C **3.** D **4.** C **5.** A

गद्यांश 17

1. B **2.** A **3.** C **4.** D **5.** D

❑ ❑ ❑

साहित्य

आदिकाल

- हेमचन्द्र अपभ्रंश व्याकरण के रचयिता थे।
- आदिकाल को 'आदिकाल' का नाम हजारी प्रसाद द्विवेदी ने दिया था।
- खड़ी बोली/कौरवी बोली का सम्बन्ध पश्चिमी हिन्दी से है।
- बघेली बोली का सम्बन्ध पूर्वी हिन्दी से है।
- खड़ी बोली का उद्भव अपभ्रंश के शौरसेनी के उत्तरी रूप से हुआ है।
- श्रावकाचार को हिन्दी की प्रथम रचना माना जाता है।
- धीरेंद्र वर्मा ने आदिकाल को 'अपभ्रंश काल' कहा है।
- 'गाथा सप्तशती' की रचना प्राकृत भाषा में हुई है।
- ब्रजभाषा का उद्भव शौरसेनी के मध्यवर्ती रूप से हुआ है।
- चंदबरदायी कृत 'पृथ्वीराज रासो' में शृंगार और वीर रस का समावेश है।
- आदिकाल में धर्म से सम्बन्धित पुस्तकों का सृजन मुख्यतः अपभ्रंश भाषा में मिलता है।
- आदिकाल में खड़ी बोली को काव्य का आधार सर्वप्रथम 'अमीर खुसरो' ने बनाया था।
- अमर खुसरो की रचनाओं को देशी भाषा काव्य के अन्तर्गत माना जाता है।
- आदिकालीन हिन्दी साहित्य को मुख्यतः अपभ्रंश-हिन्दी के वर्ग में रखा जाता है।
- 'मैथिल कोकिल' के नाम से प्रसिद्ध विद्यापति का समय सम्वत् 1460 माना जाता है।
- आदिकाल में 'अवधूत संप्रदाय' का सम्बन्ध नाथों से है।
- आदिकाल में जैनों द्वारा रचित साहित्य को सर्वाधिक प्रमाणिक माना जाता है।
- रामायण में संस्कृत भाषा का प्रयोग किया गया है।
- अमीर खुसरो ने फारसी तथा खड़ी बोली दोनों में रचना की है।
- मैथिल कोकिल 'विद्यापति' संस्कृत, अपभ्रंश तथा मैथिली तीनों में रचना की है।
- वर्णरत्नाकर मैथिली की पहली गद्य रचना है। इसके लेखक ज्योतिरीश्वर ठाकुर हैं।
- 'ढ़ोला मारू रा दूहा' के रचयिता कल्लोल कवि हैं।
- 'कीर्तिलता' की भाषा मिश्रित अपभ्रंश है।
- 'पृथ्वीराज विजय' की रचना जयानक ने की थी।

आदिकाल के प्रमुख रचनाकार तथा उनकी रचनायें

क्र.सं	रचनाकार	रचनायें
1.	सहरपा	दोहाकोष
2.	ज्योतिरिश्वर ठाकुर	वर्णरत्नाकर
3.	शबरपा	चर्यापद
4.	श्रीधर	रणमल्ल छंद
5.	जगनिक	परमाल रासो
6.	हाल कवि	गाथा सप्तशती
7.	नल्ल सिंह	विजयपाल रासो
8.	विद्यापति	पदावली, कीर्तिपताका, कीर्तिलता, भूपरिक्रमा
9.	अमीर खुसरो	खालिकबारी, पहेलियां, दो सुखने, गजल
10.	राजशेखर	कर्पूर मंजरी
11.	चन्दबरदायी	पृथ्वीराज रासो
12.	नरपति नाल्ह	बीसलदेव रासो
13.	कल्लोल	ढोला मारू रा दूहा

भक्तिकाल

- 'हरडेवानी' दादू की रचनाओं का संग्रह है।
- 'चित्रावली' की रचना उस्मान ने की थी।
- भक्तिकालीन 'प्रेमाश्रयी शाखा' पर सूफी मत का प्रभाव सर्वाधिक है।
- 'मधुमालती' के रचयिता मंझन हैं।
- तुलसीदास जी के गुरु का नाम 'नरहरि दास' था।
- गोस्वामी तुलसीदास ने 'रामचरित मानस' की रचना दोहा-चौपाई पद्धति पर की है।
- तुलसीदास की रचना 'विनय पत्रिका' गीत पद्धति पर आधारित है।
- 'बीजक' ग्रंथ का प्रणयन सधुक्कड़ी भाषा में किया गया है।
- 'विनय-पत्रिका' की भाषा ब्रजभाषा है।
- चंदायन की रचना मुल्ला दाऊद ने की थी।
- चंदायन की रचना से हिन्दी में सूफी काव्य परम्परा का सूत्रपात होता है।
- पद्मावत की भाषा अवधी है।

- रामचरित मानस की भाषा अवधी है।
- ब्रज भक्तिकालीन हिन्दी काव्य की सर्वाधिक प्रमुख भाषा है।
- तुलसीदास की 'गीतावली' ब्रजभाषा में लिखी गयी है।
- मीराबाई पर सूफियों का प्रभाव था।
- 'गीत-गोविंद' के रचयिता जयदेव हैं।

भक्तिकाव्य के प्रमुख रचनाकार तथा उनकी रचनायें

क्र.सं	रचनाकार	रचनायें
1.	कबीर	बीजक
2.	नाभादास	भक्तमाल
3.	दादू	हरडेवानी
4.	मूल्ला दाउद	चंदायन
5.	मंझन	मधुमालती
6.	उसमान	चित्रावली
7.	जायसी	पद्मावत, चित्रलेखा, अखरावट, कहरनामा
8.	नरपति व्यास	नल दमयन्ती
9.	तुलसीदास	दोहावली, जानकी मंगल, रामचरितमानस
10.	जयदेव	गीत-गोविन्द
11.	सूरदास	सूरसागर, साहित्य लहरी
12.	रसखान	प्रेमवाटिका, सुजान खान

रीतिकाल

- आचार्य रामचंद्र शुक्ल के अनुसार रीतिकाल की समय सीमा 1643 ई. से 1843 ई. के बीच है।
- मतिराम की रचना 'छंदसार' पिंगल ग्रंथ का उदाहरण है।
- रीतिकाल के प्रसिद्ध कवि भूषण की रचना 'शिवराज भूषण' अलंकार ग्रंथ का प्रमुख उदाहरण है।
- केशवदास को अलंकारवादी आचार्य कहा जाता है।
- **'करणा भरण श्रुतिभरण'** नामक काव्य का सम्बन्ध अलंकार विद्या से है।
- रीतिकाल के अधिकांश कवियों की भाषा थी–ब्रजभाषा।
- रीतिकाल के कवि घनानंद को 'साक्षात् रस मूर्ति' माना जाता है।
- 'विज्ञान गीता' उपदेशात्मक है।
- रीतिकाल के कवि पद्माकर ने भक्ति, शृंगार और वीर तीनों में समान अधिकार से रचना की है।
- सिखों के दसवें गुरु 'गुरु गोविंद सिंह' को रीतिकाल के रीतिमुक्त काव्य धारा का माना गया है।

रीतिकाल के प्रमुख रचनाकार तथा उनकी रचनायें

क्र.सं	रचनाकार	रचनायें
1.	चिंतामणि	पिंगल, कविकुल-कल्पतरु, रसमंजरी, काव्य-प्रकाश
2.	केशवदास	कवि प्रिया, रसिक प्रिया
3.	कृपाराम	हिततरंगिणि, रस तरंगिणि
4.	करनेस	कर्णाभरण, श्रुतिभूषण, भूपभूषण
5.	रहीम	रहीम सतसई, मदनाष्टक, शृंगार सोरठा, नगरशोभा
6.	मतिराम	छन्दसार, रसराज, साहित्यसार, अलंकार पंचाशिका
7.	भूषण	शिवराज भूषण, शिवा बावनी, छत्रसाल दशक, भूषण उल्लास
8.	बिहारी	बिहारी सतसई
9.	कुलपति मिश्र	रस रहस्य
10.	सुखदेव मिश्र	वृत्त विचार, छन्द विचार, रसार्णव, शृंगार लता
11.	पद्माकर	जगत विनोद, पद्माभरण, गंगा लहरी, प्रबोध पचासा
12.	घनानंद	इश्कलता, विरहलीला, सुजानसागर, कृपाकांड
13.	जोधराण	हम्मीर रासो
14.	गुरु गोविंद सिंह	चण्डी चरित्र, सुनीति प्रकाश, बुद्धिसागर
15.	रसखान	प्रेमवाटिका, सुजान रसखान

रीतिकाल का नामकरण करने वाले विभिन्न विद्वान

क्र.सं	विद्वान	नामकरण
1.	आचार्य शुक्ल	रीतिकाल
2.	मिश्रबंधु	अलंकृत मध्यकाल
3.	ग्रियर्सन	रीतिकाव्य
4.	विश्वनाथ प्रसाद मिश्र	शृंगार काल

आधुनिक काल

- आधुनिक काल में सम्मिलित हैं–भारतेन्दु युग, द्विवेदी युग, छायावादी युग, प्रगतिवादी युग तथा प्रयोगवादी युग।
- भारतेन्दु युग के प्रमुख रचनाकार हैं–भारतेन्दु हरिश्चन्द्र, बालकृष्ण भट्ट, प्रताप नारायण मिश्र, बद्रीनारायण चौधरी
- द्विवेदी युग के प्रमुख रचनाकार हैं–आचार्य महावीर प्रसाद द्विवेदी, श्रीधर पाठक, रामनरेश त्रिपाठी, अयोध्या सिंह उपाध्याय 'हरिऔध', मैथिलीशरण गुप्त, श्यामसुन्दर दास।
- छायावादी युग के प्रमुख रचनाकार हैं–जयशंकर प्रसाद, सूर्यकान्त त्रिपाठी 'निराला', सुमित्रानन्दन पंत तथा महादेवी वर्मा।

हिन्दी साहित्य के गद्य एवं पद्य से सम्बन्धित कुछ महत्त्वपूर्ण रचनाकार

सूरदास

महाप्रभु वल्लभाचार्य के शिष्य सूरदास अष्टछाप के कवियों में सर्वाधिक प्रसिद्ध हैं। उनके तीन ग्रंथो सूरसागर, साहित्य लहरी और सूर सारावली में सूरसागर सर्वाधिक लोकप्रिय ग्रंथ है। सूर 'वात्सल्य' और 'शृंगार' के श्रेष्ठ कवि माने जाते हैं। उनकी कविता में ब्रजभाषा का निखरा हुआ रूप है।

तुलसीदास

तुलसीदास का जन्म उत्तर प्रदेश के बाँदा जिले के राजापुर गाँव में सन् 1532 में हुआ था। रामचरितमानस, कवितावली, गीतावली, दोहावली, कृष्णगीतावली तथा विनयपत्रिका उनकी प्रमुख रचनाएं हैं। तुलसीदास ने रामचरितमानस की रचना अवधी में और विनय पत्रिका तथा कवितावली की रचना ब्रजभाषा में की। विनय पत्रिका की रचना गेय पदों में हुई है।

देव

देव का जन्म इटावा में सन् 1673 में हुआ था। रसविलास, भावविलास, काव्यरसायन, भवानीविलास आदि देव के प्रमुख ग्रंथ माने जाते हैं। देव रीतिकाल के प्रमुख कवि हैं। रीतिकालीन कविता का सम्बन्ध दरबारों, आश्रयदाताओं से था। इस कारण उसमें दरबारी संस्कृति का चित्रण अधिक हुआ है। आलंकारिकता और शृंगारिकता उनके काव्य की प्रमुख विशेषताएं हैं।

जयशंकर प्रसाद

जयशंकर प्रसाद का जन्म सन् 1889 में वाराणसी में हुआ। छायावादी काव्य प्रवृत्ति के प्रमुख कवियों में एक जयशंकर प्रसाद का सन् 1937 में निधन हो गया। उनकी प्रमुख काव्य-कृतियाँ हैं—चित्राधार, कानन-कुसुम, झरना, आँसू, लहर और कामायनी। अजातशत्रु, चन्द्रगुप्त, स्कंदगुप्त और ध्रुवस्वामिनी उनके नाटक हैं तथा कंकाल, तितली और इरावती उनके उपन्यास हैं।

सूर्यकांत त्रिपाठी 'निराला'

सूर्यकांत त्रिपाठी 'निराला' का जन्म बंगाल के महिषादल में सन् 1899 में हुआ। उनकी प्रमुख काव्य रचनाएं हैं—अनामिका, परिमल, गीतिका, कुकुरमुत्ता और नए पत्ते। छायावादी रचनाकारों में उन्होंने सबसे पहले मुक्त छंद का प्रयोग किया।

नागार्जुन

नागार्जुन का जन्म बिहार के दरभंगा जिले के सतलखा गाँव में सन् 1911 में हुआ। उनका मूल नाम बैद्यनाथ मिश्र था। नागार्जुन की प्रमुख काव्य-कृतियां हैं—युगधारा, सतरंगे पंखों वाली, हजार-हजार बाँहों वाली, तुमने कहा था, पुरानी जुतियों का कोरस, मैं मिलटरी का बूढ़ा घोड़ा। उनको आधुनिक कबीर भी कहा जाता है। छायावादोत्तर दौर के वे ऐसे अकेले कवि हैं, जिनकी कविता गाँव की चौपालों और साहित्यिक दुनिया में समान रूप से लोकप्रिय रही। उन्होंने छंदों में काव्य-रचना की और मुक्त छंद में भी।

रामवृक्ष बेनीपुरी

रामवृक्ष बेनीपुरी का जन्म बिहार के मुजफ्फरपुर जिले के बेनीपुर गाँव मे सन् 1899 में हुआ। उन्होंने अनेक दैनिक, साप्ताहिक एवं मासिक पत्र-पत्रिकाओं का संपादन किया। उनकी रचना-यात्रा के महत्त्वपूर्ण पड़ाव हैं—पतितो के देश में (उपन्यास); चिंता के फूल (कहानी), आम्रपाली (नाटक); माटी की मूरतें (रेखाचित्र); पैरों में पंख बांध कर (यात्रा-वृत्तांत); जंजीरें और दीवारें (संस्मरण) आदि। विशिष्ट शैलीकार होने के कारण उन्हें 'कलम का जादूगर' कहा जाता है।

महावीर प्रसाद द्विवेदी

महावीर प्रसाद द्विवेदी का जन्म सन् 1864 में ग्राम दौलतपुर, जिला राय बरेली (उत्तर प्रदेश) में हुआ। वे हिन्दी के पहले व्यवस्थित संपादक, भाषावैज्ञानिक, इतिहासकार, पुरातत्ववेत्ता अर्थशास्त्री, समाजशास्त्री एवं लेखक थे। उनकी प्रमुख कृतियां हैं—रसज्ञ रंजन, साहित्य-सीकर, साहित्य-संदर्भ, अद्‌भुत आलाप (निबंध संग्रह)। संपत्तिशास्त्र उनकी अर्थशास्त्र से सम्बन्धित पुस्तक है। उन्होंने कविता की भाषा के रूप में ब्रजभाषा के बदले खड़ी बोली को प्रतिष्ठित किया। हिन्दी में पहली बार समालोचना को स्थापित करने का श्रेय भी उनको जाता है।

कबीर

कबीर का जन्म काशी में हुआ था। कबीर गुरु रामानंद के शिष्य थे। उन्होंने जनचेतना और जनभावनाओं को अपने सबद और साखियों के माध्यम से जन-जन तक पहुँचाया। कबीर की भाषा को सधुक्कड़ी कहा जाता है।

मीरा

मीराबाई का जन्म जोधपुर के चोकड़ी गाँव में 1503 में हुआ माना जाता है। 13 वर्ष की आयु में मेवाड़ के महाराणा सांगा के कुंवर भोजराज से उनका विवाह हुआ। विवाह के कुछ ही वर्ष पश्चात् पहले पति, फिर पिता और एक युद्ध के दौरान स्वसुर का भी देहांत हो गया। मध्यकालीन भक्ति आंदोलन की आध्यात्मिक प्रेरणा ने जिन कवियों को जन्म दिया उनमें मीराबाई का विशिष्ट स्थान है। मीरा हिन्दी और गुजराती दोनों की कवयित्री मानी जाती हैं। मीरा संत रैदास की शिष्या थीं। मीरा की भक्ति दैन्य और माधुर्यभाव की है।

बिहारी

बिहारी का जन्म 1595 में ग्वालियर में हुआ था। बिहारी ने आचार्य केशवदास से काव्य शिक्षा पायी थी। बिहारी सतसई बिहारी की

रचना है। रीति का उन्हें भरपूर ज्ञान था। इनकी कविता श्रृंगार रस की है। बिहारी की भाषा बहुत कुछ शुद्ध ब्रज है पर है वह साहित्यिक। ओरक्षा में बिहारी रहीम के संपर्क में आए।

मैथिलीशरण गुप्त

1886 में झाँसी के चिरगाँव में जन्मे मैथिलीशरण गुप्त अपने जीवनकाल में ही राष्ट्रकवि के रूप में विख्यात हुए। गुप्त जी रामभक्त कवि थे। गुप्त जी की कविता की भाषा विशुद्ध खड़ी बोली है। गुप्त जी की प्रमुख कृतियां हैं–साकेत, यशोधरा, जयद्रथ वध।

सुमित्रानंदन पंत

सुमित्रानंदन पंत का जन्म 1900 ई. में वर्तमान उत्तराखंड के कौसानी-अलमोड़ा में हुआ था। वे छायावाद के प्रमुख स्तंभ माने जाते हैं। इनकी प्रमुख कृतियां हैं–वीणा, पल्लव, युगवाणी, ग्राम्या, स्वर्ण किरण, कला और बूढ़ा चांद और लोकायतन।

महादेवी वर्मा

महादेवी वर्मा का जन्म 1907 ई. में उत्तर प्रदेश के फर्रुखाबाद में हुआ था। महादेवी ने छायावाद के चार प्रमुख रचनाकारों में औरों से भिन्न अपना एक विशिष्ट स्थान बनाया। महादेवी का समस्त काव्य वेदनामय है। महादेवी की प्रमुख काव्य कृतियां हैं–नीहार, रश्मि, नीरजा, सांध्य गीत, दीपशिखा, प्रथम आयाम और अग्निरेखा तथा गद्य रचनाएं हैं–अतीत के चलचित्र, श्रृंखला की कड़ियाँ, स्मृति की रेखाएं, पथ के साथी, मेरा परिवार और चिंतन के क्षण।

प्रेमचंद

31 जुलाई 1880 को बनारस के करीब लमही गाँव में जन्मे धनपत राय ने उर्दू में गुलाब राय और हिन्दी में प्रेमचंद नाम से लेखन कार्य किया। उनके प्रमुख उपन्यास हैं–गोदान, गबन, प्रेमाश्रम, सेवासदन, निर्मला, कर्मभूमि, रंगभूमि, कायाकल्प, प्रतिज्ञा और मंगल सूत्र।

प्रसिद्ध रचनाएँ एवं रचनाकार

रचनाएँ	रचनाकार
राग गोविन्द	मीरा बाई
दीपशिखा	महादेवी
आखिरी कलाम	जायसी
इन्द्र धनुष रौंदे हुए	अज्ञेय
साहित्य लहरी	सूरदास
द्वापर	मैथिली शरण गुप्त
रामचरित मानस	तुलसीदास
कर्ण	केदारनाथ मिश्र 'प्रभात'
बिहारी सतसई	बिहारी लाल
प्रेम पत्रिका	घनानन्द
पद्मावत	जायसी
रंगभूमि	प्रेमचन्द
विनय पत्रिका	तुलसीदास
सन् बयालिस के संस्मरण	श्रीराम शर्मा
यामा	महादेवी वर्मा
श्रृंखला की कड़ियाँ	महादेवी
उर्वशी	दिनकर
बाबरा अहेरी	अज्ञेय
बलचनमा	नागार्जुन
साधना के पथ पर	हरिभाऊ उपाध्याय
भारत भारती	मैथिलीशरण गुप्त
पैरों में पंख बाँधकर	बेनीपुरी
पृथ्वी राज रासो	चन्दवरदाई
लाल चीन	भगवत शरण उपाध्याय
प्रेम वाटिका	रसखान
नवरस	बाबू गुलाबराय
प्रेम माधुरी	भारतेन्दु हरिश्चन्द्र

रचनाएँ	रचनाकार
माटी हो गई सोना	कन्हैया लाल मिश्र प्रभाकर
साकेत	मैथिलीशरण गुप्त
गीता-प्रवचन	विनोबा भावे
चन्द्रकान्ता	देवकीनन्दन खत्री
अंधा युग	धर्मवीर भारती
कुकुरमुत्ता	निराला
शेष स्मृतियाँ	डॉ. रघुवीर सिंह
अतीत के चलचित्र	महादेवी
तितली	प्रसाद
जानकी मंगल	तुलसीदास
रास पंचाध्यायी	नन्ददास
लोकायतन	पंत
हिततरंगिणी	कृपाराम
बरवै नायिका भेद	रहीम
रसिकप्रिया	केशव दास
श्रृंगार शिला	वृन्द
कर्णाभरण	करनेस बन्दीजन
प्रिय प्रवास	हरिऔध
रामचन्द्रिका	केशवदास
कला और बूढ़ा चाँद	पंत
चिंतामणि	आचार्य शुक्ल
श्रृंगार सतसई	रहीम
ललित ललाम	मतिराम
वैदेही वनवास	हरिऔध
छत्रसाल दशक	भूषण
कंकाल	प्रसाद

रचनाएँ	रचनाकार
भाव विलास	देव
अणिमा	निराला
काव्य निर्णय	भिखारीदास
रमैनी	कबीरदास
गंगा लहरी	पद्माकर
भरतेश्वर बाहुवली रास	शालिभद्र सूरि
रसकेलिवल्ली	घनानन्द
पउम चरिउ	स्वयं भू
मदनाष्टक	रहीम
प्राकृत व्याकरण	जैनाचार्य हेमचन्द्र
जगद्विनोद	पद्माकर
वीसलदेव रास	नरपति नाल्ह
प्रेम फुलवारी	भारतेन्दु हरिश्चन्द्र
संदेश रासक	अद्द हयाण
रस कलश	हरिऔध
सुकवि कीर्तन	महावीर प्रसाद द्विवेदी
उद्धव शतक	रत्नाकर
कश्मीर सुषमा	श्रीधर पाठक
कबीर का रहस्यवाद	डॉ. राम कुमार वर्मा
पथिक	रामनरेश त्रिपाठी
मधुशाला	बच्चन
कामायनी	प्रसाद
टेढ़े-मेढ़े रास्ते	भगवती चरण वर्मा
तुलसीदास	निराला
प्रभात फेरी	नरेन्द्र शर्मा
सांध्यगीत	महादेवी
हिम किरीटिनी	माखन लाल चतुर्वेदी
युगाधार	सोहन लाल द्विवेदी
हम विषपायी जनम के	बालकृष्ण शर्मा नवीन
मौर्य विजय	सियाराम शरण गुप्त
हुँकार	दिनकर
इत्यलम्	अज्ञेय
भस्मांकुर	नागार्जुन
मैला आँचल	फणीश्वर नाथ रेणु
सिन्दूर की होली	लक्ष्मी नारायण मिश्र
छठा बेटा	उपेन्द्रनाथ अश्क
नूतन ब्रह्मचारी	बाल कृष्ण भट्ट
मादा कैक्टस	लक्ष्मी नारायण लाल
कुसुम कुमारी	किशोरी लाल गोस्वामी
ठेठ हिन्दी का ठाठ	हरिऔध
आदर्श हिन्दू	लज्जाराम मेहता
चित्रलेखा	भगवती चरण वर्मा
दादा कामरेड	यशपाल
जहाज का पंछी	इलाचन्द्र जोशी
गिरती दीवारें	उपेन्द्रनाथ अश्क

रचनाएँ	रचनाकार
मानस का हंस	अमृत लाल नागर
ब्रह्मपुत्र	देवेन्द्र सत्यार्थी
वैशाली की नगर वधू	आचार्य चतुरसेन शास्त्री
नदी यशस्वी है	नरेश मेहता
गढ़कुण्डार	वृन्दावन लाल वर्मा
राग दरबारी	श्रीलाल शुक्ल
शेखर : एक जीवनी	अज्ञेय
एक पति के नोट्स	महेन्द्र भल्ला
झूठा सच	यशपाल
दिल्ली का दलाल	पाण्डेय बेचन शर्मा 'उग्र'
नदी के द्वीप	अज्ञेय
सेवासदन	प्रेमचन्द
चुटकी भर चाँदनी	केशनी प्रसाद चौरसिया
उत्तराधिकारी	यशपाल
जहाँ लक्ष्मी कैद है	राजेन्द्र यादव
माँस का दरिया	कमलेश्वर
शिव शम्भु का चिट्ठा	बाल मुकुन्द गुप्त
अशोक के फूल	आचार्य हजारी प्रसाद द्विवेदी
लिफाफा देखकर	शैलेन्द्र नाथ श्रीवास्तव
नई पौध	नागार्जुन
नई कविता के प्रतिमान	लक्ष्मीकान्त वर्मा
डूबते मस्तूल	प्रियंवदा
साये में धूप	दुष्यन्त कुमार
कलम का सिपाही	अमृत राय
बाबा बटेसर नाथ	नागार्जुन
रश्मिरथी	दिनकर
आवारा भीड़ के खतरे	हरिशंकर परसाई
डाक बंगला	कमलेश्वर
एक चिथड़ा सुख	निर्मल वर्मा
नेताजी कहिन	मनोहर श्याम जोशी
युगवाणी	पंत
नहुष	मैथिली शरण गुप्त
ठण्डा लोहा	धर्मवीर भारती
संस्कृति के चार अध्याय	दिनकर
लहरों का राजहंस	मोहन राकेश
सुखदा	जैनेन्द्र कुमार
परशुराम की प्रतीक्षा	दिनकर
शिवा बावनी	भूषण
भारत की खोज	पं. जवाहर लाल नेहरू
मृगनयनी	वृन्दावन लाल वर्मा
जहाँगीर जस चन्द्रिका	केशवदास
तमस	भीष्म साहनी
त्याग पत्र	जैनेन्द्र कुमार
रेणुका	दिनकर

वस्तुनिष्ठ प्रश्न

1. हिन्दी साहित्य में गद्य का विकास–
   A. पद्य के साथ-साथ हुआ
   B. पद्य से पहले हुआ
   C. पद्य के बाद हुआ
   D. उपरोक्त में से कोई नहीं

2. आधुनिक काल में कुल मिलाकर–
   A. पद्य और गद्य बराबर लिखा गया
   B. पद्य अधिक लिखा गया
   C. गद्य अधिक लिखा गया
   D. उपरोक्त में से कोई नहीं

3. हिन्दी में गद्य का प्राचीनतम रूप किस ग्रंथ में मिलता है?
   A. चौरासी वैष्णवन की वार्ता B. चन्द छंद बरनन की महिमा
   C. पद्मपुराण D. सुख सागर

4. 'चौरासी वैष्णवन की वार्ता' का रचयिता कौन था?
   A. विट्ठलनाथ जी B. गोकुलनाथ जी
   C. नाभादास जी D. गंग कवि

5. 'अष्टयाम' किसकी रचना है?
   A. गोकुलनाथ जी B. विट्ठलनाथ जी
   C. नाभादास जी D. रामप्रसाद निरंजनी

6. प्रारम्भिक गद्य की भाषा क्या थी?
   A. अपभ्रंश B. खड़ी बोली
   C. अवधी D. ब्रजभाषा

7. जैन 'पद्म पुराण' का अनुवाद किसने किया था?
   A. लक्ष्मण सिंह B. दौलत राम
   C. श्रद्धाराम फिल्लौरी D. रामप्रसाद निरंजनी

8. 19वीं शताब्दी के आरम्भ में हिन्दी गद्य के चार मुख्य लेखक हुए। उनमें से एक ने 'सुखसागर' लिखा। उसका नाम क्या था?
   A. सदल मिश्र B. लल्लू लाल
   C. सदासुख लाल D. इंशाअल्ला खां

9. 'रानी केतकी की कहानी' किसने लिखी थी?
   A. इंशाअल्ला खां B. लक्ष्मण सिंह
   C. बालकृष्ण भट्ट D. प्रताप नारायण मिश्र

10. नीचे पुस्तकों और लेखकों के जोड़े दिये गए हैं। इनमें एक जोड़ा गलत है। बताइये कौन-सा जोड़ा गलत है?
   A. भाषा योगवशिष्ट – नाभादास
   B. नासिकेतोपाख्यान – सदल मिश्र
   C. शृंगार रस मंडन – विट्ठल नाथ
   D. प्रेमसागर – लल्लू लाल

11. ईसाई पादरियों ने किस प्रकार हिन्दी गद्य के प्रसार में योगदान किया?
   A. उन्होंने गद्य लेखन पर पुरस्कार दिये
   B. स्वयं हिन्दी गद्य में लिखा
   C. बाइबिल का हिन्दी में अनुवाद कराया और उसे बांटा
   D. उपरोक्त सभी

12. 'सितारे हिन्द' किसकी उपाधि थी?
   A. राजा शिवप्रसाद B. राजा लक्ष्मण सिंह
   C. देवकीनंदन खत्री D. श्रीनिवास दास

13. 'इतिहास तिमिर नाशक' ग्रंथ का रचयिता कौन है?
   A. भारतेन्दु हरिश्चन्द्र
   B. बालकृष्ण भट्ट
   C. राजा शिवप्रसाद 'सितारे हिन्द'
   D. राजा लक्ष्मण सिंह

14. भारतेन्दु हरिश्चन्द्र के समय में हिन्दी गद्य की बड़ी उन्नति हुई। इसमें इनके दो सहयोगियों की प्रमुख भूमिका थी, जिनमें एक का नाम था प्रतापनारायण मिश्र और दूसरे का नाम था–
   A. देवकीनंदन खत्री B. श्यामसुंदर दास
   C. श्रीनिवास दास D. बालकृष्ण भट्ट

15. भारतेन्दु हरिश्चन्द्र के काल में हिन्दी गद्य में–
   A. नाटक लिखे गये B. निबंध लिखे गये
   C. आलोचना लिखी गई D. उपरोक्त तीनों लिखे गये

16. द्विवेदी युग में हिन्दी गद्य–
   A. का रूप पूर्णतः स्थिर हो गया
   B. उर्दू मिश्रित हो गया
   C. की उपेक्षा हुई
   D. में केवल कुछ कहानियां लिखी गईं

17. द्विवेदी-युग में रामचन्द्र शुक्ल ने साहित्य के किस क्षेत्र में मूल्यवान योगदान किया?
   A. उपन्यास के क्षेत्र में B. कहानी के क्षेत्र में
   C. नाटक के क्षेत्र में D. आलोचना के क्षेत्र में

18. मिश्र बंधु का योगदान गद्य के किस क्षेत्र में रहा?
   A. नाटक के क्षेत्र में B. कहानी के क्षेत्र में
   C. आलोचना के क्षेत्र में D. उपन्यास के क्षेत्र में

19. द्विवेदी युग में ही हिन्दी के महान् उपन्यासकार की रचनायें प्रकाश में आईं। वह उपन्यासकार थे–
   A. जैनेन्द्र कुमार B. यशपाल
   C. प्रेमचन्द D. इलाचन्द जोशी

20. छायावादी कवियों में जयशंकर प्रसाद ने गद्य की किस विधा को समृद्ध बनाया?

A. नाटक B. उपन्यास
C. निबन्ध D. कहानी

21. छायावादी कवि निराला का प्रसिद्ध उपन्यास है–

A. अलका B. चन्द्रकला
C. सावित्री D. इन्द्रा

22. महादेवी वर्मा की रचना 'अतीत के चलचित्र'–

A. कहानी संग्रह है B. उपन्यास है
C. निबन्ध-संग्रह है D. संस्मरणों का संग्रह है

23. 'भारत दुर्दशा' नाटक का लेखक कौन है?

A. भारतेन्दु हरिश्चन्द्र B. देवकीनंदन खत्री
C. बालकृष्ण भट्ट D. प्रतापनारायण मिश्र

24. 'चन्द्रकान्ता संतति' उपन्यास के कितने खण्ड निकले थे?

A. 14 खण्ड B. 8 खण्ड
C. 3 खण्ड D. 24 खण्ड

25. तिलिस्म और ऐयारी से भरे 'चंद्रकान्ता संतति' उपन्यास का सबसे बड़ा योगदान यह रहा कि–

A. उपन्यास के नए क्षेत्र खुल गए
B. हिन्दी गद्य का रूप निखर गया
C. इसी किस्म के बहुत-से उपन्यास लिखे गये
D. असंख्य लोगों ने इस उपन्यास को पढ़ने के लिए हिन्दी भाषा सीखी

26. मुंशी प्रेमचंद के 'गोदान' उपन्यास में मुख्य पात्र (हीरो) का नाम क्या है?

A. मधुवा B. होरी
C. विशाल देव D. दिव्या

27. निराला के उपन्यास 'निरूपमा' में किस समस्या का वर्णन है?

A. ग्राम्य-जीवन की वास्तविकतायें
B. दहेज प्रथा
C. मध्यवर्गीय समाज की आर्थिक विपन्नता
D. प्रादेशिक भेदभाव और सामाजिक कुरीतियां

28. कुछ विद्वान 'परीक्षा गुरु' को हिन्दी का प्रथम उपन्यास मानते हैं। इसके लेखक हैं–

A. रामचन्द्र शुक्ल B. श्रीनिवास दास
C. बालकृष्ण भट्ट D. बाबू राधाकृष्ण दास

29. बालकृष्ण भट्ट का उपन्यास 'सौ अजान एक सुजान' कैसा उपन्यास है?

A. सांस्कृतिक B. ऐतिहासिक
C. तिलिस्मी D. उपदेशात्मक

30. निम्नलिखित उपन्यासों में से कौन-सा उपन्यास अम्बिकादत्त व्यास का है?

A. नूतन ब्रह्मचारी B. मरता क्या न करता
C. मृण्मयी D. आश्चर्य वृतान्त

31. उपन्यासों के विकास के प्रारम्भिक चरण के सम्बन्ध में कौन-सा कथन सही है?

A. कुछ उपन्यास मौलिक हैं
B. कुछ उपन्यास अनूदित हैं
C. इनका लाभ यह हुआ कि मौलिक उपन्यास लेखन की प्रवृति बढ़ी
D. उपरोक्त सभी

32. निम्नलिखित उपन्यासों में से कौन-सा उपन्यास अयोध्या सिंह उपाध्याय 'हरिऔध' का नहीं है?

A. वेनिस का बाँका B. ठेठ हिन्दी का ठाठ
C. अधलिखा फूल D. रसिक लाल

33. हिन्दी के प्रथम मौलिक उपन्यासकारों में देवकीनंदन खत्री विख्यात हैं। इनका सर्वाधिक लोकप्रिय उपन्यास 'चन्द्रकान्ता संतति' है। इसके अलावा भी इनका एक अन्य उपन्यास है, जिसका नाम है–

A. अंगूठी का नगीना B. भूतनाथ
C. दिल्ली के दलाल D. युगान्तर

34. 'संन्यासी' एक प्रसिद्ध उपन्यास है। इसके लेखक का नाम है–

A. वृन्दावनलाल वर्मा B. यशपाल
C. उपेन्द्रनाथ अश्क D. इलाचन्द्र जोशी

35. निम्नलिखित उपन्यासों में से कौन-सा उपन्यास यशपालजी का नहीं है?

A. दादा कामरेड B. दिव्या
C. देशद्रोही D. भिखारिणी

36. किसको 'उपन्यास सम्राट' माना जाता है?

A. जैनेन्द्र कुमार B. यशपाल
C. उपेन्द्रनाथ अश्क D. प्रेमचंद

37. 'चित्रलेखा' एक अति लोकप्रिय उपन्यास है। इसके लेखक का नाम है–

A. चतुरसेन शास्त्री B. पाण्डेय बेचन शर्मा 'उग्र'
C. वृन्दावनलाल वर्मा D. भगवतीचरण वर्मा

38. जयशंकर प्रसाद के दो उपन्यासों में एक का नाम 'कंकाल' है, और दूसरे का–

A. तीन वर्ष B. मां
C. तितली D. वैशाली की नगरवधू

39. मुंशी प्रेमचंद के उपन्यास–

A. ऐतिहासिक हैं B. सामाजिक हैं
C. रोमांटिक हैं D. मनोवैज्ञानिक हैं

40. निम्नलिखित उपन्यासों में से कौन-सा उपन्यास प्रेमचंदजी का नहीं है?

A. गबन B. निर्मला
C. गोदान D. विसर्जन

41. 'वैशाली की नगरवधू' किसका उपन्यास है?

A. जैनेन्द्र कुमार B. चतुरसेन शास्त्री
C. वृन्दावनलाल वर्मा D. इलाचन्द्र जोशी

42. ऐतिहासिक उपन्यासों के लिए कौन-सा नाम विख्यात है?
A. यशपाल B. अज्ञेय
C. उपेन्द्रनाथ अश्क D. वृन्दावनलाल वर्मा

43. 'शेखर-एक जीवनी' किसका बहुचर्चित उपन्यास है?
A. राहुल सांकृत्यायन B. धर्मवीर भारती
C. अमृतलाल नागर D. अज्ञेय

44. नीचे कुछ उपन्यासों और उनके लेखकों के नामों के जोड़े दिये गए हैं। इनमें से कौन-सा जोड़ा सही नहीं है?
A. जयशंकर प्रसाद – तितली
B. देवकीनंदन खत्री – भूतनाथ
C. जैनेन्द्र कुमार – सुनीता
D. अज्ञेय – दिव्या

45. 'मैला आँचल' उपन्यास का लेखक कौन है?
A. फणीश्वरनाथ रेणु B. धर्मवीर भारती
C. अज्ञेय D. नरेश मेहता

46. 'शेखर-एक जीवनी' अज्ञेय का लिखा हुआ उपन्यास है। यह–
A. अपनी ऐतिहासिक पृष्ठभूमि के लिए विख्यात है
B. अपने सांस्कृतिक मूल्यों के लिए विख्यात है
C. नवीन शैली व पैनी मनोवैज्ञानिक दृष्टि के लिए विख्यात है
D. सामाजिक कुरीतियों का पर्दाफाश करने के लिए विख्यात है

47. प्रेमचन्द जी के 'गोदान' में–
A. जीवन के जीते-जागते चित्र हैं
B. जीवन की कठोर वास्तविकता का सूक्ष्म विवेचन है
C. ग्राम-जीवन की रीतियों का सूक्ष्म विवेचन है
D. उपरोक्त सभी

48. प्रसादजी के 'कंकाल' उपन्यास में–
A. सामाजिक बंधनों की विषमता और व्यक्ति की सहज प्रवृत्तियों का संघर्ष अंकित है
B. समाज-व्यवस्था प ीखा व्यंग्य है
C. आदर्श और यथार्थ के बीच खड़ी खाई का रूप है
D. उपरोक्त सभी

49. निम्नलिखित में कौन-सा एक उपन्यास वृन्दावनलाल वर्मा का नहीं है?
A. गढ़ कुण्डार B. झांसी की रानी
C. विराटा की पद्मिनी D. देशद्रोही

50. 'बूंद और समुद्र' किसका विख्यात उपन्यास है?
A. उदय शंकर भट्ट B. फणीश्वरनाथ रेणु
C. शैलेश मटियानी D. अमृतलाल नागर

51. निम्नलिखित आंचलिक उपन्यासों में से एक फणीश्वरनाथ रेणु का नहीं है। वह है–
A. मैला आँचल B. परती परिकथा
C. द्वामा D. पल्टू बाबू रोड

52. 'चिट्टीरसैनी' किसका प्रसिद्ध उपन्यास है?
A. उपेन्द्रनाथ अश्क B. हरिकृष्ण प्रेमी
C. शैलेश मटियानी D. यशपाल

53. 'चित्रलेखा' और 'तीन वर्ष' के अतिरिक्त भगवतीचरण वर्मा के अन्य उपन्यास हैं–
A. टेढ़े-मेढ़े रास्ते B. भूले-बिसरे चित्र
C. सीधी-सच्ची बातें D. उपरोक्त सभी

54. 'गिरती दीवारें' किसका उत्तम उपन्यास है?
A. उपेन्द्रनाथ अश्क B. धर्मवीर भारती
C. अमृतलाल नागर D. नागार्जुन

55. 'मृगनयनी' किसका उपन्यास है?
A. जैनेन्द्र कुमार का B. वृन्दावनलाल वर्मा का
C. अमृतलाल नागर का D. उषरोक्त में से कोई नहीं

56. निम्नलिखित सूची-I का सूची-II से मिलान कीजिए तथा नीचे दिए गए कूट की सहायता से सही उत्तर का चयन कीजिए :

सूची-I	**सूची-II**
(*a*) अपने-अपने अजनबी	1. धर्मवीर भारती
(*b*) सूरज का सातवां घोड़ा	2. अज्ञेय
(*c*) खाली कुर्सी की आत्मा	3. इलाचंद जोशी
(*d*) प्रेत और छाया	4. लक्ष्मीकान्त वर्मा

कूट :

	(*a*)	(*b*)	(*c*)	(*d*)
A.	2	1	4	3
B.	1	2	4	3
C.	1	2	3	4
D.	3	4	2	1

57. हरिवंश राय बच्चन की रचना "क्या भूलूं क्या याद करूं" किस कोटि के अन्तर्गत आती है?
A. आत्मकथा B. यात्रा वृत्तान्त
C. इंटरव्यू D. रेखाचित्र

58. महादेवी वर्मा की रचना 'पथ के साथी' किस कोटि के अन्तर्गत आती है?
A. संस्मरण B. रेखाचित्र
C. यात्रा वृत्तान्त D. जीवनी

59. नीचे कुछ रचनायें दी हुई हैं और उनके सामने उनके लेखकों के नाम हैं। कौन-सा जोड़ा गलत है?
A. अरे यायावर याद रहेगा – अज्ञेय
B. मैं इनसे मिला – पद्मसिंह शर्मा कमलेश
C. जंजीरें और दीवार – रामवृक्ष बेनीपुरी
D. माटी हो गई सोना – महादेवी वर्मा

60. धर्मवीर भारती की रचना 'ठेले पर हिमालय' किस कोटि की है?
A. जीवनी B. यात्रा वृत्तान्त
C. संस्मरण D. इंटरव्यू

61. 'एक बूंद सहसा उछली' किसका विख्यात यात्रा संस्मरण है?
A. निर्मल वर्मा का B. रामवृक्ष बेनीपुरी का
C. अज्ञेय का D. डा. रघुवंश का

62. हिन्दी की सर्वप्रथम मौलिक कहानी किसे माना जाता है?
A. इन्दुमती B. आकाशदीप
C. ग्यारह वर्ष का समय D. उसने कहा था

63. हिन्दी की सर्वप्रथम मौलिक कहानी 'इन्दुमती' का लेखक कौन था?
A. गिरिजादत्त वाजपेयी B. किशोरी लाल गोस्वामी
C. रामचन्द्र शुक्ल D. प्रताप नारायण मिश्र

64. चन्द्रधर शर्मा 'गुलेरी' की सुविख्यात कहानी कौन-सी है?
A. छाया B. उसने कहा था
C. बड़े घर की बेटी D. शतरंज के खिलाड़ी

65. प्रेमचंद का सर्वोत्कृष्ट उपन्यास कौन-सा है?
A. निर्मला B. सेवासदन
C. रंगभूमि D. गोदान

66. मुंशी प्रेमचंद ने अपने उपन्यासों में किस समस्या को प्रस्तुत किया है?
A. विधवा विवाह B. अनमेल विवाह
C. दहेज प्रथा D. उपरोक्त तीनों

67. 'मधुआ' कहानी किसकी है?
A. प्रेमचन्द की B. प्रसादजी की
C. यशपाल की D. अज्ञेय की

68. 'जार्ज पंचम की नाक' कहानी का लेखक कौन है?
A. कमलेश्वर B. हरिकृष्ण प्रेमी
C. भीष्म साहनी D. अज्ञेय

69. प्रेमचंद की 'पूस की रात' कहानी–
A. भारतीय किसान की टूटन की कहानी है
B. भारतीय मध्यवर्ग के मिथ्याभिमान की कहानी है
C. वर्ग संघर्ष की कहानी है
D. अशिक्षा के अभिशाप की कहानी है

70. प्रसादजी की मधुआ कहानी एक–
A. शराबी के हृदय-परिवर्तन की कहानी है
B. रईस की हृदयहीनता की कहानी है
C. बालक के शोषण की कहानी है
D. उपरोक्त में से कोई नहीं

71. यशपाल ने अपनी कहानी 'खच्चर और आदमी' में क्या बताया है?
A. खच्चर आदमी से श्रेष्ठ है
B. आदमी खच्चर से श्रेष्ठ हैं
C. जो अपने को परिस्थितियों में ढाल ले वही बच पाता है
D. मनुष्य परिस्थितियों का दास है

72. अज्ञेय की 'शरणदाता' कहानी–
A. मानव संघर्ष की कहानी है
B. साम्प्रदायिकता-विरोधी कहानी है
C. नारी ममता की कहानी है
D. उपरोक्त तीनों

73. 'कानों में कंगना' नामक कहानी का लेखक कौन है?
A. विश्वम्भर नाथ शर्मा 'कौशिक'
B. राधिकारमण प्रसाद
C. पदुमलाल पुन्नालाल बख्शी
D. रायकृष्ण दास

74. 'ताई' कहानी का लेखक कौन है?
A. वृन्दावनलाल वर्मा B. राजेन्द्र यादव
C. मन्नू भंडारी D. विश्वम्भर नाथ शर्मा 'कौशिक'

75. निम्नलिखित कहानियों में से कौन-सी कहानी उषा देवी मित्रा की लिखी हुई है?
A. भाई-बहन B. लछमा
C. अधूरा चित्र D. सान्ध्य तारा

76. 'आत्माराम' और 'पंच परमेश्वर' किसकी कहानियां हैं?
A. सुदर्शन B. शिवपूजन सहाय
C. चंडी प्रसाद 'हृदयेश' D. प्रेमचंद

77. गिरिजादत्त वाजपेयी की एक उत्तम कहानी है–
A. रानी सारंधा B. प्रतिध्वनि
C. हार की जीत D. पंडित और पंडितानी

78. 'पुरस्कार' और 'आकाशदीप' कहानियां किसकी हैं?
A. रायकृष्ण दास B. सुदर्शन
C. चन्द्रकिरण सौनरिक्सा D. जयशंकर प्रसाद

79. 'हार की जीत' नामक अत्यन्त लोकप्रिय और महान् चरित्र वाली कहानी का लेखक कौन है?
A. सुदर्शन B. चतुरसेन शास्त्री
C. विष्णु प्रभाकर D. यशपाल

80. गुलेरीजी की 'उसने कहा था' कहानी का सार क्या है?
A. अमृतसर का जन-जीवन B. युद्ध की निस्सारता
C. निःस्वार्थ बलिदान D. अपराध का मनोविज्ञान

81. 'बैताल पचीसी' और 'सिंहासनबत्तीसी' कहानियों को हिन्दी में किसने अनूदित किया?
A. लल्लू लाल B. शिवप्रसाद 'सितारे हिन्द'
C. भारतेन्दु हरिश्चन्द्र D. उपरोक्त में से कोई नहीं

82. 'रानी केतकी की कहानी' कहानी के बारे में कौन-सा कथन सही नहीं है?
A. यह कहानी ठेठ हिन्दी में है
B. इसमें रानी केतकी और उदयभान की प्रेम-कथा का वर्णन है
C. इसके लेखक सदल मिश्र हैं
D. इसके लेखक इंशाअल्ला खां हैं

83. 'राजा भोज का सपना' किसकी कहानी है?
A. शिवप्रसाद 'सितारे हिन्द' B. चतुरसेन शास्त्री
C. उषा देवी मित्रा D. सुदर्शन

84. मनोवैज्ञानिक कहानीकारों में किसकी गणना नहीं की जाती?
A. राजेन्द्र यादव B. अज्ञेय
C. इलाचन्द्र जोशी D. पाण्डेय बेचन शर्मा 'उग्र'

85. जैनेन्द्रजी कहानी के सम्बन्ध में प्रेमचंद की परिपाटी में आते हैं; क्योंकि उन्होंने अपनी कहानियों के लिए
A. मनोवैज्ञानिक विषय चुने
B. सामाजिक और पारिवारिक विषय चुने
C. राष्ट्र निर्माण के विषयों को अपनाया
D. उपरोक्त तीनों

86. 'मिठाई वाला' कहानी का लेखक कौन है?
A. भगवतीचरण वर्मा B. भगवती प्रसाद वाजपेयी
C. यशपाल D. सुदर्शन

87. निम्नलिखित कहानियों में से कौन-सी कहानी रायकृष्ण दास की है?
A. रमणी का रहस्य B. अपना-अपना भाग्य
C. नन्दिनी D. कमल की बेटी

88. प्रसाद जी की प्रथम कहानी कौन-सी थी?
A. ग्राम B. मधुआ
C. आकाशदीप D. पुरस्कार

89. निम्नलिखित में से कौन-सा कहानी संग्रह प्रसाद जी का नहीं है?
A. छाया B. आकाशदीप
C. कोठरी की बात D. प्रतिध्वनि

90. 'रक्षा बन्धन' किसकी कहानी है?
A. शिवपूजन सहाय की B. जैनेन्द्र की
C. सुदर्शन की D. कौशिक की

91. निम्नलिखित में से कौन-सा कहानी संग्रह वृन्दावनलाल वर्मा का नहीं है?
A. हर सिंगार B. दबे पांव
C. कलाकार का दण्ड D. मानुषी

92. 'नई कहानी' वर्ग के कहानीकारों में निम्न में से किसका नाम नहीं आता?
A. मोहन राकेश का B. राजेन्द्र यादव का
C. कमलेश्वर का D. विष्णु प्रभाकर का

93. 'दुलाई वाली' कहानी किसकी थी?
A. रामचन्द्र शुक्ल की
B. विश्वम्भर नाथ शर्मा 'कौशिक' की
C. प्रेमचंद की
D. वंग महिला की

94. कहानी के विकास-क्रम में महत्वपूर्ण भूमिका निभाने वाली पत्रिका का नाम है–
A. सरस्वती B. इन्दु
C. उपरोक्त दोनों D. इन्दुमती

95. जैनेन्द्रजी का चिन्तन एवं दृष्टिकोण–
A. गांधीवादी B. प्रगतिशील
C. यथार्थवादी D. साम्यवादी

96. आंचलिक कहानी संग्रह 'ठुमरी' किसका है?
A. उपेन्द्र नाथ 'अश्क' B. शैलेश मटियानी
C. रघुवीर सहाय D. फणीश्वर नाथ 'रेणु'

97. विष्णु प्रभाकर की 'अधूरी कहानी' का उद्देश्य–
A. साम्प्रदायिक सद्भाव है B. नारी-उत्थान है
C. कुंठा-उन्मूलन है D. अहंकार का पतन है

98. 'काकी' कहानी किसकी है?
A. सुदर्शन B. कौशिक
C. सियारामशरण गुप्त D. प्रेमचन्द

99. 'परदा' कहानी में यशपालजी का उद्देश्य–
A. मध्यम वर्ग की निर्धनता का वर्णन करना है
B. उन्माद की निंदा करना है
C. झूठी प्रतिष्ठाप्रियता की पोल खोलना है
D. परदा-प्रथा की बुराइयां बताना है

100. 'दो बांके' किसका कहानी संग्रह है?
A. भगवती प्रसाद वाजपेयी B. भगवतीचरण वर्मा
C. मन्नू भंडारी D. होमवती देवी

101. कालिदास के 'शकुन्तला' नाटक का हिन्दी अनुवाद किसने किया?
A. भारतेन्दु हरिश्चन्द्र B. राजा लक्ष्मण सिंह
C. बाबू गोपाल चन्द्र D. प्रताप नारायण मिश्र

102. निम्नलिखित नाटकों में से कौन-सा नाटक भारतेन्दुजी द्वारा लिखित नहीं है?
A. भारत दुर्दशा B. भारत-सौभाग्य
C. नील देवी D. अन्धेर नगरी

103. भारतेन्दुजी के 'चन्द्रावली' नाटक में–
A. भारत की दयनीय दशा का चित्रण है
B. शासन-व्यवस्था पर व्यंग्य है
C. आदर्श प्रेम का चित्रण है
D. ऐतिहासिक खोज है

104. 'दुखिनी बाला' किसका नाटक है?
A. भारतेन्दु बाबू B. राधाकृष्ण दास
C. प्रतापनारायण मिश्र D. अम्बिकादत्त व्यास

105. द्विवेदी युग में–
A. मौलिक नाटक खूब लिखे गए
B. नाटकों के अनुवाद खूब हुए
C. नाटकों का मनुष्य के जीवन में निकट का सम्बन्ध रहा
D. उपरोक्त सभी

106. द्विजेन्द्र लाल राय के बंगला नाटकों का हिन्दी अनुवाद किसने किया?
A. श्रीनिवास दास B. बाबू सीताराम
C. सत्य नारायण D. रूप नारायण

107. प्रसाद युग से पूर्व मैथिलीशरण गुप्त का कौन-सा नाटक आया था?
A. चन्द्रगुप्त B. चन्द्रहास
C. चन्द्रकला D. चन्द्रोदय

108. प्रसादजी के नाटकों में–
A. साहित्यिक भाषा है
B. ऐतिहासिक पुट है
C. भारतीय सभ्यता और संस्कृति के गौरव का चित्रण है
D. उपरोक्त सभी

109. निम्नलिखित नाटकों में से कौन-सा नाटक प्रसादजी द्वारा लिखित नहीं है?
A. राज्यश्री B. स्कन्दगुप्त
C. अजातशत्रु D. विश्वामित्र

110. उदयशंकर भट्टजी के नाटक–
A. राष्ट्रीयता प्रधान हैं B. पौराणिक हैं
C. ऐतिहासिक हैं D. अन्तर्द्वन्द्व प्रधान हैं

111. 'अम्बा' और 'मतस्यगंधा' किसके नाटक हैं?
A. हरिकृष्ण प्रेमी B. विश्वम्भर नाथ शर्मा 'कौशिक'
C. सुदर्शन D. उदय शंकर भट्ट

112. 'सिन्दूर की होली' किसका विख्यात नाटक है?
A. लक्ष्मीनारायण मिश्र B. उपेन्द्रनाथ अश्क
C. सेठ गोविन्द दास D. माखनलाल चतुर्वेदी

113. मोहन राकेश की ख्याति किस नाटक से फैली?
A. शशिगुप्त B. कर्तव्य
C. आषाढ़ का एक दिन D. रेशमी टाई

114. निम्नलिखित में से कौन-सा नाटक लक्ष्मी नारायण लाल का नहीं है?
A. अंधा कुआं B. मादा कैक्टस
C. सूखा सरोवर D. लहरों का राजहंस

115. हिन्दी का प्रथम एकांकी नाटककार कौन था?
A. प्रसादजी B. रामकुमार वर्मा
C. भगवतीचरण वर्मा D. उपेन्द्र नाथ अश्क

116. हिन्दी का सर्वप्रथम एकांकी नाटक किसे माना जाता है?
A. बड़ा आदमी B. एक बूंद
C. कारवां D. दस मिनट

117. 'देवताओं की छाया में' किसका एकांकी-संग्रह है?
A. उपेन्द्रनाथ अश्क B. रामकुमार वर्मा
C. भुवनेश्वर मिश्र D. सेठ गोविन्द दास

118. 'सबसे बड़ा आदमी' किसका एकांकी है?
A. भगवतीचरण वर्मा B. विष्णु प्रभाकर
C. जगदीश चन्द्र माथुर D. उदय शंकर भट्ट

119. 'गरुड़ध्वज' और 'दशाश्वमेध' किसके विख्यात ऐतिहासिक नाटक हैं?
A. रामकुमार वर्मा B. हरिकृष्ण प्रेमी
C. उपेन्द्रनाथ अश्क D. लक्ष्मीनारायण मिश्र

120. 'युगे-युगे क्रान्ति' नाटक किसका है?
A. जगदीशचन्द्र माथुर B. सेठ गोविन्द दास
C. विष्णु प्रभाकर D. देवराज दिनेश

121. जगदीश चन्द्र माथुर का एकांकी संकलन है–
A. कुलीनता B. रंगमंच
C. भोर का तारा D. मां का बेटा

122. 'आधे-अधूरे' किसका नाटक है?
A. नरेश मेहता B. देवराज दिनेश
C. विपिन अग्रवाल D. मोहन राकेश

123. निम्नलिखित नाटकों में से कौन-सा लक्ष्मीकांत वर्मा का है?
A. आदमी का जहर B. तीन अपाहिज
C. नया-पुराना D. उपरोक्त में से कोई नहीं

124. 'पृथ्वीराज की आँखें' और 'कैलेण्डर का आखिरी पन्ना' किसके विख्यात एकांकी हैं?
A. सेठ गोविन्द दास B. विष्णु प्रभाकर
C. रामकुमार वर्मा D. उदय शंकर भट्ट

125. सेठ गोविन्द दास के एकांकियों में–
A. गांधीवादी विचारधारा है
B. राजनैतिक एवं सामाजिक समस्याओं का चित्रण है
C. ऐतिहासिक पृष्ठभूमि है
D. उपरोक्त A और B दोनों

126. सेठ गोविन्ददास के प्रसिद्ध कहानी संग्रह हैं–
A. नवरस B. एकादशी
C. स्पर्द्धा D. उपरोक्त तीनों

127. उदय शंकर भट्ट के एकांकियों में–
A. मनोविश्लेषणात्मक शैली है B. अन्तर्द्वन्द्व का चित्रण है
C. भाषा पात्रों के अनुकूल है D. उपरोक्त तीनों

128. 'एकला चलो रे' किसका विख्यात एकांकी है?
A. उदय शंकर भट्ट B. हरिकृष्ण प्रेमी
C. उपेन्द्र नाथ अश्क D. विष्णु प्रभाकर

129. 'अधिकार का रक्षक' और 'लक्ष्मी का स्वागत' किसके विख्यात एकांकी हैं?
A. हरिकृष्ण प्रेमी B. रेवती शरण शर्मा
C. धर्मवीर भारती D. उपेन्द्र नाथ अश्क

130. लोकप्रिय एकांकी 'रीढ़ की हड्डी' किसकी रचना है?
A. गिरजा कुमार माथुर B. लक्ष्मीकान्त वर्मा
C. भारत भूषण अग्रवाल D. जगदीश चन्द्र माथुर

131. 'मुझे जीने दो' किसका लोकप्रिय एकांकी है?
A. लक्ष्मीकान्त मिश्र B. जयनाथ नलिन
C. रेवती शरण शर्मा D. उपरोक्त में से कोई नहीं

132. 'लस्सी का गिलास' एकांकी का लेखक कौन है?
A. सद्गुरु शरण अवस्थी B. विष्णु प्रभाकर
C. जयनाथ नलिन D. विनोद रस्तोगी

133. निम्नलिखित में से कौन-सा एकांकी विमला लूथरा का नहीं है?
A. लाइन क्लीअर B. मुन्ने का नामकरण
C. प्रीतिभोज D. डाक्टर बीबी

134. 'रसोईघर में प्रजातंत्र' विष्णु प्रभाकर का एकांकी है, जिसमें–
A. व्यंग्य है B. क्षोभ है
C. उद्बोधन है D. निराशा है

135. निम्नलिखित में से किसे हिन्दी का सशक्त नाटककार माना जाता है?
A. मुंशी प्रेमचंद B. सेठ गोविन्द दास
C. जयशंकर प्रसाद D. भारतेन्दु हरिश्चन्द्र

136. 'विशाख' और 'एक घूंट' नाटकों का लेखक कौन है?
A. हरिकृष्ण प्रेमी B. लक्ष्मी नारायण लाल
C. जयशंकर प्रसाद D. उदय शंकर भट्ट

137. 'लहरों का राजहंस' किसका प्रसिद्ध नाटक है?
A. मोहन राकेश B. जगदीश चन्द्र माथुर
C. जयशंकर प्रसाद D. उदय शंकर भट्ट

138. 'आनरेरी मजिस्ट्रेट' का लेखक कौन है?
A. भगवती प्रसाद वाजपेयी B. रामकुमार वर्मा
C. देवकीनंदन खत्री D. हरिकृष्ण प्रेमी

139. 'अम्बपाली' किसकी रचना है?
A. श्रीनिवास दास B. उदय शंकर भट्ट
C. रामवृक्ष बेनीपुरी D. उपेन्द्र नाथ अश्क

140. ऐतिहासिक तथ्यों और काल्पनिक प्रसंगों के मिश्रण से जगदीश चन्द्र माथुर ने किस नाटक की रचना की?
A. क्षत्राणी B. शिवानी
C. कोणार्क D. सूर्यरथ

141. 'धूर्त रसिक लाल' का लेखक कौन है?
A. गोपालराम गहमरी B. भगवतीचरण वर्मा
C. शिवपूजन सहाय D. पं. लज्जा राम मेहता

142. प्रेमचंद रचित 'मान सरोवर' के कितने भाग हैं?
A. तीन भाग B. पांच भाग
C. सात भाग D. आठ भाग

143. 'वयं रक्षामः' किसका उपन्यास है?
A. गुरुदत्त का B. चतुरसेन शास्त्री का
C. भगवतीचरण वर्मा का D. इलाचन्द्र जोशी का

144. 'मुण्डमाल' किसकी रचना है?
A. कौशिक B. रामकुमार वर्मा
C. शिवपूजन सहाय D. उपरोक्त में से कोई नहीं

145. 'कोठरी की बात' कहानी-संग्रह किसका है?
A. यशपाल का B. जैनेन्द्र का
C. अज्ञेय का D. धर्मवीर भारती का

146. 'चारुमित्रा' और 'तैमूर की हार' किस लेखक के एकांकी हैं?
A. उपेन्द्र नाथ अश्क B. भुवनेश्वर प्रसाद
C. विष्णु प्रभाकर D. रामकुमार वर्मा

147. उपेन्द्रनाथ अश्क के अधिकांश एकांकी–
A. आदर्शवादी हैं B. राजनैतिक हैं
C. सामाजिक व पारिवारिक हैं D. मनोवैज्ञानिक हैं

148. 'यशस्वी भोज' किसका एकांकी है?
A. लक्ष्मी नारायण लाल B. देवराज दिनेश
C. उदय शंकर भट्ट D. सेठ गोविन्द दास

149. 'चिरंजीव' का विख्यात एकांकी है–
A. दो कलाकार B. माटी की मूरत
C. पंचकन्या D. दादी मां जागी

150. 'ध्रुवस्वामिनी' प्रसादजी का–
A. सामाजिक नाटक है B. ऐतिहासिक नाटक है
C. पारिवारिक नाटक है D. पौराणिक नाटक है

151. 'बादल की मृत्यु' एकांकी के रचनाकार हैं–
A. रामकुमार वर्मा B. आचार्य शुक्ल
C. प्रसाद D. विष्णु प्रभाकर

152. धर्मवीर भारती के एकांकी का नाम है–
A. निशानेबाज B. नदी प्यासी थी
C. उपर्युक्त दोनों D. इनमें से कोई नहीं

153. अमृतराय की एकांकी है–
A. राह चलते B. रूसी लोग
C. उपर्युक्त दोनों D. इनमें से कोई नहीं

154. 'एक साहित्यिक की डायरी' के लेखक हैं–
A. अज्ञेय B. मुक्तिबोध
C. धर्मवीर-भारती D. अमृतराय

155. उपन्यास और रचनाकारों को सुमेलित करें–

रचनाकार	उपन्यास
(*i*) राजेन्द्र यादव	(*a*) अंधेरे बंद कमरे
(*ii*) मोहन राकेश	(*b*) एक सड़क सत्तावन गलियाँ
(*iii*) कमलेश्वर	(*c*) आँचल में कोई
(*iv*) वृन्दावन लाल वर्मा	(*d*) कुलटा

कूट :

	(*i*)	(*ii*)	(*iii*)	(*iv*)
A.	(*a*)	(*d*)	(*c*)	(*b*)
B.	(*b*)	(*d*)	(*c*)	(*a*)
C.	(*d*)	(*a*)	(*b*)	(*c*)
D.	(*b*)	(*a*)	(*d*)	(*c*)

156. 'टेढ़े-मेढ़े रास्ते' उपन्यास के लेखक हैं–
A. रांगेय राघव B. अमृतराय
C. मन्नू भंडारी D. भगवती चरण वर्मा

157. 'निशिकान्त' उपन्यास के लेखक हैं–
A. विष्णु प्रभाकर B. प्रभाकर माचवे
C. नरेश मेहता D. राम नरेश त्रिपाठी

158. 'अपने-अपने अजनबी' उपन्यास लिखा है–
A. मुक्तिबोध B. अज्ञेय
C. चतुरसेन शास्त्री D. शमशेर

159. 'नागार्जुन' के उपन्यास का नाम है–
A. हीरक जयंती B. मशाल
C. जंजीरे D. उपर्युक्त सभी

160. 'दीर्घतपा' उपन्यास लिखा है–
A. नरेश मेहता B. रांगेय राघव
C. रेणु D. मन्नू भण्डारी

161. उषा प्रियंवदा के उपन्यास का नाम है–
A. हम तिनके B. पचपन खम्भे, लाल दीवारें
C. जंगल के फूल D. धूमकेतु

162. भीष्म साहनी का उपन्यास है–
A. सोनल का फूल B. वृषित
C. गंगामैया D. बसन्ती

163. अमृतराय के उपन्यास का नाम है :
A. धुँआ B. छोटे-छोटे पक्षी
C. कुरू-करू स्वाहा D. नई ईमारत

164. 'नवनिधी' किसका कहानी संग्रह है?
A. पंकज बिष्ट B. नागार्जुन
C. प्रेमचंद D. अज्ञेय

165. 'कोठरी की बात' कहानी संग्रह के रचयिता हैं–
A. मुक्तिबोध B. अज्ञेय
C. लाला श्रीनिवासदास D. प्रभाकर माचवे

166. यशपाल के कहानी संग्रह का नाम है–
A. फूलों का कुर्ता B. पिंजड़े की उड़ान
C. उपर्युक्त दोनों D. इनमें से कोई नहीं

167. 'संगीनों का साया' किसका काव्य संग्रह है?
A. प्रभाकर माचवे B. राहुल सांकृत्यायन
C. यशपाल D. अज्ञेय

168. कहानी संग्रह और लेखकों के नाम को सुमेलित करें–

लेखक	कहानी संग्रह
(*i*) मोहन राकेश	(*a*) फिर बसन्त आया
(*ii*) कमलेश्वर	(*b*) पहला पाठ
(*iii*) भीष्म साहनी	(*c*) नए बादल
(*iv*) उषा प्रियंवदा	(*d*) मांस का दरिया

कूट :

	(*i*)	(*ii*)	(*iii*)	(*iv*)
A.	(*d*)	(*a*)	(*c*)	(*b*)
B.	(*d*)	(*c*)	(*d*)	(*a*)
C.	(*c*)	(*d*)	(*b*)	(*a*)
D.	(*a*)	(*c*)	(*b*)	(*d*)

169. 'मेरी जीवन रेखा' आत्मकथा के रचयिता हैं–
A. हजारी प्रसाद द्विवेदी B. महावीर प्रसाद द्विवेदी
C. राहुल सांकृत्यायन D. प्रभाकर माचवे

170. 'मेरा जीवन साथी' किसकी आत्मकथा है?
A. नंद दुलारे वाजपेयी B. अज्ञेय
C. राम कुमार वर्मा D. प्रेमचंद

171. 'मेरी जीवन यात्रा' किसकी रचना है?
A. नागार्जुन B. राहुल सांकृत्यायन
C. महावीर प्रसाद द्विवेदी D. मुक्तिबोध

172. 'आत्मकथा' किसकी रचना है?
A. महात्मा गाँधी B. जवाहर लाल नेहरू
C. डॉ॰ राजेन्द्र प्रसाद D. लाल बहादुर शास्त्री

173. 'मेरी आत्म कहानी' आत्मकथा किसने लिखी है?
A. चतुरसेन शास्त्री B. महावीर प्रसाद द्विवेदी
C. राहुल सांकृत्यायन D. महात्मा गाँधी

174. 'सौष्ठववादी' किसकी समीक्षा पद्धति को कहा जाता है?
A. डॉ॰ नगेन्द्र B. हजारी प्रसाद द्विवेदी
C. आचार्य शुक्ल D. नंद दुलारे वाजपेयी

175. रामविलास शर्मा द्वारा लिखित है–
A. प्रगति और परम्परा B. भाषा, युगबोध और कविता
C. परम्परा का मूल्यांकन D. उपर्युक्त सभी

176. 'भारतीय साहित्य के इतिहास की समस्याएँ' लिखा है–
A. राम कुमार वर्मा B. राम विलास शर्मा
C. नंद दुलारे वाजपेयी D. हजारी प्रसाद द्विवेदी

177. 'पाप के पुजारी' नाटक के रचयिता हैं–
A. प्रभाकर माचवे B. दिनकर
C. रामविलास शर्मा D. नरेश मेहता

178. 'आचार्य रामचन्द्र शुक्ल और हिन्दी आलोचना' लिखा है–
A. डॉ॰ नगेन्द्र B. रामविलास शर्मा
C. हजारी प्रसाद द्विवेदी D. नामवर सिंह

179. 'मार्क्स, त्रात्सकी और एशियाई समाज' लिखा है–
A. रामकुमार वर्मा B. डॉ॰ नगेन्द्र
C. हजारी प्रसाद द्विवेदी D. राम विलास शर्मा

180. 'ऐन्दुई हिन्दुस्तानी' का प्रकाशन हुआ–
A. 1849 ई॰ B. 1839 ई॰
C. 1832 ई॰ D. 1843 ई॰

181. रीतिकाव्य की भूमिका किसने लिखी?
A. रामविलास शर्मा B. डॉ॰ राम कुमार वर्मा
C. आचार्य शुक्ल D. डॉ॰ नगेन्द्र

182. शुक्ल जी ने रासो शब्द की उत्पत्ति किसके द्वारा मानी है?
A. रास शब्द से B. रासक शब्द से
C. रसायण शब्द से D. रस शब्द से

183. रोमांस शब्द आया है–
A. अंग्रेजी भाषा में B. यूनानी भाषा में
C. जर्मन भाषा में D. फ्रांसीसी भाषा में

184. भारत में रोमांटिक कथाओं का उद्‌भव काल माना जाता है–
A. हड़प्पा काल से B. वेद काल से
C. महाभारत काल से D. आदि काल से

185. 'विकलांग श्रद्धा का दौर' के लेखक हैं–
A. प्रभाकर माचवे B. नरेश मेहता
C. बालकृष्ण भट्ट D. हरिशंकर परसाई

186. परसाई जी की कृति है–
A. निठल्ले की डायरी B. तुलसी भूषण
C. राम रत्नाकर D. रुक्मिणी परिणय

187. भारतेन्दु की भक्तिपरक रचना का नाम है–
A. भक्त सर्वस्त B. रुक्मिणी परिणय
C. उपर्युक्त दोनों D. इनमें से कोई नहीं

188. भारतेन्दु की प्रेम संबंधी रचना का नाम है–
A. प्रेम सरोवर B. प्रेम मालिका
C. उपर्युक्त दोनों D. इनमें से कोई नहीं

189. अम्बिका दत्त व्यास की प्रसिद्ध कृति का नाम है–
A. षटऋतु
B. प्रेमतरंग
C. प्रेम माधुरी
D. बिहारी बिहार

190. 'प्रेम पथिक' के रचनाकार हैं–
A. अम्बिकादत्त व्यास
B. नरेश मेहता
C. ठाकुर जगमोहन सिंह
D. वियोगी हरि

191. 'बैशाख माहात्म्य' रचना है–
A. बालकृष्ण भट्ट
B. भारतेन्दु
C. वियोगी हरि
D. ठाकुर जगमोहन सिंह

192. 'नये जमाने की मुकरी' के रचनाकार का नाम है–
A. अम्बिकादत्त व्यास
B. प्रताप नारायण मिश्र
C. बद्रीनारायण चौधरी
D. भारतेन्दु

193. 'हिन्दी हिन्दू, हिन्दुस्तान' के रचयिता हैं–
A. भारतेन्दु
B. प्रतापनारायण मिश्र
C. वियोगी हरि
D. अम्बिकादत्त व्यास

194. नीचे कुछ रचनाकारों और रचनाओं के नाम दिए जा रहे हैं, उन्हें सुमेलित करें।

रचनाकार	रचना
(i) प्रताप नारायण मिश्र	*(a)* युगल स्त्रोत
(ii) राधाचरण गोस्वामी	*(b)* शिवशम्भू के चिट्ठे
(iii) बालमुकुन्द गुप्त	*(c)* नव भक्त माल
(iv) बद्री नारायण चौधरी	*(d)* मन की लहर

कूट :

	(i)	*(ii)*	*(iii)*	*(iv)*
A.	*(d)*	*(b)*	*(a)*	*(c)*
B.	*(d)*	*(c)*	*(b)*	*(a)*
C.	*(b)*	*(c)*	*(a)*	*(d)*
D.	*(a)*	*(b)*	*(c)*	*(d)*

195. खड़ी बोली के लिए सशक्त आंदोलन चलाया–
A. आचार्य शुक्ल
B. हजारी प्रसाद द्विवेदी
C. महावीर प्रसाद द्विवेदी
D. नंद दुलारे वाजपेयी

196. 'विरहिणी ब्रजांगना' के रचयिता हैं–
A. माखनलाल चतुर्वेदी
B. मैथिलीशरण गुप्त
C. दिनकर
D. श्रीधर पाठक

197. 'मिलन' किसकी रचना है?
A. राम नरेश त्रिपाठी
B. रामचरित उपाध्याय
C. श्रीधर पाठक
D. मैथिलीशरण गुप्त

198. 'शाकुन्तलम्' के रचयिता हैं–
A. दिनकर
B. केदारनाथ अग्रवाल
C. माखनलाल चतुर्वेदी
D. मैथिलीशरण गुप्त

199. 'काव्य मंजूषा' और 'सुमन' किसकी पद्य रचनाएँ हैं?
A. महावीर प्रसाद द्विवेदी
B. प्रसाद
C. मैथिलीशरण गुप्त
D. अज्ञेय

200. मैथिलीशरण गुप्त की पद्य रचना है–
A. किसान
B. स्वर्गीय पीपा
C. प्रेम प्रबंध
D. रस कलश

201. 'पारिजात' महाकाव्य किसके द्वारा रचित है?
A. मैथिलीशरण गुप्त
B. सियाराम शरण गुप्त
C. हरिऔध
D. श्रीधर पाठक

202. प्रिय प्रवास आधारित है–
A. स्कंध पुराण पर
B. उपनिषद पर
C. महाभारत पर
D. भागवत पुराण पर

203. 'दिवस का अवसान समीप था' कहाँ से उद्धृत है?
A. प्रिय प्रवास से
B. करुणालय से
C. झरना से
D. युगांत से

204. सियाराम शरण गुप्त की रचना है–
A. मौर्य विजय
B. रसिक रहस्य
C. विष्णुप्रिया
D. स्वदेश संगीत

205. 'वीर क्षत्राणी' के रचनाकार हैं–
A. देवी प्रसाद पूर्ण
B. सियाराम शरण गुप्त
C. लाला भगवानदीन
D. रामचरित उपाध्याय

206. 'महामानव' प्रबंध काव्य किसने लिखा?
A. मोहन लाल महतो वियोगी
B. गुरुभक्त सिंह
C. मैथिलीशरण गुप्त
D. ठाकुर प्रसाद सिंह

207. 'छायावाद को स्थूल के प्रति सूक्ष्म का विद्रोह' किसने माना है–
A. आचार्य शुक्ल
B. हजारी प्रसाद द्विवेदी
C. नंद दुलारे वाजपेयी
D. डॉ॰ नगेन्द्र

208. छायावाद पर किसका प्रभाव है?
A. द्वैतवाद का
B. अद्वैतवाद का
C. विशिष्ट द्वैतवाद का
D. मार्क्सवाद का

209. किसे 'भारतीय आत्मा' कहा जाता है?
A. दिनकर
B. मैथिलीशरण गुप्त
C. प्रसाद
D. माखनलाल चतुर्वेदी

210. 'उच्छ्वास' किसका काव्य संग्रह है?
A. प्रसाद
B. निराला
C. हरिऔध
D. पंत

211. छायावाद की प्रथम कृति का नाम है–
A. आँसू
B. गुंजन
C. झरना
D. पल्लव

212. रजत शिखर और शिल्पी किसके द्वारा लिखे गए?
A. निराला द्वारा
B. प्रसाद द्वारा
C. पंत द्वारा
D. महादेवी वर्मा

213. 'ग्रंथि' काव्य संग्रह के रचयिता हैं–
A. निराला
B. पंत
C. मैथिलीशरण गुप्त
D. प्रसाद

214. 'चित्रलेखा' के रचयिता हैं–
A. चन्द्रधर शर्मा 'गुलेरी' B. भगवती चरण वर्मा
C. जैनेन्द्र D. प्रसाद

215. बच्चन जी की प्रमुख काव्य कृति है–
A. निशा निमंत्रण B. अभिशाप
C. चित्राधार D. महाराणा का महत्व

216. 'सृजन के क्षण' किसका प्रमुख काव्य है?
A. अज्ञेय B. मुक्तिबोध
C. भगवतीचरण वर्मा D. दिनकर

217. 'महाराणा का महत्व' किसकी रचना है?
A. निराला B. प्रसाद
C. पंत D. केदारनाथ अग्रवाल

218. 'हिमकिरीटिनी' किसका प्रसिद्ध काव्य संग्रह है?
A. धूमिल B. आरसी प्रसाद सिंह
C. माखनलाल चतुर्वेदी D. दिनकर

219. 'उर्मिला' किसका काव्य संग्रह है?
A. प्रेमचंद B. भारतेंदु
C. मैथिलीशरण गुप्त D. नवीन जी

220. द्वन्द्व गीत किसका काव्य संग्रह है?
A. जगन्नाथ प्रसाद मिलिन्द B. दिनकर
C. माखनलाल चतुर्वेदी D. देवराज दिनेश

221. 'इतिहास के आँसू' काव्य संग्रह के रचयिता हैं–
A. दिनकर B. माखनलाल चतुर्वेदी
C. मैथिलीशरण गुप्त D. हरिवंश राय बच्चन

222. 'स्वर्णोदय' और 'कर्ण' किसका काव्य संग्रह है?
A. हरिऔध B. श्रीधर पाठक
C. मुक्तिबोध D. केदारनाथ मिश्र

223. 'ऋतुम्भरा' किसका काव्य संग्रह है?
A. माखन लाल चतुर्वेदी B. प्रसाद
C. सुभद्रा कुमारी चौहान D. दिनकर

224. 'मेघगीत' व 'अवन्तिका' किसका काव्य संग्रह है?
A. देवकी नंदन विभव B. जानकी वल्लभ शास्त्री
C. महेश चंद प्रसाद D. सुभद्रा कुमारी चौहान

225. 'रूप रश्मि' किसका काव्य संग्रह है?
A. हरिकृष्ण B. शम्भूनाथ सिंह
C. देवकी नंदन विभव D. नवीन

226. कवि और उनके काव्य संग्रह को सुमेलित करें–

कवि	काव्य संग्रह
(*i*) नरेन्द्र शर्मा	(*a*) प्रवास के गीत
(*ii*) उपेन्द्रनाथ 'अश्क'	(*b*) उर्मियां
(*iii*) विद्यावती कोकिल	(*c*) कुसुमांजलि
(*iv*) देवकी नंदन विभव	(*d*) सुहागिन

कूट :

	(*i*)	(*ii*)	(*iii*)	(*iv*)
A.	(*a*)	(*b*)	(*c*)	(*d*)
B.	(*d*)	(*a*)	(*c*)	(*b*)
C.	(*a*)	(*b*)	(*d*)	(*c*)
D.	(*b*)	(*d*)	(*c*)	(*a*)

227. 'आधुनिक कवि' किसका काव्य संग्रह है?
A. दिनकर B. भारतेन्दु
C. हरिऔध D. उपेन्द्रनाथ 'अश्क'

228. पेरिस में प्रगतिशील लेखक संघ की स्थापना कब हुई?
A. 1931 ई॰ B. 1932 ई॰
C. 1934 ई॰ D. 1935 ई॰

229. निराला की भिक्षुक, विधवा और बादल कविताएँ संग्रहीत हैं–
A. अनामिका में B. परिमल में
C. गीतिका में D. तुलसीदास में

230. 'मधुकण' किसका काव्य संग्रह है?
A. दिनकर B. भगवती चरण वर्मा
C. पंत D. प्रसाद

231. कालक्रम से हिन्दी के प्रथम प्रगतिवादी कवि हैं–
A. केदारनाथ अग्रवाल B. रांगेय राघव
C. रामेश्वर करूण D. रामविलास शर्मा

232. कवि और उनके द्वारा रचित काव्य संग्रह को सुमेलित करें।

कवि	काव्य संग्रह
(*i*) केदारनाथ अग्रवाल	(*a*) युगधारा
(*ii*) नागार्जुन	(*b*) रूप तरंग
(*iii*) रामविलास शर्मा	(*c*) नींद के बादल
(*iv*) शिवमंगल सिंह	(*d*) कल्लोल

कूट :

	(*i*)	(*ii*)	(*iii*)	(*iv*)
A.	(*a*)	(*b*)	(*d*)	(*c*)
B.	(*a*)	(*c*)	(*b*)	(*d*)
C.	(*d*)	(*a*)	(*c*)	(*b*)
D.	(*b*)	(*c*)	(*a*)	(*d*)

233. 'अजेय खण्डहर' काव्य संग्रह है–
A. रांगेय राघव B. नागार्जुन
C. रामविलास शर्मा D. माखनलाल चतुर्वेदी

234. 'दूब के आंसू' किसका काव्य संग्रह है?
A. रणजीत B. सुदर्शन
C. कमलेश D. मुक्तिबोध

235. 'नई कविता' नाम का प्रचार किया–
A. कमलेश ने B. डॉ॰ जगदीश गुप्त ने
C. हरिनारायण विद्रोही D. अज्ञेय ने

236. 'नई कविता' पत्रिका का संपादन वर्ष है–
A. 1952 ई॰ B. 1953 ई॰
C. 1954 ई॰ D. 1955 ई॰

237. नकेनवादी परम्परा के प्रतिनिधि कवि हैं–
A. नलिन विलोचन शर्मा B. केसरी कुमार
C. नरेश मेहता D. उपर्युक्त सभी

238. प्रतीकवाद की स्थापना कहाँ हुई?
A. इटली B. फ्रांस
C. जर्मनी D. यूनान

239. बिम्बवाद की स्थापना हुई–
A. इंग्लैंड B. यूनान
C. जर्मनी D. फ्रांस

240. दादावाद के विकसित रूप को कहते हैं–
A. प्रयोगवाद B. यथार्थवाद
C. अतियथार्थवाद D. आदर्शवाद

241. 'भग्नदूत' किसका काव्य संग्रह है?
A. मुक्तिबोध B. अज्ञेय
C. माखन लाल चतुर्वेदी D. कमलेश

242. 'मंजीर' काव्य संग्रह के रचयिता हैं–
A. प्रयाग नारायण त्रिपाठी B. दिनकर
C. गिरिजा कुमार माथुर D. रामस्वरूप चतुर्वेदी

243. 'सात गीत वर्ष' किसका काव्य संग्रह है?
A. गिरिजा कुमार माथुर B. नलिन विलोचन
C. लक्ष्मीकांत वर्मा D. धर्मवीर भारती

244. 'जागते रहो' किसका काव्य-संग्रह है?
A. गिरिजा कुमार माथुर B. केदारनाथ अग्रवाल
C. भारतभूषण अग्रवाल D. दिनकर

245. नीचे कवि और उसके काव्य संग्रह को सुमेलित करें।

कवि	काव्य संग्रह
(*i*) शमशेर	(*a*) मेपल
(*ii*) डॉ॰ रघुवीर सहाय	(*b*) कुछ कविताएँ, कुछ और कविताएँ
(*iii*) दुष्यंत कुमार	(*c*) लोग भूल गए हैं
(*iv*) प्रभाकर माचवे	(*d*) सूर्य का स्वागत

कूट :

	(*i*)	(*ii*)	(*iii*)	(*iv*)
A.	(*a*)	(*b*)	(*d*)	(*c*)
B.	(*b*)	(*c*)	(*a*)	(*d*)
C.	(*d*)	(*b*)	(*c*)	(*a*)
D.	(*b*)	(*c*)	(*d*)	(*a*)

246. 'चन्द्रगुप्त मौर्य' रचना की–
A. बालकृष्ण शर्मा B. श्याम नारायण प्रसाद
C. नटवर लाल सनेही D. राम खेलावन

247. 'संशय की एक रात' के रचनाकार हैं–
A. नवीन B. नरेश मेहता
C. दिनकर D. मुक्तिबोध

248. 'दिग्विजय' के रचयिता हैं–
A. अरूण पोद्धार B. आचार्य तुलसी
C. कमलेश D. बलदेव प्रसाद मिश्र

249. नीचे रचनाकार और रचनाओं को सुमेलित करें–

रचनाकार	रचना
(*i*) नागार्जुन	(*a*) सुवर्णा
(*ii*) नरेन्द्र शर्मा	(*b*) भस्मांकुर
(*iii*) परमानंद	(*c*) उत्तरायण
(*iv*) रामकुमार वर्मा	(*d*) निष्कासिका

कूट :

	(*i*)	(*ii*)	(*iii*)	(*iv*)
A.	(*b*)	(*a*)	(*c*)	(*d*)
B.	(*b*)	(*a*)	(*d*)	(*c*)
C.	(*a*)	(*d*)	(*c*)	(*b*)
D.	(*c*)	(*a*)	(*d*)	(*b*)

250. नीचे रचनाकार और रचनाओं को सुमेलित करें–

रचनाकार	रचना
(*i*) नरेश मेहता	(*a*) सत्यकाम
(*ii*) सुमित्रानंदन पंत	(*b*) प्रणभंग
(*iii*) दिनकर	(*c*) महाप्रस्थान
(*iv*) भारतभूषण अग्रवाल	(*d*) अग्निलीक

कूट :

	(*i*)	(*ii*)	(*iii*)	(*iv*)
A.	(*a*)	(*b*)	(*c*)	(*d*)
B.	(*b*)	(*a*)	(*d*)	(*c*)
C.	(*a*)	(*d*)	(*c*)	(*b*)
D.	(*c*)	(*a*)	(*d*)	(*b*)

251. नीचे दिए गए रचनाकार और रचनाओं को सुमेलित करें–

रचनाकार	रचना
(*i*) भवानी प्रसाद मिश्र	(*a*) कालजयी
(*ii*) पंत	(*b*) पुरूषोत्तम राम
(*iii*) नरेंद्र शर्मा	(*c*) द्रौपदी
(*iv*) केदार नाथ मिश्र	(*d*) ऋतुम्भरा

कूट :

	(*i*)	(*ii*)	(*iii*)	(*iv*)
A.	(*a*)	(*d*)	(*c*)	(*b*)
B.	(*a*)	(*b*)	(*d*)	(*c*)
C.	(*c*)	(*a*)	(*d*)	(*b*)
D.	(*a*)	(*b*)	(*c*)	(*d*)

252. 'सारथी' के रचनाकार हैं–
A. अनूप शर्मा B. भारतभूषण अग्रवाल
C. राम गोपाल शर्मा D. नरेन्द्र शर्मा

253. नीचे रचनाकारों और रचनाओं को सुमेलित करें?

रचनाकार	रचना
(*i*) बालकृष्ण शर्मा नवीन	(*a*) कालजयी (प्रबंध काव्य)
(*ii*) देवेन्द्र शर्मा	(*b*) प्राण अपर्ण
(*iii*) उपेन्द्रनाथ 'अश्क'	(*c*) सुनंदा (प्रबंध काव्य)
(*iv*) सियाराम शरण गुप्त	(*d*) चांदनी रात

कूट :

	(i)	(ii)	(iii)	(iv)
A.	(a)	(b)	(d)	(c)
B.	(b)	(a)	(d)	(c)
C.	(c)	(a)	(d)	(b)
D.	(d)	(b)	(a)	(c)

254. 'नई कविता' के प्रमुख कवि हैं-
A. दिनकर
B. प्रसाद
C. निराला
D. अज्ञेय

255. नवगीत के प्रवर्तन का श्रेय किसे है?
A. राजेन्द्र प्रसाद सिंह
B. अज्ञेय
C. डॉ॰ देवराज
D. शमशेर

256. प्रज्ञा नामक साहित्यिक संस्था है–
A. कोलकाता में
B. इलाहाबाद में
C. दिल्ली में
D. मेरठ में

257. रंगायन संस्था है–
A. मुम्बई में
B. कोलकाता में
C. दिल्ली में
D. हैदराबाद में

258. साहित्यिक संस्था कहाँ है?
A. मुम्बई
B. दिल्ली
C. बनारस
D. कोलकाता

259. नवगीत परम्परा में सर्वाधिक प्रसिद्धि किसे मिली?
A. राजेन्द्र प्रसाद सिंह
B. अज्ञेय
C. नीरज
D. इनमें से कोई नहीं

260. नीचे दिए गए कवि और उनके काव्य संग्रह को सुमेलित करें।

कवि	काव्य संग्रह
(i) नीरज	(a) संघर्ष
(ii) रवीन्द्र भ्रमर	(b) सोन मछरी मन बसो
(iii) राजेन्द्र प्रसाद सिंह	(c) मिट्टी बोलती है
(iv) रमेश रंजक	(d) संजीवनी कहाँ

कूट :

	(i)	(ii)	(iii)	(iv)
A.	(a)	(b)	(c)	(d)
B.	(a)	(d)	(b)	(c)
C.	(b)	(c)	(a)	(d)
D.	(a)	(b)	(d)	(c)

261. भाषा किसका साधन है?
A. लिखने का
B. बोलने का
C. अध्ययन का
D. अभिव्यक्ति का

262. भाषा—
A. जड़ होती है
B. विकासोन्मुख होती है
C. बोधगम्य होती है
D. उपर्युक्त तीनों

263. भाषा में किन शब्दों का बाहुल्य होता है?
A. तत्सम
B. तद्भव
C. विदेशी
D. लोक व्यवहार के

264. हिन्दी के विकास के आदिकाल में इस पर किसका प्रभाव रहा?
A. संस्कृत का
B. देशज शब्दों का
C. ब्रज भाषा का
D. अपभ्रंश का

265. खड़ी बोली का विकास कब हुआ?
A. आधुनिक युग में
B. मध्य युग में
C. आदिकाल में
D. उपर्युक्त में से कोई भी नहीं

266. अपभ्रंश भाषा का व्याकरण किसने लिखा?
A. हेमचन्द्र
B. चन्द्रनाथ
C. उमानाथ
D. धर्मेन्द्र

267. निम्नलिखित में से कौन-सी बिहारी बोली है?
A. ब्रज
B. मैथिली
C. बुन्देली
D. अवधी

268. भाषा को बोलने में किसका प्रयोग किया जाता है?
A. लिपि का
B. ध्वनियों का
C. दोनों का
D. दोनों में से कोई भी नहीं

269. व्याकरण—
A. भाषा की लिपि निर्धारित करता है
B. भाषा को सुबोध बनाता है
C. भाषा का रूप निर्धारित करता है
D. भाषा के वर्णों का अध्ययन करता है

270. वर्ण—
A. स्वर हैं
B. व्यंजन हैं
C. ध्वनियाँ हैं
D. उच्चारण हैं

271. हिन्दी में कितने वर्ण हैं?
A. 56
B. 26
C. 44
D. 36

272. स्वर/स्वरों—
A. मूल ध्वनियाँ हैं
B. को किसी अन्य ध्वनि की सहायता के बिना उच्चरित किया जा सकता है
C. की संख्या 11 है
D. उपरोक्त सभी

273. जिन स्वरों के उच्चारण में 'अ' के उच्चारण के बराबर समय लगता है, उन्हें क्या कहते हैं?
A. दीर्घ स्वर
B. ह्रस्व स्वर
C. प्लुत स्वर
D. पूर्ण स्वर

274. संयुक्त स्वर का एक उदाहरण है—
A. आ
B. अ
C. इ
D. उ

275. क् + ष =
A. श
B. क्ष
C. ष
D. उपर्युक्त में से कोई नहीं

276. व्यंजन तीन प्रकार के होते हैं–

(i) स्पर्श, (ii) अन्तस्थ और (iii) ....

A. ऊष्म B. कन्ठ्य

C. दन्तोष्ठ D. नासिका

277. त, थ, द, ध, का उच्चारण—

A. दाँतों के साथ जिह्वा के मेल से होता है

B. कंठ और ओठों के मेल से होता है

C. केवल ओठों से होता है

D. जीभ के प्रयोग के बिना होता है

278. एक या एक से अधिक वर्णों के संयोग से बनी ध्वनियों को क्या कहते हैं?

A. स्वर B. व्यंजन

C. शब्द D. रूढ़ि

279. व्युत्पत्ति के आधार पर शब्दों के तीन भेद होते हैं—

(i) रूढ़ि, (ii) यौगिक और (iii) ....

A. मिश्र B. योगरूढ़ि

C. तद्भव D. उपर्युक्त में से कोई भी नहीं

280. 'पाठशाला' शब्द किस वर्ग का है?

A. यौगिक B. रूढ़ि

C. योगरूढ़ि D. उपर्युक्त में से कोई भी नहीं

281. 'नीलकंठ' शब्द किस वर्ग का है?

A. यौगिक B. रूढ़ि

C. योगरूढ़ि D. उपर्युक्त में से कोई भी नहीं

282. जो शब्द संस्कृत के हैं और जिन्हें हिन्दी में ज्यों-का-त्यों इस्तेमाल किया जाता है, क्या कहलाते हैं?

A. तत्सम B. तद्भव

C. देशज D. उपर्युक्त में से कोई भी नहीं

283. 'अग्नि' शब्द किस वर्ग का है?

A. तत्सम B. तद्भव

C. देशज D. उपरोक्त में से कोई नहीं

284. संस्कृत मूल वाले शब्दों को जब हिन्दी में कुछ परिवर्तन के साथ इस्तेमाल किया जाता है, तो उन्हें क्या नाम दिया जाता है?

A. अविकारी B. तद्भव

C. तत्सम D. देशज

285. 'खेत' शब्द किस वर्ग का है?

A. देशज B. तत्सम

C. तद्भव D. विदेशी

286. काव्य में कितने स्थायी भाव प्रधान माने गए हैं?

A. पाँच B. सात

C. नौ D. ग्यारह

287. मन में जिसके प्रति भाव (स्थायी भाव) प्रकट होता है, इसे कहते हैं–

A. आलम्बन B. आश्रय

C. उद्दीपन D. संचारी भाव

288. संचारी भाव कितने माने गए हैं?

A. ग्यारह B. बाईस

C. तैंतीस D. सात

289. शृंगार रस का स्थायी भाव क्या है?

A. उत्साह B. शोक

C. रति D. विनोद

290. संचारी भाव

A. स्थायी भाव को पुष्ट करता है

B. स्थायी भाव के सहयोगी का काम करता है

C. अपना काम करने के बाद स्थायी भाव में ही लुप्त हो जाता है

D. उपरोक्त तीनों

291. रौद्र रस का स्थायी भाव क्या है?

A. शोक B. जुगुप्सा

C. क्रोध D. भय

292. वात्सल्य रस का स्थायी भाव क्या है?

A. स्नेह B. उत्साह

C. प्रेम D. जुगुप्सा

293. जिसके कारण हृदय में भाव प्रवृत्त होता है, वह क्या कहलाता है?

A. विभाव B. आलम्बन

C. उद्दीपन D. आश्रय

294. हास्य रस के कितने भेद हैं?

A. दो B. तीन

C. छह D. आठ

295. करुण रस का स्थायी भाव क्या है?

A. क्रोध B. भय

C. जुगुप्सा D. शोक

296. रस का आधार क्या है?

A. अनुभूति B. काव्य

C. संचारी भाव D. अलंकार

297. एक ओर अजगरहिं लखि एक ओर मृग राय।
विकल बटोही बीच ही परयौ मूरछा खाय।

उक्त पद में रस कौन-सा है?

A. करुण रस B. रौद्र रस

C. वीभत्स रस D. भयानक रस

298. जशोदा हरि पालने झुलावै।
हलरावै दुलरावै जोई सोई कछु गावै।

उक्त पद में रस कौन-सा है?

A. शृंगार रस B. वात्सल्य रस

C. वीभत्स रस D. वीर रस

299. 'क्या भाग रहा है भार देख?
तू मेरी ओर निहार देख
मैं त्याग चला निस्सार देख
अटकेगा मेरा कौन काम?

उक्त पद में रस कौन-सा है?

A. शांत रस B. वात्सल्य रस
C. रौद्र रस D. करुण रस

300. 'अखिल भुवन चर-अचर सब, हरि मुख में लखि मातु।
चकित भई गद्गद् वचन, विकसित दृग पुलकातु।'

उक्त पद में रस कौन-सा है?

A. शांत रस B. वात्सल्य रस
C. अदभुत रस D. वीभत्स रस

301. इसमें रस कौन-सा है–

'बरतस लालच लाल की मुरली धरी लुकाय।
सौंह करै, भौंहन हँसे, दैन कहै, नटिं जाय।।'

A. करुण रस B. हास्य रस
C. श्रृंगार रस D. रौद्र रस

302. 'सभय बिलोके लोग सब जानि जानकी भीर।
हृदय न हरप विषाद कछु बोले श्रीरघुवीर।।

उक्त पद में रस कौन-सा है?

A. शांत रस B. श्रृंगार रस
C. वीर रस D. करुण रस

303. वीर रस कितने प्रकार के होते हैं?

A. तीन B. चार
C. पाँच D. छह

304. रस की भांति भाव के भी शुद्ध रूप में न होने और किसी विकार या दोष से युक्त होने के कारण उसे कहा जाता है–

A. रसाभाव B. भावाभाव
C. भाव-सन्धि D. भाव सबलता

305. जहाँ किसी भाव के शांत होते ही सहसा किसी दूसरे भाव के उदय होने का वर्णन होता है, वहां–

A. भावोदय होता है B. भाव-संधि होती है
C. भावसबलता होती है D. रसाभाव होता है

306. 'चेतक के पीछे दो काल, पड़े हुए ये ले असि ढाल।
उसके पथ में उनको मार, पावन की अपनी करवान।'

उक्त पंक्तियों में क्या है?

A. भाव-संधि B. भावोदय
C. भाव-शांति D. भावाभास

307. जहाँ दो भावों का संचार एक ही साथ वर्णन किया जाए, वहाँ क्या होता है?

A. भावाभास B. रसाभाव
C. भाव-शांति D. भाव-संधि

308. जहाँ दो से अधिक परस्पर विरोधी व उदासीन भावों के गड्डमड्ड होने अथवा एक साथ उदय होने का भाव हो, वहाँ क्या होता है–

A. भावाभास B. भाव-संधि
C. भाव-शांति D. भावसबलता

309. रस में विरोध कितने प्रकार का माना जाता है?

A. दो B. तीन
C. चार D. पाँच

310. जो स्वर दो स्वरों के योग से उच्चारित होते हैं, वे क्या कहलाते हैं?

A. ह्रस्व B. दीर्घ
C. व्यंजन D. गुरु

311. स्वर के उच्चारण में जो समय लगता है, उस अवधि को क्या कहते हैं?

A. मात्रा B. ह्रस्व
C. लघु D. वर्ण

312. लघु वर्ण की कितनी मात्रा होती है?

A. एक B. दो
C. चार D. पाँच

313. गुरु वर्ण की कितनी मात्रा होती है?

A. एक B. दो
C. चार D. तीन

314. 'मान्धाता' शब्द में तीनों मात्राएँ क्या हैं?

A. लघु B. गुरु
C. ह्रस्व D. दीर्घ

315. छंदों में प्रवाह होना चाहिए, जिससे पढ़ने में रुकावट न हो। इस प्रवाह को क्या कहते हैं?

A. क्रम B. यति
C. गण D. गति

316. चरणों में रुकावट, विराम, विश्राम को क्या कहते हैं?

A. गण B. क्रम
C. गति D. यति

317. छंद में गण शब्द का क्या तात्पर्य है?

A. दो अक्षरों का समूह B. तीन अक्षरों का समूह
C. पाँच अक्षरों का समूह D. छह अक्षरों का समूह

318. छंदों में त्रि-वर्ण के कितने समूह हैं?

A. तीन B. चार
C. सात D. आठ

319. छंद के दो या चार चरणों के अन्त में जब कोई एक स्वर आता है, तब उस अक्षर की एकता को क्या कहते हैं?

A. यति B. गति
C. क्रम D. तुक

320. छंदों के कितने भेद हैं?

A. दो B. तीन
C. चार D. आठ

321. चौपाई छंद के एक चरण में कितनी मात्राएँ होती हैं?
A. 16 B. 14
C. 17 D. 13

322. 'खंजन मंजु तिरीछे नयननि, निज पति कहेऊ तिन्हहि सिय सयननि।'
प्रस्तुत छंद क्या है?
A. चौपाई B. सोरठा
C. दोहा D. रोला

323. वर्णों के अनुसार गणों का मिलान कीजिए तथा दिए गए कूट की सहायता से सही उत्तर का चयन कीजिए–

गण	वर्ण
(*a*) रगण	1. सावन
(*b*) तगण	2. सौतेला
(*c*) भगण	3. साधना
(*d*) मगण	4. साकार

कूट :

	(*a*)	(*b*)	(*c*)	(*d*)
A.	3	4	1	2
B.	1	2	4	3
C.	1	2	3	4
D.	3	4	2	1

324. वर्णों के अनुसार गणों का मिलान कीजिए तथा दिए गए कूट की सहायता से सही उत्तर का चयन कीजिए–

गण	वर्ण
(*a*) नगण	1. सुभाषा
(*b*) यगण	2. सुजाता
(*c*) जगण	3. सरिता
(*d*) सगण	4. सरल

कूट :

	(*a*)	(*b*)	(*c*)	(*d*)
A.	2	1	4	3
B.	4	2	1	3
C.	1	2	3	4
D.	3	4	2	1

325. मगण गण में गण का क्या लक्षण है?
A. पहला वर्ण गुरु B. बीच वर्ण गुरु
C. अन्त वर्ण गुरु D. तीनों वर्ण गुरु

326. तगण गण में गण का क्या लक्षण है?
A. अन्त का वर्ण लघु B. बीच का वर्ण लघु
C. तीनों वर्ण लघु D. पहला वर्ण लघु

327. जगण गण में गण का क्या लक्षण है?
A. बीच का वर्ण लघु B. बीच का वर्ण गुरु
C. अन्त का वर्ण लघु D. अन्त का वर्ण गुरु

328. निम्न में अर्द्धमात्रिक छद कौन-सा है?
A. दोहा B. रोला
C. सोरठा D. चौपाई

329. निम्न में अर्द्धसममात्रिक छंद कौन-सा है?
A. दोहा B. रोला
C. सोरठा D. कुण्डलिया

330. छंदों में विषम चरणों से तात्पर्य है–
A. पहला और दूसरा चरण
B. दूसरा और तीसरा चरण
C. पहला और चौथा चरण
D. पहला और तीसरा चरण

उत्तरमाला

1	**2**	**3**	**4**	**5**	**6**	**7**	**8**	**9**	**10**
C	C	A	B	C	D	B	C	A	A
11	**12**	**13**	**14**	**15**	**16**	**17**	**18**	**19**	**20**
C	A	C	D	D	A	D	C	C	A
21	**22**	**23**	**24**	**25**	**26**	**27**	**28**	**29**	**30**
A	D	A	D	D	B	D	B	D	D
31	**32**	**33**	**34**	**35**	**36**	**37**	**38**	**39**	**40**
D	D	B	D	D	D	D	C	B	D
41	**42**	**43**	**44**	**45**	**46**	**47**	**48**	**49**	**50**
B	D	D	D	A	C	D	A	D	D
51	**52**	**53**	**54**	**55**	**56**	**57**	**58**	**59**	**60**
C	C	D	A	B	A	A	A	D	B
61	**62**	**63**	**64**	**65**	**66**	**67**	**68**	**69**	**70**
C	A	B	B	D	D	B	A	A	A
71	**72**	**73**	**74**	**75**	**76**	**77**	**78**	**79**	**80**
C	A	B	D	D	D	D	D	A	C
81	**82**	**83**	**84**	**85**	**86**	**87**	**88**	**89**	**90**
A	C	A	A	B	B	A	A	C	D

91	92	93	94	95	96	97	98	99	100
D	D	D	C	A	D	A	C	C	B
101	102	103	104	105	106	107	108	109	110
B	B	C	B	B	D	B	D	D	B
111	112	113	114	115	116	117	118	119	120
D	A	C	D	A	B	A	A	D	C
121	122	123	124	125	126	127	128	129	130
C	D	A	C	D	D	D	A	D	D
131	132	133	134	135	136	137	138	139	140
C	C	D	A	C	C	A	A	C	C
141	142	143	144	145	146	147	148	149	150
D	D	B	C	C	D	C	B	D	B
151	152	153	154	155	156	157	158	159	160
A	B	C	B	C	D	A	B	A	C
161	162	163	164	165	166	167	168	169	170
B	D	A	C	B	C	A	C	B	D
171	172	173	174	175	176	177	178	179	180
B	C	A	D	D	B	C	B	D	B
181	182	183	184	185	186	187	188	189	190
D	C	D	C	D	A	A	C	D	D
191	192	193	194	195	196	197	198	199	200
B	D	B	B	C	B	A	D	A	A
201	202	203	204	205	206	207	208	209	210
C	D	A	A	C	D	D	B	D	D
211	212	213	214	215	216	217	218	219	220
C	C	B	B	A	A	B	C	D	B
221	222	223	224	225	226	227	228	229	230
A	D	C	B	B	C	C	D	B	B
231	232	233	234	235	236	237	238	239	240
C	B	A	C	B	C	D	B	A	C
241	242	243	244	245	246	247	248	249	250
B	C	D	C	D	D	B	C	B	C
251	252	253	254	255	256	257	258	259	260
D	C	B	D	A	C	A	D	C	D
261	262	263	264	265	266	267	268	269	270
D	B	D	D	A	A	B	B	C	C
271	272	273	274	275	276	277	278	279	280
C	D	B	A	B	A	A	C	B	A
281	282	283	284	285	286	287	288	289	290
C	A	A	B	C	C	A	C	C	D
291	292	293	294	295	296	297	298	299	300
C	A	C	C	D	A	D	B	A	C
301	302	303	304	305	306	307	308	309	310
B	C	B	B	A	B	D	D	B	B
311	312	313	314	315	316	317	318	319	320
A	A	B	B	D	D	B	D	D	C
321	322	323	324	325	326	327	328	329	330
A	A	A	B	D	A	B	A	C	D

❑❑❑

QUANTITATIVE APTITUDE

NUMBER SYSTEM

1. There are four numbers A, B, C and D. Average of the first three *i.e.*, A, B and C is 15 and that of B, C and D is 16. If the last number, *i.e.*, D is 19, then the first number is—

A. 15 B. 16
C. 17 D. 18

2. Of the three numbers, the first is twice the second and thrice the third. If the average of three is 22, the three numbers are—

A. 12, 18, 36
B. 18, 12, 36
C. 36, 12, 18
D. 36, 18, 12

3. If a person is standing on the sixth number in the queue from both the ends, the total persons in the queue are—

A. 9 B. 11
C. 12 D. 13

4. A number 'x' when multiplied by 5 and added to three times its own gives 64, the number is—

A. 8 B. 12
C. 14 D. 18

5. A number which when multiplied by 11 is as much above 180 as it was originally below it. The number is—

A. 25 B. 30
C. 40 D. 45

6. The sum of a number and its reciprocal is thrice the difference of the number and its reciprocal. Find the number.

A. $\sqrt{2}$ B. $\sqrt{3}$
C. $\sqrt{5}$ D. $\sqrt{7}$

7. A boy was asked to find $\frac{7}{9}$ of a fraction. He made a mistake of dividing the fraction by $\frac{7}{9}$ and so got an answer which exceeded the correct answer by $\frac{8}{21}$. Find the correct answer.

A. $\frac{2}{3}$ B. $\frac{5}{7}$
C. $\frac{7}{12}$ D. $\frac{7}{15}$

8. There are 408 boys and 312 girls in a school, which are to be divided into equal sections of either boys or girls alone. Find the maximum number of boys or girls that can be placed in a section. Also find the total number of sections thus formed.

A. 10, 20 B. 24, 30
C. 24, 40 D. 30, 30

9. The sum of all possible two-digit number formed from three different one-digit natural numbers, when divided by the sum of the original three numbers is equal to—

A. 11 B. 18
C. 22 D. 36

10. There are four prime numbers written in ascending order. The product of the first three is 385 and that of the last three is 1001. The last number is—

A. 19 B. 17
C. 13 D. 11

11. If the number 357 ★ 25 ★ is divisible by both 3 and 5, then the missing digits in the unit's place and thousandth place respectively are—

A. 0, 4 B. 5, 4
C. 5, 6 D. 0, 6

12. The difference between two numbers is 1365. When the larger number is divided by the smaller one, the quotient is 6 and the remainder is 15. The smaller number is:

A. 360 B. 295
C. 270 D. 240

13. When a number is divided by 31, the remainder is 29. When the same number is divided by 16, what will be the remainder?

A. 15 B. 13
C. 11 D. Data inadequate

14. In dividing a number by 585, a student applied the method of short division. He divided the number successively by 5, 9 and 13 (factor of 585) and got the remainders 4, 8 and 12. If he had divided the number by 585, the remainder would have been:

A. 584 B. 292
C. 144 D. 24

15. When a number divided by 6 leaves a remainder 3. When the square of the same number is divided by 6, the remainder is:

A. 3 B. 2
C. 1 D. zero

ANSWERS

1	2	3	4	5	6	7	8	9	10
B	D	B	A	B	A	C	B	C	C
11	**12**	**13**	**14**	**15**					
C	C	D	A	A					

EXPLANATORY ANSWERS

1. $\dfrac{A+B+C}{3} = 15,$

or, $A + B + C = 15 \times 3 = 45$ ... (*i*)

$\dfrac{B+C+D}{3} = 16,$

or $B + C + D = 48$ ... (*ii*)

$D = 19$

$\therefore$ $B + C + 19 = 48$ or, $B + C = 48 - 19 = 29$

But, $A + B + C = 45$

Putting the value of $B + C = 29$ in the above equation (*i*), we get $A + 29 = 45$

$\therefore A = 45 - 29 = 16.$

2. Let the third number $= x$

$\therefore$ First number $= 3x$

Second number $= \dfrac{3x}{2}$

$\therefore \dfrac{1}{3}\left[x+3x+\dfrac{3x}{2}\right] = 22 \Rightarrow \dfrac{11}{2}x = 66$

$\Rightarrow x = \dfrac{66\times 2}{11} = 12 =$ Third number,

$12 \times 3 = 36 =$ First number,

$\dfrac{12\times 3}{2} = 18 =$ Second number.

3. If the person is standing at sixth number in the queue from both sides, that means there are five persons ahead and five persons behind him. Hence, total number of persons in the queue is $5 + 1 + 5 = 11$.

4. $5 \times x + 3x = 64 \quad \Rightarrow 8x = 64$

$\therefore \quad x = \dfrac{64}{8} = 8.$

5. Let the number is x

$\therefore \quad 180 - x = 11x - 180$

$\Rightarrow \quad 180 + 180 = 11x + x$

$\Rightarrow \quad 360 = 12x,$

$\Rightarrow \quad x = \dfrac{360}{12} = 30.$

6. Let the no. $= x$ then its reciprocal $= \dfrac{1}{x}$.

By the question, $\left(x+\dfrac{1}{x}\right) = 3\left(x-\dfrac{1}{x}\right)$

$\Rightarrow \quad \dfrac{x^2+1}{x} = \dfrac{3\left(x^2-1\right)}{x}$

$\Rightarrow \quad x^2 + 1 = 3x^2 - 3$

$\Rightarrow \quad 3x^2 - x^2 = 3 + 1$

$\therefore \quad x = \sqrt{2}.$

7. Let the required fraction $= x$

then, by the question $x \div \dfrac{7}{9} - x \times \dfrac{7}{9} = \dfrac{8}{21}$

$\Rightarrow \quad x \times \dfrac{9}{7} - \dfrac{7x}{9} = \dfrac{8}{21}$

$\Rightarrow \quad \dfrac{32x}{63} = \dfrac{8}{21}$

$\Rightarrow \quad x = \dfrac{8}{21} \times \dfrac{63}{32} = \dfrac{3}{4}$

Hence, the correct answer $= \dfrac{3}{4} \times \dfrac{7}{9} = \dfrac{7}{12}$.

8.
```
312) 408(1
     312
     96) 312 (3
         288
         24) 96 (4
             96
             ×
```

$\therefore$ Maximum number of girls or boys that can be placed in a section = 24 and total number of such

section $= \dfrac{408}{24} + \dfrac{312}{24}$

$= 17 + 13 = 30$

9. Let three different one digit natural numbers be x, y and z.

Then, sum of all possible two digits numbers

$= (10x + y) + (10y + x) + (10x + z)$

$+ (10z + x) + (10y + z) + (10z + y)$

$= 22x + 22y + 22z = 22\,(x + y + z)$

Hence, required number = 22.

10. Let four prime numbers be a, b, c and d respectively.

Now, $\frac{abc}{bcd} = \frac{385}{1001}$

$\Rightarrow \quad \frac{c}{d} = \frac{5}{13}$

Hence, $a = 5$ and $d = 13$

11. 357 ★ 25 ★

For divisible by 5, the last digit must be either 0 or 5.

If last digit is 0, then other required digit will be 2 or 5 or 8

Hence, the numbers are (0, 2) or (0, 5) or (0, 8)

If last digit is 5, then other required digit will be 0 or 3 or 6 or 9

Hence, the numbers are (5, 0) or (5, 3) or (5, 6) or (5, 9)

So, correct option is (c).

12. Here, $(x + 1365) = 6x + 15$

$\Rightarrow 5x = 1350$

$\therefore \; x = \frac{1350}{5} = 270$

Hence, the smaller number = 270.

13. The number = $31x + 29$.

Here, given data is inadequate.

14.

5	a
9	$b - 4$
13	$c - 8$
	$1 - 12$

Now, $c = 13 \times 1 + 12 = 25$

$b = 9c + 8 = 9 \times 25 + 8 = 233$

$a = 5b + 4 = 5 \times 233 + 4$

$= 1165 + 4 = 1169$

$1169 = 585 \times 1 + 584$

Hence, required remainder = 584.

15. The number = $6x + 3$

Now, $(6x + 3)^2 = 36x^2 + 36x + 9$

$= (36x^2 + 36x + 6) + 3$

$= 6(6x^2 + 6x + 1) + 3$

Hence, required remainder = 3.

LCM AND HCF

1. The L.C.M. and H.C.F. of two numbers are 4284 and 32 respectively. If one of the numbers is 204, the other is

A. 672 B. 576
C. 676 D. 572

2. Two numbers are in the ratio of 8 : 15. If their H.C.F. is 4, the numbers are

A. 32 and 60 B. 16 and 30
C. 80 and 150 D. 64 and 120

3. The greatest number that will divide 366, 513 and 324 leaving the same remainder in each case is

A. 21 B. 18
C. 27 D. 42

4. The L.C.M. of two numbers is 45 times their H.C.F. If the sum of the L.C.M. and the H.C.F. of these two numbers is 1150 and one of the numbers is 125, then the other number is

A. 256 B. 225
C. 250 D. 255

5. The H.C.F. and the L.C.M. of two numbers are 50 and 250 respectively. On dividing one of these numbers by 2, 50 is obtained as quotient. The numbrs are

A. 100, 125 B. 80, 100
C. 125, 100 D. 200, 250

6. Three bells ring respectively at an interval of 15 seconds, 20 seconds and 24 seconds. If they ring continuously for 12 minutes then how many times, during this period, will they ring together?

A. 2 times B. 6 times
C. 5 times D. 3 times

7. If the sum of two numbers is 55 and the H.C.F. and L.C.M. of these numbers are 5 and 120 respectively. Find the sum of their reciprocals.

A. $\frac{120}{11}$ B. $\frac{11}{120}$

C. $\frac{601}{55}$ D. $\frac{55}{601}$

8. The LCM of two numbers is 48. The numbers are in the ratio of 2 : 3. The sum of the numbers is

A. 64 B. 40
C. 32 D. 28

9. Find the greatest number that will divide 43, 91 and 183 so as to leave the same remainder in each case.

A. 13 B. 9
C. 7 D. 4

10. The greatest possible length which can be used to measure exactly the length 7m, 3m 85cm, 12m 95 cm is

A. 42 cm B. 35 cm
C. 25 cm D. 15 cm

11. A, B and C start at the same time in the same direction to run around a circular park. A completes a round in 252 seconds, B in 308 seconds and C in 198 seconds, all starting at the same point. After what time will they meet again at the starting point?
A. 46 minutes 12 seconds
B. 45 minutes
C. 42 minutes 36 seconds
D. 26 minutes 18 seconds

12. Which of the following has most numbers of divisors?
A. 182 B. 176
C. 101 D. 99

13. Which is of the following is a co-primes?
A. (23, 92) B. (21, 35)
C. (18, 25) D. (16, 62)

14. Let N be the greatest number that will divide 1305, 4665 and 6905, leaving the same remainder in each case. Then find the sum of the digits in N.
A. 8 B. 6
C. 5 D. 4

15. The greatest number which one dividing 1657 and 2037 leaves remainder 6 and 5 respectively, is:
A. 305 B. 235
C. 127 D. 123

ANSWERS

1	2	3	4	5	6	7	8	9	10
A	A	A	B	A	B	B	B	D	B
11	**12**	**13**	**14**	**15**					
A	B	C	D	C					

EXPLANATORY ANSWERS

1. 1st number × 2nd number = LCM × HCF
$\therefore$ 204 × 2nd number = 4284 × 32
$\therefore$ 2nd number $= \frac{4284 \times 32}{204} = 672$
$\therefore$ 2nd number = 672

2. Let the numbers be $8x$ and $15x$
$8x = 2 \times 2 \times 2 \times x$
$15x = 3 \times 5 \times x$
$\therefore$ LCM of $8x$ and $15x = 2 \times 2 \times 2 \times x \times 3 \times 5 = 120x$
Now, 1st number × 2nd number = HCF × LCM
$\Rightarrow 8x \times 15x = 4 \times 120x$
$\Rightarrow 120x^2 = 4 \times 120x$
$\Rightarrow x = 4$
$\therefore$ Numbers are 8 × 4 = 32 and 15 × 4 = 60

3. Difference between 366 and 513 = 513 – 366 = 147
and difference between 513 and 324 = 513 – 324 = 189
$\therefore$ HCF of 147 and 189

```
147) 189 (1
     147
     × 42) 147 (3
           126
           × 21) 42 (2
                 42
                 ×
```

$\therefore$ The required largest number is 21.

4. LCM of the two numbers = 45 × HCF
and LCM + HCF = 1150
$\Rightarrow$ 45 × HCF + HCF = 1150
$\Rightarrow$ HCF(45 + 1) = 1150
$\Rightarrow$ HCF $= \frac{1150}{46} = 25$
$\therefore$ LCM = 45 × 25 = 1125
$\because$ 1st number × 2nd number = LCM × HCF
$\therefore$ 125 × 2nd number = 1125 × 25
$\therefore$ 2nd number $= \frac{1125 \times 25}{125} = 225.$

5. According to the condition of the problem, 50 is obtained on dividing one of the numbers by 2
$\therefore$ One of the numbers = 50 × 2 = 100
Now, 1st number × 2nd number = LCM × HCF
$\therefore$ 100 × 2nd number = 250 × 50
$\therefore$ 2nd number $= \frac{250 \times 50}{100} = 125$
Hence, numbers are 100 and 125.

6. LCM of 15, 20 and 24

5	15,	20,	24
4	3,	4,	24
3	3,	1,	6
	1,	1,	2

LCM = 5 × 4 × 3 × 2 = 120
$\because$ 12 minutes = 12 × 60 = 720 seconds
$\therefore$ Number of times the bells will ring together during 12 minutes
$= \frac{720}{120} = 6$ times.

7. Let the number be x and y.
Then, $x + y = 55$;
$xy = \text{HCF} \times \text{LCM} = 5 \times 120$
$\therefore$ Sum of their reciprocals

$$= \frac{1}{x} + \frac{1}{y} = \frac{x+y}{xy} = \frac{55}{5 \times 120} = \frac{11}{120}.$$

8. Let the two numbers be $2x$ and $3x$;
their LCM $= 6x$
Now, $6x = 48$ $\therefore$ $x = 8$
Hence, the numbers are $2 \times 8,\ 3 \times 8 = 16, 24$
Their sum $= 16 + 24 = 40$.

9.
```
2240) 3360 (1          1120) 5600 (5
      2240                   5600
      1120 ) 2240 (2         ×
             2240
              ×
```
Hence, N = HCF of 3360, 2240 and 5600 = 1120
Sum of digits in N = 1 + 1 + 2 + 0 = 4.

10. 7m = 700 cm;
3m 85 = 385 cm;
12m 95cm = 1295 cm
```
385) 700 (1
     385
     315) 385 (1
          315
           70) 315 (4
               280
                35 ) 70 (2
                     70
                     ×

35) 1295 (37
    105
     245
     245
      ×
```
Hence, required length = HCF of 700 cm, 385 cm, 1295 cm = 35 cm.

11.

2	252, 308, 198
2	126, 154, 99
3	63, 77, 99
3	21, 77, 33
7	7, 77, 11
11	1, 11, 11
	1, 1, 1

Hence, LCM $= 2 \times 2 \times 3 \times 3 \times 7 \times 11 = 2772$
Hence, A, B, C will meet again at the starting point after 2772 sec. = 46 min 12 sec.

12. ***Numbers*** ***Their divisors***
182 → 1, 2, 7, 13, 14, 26, 91 and 182
176 → 1, 2, 4, 8, 16, 22, 44, 88 and 176
101 → 1 and 101
99 → 1, 3, 9, 11, 33 and 99
Therefore, 176 has the most number of divisors.

13. HCF of 23 and 92 = 23
HCF of 21 and 35 = 7
HCF of 18 and 25 = 1
HCF of 16 and 62 = 2
Hence, 18 and 25 are co-prime numbers.

14. N = HCF of (4665 – 1305), (6905 – 4665) and (6905 – 1305)
= HCF of 3360, 2240 and 5600 = 112
Sum of digit of 1 + 1 + 2 = 4.

15. Required number = HCF of (1657 – 6) and (2037 – 5)
= HCF of 1651 and 2032 = 127.
```
1651) 2032 (1
      1651
       381) 1651 (4
            1524
             127) 381 (3
                  381
                   ×
```

AVERAGE

1. One-third of a certain journey was covered at the rate of 25 km per hour, one-fourth at the rate of 30 km per hour and the rest at the 50 km per hour. What is the average speed per hour for whole journey?

A. $33\frac{1}{3}$ kmph B. $44\frac{1}{4}$ kmph
C. $22\frac{1}{2}$ kmph D. 33 kmph

2. A batsman has a certain average of runs for 16 innings. In the 17th innings, he makes a score of 85 runs thereby increasing his average by 3. What is the average after the 17th inning?

A. 33 runs B. 34 runs
C. 37 runs D. 36 runs

3. The average of 6 observations is 12. A new seventh observation is included and the new average is decreased by 1. The seventh observation is

A. 1 B. 3
C. 5 D. 6

4. The average age of 30 students in a class is 12 years. The average age of a group of 5 of the students is 10 years and that of another group of 5 of them is 14 years. The average age of the remaining students is
A. 8 years B. 10 years
C. 12 years D. 14 years

5. Out of the three given numbers, the first number is twice the second and thrice the third. If the average of three numbers is 121, what is the difference between the first and third number?
A. 144 B. 77
C. 99 D. 132

6. If the average marks of three batches of 55, 60 and 45 students is 50, 55 and 60, then average marks of all the students is:
A. 55 B. 54
C. 54.68 D. 55.68

7. The average of 8 numbers is 20. The average of first two numbers is $15\frac{1}{2}$ and that of the next three is $21\frac{1}{3}$. If the sixth number is less than the seventh and eighth numbers by 4 and 7 respectively, then the eighth number is:
A. 27 B. 25
C. 22 D. 18

8. A pupil's marks were wrongly entered as 83 instead of 63. Due to that the average marks for the class got increased by half. What is the number of pupils in the class?
A. 73 B. 40
C. 40 D. 10

9. A cricketer whose bowling average is 12.4 runs per wicket takes 5 wickets for 26 runs and thereby decreases his average by 0.4. The number of wickets taken by him till the last match was:
A. 85 B. 80
C. 72 D. 64

10. The average weight of a class of 24 students is 35 kg. If the weight of the teacher is included, the average rises by 400 g. What is the weight of the teacher?
A. 55 kg B. 53 kg
C. 50 kg D. 45 kg

11. Nine men went to a hotel. Eight of them spent Rs. 3 for each over their meals and the ninth spent Rs. 2 more than the average expenditure of all the nine. What is the total money spent by them?
A. Rs. 29.25 B. Rs. 29.50
C. Rs. 29 D. Rs. 30

12. The average age of 24 students in a class is 10. If the teacher's age is included, the average increases by one. The age of the teacher is
A. 25 B. 30
C. 35 D. 40

13. The average of 5 consecutive even numbers A, B, C, D and E is 34. What is the product of B and D?
A. 1152 B. 1368
C. 1224 D. 1088

14. The average of 50 numbers is 30. If two numbers, 35 and 40 are discarded, then the average of the remaining numbers is nearly:
A. 29.68 B. 29.27
C. 28.78 D. 28.32

15. The average monthly salary of 20 employees of an organisation is Rs. 1500. If the manager's salary is added, then the average salary increases by Rs. 100. Find the manager's monthly salary?
A. Rs. 4800 B. Rs. 3600
C. Rs. 2400 D. Rs. 2000

ANSWERS

1	2	3	4	5	6	7	8	9	10
A	C	C	C	D	C	B	B	A	D
11	**12**	**13**	**14**	**15**					
A	C	A	A	B					

EXPLANATORY ANSWERS

1. Let the total distance covered during journey = 60 km

$\frac{1}{3}$ of the distance covered during journey

$$= 60 \times \frac{1}{3} = 20 \text{ km}$$

$\frac{1}{4}$ of the distance covered during journey

$$= \frac{1}{4} \times 60 = 15 \text{ km}$$

∴ The distance covered during the rest of journey = 60 – (20 + 15) = 25 km

Time taken to cover 20 km at 25 km/h

$$= \frac{20}{25} \text{ hours} = \frac{4}{5} \text{ hour}$$

Time taken to cover 15 km at 30 km/h

$$= \frac{15}{30} \text{ hours} = \frac{1}{2} \text{ hour}$$

Time taken to cover 25 km at 50 km/h

$$= \frac{25}{50} \text{ hours} = \frac{1}{2} \text{ hour}$$

$$\text{Total time taken} = \frac{4}{5} + \frac{1}{2} + \frac{1}{2}$$

$$= \frac{9}{5} \text{ hours}$$

$$\text{Hence average speed per hour} = 60 \div \frac{9}{5}$$

$$= \frac{60 \times 5}{9} = \frac{100}{3} \text{ km/h}$$

$$= 33\frac{1}{3} \text{ km/h}$$

2. Average increase in the score of 17 innings $= 3$ runs

Total increase in the score of 17 innings $= 3 \times 17 = 51$ runs

$\therefore$ His average of 16 innings $= 85 - 51 = 34$ runs

Hence, average after the 17th innings $= 34 + 3 = 37$ runs

3. Seventh observation $= (7 \times 11 - 6 \times 12) = 5$

4. Let, the required average age be x

Then, $5 \times 10 + 5 \times 14 + 20 \times x = 30 \times 12$

$\Rightarrow \quad 20x = 360 - 120$

$\Rightarrow \quad 20x = 240$

$\Rightarrow \quad x = 12$

5. Let the three numbers be x, $\frac{x}{2}$ and $\frac{x}{3}$ respectively,

$$\text{Now, } \frac{1}{3}\left(x + \frac{x}{2} + \frac{x}{3}\right) = 121$$

$$\Rightarrow \frac{11x}{6} = 121 \times 3$$

$$\therefore \ x = \frac{121 \times 3 \times 6}{11} = 198$$

$$\text{Hence, required difference} = x - \frac{x}{3} = \frac{2x}{3}$$

$$= \frac{2}{3} \times 198 = 132$$

6. Required average Marks

$$= \frac{55 \times 50 + 60 \times 55 + 45 \times 60}{55 + 60 + 45} = \frac{8750}{160} = 54.68$$

7. Let the sixth, seventh and eighth numbers are x, $x + 4$ and $x + 7$.

Sum of last three numbers

$$= 8 \times 20 - (2 \times \frac{31}{2} + 3 \times \frac{64}{3})$$

$\Rightarrow x + x + 4 + x + 7 = 160 - 95$

$\Rightarrow 3x + 11 = 65$

$\Rightarrow 3x = 54 \qquad \therefore x = 18$

New eighth number $= x + 7 = 18 + 7 = 25$

8. Let the total number of pupils in the class be x; then,

$$\frac{83 - 63}{x} = \frac{1}{2} \Rightarrow \frac{20}{x} = \frac{1}{2} \qquad \therefore x = 40$$

9. Let the number of wickets taken by him be x till the last match.

$$\text{Then, } \frac{x \times 12.4 + 26}{x + 5} = 12$$

$\Rightarrow 12.4x + 26 = 12x + 60$

$$\Rightarrow 0.4x = 34 \quad \therefore \ x = \frac{340}{4} = 85$$

10. Let the weight of the teacher be x kgs, then

$$\frac{24 \times 35 + x}{25} = 35.4$$

$\Rightarrow \ 840 + x = 885 \qquad \therefore \ x = 45$ kgs

12. Age of the teacher $= (25 \times 11 - 24 \times 10)$ years $= 35$ years

13. Let 5 consecutive even numbers A, B, C, D and E be x, $x + 2$, $x + 4$, $x + 6$ and $x + 8$ respectively.

$$\text{Now, } \frac{x + x + 2 + x + 4 + x + 6 + x + 8}{5} = 34$$

$\Rightarrow 5x + 20 = 170$

$\Rightarrow 5x = 150 \qquad \therefore x = 30$

Then, $B = x + 2 = 30 + 2 = 32$;

$D = x + 6 = 30 + 6 = 36$

Hence, their product $= 32 \times 36 = 1152$

14. The average of remaining 48 numbers

$$= \frac{50 \times 30 - (35 + 40)}{48} = \frac{1500 - 75}{48}$$

$$= \frac{1425}{48} = 29.68$$

15. Let manager's salary be Rs. x, then

$$\frac{20 \times 1500 + x}{21} = 1600$$

$\Rightarrow \ 30{,}000 + x = 33600$

$\therefore \ x =$ Rs. 3600

PROBLEMS BASED ON AGES

1. The ratio of ages of A and B is 3 : 11. After 3 years the ratio becomes 1 : 3. What are the ages of A and B?

A. 9 years, 33 years
B. 10 years, 40 years
C. 9 years, 27 years
D. None of these

2. Two years ago, the ratio of Ram's and Mohan's age was 3 : 2 and at present 7 : 5. What are their present ages?

A. 14 years, 10 years B. 15 years, 10 years
C. 13 years, 9 years D. None of these

3. The ages of Samir and Saurabh are in the ratio of 8 : 15 respectively. After 9 years the ratio of their ages will be 11 : 18. What is the difference between their ages in years?

A. 20 years B. 21 years
C. 22 years D. 24 years

4. The present age of father is 34 years more than that of his son. 12 years ago, father's age was 18 times the age of his son. The present age of son in years is:

A. 12 B. 14
C. 16 D. 18

5. A mother is 25 years older than her daughter. Five years ago, the age of the mother was 6 times the age of the daughter. What is the present age of mother?

A. 25 years B. 29 years
C. 32 years D. 35 years

6. The difference between the present ages of P and Q is 4 years. The ratio of their ages after 5 years will be 9 : 8. The present age of P is:

A. 24 years B. 30 years
C. 32 years D. None of these

7. Ten years ago, the age of Divya was half of the age of Namrata. If the ratio of present ages of both is 3 : 4, the sum of their present ages is:

A. 35 years B. 30 years
C. 25 years D. 18 years

8. The ratio between the present ages of A and B is 5 : 3 respectively. The ratio between A's age 4 years ago and B's age 4 years hence is 1 : 1. The ratio between A's age 4 years hence and B's age 4 years ago is:

A. 4 : 1 B. 3 : 1
C. 2 : 1 D. 1 : 3

9. Ram got married 8 years ago. His present age is $\frac{6}{5}$ times his age at the time of marriage. Ram's sister was 10 years younger to him at the time of his marriage. What is the present age of Ram's sister?

A. 40 years B. 38 years
C. 36 years D. 32 years

10. A father said to his son, "I was as old as you are at present at the time of your birth." If the father's age is 38 years now. Five years ago the age of son was:

A. 38 years B. 33 years
C. 19 years D. 14 years

ANSWERS

1	2	3	4	5	6	7	8	9	10
A	A	B	B	D	D	A	B	B	D

EXPLANATORY ANSWERS

1. Let the ages of A and B be $3x$ and $11x$ years; then

$$\frac{3x+3}{11x+3} = \frac{1}{3} \quad \Rightarrow \quad 9x + 9 = 11x + 3$$

$\Rightarrow 2x = 6 \quad \therefore \quad x = 3$

Hence, their present age, $3x = 3 \times 3 = 9$ years; $11x = 11 \times 3 = 33$ years

2. Let the present ages of Ram and Mohan are $7x$ and $5x$ years; then

$$\frac{7x-2}{5x-2} = \frac{3}{2} \quad \Rightarrow \quad 14x - 4 = 15x - 6 \quad \therefore x = 2$$

Hence, their present ages : $7 \times 2 = 14$ years and $5 \times 2 = 10$ years

3. Let the present ages of Samir and Saurabh are $8x$ and $15x$ years respectively; then

$$\frac{8x+9}{15x+9} = \frac{11}{18} \quad \Rightarrow \quad 144x + 162 = 165x + 99$$

$\Rightarrow 21x = 63 \quad \therefore \quad x = 3$

Hence, difference of their ages $= 15x - 8x = 7x$
$= 7 \times 3 = 21$ years

4. Let the present ages of father and his son be $x + 34$ and x years respectively; then
$18(x - 12) = x + 34 - 12$
$\Rightarrow 18x - 216 = x + 22$
$\Rightarrow 17x = 238 \quad \therefore x = 14$
Hence, present age of his son = 14 years

5. Let the present ages of mother and her daughter are $(x + 25)$ and x years respectively; then
$6(x - 5) = x + 25 - 5$
$\Rightarrow 6x - 30 = x + 20$
$\Rightarrow 5x = 50 \quad \therefore x = 10$
Hence, the age of the mother = 10 + 25
= 35 years

6. Let the present ages of P and Q be $(x + 4)$ and x years;
then, $\frac{x+4+5}{x+5} = \frac{9}{8} \Rightarrow 8x + 72$
$= 9x + 45 \quad \therefore x = 27$
Hence, present age of P = 27 + 4 = 31 years

7. Let the present ages of Divya and Namrata are $3x$ and $4x$ years respectively; then
$\frac{3x-10}{4x-10} = \frac{1}{2}$
$\Rightarrow 6x - 20 = 4x - 10$
$\Rightarrow 2x = 10 \quad \therefore x = 5$
Hence, sum of their ages = $3x + 4x = 7x$
= 7 × 5 = 35 years

8. Let the present ages of A and B are $5x$ and $3x$ years respectively; then,
$\frac{5x-4}{3x+4} = 1 \Rightarrow 5x - 4 = 3x + 4$
$\Rightarrow 2x = 8 \quad \therefore x = 4$
Hence, their present ages are 20 years and 12 years.
So, required ratio = (20 + 4) : (12 – 4)
= 24 : 8 = 3 : 1

9. Let the present age of Ram be x years; then
$\frac{x}{x-8} = \frac{6}{5} \Rightarrow 5x = 6x - 48$
$\therefore x = 48$
Hence, present age of Ram's sister
= 48 – 10 = 38 years.

10. Let the age of father was x years at the time of his son's birth, then present age of father and his son will be $2x$ and x years,
Now, $2x = 38 \quad \therefore x = 19$ years
Hence, 5 years ago the age of son was
19 – 5 = 14 years

CHAIN RULE

1. A fort has provision for 50 days. After 15 days a reinforcement of 150 men arrives and the provision now lasts 25 days. How many men were there in the fort?
A. 300 B. 225
C. 275 D. 200

2. In a fort there is provisions for 40 days for 275 persons. If after 16 days 125 persons leave the fort for how many more days the provisions will last?
A. 35 days B. 44 days
C. 45 days D. 53 days

3. 60 men could complete a work in 250 days. They worked together for 200 days. After that the work had to be stopped for 10 days due to bad weather. How many more men should be engaged to complete the work in time?
A. 20 B. 18
C. 15 D. 10

4. A contractor undertook to complete a project in 90 days and employed 60 men on it. After 60 days, he found that $\frac{3}{4}$ of the work has already been completed. How many men can he discharge so that the project may completed exactly on time?
A. 15 B. 20
C. 30 D. 40

5. A flagstaff 17.5 m high casts a shadow of length 40.25 m. The height of the building, which casts a shadow of length 28.75m under similar condition will be:
A. 21.25 m B. 17.5 m
C. 12.5 m D. 10 m

6. If 5 men or 9 women can do a piece of work in 19 days, then 3 men and 6 women will do the same work in how many days?
A. 21 B. 18
C. 15 D. 12

7. A certain number of men can finish a piece of work in 100 days. If there were 10 men less, it will take 10 days more for the work to be finished. How many men were there originally?
A. 110 B. 100
C. 82 D. 75

8. Some persons can do a piece of work in 12 days. Two times the number of such persons will do half of that work in:

A. 12 days B. 3 days
C. 6 days D. 4 days

9. 2 men and 7 boys can do a piece of work in 14 days; 3 men and 8 boys can do the same in 11 days. Then 8 men and 6 boys can do three times of this work in

A. 30 days B. 4 days
C. 21 days D. 18 days

10. If 3 men or 6 boys, working 7 hours a day can do a piece of work in 10 days; how many days will it take to complete a piece of work twice as large with 6 men and 2 boys working together for 8 hours a day?

A. 9 B. $8\frac{1}{2}$
C. $7\frac{1}{2}$ D. $6\frac{1}{2}$

11. If 15 men can do a certain amount of work in 20 days working 8 hours a day, in how many days will 10 men do three times the work working 6 hours a day?

A. 120 days B. 70 days
C. 100 days D. None of these

12. 40 men consume 60 kgs of rice in 15 days, then in how many days will 30 men consume 12 kgs of rice?

A. 9 days B. $6\frac{1}{4}$ days
C. 4 days D. $3\frac{1}{4}$ days

13. 56 men can complete a piece of work in 24 days. In how many days can 42 men complete the same piece of work?

A. 48 B. 32
C. 20 D. 16

14. Running at the same constant rate, 6 identical machines can produce a total of 270 bottles per minute. At this rate, how many bottles could 10 such machines produce in 4 minutes?

A. 1400 B. 1600
C. 1800 D. 2000

15. 400 persons, working 9 hours a day complete $\frac{1}{4}th$ of the work in 10 days. The number of additional persons, working 8 hours a day, required to complete the remaining work in 20 days, is:

A. 275 B. 250
C. 675 D. 200

ANSWERS

1	2	3	4	5	6	7	8	9	10
B	B	C	B	C	C	A	B	C	C
11	**12**	**13**	**14**	**15**					
A	C	B	C	C					

EXPLANATORY ANSWERS

1.

Days	Men
35 ↑	x ↓
25	$x + 150$

$$\Rightarrow \frac{x+150}{x} = \frac{35}{25} \quad \Rightarrow 1 + \frac{150}{x} = \frac{35}{25}$$

$$\Rightarrow \frac{150}{x} = \frac{10}{25}$$

$$\therefore x = \frac{25}{10} \times 150 = 375$$

Required number of men = 375 – 150 = 225

2.

Persons	Days
275 ↑	24 ↓
150	x

$$\Rightarrow \frac{x}{24} = \frac{275}{150} \quad \therefore x = \frac{275}{150} \times 24 = 44 \text{ days}$$

3.

Days	Men
50 ↑	60 ↓
40	x

$$\Rightarrow \frac{x}{60} = \frac{50}{40} \quad \therefore x = \frac{50}{40} \times 60 = 75 \text{ men}$$

Hence, number of additional men = 75 – 60 = 15

4.

Work	Days	Men
$\frac{3}{4}$ ↓	60 ↑	60 ↓
$\frac{1}{4}$	30	x

$$\Rightarrow \frac{x}{60} = \frac{60}{30} \times \frac{1/4}{3/4}$$

$$\therefore x = \frac{60}{30} \times \frac{1}{3} \times 60 = 40 \text{ days}$$

Hence, number of men to be discharged

$= 60 - 40 = 20$

5. Shadow (m)   Object (m)

$40.25 \downarrow$ $17.5 \downarrow$

28.75 x

$$\Rightarrow \frac{x}{17.5} = \frac{28.75}{40.25}$$

$$\therefore x = \frac{28.75 \times 17.5}{40.25} = 12.5 \text{ m}$$

6. 5 men $\equiv$ 9 women

$$\therefore 3 \text{ men} = \frac{9}{5} \times 3 = \frac{27}{5} \text{ women}$$

$$\text{Hence, 3 men and 6 women} = \frac{27}{5} + 6$$

$$= \frac{57}{5} \text{ women}$$

Women   Days

$9 \uparrow$ $19 \downarrow$

$\frac{57}{5}$ x

$$\Rightarrow \frac{x}{19} = \frac{9 \times 5}{57}$$

$$\therefore x = \frac{9 \times 5}{57} \times 19$$

$= 15$ days

7. Days   Men

$100 \uparrow$ $x \downarrow$

110 $x - 10$

$$\Rightarrow \frac{x-10}{x} = \frac{100}{110}$$

$\Rightarrow 110x - 1100 = 100x$

$\Rightarrow 10x = 1100 \quad \therefore x = 110$

Hence, initially the number of men = 110

8. Work   Persons   Days

$1 \downarrow$ $x \uparrow$ $12 \downarrow$

$\frac{1}{2}$ $2x$ a

$$\Rightarrow \frac{a}{12} = \frac{x}{2x} \times \frac{1}{2} \quad \therefore \quad a = \frac{1}{4} \times 12 = 3 \text{ days}$$

9. Here, 14×2 men + 14×7 boys $\equiv$ 11×3 men + 11×8 boys

$\Rightarrow$ 28 men + 98 boys $\equiv$ 33 men + 88 boys

$\Rightarrow$ 5 men = 10 boys

$\therefore$ 1 man = 2 boys

Then, 2 men and 7 boys $\equiv$ 4 boys + 7 boys

= 11 boys

& also, 8 men and 6 boys $\equiv$ 16 boys + 6 boys

= 22 boys

Work   Boys   Days

$1 \downarrow$ $11 \uparrow$ $14 \downarrow$

3 22 x

$$\Rightarrow \frac{x}{14} = \frac{11}{22} \times \frac{3}{1}$$

$$\therefore x = \frac{1}{2} \times 3 \times 14$$

$= 21$ days

12. Men   Rice (kgs)   Days

$40 \uparrow$ $60 \downarrow$ $15 \downarrow$

30 12 x

$$\Rightarrow \frac{x}{15} = \frac{12}{60} \times \frac{40}{30}$$

$$\therefore x = \frac{12}{60} \times \frac{40}{30} \times 15 = 4 \text{ days}$$

14. Machines   Time (minutes)   Bottles

$6 \downarrow$ $1 \downarrow$ $270 \downarrow$

10 4 x

$$\Rightarrow \frac{x}{270} = \frac{4}{1} \times \frac{10}{6}$$

$$\therefore x = \frac{4 \times 10}{6} \times 270$$

$= 1800$ bottles

15. Work   Hours   Days   Persons

$\frac{1}{4} \downarrow$ $9 \uparrow$ $10 \uparrow$ $400 \downarrow$

$\frac{3}{4}$ 8 20 x

$$\Rightarrow \frac{x}{400} = \frac{10}{20} \times \frac{9}{8} \times \frac{3/4}{1/4}$$

$$\therefore x = \frac{1}{2} \times \frac{9}{8} \times 3 \times 400 = 675$$

Hence, number of additional persons

$= 675 - 400 = 275$

TIME AND DISTANCE

1. Starting from a point at a speed of 4 km/hr a man reaches at a cerain place and returns back to the point from where he had started journey on bicycle at the speed of 16 km/hr. His average speed during the entire journey will be :

A. 6.4 km/h B. 8.4 km/h
C. 5.4 km/h D. 10 km/h

2. A motorist covers a certain distance at a average speed of 48 km/h in 45 minutes. What speed in km/h he must maintain to cover the same distance in 30 minutes?

A. 66 km/h B. 79 km/h
C. 80 km/h D. 72 km/h

3. A policeman saw a thief at a distance of 200 m. The policeman and the thief started running at the same time. If the policeman runs at a speed of $4\frac{1}{6}$ m per second and the thief at a speed of $3\frac{1}{3}$ m per second, after what time the policeman will catch the thief?

A. 12 min B. 10 min
C. 9 min D. 4 min

4. A monkey wants to climb up a glazed pole. He climbs 12 metres in 1 minute and then he slips back 3 metres in the next minute. If the pole is 63 metre high, how long does he take to climb at the top of the pole?

A. $11\frac{1}{4}$ min B. $12\frac{1}{2}$ min
C. $12\frac{3}{4}$ min D. $14\frac{3}{4}$ min

5. The distance between two stations A and B is 300 km. A train leaves the station A with a speed of 40 km/hr. At the same time another train departs from the station B with a speed of 50 km/hr. How much time will these two trains take to cross each other?

A. 3 hrs 40 min B. 3 hrs 20 min
C. 2 hrs 20 min D. 3 hrs 45 min

6. Nilesh goes to school from his village at the speed of 4 km/hr and returns from school to village at the speed of 2 km/hr. If he takes 6 hours in all, then what is the distance between the village and the school?

A. 8 km B. 6 km
C. 5 km D. 4 km

7. By increasing the speed of the bus by 10 km/hr the time of journey for 72 km is reduced by 36 minutes. What was the original speed of the bus?

A. 30 km/hr B. 35 km/hr
C. 40 km/hr D. 45 km/hr

8. A train covers a distance in 50 minutes, if it runs at a speed of 48 km/hr on an average. The speed at which the train must run to reduce the time of journey to 40 minutes will be:

A. 70 km/hr B. 60 km/hr
C. 55 km/hr D. 50 km/hr

9. A certain distance is covered by a vehicle at a certain speed. If half of this distance is covered by another vehicle in double the time, the ratio of the speeds of the two vehicles is:

A. 4 : 1 B. 1 : 4
C. 2 : 1 D. 1 : 2

10. A is faster than B. A and B each walk 24 km. The sum of their speeds is 7 km/hr and sum of times taken by them is 14 hours. What is the speed of A?

A. 7 km/hr B. 5 km/hr
C. 4 km/hr D. 3 km/hr

ANSWERS

1	2	3	4	5	6	7	8	9	10
A	D	D	C	B	A	A	B	A	C

EXPLANATORY ANSWERS

1. Average speed during the entire journey

$$= \frac{2xy}{x+y} = \frac{2\times4\times16}{4+16} = \frac{8\times16}{20} = 6.4 \text{ km/hr.}$$

2. Let required speed be x km/hr; then

$$x \times \frac{1}{2} = 48 \times \frac{3}{4} \quad \therefore \; x = 48 \times \frac{3}{4} \times 2$$
$$= 72 \text{ km/hr}$$

3. Suppose the policeman will catch the thief after t seconds then, $\left(\frac{25}{6}-\frac{10}{3}\right)t = 200 \Rightarrow \frac{5}{6}t = 200$

$\therefore\ t = \frac{200 \times 6}{5} = 240$ sec = 4 min.

4. The monkey climbs 12 metres in 1 minute and then he slips back 3 metres in the next minute

∴ The monkey climbs in the first 2 minutes = 12 – 3 = 9 metres

∴ In the first 12 minutes the monkey climbs = 9 × 6 = 54 metres

Remaining height of the pole to be covered by the monkey = 63 – 54 = 9 metre

∴ The monkey will climb the height of 9 metres in the 13th minute

∵ The monkey climbs 12 metres in 1 minute

∴ The monkey will climb 9 metres in $\frac{1}{12} \times 9$

$= \frac{3}{4}$ minute

∴ Time spent in climbing at the top of the pole

$= \left(12+\frac{3}{4}\right)$ minutes $= 12\frac{3}{4}$ minutes

5. The two trains are moving in the opposite directions

∴ Relative speed = 40 + 50 = 90 km/hr.

∴ Time taken to cross each other $= \frac{300}{90} = 3\frac{1}{3}$ hours

or, 3 hours 20 minutes.

6. Let x km be the distance between village and the school; then

$\frac{x}{4}+\frac{x}{2}=6 \quad \Rightarrow \frac{3x}{4}=6$

$\therefore\ x = \frac{6 \times 4}{3} = 8$ km

8. Let x km/hr be the required speed of the train; then

$x \times \frac{40}{60} = 48 \times \frac{50}{60}$

$\therefore\ x = \frac{48 \times 50}{40} = 60$ km/hr

9. Let x km/hr and t hr be the certain speed and certain time.

Then, ratio of their speeds $= \frac{x}{t} : \frac{x}{2 \times 2t} = 1 : \frac{1}{4} = 4 : 1$

10. Let speeds of A and B are x_1 and x_2 km/hr and times taken by them are t_1 and t_2 hrs, then

$x_1 + x_2 = 7$ km/hr ...(i)

$t_1 + t_2 = 14$ hrs ...(ii)

Now, $\frac{24}{x_1}+\frac{24}{x_2} = 14 \Rightarrow \frac{24(x_1+x_2)}{x_1x_2} = 14$

$\therefore\ x_1x_2 = \frac{24 \times 7}{14} = 12$

Then, $x_1 - x_2 = \sqrt{(x_1+x_2)^2 - 4x_1x_2}$

$= \sqrt{(7)^2 - 4 \times 12} = 1$ ...(iii)

Solving *(i)* and *(iii)* we get $x_1 = 4$ km/hr

TIME AND WORK

1. A and B working together complete a work in 35 days. If A takes 60 days to complete it, how long would B alone take to complete it?

A. 64 days B. 72 days
C. 81 days D. 84 days

2. A few children working together can do a piece of work in 18 days. If the number of children employed on the work is made double, how long would they take to complete half of the work?

A. $4\frac{1}{2}$ days B. $2\frac{1}{3}$ days
C. $8\frac{3}{4}$ days D. $6\frac{1}{2}$ days

3. 10 men or 18 boys can do a piece of work in 15 days. In how many days would 25 men and 15 boys complete the same work working together?

A. $5\frac{1}{2}$ days B. $4\frac{1}{2}$ days
C. $6\frac{2}{3}$ days D. $2\frac{1}{3}$ days

4. A cistern is filled by a tap in $3\frac{1}{2}$ hours. Due to a leak in the bottom of the cistern, it takes half an hour longer to fill the cistern. If the cistern is full, how long will it take the leak to empty it?

A. 28 hours B. 29 hours
C. $31\frac{1}{3}$ hours D. 38 hours

5. A is twice as good a workman as B and thrice as good a workman as C. If C alone can do a piece of work in 24 days, how long would the three persons take to finish the work working together?

A. $3\frac{3}{11}$ days B. $4\frac{4}{7}$ days

C. $4\frac{4}{11}$ days D. $3\frac{4}{11}$ days

6. If 3 men and 5 women can do a piece of work in 8 days and 2 men and 7 boys can do the same work in 12 days. Find the number of boys, the work done by whom can equate the work done by 10 women.

A. 19 boys B. 21 boys
C. 23 boys D. 15 boys

7. 8 men alone can complete a piece of work in 12 days. 4 women alone can complete the same piece of work in 48 days and 10 children alone can complete the piece of work in 24 days. In how many days can 10 men, 4 women and 10 children together complete the piece of work?

A. 6 B. 8
C. 10 D. 15

8. A works twice as fast as B. If B can complete a piece of work independently in 12 days. Find in how many days A and B together can complete the work?

A. 8 days B. 6 days
C. 4 days D. 18 days

9. A contractor undertook to complete a project in 90 days and employed 60 men on it. After 60 days, he found that $\frac{3}{4}$ of the work has already been completed. How many men can he discharge so that the project may be completed exactly on time?

A. 15 B. 20
C. 30 D. 40

10. A can do a piece of work in 25 days and B can do it in 20 days. They work together for 5 days and then A goes away. In how many days will B finish the remaining work?

A. 33 days B. 20 days
C. 11 days D. 10 days

ANSWERS

1	2	3	4	5	6	7	8	9	10
D	A	B	A	C	B	A	C	B	C

EXPLANATORY ANSWERS

1. (A + B)'s 1 day's work = $\frac{1}{35}$

and also, A's 1 day's work = $\frac{1}{60}$

Hence, B's 1 day's work = $\frac{1}{35}-\frac{1}{60}=\frac{5}{420}=\frac{1}{84}$

So, B will do the whole work in 84 days.

3. 10 men ≡ 18 boys

25 men ≡ $\frac{18}{10}\times 25 = 45$ boys

Hence, 25 men + 15 boys = 45 + 15 = 60 boys

Now, 18 boys can do a piece of work in 15 days.

Hence, 60 boys will do a piece of work in $\frac{15\times 18}{60}=\frac{9}{2}$ days = $4\frac{1}{2}$ days.

4. In 1 hour $\frac{2}{7}$ cistern is filled by the tap.

Hence, in $\frac{1}{2}$ hour $\frac{2}{14}=\frac{1}{7}$ cistern is filled by the tap.

So, $\frac{1}{7}$ cistern is emptied by the leakage in 4 hours.

So, 1 cistern will be emptied by the leakage in 28 hours.

6. Here, (3 men + 5 women) × 8

≡ (2 men + 7 boys) × 12

⇒ 40 women ≡ 84 boys

∴ 10 women ≡ $\frac{84}{40}\times 10$ = 21 boys

Hence, work done by 10 women

= work done of 21 boys.

7. B's 1 day's work = $\frac{1}{4}-\frac{1}{12}=\frac{2}{12}=\frac{1}{6}$

Hence, B alone will complete the work in 6 days.

8. Ratio of efficiency of A and B = 2 : 1

Then, ratio of their time taking = 1 : 2

Hence, if B can complete the work in 12 days, then A in 6 days.

Now, (A + B)'s 1 day's work = $\frac{1}{6}+\frac{1}{12}=\frac{3}{12}=\frac{1}{4}$

So, A and B together can complete the work in 4 days.

9. After 60 days remaining work = $1-\frac{3}{4}=\frac{1}{4}$

In 60 days $\frac{3}{4}$ work has been done by 60 men

In 30 days $\frac{1}{4}$ work will be done by $60\times\frac{4}{3}\times\frac{1}{4}\times\frac{60}{30}$ = 40 men.

Hence, required number of men = 60 – 40 = 20 (which are to be discharged).

BOATS AND STREAMS

1. A boat goes 6 km upstream and back to the starting point in 2 hours. If the current of the stream runs at the rate of 4 km/hr, find the speed of the boat in still water.

A. 6 km/hr B. 8 km/hr
C. 10 km/hr D. 12 km/hr

2. A boat covers 24 km upstream and 36 km downstream in 6 hours, while it covers 36 km upstream and 24 km downstream in 6½ horus. Find the speed of the current.

A. 2 km/hr B. 4 km/hr
C. 6 km/hr D. 8 km/hr

3. A man can row 5 km/hr in still water and the speed of the stream is 1.5 km/hr. He takes an hour when he travels upstream to a place and back again to the starting point. How far is the place from the starting point?

A. 2.275 km B. 3.5 km
C. 1.5 km D. None of these

4. The speed of a boat in still water is 6 km/hr and the speed of the stream is 1.5 km/hr. A man rows to a place at a distance of 22.5 km and comes back to the starting point. Find the total time taken by him.

A. 8 hours B. 10 hours
C. 12 hours D. 4 hours

5. A boat covers 20 km downstream and 6 km upstream in 3 hours, while it covers 30 km downstream and 12 km upstream in 5 hours. What is the speed of boat in still water?

A. 6 km/hr B. 8 km/hr.
C. 10 km/hr D. 12 km/hr.

6. Samir can travel 12 miles downstream in a certain river in 6 hours less than it takes him to travel the same distance upstream. But when he could double his rowing rate for his 24-mile round trip, the downstream 12 miles would then take only one hour less than the upstream 12 miles. Find the speed of the current in miles/hour.

A. $2\frac{2}{3}$ B. $2\frac{1}{3}$
C. $1\frac{2}{3}$ D. $1\frac{1}{3}$

7. A boat takes 6 hours to travel from place M to N downstream and back from N to M upstream. If the speed of the boat in still water is 4 km/hr; what is the distance between two places?

A. 6 kms B. 8 kms
C. 12 kms D. Data inadequate

8. A man can row upstream at 8 km/hr and downstream at 13 km/hr. The speed of the stream is:

A. 2.5 km/hr B. 4.2 km/hr
C. 5 km/hr D. 10.5 km/hr

9. A man's speed with the current is 15 km/hr and the speed of the current is 2.5 km/hr. The man's speed against the current is:

A. 12.5 km/hr B. 10 km/hr
C. 9 km/hr D. 8.5 km/hr

10. A motorboat, whose speed is 15 km/hr in still water goes 30 km downstream and comes back in a total of 4 hours 30 minutes. What is the speed of the stream (in km/hr)?

A. 10 B. 6
C. 5 D. 4

ANSWERS

1	2	3	4	5	6	7	8	9	10
B	A	A	A	B	B	D	A	B	C

EXPLANATORY ANSWERS

1. Let the speed of a boat in still water = x km/hr; then

$\frac{6}{x-4}+\frac{6}{x+4}=2 \Rightarrow \frac{2x}{x^2-16}=\frac{1}{3}$

$\Rightarrow x^2 - 6x - 16 = 0$

$\Rightarrow (x - 8)(x + 2) = 0$

Hence, the speed of the boat = 8 km/hr.

2. Let x km/hr and y km/hr be the speeds of the boat in still water and the speed of the current respectively, then

$\frac{24}{x-y}+\frac{36}{x+y}=6 \Rightarrow \frac{4}{x-y}+\frac{6}{x+y}=1$ ...(i)

And, $\frac{36}{x-y}+\frac{24}{x+y}=\frac{13}{2}$ ...(ii)

Solving these two equations, we get

$x + y = 12;\ x - y = 8$

Hence, $y = \frac{1}{2}(12-8) = 2$ km/hr.

3. Let required distance be x km, then

$\frac{x}{5-1.5}+\frac{x}{5+1.5}=1 \Rightarrow \frac{x\times 2}{7}+\frac{x\times 2}{13}=1$

$\Rightarrow 40x = 91 \quad \therefore x = 91/40 = 2.275$ km

4. Required time period $= \frac{22.5}{6+1.5}+\frac{22.5}{6-1.5}$

$= \frac{45}{15}+\frac{45}{9} = 8$ hours.

5. Let x km/hr and y km/hr be the speed of boat in still water and speed of current respectively; then

$\frac{20}{x+y}+\frac{6}{x-y}=3$ ...(i)

and also, $\frac{30}{x+y}+\frac{12}{x-y}=5$

$\Rightarrow \frac{15}{x+y}+\frac{6}{x-y}=\frac{5}{2}$ ...(ii)

Solving equations *(i)* & *(ii)*, we get $x + y = 10$ and $x - y = 6$

Since, $x = \frac{1}{2}(10 + 6) = 8$ km/hr.

6. Let x km/hr and y km/hr be the speed of rowing in still water and speed of the current respectively; then

$\frac{12}{x-y}-\frac{12}{x+y}=6 \Rightarrow \frac{24y}{x^2-y^2}=6$

$\Rightarrow x^2 = y^2 + 4y$ ...(i)

Again, $\frac{12}{2x-y}-\frac{12}{2x+y}=1$

$\Rightarrow \frac{24y}{4x^2-y^2}=1 \Rightarrow x^2=\frac{y^2+24y}{4}$ ...(ii)

From equations (i) and (ii), we get

$y^2 + 4y = \frac{y^2+24y}{4} \Rightarrow 3y^2 = 8y$

$\therefore\ y = \frac{8}{3} = 2\frac{1}{3}$ miles/hr.

8. The speed of the stream $= \frac{1}{2}(13 - 8) = \frac{5}{2}$

$= 2.5$ km/hr.

9. The man's speed in still water

$= 15 - 2.5 = 12.5$ km/hr

Hence, the men's speed against the current

$= 12.5 - 2.5 = 10$ km/hr

10. Let speed of the stream be x km/hr, then

$\frac{30}{15+x}+\frac{30}{15-x}=4\frac{1}{2} \Rightarrow \frac{30\times 30}{225-x^2}=\frac{9}{2}$

$\Rightarrow \frac{200}{225-x^2}=1 \quad \Rightarrow x^2 = 225 - 200$

$\Rightarrow x^2 = 25 \quad \therefore\ x = 5$ km/hr.

ALLIGATION OR MIXTURE

1. A shopkeeper buys 26 kgs of milk @ Rs. 16 per kg. He also buys from another source an inferior quality of milk @ Rs. 10 per kg. How much quantity of the latter should he buy to mix it with the former so that he can sell the mixture @ Rs. 14 per kg without making any loss?

A. 13 kgs B. 12 kgs
C. 14 kgs D. 16 kgs

2. Two vessels A and B contain mixture of milk and water in the ratio 4 : 1 and 9 : 11 respectively. They are mixed in the ratio of 3 : 2. Find the ratio of milk : water in the resulting mixture.

A. 34 : 16 B. 33 : 17
C. 16 : 34 D. 17 : 33

3. A shopkeeper has 50 kgs of rice. He sells a part of it at 20% profit and the rest at 40% profit. If he gains 25% on the whole, find the quantity of each part.

A. 12.5 kgs and 37.5 kgs
B. 37.5 kgs and 12.5 kgs
C. 23.5 kgs and 21.5 kgs
D. 21.5 kgs and 23.5 kgs

4. A man bought a certain quantity of sugar for Rs. 8000. He sells one-fourth of it at 20% loss. At what per cent profit should he sell the remainder stock so as to make an overall profit of 20%?

A. 20% B. 30%
C. 35% D. 40%

5. Rs. 675 was divided among 75 boys and girls. Each boy gets Rs. 20 whereas a girl gets Rs. 5. Find the number of boys and girls.

A. 20, 55 B. 15, 60
C. 25, 50 D. 30, 45

6. A vessel contains mixture of liquids A and B in the ratio 3 : 2. When 20 litres of the mixture is taken out and replaced by 20 litres of liquid B, the ratio changes to 1 : 4. How many litres of liquid A was there initially present in the vessel?

A. 12 litres B. 18 litres
C. 24 litres D. 22 litres

7. A container is full of milk. One-third of milk is taken out of it and replaced by same quantity of water. Then again one-third of the mixture is taken out of it and replaced by the same quantity of water. The process is repeated 4 times. If 16 litres of milk is left in the container at the end of 4th operation, find the capacity of the container.

A. 76 litres B. 81 litres
C. 82 litres D. 85 litres

8. The cost of type-I rice is Rs. 15 per kg and type-II is Rs. 20 per kg. If both type I and type II are mixed in the ratio of 2 : 3, then find the price per kg of the mixed variety.

A. Rs. 19.50 B. Rs. 19
C. Rs. 18.50 D. Rs. 18

9. In what ratio must a grocer mix two varieties of tea worth Rs. 60 a kg and Rs. 65 a kg so that by selling the mixture at Rs. 68.20 a kg he may gain 10%?

A. 4 : 5 B. 3 : 5
C. 3 : 4 D. 3 : 2

10. A vessel contains 80 litres of milk. 16 litres of milk was taken out of the vessel and replaced by water. Then 16 litres of mixture was withdrawn and again replaced by water. The operation was repeated for third time. How much milk is now left in the vessel?

A. 96.40 litres
B. 50.36 litres
C. 40.96 litres
D. 32.76 litres

ANSWERS

1	2	3	4	5	6	7	8	9	10
A	B	B	B	A	B	B	D	D	C

EXPLANATORY ANSWERS

1.

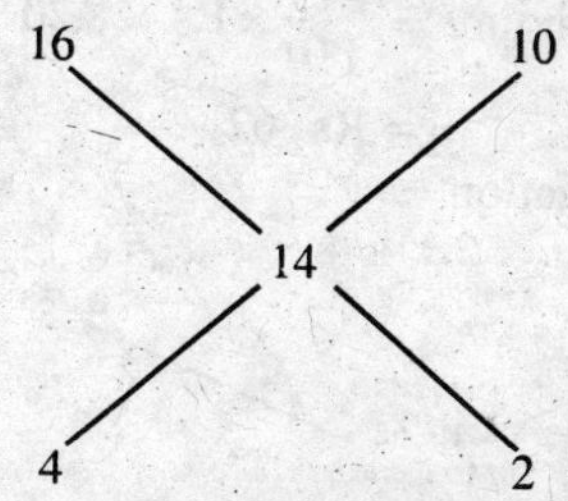

or 2 : 1 $\dfrac{\text{Quantity of milk @ Rs.10 per kg}}{\text{Quantity of milk @ Rs. 16 per kg}} = \dfrac{1}{2}$

So, quantity of milk @ Rs. 10 per kg. $= \dfrac{26}{2} = 13$ kgs.

2. Fraction is

	Milk	*Water*
A :	$\dfrac{4}{5}$	$\dfrac{1}{5}$
B :	$\dfrac{9}{20}$	$\dfrac{11}{20}$

$(3A + 2B) = A \text{ and } B : \left(\dfrac{12}{5} + \dfrac{9}{10}\right) \left(\dfrac{3}{5} + \dfrac{11}{10}\right)$

$\dfrac{33}{10} \quad \dfrac{17}{10}$

So, Ratio of milk : water in the resulting mixture = 33 : 17.

3.

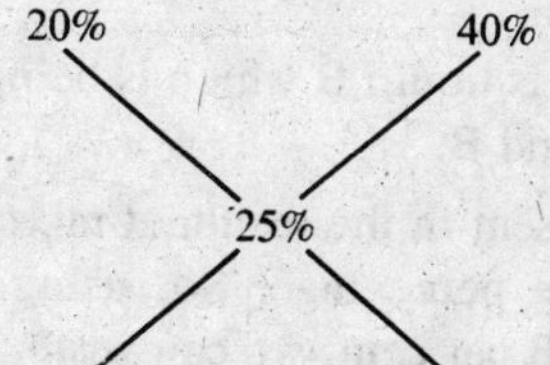

or 3 : 1

Quantity sold at 20% profit = $\frac{3}{3+1} \times 50$

$= 37.5$ kgs.

Quantity sold at 40% profit = (50 – 37.5)

$= 12.5$ kgs.

4. Let the remainder stock be sold at x% profit.

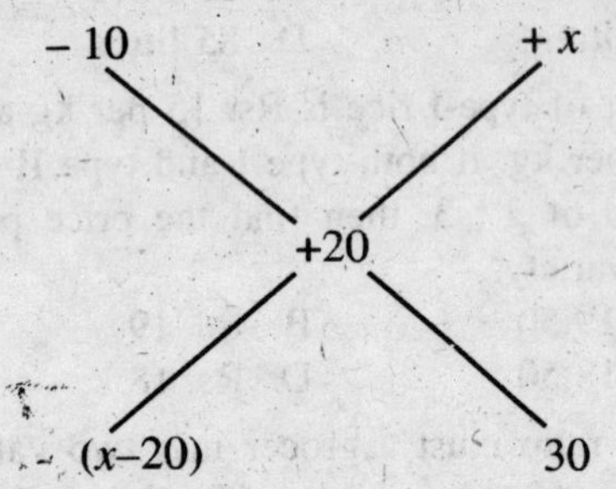

$$\frac{x-20}{30} = \frac{1/4}{3/4}$$

or $\quad x - 20 = 30 \times \frac{1}{3}$

or $\quad x = 20 + 10$

$x = 30\%$ profit.

5. Average money per head (boy or girl)

$= \text{Rs. } \frac{675}{75} = \text{Rs. } 9$

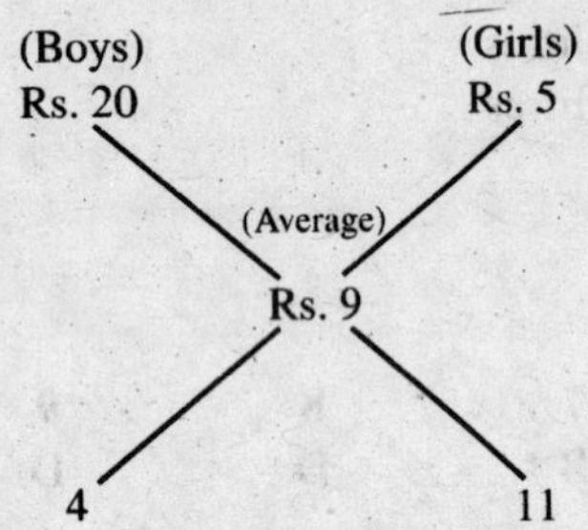

Number of boys $= \frac{4}{4+11} \times 75 = 20$

Number of girls $= \frac{11}{4+11} \times 75 = 55.$

6. % of liquid B initially present in the vessel

$= \frac{2}{3+2} \times 100 = 40\%$

% of liquid B finally present in the vessel

$= \frac{4}{1+4} \times 100 = 80\%$

The second solution is liquid B which is being mixed and it has 100% liquid B.

80% of liquid B present in the resultant mixture may be taken as average percentage. So, using rule of alligation on liquid B per cent, we can write,

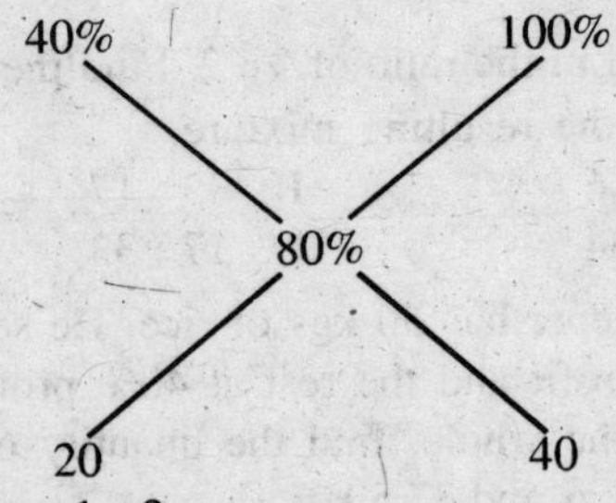

or $\quad$ 1 : 2

The ratio of liquid left in the vessel to liquid B being mixed = 1 : 2

Since the quantity of liquid B being mixed is 20 litres, the quantity of liquid left in the vessel is 10 litres. Therefore, the total quantity of liquid initially present in the vessel

$= 10 + 20 = 30$ litres

Quantity of liquid A $= \frac{3}{2+3} \times 30 = 18$ litres.

7. Let capacity of the container be x litre; then

$x(1 - 1/3)^4 = 16 \Rightarrow x\left(\frac{2}{3}\right)^4 = 16$

$\Rightarrow x \times \frac{16}{81} = 16 \quad \therefore \; x = 81$ litres

8. Let the price per kg of mixed variety be Rs. x; then

By the rule of alligation,

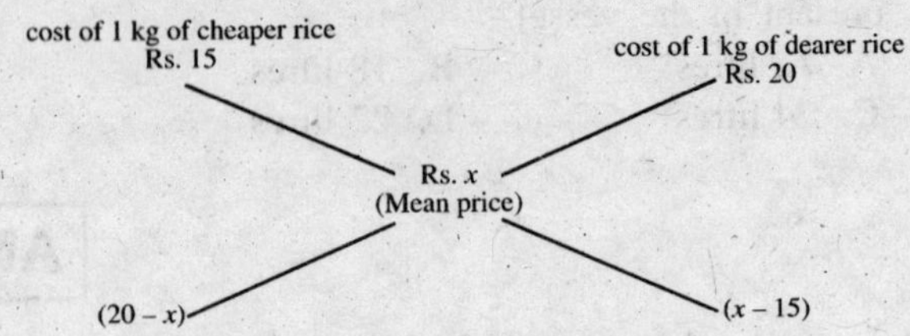

Now, $\frac{20-x}{x-15} = \frac{2}{3} \Rightarrow 60 - 3x = 2x - 30$

$\Rightarrow 5x = 90 \quad \therefore \; x = \text{Rs. } 18$

9. S.P. of 1 kg mixture = Rs. 68.20, Gain % = 10%

Hence, C.P. of 1 kg mixture $= \frac{100}{110} \times \text{Rs. } 68.20$

$= \text{Rs. } 62$

By the rule of alligation

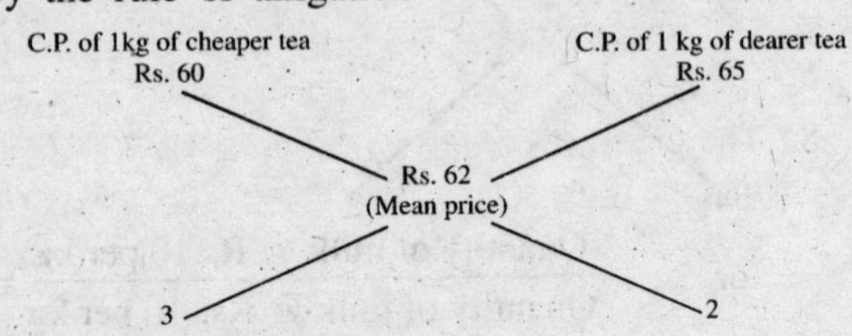

Hence, required ratio = 3 : 2

10. Amount of milk left $= 80\left(1-\frac{16}{80}\right)^3 = 80\left(\frac{4}{5}\right)^3$

$80 \times \frac{64}{125} = 40.96$ litres.

PERCENTAGE

1. A student who secures 20% marks in an examination fails by 30 marks. Another student who secures 32% gets 42 marks more than those required to pass. The percentage of marks required to pass is:
A. 20 B. 25
C. 28 D. 30

2. In a college election, a candidate secured 62% of the votes and is elected by a majority of 144 votes. The total number of votes polled is:
A. 600 B. 800
C. 925 D. 1200

3. In an organisation, 40% of the employees are matriculates, 50% of the remaining are graduates and the remaining 180 are postgraduates. How many employees are graduates?
A. 360 B. 240
C. 300 D. 180

4. The population of a village is 4500. $\frac{5}{9}$th of them are males and rest females. If 40% of the males are married, then the percentage of married female is :
A. 35 B. 40
C. 50 D. 60

5. A's income is 10% more than B's. How much per cent is B's income is less than A's?
A. 10% B. 7%
C. $9\frac{1}{11}$% D. $6\frac{1}{2}$%

6. If the price of a television set is increased by 25%, then by what percentage should the new price be reduced to bring the price back to original level?
A. 15% B. 20%
C. 25% D. 30%

7. In an election one of the two candidates gets 40% votes and loses by 100 votes. Total number of votes is :
A. 500 B. 400
C. 600 D. 1000

8. The gross income of a person is Rs. 20000. 10% of his income is exempted from income tax and his net income is Rs. 19100. The rate of income tax is :
A. 3% B. 2%
C. 4% D. 5%

9. The owner of a cell phone shop charges his customer 32% more than the cost price. If a customer paid Rs. 6600 for the cell phone, then what was the cost price of the cell phone?
A. Rs. 5000 B. Rs. 5500
C. Rs. 5800 D. Rs. 6100

10. If the cost of pins reduced by Rs. 4 per dozen, 12 more pins can be purchased for Rs. 48. The cost of pins per dozen after reduction is:
A. Rs. 8 B. Rs. 12
C. Rs. 16 D. Rs. 20

11. In an examination 80% of the students passed in Mathematics and 70% passed in English, while 10% students failed in both the subjects. If 360 students passed in both the subjects, find the total number of students who appeared in the examination.
A. 400 B. 600
C. 630 D. 640

12. Electric tax is increased by 20% and its consumption is decreased by 20%. The change in the expenditure is:
A. 4% decrease B. 4% increase
C. 5% decrease D. 5% increase

13. The selling price of certain commodity was reduced by 25%. As a result of it, the sales increased by 30%. What was the effect of it on cash collected by daily sales?
A. 2.5% decrease B. 2.5% increase
C. 5% decrease D. 5% increase

14. The wheat sold by a grocer contained 10% low quality wheat. What quantity of good quality wheat should be added to 150 kgs of wheat so that the percentage of low quality wheat becomes 5%?
A. 50 kgs B. 85 kgs
C. 135 kgs D. 150 kgs

15. Nilam spends 15% of her monthly income on household expenses. She spends 17% of the monthly income in travelling and 6% on medical expenses and saves the rest Rs. 15,500. What is her monthly income?
A. Rs. 20,000 B. Rs. 25,000
C. Rs. 30,000 D. Rs. 35,000

ANSWERS

1	2	3	4	5	6	7	8	9	10
B	A	D	C	C	B	A	D	A	B
11	**12**	**13**	**14**	**15**					
B	A	A	D	B					

EXPLANATORY ANSWERS

1. $20\% \text{ of } x + 30 = 32\% \text{ of } x - 42$

$\Rightarrow \quad 12\% \text{ of } x = 72$

$\Rightarrow \quad x = \frac{72 \times 100}{12} = 600$

Pass Mark $= 20\%$ of $600 + 30 = 150$

Pass percentage $= \left(\frac{150}{600} \times 100\right)\% = 25\%$

2. $(62\% \text{ of } x - 38\% \text{ of } x) = 144$

$\Rightarrow 24\% \text{ of } x = 144 \quad \Rightarrow x = \frac{144 \times 100}{24} = 600$

3. Matriculates $= \frac{40}{100} x = \frac{2x}{5}$

Remaining $= \left(x - \frac{2x}{5}\right) = \frac{3x}{5}$

Graduates $= \frac{50}{100} \times \frac{3x}{5} = \frac{3x}{10}$

Remaining $= \frac{3x}{5} - \frac{3x}{10} = \frac{3x}{10}$

Now, $\frac{3x}{10} = 180 \quad \therefore x = \frac{10 \times 180}{3} = 600$

$\therefore$ Graduates $= \frac{3 \times 600}{10} = 180$.

4. Males $= \left(\frac{5}{9} \times 4500\right) = 2500$

Females $= 2000$

$\therefore$ Married males $= \frac{40}{100} \times 2500 = 1000$

and married females $= 1000$

$\therefore$ Percentage of married females

$= \left(\frac{1000}{2000} \times 100\right)\% = 50\%$.

5. Required percentage $= \left[\frac{10}{(100+10)} \times 100\right]\% = 9\frac{1}{11}\%$.

6. Required reduction $= \frac{25}{100+25} \times 100 = 20\%$.

7. Out of 100, difference in votes $= (60 - 40) = 20$

20% of $x = 100$

$\therefore x = \frac{100 \times 100}{20} = 500$.

8. Gross income = Rs. 20000

Income exempted from income tax = 10% of gross income

$\therefore$ Income on which income tax is chargeable $= (100 - 10\%) = 90\%$ of gross income

$= 20000 \times \frac{90}{100} =$ Rs. 18000

$\therefore$ Total income tax paid on

= Rs. 20000 – Rs. 19100 = Rs. 900

$\therefore$ Rate per cent of income tax $= \frac{900}{18000} \times 100 = 5\%$

9. Let cost price of the cell phone be Rs. x; then

$x + \frac{32}{100} \times x = 6600 \quad \Rightarrow \frac{132x}{100} = 6600$

$\therefore x = \frac{100 \times 6600}{132} =$ Rs. 5000.

10. Let reduced price by Rs. x per dozen, then

$\frac{48}{x} - \frac{48}{x+4} = 1 \quad \Rightarrow \frac{48 \times 4}{x^2 + 4x} = 1$

$\Rightarrow \quad x^2 + 4x - 192 = 0$

$\Rightarrow (x + 16)(x - 12) = 0$

$\therefore \quad x =$ Rs. 12.

11. Here, percentage of students failed in Mathematics and English be 30% and 20% respectively.

Percentage of students failed either one or both subjects $= 30 + 20 - 10 = 40\%$

Hence, percentage of pass students $= 100 - 40 = 60\%$

Now, $60\% = 360$

$\therefore 100\% = \frac{360}{60} \times 100 = 600$.

12. Let initially electric tax is Rs. 100 and consumption = 100 units

Decrease in consumption

$= 100 \times 100 - 120 \times 80 =$ Rs. 400

Hence, decrease percentage $= \frac{400 \times 100}{100 \times 100} = 4\%$.

13. Let the selling price of a commodity be Rs. 100 and number of sales = 100 units

Decrease in daily cash $= 100 \times 100 - 75 \times 130$

= Rs. 250

Hence, decrease percentage $= \frac{250 \times 100}{100 \times 100} = 2.5\%$.

14. Let x kg of good wheat be added; then

$\frac{10}{100} \times 150 = \frac{5}{100}(150 + x)$

$\Rightarrow 150 + x = 300 \quad \therefore x = 150$ kg.

15. Let her monthly income be Rs. x; then

$x - \left(\frac{15}{100} \times x + \frac{17}{100} \times x + \frac{6}{100} \times x\right) = 15{,}500$

$\Rightarrow x - \frac{38x}{100} = 15500 \quad \Rightarrow \frac{62x}{100} = 15500$

$\therefore \quad x = \frac{15500 \times 100}{62} =$ Rs. 25000.

PROFIT AND LOSS

1. Ashok bought 25 kg of rice at the rate of Rs. 6 per kg and 35 kg of rice at the rate of Rs. 7 per kg. He mixed the two and sold the mixture at the rate of Rs. 6.75 per kg. What was his gain or loss in the transaction?
   A. Rs. 16 gain B. Rs. 16 loss
   C. Rs. 10 gain D. None of these
2. Profit after selling a commodity for Rs. 425 is same as loss after selling it for Rs. 355. The cost of the commodity is :
   A. Rs. 285 B. Rs. 390
   C. Rs. 295 D. Rs. 400
3. Ram bought 4 dozen apples at Rs. 12 per dozen and 2 dozen at Rs. 16 per dozen. He sold all of them to earn 20%. At what price per dozen did he sell the apples?
   A. Rs. 14.40 B. Rs. 16.00
   C. Rs. 16.80 D. Rs. 16.20
4. At what price must Kantilal sell a mixture of 80 kg sugar at Rs. 6.75 per kg with 120 kg at Rs. 8 per kg to gain 20%?
   A. Rs. 7.50 per kg B. Rs. 8.20 per kg
   C. Rs. 8.35 per kg D. Rs. 9 per kg
5. A person bought an article and sold it at a loss of 10%. If he had bought it for 20% less and sold it for Rs. 55 more, he would have had a profit of 40%. The C.P. of the article is :
   A. Rs. 200 B. Rs. 225
   C. Rs. 250 D. None of these
6. A dealer sold a machine to a shopkeeper at 20% profit. The shopkeeper sold the machine to a customer so as to get 25% profit for himself. The difference between the selling price of the dealer and that of the shopkeeper was found to be Rs. 129. What is the initial price of the machine?
   A. Rs. 410 B. Rs. 420
   C. Rs. 430 D. Rs. 440
7. A man bought a horse and cart. If he sold the horse at 10% loss and the cart at 20% gain he would not loss anything. If he sold the horse at 5% loss and the cart at 5% gain he would lose Rs. 10 in the bargain. What did he pay for each?
   A. Rs. 400, Rs. 200 B. Rs. 300, Rs. 300
   C. Rs. 250, Rs. 350 D. Rs. 350, Rs. 250
8. The marked price of a radio is 20% more than its cost price. If a discount of 10% is given on the marked price, the gain percentage is:
   A. 8 B. 10
   C. 12 D. 15
9. A dishonest dealer sells his goods at the cost price and still earns a profit of 60% by underweight. What weight does he use for a kg?
   A. 625 gms B. 750 gms
   C. 800 gms D. 850 gms
10. A man sells two horses for Rs. 990 each. On one he gains 10% and the other he loses 10%. What is his total percentage of gain or loss in the transaction?
   A. 1% gain B. 1% loss
   C. 2% gain D. 2% loss

ANSWERS

1	2	3	4	5	6	7	8	9	10
C	B	B	D	C	C	A	A	A	B

EXPLANATORY ANSWERS

1. C.P. of 60 kg mixture = Rs. $(25 \times 6 + 35 \times 7)$ = Rs. 395

S.P. of 60 kg mixtire = Rs. (60×6.75) = Rs. 405

$\therefore$ Gain = Rs. $(405 - 395)$ = Rs. 10

2. Let C.P. = Rs. x

Then, $425 - x = x - 355 \Rightarrow 2x = 780$

$\therefore$ x = Rs. 390

3. C.P. of 6 dozen apples = Rs. $(12 \times 4 + 16 \times 2)$ = Rs. 80

$$\therefore \quad \text{S.P.} = \text{Rs.}\left(\frac{120}{100} \times 80\right) = \text{Rs. } 96$$

$$\therefore \quad \text{S.P. per dozen} = \text{Rs.}\left(\frac{96}{6}\right) = \text{Rs. } 16$$

4. C.P. of 1 kg sugar $= \dfrac{80 \times 6.75 + 120 \times 8}{200}$

$= \text{Rs. } 7.50$

$\therefore$ S.P. of 1 kg $= \text{Rs.}\left(\dfrac{120}{100} \times 7.50\right)$

$= \text{Rs. } 9 \text{ per kg}$

5. Let, C.P. = Rs. x,

then, S.P. $= \dfrac{90}{100} \times x = \text{Rs. } \dfrac{9x}{10}$

Now, when C.P. = Rs. $\dfrac{80x}{100} = \text{Rs. } \dfrac{4x}{5}$;

then, S.P. $= \dfrac{140}{100} \times \dfrac{4x}{5} = \text{Rs. } \dfrac{28x}{25}$

But, $\dfrac{28x}{25} - \dfrac{9x}{10} = 55 \Rightarrow \dfrac{11x}{50} = 55$

$\therefore$ $x = \text{Rs. } 250$

6. Let the initial price = Rs. x; then C.P. for dealer

$= \dfrac{120}{100} \times x = \text{Rs. } \dfrac{6x}{5}$

Again, C.P. for shopkeeper $= \dfrac{125}{100} \times \dfrac{6x}{5}$

$= \text{Rs. } \dfrac{3x}{2}$

Now, $\dfrac{3x}{2} - \dfrac{6x}{5} = 129 \Rightarrow \dfrac{3x}{10} = 129$

$\therefore x = \dfrac{10 \times 129}{3} = \text{Rs. } 430$

7. Here, 10% C.P. of horse = 20% C.P. of cart; Hence, C.P. of horse = 2 × C.P. of cart;

Let C.P. of cart and horse be Rs. x and Rs. $2x$ respectively; then,

$\dfrac{5}{100} \times 2x - \dfrac{5}{100} \times x = 10 \Rightarrow \dfrac{1}{20}x = 10$

$\therefore x = 200$

Hence, C.P. of a cart = Rs. 200 and C.P. of a horse $= 2 \times 200 = \text{Rs. } 400$

8. Let C.P. be Rs. 100; then marked price = Rs. 120

Since, S.P. $= \dfrac{90}{100} \times 120 = \text{Rs. } 108$

$\therefore$ Profit = 108 – 100 = Rs. 8, Hence, gain = 8%.

9. Required weight $= \dfrac{100}{160} \times 1000 = 625$ gms.

10. Here, loss % $= \left(\dfrac{10}{10}\right)^2 = 1\%$.

SIMPLE INTEREST

1. A lent a sum of Rs. 1250 to B at a certain rate of interest for 3 years and a sum of Rs. 1500 to C at the same rate of interest for 2 years. If he was paid total Rs. 258.75 as interest in both cases, find the rate of interest at which money was lent by him.

A. $4\frac{1}{6}\%$ B. $6\frac{1}{4}\%$
C. $2\frac{1}{7}\%$ D. $3\frac{5}{6}\%$

2. A invested Rs. 5000 at a certain rate of simple interest and Rs. 4000 for the same period at 1% higher rate of interest. If the interest in both cases is same, the former rate of interest is :

A. 3% B. 4%
C. 6% D. 5%

3. If a certain sum of money at simple interest amounts to Rs. 1900 in 3 years and to Rs. 2050 in 5 years, the rate per cent per annum is :

A. 4½% B. 3½%
C. 2½% D. 5¼%

4. A certain sum of money lent out on simple interest amounts to Rs. 1760 in 2 years and to Rs. 2000 in 5 years. Find the sum.

A. Rs. 1650 B. Rs. 1500
C. Rs. 1580 D. Rs. 1600

5. Out of the sum of Rs. 1550, a part was lent out at 5% p.a. simple interest and the remaining at 8% p.a. simple interest. If the total interest in both cases after 3 years is Rs. 300, the sum of money lent out at 8% p.a. simple interest was:

A. Rs. 760 B. Rs. 775
C. Rs. 750 D. Rs. 780

6. If simple interest on a certain sum of money for 4 years at 5% p.a. is same as the simple interest on Rs. 840 for 10 years at the rate of 4% p.a., the sum of money is:

A. Rs. 1780 B. Rs. 1660
C. Rs. 1680 D. Rs. 1620

7. What equal instalment of annual payment will discharge a debt which is due as Rs. 848 at the end of 4 years at 4% per annum simple interest?

A. Rs. 200 B. Rs. 212
C. Rs. 225 D. Rs. 250

8. Madhavi lent Rs. 5000 to Kamla for 5 years and Rs. 3000 to Vimla for 4 years. Find the rate of interest, if Madhavi gets an interest of Rs. 600 in the end.
A. 1.62% B. 2.5%
C. 3% D. 4%

9. A sum of money doubles itself in 7 years at simple interest. In how many years it will become four fold?
A. 10 years B. 14 years
C. 21 years D. 35 years

10. An amount doubles itself at the end of 8 years with a certain rate of simple interest. What will be the total simple interest on Rs. 8000 at that rate at the end of 4 years?
A. Rs. 2000 B. Rs. 4000
C. Rs. 6000 D. None of these

ANSWERS

1	2	3	4	5	6	7	8	9	10
D	B	A	D	C	C	A	A	C	B

EXPLANATORY ANSWERS

1. $\frac{1250 \times R \times 3}{100} + \frac{1500 \times R \times 2}{100} = 258.75$

$\Rightarrow 6750\ R = 25875$

$\therefore \quad R = \frac{25875}{6750} = \frac{23}{6} = 3\frac{5}{6}\%$

2. Here, $\frac{5000 \times R \times T}{100} = \frac{4000 \times (R+1) \times T}{100}$

$\Rightarrow 5R = 4R + 4 \quad \therefore \ R = 4\%$

3. Simple interest for 2 years
= Rs. 2050 – Rs. 1900 = Rs. 150

$\therefore$ Simple interest for 1 year = Rs. $\frac{150}{2}$ = Rs. 75

Since simple interest for 3 years = Rs. 75 × 3
= Rs. 225

$\therefore$ Principal = Rs. 1900 – Rs. 225 = Rs. 1675

Hence, Rate = $\frac{75 \times 100}{1675 \times 1} = 4½\%$

4. Interest for 3 years = Rs. 2000 – Rs. 1760
= Rs. 240

$\therefore$ Interest for 1 year = Rs. $\frac{240}{3}$ = Rs. 80

And interest for 2 years = Rs. 80 × 2 = Rs. 160

$\therefore$ Principal = Rs. 1760 – Rs. 160 = Rs. 1600

5. Let Rs. x and Rs $(1550 - x)$ were lent out at 8% and 5% respectively; then

$\frac{x \times 8 \times 3}{100} + \frac{(1550 - x) \times 5 \times 3}{100} = 300$

$\Rightarrow 24x + 23250 - 15x = 30000$

$\Rightarrow 9x = 6750 \quad \therefore \ x = \frac{6750}{9}$ = Rs. 750

6. Here, $\frac{P \times 5 \times 4}{100} = \frac{840 \times 4 \times 10}{100} \Rightarrow 5P = 8400$

$\therefore \quad P = \frac{8400}{5}$ = Rs. 1680

7. Let equal instalment be Rs. x; then

$x + \frac{x \times 4 \times 3}{100} + x + \frac{x \times 4 \times 2}{100} + x + \frac{x \times 4 \times 1}{100} + x = 848$

$\Rightarrow 4x + \frac{24x}{100} = 848 \quad \Rightarrow \quad \frac{106x}{25} = 848$

$\therefore x = \frac{848 \times 25}{106}$ = Rs. 200

8. $\frac{5000 \times R \times 5}{100} + \frac{3000 \times R \times 4}{100} = 600$

$\Rightarrow \quad 250\ R + 120\ R = 600$

$\Rightarrow \quad 370R = 600$

$\therefore \quad R = \frac{600}{370} = 1.62\%$

9. Let principal be Rs. x; then amount = Rs. $2x$, Hence, I = $2x - x$ = Rs. x.

$R = \frac{x \times 100}{x \times 7} = \frac{100}{7}\%$ p.a.

Now, amount = Rs. $4x$; then I = $4x - x$ = Rs. $3x$

Hence, $T = \frac{3x \times 100}{x \times \frac{100}{7}} = \frac{3 \times 100 \times 7}{100} = 21$ years

10. Let principal = Rs. x; then amount = Rs. $2x$; I
= $2x - x$ = Rs. x

$R = \frac{x \times 100}{x \times 8} = \frac{25}{2}\%$

Again, $I = \frac{8000 \times 25 \times 4}{100 \times 2}$ = Rs. 4000

COMPOUND INTEREST

1. The compound interest on a certain sum of money invested for 3 years at 5% per annum is Rs. 1891.50. What will be the simple interest on the same sum at the same rate for 2 years?

A. Rs. 1700 B. Rs. 1200
C. Rs. 1500 D. Rs. 2100

2. A sum of money lent out at a certain rate of simple interest amounts to Rs. 6600 in 2 years and to Rs. 6900 in 3 years. What will be the compound interest on the same sum of money if lent out at the same rate for 2 years?

A. Rs. 605 B. Rs. 715
C. Rs. 615 D. Rs. 595

3. A man deposits Rs. 1200 in a bank on the 1st day of each year. If the bank pays 5% per annum compound interest on deposited sum of money, what will be the amount to his credit on the 10th day of the second year?

A. Rs. 2560 B. Rs. 2460
C. Rs. 2370 D. Rs. 2860

4. If the difference between compound and simple interest on a certain sum of money for 3 years at 5% per annum is Rs. 244, the sum is :

A. Rs. 40000 B. Rs. 25000
C. Rs. 30000 D. Rs. 32000

5. A man purchased a sewing machine for Rs. 5000. If due to sustained use value of this sewing machine depreciates by 6% annually, find its value after 3 years.

A. Rs. 3775.67 B. Rs. 4152.92
C. Rs. 4250.25 D. Rs. 4356.25

6. Find the sum on which the difference between compound and simple interest for 3 years at 10% per annum will be Rs. 868.

A. Rs. 29500 B. Rs. 27625
C. Rs. 28500 D. Rs. 28000

7. Samir invested Rs. 15000 at the rate of interest 10% p.a. for 1 year. If the interest compound six months. What amount will Samir get at the end of the year?

A. Rs. 16,500 B. Rs. 16525.50
C. Rs. 16537.50 D. Rs. 18,150

8. The compound interest on a certain sum for 2 years at 10% per annum is Rs. 525. The simple interest on the same sum for double the time at half the rate per cent per annum is:

A. Rs. 800 B. Rs. 600
C. Rs. 500 D. Rs. 400

9. The least number of complete years in which a sum of money put at 20% compound interest will be more than doubled is:

A. 6 B. 5
C. 4 D. 3

10. On a sum of money, the simple interest for 2 years is Rs. 660, while the compound interest is Rs. 696.30, the rate of interest being the same in both cases. Find the rate of interest.

A. Rs. 12% B. 11%
C. 10% D. 9%

ANSWERS

1	2	3	4	5	6	7	8	9	10
B	C	B	D	B	D	C	C	C	B

EXPLANATORY ANSWERS

1. Here, $1891.50 = P\left[\left(1+\frac{5}{100}\right)^3 - 1\right]$

$\Rightarrow \quad 1891.50 = P\left[\left(\frac{21}{20}\right)^3 - 1\right]$

$\Rightarrow \quad 1891.50 = P\left(\frac{1261}{8000}\right)$

$\therefore \; P = \frac{1891.50 \times 8000}{1261} = \text{Rs. } 12000$

Now, $\text{S.I.} = \frac{12000 \times 5 \times 2}{100} = \text{Rs. } 1200$

2. Here, 1 year's S.I. = Rs. 6900 – Rs. 6600 = Rs. 300

$\therefore$ 2 year's S.I. = 300 × 2 = Rs. 600

$\therefore$ Principal = Rs. 6600 – Rs. 600 = Rs. 6000

Hence, $\text{Rate} = \frac{600 \times 100}{6000 \times 2} = 5\%$

$\therefore$ $$\text{C.I.} = 6000\left[\left(1+\frac{5}{100}\right)^2 - 1\right]$$

$$= 6000\left[\left(\frac{21}{20}\right)^2 - 1\right] = \frac{6000 \times 41}{400} = \text{Rs. } 615$$

3. Required amount $= 1200\left(1+\frac{5}{100}\right) + 1200$

$$= 1200 \times \frac{21}{20} + 1200 = 1260 + 1200 = \text{Rs. } 2460$$

4. Here, $P\left[\left(1+\frac{5}{100}\right)^3 - 1\right] - \frac{P \times 5 \times 3}{100} = 244$

$$\Rightarrow P \times \frac{1261}{8000} - \frac{3P}{20} = 244 \Rightarrow P \times \frac{61}{8000} = 244$$

$$\therefore P = \frac{244 \times 8000}{61} = \text{Rs. } 32000$$

5. Here, value of the machine after 3 years

$$= 5000\left(1-\frac{6}{100}\right)^3 = 5000 \times \frac{47}{50} \times \frac{47}{50} \times \frac{47}{50}$$

= Rs. 4152.92.

6. Here, $P\left[\left(1+\frac{10}{100}\right)^3 - 1\right] - \frac{P \times 10 \times 3}{100} = 868$

$$\Rightarrow P \times \frac{331}{1000} - \frac{3P}{10} = 868$$

$$\Rightarrow P \times \frac{31}{1000} = 868 \therefore P = \frac{868 \times 1000}{31}$$

$= \text{Rs. } 28000$

7. $A = 15000\left(1+\frac{5}{100}\right)^2 = 15000 \times \frac{441}{400}$

$= \text{Rs. } 16537.50$

8. Here, $P\left[\left(1+\frac{10}{100}\right)^2 - 1\right] = 525$

$$\Rightarrow P\left[\frac{121}{100} - 1\right] = 525 \Rightarrow P \times \frac{21}{100} = 525$$

$$\therefore P = \frac{525 \times 100}{21} = \text{Rs. } 2500$$

Hence, required S.I. $= \frac{2500 \times 5 \times 4}{100} = \text{Rs. } 500$

9. Here, $P\left(1+\frac{20}{100}\right)^n > 2P \Rightarrow \left(\frac{6}{5}\right)^n > 2$

Hence, if $n = 4$ then, $\left(\frac{6}{5}\right)^4 = \frac{1296}{625} > 2$

So, $n = 4$ years

10. Here, S.I. for 1 year = Rs. 330
Since, simple interest of Rs. 330 for 1 year
= 696.30 − 660 = Rs. 36.30

Hence, required rate $= \frac{36.30 \times 100}{330 \times 1} = \frac{3630}{330} = 11\%$

AREA AND PERIMETER

1. If side of a square is reduced by 50%, its area will be reduced by

A. 50% B. 75%
C. 80% D. 60%

2. If each side of a square is doubled, its area will become

A. double B. four times
C. three times D. eight times

3. Three sides of a triangle are in the ratio of 17 : 15 : 8. If the perimeter of this triangle is 40 m, find its area

A. 50 sq. m. B. 49 sq. m.
C. 60 sq. m. D. 69 sq. m.

4. If the length of a rectangle is increased by 20% and width is decreased by 15%, then its area

A. decreases by 4% B. increases by 2%
C. decreases by 2% D. increases by 3%

5. If the length of a rectangle is increased by 20%, then by how much per cent its breadth must be decreased so as to keep its area unaltered?

A. 25% B. $8\frac{1}{3}\%$
C. $16\frac{2}{3}\%$ D. 20%

6. The ratio of length and breadth of a rectangular plot is 71 : 61 respectively. The area of the plot is 17324 m^2. What is perimeter of the plot?

A. 264 m B. 284 m
C. 528 m D. 614 m

7. If the length and breadth of a rectangular field are increased, the area increases by 50%. If the increase in length was 20%, by what percentage was the breadth increased?

A. 20% B. 25%
C. 30% D. 40%

8. The length and breadth of a varandah is 40 m and 15 m respectively. How many stone slabs of size 6 decimetre × 5 decimetre each are needed in flooring it:
A. 1000 B. 2000
C. 3000 D. 4000

9. The circumference of a circular plot is 396 m. What is the area of the circular plot?
A. 9,446 m^2 B. 9,856 m^2
C. 12,474 m^2 D. 18,634 m^2

10. If the sides of an equilateral triangle are increased by 20%, 30% and 50% respectively to form a new triangle, the increase in the perimeter of the equilateral triangle is:
A. 25% B. $33\frac{1}{3}\%$
C. 50% D. 100%

ANSWERS

1	2	3	4	5	6	7	8	9	10
B	B	C	B	C	C	B	B	C	B

EXPLANATORY ANSWERS

1. Area of the square = x^2 sq. m.

Side of the new square = $x - 50\%$ of $x = \frac{x}{2}$ m

$\therefore$ Area of the new square $= \left(\frac{x}{2}\right)^2 = \frac{x^2}{4}$ sq. m.

$\therefore$ Reduction in area of the square $= x^2 - \frac{x^2}{4}$

$= \frac{3x^2}{4}$ sq. m.

$\therefore$ Percentage reduction $= \frac{3x^2/4}{x^2} \times 100 = 75\%$

2. Area of the square = x^2 sq. m
Now, area of the new square = $(2x)^2 = 4x^2$ sq. m
Hence, it is clear that if side of a square is doubled, its area becomes four times.

3. Suppose sides of the triangle are $17x$ m, $15x$ m and $8x$ metres
$\therefore$ Perimeter $= 17x + 15x + 8x = 40x$
Now, $40x = 40$
$\Rightarrow x = 1$ m
Therefore, the sides are $17 \times 1 = 17$ m, $15 \times 1 = 15$ m and $8 \times 1 = 8$ m
$\because (17)^2 = (15)^2 + (8)^2$,
i.e., it is a right angled triangle
$\therefore$ Area of the right angled triangle
$= \frac{1}{2} \times 8 \times 15 = 60$ sq.m.

4. Area of the rectangle = xy sq. metre

Area of the new rectangle $= \frac{120}{100} x \times \frac{85}{100} y$

$= 1.020\, xy$ sq. metre

$\therefore$ Increase in the area $= 1.02\, xy - xy = .02\, xy$ sq. m.

$\therefore$ Percentage increase $= \frac{.02xy}{xy} \times 100 = 2\%$

5. Area of the rectangle = xy
On reducing the breadth by A% and increasing the length by 20%

Length of the new rectangle $= \frac{120x}{100} x = 1.2x$

Breadth of the new rectangle $= y - A\%$ of $y = y\left(1 - \frac{A}{100}\right)$

$\therefore$ Area of the new rectangle $= 1.2x \times y\left(1 - \frac{A}{100}\right)$

Now, $xy = 1.2\, xy\left(1 - \frac{A}{100}\right) \Rightarrow 1 = 1.2 \frac{(100 - A)}{100}$

$\Rightarrow 1.2\, A = 120 - 100$

$\therefore A = \frac{20}{1.2} = 16\frac{2}{3}\%$

6. Let length and breadth of a rectangle be $71x$ and $61x$ m; then

$71x \times 61x = 17324 \Rightarrow x^2 = \frac{17324}{71 \times 61} = 4$

$\therefore x = 2$
Hence, length $= 71 \times 2 = 142$ m; breadth $= 61 \times 2 = 122$ m
Since, perimeter $= 2(142 + 122) = 2 \times 264 = 528$ m

7. Here, $20 + x + \frac{20 \times x}{100} = 50 \Rightarrow x + \frac{x}{5} = 30$

$\Rightarrow \frac{6x}{5} = 30 \quad \therefore x = \frac{5 \times 30}{6} = 25$

Hence, breadth was increased by 25%

8. Required number of stone slabs $= \frac{40 \times 15}{\frac{6}{10} \times \frac{5}{10}}$

$= \frac{40 \times 15 \times 100}{6 \times 5} = 2000$

VOLUME AND SURFACE AREA

1. If a solid sphere of 3 cm radius is melted and recast into a right circular cone whose base radius is same as that of the sphere, the height of the cone will be

A. 8 cm B. 12 cm
C. 6 cm D. 5 cm

2. Diameter of a roller is 2.4 m and it is 1.68 m long. If it takes 1000 complete revolutions once over to level a field, the area of the field is

A. 12672 sq. m B. 12671 sq. m
C. 12762 sq. m D. 11768 sq. m

3. If each edge of a cube is increased by 10%, then by how much per cent will the surface area of this cube be increased?

A. 21% B. 18%
C. 15% D. 20%

4. Height and base radius of a solid cylinder are 14 m and 4 m respectively. It is melted and recast into a solid cone of the same base radius as that of the cylinder, what will be the height of the cone?

A. 21 m B. 42 m
C. 48 m D. 54 m

5. A room is in the form of a cube of side 10 m. How many bales of cotton can be kept in it if each bale covers 5 cu m space?

A. 100 B. 175
C. 200 D. 225

6. Three cubes having side 2 cm, 3 cm and 4 cm respectively are melted together to form a new cube. The side of the new cube will be

A. 3.526 cm B. 4.628 cm
C. 4.626 cm D. 4.528 cm

7. If base diameter of a cylinder is increased by 50%, then by how much per cent its height must be decreased so as to keep its volume unaltered?

A. 45.56% B. 55.56%
C. 50.16% D. 62.33%

8. The surface area of a cube is 600 sq. m. Its diagonal is

A. $10\sqrt{3}$ cm B. $5\sqrt{3}$ cm
C. $4\sqrt{2}$ cm D. $10\sqrt{2}$ cm

9. The base diameter of a conical tomb is 28 m and its slant height is 50 m. Find the cost of white washing its curved surface at the rate of 80 paise per sq. m?

A. Rs. 1860 B. Rs. 1760
C. Rs. 1950 D. Rs. 1875

10. The volume of a cuboid is 1120 cu cm and its height is 5 cm while the length and the breadth of the cuboid are in the ratio 8 : 7. The length of this cylinder exceeds the breadth by

A. 4 cm B. 2 cm
C. 7 cm D. 5 cm

ANSWERS

1	2	3	4	5	6	7	8	9	10
B	A	A	B	C	C	B	A	B	B

EXPLANATORY ANSWERS

1. Volume of the cone = Volume of the sphere

$$\therefore \quad \frac{1}{3}\pi(3)^2 \times h = \frac{4}{3}\pi \times 3^3 \Rightarrow h = 12 \text{ cm}$$

Hence, height of the cone = 12 cm.

2. Surface area of the roller = $2\pi rh$

$$= 2 \times \frac{22}{7} \times 1.2 \times 1.68 = 12.672 \text{ sq. m}$$

In one complete revolution, the roller covers 12.672 sq. m.

∴ It will cover in 1000 revolutions

= 12.672 × 1000 = 12672 sq. m

Hence, area of the field = 12672 sq. m.

3. Percentage increase in the surface area of the cube

$$= \left(x + y + \frac{xy}{100}\right)\%$$

$$= \left(10 + 10 + \frac{10 \times 10}{100}\right)\% = 21\%.$$

4. Here,

volume of the cone = Volume of the cylinder

$$\Rightarrow \quad \frac{1}{3}\pi r^2 \times \text{height} = \pi r^2 \times 14$$

$$\therefore \quad \text{Height} = 14 \times 3 = 42 \text{ m}$$

Thus, height of the cone = 42 m.

5. Volume of the cubical room = $(10)^3$
= 1000 cu m

Number of cotton bales which can be placed in the room

$$= \frac{\text{Volume of the room}}{\text{Volume of each cotton bale}} = \frac{1000}{5} = 200.$$

6. Volume of the new cube = $2^3 + 3^3 + 4^3$
= 8 + 27 + 64 = 99cu cm

$\therefore$ Side of the new cube = $\sqrt[3]{99}$ = 4.626 cm.

7. Change in the volume of the cylinder

$$= \left(x + y + (-z) + \frac{xy + y(-z) + (-zx)}{100} + \frac{xy(-z)}{100^2}\right)\%$$

Since volume of the cylinder remains unchanged.

$\therefore$ Change = 0%

Now, $\left(50 + 50 + (-z) + \frac{50 \times 50 - 50z - 50z}{100} + \frac{50 \times 50 \times (-z)}{100^2}\right) = 0$

$\therefore$ 100 − z + 25 − z − .25z = 0

$\Rightarrow 2.25z = 125 \Rightarrow z = \frac{125}{2.25} = 55.56$

$\therefore$ Height of the cylinder should be decreased by 55.56%.

8. Here, $6 \times (\text{side})^2 = 600$

$\Rightarrow$ $\text{side}^2 = 100$

$\Rightarrow$ side = $\sqrt{100}$ = 10 cm

$\therefore$ Diagonal of the cube= $\sqrt{3} \times \text{side}$

$= \sqrt{3} \times 10$

$= 10\sqrt{3}$ cm.

9. Area of the curved surface of the cone

$$= \frac{22}{7} \times \frac{28}{2} \times 50 = 2200 \text{ sq. m.}$$

$\therefore$ Cost of white washing at 80 paise per sq. m

$$= 2200 \times \frac{80}{100} = \text{Rs. } 1760.$$

10. Suppose the length and the breadth of the cuboid are $8x$ cm and $7x$ cm

$\therefore$ Here, $8x \times 7x \times 5 = 1120$

$\Rightarrow x^2 = \frac{1120}{280} = 4 = (2)^2 \quad \Rightarrow \quad x = 2$

$\therefore$ Length of the cuboid = 8 × 2 = 16 cm

Breadth of the cuboid = 7 × 2 = 14 cm

Hence, it is clear that length of the cuboid exceeds the breadth by 2 cm.

SERIES

Directions (Qs. 1 to 7) : *In the following number series, one of the numbers does not fit into the series. Find the wrong number.*

1. 2, 5, 10, 18, 26, 37, 50
A. 2 B. 5
C. 37 D. 18

2. 3 , 18, 38, 78, 123, 178, 243
A. 123 B. 178
C. 3 D. 38

3. 380, 188, 92, 48, 20, 8, 2
A. 188 B. 92
C. 48 D. 20

4. 5, 11, 23, 47, 96, 191, 383
A. 11 B. 23
C. 47 D. 96

5. 89, 78, 86, 80, 85, 82, 83
A. 78 B. 86
C. 80 D. 85

6. 58, 57, 54, 50, 42, 33, 32
A. 57 B. 54
C. 50 D. 32

7. 2, 20, 27, 44, 64
A. 27 B. 8
C. 20 D. 44

Directions (Qs. 8 to 10) : *Complete the following series.*

8. 1 4 9 16 25 36 49 ....
A. 54 B. 56
C. 64 D. 81

9. 11 13 17 19 23 29 31 37 41 ....
A. 43 B. 47
C. 53 D. 51

10. 3 7 6 5 9 3 12 1 15 ....
A. 18 B. 13
C. −1 D. 3

ANSWERS

1	2	3	4	5	6	7	8	9	10
D	C	C	D	A	C	C	C	A	C

EXPLANATORY ANSWERS

1. 2 5 10 18 26 37 50

1^2+1 2^2+1 3^2+1 4^2+1 5^2+1 6^2+1 7^2+1

Wrong no. = 18, Correct no. = 17.

2. Only 3 is a prime number.

3. Wrong no. = 48, Correct no. = 44

Each term will be four more than two times the next term.

4. 5 11 23 47 [96] 191 383

+6 +12 +24 +48 +96 +192

Wrong no. = 96, Correct no. = 95.

5. If 87 is written in place of 78 then tens digit of each term will be 8.

6. 58 57 54 [50] 42 33 22

−1 −3 −5 −7 −9 −11

Wrong no. = 50, Correct no. = 49.

7. 2 [20] 27 44 64

+11 +14 +17 +20

Wrong no. = 20, Correct no. = 13.

8. Numbers are $1^2, 2^2, 3^2, 4^2, 5^2, 6^2, 7^2$.
So, the next number is $8^2 = 64$.

9. Numbers are all primes. The next prime is 43.

10. There are two series, beginning respectively with 3 and 7. In one 3 is added and in another 2 is subtracted. The next number is $1 - 2 = -1$.

APPROXIMATE VALUES

1. $85432 \div 2106 + 59.5614 = ?$
(*a*) 100 (*b*) 60
(*c*) 80 (*d*) 140

2. $\sqrt{67621} = ?$
(*a*) 320 (*b*) 260
(*c*) 200 (*d*) 280

3. 9.7 % of 5011 + 55.03 % of 4991
(*a*) 5500 (*b*) 7200
(*c*) 6000 (*d*) 4200

4. $730 \times 199 = ?$
(*a*) 350000 (*b*) 335000
(*c*) 300000 (*d*) 34600

5. $.0144 \times 0.36 = ?$
(*a*) 0.5 (*b*) 0.005
(*c*) 0.05 (*d*) 0.005

6. 31% of 1508 + 26% of 2018
(*a*) 1500 (*b*) 2000
(*c*) 1000 (*d*) 1200

7. $3015 + 13594 + 3738 = ?$
(*a*) 40000 (*b*) 36000
(*c*) 42000 (*d*) 46000

8. $6012 \times 119 = ?$
(*a*) 560000 (*b*) 448000
(*c*) 900000 (*d*) 720000

9. $2712.1563 \div 1805.4018 + 3.4982 = ?$
(*a*) 9 (*b*) 8
(*c*) 4 (*d*) 5

10. $4182.365 \div 20.886 = ?$
(*a*) 300 (*b*) 200
(*c*) 150 (*d*) 250

ANSWERS

1	2	3	4	5	6	7	8	9	10
A	B	D	A	B	C	A	D	D	B

EXPLANATORY ANSWERS

1. $85432 \div 2106 + 60 = 40 + 60 = 100$
Therefore, (B) is the correct answer.

2. $\sqrt{67621} = \sqrt{67600} = 260$
Therefore, (B) is the correct answer.

3. 29.7 % of 5011 + 55.03 % of 4991
= 30 % of 5000 + 55 % of 5000

$$= \frac{30}{100} \times 5000 + \frac{55}{100} \times 5000$$

$= 1500 + 2750 = 4250 \Rightarrow 4200$
Therefore, (D) is the correct answer.

4. $1730 \times 199 = 1730 \times 200$
$= 346000 \Rightarrow 350000$
Therefore, (B) is the correct answer.

5. $0.0144 \times 0.36 = 0.0140 \times 0.36 = .005040$
$\Rightarrow .005$
Therefore, (B) is the correct answer.

6. 31% of 1508 + 26% of 2018
= 30% of 1500 + 25% × 2000

$$= \frac{30}{100} \times 1500 + \frac{25}{100} \times 2000$$

$= 450 + 500 = 950 \Rightarrow 1000$
Therefore, (C) is the correct answer.

7. $23015 + 13594 + 3738$
$= 23000 + 13600 + 3700$
$= 40300 \Rightarrow 40000$
Therefore, (A) is the correct answer.

8. $6012 \times 119 = 6000 \times 120 = 720000$
Therefore, (D) is the correct answer.

9. $2712.1563 \div 1805.4018 + 3.4982$
$= 2700 \div 1800 + 3.5 = 1.5 + 3.5 = 5$
Therefore, (D) is the correct answer.

10. $4182.365 \div 20.886 = 4200 \div 21 = 200$
Therefore, (B) is the correct answer.

REASONING ABILITY

SERIES

Directions : *In each of the following series determine the order of the letters. Then from the given options select the one which will complete the given series.*

1. BMK, DLM, FKO, HJQ, ?

A. JIR B. JIT C. JHS D. JIS

2. A, CD, FGH, ?

A. IJKL B. KLMN C. JKLM D. LMNO

3. BXJ, ETL, HPN, KLP, ?

A. PHR B. NIR C. NHR D. MHR

4. PUF, QVG, RWH, ?

A. SXI B. SYZ C. SXJ D. SVI

5. DEF, HIJ, MNO, ?

A. RTV B. STU C. PTU D. SRU

Directions : *Which of the following groups of letters will complete the given series?*

6. ab---b-bbaa-

A. babba B. abaab C. abbab D. baaab

7. aa-ab--aaa-a

A. baaa B. abab C. aaab D. aabb

8. -baa-aab-a-a

A. baab B. abab C. aaba D. aabb

9. -a cca-ccca-acccc-aaa

A. ccaa B. acca C. caac D. caaa

10. c-bbb--abbbb-abbb-

A. abccb B. bacbb C. aabcb D. abacb

Directions : *In the following questions, select the number(s) from the given options for completing the given series.*

11. 3, 9, 27, 81, 243, ?

A. 486 B. 729 C. 972 D. 359

12. 1, 6, 12, 19, 27, ?

A. 38 B. 35 C. 36 D. 54

13. 2, 6, 14, 30, 62, ?

A. 126 B. 128 C. 120 D. 130

14. 8, 48, 16, 96, 32, ?

A. 192 B. 150 C. 64 D. 288

15. 2, 8, 14, 24, 34, 48, ?

A. 66 B. 62 C. 58 D. 64

Directions : *In the given series find the number which is wrong.*

16. 5, 25, 120, 625, 3125, 15625

A. 15625 B. 625 C. 120 D. 5

17. 4, 8, 11, 22, 18, 36, 24, 50

A. 8 B. 22 C. 36 D. 24

18. 2, 4, 12, 24, 72, 142, 432

A. 432 B. 12 C. 142 D. 72

19. 2, 3, 4, 4, 6, 8, 9, 12, 16

A. 3 B. 9 C. 6 D. 12

20. 97, 91, 86, 83, 79, 77, 76, 76

A. 86 B. 76 C. 91 D. 83

ANSWERS

1	2	3	4	5	6	7	8	9	10
D	C	C	A	B	D	C	B	D	A
11	**12**	**13**	**14**	**15**	**16**	**17**	**18**	**19**	**20**
B	C	A	A	B	C	D	C	B	D

EXPLANATORY ANSWERS

1. The letters in one group correspond to the letters in the next group in the manner +2, –1, +2 respectively.

BMK DLM FKO HJQ JIS

+2 +2 +2 +2

–1 –1 –1 –1

+2 +2 +2 +2

2. The letters are in natural sequence and from one group to the next one letter is dropped. Also the number of letters in groups is increased by one.

A CD FGH JKLM

↓ ↓ ↓

B E I

3. The letters in one group correspond to the letters in the next group in the manner +3, – 4, +2 respectively, *i.e.*,

BXJ ETL HPN KLP NHR

+3 +3 +3 +3

–4 –4 –4 –4

+2 +2 +2 +2

4. The three letters in each group are moved one step forward.

PUF QVG RWH SXI

+1 +1 +1

+1 +1 +1

+1 +1 +1

5. The letters are in natural order. The number of letters dropped in between the groups is increased by one at each step.

DEF HIJ MNO STU

↓ ↓ ↓

G KL PQR

6. The series is abbaab, abbaab

7. The series is aaaaba, aaaaba

8. The series is aba, aba, aba, aba

9. The series is c,a,cc,aa, ccc, aaa, cccc, aaaa

10. The series is cabbbb, cabbbb, cabbbb

11. The numbers in the series are multiplied by 3 to get the next numbers.

12. The difference between the numbers in the series increases by 1, after beginning from 5, *i.e.*,

1 6 12 19 27 36

+5 +6 +7 +8 +9

13. The difference between the numbers in the series doubles each time, after beginning from 4, *i.e.*,

2 6 14 30 62 126

+4 +8 +16 +32 +64

14. *Explanation I* : The sequence in the series is × 6, ÷ 3 which is repeated.

8 48 16 96 32 192

× 6 ÷ 3 × 6 ÷ 3 × 6

Explanation II : There are two alternate series and the numbers are multiplied by 2.

× 2 × 2

8 48 16 96 32 192

× 2 × 2

Series I : 8, 16, 32

Series II : 48, 96, 192

15. The sequence in the series is :

2 8 14 24 34 48 62

+6 +6 +10 +10 +14 +14

The difference increases by 4 at alternate step.

16. The numbers in the series are multiplied by 5 to get the next number.

∴ 125 should be in place of 120.

17. Two numbers form a pair. The first number increases by 7 for the next pair and the second number is the double of first number.

4 8 11 22 18 36 25 50

× 2 × 2 × 2 × 2

+7 +7 +7

∴ 25 should be in place of 24.

18. There are two alternate series and in each series, the numbers are multiplied by 6 to get the next number.

× 6 × 6 × 6

2 4 12 24 72 144 432

× 6 × 6

∴ 144 should be in place of 142.

19. There are three alternate series and in each series, the numbers are multiplied by 2 to get the next number.

× 2 × 2

2 3 4 4 6 8 8 12 16

× 2 × 2

× 2 × 2

Series I : 2, 4, 8

Series II : 3, 6, 12

Series III : 4, 8, 16

∴ 8 should be in place of 9.

20. The difference between the consecutive numbers in the series decreases by 1 at each step.

97 91 86 82 79 77 76 76

–6 –5 –4 –3 –2 –1 –0

∴ 82 should be in place of 83.

ANALOGIES OR RELATIONSHIPS

Directions : *In the questions given below establish the relationship between the two words. Then from the given options select one which has the same relationship as of the given two words.*

1. ADULT : BABY : : FLOWER : ?
A. Seed B. Bud
C. Fruit D. Butterfly

2. WRITER : READER : : PRODUCER : ?
A. Creator B. Contractor
C. Creature D. Consumer

3. ENTRANCE : EXIT : : LOYALTY : ?
A. Treachery B. Patriotism
C. Fidelity D. Reward

4. MOTHER : MATERNAL : : FATHER : ?
A. Eternal B. Detrimental
C. Paternal D. Formidable

Directions : *In the questions given below one term is missing. Based on the relationship of the two given words find the missing term from the given options.*

5. GFC : CFG : : RPJ : ?
A. JRP B. JPR
C. PJR D. RJP

6. BCF : DEG : : MNQ : ?
A. OPR B. PQS
C. OPP D. QRT

7. NATION : ANITNO : : HUNGRY : ?
A. HNUGRY B. UNHGYR
C. YRNGUH D. UHGNYR

8. SSTU : MMNO : : AABC : ?
A. GGHH B. IJKK
C. XXYZ D. NOOP

ANSWERS

1	2	3	4	5	6	7	8
B	D	A	C	B	A	D	C

EXPLANATORY ANSWERS

1. The youngone of an adult is a baby and that of a flower is a bud.

2. A writer aims to please the readers by his writings, a producer aims to please the consumers by his products.

3. The related words are opposites.

4. Relations on the mother's side are maternal and on the father's side paternal.

5. The letters of the first group are reversed.

GFC : CFG : : RPJ : JPR

6. The three letters are moved 2, 2 and 1 steps forward respectively.

BCF : DEG : : MNQ : OPR
(+2, +2, +1) (+2, +2, +1)

7. The word is divided in sections of two letters and the letters are reversed.

NATION : ANITNO : : HUNGRY : UHGNYR

8. The first letter in each group is repeated and followed by two consecutive letters.

ODD ONE OUT

Directions : *Three of the following four in each question are alike in a certain way and so form a group. Select the group of letters that does not belong to that group.*

1. A. ACE B. LOR
C. GIK D. VXZ

2. A. TSR B. LKJ
C. PQO D. HGF

3. A. EF LM B. KJ SR
C. XW HG D. ED YX

4. A. JOPK B. BOPC
C. QOPR D. TOPS

5. A. DfH B. MoQ
C. UwY D. lnO

6. A. JKkL B. OPpQ
C. DEEf D. VWwX

7. A. BdfH B. FHJL
C. RTvX D. uVwX

8. A. DFHEG B. TWXUV
C. OQSPR D. JLNKM

9. A. FEUV B. DCXW
C. BAZY D. HGTS

10. A. UTSR B. XYZW
C. ONML D. IHGF

ANSWERS

1	2	3	4	5	6	7	8	9	10
B	C	A	D	D	C	D	B	A	B

EXPLANATORY ANSWERS

1. The sequence in each group is +2. Only option B has sequence in +3, *i.e.*,

ABCDE (+2 +2) LMNOPQR (+3 +3)

GHIJK (+2 +2) VWXYZ (+2 +2)

2. The sequence of alphabet in each group is in reverse order. Only option C has sequence in disturbed order.

3. Two consecutive alphabet in each group are in reverse sequence (–1), *i.e.*,

KJ SR; XW HG; ED YX
–1 –1 –1 –1 –1 –1

Only in option (A) the sequence is in natural order (+1), *i.e.*,

E F (+1) L M (+1)

4. In each group, letters 'OP' are common. The two corner alphabet are in natural order (+1); *i.e.*,

JOPK ; BOPC ; QOPR
+1 +1 +1

Only in option (D) they are in reverse order (–1); *i.e.*,

TOPS
–1

5. In other groups, only the alphabet in the centre is of lower case. In this option letter 'L' on the left is also in lower case.

6. In other groups, the third letter which is a repeat of the second alphabet is in lower case.

7. In each group, the sequence of the alphabet, irrespective of the case, is +2; *i.e.*,

B D f H ; F H J L ; R T v X
+2 +2 +2 +2 +2+2 +2 +2 +2

Only in option (D) the sequence is in natural order (+1), *i.e.*,

uV w X
+1 +1 +1

8. In each group; the alphabet at positions-first, fourth, second, fifth and third, form a natural sequence.

In option (B), the alphabet at positions first, fourth, fifth, second and third, form the natural sequence.

9. In each group, two alphabets in the corner and two alphabets in the centre correspond to their reverse order positioned alphabet. *i.e.*,

natural order → A B C D E F G H I J K L M
reverse order → Z Y X W V U T S R Q P O N
natural order → N O P Q R S T U V W X Y Z
reverse order → M L K J I H G F E D C B A

As such—

D corresponds with W and
C corresponds with X.
B corresponds with Y and
A corresponds with Z.
H corresponds with S and
G corresponds with T.

Similarly,

F should correspond with U and
E should correspond with V;
i.e. letters 'UV' should be written as 'VU'

10. In each group, the alphabet are in reverse order.

In option (B), the order is disturbed.

CODING AND DECODING

Directions : *In the following questions select the right option which indicates the correct code for the word or letter given in the question.*

1. If CHAIR is coded as FKDLU then RAID is coded as:
   A. ULGD B. ULKG
   C. ULDG D. UDLG

2. If CONDEMN is coded as CNODMEN, then TEACHER is coded as :
   A. TEACHER B. TAEECHR
   C. TCAEEHR D. TAECEHR

3. In a code language COME is written as XLNV and ABLE as ZYOV. How will MOLLY be written in that code?
   A. NLOBO B. NLBOO
   C. LNOOB D. NLOOB

4. In a certain code PROFESSION is written as EFORPNOISS. In the same code DICTIONARY will be written as :
   A. YRANOITCID B. ITCIDYRANO
   C. ITCIDYRNAO D. ITCDIYARNO

5. JUNE is coded as NXPF, how will STAY be coded in the same manner?
   A. WWCZ B. WVCZ
   C. WWDB D. VWZC

Directions : *In the following questions study the coded patterns and then select the right option from the given alternatives.*

6. In a certain language, (a) 'go ju mi' stands for 'plenty of money'; (b) pao ju go nei vu' for 'money creates lots of problems'; (c) 'kol vu nei' for 'problems create tension'; and (d) 'sol tun ju haw' for 'still money is needed'. Which of the following words stand for 'money'?
   A. nei B. ju
   C. haw D. go

7. In a certain language, (a) 'FOR' stands for 'old is gold'; (b) 'ROT' stands for 'gold is pure'; (c) 'ROM' stands for 'gold is costly'. How will 'pure old gold is costly' be written?
   A. TFROM B. FOTRM
   C. FTORM D. TOMRF

8. In a certain code '415' means 'milk is hot'; '18' means 'hot soup'; and '895' means 'soup is tasty'. What number will indicate the word 'tasty'?
   A. 9 B. 8
   C. 5 D. 4

9. In a certain code '643' means 'she is beautiful', '593' means 'he is handsome', and '567' means 'handsome meets beautiful'. What number will indicate the word 'meets'?
   A. 5 B. 3
   C. 7 D. 6

10. In a certain code language, (a) 'dugo hui mul zo' stands for 'work is very hard'; (b) 'hui dugo ba ki' for 'Bingo is very smart'; (c) 'nano mul dugo' for 'cake is hard', and (d) 'mul ki qu' for 'smart and hard'. Which of the following words stand for 'Bingo'?
    A. jalu B. dugo
    C. ki D. ba

ANSWERS

1	2	3	4	5	6	7	8	9	10
D	D	D	B	A	B	A	A	C	D

EXPLANATORY ANSWERS

2. In this word, the second and third letters interchange their places and the fifth and sixth letters do the same. Other letters retain their position.

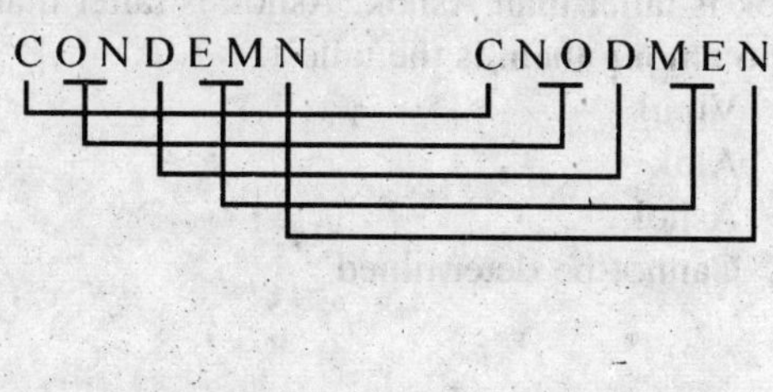

3. The letters of the word are coded by their represented letters in the reverse series.

C O M E → letters in natural series
X L N V → letters in reverse series
↓ ↓ ↓ ↓
3rd 15th 13th 5th → position of letters
A B L E → letters in natural series
Z Y O V → letters in reverse series
↓ ↓ ↓ ↓
1st 2nd 12th 5th → position of letters

Similarly,
M O L L Y → letters in natural series
N L O O B → letters in reverse series
↓ ↓ ↓ ↓ ↓
13th 15th 12th 12th 25th → position of letters

4. The word is divided into two equal parts and the letters of each part are written backwards.

PROFE SSION → EFORP NOISS

Similarly,

DICTI ONARY → ITCID YRANO

5. The word is coded by moving the letters +4, +3, +2, and +1 steps respectively.

J U N E → N X P F (+4, +3, +2, +1)

Similarly,

S T A Y → W W C Z (+4, +3, +2, +1)

6.

	Code	*Sentence*
1.	go *ju* mi	plenty of *money*
2.	pao *ju* go nei vu	*money* creates lots of problems
3.	kol vu nei	problems create tension
4.	sol tun *ju* haw	still *money* is needed

In 1st, 2nd and 4th codes and their sentences the word 'ju' is repeated and so is 'money'.

8.

	Code	*Sentence*
1.	415	milk is hot
2.	18	hot soup
3.	895	soup is *tasty*

From 3rd code and its sentence neither number '9' is repeated nor the word 'tasty'.

9.

	Code	*Sentence*
1.	643	she is beautiful
2.	593	he is handsome
3.	567	handsome *meets* beautiful

From 3rd code and its sentence, neither number '7' nor the word 'meets' is repeated.

10.

	Code	*Sentence*
1.	*dugo hui* mul zo	work *is very* hard
2.	*hui dugo* **ba** *ki*	**Bingo** *is very smart*
3.	nano mul *dugo*	cake is *hard*
4.	mul *ki* qu	*smart* and hard

From 2nd code and its sentence, neither 'ba' nor 'Bingo' is repeated.
(Words repeated are in italics)

STATEMENT ANALYSIS

1. Among five friends, A is heavier than B; C is lighter than D; B is lighter than D but heavier than E. Who among them is the heaviest?

A. B B. C
C. A D. Can't say

2. Pune is bigger than Jhansi, Sitapur is bigger than Chittor. Raigarh is not as big as Jhansi, but is bigger than Sitapur. Chittor is not as big as Sitapur. Which is the smallest?

A. Jhansi B. Pune
C. Chittor D. Sitapur

3. Ajay works more than Ram. Alok works as much as Raju. Pankaj works less than Alok. Ram works more than Alok. Who works the most of all?

A. Ajay B. Ram
C. Alok D. Raju

4. Vipul is taller than Hans. Hans is taller than Anand. Alok is taller than Ashok. Ashok is taller than Hans. Who among them is the tallest?

A. Vipul
B. Alok
C. Ashok
D. Cannot be determined

5. Pramod is taller than Gopal. Gopal is shorter than Madhu. To find out who among them is the tallest, which of the following further informations is necessary?
A. Madhu is taller than Gopal.
B. Madhu is shorter than Pramod's brother
C. Pramod is taller than Madhu.
D. Pramod is taller than Madhu's brother.

6. Among five friends P, Q, R, S and T, who is the youngest? To arrive at the answer which of the following information given in the statements (*a*) and (*b*) is sufficient?
(*a*) R is younger than P and T.
(*b*) S is younger than Q.
A. Only (*a*) alone is sufficient
B. Either (*a*) or (*b*) is sufficient
C. Both (*a*) and (*b*) together are needed
D. Both (*a*) and (*b*) together are not sufficient

7. Sushma is richer than Rashmi whereas Anand is richer than Priya. Arun is as rich as Rashmi. Shoba is richer than Sushma.
Which of the following statements is correct according to the above propositions?
A. Rashmi is poorer than Priya.
B. Priya is richer than Arun
C. Arun is poorer than Sushma.
D. Anand is richer than Rashmi

8. A is elder to B while C and D are elder to E who lies between A and B. If C be elder to B, which one of the following statements is necessarily true?
A. E is elder to B
B. A is elder to C
C. C is elder to D
D. D is elder to C

9. Vikram is taller than Rajan but shorter than Annie. Jamal is taller than Annie. Sita is taller than Vikram. Rajan is shorter than Sita. Who is the shortest of all in the group?
A. Sita
B. Rajan
C. Vikram
D. Cannot be determined

10. Suresh is as much older than Kamal as he is younger than Prabodh. Navin is as old as Kamal. Which of the following statements is wrong?
A. Suresh is older than Navin
B. Kamal is younger than Suresh
C. Prabodh is not the oldest
D. Navin is younger than Prabodh

ANSWERS

1	2	3	4	5	6	7	8	9	10
D	C	A	D	C	D	C	A	B	C

EXPLANATORY ANSWERS

1. The five friends in descending order of weight are : A/D, B/C, E or A/D, B, C/E. Either A or D is the heaviest.

2. The order of cities in descending order of size is : Pune, Jhansi, Raigarh, Sitapur, Chittor.

3. On the basis of doing work, the descending order will be : Ajay, Ram, Alok/Raju, Pankaj.

4. On the basis of height, the descending order will be Vipul/Alok, Ashok, Hans, Anand. Either Vipul or Alok is the tallest.

5. According to the information both Pramod and Madhu are taller than Gopal. Option (c) decides who is the tallest.

6. Statements are not inter-related.

7. On the basis of wealth, the descending order will be :
   1. Shobha, Sushma, Rashmi/Arun
   2. Anand, *and* Priya

(The two statements are not inter-related.)

8. The order in descending seniority will be : A/C/D, E, B.

9. On the basis of height the descending order will be :
Jamal/Sita, Annie, Vikram, Rajan.
or
Jamal, Sita/Annie, Vikram, Rajan.

10. On the basis of age the descending order will be : Prabodh, Suresh, Kamal/Navin.

PLACE ARRANGEMENT

Directions: *In the following questions, understand the arrangement pattern and then select the right answer from the given options :*

1. Five boys are sitting in a row. Raghu is not adjacent to Shyam or Amit. Ajay is not adjacent to Shyam. Raghu is adjacent to Mayank. If Mayank is at the middle in the row, then Ajay is adjacent to whom out of the following?

A. Amit B. Raghu
C. Mayank D. Shyam

2. Mini is to the right of Rajni but to the left of Ananta. Saya is to the right of Mini but to the left of Jaya. Who is on the extreme left if all the girls are facing North?

A. Jaya B. Mini
C. Rajni D. Saya

3. Kittu is in-between Mohan and Sohan. Raju is to the left of Sohan and Shyam is to the right of Mohan. If all of the friends are sitting facing South, then who is on their extreme right?

A. Mohan B. Sohan
C. Kittu D. Shyam

4. A, B, C, D and E are running one behind the other. C is not near E and A is not near D. B is next to A and E is not near D. Who is in the middle?

A. B B. E
C. A D. Cannot be said

5. O, P, Q, R, S and T are standing on a bench according to their height. P is taller than O but shorter than S. Only S is taller than T. R is shorter than P but taller than Q. Who is the shortest?

A. O B. Q
C. P D. Cannot be said

ANSWERS

1	2	3	4	5
B	C	D	A	D

EXPLANATORY ANSWERS

1. The order of sitting is :
Amit, Shyam, Mayank, Ajay, Raghu
or
Ajay, Raghu, Mayank, Amit, Shyam

2. The order in which the girls are positioned is :
Rajni, Mini, Ananta, Saya, Jaya
or
Saya, Jaya, Ananta
or
Saya, Ananta, Jaya

3. The order of sitting while facing South is:
Shyam, Mohan, Kittu, Sohan, Raju.

4. The positions while running behind the other is :

E E
A A
B *or* B
C D
D C

5. In descending order of height, the standing positions are :

S S
T T
P *or* P
R R
O Q
Q O

Either O or Q is the shortest. The information given is not enough to clarify the answer.

DIRECTION SENSE

Directions : *In the following questions, select the right answer from the given options to depict the correct direction/distance.*

1. Kittu walks towards East and then towards South. After walking some distance he turns towards West and then turns to his left. In which direction is he walking now?

A. North B. South
C. East D. West

2. A person is driving towards West. What sequence of directions should he follow so that he is driving towards South?

A. left, right, right
B. right, right, left
C. left, left, left
D. right, right, right

3. Richa drives 8 km to the South, turns left and drives 5 km. Again, she turns left and drives 8 km. How far is she from her starting point?

A. 3 km B. 5 km
C. 8 km D. 13 km

4. Dingi runs 40 km towards North then turns right and runs 50 km. He turns right and runs 30 km, and once again turns right and runs 50 km. How far is he from his starting point?

A. 90 km B. 50 km
C. 10 km D. 5 km

5. Debu walks towards East then towards North and turning 45° right walks for a while and lastly turns towards left. In which direction is he walking now?

A. North B. East
C. South-East D. North-West

ANSWERS

1	2	3	4	5
B	D	B	C	D

EXPLANATORY ANSWERS

1.
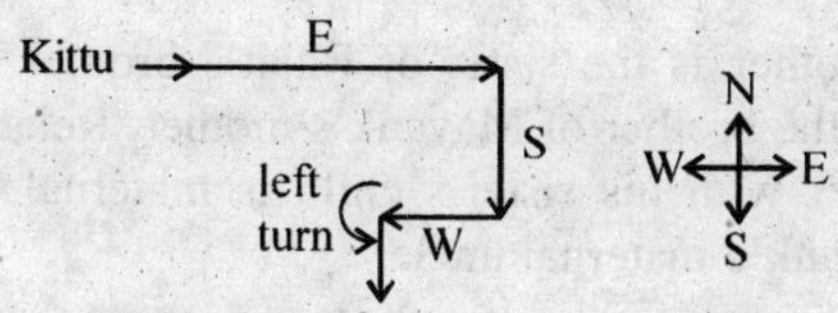

2.
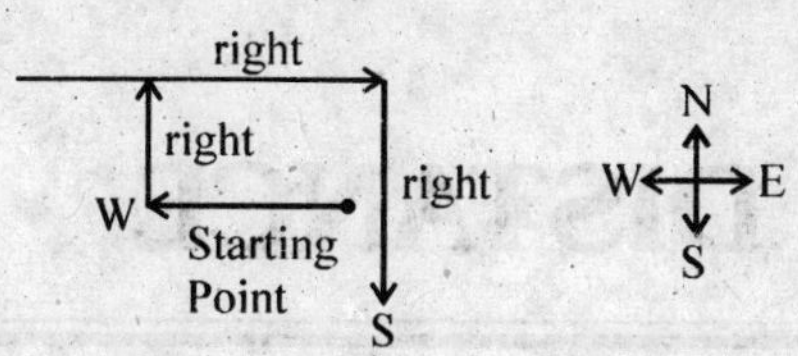

3.
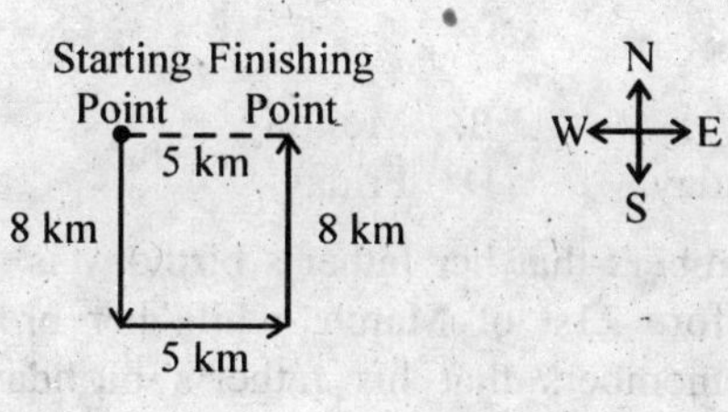

4.
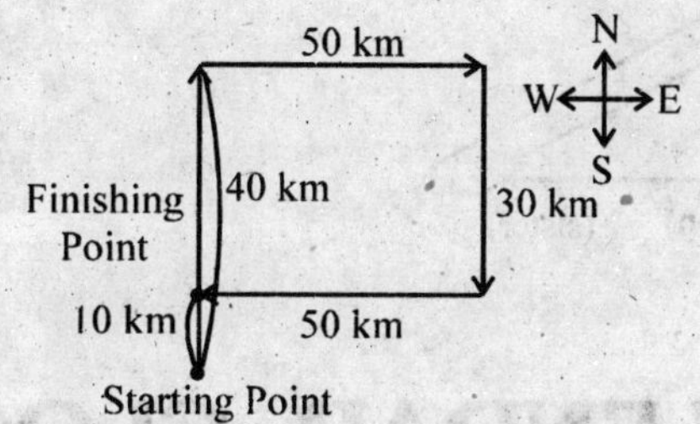

5.
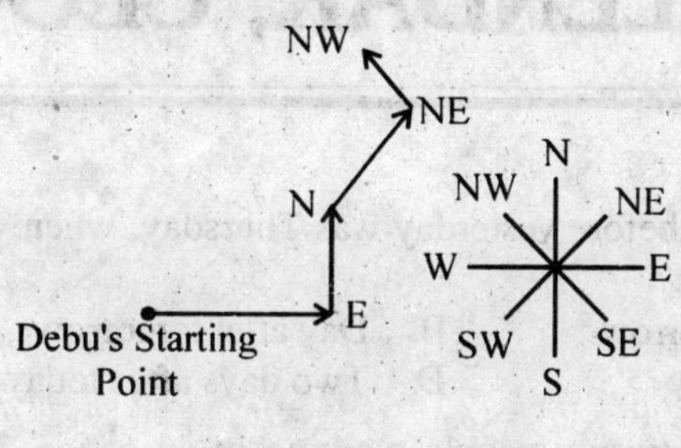

BLOOD RELATIONSHIPS

Directions : *In each of the following questions keenly study the relationship mentioned between the persons, and then from the given options select the right relationship as the answer.*

1. 'A' is the father of 'B' and 'C'. 'B' is the son of 'A' but 'C' is not the son of 'A'. What is 'C's' relation with 'A'?

A. Daughter B. Son
C. Niece D. Nephew

2. A lady said, "The person standing there is my grandfather's only son's daughter". How is the lady related to the standing person?

A. Sister B. Mother
C. Aunt D. Cousin

3. Ravi is the brother of Amit's son's son. What is Amit's relation to Ravi?

A. Cousin B. Father
C. Grandfather D. Son

4. Mayank said, "My mother is the sister of Rajat's brother." What is Rajat's relation with Mayank?
   A. Cousin B. Maternal uncle
   C. Uncle D. Brother-in-law

5. Introducing Lily, Raghav said, "Her father is my mother's only son". How is Lily related to Raghav?
   A. Aunt B. Daughter
   C. Mother D. Sister

ANSWERS

1	2	3	4	5
A	A	C	B	B

EXPLANATORY ANSWERS

1. 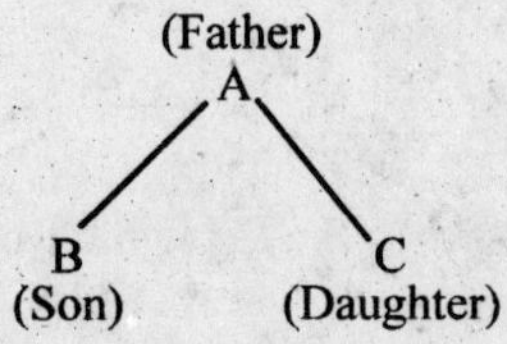

'C' is not the son of 'A', but 'A' is the father of 'C'. So, 'C' is the daughter of 'A'.

2. 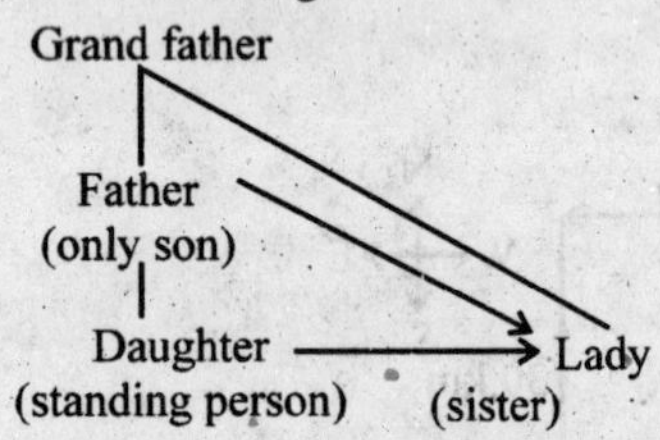

Lady's grandfather's son is lady's father and father's daughter will only be lady's sister.

4. 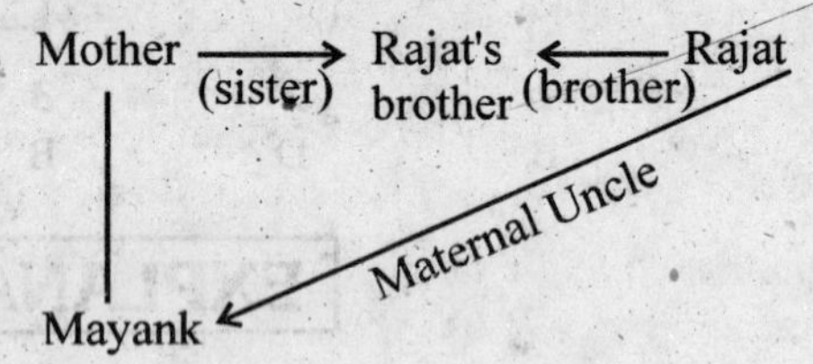

Mayank's mother is the sister of Rajat's brother. So Rajat is also the brother of Mayank's mother. Relation of the brother with his sister's child is maternal. So Rajat is Mayank's maternal uncle.

CALENDAR, CLOCK, TIME, DISTANCE

1. If the day before yesterday was Thursday, when will Sunday be?
   A. Tomorrow B. Day after tomorrow
   C. Today D. Two days after today

2. There are twenty people working in an office. The first group of five works between 8:00 A.M. and 2:00 PM. The second group of ten works between 10:00 AM to 4:00 PM. And the third group of five works between 12 noon to 6:00 PM. There are three computers in the office which all the employees frequently use. During which of the following hours the computers are likely to be used most?
   A. 1:00 PM - 3:00 PM
   B. 12 noon - 2:00 PM
   C. 2:00 PM - 4:00 PM
   D. 10:00 AM - 12 noon

3. If the seventh day of a month is three (3) days earlier than Friday, what day will it be on the nineteenth day of the month?
   A. Sunday B. Monday
   C. Wednesday D. Friday

4. Radha remembers that her father's birthday is after 16th but before 21st of March, while her brother Mangesh remembers that his father's birthday is before 22nd but after 19th of March. On which date is the birthday of their father?
   A. 19th
   B. 20th
   C. 21st
   D. Cannot be determined

5. A man is three (3) years older than his wife and four (4) times as old as his son. If the son attains an age of fifteen (15) years after three (3) years, what is the present age of the mother?
   A. 45 years B. 51 years
   C. 48 years D. 60 years

6. A clock is so placed that at 12 noon its minute hand points towards north-east. In which direction does its

hour hand point at 1.30 P.M.?

A. East B. West
C. North D. South

7. If in the above question clock is turned through an angle of 135º in an anticlockwise direction, in which direction will its minute hand point at 8.45 P.M.?

A. East B. West
C. North D. South

8. A couple married in 1980 had two children, one in 1982 and the other in 1984. Their combined ages will equal the years of the marriage in?

A. 1986 B. 1985
C. 1987 D. 1988

9. Manoj left home for the bus stop 15 minutes earlier than the usual time. It takes 10 minutes to reach the stop. He reached the stop at 8.40 a.m. What time does he usually leave home for the bus stop?

A. 8.30 a.m. B. 8.55 a.m.
C. 8.45 p.m. D. None of these

10. Mamuni went to the movies nine days ago. She goes to the movies only on Thursday. What day of the week is today?

A. Sunday B. Tuesday
C. Thursday D. Saturday

11. If Thursday was the day after the day before yesterday five days ago, what is the least number of days ago when Sunday was three days before the day after tomorrow?

A. Two days ago B. Three days ago
C. Four days ago D. Five days ago

12. 1.12.91 is the first Sunday. Which is the fourth Tuesday of December 91?

A. 31.12.91 B. 24.12.91
C. 17.12.91 D. 26.12.91

13. If the third day of a month is Monday, which of the following will be the fifth day from 21st of that month?

A. Tuesday B. Monday
C. Wednesday D. Thursday

14. Keshav runs a factory in three shifts of eight hours each with 210 employees. In each shift minimum of 80 employees are required to run the factory effectively. No employee can be allowed to work for more than 16 hours a day. At least how many employees will be required to work for 16 hours every day?

A. 30 B. 60
C. Data inadequate D. None of these

15. If 15 horses eat 15 bags of gram in 15 days, in how many days will one horse eat one bag of grain?

A. 15 days B. 1/15 days
C. 1 day D. 30 days

16. A century leap year is divisible by :

A. 4 B. 16
C. 40 D. 400

17. If the fifth day of a month is Friday, which of the following will be the Seventh day from 10th of that month?

A. Tuesday B. Monday
C. Wednesday D. Thursday

18. Day after tomorrow is my birthday. On the same day next week falls 'Holi'. Today is Monday. What will be the day after 'Holi'?

A. Wednesday B. Thursday
C. Friday D. Saturday

19. A clock shows the time as 3 : 30 p.m. If the minute hand gains 2 minutes every hour, how many minutes will the clock gain by 4 a.m.?

A. 23 Minutes B. 24 Minutes
C. 25 Minutes D. 26 Minutes

20. Two brothers were expected to return home on the same day. Rajat returned 3 days earlier but Rohit returned 4 days later. If Rajat returned on Thursday, what was the expected day when both the brothers were to return home and when did Rohit Return?

A. Wednesday, Sunday
B. Thursday, Monday
C. Sunday, Thursday
D. Monday, Friday

ANSWERS

1	2	3	4	5	6	7	8	9	10
A	B	A	B	A	A	D	A	D	D
11	**12**	**13**	**14**	**15**	**16**	**17**	**18**	**19**	**20**
A	B	C	D	A	D	C	B	C	C

EXPLANATORY ANSWERS

1. Thursday —Day-before-yesterday
Friday —Yesterday
Saturday —Today
Sunday — Tomorrow

2. 1. 5 people work between 8 a.m. to 2 p.m.

2. 10 people work between 10 a.m. to 4 p.m.

3. 5 people work between 12 noon to 6 p.m.

So, computers are used most between 12 noon to 2 p.m.

3. 7th day is 3 days earlier than Friday so, 10th day is Friday, so also is 17th.

∴ 19th day will be 2nd day ahead of Friday, *i.e.,* Sunday.

4. Father's birthday

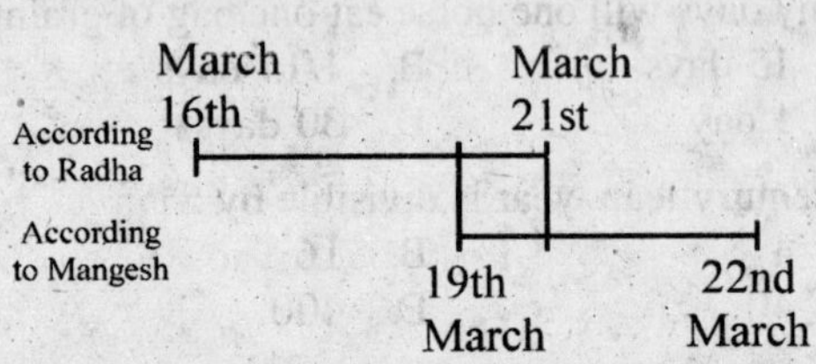

∴ Their father's birthday is on 20th March.

5. Present age of son is 15 – 3 = 12 years. Age of the man is 4 times the age of son, *i.e.,*

12 × 4 = 48 years

Man is 3 years elder to his wife/son's mother.

So Age of the mother is 48 – 3 = 45 years

6.

At 12 noon

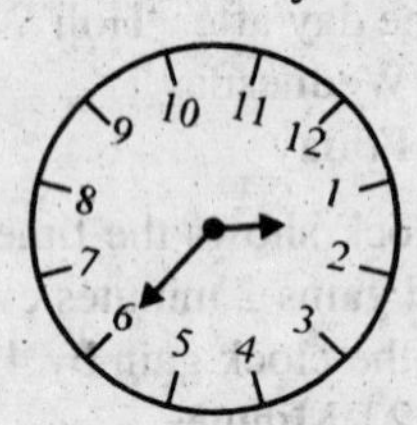

At 1.30 p.m. the hour hand will point towards East.

7.

After rotating the clock in earlier question, its minute hand will point towards South at 8:45 p.m.

8. 1982 — 2 years later — 1st child

1984 — 4 years later — 2nd child

Total age of children — 2 years.

1985 — 5 years later — Total age of children: 4 years.

1986 — 6 years later — Total age of children : 6 years.

9. Manoj reached the bus stop at 8.40 a.m. He left his home at 8:40 – 10 minutes = 8:30 a.m. He left 15 minutes earlier than usual, so his actual time of leaving home is 8:30 am + 15 minutes = 8:45 a.m.

10. Mamuni goes to the movies on Thursday, so nine days ago was Thursday.

∴ Two days ago was also Thursday. So, today is Saturday.

11. Day after the day-before-yesterday five days ago is the 6th day which is Thursday. And so, the 3rd day will be Sunday. Three days before the day-after-tomorrow is Yesterday which is the 1st day of the five days. So, two days ago was Sunday.

12. First Sunday is on 1st December

First Tuesday is on 3rd December

3 weeks later, Fourth Tuesday will be on 3 + (7 × 3) = 24th December.

13. 3rd day of the month is Monday

5th day from 21st is 26th

26 – 3 = 23 days

23 days later, 23/7 leaves 2 days.

So, two days ahead of Monday will be Wednesday.

14. 80 employees are required for double shift.

15. 15 horses eat 15 bags of grain in 15 days

15 horses eat 1 bag of grain in 1 day

1 horse eats 1 bag of grain in 15 days

16. A leap year is divisible by 4 and a century leap year is divisible by 400.

17. Seventh day from 10th is 17th.

5th day is Friday. Next Friday is on 12th, 17 – 12 = 5, 5 days ahead of Friday will be Wednesday. So, 17th is Wednesday.

18. Today is Monday

Day-after-tomorrow is Wednesday

Next week 'Holi' is also on Wednesday

So, Day after Holi is Thursday.

19. Hours between 3:30 p.m. and 4 a.m. are — 12½ hours. Number of minutes gained will be 12½ × 2 = 25 minutes.

20. Rajat returned on Thursday. 3 days later was the day of expected return, *i.e.,* Sunday. Rohit returned 4 days after Sunday, *i.e.,* Thursday.

ROWS AND RANKS

1. In a row of trees, one tree is fifth from either end of the row. How many trees are in the row?

A. 11 B. 8
C. 10 D. 9

2. Jaya ranks 5th in a class of 53. What is her rank from the bottom in the class?

A. 49th B. 48th
C. 47th D. 50th

3. Mohan ranks twenty-first in a class of sixty-five students. What will be his (Mohan's) rank if the lowest candidate is assigned rank 1?

A. 44th B. 45th
C. 46th D. Data inadequate

4. If Rahul finds that he is 12th from the right in a line of boys and 4th from the left, how many boys should be added to the line such that there are 28 boys in the line?

A. 12 B. 14
C. 20 D. 13

5. In a row of boys, Rajan is tenth from the right and Suraj is tenth from the left. When Rajan and Suraj interchange their positions, Suraj will be twenty-seventh from the left. Which of the following will be Rajan's position from the right?

A. Tenth B. Twenty-sixth
C. Twenty-ninth D. None of these

6. Mahesh and Suresh are ranked 11th and 12th respectively from the top in a class of 41 students. What will be their respective ranks from the bottom?

A. 32nd and 33rd B. 29th and 30th
C. 30th and 31st D. 31st and 30th

7. Uma ranked 8th from the top and 37th from bottom in a class. How many students are there in the class?

A. 47 B. 46
C. 45 D. None of these

8. In a queue, Sadiq is 14th from the front and Joseph is 17th from the end, while Jane is in between Sadiq and Joseph. If Sadiq be ahead of Joseph and there be 48 persons in the queue, how many persons are there between Sadiq and Jane?

A. 5 B. 6
C. 7 D. 8

9. Rohan ranked eleventh from the top and twenty-seventh from the bottom among the students who passed the annual examination in a class. If the number of students who failed in the examination was 12, how many students appeared for the examination?

A. 48
B. 49
C. 50
D. Cannot be determined

10. Some boys are sitting in a row. P is sitting fourteenth from the left and Q is seventh from the right. If there are four boys between P and Q, how many boys are there in the row?

A. 19 B. 21
C. 25 D. 23

ANSWERS

1	2	3	4	5	6	7	8	9	10
D	A	B	D	D	D	D	C	B	C

EXPLANATORY ANSWERS

1.

Total number of trees in the row are :
(5 + 5) – 1 = 9

2.
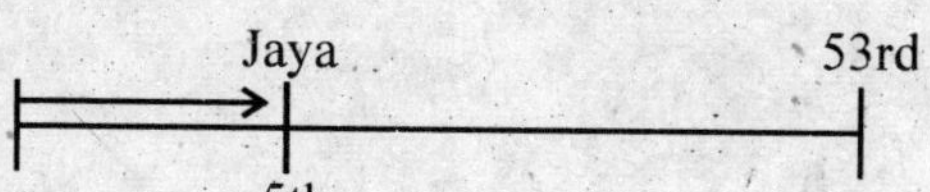

Jaya's rank from the bottom is :
(53 – 5) + 1 = 49th.

3.
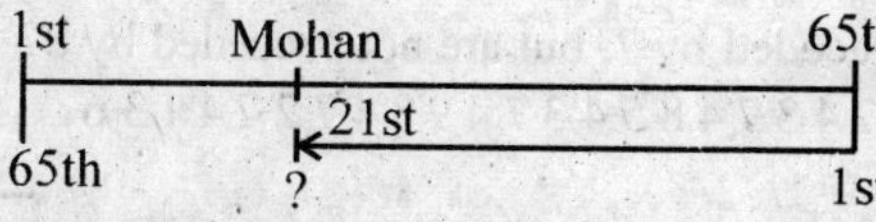

Note : Mohan's rank from the last or the question asked means the same.

Mohan's rank is (65 – 21) + 1 = 45th

4.
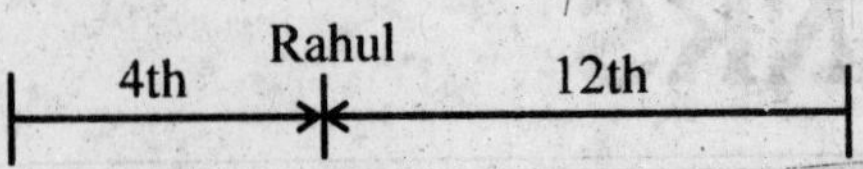

The number of boys in the line are :
(4 + 12) – 1 = 15
To make a line of 28 boys, (28 –15) *i.e.* 13 more boys are needed.

5.
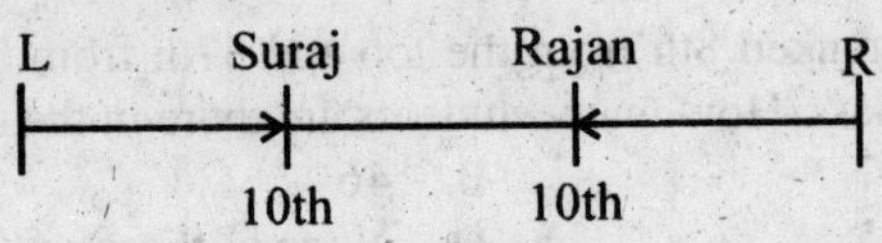

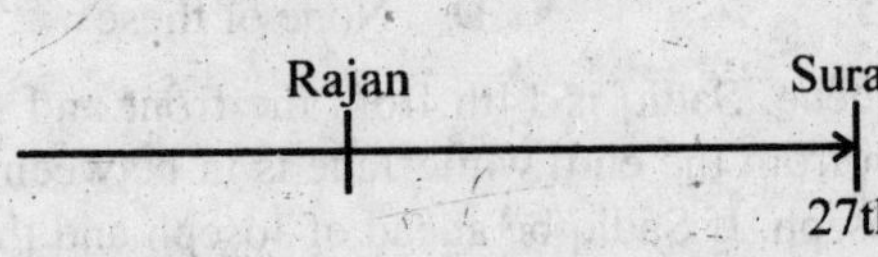

As the position of boys is equal from both ends, Rajan will also be 27th from the right after changing positions.

6.
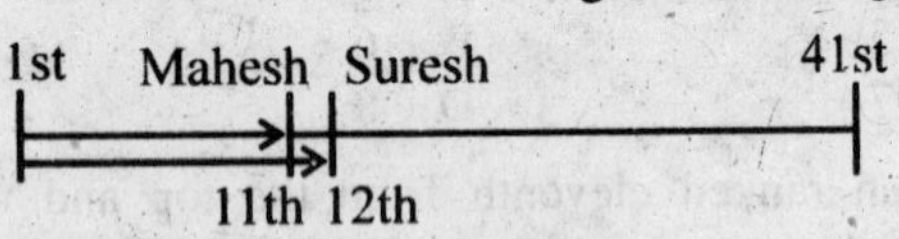

Mahesh's position from bottom is :
(41 – 11) + 1 = 31st
Suresh's position from bottom is :
(41 – 12) +1 = 30th

7.
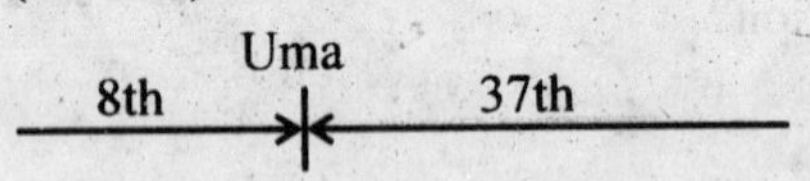

Total number of students in the class are :
(8 + 37) – 1 = 44

8.
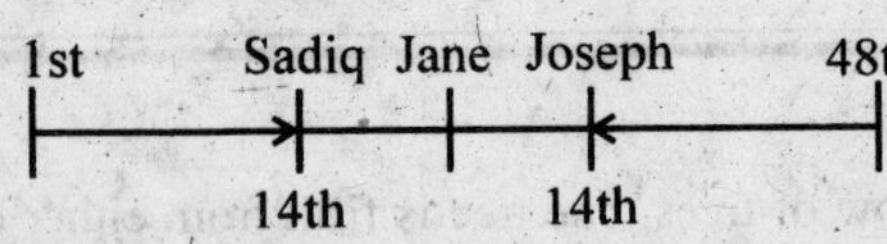

Sadiq's position from last is :
(48 – 14) + 1 = 35th
Number of persons between Sadiq and Joseph are (35 – 17) – 1 = 17
Jane is in-between Sadiq and Joseph *i.e.,* she's at 9th position from both the boys.
∴ there are 8 persons between Sadiq and Jane.
Note : (8 + 8) – 1 = 17

9.
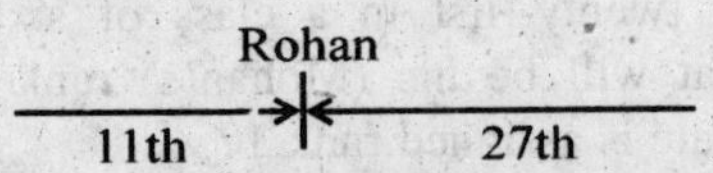

Number of students who passed the examination (11+ 27) – 1 = 37
Those who failed = 12
Total number of students who appeared in the examination = 37 + 12 = 49.

10.
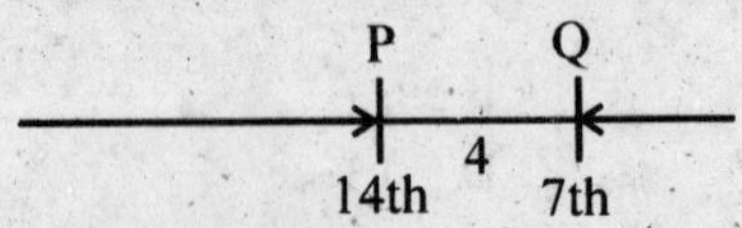

The number of boys in the row are :
(14 + 4 + 7) = 25

NUMBER PROBLEMS

1. How many 6's are there in the following series of numbers which are preceded by 7 but not immediately followed by 9?
6 7 9 5 6 9 7 6 8 7 6 7 8 6 9 4 6 7 7 6 9 5 7 6 3

A. One B. Two
C. Three D. Four

2. In a chess tournament each of six players will play every other player exactly once. How many matches will be played during the tournament?

A. 12 B. 15
C. 30 D. 36

3. How many 4's are there in the following series which are preceded by 7, but are not preceded by 8?
3 4 5 7 4 3 7 4 8 5 4 3 7 4 9 8 4 7 2 7 4 1 3 6

A. 1 B. 2
C. 3 D. 4

4. How many even numbers are there in the following series of numbers, each of which is immediately preceded by an odd number, but not immediately followed by an even number?
5 3 4 8 9 7 1 6 5 3 2 9 8 4 3 5

A. Nil B. 1
C. 2 D. 3

5. If all the numbers from 1 to 51 which are exactly divisible by 3 are arranged in descending order, which of the following numbers will come at the seventh and tenth places from the top?

A. 33 & 27 B. 33 & 21
C. 21 & 30 D. 33 & 24

ANSWERS

1	2	3	4	5
C	B	D	C	D

EXPLANATORY ANSWERS

1. 6 7 9 5 6 9 $\underline{7\,6\,8}$ $\underline{7\,6\,7}$ 8 6 9 4 6 7 7 6 9 5 $\underline{7\,6\,3}$
   1 2 3

2. When all the players have to play with each other then the method of calculating the number of matches to be played is $\frac{n(n-1)}{2}$ where 'n' is the number of players playing the match. So, the number of matches played will be :
   $(6 \times 5) \div 2 = 30 \div 2 = 15$

3. 3 4 5 $\underline{7\,4}$ 3 $\underline{7\,4}$ 8 5 4 3 $\underline{7\,4}$ 9 8 4 7 2 $\underline{7\,4}$ 1 3 6
   1 2 3 4

4. 5 3 4 8 9 7 $\underline{1\,6\,5}$ $\underline{3\,2\,9}$ 8 4 3 5
   1 2

5. The numbers divisible by 3 in descending order are :
   51, 48, 45, 42, 39, 36, 33, $\underline{30}$ (7th), 27, $\underline{24}$ (10th), 21, 18, 15, 12, 9, 6, 3.

SYMBOL SUBSTITUTION

1. If "+" means "–"; "–" means "×"; "×"means "÷" and "÷" means "+", then
   $15 \times 5 \div 10 + 5 - 3 = ?$
   A. 9.5 B. 0
   C. – 2 D. 24
2. If "+" means "–"; "–" means "×"; "×"means "÷" and "÷" means "+", then
   $15 \times 3 \div 15 + 5 - 2 = ?$
   A. 0 B. 10
   C. 20 D. 6
3. If "+" means "÷";"×" means "–"; "÷"means "+" and "–" means "×", then
   $16 \div 8 \times 6 - 2 + 12 = ?$
   A. 22 B. 24
   C. 23 D. 20
4. If "+" means "×"; "–" means "÷"; "÷"means "+" and "×" means "–", then what will be the value of $20 \div 40 - 4 \times 5 + 6 = ?$
   A. 60 B. 1.67
   C. 150 D. 0
5. If "+" means "×"; "–" means "÷"; "×"means "–" and "÷" means "+", then
   $5 + 8 - 4 \times 2 \div 9 = ?$
   A. 15 B. 13
   C. 17 D. 11

ANSWERS

1	2	3	4	5
C	B	C	D	C

EXPLANATORY ANSWERS

1. $15 \div 5 + 10 - 5 \times 3$
   $3 + 10 - 15 = -2$
2. $15 \div 3 + 15 - 5 \times 2$
   $5 + 15 - 10 = 10$
3. $16 + 8 - 6 \times 2 \div 12$
   $16 + 8 - 1 = 23$
4. $20 + 40 \div 4 - 5 \times 6$
   $20 + 10 - 30 = 0$
5. $5 \times 8 \div 4 - 2 + 9$
   $10 - 2 + 9 = 17$

MISSING NUMBERS

Directions: *In each question given below which one number can be placed at the sign of interrogation?*

1.

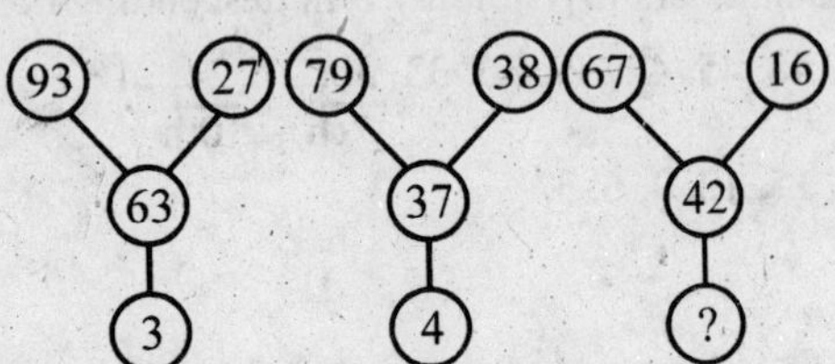

A. 5 B. 6
C. 8 D. 9

2.

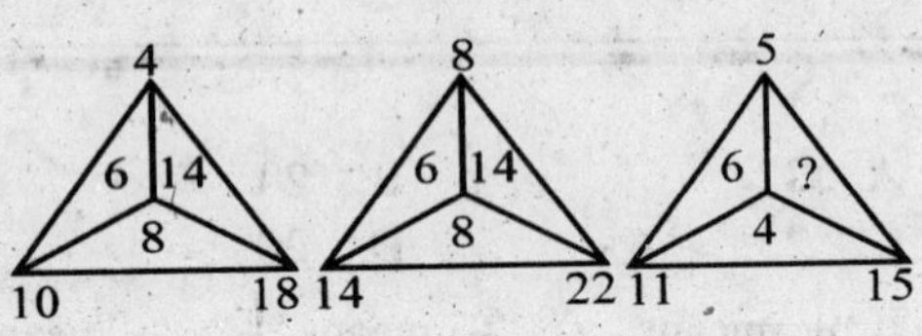

A. 8 B. 14
C. 10 D. 6

3.

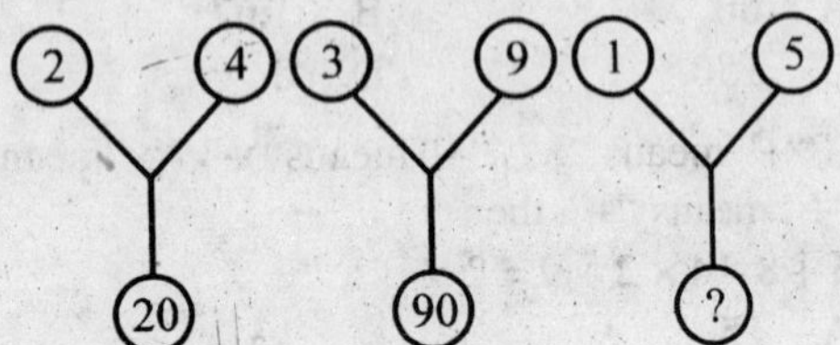

A. 20 B. 25
C. 26 D. 75

4. 27 22 50
13 12 26
9 2 ?

A. 12 B. 39
C. 18 D. 24

5.

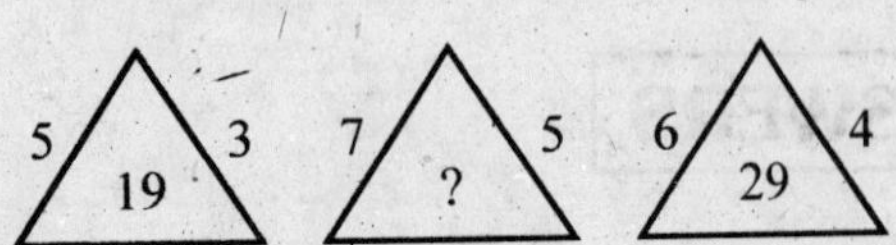

A. 25 B. 47
C. 37 D. 41

6.

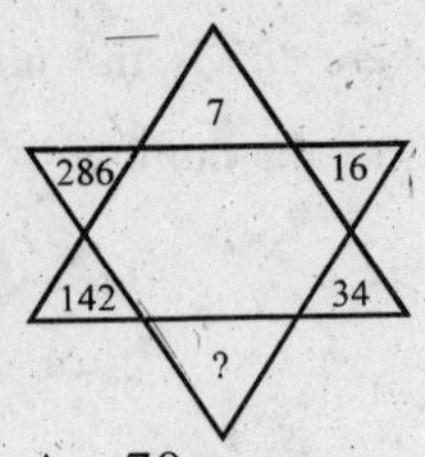

A. 70 B. 68
C. 56 D. 92

7.

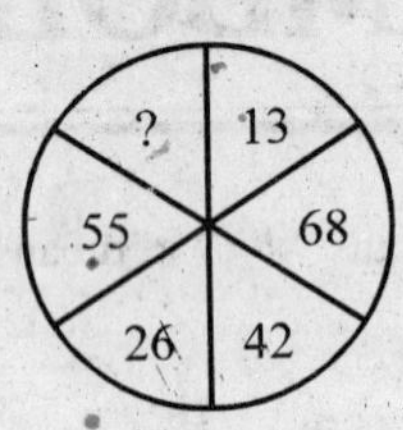

A. 41 B. 37
C. 29 D. 25

8.

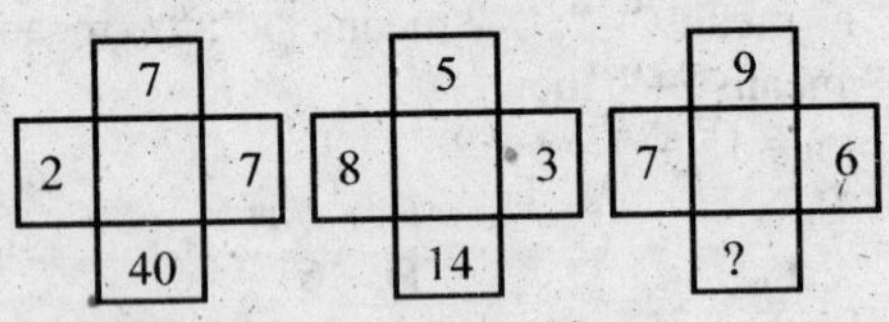

A. 72 B. 68
C. 82 D. 96

9. 42 (21) 22
78 (?) 84
162 (18) 99

A. 12 B. 13
C. 60 D. 72

10.

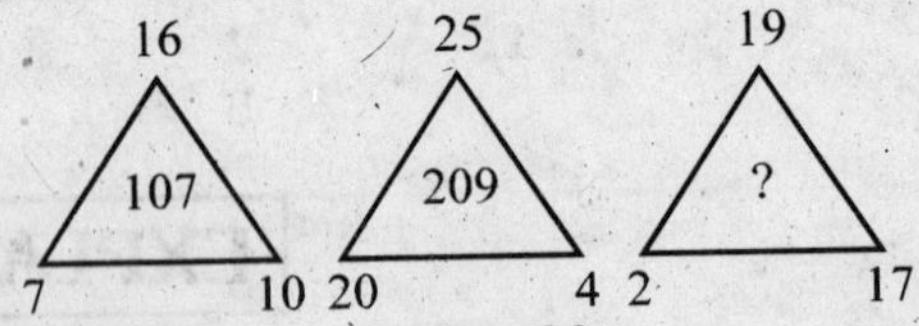

A. 68 B. 93
C. 175 D. 217

ANSWERS

1	2	3	4	5	6	7	8	9	10
D	C	C	A	D	A	C	B	B	A

EXPLANATORY ANSWERS

1. The sum of numbers on right and centre subtracted from the number on the left gives the number at the bottom, *i.e.,*

$93 - (27 + 63) = 3$
$79 - (38 + 37) = 4$

Similarly,
$67 - (16 + 42) = 9$

2. The number inside each triangle is the difference of the numbers at its base *i.e.*
$10 - 4 = 6$, $18 - 4 = 14$ and $18 - 10 = 8$
$14 - 8 = 6$, $22 - 8 = 14$ and $22 - 14 = 8$, similarly
$11 - 5 = 6$, $15 - 5 = 10$ and $15 - 11 = 4$.

3. The sum of squares of two numbers at the top gives the third number below, *i.e.*,
$2^2 + 4^2 = 20$
$3^2 + 9^2 = 90$, similarly
$1^2 + 5^2 = 26$

4. The sum of numbers in 1st and 2nd column plus 1 is the number in the 3rd column, *i.e.*,
$27 + 22 + 1 = 50$
$13 + 12 + 1 = 26$, similarly
$9 + 2 + 1 = 12$

5. The product of numbers on either side of the triangle plus the number at the base is the number inside the triangle, *i.e.*,
$(5 \times 3) + 4 = 19$
$(6 \times 4) + 5 = 29$, similarly
$(7 \times 5) + 6 = 41$

6. Clockwise starting from number 7, the next number is obtained by doubling the number and adding 2, *i.e.*,
$(7 \times 2) + 2 = 16$
$(16 \times 2) + 2 = 34 \ldots$, similarly
$(34 \times 2) + 2 = 70$
$(70 \times 2) + 2 = 142$
$(142 \times 2) + 2 = 286$

7. The difference between the numbers in opposite sectors is 13, *i.e.*,
$26 - 13 = 13$
$68 - 55 = 13$, similarly
The missing number is $42 - 13 = 29$
($42 + 13 = 55$ is not given as option)

8. The number at the bottom is obtained by subtracting the sum of two numbers in the centre grid line from the square of the number at the top, *i.e.*,
$7^2 - (2 + 7) = 40$
$5^2 - (8 + 3) = 14$, similarly
$9^2 - (7 + 6) = 68$

9. The number inside the brackets is obtained by multiplying the number on the left by 2 and then dividing the product by the sum of digits of number on the right, *i.e.*,
$(42 \times 2) \div (2 + 2) = 21$
$(162 \times 2) \div (9 + 9) = 18$, similarly
$(78 \times 2) \div (8 + 4) = 13$

10. Subtracting the sum of squares of two numbers at the base from the square of number at the apex gives the number inside the triangle, *i.e.*,
$16^2 - (7^2 + 10^2) = 107$
$25^2 - (20^2 + 4^2) = 209$, similarly
$19^2 - (2^2 + 17^2) = 68$

ALPHABET PROBLEMS

Directions : *The following questions are based on alphabet series in natural or reverse order and the combinations that can be made by changing the position of alphabet in given words.*

1. Which alphabet comes immediately before the sixth alphabet from the left extreme in alphabetical series?
A. U B. E
C. F D. V

2. Which letter is midway between G and S?
A. L B. N
C. M D. No letter

3. Which letter should be ninth letter to the left of ninth letter from the right if the first half of the alphabet is reversed?
A. I B. D
C. F D. E

4. If the alphabet is in reverse order, which letter will be eighth letter to the left of the seventh letter counting from the right end?
A. O B. P
C. N D. Q

5. What will be the fifth letter to the right of the thirteenth letter from the right?
A. R B. S
C. I D. O

ANSWERS

1	2	3	4	5
B	C	D	A	B

EXPLANATORY ANSWERS

1.

Sixth letter from left is 'F' and letter immediately before 'F' is 'E'.

2.

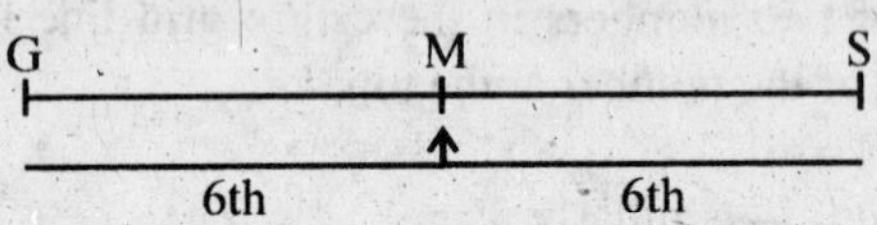

'M' is midway between G and S.

3. MLKJIHGFEDCBANOPQRSTUVWXYZ

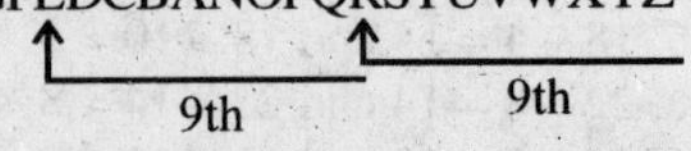

4. ZYXWVUTSRQPONMLKJIHGFEDCBA

5.

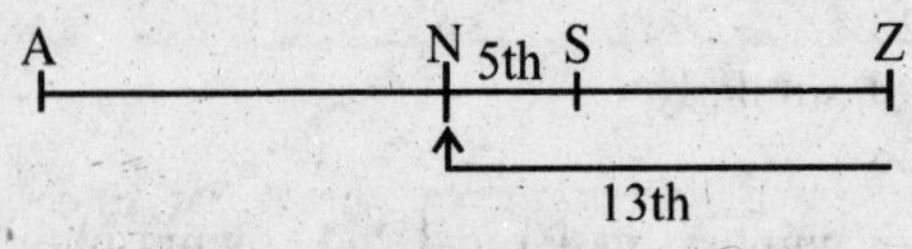

13th letter from right is 'N' and 5th letter to the right of 'N' is 'S'.

NON-VERBAL SERIES

Directions (Q. 1–10) : *In each of the following questions which one of the five answer figures given below should come after the problem figures if the sequence are continued?*

Problem Figures **Answer Figures**

1.

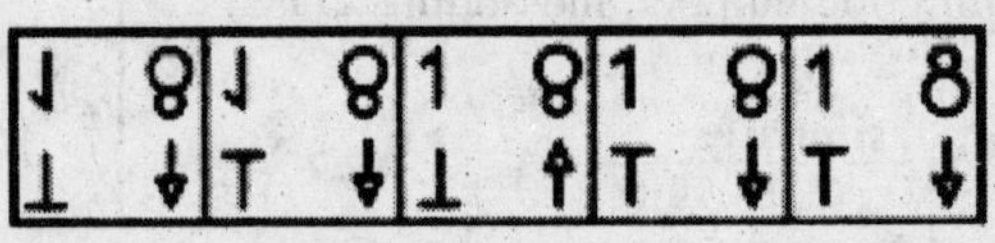

(a) (b) (c) (d) (e)

2.

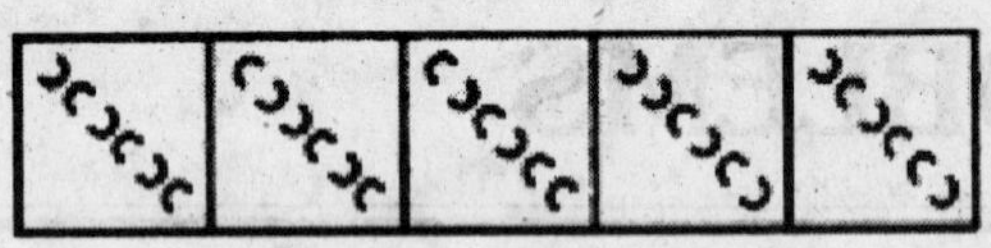

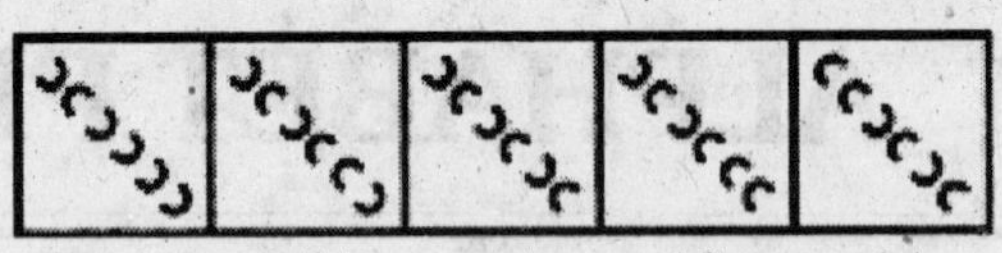

(a) (b) (c) (d) (e)

3.

(a) (b) (c) (d) (e)

4.

(a) (b) (c) (d) (e)

5.

(a) (b) (c) (d) (e)

6.

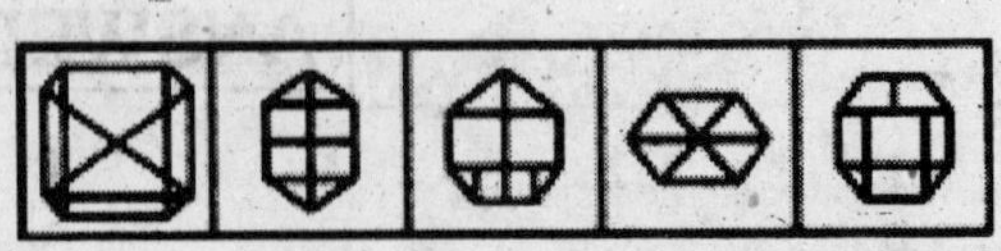

(a) (b) (c) (d) (e)

7.  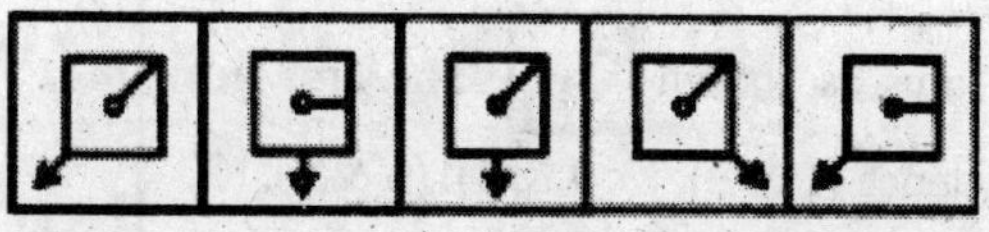

(a) (b) (c) (d) (e)

Problem Figures **Answer Figures**

8. 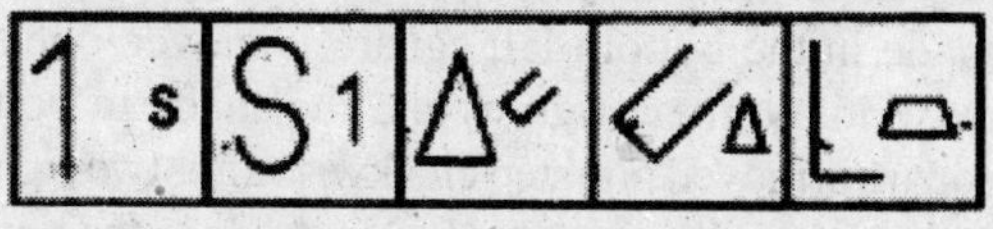 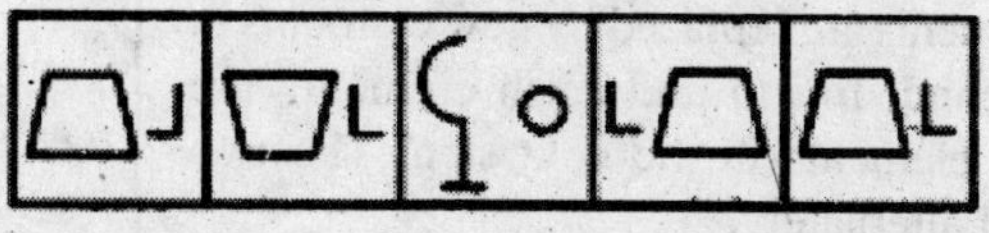

(a) (b) (c) (d) (e)

9.  

(a) (b) (c) (d) (e)

10.  

(a) (b) (c) (d) (e)

Directions (Q. 11-20) : *In each of these questions, a series begins with an unmarked figure on the extreme left in the row of figures. One and only one of the five lettered figures in the series does not fit into the series. The two unmarked figures, one on the extreme left and the other on the extreme right fit into the series. Take as many aspects into account as possible of the figures in the series and find out the one and only of the five marked figures which does not fit into the series. The letter of that figure is the answer.*

11. 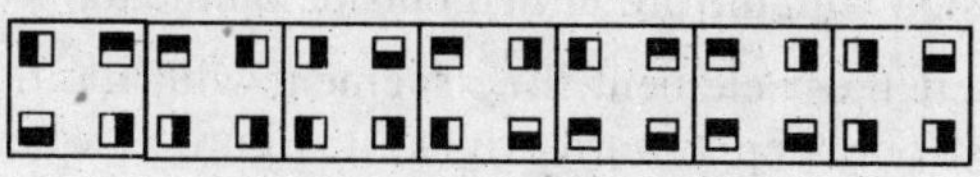

(a) (b) (c) (d) (e)

12. 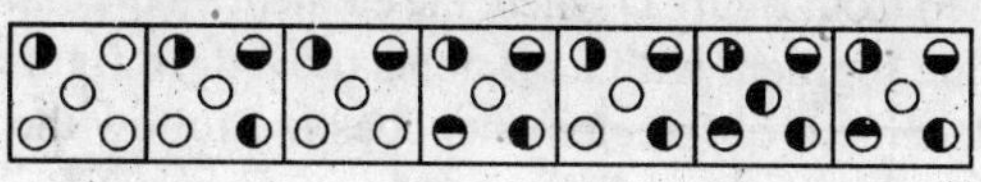

(a) (b) (c) (d) (e)

13. 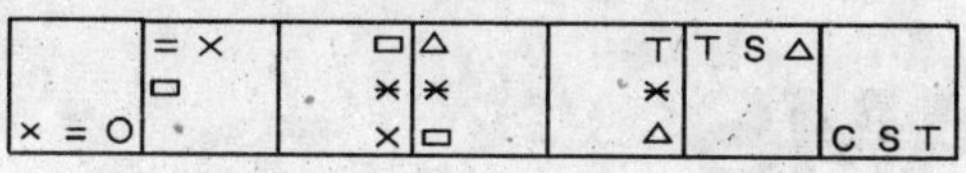

(a) (b) (c) (d) (e)

14. 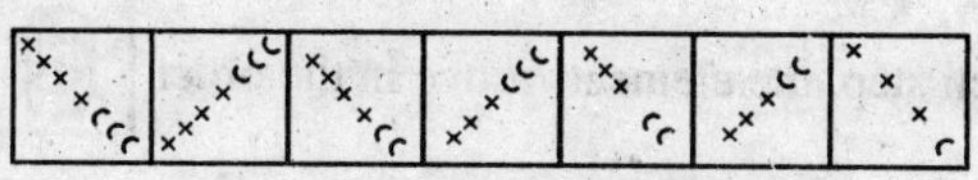

(a) (b) (c) (d) (e)

15. 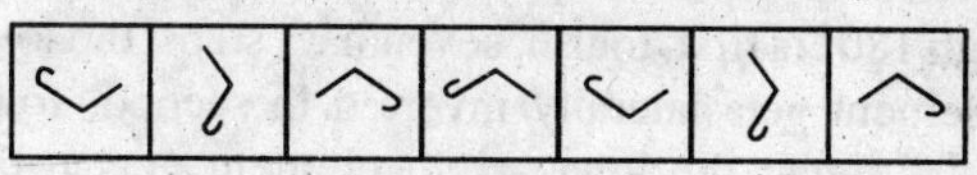

(a) (b) (c) (d) (e)

16. 

(a) (b) (c) (d) (e)

ANSWERS

1	2	3	4	5	6	7	8	9	10
D	C	D	A	C	E	C	E	C	B
11	**12**	**13**	**14**	**15**	**16**				
A	E	A	C	C	E				

EXPLANATORY ANSWERS

1. In each step, all the elements move to the adjacent corner (of the square boundary) in a CW direction and the element that reaches the upper-left corner gets vertically inverted.

2. We can label the arcs as shown . The arcs get inverted in the sequence (1 &`2), (3, 4 & 5), (6 & 1), (2, 3 & 4), (5 & 6), ...

3. All the elements move half-a-side of the square boundary in ACW direction in each step. Also, first, third and fifth elements are replaced by new elements in one step and second, fourth and sixth elements are replaced by new elements in the next step. The two steps are repeated alternately.

4. In each step, the dot moves one space CW and the arrow moves two spaces CW.

5. One arc and four arcs get inverted alternately.

6. The number of parts increases by one along with the number of sides in the figure.

7. The pin rotates 45°CW and 90°CW alternately and moves one space (each space is equal to half-a-side of the square) and two spaces CW alternately. The arrow rotates 90°ACW and 45°ACW alternately and moves two spaces and one space.

8. In one step, the two elements interchange positions and the smaller element gets enlarged while the larger element gets reduced in size. In the next step, the smaller element is replaced by a new small element and the larger element is replaced by a new large element.

9. In each step, the elements move in the order .

10. The upper-left element gets laterally inverted in first, third, fifth. .... steps; the upper-right element gets rotated through 180° is first, fourth, seventh,.... steps; the lower-left element gets laterally inverted in second, fourth, sixth, ... steps; the lower-right element gets rotated through 180° in third, sixth,... steps and the pin at the middle-right position gets laterally inverted in every second step.

11. The shade in the top left square is moved one step clockwise till figure B and then reversed, the process is repeated. The shade in the top right square is moved one step anticlockwise till figure D and then reversed. The shade in the bottom left square is moved one step clockwise in alternate figures and the shade in bottom right square is moved one step clockwise after two figures. In figure 'A' the rule is isolated by the shade in the bottom left square.

12. In alternate figures a new circle is shaded clockwise. The pattern of the shade is also moved clockwise. In figure 'E' right half of the circle in the centre should have been shaded.

13. The three elements are placed either horizontally or vertically. In option 'A' neither of the placements can be applied.

14. The placement of elements is same in alternate figures. The number and type of elements is same in two subsequent figures. In this manner, figure 'C' should have four crosses and two C shapes.

15. *(c)* : The element is moved one step anticlockwise and the arc at one end is turned outside and inside alternately. In figure 'C' the element should be on the right side with the arc turned outside on the top side.

16. The left most element, line segment with the dot is moved one step towards right till figure C where it reaches the extreme right position. This process is repeated from figure D where the element on the extreme left, line segment with a circle, is moved. In figure 'E' the placement of the elements does not follow the rule of the series.

VENN DIAGRAMS

1. What is the number which is common to only two geometrical figures?

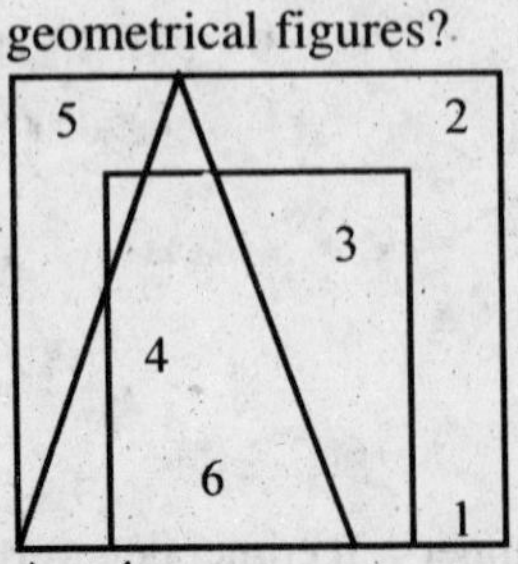

A. 4 B. 3
C. 5 D. 2

Directions (Qs. 2 and 3) : *In the following diagram, rectangle represents Hindi Announcers, circle represents English Announcers, square represents French Announcers, and triangle represents German Announcers.*

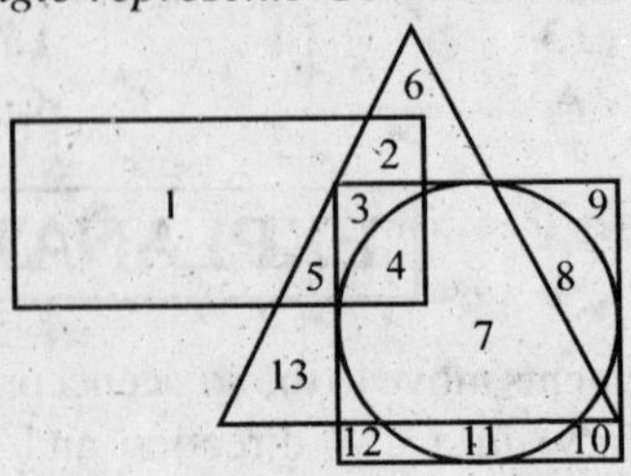

2. Which area represents those announcers who can present programmes in Hindi, French and German only?
   A. 1 B. 2
   C. 3 D. 4

3 Which area represents those announcers who can present programmes in French and English only?
   A. 7 B. 9
   C. 11 D. 13

Directions (Qs. 4 and 5) : *Study the diagram to answer these questions.*

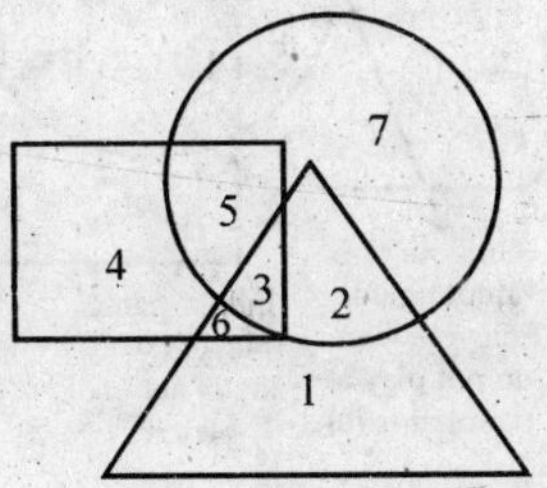

4. Which number is in all the geometrical figures?
   A. 5 B. 6
   C. 2 D. 3

5. Number 6 is in :
   A. Rectangle and triangle
   B. Circle and traingle
   C. Rectangle and circle
   D. Rectangle only

Directions (Qs. 6 to 9) : *In the following diagram*

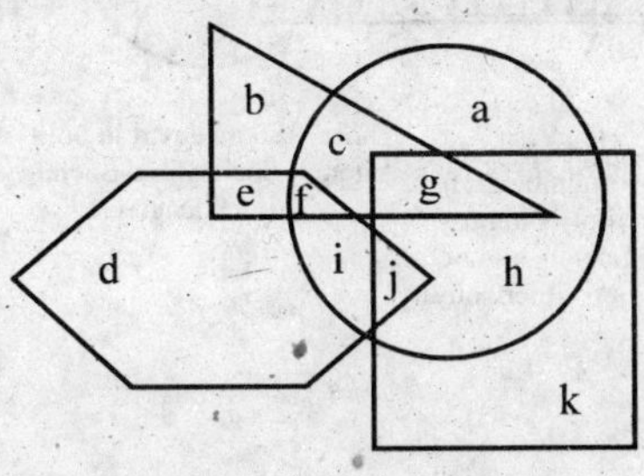

The Circle represents players
The Triangle represents outdoor games
The Hexagon represents indoor games and
The Square represents national level players
Study the diagram and answer the questions given below :

6. The letter in the section representing the players who play indoor games at national level is :
   A. f B. i
   C. j D. g

7. The letter representing the section of outdoor as well as indoor game players who do not play at the national level is :
   A. c B. f
   C. e D. i

8. The section representing national level players who do not play either outdoor or indoor games but still come under the category of players is :
   A. k B. g
   C. c D. h

9. Persons who play outdoor games but do not come under the category of players are represented in the section marked :
   A. b B. c
   C. a D. d

Directions (Qs. 10 to 13) : *Study the diagram given below.*

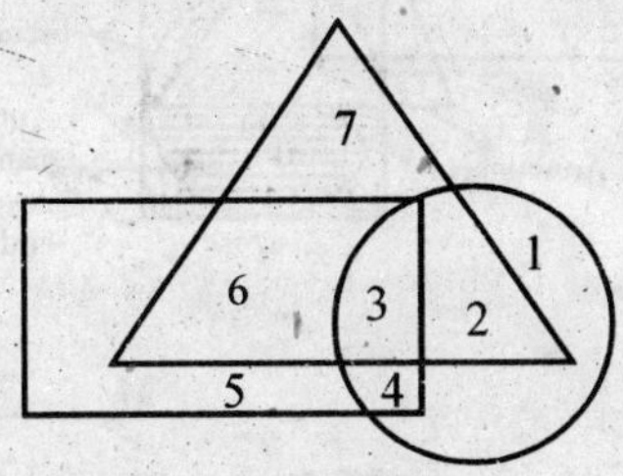

A college provides three different activities, students union represented by triangle, literary society represented by rectangle and social service league represented by circle.

10. Those who take part in both literary society and social service league but not in students union are represented by :
    A. 3 & 4 B. 5 & 6
    C. 5 & 1 D. 4

11. Those who take part in students union but not in social service league are represented by:
    A. 2 & 7 B. 6 & 7
    C. 6 D. 7

12. Those students who are members of literary society only and not of any other activity are represented by:
    A. 2 B. 5
    C. 3 & 4 D. 3

13. Those students who are members of all three groups are represented by :
    A. 2 B. 3
    C. 4 D. 6

ANSWERS

1	2	3	4	5	6	7	8	9	10
B	C	C	D	A	C	B	D	A	D
11	**12**	**13**							
B	B	B							

EXPLANATORY ANSWERS

1.

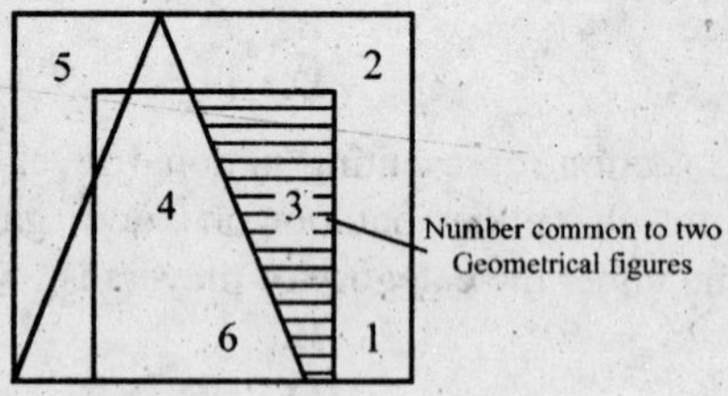

Note : Numbers 4 and 6 are common to all three geometrical figures.

Qs. 2 and 3.

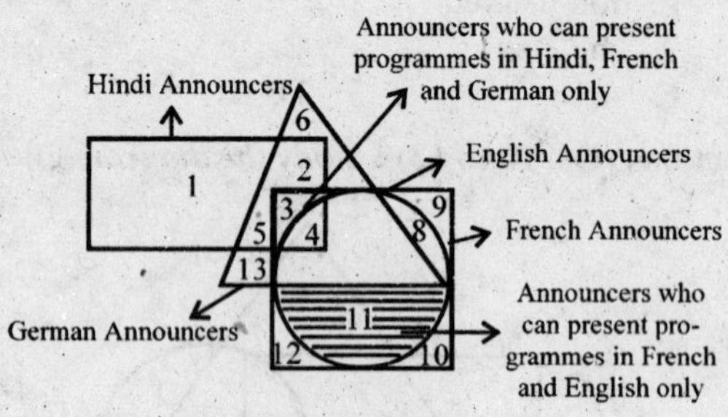

Qs. 4 and 5.

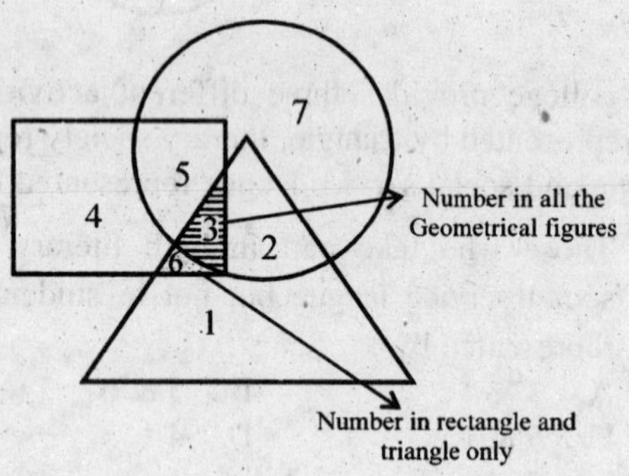

Qs. 6 to 9.

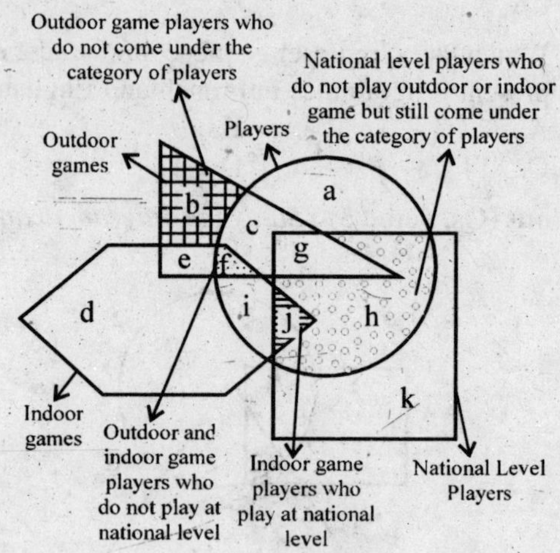

Qs. 10 to 13.

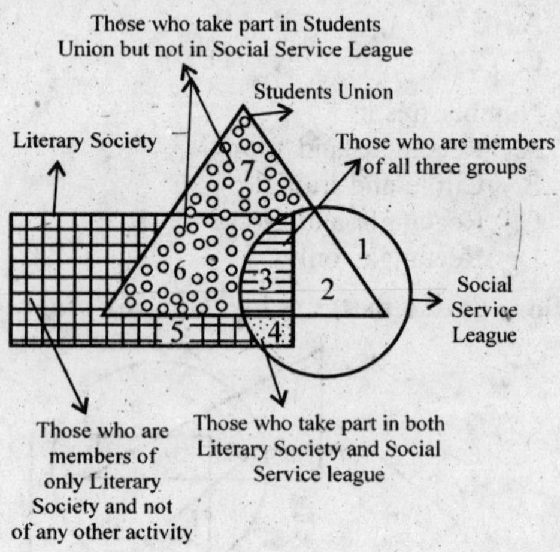

SCIENCE & ENVIRONMENT

1

SCIENCE

PHYSICS

Units and Measurement

Unit is that physical quantity which expresses the length, mass and time.

Types of Units: There are three systems of the fundamental units which are commonly used and internationally recognized these are:

(i) Metric System Unit (M.K.S.): In this system of unit 'M' stands for metre, 'K' for kilogram and S for second (time). Metre as unit of length, Kilogram as unit of mass and Second as unit of time.

(ii) C.G.S. System of unit: In this system 'C' stands for centimetre 'G' stands for gram and 'S' for Second. Centimetre is the unit of length, Gram is the unit of mass and Second is the unit of time.

(iii) F.P.S. System of Unit: In this system of unit 'F' stands for foot, 'P' stands for pound and 'S' for second. Foot is the unit of length, Pound is unit of mass, second is unit of time.

Scientific Instruments

1. **Altimeter:** It is used for measuring altitudes specially used in aircraft.
2. **Ammeter:** It is used for measuring the strength of the current in amperes.
3. **Barometer:** It is used for measuring the atmospheric pressure.
4. **Dynamo:** It is used to convert mechanical energy into electrical energy.
5. **Galvanometer:** It is used for detecting the presence of current.
6. **Hygrometer:** It is used for measuring humidity in air.
7. **Periscope:** A device to see the objects which are above the eye level of the observer.
8. **Potentiometer:** It is used for measuring or adjusting electrical potential.
9. **Sextant:** It is used for measuring angular elevation.
10. **Transformer:** It is used to decrease or increase the voltage of an alternating current.
11. **Thermocouple:** It is based on thermoelectricity used for measuring temperature.
12. **Thermometer:** It is used measuring temperature.
13. **Viscometer:** It is used for measuring viscosity of liquids.
14. **Voltmeter:** It measures the potential difference.

Mechanics

Branch of science dealing with the study of motion of object in called mechanics.

Distance: The length of path traversed by a particle in a given time is known as distance.

Displacement: The distance covered by a particle in a particular direction with respect to the point of reference is known as displacement.

Speed: The distance travelled by a particle in unit time is defined as its speed.

Average or Mean Speed: The ratio of the total distance travelled by a particle to the time taken to cover that distance is defined as its average speed.

Velocity: The ratio of the total displacement of a particle to the time taken to cover that displacement is defined as average velocity.

Acceleration: The change in velocity of a particle in unit time is defined as its average acceleration.

Retardation: The rate of decrease of velocity of a particle is defined as retardation. It is a negative acceleration.

Inertia: The property of a body by virtue of which it opposes any change in its state is defined as its inertia.

Mass: The quantity of matter contained in a body is defined as its mass.

(*a*) The mass of a body can never be zero.

(*b*) The mass of a body remains constant at all places of earth.

(*c*) It can be determined by a physical balance.

(*d*) There are two types of mass, *i.e.*, (*i*) gravitational mass, and (*ii*) inertial mass.

Gravitational Mass: The ratio of the weight of a body and acceleration due to gravity at that place is defined as gravitational mass. The mass determined by a chemical or physical balance is the gravitational mass.

Inertial Mass: The ratio of the force applied and the acceleration produced in a body at a place with zero gravity is defined as the inertial mass.

Force: The push or pull which one system exerts on another is defined as force.

Momentum: The product of mass and velocity of a moving body is known as its linear momentum.

Impulse: The product of applied force on a body and the time internal for which the force acts is defined as impulse.

Energy: The capacity of doing work is known as energy. Energy can be converted from one form to another form.

Mechanical Energy: The energy present in a body on account of its position or motion is defined as mechanical energy. This is of two type viz., (*i*) Potential energy and (*ii*) Kinetic energy.

Newton's Laws of Motion

(*i*) *First Law or Law of Inertia:* A body to be in its state of rest or of uniform motion until and unless it is acted upon by some external forces. This law defines forces.

(*ii*) *Second Law:* The force applied to a body is equal to the rate of change of its momentum.

(*iii*) *Third Law or Law of Action and Reaction:* To every action force there is an equal and opposite reaction force.

Gravitational Field: The region of space around a body in which gravitational force is experienced by other bodies is defined as the gravitational field of that body.

Newton's Law of Gravitation: Every particle in the universe attracts energy other particle with a force which is directly proportional to the product of their masses and inversely proportional to the square of distance between them.

Force of Gravity: The force with which earth attracts anybody towards its centre is defined as the force of gravity. The force exerted by earth on the body is known as the weight of the body.

Acceleration due to Gravity: The rate of change of velocity of a body falling freely due to earth's force of gravity is defined as acceleration due to gravity

Satellites: The bodies revolving around a planet in its gravitational field are defined as satellites.

Natural Satellites: The natural heavenly bodies which revolve around a planet are known as natural satellites, *e.g.*, moon is the natural satellite of earth.

Artificial Satellites: The man made bodies which are established in a particular orbit and are made to revolve around the earth are known as artificial satellites, *e.g.*, Aryabhatta, Rohini, Bhaskar.

Orbital Satellite: The satellites which always revolve in different orbits around earth are known as orbital satellites.

Communication Satellites: The satellite which remain stationary with respect to earth are known as communication satellites, *e.g.*, INSAT, 1B, 2A, 2E etc.

Power: The rate of doing work by a machine or a person is defined as power.

Law of Conservation of Momentum: In the absence of an external force, the total momentum of a system remains constant.

Deforming Force: The external force acting on a body on account of which is size or shape or both change is defined as the deforming force.

Elasticity: The property of a body, by virtue of which it regains its original form (size and shape) after the removal of external deforming force, is defined as elasticity.

Perfectly Elastic Body: The body which perfectly regains its original form on removing the external deforming force, is defined as a perfectly elastic body, *e.g.*, quartz.

Plastic Body: The body which does not have the property of opposing the external deforming force is known as a plastic body.

Elastic Limit: The maximum deforming force after which a body loses its property of elasticity and it gets permanently deformed, is defined as the elastic limit.

Stress: The internal reactional force per unit area developed as a result of applied external force is defined as stress.

Strain: The change in dimensions per unit original dimensions due to applied deforming force is defined as strain.

Hooke's Law: Within elastic limit, stress is directly proportional to strain.

Cohesive Force: The force of attraction acting between the molecules of same material is defined as cohesive force, *e.g.*, the force acting between water molecule.

Adhesive Force: The force of attraction acting between the molecules of two different materials is defined as adhesive force, *e.g.*, the force acting between the molecules of paper and ink.

Surface Tension: The property of a liquid, on account of which it lends to keep surface area in its free surface, is defined as surface tension.

Viscosity: The property of fluids, by virtue of which they oppose the relative motion between their different layers, is known as viscosity.

Heat

Temperature: Temperature of a body is that property which tells us that how much hot or cold a particular body is.

Scales of Temperature:

(*i*) Temperature in Kelvin = Temperature in Celsius + 273

(ii) 1°C temperature difference = 1° K
(iii) The temperature of –40°C is same in °C and °F
(iv) The temperature of a normal person is 37°C or 98.6°F.

Heat: Heat is a form of energy which is exchanged among various bodies or systems on account of temperature difference.

Latent Heat: The amount of heat used to change the state of matter, without changing its temperature is defined as latent heat.

Specific Heat: The amount of heat required to increase the temperature of 1 gm of material by 1°C is defined as its specific heat.

Boyles Law: At a constant temperature the volume of the given mass of gas is inversely proportional to its pressure.

Charle's Law: At constant pressure the volume of a given mass of gas is directly proportional to its absolute temperature. At constant pressure the volume of a given mass of gas increases by $\frac{1}{273}$ of its volume at 0°C for 1°C size in its temperature.

Gay Lussac's Law: At constant volume, the pressure of given mass of gas is directly proportional to its absolute temperature.

Graham's Law of Diffusion: At constant temperature and pressure, the rate of diffusion of a gas is inversely proportional to the square root of its density.

Dalton's Law of Partial Pressure: The total pressure exerted by the mixture of inactive gases in a vessel is equal to the sum of the partial pressures due to individual gas.

Avogadro's Law: If the temperature, pressure and volume of two gases are same then the number of molecules in them will also be equal.

Sound

Wave: A disturbance created in the medium which propagates in the forward direction with constant velocity without changing its shape, is defined as a wave.

Wave Motion: The mode of energy transfer in which a disturbance advances in the forward direction by affecting the medium without mass transfer, is defined as wave motion.

Characteristics of Wave Motion:

(i) The particle of the medium do not leave their mean positions rather they keep on vibrating about their mean positions.
(ii) The medium itself does not move.
(iii) The energy and momentum are transferred in the medium.
(iv) The phase of various particle of the medium keep on changing constantly.

Properties of Medium Necessary for Wave Propagation

(i) The medium should have the property of inertia.
(ii) The medium should posses the property of elasticity.
(iii) The medium should have low resistance.

Longitudinal Waves: In these waves the particles of the medium vibrate in the direction of propagation of waves.

Transverse Waves: In these waves the particles of the medium vibrate at right angles to the direction.

Ultrasonic Waves: The waves with frequency greater than that of sound, *i.e.*, 20×10^3 Hz are defined as Ultrasonic waves.

Shock Waves: When a sound source move with a velocity greater than that of sound then it leave behind it waves whose wave front is conical. These waves are defined as shock wave.

Terms Related to Wave Motion

(i) ***Displacement:*** The distance covered by a particle from mean position in a particular direction in SHM is known as displacement.
(ii) ***Amplitude:*** The maximum displacement of a particle executing SHM from its mean position, is defined as amplitude.
(iii) ***Time Period:*** The time taken by a particle in completing one vibration is defined as time period.
(iv) ***Frequency:*** The number of vibrations per second made by any particle of the medium is defined as its frequency.
(v) ***Wavelength:*** The distance between two nearest particles in one complete vibration is defined as the wavelength.
(vi) ***Wave Number:*** The number of wave present in unit length is defined as the wave number.
(vii) ***Wave Velocity:*** The velocity with which the crests and troughs or compression and rarefactions travel in medium, is defined as wave velocity.
(viii) ***Beats:*** When two waves of nearly same frequency, travelling in the same direction of the medium, superimpose over each other then the intensity at any point of the medium changes periodically with time. This phenomenon is defined as beats.
(ix) ***Beat Frequency:*** The number of beats heard per second is defined as beat frequency.
(x) ***Note:*** Any musical sound which is produced by the SHM of sound source is known as note.
(xi) ***Tone:*** Every component of musical sound is known as a tone. Every musical sound consists of a number of components of different frequencies. Every component is known as a tone.
(xii) ***Organ Pipe:*** The pipe filled with air and which when vibrated produces sound waves is known as organ pipe.
(xiii) ***Loudness:*** It is that characteristic of sound, on account of which the sound appears to be intense or slow is defined as loudness of sound or the power crossing per unit area at any point of the medium is defined as loudness.
(xiv) ***Pitch:*** It is that characteristic of sound on account of which it appears to be shrill or grave, is known as pitch.

Light

Light: The light is an electromagnetic radiation with the help of which our eyes experience the sensation of vision is known as light.

Ray of Light: The path of light energy from one point to another is known as a ray of light.

Properties of Light

(*i*) It propagates in straight line.
(*ii*) It exhibits the phenomenon of reflection, refraction, interference, diffraction, polarisation and double refraction.
(*iii*) The properties of the medium through which light passes remain unchanged.
(*iv*) Its velocity is different in different media. In rarer medium it is more and in denser medium it is less.
(*v*) Its velocity in vacuum is maximum whose value is 3×10^8 m/s.

Reflection of Light: The phenomenon of returning of incident light in the same medium is known as reflection.

Laws of Reflection:

(*i*) The incident ray, the reflected ray and the normal all lie in the same plane.
(*ii*) In regular reflection the angle of incidence is equal to the angle of reflection.
(*iii*) When light is reflected by a rarer medium then its phase remains unchanged whereas phase difference of a path difference of $\lambda/2$ or time difference T/2 is created when it is reflected by a denser medium. This is also known as Stoke's Law.

Refraction of Light: When a ray of light enters from one medium to another then at the boundary of separation it deviates from its initial path. This phenomenon is known as refraction.

Law of Refraction:

(*i*) The incident ray, the refracted ray and the normal all three lie in the same plane.
(*ii*) For given two media and for a given wavelength, the ratio of the sine of angle of incidence to the sine of angle of refraction always remain constant.
(*iii*) Light bends towards the normal if passes through rarer medium to denser medium.
(*iv*) Light bends away from the normal if passes through denser medium to rarer medium.

Critical Angle: When a ray of light enters from denser to rarer medium, then the angle of incidence corresponding to which the angle of refraction is 90°, is defined as the critical angle.

Total Internal Reflection: When a ray of light passes from a denser to rarer medium at an angle greater than the critical angle, then it gets totally reflected. This phenomenon is known as total internal reflection.

Refractive Index: The ratio of velocities of light in two media is defined as refractive index.

Dispersion of Light: The phenomenon of splitting of a ray of light into difference colours by a prism is defined as dispersion.

Spectrum: The whole band of colours from violet to red colour is known as spectrum. There are seven colours in the spectrum in the following order Violet, Indigo, Blue, Green, Yellow, Orange and Red or VIBGYOR.

Rainbow: The seven coloured curved strip formed as a result of dispersion of light through water droplets which keep suspended in the atmosphere after rains, is known as rainbow.

LASER (Light Amplification by Stimulated Emission of Radiation)

(*i*) The light amplification by induced emission of radiation is known as laser.
(*ii*) It is highly coherent and highly monochromatic light.
(*iii*) It is perfectly unidirectional and highly intense and powerful.

Polaroids: Microcrystals of iodo-sulphate of quinine are deposited on thin sheet of nitro-cellulose and then squeezed them out through a fine slit. In this process only the crystals having axes parallel to the slit pass through it and form a sheet. These sheets are kept between ordinary glass plates and called polaroids.

Uses of Polaroids: In winds screen; Window panes of aeroplanes; Camera filters and sun glasses in 3-D movies.

Luminous Flux: The luminous flux through a given surface is the amount of luminous energy that passes through the surface in one second in a direction normal to surface.

Lumen: One lumen is the amount of luminous flux emitted per unit solid angle by a source of light of luminous intensity one candela.

Luminous Intensity: The luminous intensity of a source is defined as the luminous flux emitted per unit solid angle by the source. It is also known as illuminating power.

Candela: One candela is the luminous intensity in a given direction due to a source, which emits monochromatic radiation of frequency 5.4×10^{14} Hz and whose radiant intensity in that direction is 1/683 watt per steradian.

Mirror: The highly polished reflecting surface is known as mirror. Mirror are of three tyes: Plane mirror; Concave mirror and Convex mirror.

Properties of Image Formed by Plane Mirror

(*i*) The image formed by a plane mirror is erect, virtual laterally reversed.
(*ii*) The size of image formed by it is equal to that of the object.
(*iii*) The image is formed behind the mirror at a distance equal to the distance of the object in front of mirror.
(*iv*) When the mirror is rotated through an angle θ, then the reflected ray rotates through an angle 2θ.
(*v*) When two mirrors are kept parallel to each other, then the number of images will be infinity as

Spherical Mirror: The smooth, polished spherical surface is known as spherical mirror, or the reflecting surface which is a part of a sphere is known as spherical mirror. It is of two types: (*i*) Concave mirror and (*ii*) Convex mirror.

Magnification (m): The ratio of the size of image to size of object is defined as the magnification of spherical mirror,

$$\text{or } magnification = \frac{v}{u} = \frac{\text{Size of image}}{\text{Size of object}}$$

$$\text{or } magnification = \frac{\text{Length of image}}{\text{Length of object}}$$

Use of Plane Mirrors:

(*a*) In dressing tables

(*b*) In looking-glass

(*c*) In scientific apparatus. Plane mirrors are used to bend the paths of rays of light in scientific apparatus.

Uses of Concave Mirror:

(*a*) As shaving and hair dressing mirrors.

(*b*) As reflectors—concave mirrors are used as reflectors in search lights and head light.

(*c*) The ENT specialists use concave mirror for viewing the inner parts of ear, nose and throat.

(*d*) In lighthouses in seas.

(*e*) In a torch for hunting purpose.

Use of Convex Mirror:

(*a*) To spread light on roads.

(*b*) As side mirrors on cars in order to view the vehicle following the cars.

(*c*) For decoration purpose as these form the very small images which look beautiful.

Lens: The part of an isotropic transparent medium by two spherical, cylindrical, parabolic or one plane and another spherical surfaces is defined as lens.

Lenses are of Two types:

(*i*) Concave lens or diverging lens.

(*ii*) Convex lens or converging lens.

Concave lenses are of three types:

(*i*) *Concave-concave lens:* Both of its surfaces are concave. The radii of curvature of its two concave surfaces may be same or different.

(*ii*) *Plano-concave lens:* Its one surface is plane and second surface is concave.

(*iii*) *Convexo-concave:* One of its surfaces is convex and another surface is concave. The radii of curvature of convex and concave surfaces are different.

Convex Lenses are of Three Types:

(*i*) *Convexo-convex:* Both of its surface are convex. The radii of curvature of its convex surfaces may be same or different.

(*ii*) *Plano-convex:* One of its surfaces is convex and another one is plane.

(*iii*) *Concavo-convex:* One of its surfaces is concave and another one is convex. The radii of its concave and convex surfaces are different.

Power of Lens:

(*i*) The power of a thin lens is equal to the reciprocal of its focal length measured in meter, *i.e.*, $P = \frac{1}{f}$. The unit of power of lens is dioptre.

(*ii*) When two lenses are kept in contact then the power of compound lens is equal to the sum of power of two lenses, *i.e.*, $P = P_1 + P_2$.

(*iii*) When a concave lens and a convex lens of equal focal lengths are kept in contact then the power of the compound lens becomes zero, *i.e.*, it behaves like a plane glass plate.

(*iv*) Magnification: The ratio of the size of image formed by lens to the size of object is defined as its linear magnification.

Prism: An isotropic transparent medium closed by surfaces inclined at an angle is define as a prism.

Dispersion: The phenomen of splitting of a white ray of light into seven colours is defined as dispersion.

Visible Spectrum: The spectrum which can be viewed with the help of eye is known as visible spectrum. The spectrum spreads from violet and (wavelength 3500Å).

Magnetism

Magnet: A piece of matter, which when suspended freely rests in a particular direction (North-South) and which possesses a net magnetic moment and which attracts ferrous bodies towards it, is called a magnet.

Natural Magnet: The magnet which is found naturally in mines is called a natural magnet, *e.g.*, magnetite. Its shape and size are indefinite, hence it cannot be used for scientific purpose. Its magnetism is quite weak.

Artificial Magnet: The magnet which are artificially prepared are known as artificial magnets. There are generally made of iron, steel and nickel. Its shape and size are definite.

Bar Magnet: A system composed of two poles, equal in magnitude but opposite in polarity, plane, at a small displacement apart is known as a bar magnet. It is also known as a magnetic dipole.

Properties of a Magnet: Like pole repel and unlike pole attract each other; it can be magnetically saturated; it can be demagnetized by beating, mechanical jerks, heating and with lapse of time; it produces magnetism in other materials by induction.

Magnetism: It is the property of a magnet, by virtue of which it attracts ferromagnetic materials towards it and rests itself in North-South direction, is known as magnetism. The magnetism of materials is mainly due to the spin motion of its electrons.

Magnetic Poles: The two points at the ends of a magnet at which magnetism is maximum are defined as magnetic poles. The magnetic poles are of two types—(*i*) North pole, (*ii*) South pole.

Magnetic Axis: The imaginary line joining the two poles of a magnet is defined as magnetic axis.

Magnetic Meridian: An imaginary plane passing through the axis of a freely suspended stationary magnet is defined as magnetic meridian. It is not a particular plane rather it is the direction of earth's magnetic field.

Pole Strength: The strength of a magnetic pole to attract magnetic materials towards it is known as pole strength.

Magnetic Field: The space around a magnet in which a torque acts on a magnetic needle is known as magnetic field.

Magnetic Dipole: The structure, which tend to align along the direction of magnetic field, are known as magnetic dipoles.

Magnetic Flux: The number of lines of forces passing through a given area is defined as magnetic flux.

Magnetic Moment: The product of the pole strength of a magnet and its length is defined as its magnetic moment.

Electromagnetic Induction: The phenomenon of production of electromotive force on account of change in magnetic flux linked with a circuit, is defined as electromagnetic induction.

Induced emf: The emf generated on account of change in magnetic flux linked with a plane or a circuit, is defined as induced emf.

Induced Charge: The electric charge flowing in a closed circuit on account of induced current is defined as induced charge.

Transformer: The device based on the principle of mutual induction used to change the value of alternating voltage is defined as transformer. There are two types of transformer: (*a*) Step-up transformer, (*b*) Step-down transformer

Dynamo: The device used to convert mechanical energy into electrical energy is known as dynamo.

Electrostatics and Current Electricity

Electrostatics: The branch of physics in which we study charges at rest, is known as electrostatics.

Electric Charge: It is a fundamental property of matter which can never be isolated from matter.

Charges are of two types: (*a*) Positive charges; (*b*) Negative charges

Positive Charges: The deficiency of electron on a body or particle is known as positive charge.

Negative Charge: The excess of electrons on a body or a particle is known as negative charge. When a negative charge is given to a body then its mass some what increases.

Properties of Charges:

(*i*) Like charges repel and unlike charges attract each other.

(*ii*) A charged body attracts other uncharged light particles.

(*iii*) Total charge of an isolated physical system is always conserved.

Law of Conservation of Charge: Charges can neither be created nor be destroyed, rather these can be transferred from one body to another.

Coulomb's Law: The force of attraction or repulsion acting between two stationary point charges is directly proportional to the product of strengths of charges and inversely proportional to the square of distance between two charges. Its direction is along the line joining the two charges.

Electric Field: The region of space around a charge in which any other charge experiences coloumb forces is known as electric field.

Electric Intensity: The resultant coulomb force per unit test charge at any point in an electric field is defined as the intensity of electric field at that point.

Electromotive Force: The total work done in carrying a unit positive test charge around a closed path in an electric field, is defined as electromotive force.

Electric Potential: The work done against electric field in carrying a unit positive test charge from infinity to any point in electric field is defined as electric potential at that point.

Potential Difference: The negative of work done in carrying a unit positive test charge from one point to another point in an electric field is defined as electric potential difference between those two points.

Capacitance: It is numerically equal to that electric charge which raises its potential by unity. Unit of capacitance is farad.

Condenser: The pair of conductors of opposite charges, on which sufficient quantity of charge may be accommodated is defined as condenser.

Current: The rate of flow of charge in a circuit is defined as current. Electric current is equal to the charge that flow in one second.

Conductor: The materials, in which the number of free electron is very large are defined as conductors, *e.g.*, silver, copper, aluminium, etc.

Insulator: The materials, in which the number of free electrons at ordinary temperatures is negligible, are defined as insulators.

Resistance: The property of a conductor by virtue of which it opposes the flow of current in it is defined as resistance.

Ohm's Law: If the physical circumstances of the conductor (temperature, etc.) remains constant, then the applied potential difference is directly proportional to the current flowing in it.

Resistivity: The resistivity of a material is equal to the resistance of the wine of that material with unit cross-sectional area and unit length.

Conductivity : The reciprocal of specific resistance is defined as specific conductance.

Nuclear Physics

Isotopes: The elements which have same atomic number, same chemical properties, same electron number and same structure, but different mass is called isotopes.

Isobars: The elements which have same atomic mass, but different atomic number, physical and chemical properties is called isobars.

Photo-electric Cell: The device, by which light energy is directly converted into electrical energy, is known as the photo-electric cell.

X-rays: There are electromagnetic waves whose wavelength is more than that of γ-rays but less than that of ultraviolet rays, *i.e.*, these rays lie in between the ultraviolet region and γ-rays region of electromagnetic spectrum.

Mass Defect: When neutrons and protons combine to form a nucleus, then the mass of the nucleus is some what less than the sum of masses of its constituent particles.

Mass defect (Δm) = total mass of all the neutrons present inside nucleus + total mass of protons – mass of the nucleus.

Binding Energy: The minimum energy required to keep the neutrons and protons bound inside the nucleus, is defined as binding energy.

Nuclear Fission: The phenomenon in which a heavy unstable nuclear breaks into two parts of nearly same mass, is defined as nuclear fission.

Chain Reaction: The process of nuclear fission, which when once started, continues spontaneously is defined as chain reaction.

Nuclear Reactor: The device in which energy is generated by chain reaction of nuclear fission is known as nuclear reactor.

Nuclear Fusion: The process in which two or more than two lighter nuclei combine to form a heavier nucleus, is known as nuclear fusion.

Radioactivity: The phenomenon of spontaneous disintegration of nuclei of unstable atoms is defined as radioactivity.

***Decay Constant*:** It is equal to the reciprocal of that time in which the number of radioactive atoms remains its initial value.

***Half-life*:** The time, in which the number of atoms (N) reduces to half of its initial value is defined as the half-life of the element.

***Mean-life*:** The time, for which a radioactive remains active, is defined as mean life of that material.

CHEMISTRY

Atoms and its Structure

Nucleus: The nucleus (atomic nucleus) is the center of an atom. It is composed of one or more protons and usually some neutrons as well. The simplest atom of all, hydrogen, has one proton in its nucleus.

Proton is a subatomic particle with a positive electric charge of 1.6×10^{-19} coulomb and a mass of 938 MeV ($1.6726231 \times 10^{-27}$ kg, or about 1800 times the mass of an electron).

Neutron is a subatomic particle with no net electric charge and a mass of 940 MeV (very slightly more than a proton). The nucleus of most atoms consists of protons and neutrons.

Electron is a subatomic particle with a negative charge. In an atom the electrons surround the nucleus of protons and neutrons. The electron has a negative electric charge of -1.6×10^{-19} coulombs, and a mass of about 9.10×10^{-31} kg, which is 1/1800 of the proton mass.

Famous Inventions

Atomic Theory	**John Dalton**
Electron	**J.J. Thomson**
Proton	**Rutherford**
Neutron	**Masley**
Dynamite	**Alfred Nobel**
Atomic Number	**Chadwick**
Periodic Table	**Dmitry Mendeleyev**
Radioactivity	**Henri Becquerel**
Oxygen	**J. Priestly**
Hydrogen	**Cavendish**

Atomic Number: The number of protons in an atoms nucleus is called the atomic number (Z), and determines the element (for example, hydrogen, carbon, oxygen, etc.).

Atomic Weight (A): The atomic weight is the sum of neutrons and protons in the nucleus of the atom also called Mass Number.

Molecular Weight: The molecular weight of a molecule is the sum of the atomic weights of the atoms making up that molecule.

Isotopes: Isotopes are atoms of a chemical element whose nuclei have the same atomic number, Z, but different atomic weights, A.

Isobars: Isobars have the same isotopic mass but different atomic number, *e.g.*, Argon, Potassium and Calcium $^{18}Ar_{40}$, $^{19}K_{40}$, $^{20}Ca_{40}$.

Isotone : Isotone contains the same number of neutrons but different numbers of protons.

Elements

Elements are substances compose of same type of atom. Hydrogen, oxygen, chlorine, sodium, and iron are examples of elements. Ninety-two elements are known to occur in nature, and 22 more have been made artificially.

Some Common Elements and their Applications

Nitrogen: Nitrogen is the most abundant constituent in the atmosphere composes about four-fifths (78.03 per cent) by volume of the atmosphere. Nitrous oxide is known as laughing gas. Nitrous oxide is used as an anesthesia. Liquid nitrogen is used as coolant in cryogenics.

Oxygen: It was discovered by Joseph priestly. Oxygen composes 21 percent by volume of atmosphere. It is used in high-temperature welding torches, administered to patients whose breathing is impaired and oxygen-enriched air is used in open-hearth furnaces for steel manufacture. High-purity oxygen is used also in the metal-fabrication industries; in liquid form it is used in a propellant for guided missiles and rockets.

Argon: Argon is the third most prevalent gas in the earth atmosphere. Argon is also used in one type of neon lamp giving blue light whereas pure neon gives a red light. It is preferred because it requires a lower voltage than neon.

Hydrogen: Hydrogen exits as a gas at room temperature and is highly flammable. In stars, hydrogen nuclei combine with each other in nuclear reactions to form helium atoms. The isotopes of Hydrogen are Deuterium and Tritium. Spacecrafts use hydrogen as fuel that reacts with fluorine or oxygen. Nuclear plants use D_2O as a moderator.

Carbon dioxide: Carbon dioxide does not burn and support ordinary combustion; it is used in fire extinguishers. Solid carbon dioxide is known as Dry ice widely used as refrigerant. The presence of carbon dioxide in the blood stimulates breathing. For this reason, CO_2 is added to the oxygen in artificial respiration.

Methane: Methane also know as marsh gas, gas composed of carbon and hydrogen with formula CH_4, the first member of the paraffin or alkane series of hydrocarbons. It is lighter than air, colourless, odourless, and flammable. It occurs in natural gas, in coal mines, as a by-product of petroleum refining, and as a product of decomposition of matter in swamps.

Iron: Iron is a metal extracted from iron ore, and is hardly ever found in the free (elemental) state. Depending upon the carbon content Iron can be classified into: Pig Iron (4%–5%), Cast iron (2–3.5%), carbon steel (0.5–1.5%) and Wrought Iron (< 0.5%).

Sodium: Sodium is a constituent of table salt and baking soda. Sulfur, however, is a common impurity in fossil fuels used for home heating and the production of electricity. Large amounts of SO_2 are causing both local air pollution as well as acid rain.

The halogens: The halogens are: fluorine, chlorine, bromine, iodine, and astatine..

- Chlorine gas is greenish yellow. It is a powerful bleaching, and disinfecting agent. Chlorine is an important chemical in water purification.
- Bromine is a red volatile liquid at room temperature.
- Astatine is radioactive and heaviest of Halogens.
- Iodine is a bluish-black, lustrous solid. Potassium Iodide is used in Photography. Iodine 131 is used as a tracer in medicine.

Compound

Compound is a substance formed from two or more elements, *e.g.*, Water. **Mixture** is the product of a mechanical blending or mixing of chemical substances without other chemical change, so that each ingredient substance retains its own chemical properties. While there are no chemical changes in a mixture, physical properties of a mixture, such as its melting point, may differ from those of its components. Mixtures can usually be separated by mechanical means. There are different types of Compounds are Acids, Bases, Salts, Oxides and organic compounds.

Acids: An acid is a water-soluble, sour-tasting chemical compound. An acid always has a pH of less than 7 and turns litmus red. An acid reacts with a base in a neutralization reaction to form a salt.

Acid	Used as
Ascetic Acid	Vinegar
Amino Acid	Basis of protein
Ascorbic Acid	Vitamin C
Carbolic Acid/Phenol	Disinfectant
Citric Acid	Citrus fruits
Nitrohydrochloric Acid (Aqua Regia)	Dissolving gold and platinum
Tartaric Acid	Used in baking powder
Carbonic Acid	Carbonated beverages
Formic Acid	Ants
Lactic Acid	Sour milk
Malic Acid	Unripe apples
Nitric Acid/Aqua Fortis	Used in explosives and rocket fuels
Prussic Acid/ Hydrocynic Acid	Poison
Salicylic Acid	Basis of aspirin
Tannic Acid/Tannin	Found in tea
Uric Acid	In the urine of birds and reptiles
Oxalic Acid	Spinach

Bases : A base is a chemical compound that will neutralize an acid and form a salt and water. Bases are typically water-soluble, bitter tasting, turns litmus blue and always have a pH greater than 7 in solution, *e.g.*, baking soda , sodium carbonate etc.

Litmus: A mixture of pigments extracted from certain lichens that turns blue in basic solution and red in acidic solution.

Salt: A salt is a neutral compound composed of cations bound to anions. A cation is a positively charged ion. Metals typically form cations where as anions are negatively charged ion.

Organic compound: These contain carbon chemically bound to hydrogen. They often contain other elements (particularly O, N, halogens, or S).

Metals and Non-metals

Metals: Metals are shiny (lustre), high density, ductile and malleable, high melting point, hard, and conduct electricity and heat.

Ores: An ore is a mineral containing a metal as a proportion of its content, which is economical to extract its metallic component.

Substance	Important Ores
Aluminium	Bauxite
Antimony	Stibnite
Beryllium	Beryl, Crysoberyl
Calcium	Lime stone, Marble, Chalk, Gypsum, Flurosper
Chromium	Chromite
Cobalt	Smaltite
Copper	Cuprite, Bornite
Iron	Hematite, Magnatite
Lead	Galena, Masicot, Serusite
Magnicium	Magnesite, Dolomite, Carnallite
Manganese	Pyrolusite, Hausmannite
Mercury	Cinnabar
Molybdenum	Molybdenite and wulfenite
Nickel	Pantilandite and Gargnierite
Phosphorous	Phosphorite Apatite, Chlorapatite
Potassium	Carnelite, Saltpetre
Silver	Argentite
Sodium	Rock Salt, Chile Saltpetre
Sulphur	Galena, Copper Pyrites and Iron Pyrites
Tin	Cassiterite, Tin stone
Titanium	Rutile, Ilmenite
Uranium	Pitchblende
Zinc	Zinc Blends,Calamine

Some Important Processes

(*a*) ***Gravity separation:*** The heavier metal or metallic mineral particles separated from the lighter gangue. Gold and magnetite are separated in this way.

(*b*) ***Flotation:*** In this method, finely ground ore is mixed with a liquid. The metal or metallic mineral floats while the gangue sinks.

(*c*) ***Magnetic separation:*** Metals that have magnetic properties are separated from the gangue, *e.g.*, magnetite.

(*d*) ***Smelting:*** The ore is heated with a reducing agent and a flux to a high temperature. The reducing agent combines with the oxygen in a metallic oxide, leaving pure metal; and the flux combines with the gangue to form a slag that is liquid poured away from the metal. The production of pig iron extract copper, lead, nickel use this process.

(*e*) ***Amalgamation*** is a metallurgical process that utilizes mercury to dissolve silver or gold to form an amalgam.

(*f*) ***Electrolysis:*** In this process, the metal is deposited at the cathode from aqueous solutions or in an electrolytic furnace. Copper, nickel, zinc, silver, and gold are several examples of metals that are refined by deposition from aqueous solutions. Aluminium, barium, calcium, magnesium, beryllium, potassium, and sodium are metals that are processed in electrolytic furnaces.

Some Interesting Points

Osmium and iridium are the most dense metals, and lithium is the least dense. Bismuth has the lowest electrical conductivity of the metallic elements, and silver the highest at ordinary temperatures. Gallium, mercury, cesium, and rubidium are the only metal elements that melt near room temperature.

Metalloids have intermediate in properties between the metals and the non-metals. Most common is that metalloids are usually semiconductors rather than conductors. They are boron, silicon, germanium, arsenic, antimony, tellurium, polonium.

Non-metal: A non-metal is a substance that conducts heat and electricity poorly, is brittle or waxy or gaseous, and cannot be hammered into sheets or drawn into wire. The non-metals are: nitrogen, oxygen, fluorine, phosphorus, sulfur, chlorine, selenium.

Alkali metals: They are soft compared to other metals, have low melting points, and are so reactive that they are never found freely in nature, *e.g.*, lithium, sodium, potassium, rubidium, cesium, and francium. Francium exists only in a radioactive form.

Alkaline Earth Metals: They are brittle, the alkaline earth metals are malleable, conduct electricity and when heated, burn readily in air, *e.g.*, beryllium, magnesium, calcium, strontium, barium, and radium.

Alloys

An alloy is a compound, of two or more elements, at least one of which is a metal.

Alloy	Composition
Duraluminium	Aluminium, copper, magnesium, and manganese
Gun Metal	Copper, Tin
Steel	Iron, Carbon
Stainless Steel	Iron, carbon, chromium, tunsten
Petwar	Tin, Antimony and Copper
Bronze	Copper, Tin and Zinc
German Silver	Copper, Zinc and Nickel
Electrum	Gold and Silver
18 carat Gold	Gold, Silver and Copper

Dentist Amalgam	Mercury Copper
Yellow Brass	Copper Zinc
Brass	Copper and Zinc
Nichrome	Nickel and Chromium
Plumbers Solder	Lead and tin

Common Chemicals and their Chemical Names

Common Name	Chemical Name
grain alcohol	ethyl alcohol
wood Alcohol	methyl alcohol
alum	aluminum potassium sulfate
alumina	aluminum oxide
baking soda	sodium bicarbonate
bleaching powder	chlorinated lime
blue vitriol	copper sulfate
brimstone	sulfur
carbolic acid	phenol
carbonic acid gas	carbon dioxide
epsom salts	gypsum
hypo (photography)	sodium thiosulfate solution
gypsum	natural calcium sulfate
lime	calcium oxide
lime, slaked	calcium hydroxide
limewater	calcium hydroxide
lunar caustic	silver nitrate
magnesia	magnesium oxide
mercury oxide, black	mercurous oxide
methanol	methyl alcohol
methylated spirits	methyl alcohol
pearl ash	potassium carbonate

Important Points to Remember

- Temporary hardness of water is due to the presence of bicarbonates of calcium and magnesium in water. Whereas the permanent hardness is due to the presence of Calcium Sulphate, which can be eliminated by the use of Zeolites.
- The gas used in balloons is helium.
- Gobar gas is obtained by decomposition of vegetable matter and animal dung.
- L.P.G. (liquefied petroleum gas) consists of mainly propane and butane.
- Natural gas is composed primarily of methane and other light hydrocarbons.
- Ethylene gas is used for artificial fruit ripening.
- Sodium and potassium react vigorously with cold water so it is preserved under kerosene while phosphorus is spontaneously inflammable in air so preserved under water.
- Nitrous oxide is called laughing gas, in mild doses it is used as anesthetic.
- Nitric acid is used as fertilizers and explosives.
- Tri-nitro toluene and nitro glycerene are common explosives.
- Smelling salt is ammonium carbonate.
- Potassium nitrate or Nitre or Indian salt petre is used as Gun powder.
- The paste applied to the side of a match box is a mixture of Phosphorous Trisulphide, glass powder and sand to cause frictions and glue. The match head contains a readily combustible substance like atimony trisulphide, potassium chlorate which maintain the combustion and a binding material like glue.
- Marble is calcium carbonate.
- Methylated spirit is a mixture of methyl alcohol and ethyl alcohol.
- Urea is the first organic compound prepared in the laboratory.
- Carbonic acid is soda water.
- Mercaptans leakage in L.P.G. cylinders is easily detected.
- Hydrazine is used to propei rockets.
- Coke is obtained by healthy wood out of contact with air.
- Terylene and nylon are synthetic fibres produced by a process of polymerization. Terylene is a polyester and Nylon a polymide.
- Pyrene is carbon tetrachloride specially used to extinguish electrical fires.
- Tincture iodine is a solution of iodine in alcohol.
- Nickel is used in conversion of oil into solid fat.
- Coal gas is the product of destructive distillation of coal *i.e.*, heating coal out of contact of air.
- Rust is hydrated ferric oxide.
- The chief component of pearl is ferric component.

BIOLOGY

The term *biology* derived from the Greek work, bios, "life" and the suffix-*logia*, "study of." **Biology** is a natural science concerned with the study of life and living organisms.

Branches of Biology

Apiculture	Culture of Bee
Cytology	Study of Cells
Dermatology	Study of Skin
Entomology	Study of Insects
Evolution	Study of Origin of new from old
Floriculture	Study of Flower Yielding Plants
Genetics	Study of Heredity and Variations
Gynaecology	Study of Female Reproductive Organ
Horticulture	Study of Garden Cultivation

Haematology	Study of Blood
Mycology	Study of Fungi
Nephrology	Study of Kidneys
Neurology	Study of Nervous System
Obstetrics	Branch of Medicine Dealing with Pregnancy
Ophthalmology	Study of Eyes
Ornithology	Study of Birds
Osteology	Study of Bones
Palaeontology	Study of Fossils
Phycology	Study of Algae
Pisciculture	Study of Fish
Pomology	Study of Fruits
Sericulture	Culture of Silk Moth and Pupa
Serpentology	Study of Snakes
Virology	Study of Virus

Cell

1. **Cell Membrane:** Cells are enclosed by a thin film like membrane called plasma membrane, cytoplasmic membrane or plasma lemma.
   Endocytosis: Taking substance inside the cell by the plasma membrane. It is of two types : *Phagocytosis :* Cell Eating. *Pinocytosis :* Cell drinking. *Exocytosis:* Reverse of Endocytosis.
2. **Cytoplasm:** It is a part of protoplasm lying between plasma membrane and nucleus.
3. **Cell Wall :** Cells of most fungi, prokaryotes (bacteria and blue-green algae) and plants (except gametes) are surrounded by the cell wall. It is absent in animals.
4. **Nucleus:** Discovered by Robert Brown. Nucleus controls the metabolic activities of the cell by controlling the synthesis of enzymes.
   - Contains nucleoplasm (nuclear sap) which contains chromatin.
   - Chromatin organizes itself into thread like structures called Chromosomes.
   - The function of chromosomes is to carry genetic information from one cell generation to another.
   - Nucleolus is also present which helps in the production of ribosomes.
5. **Chromosomes :** Waldeyer coined the term chromosome. Each chromosome is made up of DNA.
   - Chromosome number is constant for a particular species. Diploid number (2n) of chromosomes are present in somatic cells and haploid number (n) of chromosomes are there in gametes.
   - In humans, the diploid number is 46.
6. **Mitochondria :** Powerhouse of the cell and energy is stored as ATP
   - They are semi-autonomous organelles. They contain DNA.
   - Mitochondria is enclosed by a double-membraned envelope.
7. **Endoplasmic Reticulum :** Provides an increased surface area for various metabolic activities within the cell. Types: Rough ER and smooth ER.
8. **Golgi Complex :** Main function is secretion. Secretions are in the form of granules in cytoplasm.
9. **Lysosomes :** Also called Suicidal bags. Contain enzymes acid hydrolases which digest worn - out or unnecessary parts of the cell, or even whole cells by process called 'Autophagy'.
10. **Ribosomes :** Made of RNA and proteins in equal amounts. Sites of protein synthesis.
11. **Vacuoles :** Large vacuole found in plant cells. Membrane surrounding the vacuole is tonoplast. Regulation of water, in osmoregulation, in storage and in digestion.
12. **Plastids :** Found only in plant cells.
    - ***Chloroplast :*** Green contains the pigment chlorophyll.
    - ***Leucoplasts :*** Colourless, occur in large number in cells of fruits, seeds, etc. They store nutrients (*e.g.*, amyloplasts of potato store starch).
    - ***Chromoplasts :*** Coloured, containing fat soluble yellow, orange and red pigments. Found in flowers and fruits.
13. **Centrosome :** Found in animal cells and cells of lower plants (*e.g.*, Algae) only. The first indication that the cell is about to divide is generally given by the centrosome.

Balanced Diet

A Balanced Diet comprising of healthy and diverse foods is key to promoting good health. The components of food are:

1. **Carbohydrates:** Constitutes 3 elements: Carbon, Hydrogen and Oxygen. 1 gm gives 17 kJ of energy (or 4.1 kcal of energy). Carbohydrates form a better fuel than proteins and fats because their molecules have relatively more oxygen.
   - Cellulose is present in the cell-wall of plants.
   - D-fructose is the sweetest of sugars. It is found in Fruit Juices, Honey, etc.
   - Excess Sugar is stored as Glycogen in liver.
   - ***Sources of Carbohydrates are:*** Cereals (Wheat, Rice and Maize), Sugarcane, Milk (contains Lactose — a type of Sugar), Fruits, Honey, Beet, etc.
   - ***Types of Carbohydrates:*** (*i*) **Monosaccharides :** They are the simplest carbohydrates consist of one unit (*e.g.*, glucose, fructose, galactose). ***(ii)*** **Disaccharides :** Consist of 2 units of monosaccharides (*e.g.*, sucrose, lactose and 1 maltose). ***(iii)*** **Polysaccharides :** Consist of more than three monosaccharide units (*e.g.*, starch in plants and glycogen in animals).
2. **Fats:** Provides twice the energy of carbohydrates (1 gm provides 37 kJ or 9 kcal of energy). Acts as the

reserve food material, excess fat is stored in the liver and adipose tissue.

- ***Types of fatty acids :*** Saturated and Unsaturated. (*i*) **Saturated Fatty Acids :** Solids at room temperature. **(*ii*) Unsaturated Fatty Acids :** Liquids at room temperature.
- Excess of saturated fats increases the blood — cholesterol level and may cause arteriosclerosis (hardening of arteries). This may lead to heart attack.
- Essential Fatty Acids include Linoleic, Linolenic and Arachidonic Acids are present in Groundnut Oil, Sunflower Oil.
- ***Hydrogenation :*** Process by which unsaturated fatty acids are converted into saturated fatty acids by the addition of Hydrogen.

3. Proteins : Made up of Carbon, Hydrogen, Oxygen, Nitrogen and Sulphur. Important for growth and repair of the body (75% of our body is proteins only).

- ***Types of Amino acids are:*** **(*i*) Essential Amino Acids :** They cannot be synthesised in the body, *e.g.*, isoleucine, leucine, lysine, methionine, phenylalanine, threonine, tryptophan and valine. (*ii*) **Non - Essential Amino Acids :** They are synthesized in the body, *e.g.*, Alanine, Arginine, Asparagine, Aspartic Acid, Cysteine, Glutamine, Glutamic Acid, Glycine, Histidine, Proline, Serine and Tyrosine.
- ***Some Important Proteins are: Enzymes:*** *e.g.*, Pepsin, Trypsin. **Hormone:** *e.g.*, Insulin, Glucogon, **Carrier:** *e.g.*, Haemoglobin — Transports O_2 in blood, Myoglobin — Stores O_2 in muscles. **Contractile Proteins:** *e.g.*, Actin and Myosin. **Structural Proteins:** *e.g.*, Collagen — Component of Bones, Tendons, Cartilage. Keratin — Component of Skin, Feathers, Nails, Hair, Horn. **Protective Proteins:** *e.g.*, Gamma globulins. **Visual Proteins :** Rhodopsin and Iodopsin of rods and cones. (present in Retina of the eye).
- ***Protein Energy Malnutrition:*** (*i*) **Kwashiorkar :** Due to deficiency of protein. Abdomen and feet swells, Skin becomes Dark and Scaly, Enlarged Liver, Anaemia. (*ii*) **Marasmus :** Deficiency of Proteins. Losing of body weight, wasting of muscles, ribs look prominent. (Oedema and skin pigmentation absent).

4. Minerals: Minerals maintain water balance and nutrition in the body

- Although needed in very small quantities, mineral salts of various kinds are essential for the proper functioning of the body.
- They yield no energy but are important constituents of certain tissues, besides playing a major role in the regulation of metabolic activities.
- Calcium is the principal component of the skeleton.
- Meat, eggs, milk, cheese and vegetables are important sources of minerals, and usually, the body gets adequate amounts of them from a normal diet.

Minerals Required in Human beings

Minerals	Sources	Functions	Deficiency
Macro Elements			
Calcium	Milk, Cheese	Formation of Teeth and Bones	Weak Teeth and Bones
Phosphorus	Milk, Meat	Component of ATP, DNA, RNA	Weak Teeth and Bones; Retarded Growth
Sulphur	Proteins of Food	Component of Amino Acids	Disturbed Protein Metabolism.
Potassium	Meat, Milk, Cereals, Fruits	Water Regulation	Weak Muscles; Risk of Paralysis
Chlorine	Table salt	Acid-Base Balance	Loss of Appetite; Muscle Cramps.
Sodium	Table salt	Acid - Base and Water Balances	Low Blood Pressure, Loss of Appetite;
Magnesium	Cereals, Green Vegetables	Cofactor of Enzymes	Affects Nervous Functions.
Iron	Meat, Eggs, Cereals	Component of haemoglobin	Anaemia, Weakness
Iodine	Sea Food, Iodized Salt	Component of Thyroxine	Goitre, Cretinism
Micro Elements			
Flourine	Drinking Water, Tea, Sea Food	Maintenance of Bones and Teeth	Weak Teeth,
Manganese	Dry Fruits, Cereals,	Cofactor of some Enzymes	Irregular Growth of Bones, Cartilages

Vitamins Required in Human beings

Vitamins : Discovered by Funk. It do not provide energy but help in different physiological processes.

Vitamin	Sources	Effect of Deficiency
Water - Soluble Vitamins		
B_1 (Thiamine)	Rice Bran, Whole Wheat Flour	Beri - beri
B_2 (Riboflavin)	Cheese, Eggs, Yeast,	Cheilosis Keratitis of Cornea
B_3 (Nicotinic Acid)	Fresh Meat, Liver, Fish,	Pellagra, Muscle Atrophy,
B_6 (Pyridoxine)	Milk, Cereals, Fish, Meat, Liver	Dermatitis, Convulsions, Nausea, Mental Disorders
B_5 (Pantothenic Acid)	Yeast, Liver, Kidneys, Eggs, Meat,	Dermatitis, Anaemia, Fatigue, Nausea.
H (Biotin)	Yeast, Vegetables, Fruits, Eggs,	Skin Lesions, Loss of Appetite, Hair Fall.
Folic Acid Group	Green Vegetables, Soyabean,	Retarded Growth.
B_{12} (Cyanocobabmine)	Meat, Fish, Liver, Eggs,	Pernicious Anaemia
C (Ascorbic acid)	Lemon, Orange	Scurvy
Fat - Soluble Vitamins		
A (Retinol)	Milk, Butter, Egg Yolk, Liver,	Xerophthalmia
D (Cholecalciferol)	Synthesized in skin cells	Rickets, Osteomalacia.
E (Tocopherol)	Green Vegetables	Causes sterility, Muscular dystrophy,
K (Phylloauinone)	Carrots, Lettuce	Haemorrhages, delayed blood clotting

Digestive System of Humans

The process of converting food into energy giving substances is carried out by this system.

1. **Buccal Cavity :** In the mouth salivary glands secrete saliva which contains the enzyme Ptyalin
   - ***Teeth :*** They are produced in two sets — Temporary and Permanent. The teeth are of four types : Incisors, Canines, Premolars and Molars.
   - ***Structure of a Tooth :*** A tooth consists of 3 Regions: Crown, Neck and Root. Enamel is the hardest substance in the human body.
   - ***Dental Formula :*** 2123 / 2123, means that there are 2 incisors, 1 canine, 2 Premolars and 3 molars in half of the upper jaw and exactly the same arrangement in half of the lower jaw.
   - In elephants, incisors of the upper jaw grow into huge tusks.
   - Canines are very large in predators such as cat, dog and lion.
   - Rabbit and squirrel lack canines. In walrus, the upper canines are enlarged into projecting tusks.
   - The last molars are called the wisdom teeth.
2. **Pharynx:** Links Buccal Cavity to Oesophagus. Food is carried by peristaltic movement. Trachea opens into Pharynx through an aperture called Glottis.
3. **Oesophagus:** 25 cm long tube. Longitudinal folds keep its cavity almost closed, except during swallowing of food.
4. **Stomach:** Oesophagus opens into it. In stomach, the food is called chyme. Has 3 Parts: Fundus, Cardiac and Pyloric. Gastric juices produced in the stomach help in digestion of food. Also contains HCl which provides acidic medium. Besides it activates pepsinogen to pepsin and prorennin to rennin.
   - Ruminents (Cattle, Buffaloes, Goats, Sheep, Deer, Camel) have their stomach consisting of 4 Chambers: Rumen, Reticulum, Omasum and Abomasum.
5. **Small Intestine:** Here the food from the stomach is mixed with bile and pancreatic juice.
   - Duodenum receives the bile — pancreatic duct formed by the union of bile duct and pancreatic duct.
   - Both jejunum and ileum have numerous figure like projections called the villi. The villi contain blood vessels to absorb digested food.
6. **Large Intestine:** It receives undigested material from the small intestine and absorbs water.
   - Caecum is the diverted part of intestine. Cellulose digestion takes place in it. It is very large in herbivores.
   - Vermiform appendix is a part of caecum. Both caecum and appendix are vestigial in humans.

Blood in Human Body

Blood is a fluid connective tissue. It is 6.8 litres in man and 500 ml less in woman. 6-8% of body weight (pH 7.4).

1. **Red Blood Corpuscles:** Also called Erythrocytes, disc - shaped (for increased Surface Area), no nucleus contains a pigment called Haemoglobin, which gives blood its Red Colour.
   - ***Amount of Haemoglobin*** is 14-15.6 gm/ 100 cc of blood (11-14 in woman).
   - Life of RBC is 120 days after which they are broken down in spleen or liver.

- Product of breakdown of haemoglobin is a pigment (yellow colour), called bilirubin. Retention of bilirubin leads to jaundice.

2. **White Blood Corpuscles:** Also called Leucocytes, rounded, with a nucleus, far less numerous than RBCs, life 3-4 days.
   - ***Types:*** Granulocytes (Basophils, Eosinophils, Neutrophils) and Agranulocytes (Monocytes, Lymphocytes).
   - ***Basophils :*** Take up basic stains. Have an S-shaped nucleus. Secrete an anti-coagulant Heparin, which prevents clots within the blood vessels.
   - ***Eosinophils or Acidophils :*** Take up acidic stains. Assists in defence mechanism.
   - ***Neutrophils :*** Most numerous of the WBCs (65-70%). Defence.
   - ***Monocytes :*** Largest of all. Very motile. Defence.
   - ***Lymphocytes :*** 25% of the WBC. Takes part in antigen and antibody formation.
3. **Platelets :** Also called Thrombocytes, formed in bone marrow, life 3-7 days, sets off blood clotting.

   Plasma (65%) : Watery part of blood, clear, yellow fluid. Contains about 90% water, proteins and organic salts.
   - ***Lymph :*** Lymph = Blood - RBC, *i.e.*, Plasma + WBC. All interchanges of nutrients and waste products between blood and tissue takes place through lymph only.
   - Spleen produces lymph. At the same time it also acts as the graveyard of lymph.

   Blood Groupings
   - ***Father of Blood Grouping:*** Karl Landsteiner. He discovered A, B and O blood groups in 1900.
   - Decastello and Sturle in 1902 discovered AB blood group.
   - ABO system of blood groups is based on antigens and antibodies.
   - AB: Universal recipient.
   - O: Universal donor.

RH Factor: It is based on Rh antigen. Discovered in 1940 by Landsteiner and A.S. Veiner. It discovered in Rhesus monkey. A person can be Rh^+ or Rh^-.

- In world population Rh^+ are 85% and Rh^- are 15% only.
- Blood transfusion technique was first developed by James Blundell in 1825.

Excretory System of Humans

Waste materials excreted in animals are of many kinds : Nitrogenous Substances, Carbon dioxide, Pigments, Excess Water, etc.

The Nitrogenous Waste can be excreted in the following forms :

- **Ammonia :** Highly Toxic. In aquatic animals (called Ammoniotelic).
- **Urea :** Far less toxic than ammonia In Mammals, Alligators, Turtles (called Ureotelic).
- **Uric Acid :** In animals where conservation of water is needed. In Birds, Insects, Land Reptiles (called Uricotelic).

Excretory System of Mammals

1. **Kidneys :**A kidney is composed of 1.2 million microscopic structural and functional units called nephrons or uriniferous tubules.
2. **Ureters :** Open into Urinary Bladder.
3. **Urinary Bladder :** Size depends upon the amount of mine in it (up to 700-800 ml).

   The lower part is guarded by 2 Sphinctors : inner involuntary and outer voluntary.
4. **Urethra :** Leads to the exterior. In females, it carries only urine. In males it carries urine as well as spermatic fluid.

   Nephron : Functional unit of kidney. It is a long tube differentiated into 4 regions.

1. **Bowman's Capsule :** Contains a globular bunch of capillaries, the glomerulus. In glomerular filtrate: water (99%), inorganic salts, amino acids, fatty acids, glucose, urea, uric acid, hormones, vitamins are present.
2. **Proximal Convoluted Tubule :** Starts from the neck of Bowman's capsule and is highly twisted. Almost whole of the glucose and vitamins, amino acids, Na and K, Ca and Mg and water is absorbed.
3. **Loop of Henle:** U-shaped. Consist of 2 straight limbs: descending and ascending. No water is absorbed in ascending limb.
4. **Distal Convoluted Tubule :** Greatly twisted. Reabsorbs some Na and Cl. Leads to Collecting Tubules which lead to ureters.
   - The yellow colour of urine is caused by the pigment urochrome, which is a breakdown product of haemoglobin from worn out RBCs.
   - The urine gives a pungent smell due to conversion of urea into ammonia by bacteria.
   - Kidney stones: Calcium Oxalate.

Respiratory System of Humans

I. **Anaerobic Respiration :** When nutrients are oxidized without using O_2 (also called fermentation). *e.g.*, Ascaris, Fasciola, Taenia also respire anaerobically. It is a low energy yielding process.

II. **Aerobic Respiration :** Cells utilize O_2 for oxidizing nutrients. It is found in most plants and animals. It involves:

1. **External Respiration:** Gaseous exchange of O_2 and CO_2 between blood and air (or water).
2. **Internal Respiration:** Gaseous exchange between blood and tissues.
3. **Cellular Respiration:** Oxidation of nutrients in the cells and liberation of energy.

Endocrine System of Humans

Formed by endocrine glands (or Ductless Glands). They secrete hormones directly into the blood stream.

Hypothalamus : Forms a part of fore-brain, secretes neurohormones, which effect the release of hormones from pituitary.

Pituitary Gland: Also called Master Gland. It is the smallest endocrine gland. It secretes:

1. ***Somatotrophic Hormone :*** Controls the general growth of the body. Hyper-secretion leads to acromegaly and gigantism and hyposecretion leads to dwarfness.
2. ***Gonadotrophic Hormone :*** Stimulates the primary sex hormones, *i.e.*, ovaries and testes.
3. ***Lactogenic Hormone :*** Initiates milk production in the pregnant females.
4. ***Thyrotrophic Hormone :*** Aids in the regulation of thyroid secretion.
5. ***Adrenocorticotrophic Hormone :*** Influences the secretion from the cortex of adrenal glands.
6. ***Oxytocin or Pitocin :*** Stimulates smooth muscle contractions during child birth. Also helps in the secretion of milk in females.
8. ***Vasopressin (Anti-Diuretic Hormone) :*** Regulates reabsorption of water from the kidney tubules, causing increase in Blood Pressure.

Thyroid Gland : It is the largest endocrine gland located in the neck between the trachea and larynx.

1. ***Thyroxine :*** Regulates physical, mental and sexual development.
   - Poor in iodine is insufficient for the synthesis of thyroxin, leads to simple goitre.
2. ***Thyrocalcitonin :*** It controls the amount of calcium in the body.
   - *Hashimoto Disease :* Due to age factor or injury in thyroid gland secretion of thyroid reduces.

Parathyroid Gland : Secretes Parathormone. It influences calcium and phosphorus metabolism.

Thymus Gland : Situated near the heart. Produces Thymine. Preventing development of gonads.

Pancreas : It is an exocrine as well as an endocrine gland. Its endocrine part is known as Islets of Langerhans. Beta cells secrete Insulin which controls the amount of sugar in the blood.

Adrenal Glands : Consists of 2 Distinct Parts: Outer cortex and Inner medulla.

1. Adrenal Medulla secretes Adrenaline or epinephrine which effects liberation of glucose from glycogen stored in liver.
2. Adrenal Cortex secretes two types of Hormones:
   (*a*) *Mineralo Corticoids :* Maintain electrolyte balance. Its hyposecretion results in Addison's disease.
   (*b*) *Gluco Corticoids :* It influences carbohydrate metabolism. Its hypersecretion leads to Cushing Disease.

Reproductive System of Humans

It is the process by which an individual multiplies in number by producing more individuals of its own type.

I. Asexual Reproduction: Asexual Reproduction is the process of multiplication of individuals without the formation or fusion of gametes.

Binary Fission : It involves the division of the nucleus followed by that of the cytoplasm, breaking the body into two young ones. *e.g.*, Amoeba, Euglena, Paramecium, etc.

II. Sexual Reproduction : The process of sexual reproduction involves the formation and fusion of gametes (Syngamy) and results in the formation of a new organism genetically different from parent.

Mammalian Reproductive System : The reproductive system of sexually reproducing animals consists of:

Sex	Primary Sex Organs	Secondary Sex Organs
Male	Testes	Epididymis, Vas deferens, Ejaculatory duct, Urethra Seminal vesicle, Prostate Gland Cowper's gland, Penis
Female	Ovary	Fallopian tubes, Uterus, Vagina, External Genitalia/ Vulva Bartholian's Gland, Mammary glands

Sensory Organs of Humans

Eye: Eye is made up of 3 Layers : Upper Sclerotic, Middle Choroids, Inner Retina.

1. ***Sclerotic Layer :*** The Transparent bulging, circular part of sclerotic layer which lies in the front is called cornea. Cornea is covered by the thin Conjunctiva.
2. ***Choroid Layer :*** Choroid layer starts from iris which is next to cornea. The circular aperture of iris is called pupil.
   - Lens is a proteinous. It is biconvex in nature.
3. ***Retina :*** Image of the object is formed on retina. Retina is composed of 2 types of Cells:
   - *Rod Cells :* Sensitive to dim light and contain the pigment Rhodopsin (in nocturnal animals more).
   - *Cone Cells :* Colour sensitive for 3 primary colours (Red, Blue and Green). They are found more in diurnal animals.

Yellow Spot (Macula Lutea) : On retina, finest image is formed here. Favea centralis is the depression in the middle of yellow spot.

Blind Spot : No image formation takes place here as the optic nerves innervate the eyeball here.

- Cornea is donated in Eye Donation.
- Eyes glow in animals due to tapetum.

Defects of Eye

1. ***Myopia:*** Cannot see distant objects, image formed before retina, concave lens is used.
2. ***Hypermetropia :*** Cannot see near objects, image formed behind retina, convex lens is used.
3. ***Astigmatism :*** Curvature of cornea becomes irregular and image is not clear cylindrical lens is used.
4. ***Cataract :*** Due to defective protein metabolism the lens becomes opaque Operation is needed.
5. ***Gloucoma :*** Due to defect in aqueous humour.
6. ***Presbiopia :*** In this, power of accommodation of lens decreases due to age factor and defected metabolism. Can be removed by bifocai lens.

Ear : Divided into 3 Parts :

1. ***External Ear:*** Pinna + External Auditary Meatus
   - Has wax glands which produce cerumen to trap dust particles.
2. ***Middle Ear:*** It encloses 3 Ear Ossicles : Malleus (Hammer-Shaped), Incus (Anvil- Shaped), Stapes (Stirrup-Shaped)

Fanastra Ovalis : Connects middle ear to internal ear. Middle ear is connected to the pharynx by Eustachian tube.

3. ***Internal Ear (Membranous Labyrinth) :*** Most delicate part. Enclosed by parotic bone. It perform two functions : Maintenance of balance and hearing.
   - In the internal ear are 3 semi-circular canals and utriculus which are filled with a fluid, endolymph.

Diseases in Human

Human Viral Diseases	Human Bacterial Diseases
Chickenpox	Cholera
Measles	Diphtheria
Polio	Tuberculosis
Rabies	Leprosy
Mumps	Tetanus
Influenza	Typhoid
Hepatitis	Plague
Herpes	Whooping Cough
AIDS	Sore Throat
Trachoma (of Cornea)	Pneumonia
Human Protozoans Diseases	Gonorrhoea
Amoebiasis	Syphilis
Malaria	Botulism
Sleeping Sickness	**Human Fungal Diseases**
Kalazar	Ringworm
Diarrhoea	Athlete's foot
Piarrhoea	Dhobie itch

Some Important Facts of Human Body

Length of Alimentary Canal	Approximately 8 metres
Number of Cells in Body	75 trillion
Longest Bone	Femur (Thigh bone)
Smallest Bone	Ear ossicle, stapes
Weight of Brain	1400 gms
Blood Volume	6.8 litres (in 70 kg body)
Normal B.P.	120/80 mm Hg
Number of R.B.C.	(*a*) In Male : 4.5-5.0 million/cubic mm. (*b*) In Female : 4.0-4.5 million/cubic mm
Life Span of R.B.C.	120 days
Normal W.B.C. Count	5000-1000/cubic mm
Life Span of W.B.C.	3-4 days
D.L.C. (Differential Leucocyte Count)	(*a*) Basophils : 0.5-1% (*b*) Eosinophils : 1-3% (*c*) Monocytes : 3-8% (*d*) Neutrophils : 40-70% (*e*) Lymphocytes : 2-25%
Blood Platelets Count	2,00,000-4,00,000/cubic mm
Haemoglobin	(*a*) In Male : 14-15.6 gm/100 c.c. of blood (*b*) In Female : 11-14 gm/100 c.c. of blood
Hb Content in Body	500-700 gm
Universal Blood Donor	O Rh–ve
Universal Blood Recipient	AB
Blood Clotting Time	2-5 minutes
Average Body Weight	70 kg
Normal Body Temperature	98.4°F or 37°C
Breathing Rate	16-20/minute

Dental Formula	Adult : 2123/2123 = 32; Child : 2120/2120 = 22 Milk Teeth
Number of Cranial Nerves	12 pairs
Number of Spinal Nerves	31 pairs
Largest Endocrine Gland	Thyroid
Gestation Period	9 months (253-266 days)
Normal Heart Beat	72-75/minute
Largest Gland	Liver
Largest Muscle in the Body	Gluteus maximus (Buttock Muscle)
Smallest Muscle in the Body	Stapedius
Largest Artery	Abdominal Aorta
Largest Vein	Inferior Venacava
Greatest Regeneration Power	In liver
Longest Nerve	Sciatic
Longest Cell	Neuron (Nerve Cell)
Minimum Regeneration Power	In Brain Cells
pH of Gastric Juice	1.4
pH of Urine	6.0
pH of Blood	7.35-7.45
Total Number of Muscles in the Body	639
Total Number of Bones in the Body	206

MULTIPLE CHOICE QUESTIONS

1. Which of the following is an antibiotic?
A. Aspirin B. Paracetamol
C. Penicillin D. Sulphadizine

2. Digestion of food starts in:
A. mouth B. liver
C. stomach D. intestines

3. By taking the pulse rate of the human body, a doctor determines:
A. heartbeat
B. functioning of heart valves
C. the amount of blood in body
D. the condition of liver

4. A thermostat is used to:
A. purify air
B. regulate humidity
C. regulate temperature
D. regulate air pressure

5. Heat from the sun reaches the earth by:
A. reflection B. conduction
C. convection D. radiations

6. Dew forms most readily on nights that are:
A. calm and clear B. stormy
C. windy D. cloudy

7. The full moon rises in the:
A. South B. North
C. East D. West

8. An aeroplane is able to fly because;
A. it is lighter than air
B. it is heavier than air
C. it is made of very light materials
D. moving air can lift objects

9. The souring of milk is caused by the action of:
A. a protozoa B. bacteria
C. viruses D. None of these

10. The smallest living thing that can cause disease in the human body is:
A. flea B. bacteria
C. a protozoa D. viruses

11. The most abundant gas in the air is:
A. oxygen B. carbon dioxide
C. nitrogen D. hydrogen

12. Which is the element common to brass and bronze?
A. Copper B. Iron
C. Zinc D. Aluminium

13. The densest element known so far is:
A. iron B. mercury
C. osmium D. tungsten

14. The most ductile element is:
A. gold B. silver
C. iron D. aluminium

15. The metal having highest melting point is:
A. chromium B. tungsten
C. diamond D. silver

16. The gas which constitutes most of Venus's atmosphere is:
A. oxygen B. nitrogen
C. hydrogen D. carbon dioxide

17. The most common acid found in the nature is:
A. acetic acid B. citric acid
C. lactic acid D. hydrochloric acid

18. The bomb that cannot destroy the property but can damage the life only is:
A. atom bomb B. hydrogen bomb
C. fission bomb D. neutron bomb

19. The waves received by our Television sets are:
A. light waves B. radio waves
C. cosmic waves D. micro waves

20. Which of the following machines will fail to give satisfactory result in vacuum?
A. Bicycle B. Sewing machine
C. Fan D. Washing machine

21. Which of the following is the best conductor of electric current?
A. Aluminium B. Copper
C. Silver D. Gold

22. Tungsten is mainly used for making filament of electric bulbs because of its:
A. low cost
B. high melting point
C. high electrical conductivity
D. low thermal conductivity

23. The element common to bone and cement is:
A. silicon B. calcium
C. nitrogen D. phosphorus

24. The raw material common to cement and glass is:
A. soda B. rock
C. gypsum D. sand

25. What is essentially required to digest the food in stomach?
A. Air B. Water
C. Enzymes D. Minerals

26. Domestic electric meters record the consumption of electricity in:
A. Volts B. Amperes
C. Watts D. Ohms

27. Which of the following gases does not pollute air?
A. Carbon dioxide B. Carbon monoxide
C. Nitrogen dioxide D. Sulphur dioxide

28. Polio is a disease caused due to:
A. bacterial infection B. virus infection
C. protozoal infection D. food poisoning

29. Which form of gold is the softest?
A. 16 Carat B. 18 Carat
C. 20 Carat D. 22 Carat

30. Filtration of wastes from the blood in human body is done by:
A. heart B. lungs
C. kidney D. intestines

31. Speed of sound waves is maximum in:
A. vacuum B. gases
C. liquids D. solids

32. How many colours are there in the rainbow?
A. 7 B. 10
C. 12 D. 5

33. Barometer measures:
A. wind velocity B. atmospheric pressure
C. amount of rainfall D. atmospheric moisture

34. Anemometer measures:
A. amount of rainfall
B. atmospheric pressure
C. wind velocity
D. amperage of an electrical current

35. Sphygmomanometer measures:
A. specific heat, latent heat, heat of chemical combination and other thermal properties
B. intensity of light
C. distance covered, or steps taken, by a person walking
D. blood pressure

36. Meteorology is the study of:
A. meteors and meteorites
B. the climate
C. the weather
D. the measurement of length

37. Oil, water and gas can be present in a well in the ascending order of:
A. water, oil, gas B. gas, water, oil
C. water, gas, oil D. oil, water, gas

38. Vegetables can be cooked quickly in a pressure cooker because:
A. steam can boil vegetables faster than water
B. boiling point increases with the increase in pressure
C. high pressure lowers the boiling point
D. All the above

39. A person suffering from which of the following cannot see with clarity the horizontal and vertical lines simultaneously?
A. Myopia B. Hypermitropia
C. Astigmatism D. Squint

40. When a flake of ice melts in a water bowl, the level of water inside the bowl:
A. remains unchanged
B. goes down
C. increases
D. nothing can be said definitely

41. To an astronaut in a satellite the colour of the sky would appear to be:
A. black B. blue
C. grey D. white

42. A fuse wire is used for:
A. allowing high currents to flow harmlessly
B. breaking the electrical circuit
C. saving a man from receiving electric shocks
D. All the above

43. Excessive intake of alcohol damages a person's:
A. kidneys
B. liver
C. stomach
D. All the above to a certain degree

44. Which of the following is common in all acids?
A. Hydrogen B. Oxygen
C. Nitrogen D. None of the above

45. After boiling, rice grains grow in volume and weight because:
A. starch swells in water and heat
B. heat enlarges solid
C. rice is a fatty grain
D. All the above

46. Hygrometer is used for measuring:
A. temperature B. relative humidity
C. rainfall D. density of water

47. Phobos and Deimos are the satellites of:
A. Uranus B. Mars
C. Venus D. Saturn

48. Plants are grown along river banks in order to check:
A. siltage and floods B. pollution
C. rainfall D. All the above

49. Which one of the following signifies the optical technique of recording waves and amplitude?
A. Holography B. Bibliography
C. Audiography D. None of the above

50. People use iron ploughs now, instead of the old wooden ploughs. This change signifies:
A. advance technology
B. appropriate technology
C. obsolete technology
D. ultimate technology

51. Acetyl salicylic acid is used commonly as:
A. pain-reliever B. tear gas
C. chemical fertilizer D. preservative

52. In a village where fuel is not available and people are poor, which of the following measures is the most suitable to prevent disease through contaminated water from the wells?
A. Using chemicals to purify water
B. Boiling the water
C. Use of micro-organisms to purify water
D. None of the above

53. One of the main constituents of Gobar gas is:
A. thyamine B. methane
C. phosphate D. carbon monoxide

54. Quartz is softer than:
A. Diamond B. Corundum
C. Topaz D. All the above

55. Emerald and diamond are made of:
A. Beryllium and Carbon
B. Carbon
C. Silica
D. Silica and Beryllium

56. Human brain receives and sends signals as:
A. chemical impulses
B. physical impulses
C. electrical impulses
D. mechanical impulses

57. The ductless glands secreting hormones directly into human blood are known as:
A. exocrine glands B. endocrine glands
C. metabolic glands D. ductlands

58. Arrange the three forms of iron in descending order of carbon contents and other impurities in them:
I. wrought iron
II. cast iron
III. pig iron
A. III, II, I B. III, I, II
C. I, II, III D. II, I, III

59. Foot and mouth diseases attack:
A. cattle, sheep and pigs
B. cattle only
C. cattle and pigs only
D. cattle and sheep only

60. Which one of the following has maximum nitrogen content?
A. Sodium nitrate
B. Urea
C. Ammoniam sulphate
D. None of the above has enough nitrogen

61. Radio carbon dating is used for determining the age of:
A. fossils B. buildings
C. babies D. rocks

62. Pasteurization of milk means:
A. heating of milk upto 100°C
B. heating of milk at 65°C
C. cooling of milk at 100°C
D. cooling of milk upto 0°C

63. Ranikhet disease affects:
A. dogs B. cows
C. poultry D. sheep

64. Wisdom teeth appear in a human being between:
A. 17 and 20 years of age
B. 30 and 40 years of age
C. 10 and 17 years of age
D. 4 and 8 years of age

65. Decomposition of matter takes place due to the effect of:
A. bacteria B. virus
C. fungi D. algae

66. Bile is secreted by:
A. pancreas B. small intestine
C. stomach D. liver

67. Polio myelitis which causes polio is spread by:
A. mosquito B. virus
C. water D. adulterated food

68. Which of the following is a genetically transmitted disease?

A. Myopia B. Long sightedess
C. Colour blindness D. Night blindness

69. Which of the following is a metal?
A. Arsenic B. Sulphur
C. Potassium D. Carbon

70. How does weedicide remove weeds?
A. It removes the water required for growth
B. It destroys the roots of the weeds
C. It destroys the nutrients required for the growth of weeds
D. All of the above

71. A diamond is a:
A. form of fossilised mammal of ancient times
B. crystalline form of pure carbon
C. hard rolled under sea stone made into a diamond by the saliva of huge sea monsters and thereafter dug out from the mines
D. natural crystallized glass

72. High heel and/or pointed shoes are harmful because:
A. they injure the feet
B. they weaken the eyesight
C. they cause polio
D. they cause backache and sleeplessness

73. When returning to the earth, spacecrafts have a communication blackout, the reason is:
A. the returning spacecraft is doing so against the force of gravity which interferes with the radio waves
B. during the re-entry period the density of the plasma generated by the intense frictional heat is so high that the operational frequencies used for communication becomes very much less than the plasma cut-off frequency resulting in a total blackout
C. stellar X-rays attract and absorb the sound waves
D. the sounds created by the whirring of the mechanism of the spacecraft renders the sounds inaudible

74. Respiration is:
A. to change the food into energy
B. the process during which food is oxidized and its chemical energy is transformed into useful form
C. a sort of exercise
D. interconversion of food and energy

75. Dialysis is:
A. the same process as osmosis
B. the diffusion of sugar molecules through water
C. the process involved in the diffusion of toxic substance through a membrane
D. the evaporation of surplus sugar

76. Mycology is the study of:
A. Mica
B. Ants
C. Changes of a structure as a result of environment
D. Fungi

77. In human body, quantity of water is about:
A. 10% B. 20%
C. 65% D. 80%

78. What does the urine of a man contain mainly?
A. Urea B. Sugar
C. Salt D. None of the above

79. The filament of electric bulb is made of:
A. iron B. tungsten
C. nichrome D. silver

80. The lightning rod used for protecting building from lightning is made of:
A. glass B. cement
C. wood D. copper

81. When a body becomes positively charged, it:
A. loses electrons
B. gains electrons
C. loses protons
D. None of the above is correct

82. During which season our body needs more fats?
A. Summer season B. Rainy season
C. Winter season D. Spring season

83. Deficiency of insulin causes:
A. Beri-Beri B. Fever
C. Cancer D. Diabetes

84. Iron is heavier than water, still the ship floats on the sea because:
A. weight of the ship is less than the weight of water in the sea
B. weight of the ship is more than sea water
C. weight of the ship is less than the weight of water that the ship displaces
D. weight of ship is equal to the weight of water that ship displaces

85. Photosynthesis results in:
1. release of oxygen
2. release of carbon dioxide
3. formation of carbohydrates
4. intake of carbon dioxide
A. 1, 2, 3 are correct B. 1,3,4 are correct
C. 2,3,4 are correct D. only 1 is correct

86. The Pythagorean Theorem states that:
A. in any triangle the square of the longest side equals the sum of the squares of the other sides
B. in any triangle the square of the longest side equals the square of the sum of the other sides
C. in a right-angled triangle the square of the hypotenuse equals the sum of the squares of the other two sides
D. in an isosceles triangle the third side equals the sum of the two equal sides

87. The formula for inter conversion of Centigrade, Fahrenheit and Reaumur scales is:
A. $\frac{F-32}{9}=\frac{C}{5}=\frac{R}{4}$ B. $\frac{F+32}{9}=\frac{C}{5}=\frac{R}{4}$
C. $\frac{F-32}{9}=\frac{C}{9}=\frac{R}{4}$ D. $\frac{F-32}{4}=\frac{C}{9}=\frac{R}{5}$

88. Which one of the following statements is incorrect?
A. The length of the days and nights is not the same all the year round
B. The axis of the earth is inclined at an angle of 66-1/2 to the plane of its orbit
C. Water pipes are apt to burst in very cold weather
D. Evaporation produces heat

89. Which of the following statements is correct?
A. Boiling of an egg is a chemical change
B. Freezing of ice cream is a chemical change
C. Burning of a candle is a physical change
D. Extracting the juice from an orange is a chemical change

90. When a bullet is fired why does the gun kick back?
A. Because the man firing the gun is light in weight
B. Because the gun is heavier than the firing soldier
C. Because the bullet goes out very fast
D. Because to every action there is an equal and opposite reaction

91. Which one of the following definitions is wrong?
A. *Amino Acids:* Large chemical substances containing carbon and oxygen
B. *Proteins:* Giant molecules of carbon, nitrogen and oxygen which are broken into small molecules during digestion
C. *Carbohydrates:* Big molecules used for getting energy
D. *Lipids:* A group of organic compounds found in living cells

92. The depth to which a floating body sinks in pure water is a measure of its
A. Density B. Weight
C. Inertia D. Viscosity

93. Which one of the following is a contagious disease?
A. Malaria B. Small pox
C. Cholera D. Tuberculosis

94. A pure (sun) spectrum is that in which:
A. only ultra violet and infra red rays are not seen
B. all the seven colours which combine to make up the sun light are clearly, distinctly and separately visible
C. all the seven colours are found
D. where the rainbow is found

95. What do fertilisers contain?
A. Calcium B. Sodium
C. Phosphorus D. Nitrogen

96. In which the purest form of carbon is found?
A. Coke B. Diamond
C. Graphite D. Coal

97. What is Tritium?
A. Compound of hydrogen
B. Isobar of hydrogen
C. Isotope of hydrogen
D. Oxide of hydrogen

98. How do the centripetal forces pull a body?
A. Upward B. Downward
C. Inwards D. Outwards

99. What does Mycology study?
A. Minerals B. Sound
C. Insects D. Fungus

100. DNA is concentrated in the:
A. Microsome B. Nucleus
C. Chromatin D. Cell wall

101. Vinegar is obtained by the fermentation process; what does it contain?
A. Acetic acid B. Formic acid
C. Nitric acid D. Oxalic acid

102. When the leaves of a plant show chlorosis, the possible cause can be:
A. increase in nitrate content in the soil
B. increase in chloride content in the soil
C. decrease in phosphorus content in the soil
D. deficiency of trace elements in the soil

103. Which of the properties of elements is a whole number?
A. Atomic number B. Atomic weight
C. Molecular weight D. Equivalent weight

104. What does the process in which a heavy nucleus breaks to give two or more small nuclei and large amount of energy is called:
A. electrolysis B. fission
C. fusion D. ionization

105. What is the process in which two or more small nuclei join to form a large nucleus with evolution of energy is called:
A. electrolysis B. fission
C. ionization D. diffusion

106. The main endocrine gland present in the human body is:
A. Adrenal gland B. Pituitary gland
C. Thyroid gland D. Pancreas gland

107. Which one is wrongly matched?
A. Phosphorus – Match
B. Potassium Sulphate – Fertilizer
C. Methyl Isocynate – Tyre
D. Silicon – Glass

108. Which one of the following pairs is incorrect?
A. Malaria – Mosquitoes
B. Small Pox – Virus
C. Typhoid – Fungi
D. Cholera – Water

109. Which one group of the following belongs to 'lichens'?
A. Algae and bacteria B. Virus and bacteria
C. Algae and fungi D. All the above

110. Arrange the following elements, present in human body, in the descending order of their percentage:
1. Oxygen
2. Nitrogen
3. Carbon
A. 1 and 2 only B. 1 and 3 only
C. 1, 3, 2 D. 2 and 3 only

111. Which one of the following is given to a typhoid patient?
A. Chloroquin B. Vitamin A
C. Chloromycetin D. Sulphur

112. Which one of the following is called a growth gland?
A. Adrenal B. Thyroid
C. Pituitary D. None of the above

113. Which one of the following is a rich source of vitamin A?
A. Potato tuber B. Carrot root
C. Onion bulb D. Maize grains

114. Of the following the best way to put out a petrol fire is to use:
A. water
B. rugs
C. soda water fire extinguisher
D. carbon tetrachloride extinguisher

115. Which type of nerves carry impulses from the sense organs in response to stimulus?
A. Motor B. Sensory
C. Secretory D. All the above

116. The gas which helps in burning is:
A. Carbon Monoxide B. Hydrogen
C. Oxygen D. Nitrogen

117. Which one of the following best defines IQ?
A. $\frac{\text{Actual Age}}{\text{Mental Age}} \times 100$ B. $\frac{\text{Mental Age}}{\text{Actual Age}} \times 100^2$
C. $\frac{\text{Actual Age}}{\text{Mental Age}} \times 10$ D. $\frac{\text{Mental Age}}{\text{Actual Age}} \times 1000$

118. Which one of the following is called 'red planet'?
A. Mercury B. Jupiter
C. Venus D. Mars

119. The instrument used to measure radio activity is called:
A. Gyroscope B. Nephoscope
C. Machmeter D. Geiger Counter

120. Which one is the most popular fodder for poultry?
A. Barley B. Maize
C. Wheat D. Bajra

121. Hygrometer is used to measure:
A. humidity of the atmosphere
B. density of milk
C. speed of sound in water
D. None of the above

122. The process of making an object white, by destroying its colour is known as:
A. corrosion B. bleaching
C. dehydration D. pyrolysis

123. Pencillin is given to a patient in order to:
A. cure hereditary diseases
B. cure all diseases
C. prevent any rise in bodily temperature
D. prevent the growth of several types of disease-causing bacteria

124. A lectometer is used for checking the purity of:
A. milk B. oil
C. sugar D. gold

125. What are Picoplanktons?
A. Animals that are extinct now
B. Micro organisms
C. A platform in the Arabian sea off Mumbai, used for drilling
D. None of the above

126. For getting instant energy an athlete should take:
A. Carbohydrate B. Protein
C. Vitamin D. Chewing Gum

127. The amoeba type organisms in the human body, causing malaria and amoebic dysentery are known as:
A. bacteria B. virus
C. fungi D. protozoa

128. Seeds are best preserved in:
A. hot and dry condition
B. cool but dry condition
C. dry condition
D. wet and cool condition

129. When a ship enters sea from a river, its level:
A. remains same
B. rises
C. may or may not change
D. decreases

130. Kilowatt is the measuring unit of:
A. power B. current
C. work D. energy

131. Solar energy is the result of:
A. fusion of Helium
B. fusion of Hydrogen atoms
C. fission of Uranium atoms
D. fission of Hydrogen atom

132. Which among the following is least likely to catch fire?
A. Terycot B. Rayon
C. Nylon D. Cotton

133. The energy released on account of the motion of a body is termed as the:
A. potential energy B. kinetic energy
C. relative velocity D. None of these

134. The propounder of the Law of Gravitation was:
A. Faraday B. Edison
C. Newton D. Archimedes

135. Which originates from a plant?
A. Chloromycetin B. Quinine
C. Insulin D. Aspirin

136. Shortage of Vitamin A results in:
A. Beri Beri B. Rickets
C. Scurvy D. Night blindness

137. What percentage of oxygen does the atmospheric air contain?
A. 25% B. 35%
C. 21% D. 10%

138. Which metal is used for galvanising iron to immunize it against rusting?
A. Tin B. Nickel
C. Zinc D. Copper

139. The process by which plants make food is called:
A. Phototropism B. Photosynthesis
C. Transpiration D. Hydrotropism

140. The normal temperature of the human body is:
A. 32°C B. 27°C
C. 37°C D. 40°C

141. Which of the following is a gas?
A. Carbon dioxide B. Alcohol
C. Mercury D. Latex

142. The change of ice into water is a/an:
A. chemical change B. physical change
C. atomic change D. electrical change

143. The function of calcium in our body is:
A. to increase the supply of blood to the heart
B. to provide strength to the bones and teeth
C. to provide oxygen to the blood
D. to provide more sugar in our blood

144. Primary gold has a purity of .... carats
A. 14 B. 22
C. 23 D. 24

145. What is a fracture?
A. Bleeding B. Swelling
C. A broken bone D. Bruising

146. What colour does copper turn a flame?
A. Red B. Green
C. Yellow D. Mauve

147. Which of the following can build dams?
A. Otters B. Beavers
C. Water rats D. Racoons

148. Which animal fights snakes?
A. Monkey B. Mongoose
C. Tiger D. Jackal

149. In what units are light waves measured?
A. Curies B. Ohms
C. Ergs D. Angstrom

150. In a human body, the basic building block is:
A. Muscle B. Cell
C. Bones D. Nerves

ANSWERS

1	**2**	**3**	**4**	**5**	**6**	**7**	**8**	**9**	**10**
C	A	A	C	D	A	C	D	B	D
11	**12**	**13**	**14**	**15**	**16**	**17**	**18**	**19**	**20**
C	A	C	A	B	D	A	D	D	C
21	**22**	**23**	**24**	**25**	**26**	**27**	**28**	**29**	**30**
C	B	B	C	C	C	A	B	D	C
31	**32**	**33**	**34**	**35**	**36**	**37**	**38**	**39**	**40**
D	A	B	C	D	C	A	B	C	A
41	**42**	**43**	**44**	**45**	**46**	**47**	**48**	**49**	**50**
A	B	D	A	A	B	B	A	A	A
51	**52**	**53**	**54**	**55**	**56**	**57**	**58**	**59**	**60**
A	A	B	D	A	A	B	A	A	B
61	**62**	**63**	**64**	**65**	**66**	**67**	**68**	**69**	**70**
A	B	C	A	A	D	B	C	C	D
71	**72**	**73**	**74**	**75**	**76**	**77**	**78**	**79**	**80**
B	D	B	B	C	D	C	A	B	D
81	**82**	**83**	**84**	**85**	**86**	**87**	**88**	**89**	**90**
A	C	D	C	B	C	A	D	A	D
91	**92**	**93**	**94**	**95**	**96**	**97**	**98**	**99**	**100**
A	A	B	B	D	B	C	C	D	C
101	**102**	**103**	**104**	**105**	**106**	**107**	**108**	**109**	**110**
A	D	A	B	D	B	C	C	C	C
111	**112**	**113**	**114**	**115**	**116**	**117**	**118**	**119**	**120**
C	B	B	C	B	C	A	D	D	B
121	**122**	**123**	**124**	**125**	**126**	**127**	**128**	**129**	**130**
A	B	D	A	B	A	D	B	B	A
131	**132**	**133**	**134**	**135**	**136**	**137**	**138**	**139**	**140**
B	D	B	C	B	D	C	C	B	C
141	**142**	**143**	**144**	**145**	**146**	**147**	**148**	**149**	**150**
A	B	B	D	C	B	B	B	D	B

❑❑❑❑

2

ENVIRONMENT

An Environment is everything that is around us, which includes both living and nonliving things such as soil, water, animals and plants, which adapt themselves to their surroundings. It is nature's gift that helps in nourishing life on Earth.

The environment plays an important role in the existence of life on the planet earth. The word Environment is derived from the French word "Environ" which means "surrounding." An ecosystem refers to all the living and non-living things present in the environment and it is a foundation of the Biosphere, which determines the health of the entire planet earth.

Ecology and Environmental science are the branches of life science, which mainly deal with the study of organisms and their interactions with other organisms and their environment.

Ecology 'Oikos' meaning home or place to live in and 'logos' meaning study. Literally it is the study of the home of nature.

Ecology is defined "as a scientific study of the relationship of the living organisms with each other and with their environment."

It deals with the ways in which organisms are moulded by their environment, how they make use of environmental resources including energy flow and mineral cycling.

ENVIRONMENT AND ITS COMPONENT

Everything that surrounds or affects an organism during its life time is collectively known as its environment. The environment is defined as 'the sum total of living, non-living components; influences and events, surrounding an organism. All organisms (from virus to man) are obligatorily dependent on the other organism and environment for food, energy, water, oxygen, shelter and for other needs.

The relationship and interaction between organism and environment are highly complex. It comprises both living (biotic) and non-living (abiotic) components.

Components of Environment	
Abiotic	**Biotic**
Energy	Green plants
Radiation	Non-green plants
Temperature & Heat Flow	Decomposers
Water	Parasites
Atmospheric Gases and Wind	Symbionts
Fire	Animals
Gravity	Man
Topography	
Soil	
Geologic Substratum	

For Instance: Let's take the environment of the fish.

External Environment of Fish

- Its environment consists of abiotic components such as light, temperature, including the water in which nutrients, oxygen, other gases and organic matter are dissolved.
- The biotic environment consists of microscopic organisms called plankton which it assume as well as aquatic plants, animals and decomposers.

Internal Environment of Fish

- It is enclosed by the outer body surface.
- The internal environment is relatively stable as compared to the external environment.
- However, it is not absolutely constant. Injury, illness or excessive stress upsets the internal environment.
- For example, if a marine fish is transferred to a fresh water environment, it will not be able to survive.

LEVELS OF ORGANISATIONS IN ECOLOGY

The main levels of organisation of ecology are six and are as follows.

Individual: Organism is an individual living being that has the ability to act or function independently. It may be plant, animal, bacterium, fungi, etc. It is a body made up of organs, organelles, or other parts that work together to carry out on the various processes of life.

Population: Population is a group of organisms usually of the same species, occupying a defined area during a specific time. Population growth rate is the percentage variation between the number of individuals in a population at two different times. Therefore the population growth rate can be positive or negative.

Community: If we look around ourself, we will notice that population of plants and animals seldom occur by themselves. The reason for this is quite obvious. In order to survive, individuals of any one species depend on individuals of different species with which they actively interact in several ways.

Communities in most instances are named after the dominant plant form (species).

Types of Community: On the basis of size and degree of relative independence communities may be divided into two types:

(*a*) **Major Community:** These are large-sized, well organized and relatively independent. They depend only on the sun's energy from outside and are independent of the inputs and outputs from adjacent communities. E.g: tropical ever green forest in the North-East

(*b*) **Minor Communities:** These are dependent on neighbouring communities and are often called societies. They are secondary aggregations within a major community and are not therefore completely independent units as far as energy and nutrient dynamics are concerned. e.g: A mat of lichen on a cow dung pad.

Some Important Facts

- Ecology is a branch of science which studies the interactions among organisms. and between the organism and its physical environment.
- Term 'Ecology' was at first used in 1865 by Reiter.
- Ernst Haeckel used the term Oekologie instead of Ecology and explained it briefly. The word Oekologie is formed by combining two Greek words Oikos (House or living space) and logos (Science or Study).
- According to Haeckel 'Ecology is the study of the relation of the animal both to its organic as well as its inorganic environment'.
- According to Eugene Odum, 'Ecology is the study of structure and function of nature'.
- Now, ecology has been presented with a broad dimension. Now it also includes the study of Humans, society and the activities of its physical environment. It is a basic global system having biotic and abiotic components.
- In 1935, A.G. Tansley proposed the concept of Ecosystem. According to him, Ecosystem is a type of physical system formed by biotic and abiotic components. Ecosystem is am open system. These systems may differ in their size.

Ecosystem: An ecosystem is defined as a structural and functional unit of biosphere consisting of community of living beings and the physical environment, both interacting and exchanging materials between them.

It includes plants, trees, animals, fish, birds, micro-organisms, water, soil, and people. Ecosystems vary greatly in size and elements but each is a functioning unit of nature. Everything that lives in an ecosystem is dependent on the other species and elements that are also part of that ecological community. If one part of an ecosystem is damaged or disappears, it has an impact on everything else.

Components of Ecosystem: The components of ecosystem and environment are same.

1. **Abiotic Components:** Abiotic components are the inorganic and non-living parts of the world. The abiotic part consists of soil, water, air, and light energy etc. It also involves chemicals like oxygen, nitrogen etc. and physical processes including volcanoes, earthquakes, floods, forest fires, climates, and weather conditions.

   Abiotic factors are the most important determinants of where and how well an organism exists in its environment. Although these factors interact with each other, one single factor can limit the range of an organism.

   (*a*) **Energy:** Energy from the sun is essential for maintenance of life. In the case of plants, the sun directly supplies the necessary energy. Since animals cannot use solar energy directly they obtain it indirectly by eating plants or animals or both. Energy determines the distribution of organisms in the environment.

   (*b*) **Rainfall:** Water is essential for all living beings. Majority of biochemical reactions take place in an aqueous medium. Water helps to regulate body temperature. Further, water bodies form the habitat for many aquatic plants and animals.

   (*c*) **Temperature:** Temperature is a critical factor of the environment which greatly influences survival of organisms. Organisms can tolerate only a certain range of temperature and humidity.

(*d*) **Atmosphere:** The earth's atmosphere is responsible for creating conditions suitable for the existence of a healthy biosphere on this planet.

(*e*) **Substratum:** Land is covered by soil and a wide variety of microbes, protozoa, fungi and small animals (invertebrates) thrive in it. Roots of plants pierce through the soil to absorb water and nutrients. Organisms can be terrestrial or aquatic. Terrestrial animals live on land. Aquatic plants, animals and microbes live in fresh water as well as in the sea. Some microbes live even in hot water vents under the sea.

(*f*) **Materials:**

(*i*) Organic compound such as proteins, carbohydrates, lipids, humic substances are formed from inorganic compound on decomposition.

(*ii*) Inorganic compound such as carbon dioxide, water, sulphur, nitrates, phosphates, and ions of various metals are essential for organisms to survive.

(*g*) **Latitude and altitude:** Latitude has a strong influence on an area's temperature, resulting in change of climates such as polar, tropical, and temperate. These climates determine different natural biomes.

2. **Biotic Components:** Biotic components include living organisms comprising: plants, animals and microbes and are classified according to their functional attributes into producers and consumers.

(a) **Primary producers :** Autotrophs (self-nourishing)

- Primary producers are basically green plants (and certain bacteria and algae).
- They synthesise carbohydrate from simple inorganic raw materials like carbon dioxide and water in the presence of sunlight by the process of photosynthesis for themselves, and supply indirectly to other non-producers.
- In terrestrial ecosystem, producers are basically herbaceous and woody plants, while in aquatic ecosystem producers are various species of microscopic algae.

(*b*) **Consumers :** Heterotrophs or phagotrophs (other nourishing)

- Consumers are incapable of producing their own food (photosynthesis).
- They depend on organic food derived from plants, animals or both.
- Consumers can be divided into two broad groups namely micro and macro consumers.

Classification of Ecosystem:

Natural Ecosystem

- Terrestrial
  - Forests
  - Grasslands
  - Deserts
- Aquatic
  - Fresh Water
  - Saline Water
  - Marine Water

Ecotone: Ecotone is a zone of junction between two or more diverse ecosystems. For e.g. the mangrove forests represent an ecotone between marine and terrestrial ecosystem. Other examples are – grassland, estuary and river bank.

Characteristics of Ecotone

- It may be very narrow or quite wide.
- It has the conditions intermediate to the adjacent ecosystems. Hence it is a zone of tension.
- It is linear as it shows progressive increase in species composition of one in coming community and a simultaneous decrease in species of the other out going adjoining community.
- A well developed ecotones contain some organisms which are entirely different from that of the adjoining communities.
- Sometimes the number of species and the population density of some of the species is much greater in this zone than either community. This is called edge effect.

The organisms which occur primarily or most abundantly in this zone are known as edge species. In the terrestrial ecosystems edge effect is especially applicable to birds.

Niche: A niche is the unique functional role or place of a species in an ecosystem. It is a description of all the biological, physical and chemical factors that a species needs to survive, stay healthy and reproduce.

A niche is unique for a species, which means no two species have exact identical niches. Niche plays an important role in conservation of organisms.

Types of Niche

1. Habitat niche – where it lives
2. Food niche – what is eats or decomposes & what species it competes with
3. Reproductive niche – how and when it reproduces.
4. Physical & chemical niche – temperature, land shape, land slope, humidity & other requirement.

The terrestrial part of the biosphere is divisible into enormous regions called biomes, which are characterized, by climate, vegetation, animal life and general soil type.

S.No.	Name of Biome	Region	Flora and Fauna
1.	Tundra	Northern and Southern most region of world adjoining the ice bound poles	Devoid of trees except stunted shrubs in the southern part of tundra biome, ground flora includes lichen, mosses and sedges. The typical animals are reindeer, arctic fox, polar bear, snowy owl, lemming, arctic hare, ptarmigan. Reptiles and amphibians are almost absent.
2.	Taiga	Northern Europe, Asia and North America. Moderate temperature than tundra. Also known as boreal forest.	The dominating vegetation is coniferous evergreen mostly spruce, with some pine and firs. The fauna consists of birds, hawks, fur bearing carnivores, little mink, elks, puma, Siberian tiger, wolverine, wolves etc.
3.	Temperate Deciduous Forest	Extends over Central and Southern Europe, Eastern North America, Western China, Japan, New Zealand etc. Moderate average temperature and abundant rainfall.	The flora includes trees like beech, oak, maple and cherry. Most animals are the familiar vertebrates and invertebrates. These are generally the most productive agricultural areas of the earth
4.	Tropical rain forest	Tropical areas in the equatorial regions, which is abound with life. Temperature and rainfall is high.	Tropical rainforest covers about 7% of the earth's surface & 40% of the world's plant and animal species. Multiple storey of broad-leafed evergreen tree species are in abundance. Most animals and epiphytic plants are concentrated in the canopy or tree top zones.
5.	Savannah	Tropical region: Savannah is most extensive in Africa.	Grasses with scattered trees and fire resisting thorny shrubs. The fauna include a great diversity of grazers and browsers such as antelopes, buffaloes, zebras, elephants and rhinoceros; the carnivores include lion, cheetah, hyena; and mongoose, and many rodents.
6.	Grassland	North America, Ukraine, etc. Temperate conditions with low rainfall.	Grasses dominate the vegetation. The fauna include large herbivores like bison, antelope, cattle, rodents, prairie dog, wolves, and a rich and diverse array of ground nesting bird.
7.	Desert	Continental interiors with very low and sporadic rainfall with low humidity. The days are very hot but nights are cold.	The flora is drought resistance such as cactus, euphorbias, sagebrush. Fauna: Reptiles, Small Mammals and birds.

Aquatic Zones: Aquatic systems are not called biomes, however they are divided into distinct life zones, with regions of relatively distinct plant and animal life.

S. No.	Aquatic ecosystem	Characteristics
1.	Fresh Water Ecosystem	Fresh water ecosystem are classified as lotic (moving water) or lentic (still or stagnant water). Lotic water system includes freshwater streams, springs, rivulets, creeks, brooks, and rivers. Lentic water bodies include pools, ponds, some swamps, bogs and lakes. They vary considerably in physical, chemical and biological characteristics.
2.	Marine Ecosystem	Nearly three – quarter of earth's surface is covered by ocean with an average depth of 3,750 m and with salinity 35 ppt, (parts per thousand), about 90 per cent of which is sodium chloride.
3.	Estuaries	Coastal bays, river mouths and tidal marshes form the estuaries. In estuaries, fresh water from rivers meet ocean water and the two are mixed by action of tides. Estuaries are highly productive as compared to the adjacent river or sea.
4.	Coral reef	A coral reef in an underwater ecosystem characterized by reef-building corals.
5.	Mangrove	Mangrove forests are found in the lands near the coastlines in the substropical and tropical regions of the world. The trees species can tolerate highly salt concentrated water.

Biosphere: Biosphere is a part of the earth where life can exist. Biosphere represents a highly integrated and interacting zone comprising of atmosphere (air), hydrosphere (water) and lithosphere (land). It is a narrow layer around the surface of the earth. If we visualise the earth to be the size of an apple the biosphere would be as thick as its skin.

Life in the biosphere is abundant between 200 metres below the surface of the ocean and about 6,000 metres (20,000 feet) above sea level. Biosphere is absent at extremes of the North and South poles, the highest mountains and the deepest oceans, since existing hostile conditions there do not support life. Occasionally spores of fungi and bacteria do occur at great height beyond 8,000 metres, but they are not metabolically active, and hence represent only dormant life.

The energy required for the life within the biosphere comes from the sun. The nutrients necessary for living organisms come from air, water and soil. The same chemicals are recycled over and over again for life to continue. Living organisms are not uniformly distributed throughout the biosphere. Only a few organisms live in the polar regions, while the tropical rain forests have an exceedingly rich diversity of plants and animals (50% of Global Biodiversity).

ENERGY FLOW

Energy is the basic force responsible for all metabolic activities. The flow of energy from producer to top consumers is called energy flow which is unidirectional. The study of Trophic level interaction in an ecosystem gives an idea about the energy flow through the ecosystem.

Trophic Level Interaction

Trophic level interaction deals with how the members of an ecosystem are connected based on nutritional needs.

Trophic levels (Trophe = nourishment)	
I. Autotrophs	Green plants (producers)
II. Heterotrophs	Herbivore (primary consumers)
III. Heterotrophs	Carnivores (secondary consumers)
IV. Heterotrophs	Carnivore (tertiary consumers)
V. Heterotrophs	Top carnivores (Quarternary consumers)

Energy flows through the trophic levels: from producers to subsequent trophic levels. This energy always flows from lower (producer) to higher (herbivore, carnivore etc.) trophic level.

The trophic level interaction involves three concepts namely:

1. Food Chain
2. Food Web
3. Ecological Pyramids

FOOD CHAIN

Organisms in the ecosystem are related to each other through feeding mechanism or trophic levels, i.e. one organism becomes food for the other. A sequence of organisms that feed on one another, form a food chain. A food chain starts with producers and ends with top carnivores.

The sequence of eating and being eaten, produces transfer of food energy and it is known as food chain. The plant converts solar energy into chemical energy by photosynthesis.

Small herbivores consume the plant matter and convert them into animal matter. These herbivores are eaten by large carnivores.

Types of Food Chains

There are two types of food chains:

(*i*) **Grazing food chain:** The consumers which start the food chain, utilising the plant or plant part as their food, constitute the grazing food chain. This food chain begins from green plants at the base and the primary consumer is herbivore.

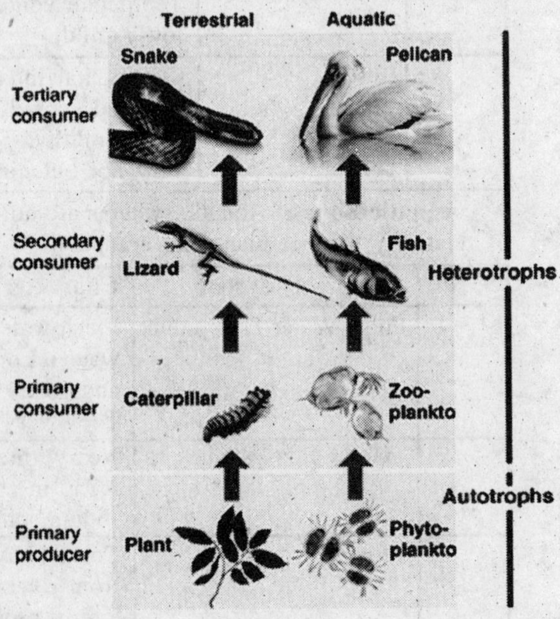

Fig. Grazing Food Chain

For example, In terestrial ecosystem, grass is eaten up by caterpillar, which is eaten by lizard and lizard is eaten by snake.

In Aquatic ecosystem phytoplanktons (primary producers) is eaten by zoo planktons which is eaten by fishes and fishes are eaten by pelicans.

(*ii*) **Detritus Food Chain:** It starts from dead organic matter of decaying animals and plant bodies consumed by the micro-organisms and then to detritus feeding organism called detrivores or decomposer and to other predators.

Litter → Earthworms → Chicken → Hawk

Fig. Detritus Food Chain

The distinction between these two food chains is the source of energy for the first level consumers. In the grazing food chain the primary source of energy is living plant biomass while in the detritus food chain the source of energy is dead organic matter or detritus. The two food chains are linked.

FOOD WEB

A food chain represents only one part of the food or energy flow through an ecosystem and implies a simple, isolated relationship, which seldom occurs in the ecosystems. An ecosystem may consist of several interrelated food chains. More typically, the same food resource is part of more than one chain, especially when that resource is at the lower trophic levels.

"A food web illustrates, all possible transfers of energy and nutrients among the organisms in an ecosystem, whereas a food chain traces only one pathway of the food".

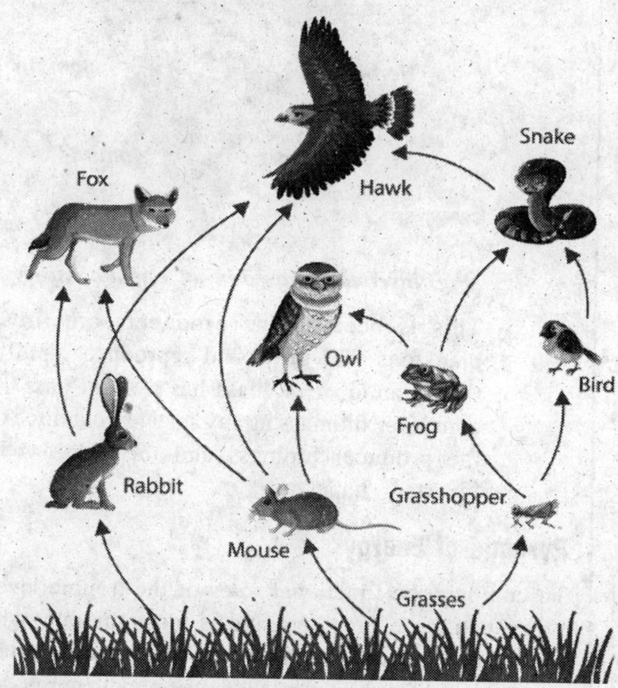

Fig. Food Web

If any of the intermediate food chain is removed, the succeeding links of the chain will be affected largely. The food web provides more than one alternative for food to most of the organisms in an ecosystem and therefore increases their chance of survival.

For example, grasses may serve food for rabbit or grasshopper or goat or cow. Similarly a herbivore may be food source for many carnivorous species.

ECOLOGICAL PYRAMIDS

The pyramid consists of a number of horizontal bars depicting specific trophic levels which are arranged sequentially from primary producer level through herbivore, carnivore onwards. The length of each bar represents the total number of individuals at each trophic level in an ecosystem.

The number, biomass and energy of organisms gradually decrease with each step from the producer level to the consumer level and the diagrammatic representation assumes a pyramid shape.

The ecological pyramids are of three categories.

1. Pyramid of numbers,
2. Pyramid of biomass, and
3. Pyramid of energy or productivity.

Pyramid of Numbers

This deals with the relationship between the numbers of primary producers and consumers of different levels. It is a graphic representation of the total number of individuals of different species, belonging to each trophic level in an ecosystem.

Depending upon the size and biomass, the pyramid of numbers may not always be upright, and may even be completely inverted.

(*a*) **Pyramid of numbers : upright**

- In this pyramid, the number of individuals is decreased from lower level to higher trophic level.
- This type of pyramid can be seen in grassland ecosystem.

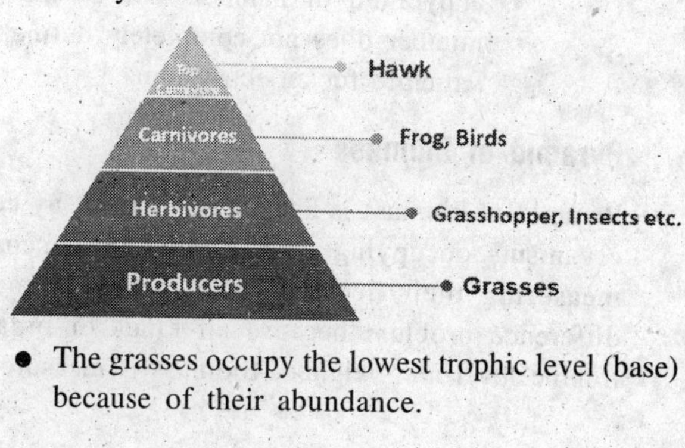

- The grasses occupy the lowest trophic level (base) because of their abundance.

- The next higher trophic level is primary consumer – herbivore (example – grasshopper).
- The individual number of grasshopper is less than that of grass. The next energy level is primary carnivore (example – rat).
- The number of rats are less than grasshopper, because, they feed on grasshopper. The next higher trophic level is secondary carnivore (example – snakes). They feed on rats.
- The next higher trophic level is the top carnivore. (Ex. Hawk).
- With each higher trophic level, the number of individual decreases.

(b) Pyramid of numbers – inverted

- In this pyramid, the number of individuals is increased from lower level to higher trophic level.
- A count in a forest would have a small number of large producers, for e.g. few number of big trees.

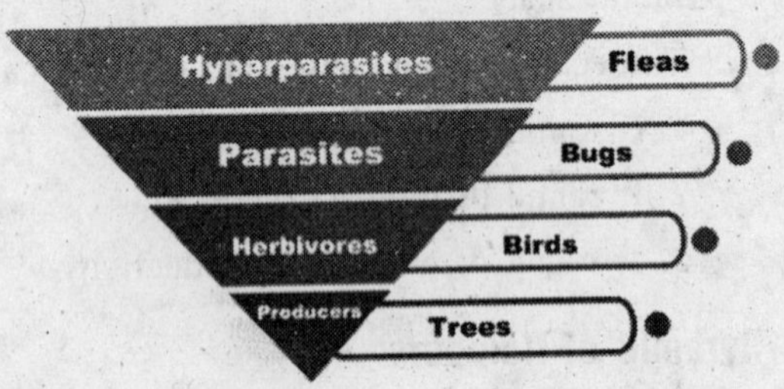

- This is because the tree (primary producer) being few in number and would represent the base of the pyramid and the dependent herbivores (for example - Birds) in the next higher trophic level and it is followed by parasites in the next trophic level. Hyper parasites being at higher trophic level represents higher in number.
- And the resulting pyramid is in inverted shape. A pyramid of numbers does not take into account the fact that the size of organisms being counted in each trophic level can vary.
- It is very difficult to count all the organisms, in a pyramid of numbers and so the pyramid of number does not completely define the trophic structure for an ecosystem.

Pyramid of Biomass

Pyramid of biomass is usually determined by collecting all organisms occupying each trophic level separately and measuring their dry weight. This overcomes the size difference problem because all kinds of organisms at a trophic level are weighed. Biomass is measured in g/m^2.

(a) Upward pyramid: For most ecosystems on land, the pyramid of biomass has a large base of primary producers with a smaller trophic level perched on top.

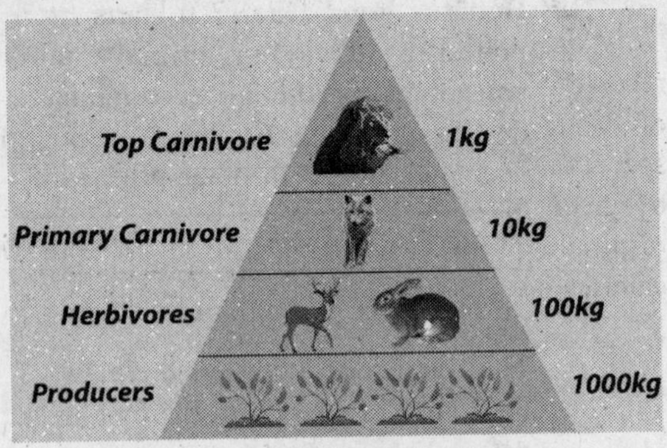

Fig. Upright Pyramid of Biomass in a Terrestrial Ecosystem

The biomass of producers (autotrophs) is at the maximum. The biomass of next trophic level i.e primary consumers is less than the producers. The biomass of next higher trophic level i.e secondary consumers is less than the primary consumers. The top, high trophic level has very less amount of biomass.

(b) Inverted pyramid: In contrast, in many aquatic ecosystems, the pyramid of biomass may assume an inverted form.

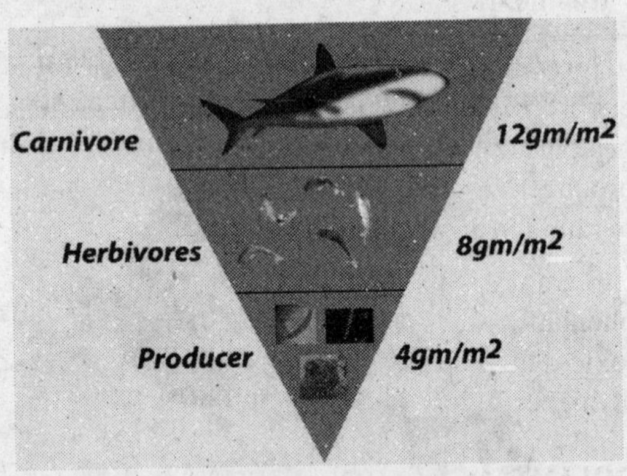

Fig. Inverted Pyramid in an Aquatic Escosystem

This is because the producers are tiny phytoplanktons that grow and reproduce rapidly. Here, the pyramid of biomass has a small base, with the consumer biomass at any instant actually exceeding the producer biomass and the pyramid assumes inverted shape.

Pyramid of Energy

To compare the functional roles of the trophic levels in an ecosystem, an energy pyramid is most suitable. An energy pyramid, reflects the laws of thermodynamics, with conversion of solar energy to chemical energy and heat energy at each trophic level and with loss of energy being depicted at each transfer to another trophic level. Hence the pyramid is always upward, with a large energy base at the bottom.

Consider the following example. Suppose an ecosystem receives 1000 calories of light energy in a given day. Most of the energy is not absorbed; some is reflected back to space; of the energy absorbed only a small portion is utilised by green plants, out of which the plant uses up some for respiration and of the 1000 calories, therefore only 100 calories are stored as energy rich materials.

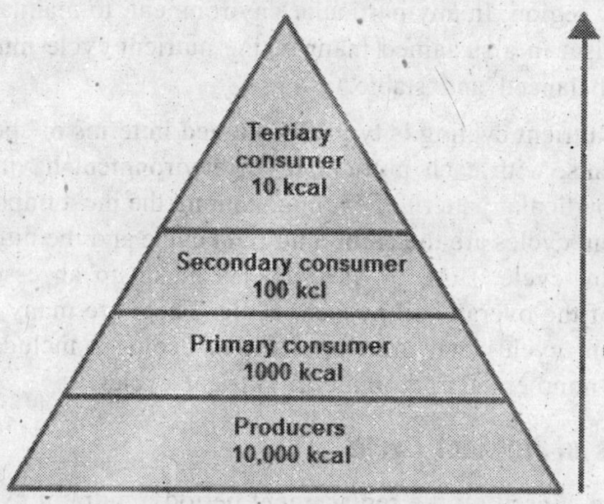

Fig. Pyramid of Energy

Now suppose an animal, say a deer, eats the plant containing 100 cal of food energy. The deer uses some of it for its own metabolism and stores only 10 cal as food energy. A lion that eats the deer gets an even smaller amount of energy. Thus usable energy decreases from sunlight to producer to herbivore to carnivore. Therefore, the energy pyramid will always be upright.

Energy pyramid concept helps to explain the phenomenon of biological magnification-the tendency for toxic substances to increase in concentration progressively at higher levels of the food chain.

POLLUTANTS AND TROPHIC LEVEL

Pollutants especially nondegradable ones move through the various trophic levels in an ecosystem. Nondegradable pollutants mean materials, which cannot be metabolized by the living organisms.

Example: chlorinated hydrocarbons.

We are concerned about these phenomena because, together they enable even small concentrations of chemicals in the environment to find their way into organisms in high enough dosages to cause problems.

Movement of these pollutants involves two main processes:

(*i*) Bioaccumulation

(*ii*) Biomagnification.

Bioaccumulation

- It refers to how pollutants enter a food chain.
- In bioaccumulation there is an increase in concentration of a pollutant from the environment to the first organism in a food chain.

Biomagnification

- Biomagnification refers to the tendency of pollutants to concentrate as they move from one trophic level to the next.

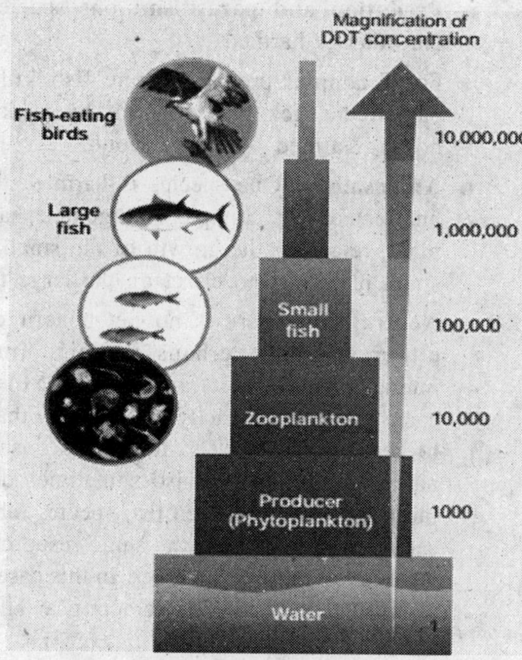

Fig. Biomagnification

- Thus in biomagnification there is an increase in concentration of a pollutant from one link in a food chain to another.

In order for biomagnification to occur, the pollutant must be: long-lived, mobile, soluble in fats, biologically active.

BIOTIC INTERACTION

- Organisms living in this earth are interlinked to each other in one way or other. The interaction between the organisms is fundamental for its survival and functioning of ecosystem as a whole.

Types of biotic interaction

- **Mutualism:** both species benefit.

  Example: in pollination mutualisms, the pollinator gets food (pollen, nectar), and the plant has its pollen transferred to other flowers for cross-fertilization (reproduction).

- **Commensalism:** one species benefits, the other is unaffected.
  For Example: cow dung provides food and shelter to dung beetles. The beetles have no effect on the cows.
- **Competition:** both species are harmed by the interaction.
  For Example: if two species eat the same food, and there isn't enough for both, both may have access to less food than they would if alone. They both suffer a shortage of food
- **Predation and parasitism:** one species benefits, the other is harmed.
  For Example: predation—one fish kills and eats parasitism: tick gains benefit by sucking blood; host is harmed by losing blood.
- **Amensalism:** One species is harmed, the other is unaffected. For Example: A large tree shades a small plant, retarding the growth of the small plant. The small plant has no effect on the large tree.
- **Neutralism:** There is no net benefit or harm to either species. Perhaps in some interspecific interactions, the costs and benefits experienced by each partner are exactly the same so that they sum to zero. It is not clear how often this happens in nature. Neutralism is also sometimes described as the relationship between two species inhabiting the same space and using the same resources, but that have no effect on each other. In this case, one could argue that they aren't interacting at all.

BIO-GEO-CHEMICAL CYCLE

The living world depends upon the energy flow and the nutrients circulation that occurs through ecosystem. Both influence the abundance of organisms, the metabolic rate at which they live, and the complexity of the ecosystem.

Energy flows through ecosystems enabling the organisms to perform various kinds of work and this energy is ultimately lost as heat forever in terms of the usefulness of the system. On the other hand, nutrients of food matter never get used up. They can be recycled again and again indefinitely.

For e.g. when we breathe we may be inhaling several million atoms of elements that may have been inhaled by our ancestors or other organisms. Carbon, hydrogen, oxygen, nitrogen and phosphorus as elements and compounds make up 97% of the mass of our bodies and are more than 95% of the mass of all living organisms. In addition to these about 15 to 25 other elements are needed in some form for the survival and good health of plants and animals.

These elements or mineral nutrients are always in circulation moving from non-living to living and then back to the non-living components of the ecosystem in a more or less circular fashion. This circular fashion is known as biogeochemical cycling (bio for living; geo for atmosphere).

Nutrient Cycling

The nutrient cycle is a concept that describes how nutrients move from the physical environment to the living organisms, and subsequently recycled back to the physical environment.

This movement of nutrients from the environment into plants and animals and again back to the environment is essential for life and it is the vital function of the ecology of any region. In any particular environment, to maintain its organism in a sustained manner, the nutrient cycle must be kept balanced and stable.

Nutrient cycling is typically studied in terms of specific nutrients, with each nutrient in an environment having its own particular pattern of cycling. Among the most important nutrient cycles are the carbon nutrient cycle and the nitrogen nutrient cycle. Both of these cycles make up an essential part of the overall soil nutrient cycle. There are many other nutrient cycles that are important in ecology, including a large number of trace mineral nutrient cycles.

Types of Nutrient Cycle

- Based on the replacement period a nutrient cycle is referred to as Perfect or Imperfect cycle.
- A perfect nutrient cycle is one in which nutrients are replaced as fast as they are utilised. Most gaseous cycles are generally considered as perfect cycles.
- In contrast sedimentary cycles are considered relatively imperfect, as some nutrients are lost from the cycle and get locked into sediments and so become unavailable for immediate cycling.
- Based on the nature of the reservoir, there are two types of cycles namely Gaseous and sedimentary cycle
- Gaseous Cycle – where the reservoir is the atmosphere or the hydrosphere, and
- Sedimentary Cycle – where the reservoir is the earth's crust.

ECOLOGICAL SUCCESSION

Succession is a universal process of directional change in vegetation, on an ecological time scale. Succession occurs when a series of communities replace one another due to large scale destruction either natural or manmade. This process continues - one community replacing another community, until a stable, mature community develops.

Succession is a progressive series of changes which leads to the establishment of a relatively stable climax community.

The first plant to colonise an area is called the pioneer community. The final stage of succession is called the climax community. The stage leading to the climax community are called successional stages or seres.

Primary Succession

In primary succession on a terrestrial site the new site is first colonized by a few hardy pioneer species that are often microbes, lichens and mosses. The pioneers over a few generations alter the habitat conditions by their growth and development.

Secondary Succession

Secondary succession occurs when plants recognize an area in which the climax community has been disturbed. Secondary succession is the sequential development of biotic communities after the complete or partial destruction of the existing community. A mature or intermediate community may be destroyed by natural events such as floods, droughts, fires, or storms or by human interventions such as deforestation, agriculture, overgrazing, etc

The differences between primary and secondary succession, the secondary succession starts on a well developed soil already formed at the site. Thus secondary succession is relatively faster as compared to primary succession which may often require hundreds of years.

Autogenic and Allogenic Succession

When succession is brought about by living inhabitants of that community itself, the process is called autogenic succession, while change brought about by outside forces is known as allogenic succession.

Autotrophic and Heterotrophic Succession

Succession in which, initially the green plants are much greater is quantity is known as autotrophic succession; and the ones in which the heterotrophs are greater in quantity is known as heterotrophic succession.

Some Important Facts

- Excess urbanisation and Industrialisation is a challenges for sustainable development, ecology & environment and Bio-Diversity Conservation.
- Green Development is a book is written by W.M. Adams.
- The full name of this Book is 'Green Development: Environment and Sustainability in a Developing World'. First edition of this book was published in the year 1990.
- Masanobu Fukuoka, the discoverer and innovator of Natural Farming, was a Japanese farmer and philosopher.
- Australia launched Green army for environmental Conservation in which 15000 youngsters of age between 17-21 years old will be recruited.
- World Environment Day is Celebrated on 5th June. The first World Environment Day was celebrated in 1973.
- Stockholm Summit was held in 1972. It was the 1st world Summit on Environment. It was decided in this summit that World Environment day will be Celebrated on 5th June every year.

MULTIPLE CHOICE QUESTIONS

1. Environmental Studies are very important for :
A. getting clean drinking water
B. hygienic living conditions
C. clean and fresh air
D. All of the above

2. Which of the following is still a very important source of energy for millions of Indians living in villages?
A. Oil B. Coal
C. Fossil fuels D. Fuel wood

3. The characteristic/s of a community is/are :
A. diversity
B. periodicity
C. dominance
D. All of these

4. National Biodiversity Strategy and Action Plan (NBSAP) was established in :
A. 1986 B. 1988
C. 1999 D. 2004

5. Major pollutants of motor vehicular emission in India are :
A. Oxides of nitrogen and lead
B. Diesel particulates and carbon monoxide
C. Ozone and carbon dioxide, other toxics
D. All of the above

6. Exposure to UV radiations cause :
A. damage to eye sight
B. sun burn
C. cancer of skin
D. All of the above

7. Sewage water treatment that involves bacteria is called:
A. Primary treatment
B. Activated sludge treatment
C. Tertiary treatment
D. Cyclic treatment

8. Air pollution effects are mostly found on :
A. leaves B. flowers
C. stems D. roots

9. Most important causative pollutant in soil is :
A. Plastic B. Glass junk
C. Iron Junk D. Detergents

10. Green Petrol is :
A. Leaded petrol
B. Unleaded petrol
C. Gasohol
D. Low sulphur Diesel

11. When was NEPA (National Environmental Policy Act) enforced in India?
A. 1968 B. 1969
C. 1985 D. 1959

12. The composition of Compressed Natural Gas (CNG) is:
A. CH_4, C_2H_6 and C_4H_8 and other gases
B. CH_4, $(CO + H_2)$
C. $CO + N_2$
D. LPG + H_2

13. Land use planning must aim at :
A. minimal loss
B. acceptable income
C. Both of the above
D. None of the above

14. The most important cause for the loss of biodiversity is :
A. global warming B. climate change
C. ozone depletion D. None of these

15. Which pigment protects plants from UV radiation damage?
A. chlorophyll B. xanthophyll
C. carotenoids D. phycocyanin

16. Green Muffler is planting of trees and shrubs to reduce noise pollution. It is done :
A. on wastelands
B. along roads
C. along canals
D. on the slopes of hills

17. A crop helpful in *Dryland reclamation* is :
A. sunflower B. paddy
C. sugarcane D. cotton

18. An ozone depleting agent being used in fire extinguishers is
A. Nitrogen oxide
B. Halon
C. Chlorofluoro carbon
D. Methyl bromide

19. The Environmental Protection Act was enacted in :
A. 1986 B. 1985
C. 1987 D. 1972

20. The major stratospheric ozone layer over Antarctica was discovered in :
A. 1983 B. 1985
C. 1987 D. 1980

21. Nitrogen oxide can be absorbed by plants like :
A. Pinus B. Quercus
C. Junipers D. All of these

22. Carbon monoxide can be absorbed by plants like :
A. Bean B. Coleus
C. Carrot D. All of these

23. Photochemical smog bring about :
A. Floral bud shedding
B. Defoliation
C. Discolouration and curling of petals
D. Bleaching and blazing of foliage

24. Where is NEERI previously known as PHERI located?
A. Nagpur B. Shimla
C. Bengluru D. Cochin

25. Photochemical smog always contain :
A. ozone B. methane
C. CO D. PAN

26. Classical smog is :
A. Dark brown
B. Yellow brown
C. Los Angeles smog
D. Smog with sec. pollutants

27. Sulphurous smog is :
A. photochemical smog
B. oxidising smog
C. classical smog
D. Los Angeles smog

28. PAN (Peroxyacylnitrate) is a secondary pollutant and is found in :
A. smog B. fertilizer
C. herbicide D. pesticide

29. DDT is banned because it :
A. affects the reproduction in birds
B. has short half life
C. is uneconomical in use
D. is dangerous to animals and man

30. *Agent orange* contains
A. 2, 4-D
B. 2, 4, 5-T
C. Dioxin as contaminant/carcinogen
D. All of the above

31. Ozone increases :
A. photosynthesis B. transpiration
C. respiration D. Both (B) and (C)

32. In hospitals sterilization is brought by :
A. spraying DDT B. UV radiation
C. infrared radiation D. alpha radiation

33. Which secondary pollutant is produced by UV rays of sun light?
A. SO_2 B. CO
C. fluorides D. ozone

34. An ecosystem is :
A. different communities of plants, animals and microbes together with their physico-chemical environments
B. an interacting system of Biotic communities and their abiotic environment
C. open and closed depending upon community
D. All of the above

35. Temperature changes in the environment affect most of the animals which are :
A. Aquatic B. Desert
C. Poikilothermal D. Homoisothermal

36. Biome is :
A. The fauna of an ocean
B. The flora of land
C. Communities of organisms interacting with one another
D. The part of the earth and its atmosphere which is inhabited by living organisms

37. Ecological niche of an organism denotes :
A. Habitat of the organism
B. On whom the organism feeds
C. The status of an organism within a particular community
D. All of the above

38. Grassland biome for its maintenance requires :
A. Periodic fire B. Intensive grazing
C. Mowing D. All of the above

39. Which of the following is a biome :
A. Wheat field B. Rain water pond
C. Grass field D. Deciduous forest

40. Total organic matter present in an ecosystem is called:
A. Biomass B. Biome
C. Litter D. Food

41. The most important organisms for an ecosystem are :
A. Herbivores B. Carnivores
C. Green plants D. Protozoa

42. A food chain consists of :
A. Producers B. Consumers
C. Decomposers D. Both A and B

43. Primary consumers are :
A. Green plants B. Herbivores
C. Carnivores D. All of the above

44. Secondary consumers are :
A. Green plants B. Herbivores
C. Carnivores D. All of the above

45. Which one is inverted pyramid :
A. Pyramid of biomass in grassland
B. Pyramid of biomass in pond ecosystem
C. Pyramid of numbers in grassland ecosystem
D. Pyramid of energy in a pond ecosystem

46. Ecological pyramid which is never inverted :
A. Pyramid of energy
B. Pyramid of biomass
C. Pyramid of numbers
D. Pyramid of species richness

47. Ecological pyramids were given by:
A. Elton B. Haeckel
C. Odum D. Reiter

48. In pond ecosystem the shape of pyramid of number is:
A. Linear B. Irregular
C. Upright D. Inverted

49. Energy flow in an ecosystem is :
A. Unidirectional B. Bidirectional
C. Multidirectional D. All of the above

50. Tree ecosystem show inverted pyramid of numbers. It shows :
A. number of organisms go on increasing
B. size of individuals go on decreasing with each trophic level
C. Both (A) and (B)
D. None of these

51. Grassland of U.S.A. is referred to as :
A. Prairies B. Steppes
C. Pampas D. Veldts

52. Plankton, Nekton and Benthos are not the components of one of ecosystems which is :
A. Oceans B. Fresh water rivers
C. Grassland D. Pond or lake

53. A man-made microecosystem is :
A. Plants grown in a pond
B. Crop field
C. Tank formed naturally in your court yard
D. Lake in a forest

54. A treeless biome is :
A. Tundra B. Grassland
C. Desert D. All of the above

55. In an ecosystem, tropic level of man is :
A. Producer B. Herbivore
C. Omnivore D. Carnivore

56. Vegetation of Delhi is predominantly :
A. Halophytic B. Xerophytic
C. Mesophytic D. Hygrophytic

57. Ecosystem has two components :
A. Animals and humans
B. Plants and animals
C. Biotic and abiotic
D. Weeds and trees

58. Tropical plants *Prosopis, Acacia* and *Capparis* belong to :
A. Evergreen forest B. Deciduous forest
C. Grassland D. Thorn forest

59. First '*Earth Summit*' at Rio-de-Janeiro (Brazil) held in 1992 was related to :
A. soil fertility
B. soil erosion
C. prevention of afforestation
D. conservation of environment

60. **Red data book** (RDB) published by IUCN provides :
A. information of threatened species of flora and fauna
B. information on wildlife
C. information on toxic plants
D. a book on biota red sea

61. International day for Biological Diversity is observed on :
A. December 21 B. December 29
C. June 5 D. December 1

62. What should we do to save the existing species of the wildlife?
A. Protection of endangered species
B. Protection of wildlife *in situ* and *ex situ*
C. Preservation of useful plants and animals in protected areas
D. All of these

63. *Ex-situ* conservation of natural resources can be obtained by :
A. controlling natural habits
B. inducing variations
C. establishing sanctuaries
D. protecting wildlife in Zoos and Botanical gardens

64. *In-situ* conservation of natural resources is :
A. protection of wildlife in natural habitat/National parks
B. control of pollution
C. control of human interference in the biosphere
D. All of the above

65. Which programme is not for preservation of wildlife/forests in India?
A. IUCN B. MAB
C. Project Tiger D. NEERI

66. Plant/animals species should be present because :
A. a species once lost can not be retrieved
B. zoologists study them
C. it can be useful to us
D. it is a creature of nature

67. National 'Wildlife Protection Act' was enacted by our government to declare hunting as unlawful act in the year :
A. 1979 B. 1972
C. 1962 D. 1982

68. The concept of biosphere reserve was evolved in 1986 by :
A. MAB programme of UNESCO
B. IUCN
C. WWF-N
D. Project Tiger

69. Where was the first biosphere reserve in India set up in 1986?
A. Nokrek B. Manas
C. Gulf of Mannar D. Nilgiri

70. National Park provides protection to :
A. fauna only B. flora only
C. Both A and B D. entire ecosystem

71. In Wildlife sanctuary :
A. only wild fauna (animals) are protected
B. private ownership is allowed
C. harvesting of trees for timber and forest products is permitted
D. All of these

72. 'Project Tiger' was launched in April 1973. It is a :
A. conservation programme
B. afforestation programme
C. biosphere reserve
D. All of the above

73. Cutch (Katha) is obtained from:
A. *Acacia arabica* B. *A. senegal*
C. *A. catechu* D. *A. melanoxylon*

74. Mulching helps in:
A. Soil conservation
B. Jhooming
C. Moisture conservation
D. All of these

75. India's largest National Park is:
A. Corbett National Park, Uttarakhand
B. Desert National Park, Rajasthan
C. Nagarjuna Sagar National Park, Hyderabad AP
D. Sunderbans, W. Bengal

76. The area of semirural, low density population is called:
A. green area B. green belt
C. greenery D. greenland

77. Lesser Panda/Red Panda (*Ailurus fulgens*) is preserved at :
A. Dachigam National Park, J and K
B. Sasan Gir National Park, Gujarat
C. Khangchend Zonga National Park, Sikkim
D. Simlipal National Park, Orissa

78. Great Indian Bustard Sanctuary is located in :
A. Rajasthan B. Maharashtra
C. Karera (MP) D. Pakistan (Lahore)

79. Shivpuri Sanctuary in MP is asylum for :
A. Birds B. Tigers
C. Lions D. Snakes

80. Sariska Tiger Project is in Rajasthan in :
A. Alwar B. Savai Madhopur
C. Jaiselmer D. Bharatpur

81. Where is Nalabana Bird Sanctuary located?
A. Sultanpur Lake B. Dal Lake
C. Chilka Lake D. Silsit Lake

82. World Environment Day is observed on :
A. March 21st B. Dec. 1st
C. May 31st D. June 5th

83. World Earth Day is observed on :
A. April 22nd B. June 5th
C. March 21st D. May 31st

84. World forest day is celebrated on :
A. March 21st
B. April 7
C. First week of October
D. April 22

85. When was the Forest Conservation Act passed in India?
A. 1960 B. 1970
C. 1980 D. 1950

86. When was the Environment Protection Act enforced in India?
A. 1980 B. 1986
C. 1982 D. 1988

87. When was the National Forest Policy formulated?
A. 1948 B. 1980
C. 1964 D. 1952

88. When was National Environment Policy Act (NEPA) was passed?
A. 1952 B. 1969
C. 1972 D. 1989

89. Which forest area in India was first brought under control and protection?
A. Malabar B. Konkan
C. Garhwal D. Sunderbans

90. Why is the *Silent Valley* so called?
A. It is silent during the night
B. It is silent during the day
C. It has nothing to do with silence
D. It is not a valley

91. Silent Valley of Kerala is preserved as :
A. it contains valuable timber trees
B. represents natural tropical rain forests with rich diversity
C. it is reservoir of rare wildlife
D. recreational value

92. Red data book is famous for :
A. extinct plants
B. endangered animals
C. endangered plants
D. endangerd plants and animals

93. The science of the relations of all organisms all their environments is:
A. Ecology B. Ecosystem
C. Toxicology D. Cytology

94. In which year the term ecology was coined?
A. 1885 B. 1886
C. 1883 D. 1884

95. Father of plant ecology is Warming. Who is revered as father of ecology in India?
A. Father H. Santapan B. W. Dudgeon
C. Ramdeo Misra D. P. Maheshwari

96. The word Ecology (Oekologie) is derived from two Greek words which means :
A. the study of wildlife
B. the study of land and life
C. the study of life
D. the study of home

97. Term **bioecology** to study plant and animal ecology as integral branch, was coined by :
A. Odum
B. Reiter
C. Shelford and Clements
D. Kormondy

98. The study of interaction between living organisms and their environment is called :
A. Ecosystem B. Phytogeography
C. Phytosociology D. Ecology

99. The aspect considered to be most important in ecology is :
A. climate B. soil
C. environment D. man

100. Broad leaved deciduous forests are typical of :
A. Mid-altitude forests
B. Mediterranean region
C. Monsoon region
D. Coniferous region

ANSWERS

1	2	3	4	5	6	7	8	9	10
D	D	D	C	D	D	B	A	D	B
11	12	13	14	15	16	17	18	19	20
B	A	C	C	C	B	A	B	A	B
21	22	23	24	25	26	27	28	29	30
D	D	D	A	A	A	C	A	C	B
31	32	33	34	35	36	37	38	39	40
D	B	D	D	C	C	C	D	D	A
41	42	43	44	45	46	47	48	49	50
C	D	B	C	B	A	A	C	A	C
51	52	53	54	55	56	57	58	59	60
A	C	B	D	C	B	C	D	D	A
61	62	63	64	65	66	67	68	69	70
B	D	D	A	D	A	B	A	D	D
71	72	73	74	75	76	77	78	79	80
D	A	B	D	C	B	C	C	B	A
81	82	83	84	85	86	87	88	89	90
C	D	A	A	C	B	D	B	A	A
91	92	93	94	95	96	97	98	99	100
D	D	A	A	C	D	C	D	C	B

❑❑❑❑

GENERAL STUDIES

1

Indian History

ANCIENT INDIA

INDUS VALLEY CIVILISATION
(2500-1750 BC)

- The earliest excavations in the Indus valley were done at Harappa in the West Punjab and Mohenjodaro in Sindh. Both places are now in Pakistan.

Important Sites

- The most important sites are Kot Diji in Sindh, Kalibangan in Rajasthan, Ropar in the Punjab, Banawali in Haryana, Lothal, Surkotada and Dhaulavira, all the three in Gujarat.
- Mohenjodaro is the largest of all the Indus cities and it is estimated to have spread over an area of 200 hectares.

Indus Valley Civilisation : An Objective Study

Major Sites	*Excavators*	*Year*	*River*	*Location*	*Important Findings*
1. Harappa	D.R. Sahni	1921	Ravi	West Punjab (Pakistan)	Granaries, Virgin Goddess, Cemetery, Stone symbol of Lingam and Yoni
2. Mohenjodaro	R.D. Banerjee	1922	Indus	Sindh (Pakistan)	Great Bath, Great Granary, Assembly Hall, Proto-Shiva, Brick Kilns, Mesopotamian seals
3. Chanhudaro	N.G. Mazumdar	1931	Indus	Sindh (Pakistan)	Bronze toy cart, Ink-pot, Lipstick, City without a citadel
4. Kalibangan	B.B. Lal & B.K. Thapar	1953	Ghaggar	Ganganagar (Rajasthan)	Decorated bricks, ploughed field surface, Firealtars
5. Lothal	S.R. Rao	1957	Bhogwa	Ahmedabad (Gujarat)	Dockyard, Rice husk, Fire altars, Double burial
6. Banawali	R.S. Bist	1973	Ghaggar	Hissar (Haryana)	Toy plough, Gridiron pattern of Town planning.
7. Dholavira	R.S. Bist	1990	Luni	Kutchh (Gujarat)	A Large well & a bath, A stadium
8. Surkotada	J. Joshi	1964	—	Gujarat	Bones of Horse, Pot burials

Salient Features of the Harappan Culture

- The Harappan Civilization was primarily Urban.
- Mohenjodaro and Harappa were the planned cities.
- The large-scale use of burnt bricks in almost all kinds of constructions are the important characteristics of the Harappan culture.
- Another remarkable feature was the underground drainage system connecting all houses to the street drains which were covered by stone slabs or bricks.
- The most important public place of Mohenjodaro is the Great Bath measuring 39 feet length, 23 feet breadth and 8 feet depth.
- Agriculture was the most important occupation. In the fertile soils, farmers cultivated two crops a year. They were the first who had grown paddy.
- Wheat and barley were the main crops grown besides sesame, mustard and cotton.
- Animals like sheep, goats and buffalo were domesticated. The use of horse is not yet firmly established.
- Bronze and copper vessels are the outstanding examples of the Harappan metal craft.
- A large number of seals numbering more than 2000 have been discovered.

Social Life

- Jewelleries such as bangles, bracelets, fillets, girdles, anklets, ear-rings and finger rings were worn by women. These ornaments were made of gold, silver, copper, bronze and semi precious stones.
- Fishing was a regular occupation while hunting and bull fighting were other pastimes.

- Manufacture of terracotta (burnt clay) was a major industry of the people.
- Figures of animals such as sacred bull and dove were discovered. The figures of Mother Goddesses were used for religious purposes.
- Most of the inscriptions were engraved on seals. It is interesting to note that the Indus script has not yet been deciphered.
- The Pipal tree was used as a religious symbol.
- The origin of the '*Swastika*' symbol can be traced to the Harrapan Civilization.
- The chief male deity was Pasupati, (proto-Siva) represented in seals as sitting in a yogic posture with three faces and two horns.

THE VEDIC PERIOD

RIG VEDIC AGE (1500 - 1000 B.C.)

- The Early Vedic period is known from the *Rig Veda*.
- The *Rig Veda* refers to Saptasindhu or the land of seven rivers. This includes the five rivers of the Punjab, namely, Jhelum, Chenab, Ravi, Beas and Sutlej along with the Indus and Saraswati.
- Historians view that the Aryans came from Central Asia. They entered India through the Khyber pass between 2000 B.C. and 1500 B.C. They first settled in seven places in the Punjab region which they called Sapta Sindhu. Slowly, they moved towards the Gangetic Valley.
- The Aryan Civilisation was a rural civilisation.

Vedic Literature

- The word 'Veda' is derived from the root 'vid', which means to know and signifies 'superior knowledge'.
- The Vedic literature consists of the four Vedas – Rig, Yajur, Sama and Atharva.
- The *Rig Veda* is the earliest of the four Vedas divided into 10 mandalas and it consists of 1028 hymns. The hymns were sung by *Hotri* in praise of various gods.
- The *Yajur Veda* consists of various details of rules to be observed at the time of sacrifice. Its hymns were recited by *Adharvayus*.
- The *Sama Veda* is set to tune for the purpose of chanting during sacrifice. It is called the book of chants and the origins of Indian music are traced in it. Its hymns were recited by *Udgatri*.
- The *Atharva Veda* contains details of rituals.
- Besides the Vedas, there are other sacred works like the Brahmanas, the Aranyakas, the Upanishads, and the epics Ramayana and Mahabharata.

Political Organisation

- During this period, the kingdom was tribal in character. Each tribe formed a separate kingdom.
- The basic unit of political organisation was *kula* or family.
- The highest political unit was called *jana* or tribe.
- There were several tribal kingdoms during the Rig Vedic period such as Bharatas, Matsyas, Yadus and Purus. The head of the kingdom was called as *rajan* or king.
- There were two popular bodies called the *Sabha* and *Samiti*. The former seems to have been a council of elders and the latter, a general assembly of the entire people.

Social Life

- Family was the basis of the society.
- The head of the family was known as *grihapathi*.

Economic Condition

- The Rig Vedic Aryans were pastoral people and their main occupation was cattle rearing. Their wealth was estimated in terms of their cattle.
- Carpentry was another important profession.

RELIGION

- The important Rig Vedic gods were Prithvi (Earth), Agni (Fire), Vayu (Wind), Varuna (Rain) and Indra (Thunder).
- Indra was the most popular among them during the early Vedic period.
- There were also female gods like Aditi and Ushas. There were no temples and no idol worship during the early Vedic period.

Rigvedic Rivers

River	Name in Rigveda
Indus	Sindhu
Jhelum	Vitasta
Chenab	Asikni
Ravi	Parushini
Beas	Vipasa
Sutlej	Sutudri
Gomati	Gomal
Saraswati	Sarasvati
Ghaggar	Prishadavati

LATER VEDIC PERIOD (1000–600 B.C.)

- This age is also called as the Epic Age because the two great epics the Ramayana and Mahabharata were written during this period.
- The Sama, Yajur, Atharva Vedas, Brahmanas, Aranyakas, Upanishads and the two epics are the sources of information for this period.

Political Organisation

- Larger kingdoms were formed during the later Vedic period.
- The king performed various rituals and sacrifices to strengthen his position.

- They include Rajasuya (consecration ceremony), Asvamedha (horse sacrifice) and Vajpeya (chariot race).
- Kingship became hereditary.
- Kings assumed titles like Ekrat, Samrat and Sarvabhauma.

Economic Condition

- Iron was used extensively in this period and this enabled the people to clear forests and to bring more land under cultivation. Agriculture became the chief occupation.
- Taxes like Bali, Sulk and Bhaga were collected from the people.
- Wealth was calculated in terms of cows.

Social Life

- The four divisions of society (Brahmins, Kshatriyas, Vaisyas and Sudras) or the Varna system was thoroughly established during the Later Vedic period.
- The Ashrama system was formed to attain 4 purusharthas. They were *Dharma*, *Artha*, *Kama* and *Moksha*.

Religion

- Gods of the Early Vedic period like Indra and Agni lost their importance. Prajapathi (the creator), Vishnu (the protector) and Rudra (the destroyer) became prominent during the Later Vedic period.

JAINISM AND BUDDHISM

JAINISM

- Jainism originated in the 6th century B.C. It rejected Vedic religion and avoided its rituals.
- Founded by Rishabha Deva. Rishabha Deva was succeeded by 23 Thirthankaras (prophets). Mahavira was the 24th Thirthankara.

Vardhamana Mahavira (540-468 B.C.)

- Vardhamana was born in a village called Kundagrama near Vaishali in Bihar.
- His father was *Siddhartha*. He was the head of a famous Kshatriya clan.
- His mother was *Trisala*. She was a princess of the Lichchhavi clan. She was the sister of the ruler of Vaishali.
- Vardhamana was married to *Yasoda,* a princess. They had a daughter.
- At the age of 30, he left his home and family. He became an ascetic (monk). He wandered from place-to-place in search of truth for 12 years.
- In the 13th year of his penance, he attained the highest spiritual knowledge called Kevalya or Jnana. Thereafter, he was called Mahavira and Jina. His followers were called Jains and his religion Jainism.
- He died at the age of 72 in 468 B.C. at a place called Pavapuri near modern Rajgir in Bihar.

Teachings of Jainism

- The three principles of Jainism, also known as Triratnas (three gems), are:
  1. right faith.
  2. right knowledge.
  3. right conduct.
- Mahavira preached his disciples to follow the five principles. They are:
  1. Ahimsa—not to injure any living beings
  2. Satya—to speak the truth
  3. Asteya—not to steal
  4. Tyag—not to own property
  5. Brahmacharia—to lead a virtuous life.

Spread of Jainism

- Mahavira preached his religion in Prakrit language which was the language of the masses.
- Chandragupta Maurya, Kharavela of Kalinga and the royal dynasties of south India such as the Gangas, the Kadambas, the Chalukyas and the Rashtrakutas patronised Jainism.
- Jainism was divided into two sects after Vallabhi Council, namely *Svetambaras* (wearing white dresses) under Sthulbhadra and *Digambaras* (naked) under Bhadrabahu.
- The first Jain Council was convened at Pataliputra by Sthulabahu, the leader of the *Digambaras*, in the beginning of the 3rd century B.C.
- The second Jain Council was held at Vallabhi in 5th century A.D. The final compilation of Jain literature called *Twelve Angas* was completed in this council.

BUDDHISM

Gautama Buddha (563-483 B.C.)

- Buddha's original name was *Siddhartha*.
- Siddhartha was born in the Lumbini Garden near Kapilavastu in Nepal. His father was Suddhodana. He was a Sakya chief of Kapilavastu. His mother, Mayadevi, died when Siddhartha was only seven days old. He was brought up by his step mother Mahaprajapati Gauthami.
- At the age of sixteen Siddhartha, married Yasodhara and gave birth to a son, Rahul.
- The sight of an old man, a diseased man, a corpse and an ascetic turned him away from worldly life. He left home at the age of twenty-nine in search of Truth.
- He wandered for seven years and at last, he sat under a bodhi tree at Bodh Gaya in Bihar and did intense penance, after which he got Enlightenment (Nirvana) at the age of thirty-five. Since then, he became known as the Buddha or 'the Enlightened One'.
- Buddha delivered his first sermon at Sarnath near Banaras (now Varanasi).
- He died at the age of 80 in 483 B.C. at Kushinagar in Uttar Pradesh.

Teachings of Buddha

- The Four Noble Truths of Buddha are:
  1. The world is full of suffering.
  2. The cause of suffering is desire.
  3. If desires are get rid off, suffering can be removed.
  4. This can be done by following the Eightfold Path.
- The Eightfold Path consists of:
  1. Right Thought.
  2. Right Belief.
  3. Right Speech.
  4. Right Action.
  5. Right Living.
  6. Right Efforts.
  7. Right Knowledge.
  8. Right Meditation.

Buddhist Literature

- In Pali language.
- Buddhist scriptures in Pali are commonly referred to as *Tripitakas, i.e.*, 'Three Baskets'.
- ***Vinaya Pitaka:*** Rules of discipline in Buddhist monasteries.
- ***Sutta Pitaka:*** Largest, contains collection of Buddha's sermons.
- ***Abidhamma Pitaka:*** Explanation of the philosophical principles of the Buddhist religion.

Main Buddhist Councils

Buddhist Council	Time	Place	Chairman	Patron
First	483 BC	Rajagriha	Mahakashyapa	Ajatasatru
Second	383 BC	Vaishali	Sabakamuni	Kalashoka
Third	250 BC	Patliputra	Moggaliputta Tissa	Ashoka
Fourth	AD 72	Kundalvana	Vasumitra, Ashwaghosa	Kanishka

The Mahajanapadas

Mahajanapadas	Capital
1. Kashi	Varanasi
2. Kosala	Shravasti
3. Anga	Champanagri
4. Magadh	Girivraj or Rajgriha
5. Vajji	Vaishali
6. Malla	Kushinagar and Pavapuri
7. Chedi	Shuktimati
8. Vatsa	Kaushambi
9. Kuru	Hastinapur, Indraprastha and Isukara
10. Panchal	Ahichhatra and Kampilya
11. Matsya	Viratnagar
12. Surasen	Mathura
13. Asmaka	Paudanya
14. Avanti	Ujjaini
15. Gandhara	Taxila
16. Kamboj	Rajpur (Hatak)

DYNASTIES OF ANCIENT INDIA

HARYANKA DYNASTY

- Bimbisara was the founder of Haryanka Dynasty.
- He was a contemporary of both Vardhamana Mahavira and Gautama Buddha.
- During his rule, Darius I, the Achaemenian emperor, conquered the Indus Valley area.
- Ajatasatru imprisoned his father Bimbisara.
- The first Buddhist Council was convened by Ajatasatru at Rajgir.
- The immediate successor of Ajatasatru was Udayin.
- Udayin laid the foundation of the new capital at Pataliputra situated at the confluence of the two rivers, the Ganges and the Sone.
- Shishunaga was the founder of Shishunaga dynasty.
- After Shishunaga, the mighty empire began to collapse. His successor was Kakavarman or Kalasoka. During his reign, the second Buddhist Council was held at Vaishali.
- Kalasoka was killed by the founder of the Nanda dynasty.

NANDAS

- The fame of Magadha scaled new heights under the Nanda dynasty.
- Mahapadmananda was the founder of Nanda rule in Magadha.
- The last Nanda ruler was Dhana Nanda. Alexander invaded India during his rule.

MAURYAN EMPIRE

CHANDRAGUPTA MAURYA (322–298 B.C.)

- Chandragupta Maurya was the founder of the Mauryan Empire. He overthrew Nanda dynasty with the help of Chanakya.
- Chandragupta defeated Seleukos Nikator, the Greek general of Alexander, in a battle in 305 B.C.
- Seleukos sent Megasthenes as Greek Ambassador to the Court of Chandragupta. Megasthenes wrote *Indica*.

- Chandragupta was a follower of Jainism.
- He came to Sravana Belgola, near Mysore with a Jain monk called Bhadrabahu. The hill in which he lived until his death is called Chandragiri.
- Chanakya served as prime minister during the reigns of Chandragupta and Bindusara.

BINDUSARA (298–273 B.C.)

- Chandragupta Maurya was succeeded by his son Bindusara.
- Bindusara was called by the Greeks as "*Amitraghatha*" meaning, slayer of enemies.

ASHOKA (273–232 B.C.)

- Ashoka was the most famous ruler of the Mauryan dynasty.
- The most important event of Ashoka's reign was his victorious war with Kalinga in 261 B.C.
- Ashoka convened the Third Buddhist Council at Pataliputra around 250 B.C. in order to strengthen the *Sangha*. It was presided over by Moggaliputta Tissa.
- Ashoka's edicts and inscriptions were deciphered by James Prinsep in 1837.
- The last Mauryan king, Brahadratha was killed by his minister Pushyamitra Sunga. It put an end to the Mauryan Empire.

SUNGAS

- The founder of the Sunga dynasty was *Pushyamitra Sunga*, who was the commander-in-chief under the Mauryas.
- He ascended the throne of Magadha in 185 B.C.
- Pushyamitra was a staunch follower of Brahmanism. He performed two asvamedha sacrifices.
- After the death of Pushyamitra, his son Agnimitra became the ruler.
- Agnimitra was a great conqueror. He was also the hero of the play *Malavikagnimitram* written by Kalidasa.

KANVA

- The last Sunga ruler was Devabhuti, who was murdered by his minister Vasudeva Kanva, the founder of the *Kanva dynasty*.
- The Kanva dynasty ruled for 45 years. After the fall of the Kanvas, the history of Magadha was a blank until the establishment of the Gupta dynasty.

SATAVAHANAS

- The founder of the Satavahana dynasty was Simuka.
- The greatest ruler of the Satavahana dynasty was *Gautamiputra Satakarni*.
- The greatest port of the Satavahanas was Kalyani on the west Deccan. Gandakasela and Ganjam on the east coast were the other important seaports.
- The fine painting at Amaravathi and Nagarjunakonda caves belong to this period.

SANGAM AGE (300 B.C. TO A.D. 300)

- The Sangam Age constitutes an important chapter in the history of South India.
- According to Tamil legends, there existed three Sangams (Academy of Tamil poets) in ancient Tamil Nadu popularly called Muchchangam. These Sangams flourished under the royal patronage of the Pandyas.
- *The first Sangam*, held at then Madurai, chaired by Agastya.
- *The second Sangam* was held at Kapadapuram, chaired by Tolkappiyar.
- *The third Sangam* at Madurai was founded by Mudathirumaran.

Political History

- The Tamil country was ruled by three dynasties namely the Chera, Chola and Pandyas during the Sangam Age.

CHERAS

- The Cheras ruled over parts of modern Kerala. Their capital was Vanji and their important seaports were Tondi and Musiris.
- The greatest Chera King was *Senguttuvan*.

CHOLAS

- The Chola kingdom of the Sangam period extended from modern Tiruchi district to southern Andhra Pradesh.
- Their capital was first located at Uraiyur and then shifted to Puhar. Kaveripattinam served as their port.

GUPTA PERIOD

- The Gupta period is considered as the *Golden Age* in the history of India because this period witnessed all round developments in Religion, Literature, Science, Art and Architecture.

CHANDRAGUPTA I (320-334 A.D.)

- In the beginning of the 4th Century A.D., Sri Gupta established a small Kingdom at Pataliputra. He is considered as the founder of the Gupta dynasty.
- The first notable ruler of the Gupta dynasty was Chandragupta I. He assumed the title *Maharajadhiraja*. The Meherauli Iron Pillar inscription mentions his extensive conquests.
- Chandragupta I is considered to be the founder of the Gupta era which starts with his accession in A.D. 320.

SAMUDRAGUPTA (335-380 A.D.)

- Samudragupta was the greatest of the rulers of the Gupta dynasty. The Allahabad Pillar inscription provides a detailed account of his reign.

- Because of his military achievements, Samudragupta was hailed as *'Indian Napoleon'*.

CHANDRAGUPTA II (380-414 A.D.)

- Samudragupta was succeeded by his son Chandragupta II Vikramaditya.
- The greatest of the military achievements of Chandragupta II was his war against the Saka *satraps* of western India.
- The famous Chinese pilgrim, Fahien visited India (A.D. 399 - A.D. 414) during the reign of Chandragupta II.

SUCCESSORS OF CHANDRAGUPTA II

- Kumaragupta (415-455) was the son and successor of Chandragupta II. His reign was marked by general peace and prosperity.
- Kumaragupta was the founder of the Nalanda University.
- Kumaragupta was followed by *Skandagupta* who ruled from A.D. 456 to A.D. 468.
- After Skandagupta's death, many of his successors like Purugupta, Narasimhagupta, Buddhagupta and Baladitya could not save the Gupta empire from the Huns. Ultimately, the Gupta power totally disappeared due to the Hun invasions and later by the rise of Yasodharman in Malwa.

PUSHYABHUTI DYNASTY (600 - 647 A.D.)

- The greatest king was *Harshavardhana*, son of Prabhakar Vardhana of Thaneshwar. He shifted the capital to *Kannauj*.
- *Hieun Tsang* visited during his reign.
- He established a large monastery at Nalanda. Banabhata adorned his court, wrote Harshacharita and Kadambari. Harsha himself wrote three plays–Priyadarshika, Ratnawali and Nagananda.

PALLAVAS

- The Pallavas established their kingdom in Tondaimandalam by Simhavishnu with its capital at Kanchipuram.
- Other great Pallava rulers were Mahendravarman I, Narasimhavarman I, and Narasimhavarman II.
- The *Kailasanatha temple* at Kanchipuram is the greatest architectural masterpiece of the Pallava art.

CHALUKYAS (543-755 A.D.)

- Pulakesin I was the founder of the Chalukya dynasty. He established a small kingdom with Vatapi or Badami as its capital.
- The structural temples of the Chalukyas exist at Aihole, Badami and Pattadakal (Virupaksha temple). Cave temple architecture was also famous under the Chalukyas. Their cave temples are found in Ajanta, Ellora and Nasik.

RASHTRAKUTAS (755-975 A.D.)

- The art and architecture of the Rashtrakutas were found at Ellora and Elephanta.

CHOLAS

- Cholas became prominent in the ninth century and established an empire comprising the major portion of South India. Their capital was Tanjore.
- The founder of the Chola kingdom was Vijayalaya.
- Rajaraja Chola built the famous Brihadeeswara temple at Tanjore.
- *Dancing Figure of Shiva* (Nataraja) belong to Chola period.

MEDIEVAL INDIA

ARAB CONQUEST OF SIND

- In 712 A.D., Muhammad bin Quasim invaded Sind. Quasim defeated Dahir, the ruler of Sind and killed him in a well-contested battle.

Mahmud of Ghazni

- In 1024, Mahmud marched from Multan across Rajaputana, defeated the Solanki King Bhimadeva I, plundered Anhilwada and sacked the famous temple of Somanatha. This was his last campaign in India. Mahmud died in 1030 A.D.
- Mahmud patronized art and literature. *Firdausi* was the poet-laureate in the court of Mahmud.

Muhammad Ghori

- Prithviraj Chauhan defeated Ghori in the first battle of Tarain near Delhi in 1191 A.D.
- In the Second Battle of Tarain in 1192, Muhammad Ghori thoroughly routed the army of Prithiviraj, who was captured and killed.
- After his brilliant victory over Prithviraj at Tarain, Muhammad Ghori returned to Ghazni leaving behind his favourite general Qutb-ud-din Aibak to make further conquests in India.

SULTANATE PERIOD

SLAVE DYNASTY (1206-1290)

- The Slave dynasty was also called Mamluk dynasty. Mamluk was the Quranic term for slave.

Qutb-ud-din Aibak

- Qutb-ud-din Aibak was a slave of Muhammad Ghori, who made him the Governor of his Indian possessions.

- After the death of Ghori in 1206, Aibak declared his independence. He assumed the title Sultan and made Lahore his capital.
- Muslim writers call Aibak Lakh Baksh or giver of lakhs because he gave liberal donations to them.
- He built the famous Quwat-Ul-Islam mosque at Delhi. He began the construction of the famous Qutb Minar at Delhi but did not live long to complete it. It was later completed by Iltutmish.

Iltutmish (1210-1236 A.D.)

- Iltutmish belonged to the Ilbari tribe and hence his dynasty was named as Ilbari dynasty.
- He shifted his capital from Lahore to Delhi.
- He organised the *Iqta system* and introduced reforms in civil administration and army.

Raziya (1236-1240 A.D.)

- She appointed an Abyssinian slave Yakuth as Master of the Royal Horses.
- In 1240, Altunia, the governor of Bhatinda revolted against her. She went in personally to suppress the revolt but Altunia killed Yakuth and took Raziya prisoner.
- Bahram Shah, son of Iltutmish killed her.

Balban (1266-1286 A.D.)

- Balban introduced rigorous court discipline and new customs such as prostration and kissing the Sultan's feet to prove his superiority over the nobles.
- He also introduced the Persian festival of *Nauroz* to impress the nobles and people with his wealth and power.
- He established a separate military department - *diwan-i-arz* – and reorganized the army.

KHILJI DYNASTY (1290-1320 A.D.)

- The founder of the Khilji dynasty was Jalaluddin Khilji.
- Ala-ud-din Khilji was the greatest ruler of the Khilji Dynasty.
- He was the first Muslim ruler to extend his empire right upto Rameshwaram in the South.
- The Sultan had built a new city called Siri near Delhi.
- Amir Khusrau the great Persian poet, patronised by Balban, continued to live in Ala-ud-din Khilji's court also.
- He introduced the system of *dagh* (branding of horses) and prepared *huliya* (descriptive list of soldiers).
- Ala-ud-din Khilji maintained a large permanent standing army and paid them in cash from the royal treasury.

TUGHLAQ DYNASTY

- Ghiyas-ud-din Tughlaq was the founder of the Tughlaq dynasty.
- To have the capital at the centre of the empire and safe from the Mongol raids, Tughlaq chose Devagiri as his new capital in A.D. 1327. The Sultan renamed the new capital Daulatabad.
- In 1329-30, Muhammad-bin-Tughlaq introduced a token currency.
- Firoz Shah Tughlaq became Sultan after the death of Muhammad-bin-Tughlaq in A.D. 1351.
- He was the first Sultan to impose irrigation tax.
- He had built new towns of Firozabad, Jaunpur, Hissar and Firozpur.
- Timur—Mongol leader of Central Asia, ordered general massacre in Delhi (AD 1398) at the time of Nasiruddin Mahmud (later Tughlaq king).

SAYYID DYNASTY

- Before his departure from India, Timur appointed Khizr Khan as governor of Multan. He captured Delhi and founded the Sayyid dynasty in 1414.
- Mubarak Shah, Mohammed Shah and Alam Shah were some of the other important noteworthy rulers of Sayyid Dynasty.

LODHI DYNASTY

- The Lodhis were Afghans.
- Bahlol Lodhi was the first Afghan ruler while his predecessors were all Turks. He died in 1489 and was succeeded by his son, Sikandar Lodhi.
- In 1504, Sikandar Lodhi founded the city of Agra and transferred his capital from Delhi to Agra.
- Babar marched against Delhi and defeated and killed Ibrahim Lodhi in the first battle of Panipat (1526).

BAHMANI AND VIJAYANAGAR KINGDOMS

- The break up of the Delhi Sultanate provided an opportunity for the rise of a number of kingdoms in the Deccan.
- After the decline of the Tughlaqs, there arose two important kingdoms in the Deccan. They were the Bahmani and Vijayanagar kingdoms.

VIJAYANAGAR EMPIRE

- The Vijayanagar Kingdom was set up in A.D. 1336. Its aim was to check the spread of Muslim power and protect Hindu Dharma in South India.
- Four dynasties – Sangama, Saluva, Tuluva and Aravidu – ruled Vijayanagar from A.D. 1336 to 1672.
- Vijayanagar was founded in 1336 by Harihara and Bukka of the Sangama dynasty.
- The Moroccan traveller, Ibn Batuta, Venetian traveller Nicolo de Conti, Persian traveller Abdur Razzak and the Portuguese traveller Domingo Paes were among them who left valuable accounts on the socio-economic conditions of the Vijayanagar Empire.

- The Hampi ruins and other monuments of Vijayanagar provide information on the cultural contributions of the Vijayanagar rulers.

KRISHNA DEVA RAYA (1509-1530)

- The Tuluva dynasty was founded by Vira Narasimha.
- The greatest of the Vijayanagar rulers, Krishna Deva Raya belonged to the Tuluva dynasty.
- Krishna Deva Raya himself authored a Telugu work, *Amukthamalyadha* and Sanskrit works, *Jambavati Kalyanam* and *Ushaparinayam*.
- He built the famous *Vittalaswamy* and *Hazara Ramaswamy* temples at Vijayanagar.
- Krishna Deva Raya renovated Virupaksha temple in A.D. 1510.
- After his death the enemies of Vijayanagar joined together and defeated the Vijayanagar ruler in the battle of Talaikota.

BAHMANI KINGDOM

- The founder of the Bahmani kingdom was Alauddin Bahman Shah also known as Hasan Gangu in 1347. Its capital was Gulbarga.
- Ahmad Wali Shah shifted the capital from Gulbarga to Bidar.
- *Gol Gumbaj* was built by *Muhammad Adil Shah*; it is famous for the so called '*Whispering Gallery*'.
- *Quli Qutub Shah* built the famous *Golcunda Fort*.

MUGHAL EMPIRE (1526-1707 AD)

BABAR (1526-1530 AD)

- Babar was the founder of the Mughal Empire in India.
- On 21st April, 1526 the first Battle of Panipat took place between Babar and Ibrahim Lodhi, who was killed in the battle.
- Babar was the first one to use guns or artillery in a battle on the Indian soil.
- Babar defeated Rana Sanga of Mewar in the battle of Kanwah in A.D. 1527.
- Babar was a soldier-scholar and wrote his own autobiography called Babar Nama in Turkish language.

HUMAYUN (1530-1556 AD)

- Sher Shah defeated Humayun at Chausa in A.D. 1539 and again at Kannauj in A.D. 1540.
- After losing his kingdom, Humayun became an exile for the next fifteen years.
- In 1555, Humayun defeated the Afghans and recovered the Mughal throne.
- After six months, he died in 1556 due to his fall from the staircase of his library.
- *Gulbadan Begum*, Humayun's half-sister wrote *Humayun-nama*.

SHER SHAH SURI

- The founder of the Sur dynasty was Sher Shah, whose original name was Farid.
- Sher Shah became the ruler of Delhi in 1540.
- Sher Shah organized a brilliant administrative system. The central government consisted of several departments.
- He built a new city on the banks of the river Yamuna near Delhi.
- Now the old fort called Purana Quila and its mosque is alone surviving.
- He built a Mausoleum at Sasaram, which is considered as one of the master pieces of Indian architecture.

AKBAR (1556-1605 AD)

- When Akbar ascended the throne in A.D. 1556 he was only 14 years old. His guardian Bairam Khan served him as a faithful minister and tutor.
- Bairam Khan, along with Akbar met Hemu in the second Battle of Panipat in 1556. Hemu was initially successful, but lost his consciousness after an arrow hit him. Akbar killed him.
- The Battle of Haldighati was fought between Rana Pratap of Mewar and Mughal army led by Man Singh and Asif Khan. Some historian say that this battle was indecisive but some say that Rana Pratap was defeated.
- Akbar abolished the pilgrim tax and in 1562, he abolished Jaziya.
- Akbar evolved a new faith called Din-i-Illahi or Divine Faith.

JAHANGIR (1605-1627 AD)

- When Akbar died, Prince Salim succeeded with the title Jahangir (Conqueror of World) in 1605.
- Jahangir's eldest son, Khusrau, rebelled against him. He was arrested and put into prison.
- *Guru Arjun Dev, the fifth Sikh Guru* was executed by Jahangir.
- In 1611, Jahangir married Mehrunnisa who was known as Nurjahan (Light of World).
- Jahangir died in A.D. 1627.

SHAHJAHAN (1628-1658 AD)

- The reign of Shahjahan is generally considered as the *Golden Age* of the Mughal period.
- Shahjahan is called as the *Prince of Builders*. He had built the Jama Masjid and Red Fort in Delhi and Taj Mahal in Agra.
- Fine arts like painting, music and literature reached high level of development during Shahjahan's time.

AURANGAZEB (1658-1707 AD)

- Aurangazeb was the last great Mughal ruler. He ascended the throne after killing his three brothers Dara, Shuja and Murad in a fratricidal war.
- Aurangazeb defeated Sikandar Shah of Bijapur and annexed his kingdom.
- Aurangazeb was against the Sikhs and he executed the ninth Sikh Guru Tegh Bahadur.
- He was called *Darvesh* or a *Zinda Pir*. He forbade *Sati*. Conquered Bijapur (AD 1686) and Golconda (AD 1687) and reimposed Jaziya and Pilgrim tax in AD 1679.
- He built *Biwi ka Makbara* on the tomb of his queen *Rabaud-Durani* at Aurangabad; *Moti Masjid* within Red Fort, Delhi; and the Jami or Badshahi Mosque at Lahore.
- Aurangazeb died in A.D. 1707.

LATER MUGHALS / FALL OF THE MUGHALS

Bahadur Shah (1707-1712)

- Assumed the title of *Shah Alam I.*

Jahandar Shah (1712-1713)

- First puppet Mughal emperor. He abolished *jaziya.*

Farrukhsiyar (1713-1719)

Mohammad Shah (1719-1748)

- Nadir Shah (*of Iran*) defeated him in the Battle of Karnal (1739) and took away *Peacock throne* and *Kohinoor diamond.*

Ahmad Shah (1748-1754)

Alamgir II (1754-1759),

Shah Alam II (1759-1806)

Akbar II (1806-1837)

- He gave Ram Mohan Roy the title '*Raja*'. He sent Raja Ram Mohan Roy to London to seek a raise in his allowance.

Bahadur Shah II (1837-1857)

- He was confined by the British to the Red Fort. During the revolt of 1857, he was proclaimed the Emperor by the rebels. He was deported to Rangoon after that.

Literature of Mughal Period

Author	Work
Babar	Tuzuk-i-Babari
Abul Fazal	Ain-i-Akbari, Akbarnamah
Jahangir	Tuzuk-i-Jahangiri
Hamid	Padshahnama
Darashikoh	Majm-ul-Bahrain
Mirza Md Qasim	Alamgirnama

THE MARATHAS

SHIVAJI (1627-1680 AD)

- Shivaji was born at Shivner in 1627. His father was Shahji Bhonsle and mother Jija Bai.
- His religious teacher was Samarth Ramdas and guardian was Dadaji Kondadev.
- In 1674, Shivaji crowned himself at Raigarh and assumed the title Chatrapathi.
- *Ashtapradhan* (eight ministers) helped in administration. These were Peshwas, Sar-i-Naubat (Military), Mazumdar or Amatya (Accounts); Waqenavis (Intelligence); Surnavis (Corres-pondence); *Dabir* or *Sumanta* (Ceremonies); *Nyayadhish* (Justice); and *Panditrao* (Charity).
- Successors of Shivaji were Shambhaji, Rajaram and *Shahu* (fought at Battle of Khed in AD 1708).

THE PESHWAS

- Balaji Vishwanath was the first Peshwa. He began his career as a small revenue official and became Peshwa in 1713. Baji Rao I was the eldest son of Balaji Vishwanath. He was considered as the "greatest exponent of guerilla tactics after Shivaji".
- It was during reign of Balaji Baji Rao (Nanasaheb) when the Marathas lost the Third Battle of Panipat.
- Baji Rao II (last Peshwa) was the first Maratha to have fled from the British attacks instead of fighting with them. Baji Rao II surrendered to Sir John Malcom.

THE SIKH

- Guru Nanak Dev was the founder of Sikhism, the religion that draws its elements from both Hinduism and Islam.
- Name of the ten Sikh Gurus and their works are given below:

1. **Guru Nanak Dev (1469-1539AD):** The founder of Sikhism.
2. **Guru Angad Dev (1504-1552AD):** Developed Gurmukhi.
3. **Guru Amar Das (1479-1574AD):** Struggled against Sati system and Purdah system.
4. **Guru Ram Das (1534-1581AD):** Founded Amritsar, the holy city of Sikhism.
5. **Guru Arjun Dev (1563-1606AD):** He built the *Swarn Mandir* (Golden Temple).
6. **Guru Hargobind (1595-1644 AD):** Established Akal Takht.
7. **Guru Har Rai (1630-1661 AD)**
8. **Guru Har Krishan (1656-1664 AD)**
9. **Guru Tegh Bahadur (1621-1675 AD)**
10. **Guru Gobind Singh (1666-1708 AD):** Founded the Khalsa and Sikh baptism, composed many poems, and nominated the Sikh sacred text as the final and enduring Guru.

MODERN INDIA

THE ADVENT OF THE EUROPEANS

THE PORTUGUESE

- Vasco-da-Gama, a Portuguese explorer, sailed through the route of Cape of Good Hope and reached near Calicut on 20th May 1498 A.D. during the reign of King Zamorin (Hindu King of Calicut).
- Vasco-da-Gama founded a factory at Cannanore on his second visit to India in 1501. In due course, Calicut, Cochin and Cannanore became the Portuguese trading centres.
- Francisco Almeida came to India in 1505. He was the first Governor of Portuguese possessions in India.
- The real founder of Portuguese power in India was *Alfonso de Albuquerque*. He captured Goa from the rulers of Bijapur in 1510. It was made their headquarters.

THE DUTCH

- The United East India Company of the Netherlands founded a factory at Masulipatnam in 1605.
- They built their first fort on the main land of India at Pulicut in 1609, near Madras (Chennai). They captured Nagapattinam from the Portuguese.
- They made Agra, Surat, Masulipatnam and Chinsura in Bengal as their trading centres.

THE DANES

- The Danish East India Company was established in 1616 in Denmark.
- They came to South India and founded a factory at Tranquebar (Tharangambadi) in 1620. They also made settlements at Serampore near Calcutta (Kolkata).

THE ENGLISH

- The English East India Company was formed in 1599 under a charter granted by Queen Elizabeth in 1600.
- The East India Company sent Sir William Hawkins to the court of the Mughal Emperor Jahangir in 1609 to obtain permission to erect a factory at Surat.
- In 1615, Sir Thomas Roe, another British merchant, came to Jahangir's court.
- He stayed for three years and succeeded in getting permission to set up their trading centres at Agra, Surat, Ahmedabad and Broach.
- In 1690, the British got permission from Aurangazeb to build a factory on the site of Calcutta. In 1696 a fort was built at that place. It was called Fort William.

THE FRENCH

- The French East India Company was established in 1664 under the inspiring and energetic leadership of Colbert, the economic adviser of the French King Louis XIV.
- In 1667, the first French factory was established at Surat by Francis Caron who was nominated as Director-General.
- French were defeated by English in the *Battle of Wandiwash* (1760).

EAST INDIA COMPANY

- After the Battle of Plassey in 1757 and the Battle of Buxar in 1764, the East India Company became a political power.
- India was under the East India Company's rule till 1858 when it came under the direct administration of the British Crown. Robert Clive was the first Governor of Fort William under the Company's rule.

GOVERNOR-GENERALS OF BENGAL

Warren Hastings (1772-85 AD)

- In 1772, the Company appointed Warren Hastings as the Governor of Fort William. The Dual System introduced by Robert Clive was abolished by Warren Hastings.
- Warren Hastings was known for his expansionist policy. His administration witnessed the Rohilla War, the First Anglo-Maratha War and the Second Anglo-Mysore War.
- Pitt's India Act (1784) was passed.

Lord Cornwallis (1786-93 AD)

- Cornwallis inaugurated the policy of making appointments mainly on the basis of merit thereby laying the foundation of the Indian Civil Service.
- Lord Cornwallis introduced Permanent Revenue Settlement.
- Tipu Sultan signed the Treaty of Srirangapatnam in 1792 with the British.

Sir John Shore (1793-98 AD)

- Played an important role in the introduction of Permanent Settlement.
- *Battle of Kharda* between the Nizams and the Marathas (1795).

Wellesley (1798-1805)

- Wellesley came to India with a determination to launch a forward policy that he adopted to achieve his object is known as the 'Subsidiary Alliance'.
- The Fourth Anglo-Mysore War started in 1799. The war was short and decisive. Tipu fought till his capital Srirangapatnam was captured and he himself was shot dead.
- Peshwa Baji Rao II signed the *Treaty* of *Bassein* with the British in 1802. It was a subsidiary treaty and the Peshwa was recognized as the head of the Maratha kingdom.
- The Treaty of Deogaon(1803) was signed between Bhonsle and Wellesley.

Lord Minto (1807-1813)

- Lord Minto concluded the Treaty of Amritsar with Ranjit Singh of Punjab in 1809.
- The Charter Act of 1813 was passed during this period.

Lord Hastings (1813-1823)

- Anglo Nepal War (1814-1816) and Treaty of Sugauli (1816).
- Third Maratha War (1817-18), dissolution of Maratha confederacy and creation of Bombay Presidency.
- He encouraged the freedom of the Press and abolished the censorship introduced in 1799.

GOVERNOR-GENERALS OF INDIA

Lord William Bentinck (1828-1835)

- Charter Act of 1833 was passed and he was made the first Governor-General of India. Before him, the designation was Governor-General of Bengal.
- The social reforms of William Bentinck made his name immortal in the history of British India. These include the abolition of *Sati*, the suppression of Thugs and the prevention of female infanticide.
- The Government Resolution in 1835 made English the official and literary language of India.

Lord Metcalfe (1835-36 AD)

- Known as liberator of press in India.

Lord Auckland (1836-42 AD)

- First Afghan War (1838-42), a disaster for the English.

Lord Ellenborough (1842-44 AD)

- Brought an end to Afghan war. War with Gwalior (1843), *Annexation of Sind* by Charles Napier (1843).

Lord Hardinge (1844-48 AD)

- First Anglo-Sikh War (1845-46) and Treaty of Lahore (1846). Gave preference to English educated persons in employment.

Lord Dalhousie (1848-1856)

- The Doctrine of Lapse was applied by Dalhousie.
- The first railway line connecting Bombay with Thane was opened in 1853.

VICEROYS OF INDIA

Lord Canning (1856-62 AD)

- Lord Canning became the first Viceroy of India in 1858.
- Revolt of 1857, Mutiny took place. Indian Penal Code 1860 was passed.

Lord Elgin (1862 AD)

- Wahabi Movement.

Lord John Lawrence (1864-69 AD)

- Established the *High Courts* at Calcutta, Bombay and Madras in 1865.
- Telegraphic communication was opened with Europe. Created the Indian Forest Department.

Lord Northbrooke (1872-76 AD)

- Kuka Rebellion in Punjab, Famine in Bihar.

Lord Lytton (1876-80)

- In 1878, the Vernacular Press Act was passed. This Act empowered a Magistrate to secure an undertaking from the editor, publisher and printer of a vernacular newspaper that nothing would be published against the English Government. This Act crushed the freedom of the Indian press. In 1878, the Arms Act was passed. This Act prevented the Indians to keep arms without appropriate license.
- Lord Lytton also held a Darbar at Delhi in 1877 in which Queen Victoria was declared as the Empress of India. This extravagant Darbar cost millions of ruppes.
- In 1878, the Statutory Civil Service was established exclusively for Indians.

Lord Ripon (1880-84 AD)

- Lord Ripon repealed the Vernacular Press Act and earned much popularity among Indians.
- Ripon appointed a Commission in 1882 under the chairmanship of Sir William Hunter.
- The Commission came to be known as the Hunter Commission. The Commission recommended for the expansion and improvement of the elementary education of the masses.
- Ripon was founder of local self-government in modern India.

Lord Dufferin (1884-88 AD)

- *Third Burmese War* (1885-86 AD). Establishment of the Indian National Congress in 1885.

Lord Lansdowne (1888-94 AD)

- Factory Act of 1891 granted weekly holiday and stipulated working hours for women and children.

Lord Elgin II (1894-99 AD)

- Southern uprisings of 1899. Great famine of 1896-1897 and Lyall Commission on famine was established.

Lord Curzon (1899-1905 AD)

- Curzon instituted in 1902, a Universities Commission to go into the entire question of university education in the country.
- On the basis of the findings and recommendations of the Commission, Curzon brought in the Indian Universities Act of 1904, which brought all the universities in India under the control of the government.

Lord Minto (1905-10 AD)

- Swadeshi Movement (1905-08); foundation of Muslim League (1906); Surat Session and split in the Congress (1907). Morley-Minto Reforms (1909).

Lord Hardinge (1910-16 AD)

- Capital shifted from Calcutta to Delhi (1911); Delhi Durbar; Partition of Bengal was cancelled.
- The Hindu Mahasabha was founded in 1915 by Pandit Madan Mohan Malaviya.

Lord Chelmsford (1916-21 AD)

- Gandhi returned to India (1915) and founded the Sabarmati Ashram (1916), Champaran Satyagraha, Satyagraha at Ahmedabad (1981), Kheda Satyagraha (1918).
- Rowlatt Act (March, 1919) and the Jallianwala Bagh Massacre (13th April, 1919).
- Khilafat Committee was formed and Khilafat Movement started (1919-20).
- Non-Cooperation Movement started (1920-22).

Lord Reading (1921-26)

- Moplah Rebellion (1921) took place. *Kakori Train* Robbery on 1st August, 1925.
- *Communal Riots* of 1923-25 in Multan, Amritsar, Delhi etc.

Lord Irwin (1926-31 AD)

- Lahore Session of Congress and *Poorna Swaraj* Declaration (1929).
- Simon Commission visited India in 1927.
- Dandi March (12th March, 1930). Civil Disobedience Movement (1930).
- First Round Table Conference was held in England in 1930. Gandhi-Irwin Pact.

Lord Willingdon (1931-36 AD)

- *Second Round Table Conference* in London in 1931 and *third* in 1932.

Lord Linlithgow (1936-43 AD)

- Congress Ministries resignation celebrated as '*Deliverance Day*' by the Muslim League (1939), the Lahore Resolution (23rd March, 1940) of the Muslim League demanding separate state for the Muslims. (It was at this session that Jinnah propounded his Two-Nation Theory). Outbreak of World War II in 1939. Cripps Mission in 1942. Quit India Movement (8th August, 1942).

Lord Wavell (1943-47 AD)

- Cabinet Mission Plan (16th May, 1946).
- First meeting of the Constituent Assembly was held on 9th December, 1946.
- Arranged the Shimla Conference on 25th June, 1945 with Indian National Congress and Muslim League but failed.

Lord Mountbatten (March to Aug, 1947)

- Last viceroy of British India and the first Governor-General of free India.
- Partition of India decided by the 3rd June Plan or Mountbatten Plan.

NATIONAL MOVEMENT (1885-1947)

INDIAN NATIONAL CONGRESS (1885)

- Allan Octavian Hume, a retired civil servant in the British Government took the initiative to form an all-India organization. Thus, the Indian National Congress was founded and its first session was held at Bombay in 1885. W.C. Banerjee was its first president. It was attended by 72 delegates from all over India.
- The second session was held in Calcutta in 1886 and the third in Madras in 1887. Between 1885 and 1905, the Congress leaders were moderates. The Moderates had faith in the British justice and goodwill. They were called moderates because they adopted peaceful and constitutional means to achieve their demands.
- In 1905, Gopal Krishna Gokhale founded the Servants of India Society to train Indians to dedicate their lives to the cause of the country.

Partition of Bengal (1905)

- By Lord Curzon on 16th October, 1905 through a royal proclamation, reducing the old province of Bengal in size by creating East Bengal and Assam out of the rest of Bengal.
- The partition of Bengal in 1905 provided a spark for the rise of extremism in the Indian National Movement.
- Curzon's real motives behind this partition were:
  - To break the growing strength of Bengali nationalism since Bengal was the base of Indian nationalism.
  - To divide the Hindus and Muslims in Bengal.
  - To show the enormous power of the British Government in doing whatever it liked.

Swadeshi Movement (1905)

- The Swadeshi Movement involved programmes like the boycott of government service, courts, schools and colleges and of foreign goods. It was both a political and economic movement.
- Lal, Bal, Pal and Aurobindo Ghosh played an important role.

Muslim League (1906)

- In December 1906, Muslim delegates from all over India met at Dacca for the Muslim Educational Conference.
- Taking advantage of this occasion, Nawab Salimullah of Dacca proposed the setting up of an organisation to look after the Muslim interests. The proposal was accepted.
- The All-India Muslim League was finally set up on December 30, 1906.

Minto Morley Reforms (1909)

- Minto, the Viceroy and Morley, the Secretary of State for India jointly proposed reforms to the Indian Councils. An Act, called the Indian Councils Act or the Minto-Morley Reforms Act was passed in 1909.
- A separate communal electorate was introduced for the Muslims.

The Lucknow Pact (1916)

- During the 1916 Congress session at Lucknow two major events occurred.
- The divided Congress became united. An understanding for joint action against the British was reached between the Congress and the Muslim League and it was called the Lucknow Pact.
- The signing of the Lucknow Pact by the Congress and the Muslim League in 1916 marked an important step in the Hindu-Muslim unity.

The Home Rule Movement (1916)

- Two Home Rule Leagues were established, one by B.G. Tilak at Poona in April 1916 and the other by Mrs. Annie Besant at Madras in September 1916.
- While Tilak's Movement concentrated on Maharashtra, Annie Besant's Movement covered the rest of the country.

August Declaration

- On 20 August, 1917, Montague, the Secretary of State in England, promised the gradual development of self-governing institutions in India.
- This August Declaration led to the end of the Home Rule Movement.

Rowlatt Act (1919)

- In 1917, a committee was set up under the presidentship of Sir Sydney Rowlatt to look into the militant Nationalist activities.
- On the basis of its report the Rowlatt Act was passed in March 1919 by the Central Legislative Council. As per this Act, any person could be arrested on the basis of suspicion. No appeal or petition could be filed against such arrests.
- This Act was called the Black Act and it was widely opposed. An all-India hartal was organized on 6 April, 1919.

Jallianwala Bagh Massacre (13 April, 1919)

- On 13th April, the Baisakhi day (harvest festival), a public meeting was organized at the Jallianwala Bagh (garden). Gen. Dyer marched in and without any warning opened fire on the crowd. The firing continued for about 10 to 15 minutes and it stopped only after the ammunition exhausted.
- According to official report 379 people were killed and 1137 wounded in the incident. There was a nationwide protest against this massacre and Rabindranath Tagore renounced his knighthood as a protest.

Khilafat Movement (1920)

- The chief cause of the Khilafat Movement was the defeat of Turkey in the First World War.
- The Muslims in India were upset over the British attitude against Turkey and launched the Khilafat Movement.
- Ali brothers, *Mohd Ali* and *Shaukat Ali* started this movement. It was jointly led by the Khilafat leaders and the Congress.

Non-Co-operation Movement (1920-22)

- Mahatma Gandhi announced his plan to begin Non-Cooperation with the government as a sequel to the Rowlatt Act, Jallianwala Bagh massacre and the Khilafat Movement.
- It was approved by the Indian National Congress at the Nagpur session in December, 1920.
- The Congress observed the Non-Co-operation movement in 1920. The main aim of this movement was to attain Swaraj through non-violent and peaceful means.
- The whole movement was abruptly called off on 11th February, 1922 by Gandhi following the Chauri-Chaura incident in the Gorakhpur district of U.P. Many top leaders of the country were stunned at this sudden suspension of the Non-Co-operation Movement.
- On 5th February an angry mob set fire to the police station at *Chauri-Chaura* and twenty two police men were burnt to death.

Swaraj Party

- Leaders like Motilal Nehru and Chittranjan Das formed a separate group within the Congress known as the Swaraj Party on 1 January, 1923.
- The Swarajists wanted to contest the council elections and wreck the government from within.

Simon Commission (1927)

- The Act of 1919 included a provision for its review after a lapse of ten years. However, the review commission under the chairmanship of Sir John Simon was appointed by the British Government two years earlier of its schedule in 1927.
- Indian leaders opposed the commission, as there were no Indians in it, they cried *Simon Go Back*.
- The government used brutal repression and at Lahore, *Lala Lajpat Rai* was severely beaten in lathi-charge.

Nehru Report (1928)

- The Secretary of State, Lord Birkenhead, challenged the Indians to produce a Constitution that would be acceptable to all. The challenge was accepted by the Congress, which convened an all party meeting on 28 February, 1928.
- A committee consisting of eight was constituted to draw up a blueprint for the future Constitution of India. It was headed by Motilal Nehru. The Report published by this Committee came to be known as the Nehru Report.

Lahore Session (1929)

- On Dec. 19, 1929, under the Presidentship of J.L. Nehru, the INC, as its Lahore session, declared Poorna Swaraj (Complete Independence) as its ultimate goal.
- On Dec. 31, 1929, the newly adopted tricolour flag was unfurled and Jan. 26, 1930 was fixed as the First Independence Day, which was to be celebrated every year.

Dandi March (1930)

- On 12th March, 1930, Gandhi began his famous March to Dandi with his chosen 79 followers to break the salt laws. He reached the coast of Dandi on 5 April, 1930 after marching a distance of 200 miles and on 6 April formally launched the Civil Disobedience Movement by breaking the salt laws.

Civil Disobedience Movement

- Countrywide mass participation by women.
- The Garhwal soldiers refused to fire on the people at Peshawar.

Round Table Conference

- The first Round Table Conference was held in November 1930 at London and it was boycotted by the Congress.
- On 8th March, 1931 the Gandhi-Irwin Pact was signed. As per this pact, Mahatma Gandhi agreed to suspend the Civil-Disobedience Movement and participate in the Second-Round Table Conference.
- In September 1931, the Second Round Table Conference was held at London. Mahatma Gandhi participated in the Conference but returned to India disappointed. In January 1932, the Civil-Disobedience Movement was resumed.

Poona Pact (1932)

- The idea of separate electorate for the depressed classes was abandoned, but seats reserved for them in the provincial legislature were increased.
- Thus, Poona Pact agreed upon a joint electorate for upper and lower castes.

Demand for Pakistan

- *Chaudhary Rehmat Ali* gave the term *Pakistan* in 1933.
- In March 1940, the Muslim League demanded the creation of Pakistan.

Cripps Mission (1942)

- The British Government in its effort to secure Indian co-operation in the Second World War sent Sir Stafford Cripps to India on 23 March, 1942. This is known as Cripps Mission. The main recommendations of Cripps was the promise of Dominion Status to India.
- Congress rejected it. Gandhi called Cripp's proposals as a "Post-dated Cheque".

Quit India Movement (1942-1944)

- The All India Congress Committee met at Bombay on 8th August, 1942 and passed the famous Quit India Resolution. On the same day, Gandhi gave his call of 'do or die'.
- On 8th and 9th August, 1942, the government arrested all the prominent leaders of the Congress. Mahatma Gandhi was kept in prison at Poona.
- Pandit Jawaharlal Nehru, Abul Kalam Azad, and other leaders were imprisoned in the Ahamednagar Fort. Quit India Movement was the final attempt for country's freedom.

Indian National Army (INA)

- On July 2, 1943, Subhash Chandra Bose reached Singapore and gave the rousing war cry of *'Dilli Chalo'*. He was made the President of Indian Independence League and soon became the supreme commander of the Indian National Army. He gave the country the slogan of *Jai Hind.*
- INA had three fighting brigades named after Gandhi, Azad and Nehru. Rani of Jhansi Brigade was an exclusive women force. INA headquarters were at Rangoon and Singapore.

Cabinet Mission (1946)

- The Cabinet Mission put forward a plan for solution of the constitutional problem. A proposal was envisaged for setting up an Interim Government, which would remain in office till a new government was elected on the basis of the new Constitution framed by the Constituent Assembly. Elections were held in July 1946 for the formation of a Constituent Assembly. Muslim league observed the *Direct Action Day* on 16 August, 1946.
- An Interim Government was formed under the leadership of Jawaharlal Nehru on 2 September, 1946.

Mountbatten Plan (1947)

- On 20 February 1947, Prime Minister Atlee announced in the House of Commons the definite intention of the British Government to transfer power to responsible Indian hands by a date not later than June 1948.
- Lord Mountbatten armed with vast powers became India's Viceroy on 24 March, 1947. The partition of India and the creation of Pakistan appeared inevitable to him.
- After extensive consultation Lord Mountbatten put forth the plan of partition of India on 3 June, 1947.
- The Congress and the Muslim League ultimately approved the Mountbatten Plan.

Indian Independence Act, 1947

- The salient features of this Act was the partition of the country into India and Pakistan would come into effect from 15 August, 1947.
- On 15th August, 1947 India, and on the 14th August Pakistan came into existence as two independent states.
- Lord Mountbatten was made the first Governor General of Independent India, whereas Mohammad Ali Jinnah became the first Governor General of Pakistan.
- C. Rajagopalachari became the first and last Indian Governor-General of India. When India became a Republic on 26 January, 1950 Dr. Rajendra Prasad became the first President of our country.

❐ ❐ ❐

2

Geography

WORLD GEOGRAPHY

THE UNIVERSE

- Existing matter and energy are together known as **Universe.**

GALAXY

- A galaxy is a huge system of billions of stars and clouds of dust and gases.
- Our solar system is a part of *Milky Way* galaxy.
- There are millions of galaxies that make the Universe.

STARS

- Stars account for 98 per cent of the matter in a galaxy. The stars nearest to the earth are *Proxima Centauri, Alpha Centauri, Barnard's Star, Sirius* and so on. Of these, *Sirius* is the brightest.

LIGHT YEAR

- Light year is the distance travelled by light in one year at a speed of 2,99,792.5 km. per second.

SOLAR SYSTEM

- The Sun, eight planets, satellites and some other celestial bodies known as asteroids and meteoroids form the solar system.

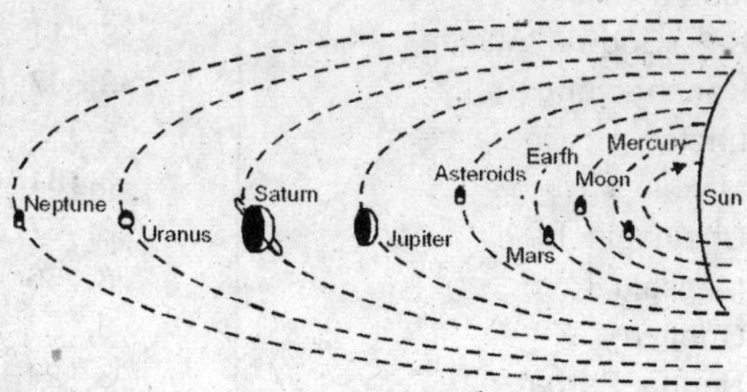

SUN

- The Sun is in the centre of the solar system.
- The Sun is a mixture of gases. It consists of 92% hydrogen, 7.8% helium and 0.2% other gases.
- The Sun is about 150 million km away from the earth.
- The sun is an ultimate source of energy for life on Earth.
- Sunlight takes 8 min 16.6 sec to reach earth.

Facts about Sun

Diameter	— 1.392×10^6 km
Volume	— 1.304 × 106 times the volume of earth
Temperature	— 6000°C at surface and 15 million degree C at the centre
Relative density	— 1.4
Gravitational Pull	— 28 times the gravitational pull of the earth

Facts about Planets

Closest to Sun	*Mercury*
Farthest from Sun	*Neptune*
Heaviest	*Jupiter*
Hottest	*Venus*
Inner	*Mercury, Venus, Earth, Mars*
Largest	*Jupiter*
Smallest	*Mercury*
Moons, None	*Mercury, Venus*
Moon; Largest	*Ganymede (Jupiter), larger than Mercury*
Nearest to Earth	*Venus*
Orbits; Order	*Mercury (closest to Sun), Venus, Earth, Mars, Jupiter, Saturn, Uranus, Neptune.*
Rings/largest number	*Saturn*
Spin; Backwards	*Venus (East to West)*

COMETS

- It has a head and a tail. Its tail originates only when it gets closer to the sun. The tail can be 20-30 million km long. It always point away from the sun because of the force exerted by solar wind and radiation on the cometory material.

THE EARTH

- The earth is the third nearest planet to the Sun.
- From the outer space, the earth appears blue because its two-thirds surface is covered by water. It is, therefore, called a blue planet. It is the densest of all planets.
- Rotation is the movement of the earth on its axis. Due to this rotation, day and night occur.
- The earth takes about 23 hours 56 minutes and 4 seconds to complete one rotation around its axis.
- Earth takes 365¼ days (one year) to revolve around the sun.

THE MOON

- Earth has only one satellite, that is, the moon.
- Its diameter is only one-quarter that of the earth. It is about 3,84,400 km away from us.
- The moon moves around the earth in about 27 days. It takes exactly the same time to complete one spin. As a result, only one side of the moon (only 59% of its surface) is visible to us on the earth.
- Moonlight takes 1.3 sec. to reach earth.

LATITUDE

- Imaginary lines drawn parallel to the equator. Measured as an angle whose apex is at the centre of the earth.
- The equator represents 0° latitude, while the North Pole is 90°N and the South Pole 90°S.
- 23½°N represents Tropic of Cancer while 23½°S represents Tropic of Capricorn.

LONGITUDE

- It is the angular distance measured from the centre of the earth. On the globe the lines of longitude are drawn as a series of semicircles that extend from the North Pole to the South Pole through the equator. They are also called meridians.
- The distance between any two meridians is not equal. At the equator, 1 degree = 111 km. At 30°N or S, it is 96.5 km. It goes on decreasing this way until it is zero at the poles.

INTERNATIONAL DATE LINE

- It is the 180° meridian running over the Pacific Ocean, deviating at Aleutian Islands, Fiji, Samoa and Gilbert Islands.
- Travellers crossing the Date Line from west to east repeat a day and travellers crossing it from east to west lose a day.

INDIAN STANDARD TIME (IST)

- Indian Standard Time is calculated on the basis of 82.5°E longitude which passes through Uttar Pradesh, Madhya Pradesh, Odisha, Chattisgarh and Andhra Pradesh.

EARTHQUAKES

- Earthquakes are a form of wave energy that is transferred through bedrock. It is transmitted from the point of the earthquake focus, as spherical seismic waves. They travel in all directions outward.
- The intensity of earthquake waves is recorded by *Seismograph*.

LANDFORMS

- There are three major landforms: mountains, plateaus and plains.

MOUNTAINS

- A mountain can be defined as an area of land that rises abruptly from the surrounding region.
- There are three types of mountains- *Fold Mountains, Block Mountains* and the ***Volcanic Mountains***.
- Himalayas, Alps, Andes, Rockies, Atlas, etc are examples of Fold Mountains. The Aravali range in India is one of the oldest **fold mountain** systems in the world.
- The Rhine valley and the Vosges mountain in Europe are examples of such mountain systems.
- Volcanic mountains are formed due to volcanic activity.
- Mt. Kilimanjaro in Africa and Mt. Fujiyama in Japan are examples of such mountains.

Major Mountain Ranges of the World

Range	Location	Highest Peak (m)	Length (km)
Andes	South America	6,960	7,200
Himalayas-Karakoram-Hindukush	South Central Asia	8,848	4,800
Rockies	North America	4,401	4,800
Great Dividing Range	East Australia	2,228	3,600
Western Ghat	Western India	2,637	1,610
Caucasus	Europe	5,642	1,200
Alaska	USA	6,194	1,130
Alps	Europe	4,808	1,050
Apennines	Europe	2,912	—
Ural	Asia	1,895	—
Atlas	North West Africa	—	1,930

PLATEAUS

- A plateau is an elevated flat land. It is a flat-topped table land standing above the surrounding area.

Principal Mountain Peaks of the World

Mountains	Height in Metres
1. Mount Everest	8,848
2. K-2 (Godwin Austen)	8,611
3. Kanchenjunga	8,597
4. Lhotse	8,511
5. Makalu I	8,481
6. Dhaulagiri I	8,167
7. Mansalu I	8,156
8. Chollyo	8,153
9. Nanga Parbat	8,124
10. Annapurna I	8,091
11. Gasherbrum I	8,068
12. Broad Peak I	8,047
13. Gasherbrum II	8,034
14. Shisha Pangma (Gosainthan)	8,014
15. Gasherbrum III	7,952

PLAINS

- A relatively low-lying and flat land surface with least difference between its highest and lowest points is called a Plain.

OCEANS

- Oceans of the world is classified into four groups: the Pacific, the Atlantic, the Arctic and the Indian.
- The Pacific is the largest ocean, being twice the size of the Atlantic. It covers about a third of the Earth's surface, and contains more than half the water on the planet.

Oceans of the World

Names	Area (Sq. Km.)	Greatest Depth
Pacific	166,240000	Mariana Trench
Atlantic	86,560000	Puerto Rico Trench
Indian	73430000	Java Trench
Arctic	13230000	—

Major Rivers of the World

River	Origin	Falls in	Length (Km.)
Nile	Victoria lake	Mediterranean Sea	6,650
Amazon	Andes (Peru)	Atlantic Ocean	6,428
Yangtze	Tibetan Kiang Plateau	China Sea	6,300
Mississippi Missouri	Itaska lake (USA)	Gulf of Mexico (USA)	6,275
Yenisei	Tannu-Ola Mts.	Arctic Ocean	5,539
Hoang Ho	Kunlun Mts.	Gulf of Chibli	5,464
Ob	Altai Mts., Russia	Gulf of Ob	5,410
Congo	Lualaba & Luapula rivers	Atlantic Ocean	4,700
Amur	Northeast China	Sea of Okhotsk	4,444
Lena	Baikal Mts	Laptev Sea	4,400
Mekong	Tibetan Highlands	South China Sea	4,350
Mackenzie	Great Slave Lake	Beaufort Sea	4,241
Niger	Guinea	Gulf of Guinea	4,200

Major Gulfs of the World

Names	Area (Sq. Km.)	Names	Areas (Sq. Km.)
Gulf of Mexico	15,44,000	Gulf of St. Lawrence	2,37,000
Gulf of Hudson	12,33,000	Gulf of California	1,62,000
Arabian Gulf	2,38,000	English Channel	89,900

Important Straits of the World

Straits	Water Bodies joined	Area
Bab-al-Mandeb	Red Sea & Arabian Sea	Arabia & Africa
Bering	Arctic Ocean & Bering Sea	Alaska & Asia
Bosphorus	Black Sea & Marmara Sea	Turkey
Dover	North Sea & Atlantic Ocean	England & Europe
Florida	Gulf of Mexico & Atlantic Ocean	Florida & Bahamas Islands
Gibralter	Mediterranean Sea & Atlantic Ocean	Spain & Africa
Malacca	Java Sea & Bay of Bengal	India & Indonesia
Palk	Bay of Bengal & Indian Ocean	India & Sri Lanka
Magellan	South Pacific & South Atlantic Ocean	Chile
Sunda	Java Sea & Indian Ocean	Indonesia

Important Lakes of the World

Lake	Location	Area (Sq. Km.)
Caspian	Russia and CIS	371000
Superior	Canada and USA	82414
Victoria	Tanzania (Africa)	69485
Huron	Canada and USA	59596
Michigan	USA	58016
Tanganyika	Africa	32892

Lake	Location	Area (Sq. Km.)
Baikal	Russia (CIS)	31502
Great Bear	Canada	31080
Malawi	Malawi (Tanzania)	30044
Great Slave	Canada	28438

Highest Waterfalls of the World

Name(s) (Foreign)	Location
Angel (Salto Angel)	Canaima Nat'l Park, Venezuela
Tugela	Natal Nat'l Park, South Africa
Utigord (Utigordsfoss)	Norway
Monge (Mongefoss)	Marstein, Norway
Gocta Cataracts	Chachapoyas, Peru
Mutarazi (Mtarazi)	Nyanga Nat'l Park, Zimbabwe
Yosemite	Yosemite Nat'l Park, California, U.S.
Espelands (Espelandsfoss)	Hardanger Fjord, Norway
Lower Mar Valley (Ostra Mardolafoss)	Eikesdal, Norway
Tyssestrengene	Odda, Norway

Continents: Some Facts

Continent	Biggest Counrty	Highest Peak	Longest River
Asia	China	Mt. Everest (8848 m)	Yangtze Kiang
Africa	Algeria	Mt. Kilimanjaro (5895 m)	Nile
North America	Canada	Mt. Mckinley (6194 m)	Mississippi Missouri
South America	Brazil	Mt. Acancagua (6960 m)	Amazon
Europe	Russia	Mt. Elbrus (5642 m)	Ob
Australia	Australia	Mt. Coscuisco (2228 m)	Darling
Antarctica	—	Vinson Massif (5140 m)	—

INDIAN GEOGRAPHY

AREA AND LOCATION

- India is in the southern parts of the Asian continent. In the west of India lies the Arabian Peninsula while in the east lies the Indo-China Peninsula.
- India extends between 8°4' N and 37°6' N latitudes and between 68°7' E and 97°2' E longitudes.
- India, has a total geographic area of 32,87,263 sq. km. This is only 2.42 % of the total geographic area of the world but holds 17.5 per cent of the world's population.
- The 23½ºN, which is the Tropic of Cancer, runs across the country.
- India has a length of 3214 km from north to south and 2933 km from east to west. It has a land frontier of 15200 km.
- The total length of the coastline of the mainland, Lakshadweep Islands and Andaman and Nicobar Islands is 7,516.6 km.
- India ranks seventh among the countries of the world, in terms of the geographical extent.
- India is bordered on three sides by water and on one by land, it is also a peninsula.
- India shares its common border with Afghanistan and Pakistan in the north-west, China and Bhutan in the north, and Bangladesh in the east. In the south, Sri Lanka is separated from India by a strait, known as the Palk Strait.
- There are 28 States, and 8 Union Territories (Delhi is National Capital Territory).
- 82°30' E longitude is considered as the Indian Standard Meridian. The local time of this longitude is taken as the Indian Standard Time (IST). This is 5½ hours ahead of the Greenwich Mean Time.

THE INDIAN STATES ON INTERNATIONAL BOUNDARIES ARE:

- ***Bordering Pakistan:*** Jammu and Kashmir, Punjab, Rajasthan, Gujarat.

- ***Bordering China:*** Jammu and Kashmir, Ladakh, Himachal Pradesh, Uttarakhand, Sikkim, Arunachal Pradesh.
- ***Bordering Nepal:*** Bihar, Uttarakhand, UP, Sikkim, West Bengal.
- ***Bordering Bangladesh:*** West Bengal, Mizoram, Meghalaya, Tripura, Assam.
- ***Bordering Bhutan:*** West Bengal, Sikkim, Arunachal Pradesh, Assam.
- ***Bordering Myanmar:*** Arunachal Pradesh, Nagaland, Manipur, Mizoram.
- ***Bordering Afghanistan:*** Jammu and Kashmir (Pakistan-occupied area).

Important Passes

Jammu & Kashmir	Burzi-La
Himachal Pradesh	Bara La, Cha-La, Shipki-La
Uttarakhand	Niti-La, Lipu-Lekh-La
Sikkim	Jelep-La, Nathu-La
Arunachal Pradesh	Bomdi-La
Ladakh	Joji-La

Heighest Mountain Peaks of India

Peaks	Elevation• (in mts.)
Godwin Austin (K2)	8611*
Kanchenjunga	8598
Nanga Parvat	8126
Gasherbrum	8068*
Broad Peak	8047*
Dastegil	7885*
Masherbrum (East)	7821
Nanda Devi	7817
Masherbrum (West)	7806*
Rakoposhi	7788*
Kamet	7756
Saser Kangdi	7672

• *Above mean sea level in metres.*

* *Situated in Pak occupied Kashmir (PoK).*

Towns at River Banks

Town	River	Town	River
Agra	Yamuna	Varanasi	The Ganges
Ayodhya	Saryu	Kolkata	Hooghly
Cuttuck	Mahanadi	Delhi	Yamuna
Dibrugarh	Brahmaputra	Ferozepur	Satluj
Guwahati	Brahmaputra	Hardwar	The Ganges
Hyderabad	Musi	Jabalpur	Narmada
Kanpur	The Ganges	Kota	Chambal
Kurnool	Tungbhadra	Lucknow	Gomti
Ludhiana	Sutlej	Nasik	Godavari
Pandharpur	Bhima	Patna	The Ganges
Sambalpur	Mahanadi	Srinagar	Jhelum
Srirangapattam	Cauveri	Prayagraj	Confluence of the Ganges and the Yamuna
Surat	Tapti		
Vijaywada	Krishna		
Ahmedabad	Sabarmati		
Ferozpur	Sutlej	Raurkela	Brahmani
Jabaplpur	Narmada	Vadodara	Vishwamitri

Waterfalls of India

Waterfall	Hgt (Mt.)	River	State
Kunchikal	455	Varahi	Karnataka
Jog/Gersoppa	260	Sharavati	Karnataka
Rakim Kund	168	Gaighat	Bihar
Chachai	127	Bihad	Madhya Pradesh
Kevti	98	Mahanadi	Madhya Pradesh
Sivasamudram	90	Cauveri	Karnataka

Important Lakes of India

Name of lake	State/UT
Pulicat Lake	Tamil Nadu & Andhra Pradesh Border
Sambhar Lake	Rajasthan
Tso Moriri Lake	Jammu & Kashmir
Vembanad Lake	Kerala
Wular & Dal Lakes	Jammu and Kashmir
Chilka Lake	Odisha
Kolleru Lake	Andhra Pradesh
Loktak Lake	Manipur
Lonar Lake	Maharashtra
Pangong Lake	Ladakh

Rivers of India

Name	Originates From	Falls Into
Yamuna	Yamunotri	Ganga
Chambal	Singar Chouri Peak, Vindhyan escarpment	Yamuna
Ghaghara	Matsatung Glacier	Ganga
Kosi	Near Gosain Dham Peak	Ganga
Sabarmati	Aravalis	Gulf of Khambat
Krishna	Western Ghats	Bay of Bengal
Godavari	Nasik district in Maharashtra	Bay of Bengal
Caurey	Brahmagir Range of Western Ghats	Bay of Bengal

Name	Originates From	Falls Into
Tungabharda	Western Ghats	Krishna
Ganges	Combines Sources	Bay of Bengal
Sutlej	Mansarovar Rakas lakes	Chenab
Indus	Near Mansarovar Lake	Arabian Sea
Ravi	Kullu Hills near Rohtang Pass	Chenab
Beas	Near Rohtang Pass	Sutlej
Jhelum	Verinag in Kashmir	Chenab
Son	Amarkantak	Ganga
Brahmaputra	Near Mansarovar Lake	Bay of Bengal
Narmada	Amarkantak	Gulf of Khambat
Tapti	Betul District in Madhya Pradesh	Gulf of Khambat
Mahanadi	Raipur District in Chhattisgarh	Bay of Bengal
Luni	Aravallis	Rann of Kuchchh
Ghaggar	Himalayas	Near Fatehabad
Betwa	Vindhyanchal	Yamuna

Geographical Surnames

Bengal's Sorrow	Damodar River	City of Lakes	Srinagar
City of Palaces	Kolkata	Twin City	Hyderabad-Secunderabad
Gateway of India	Mumbai	City of Seven Islands	Mumbai
Pink City	Jaipur	Diamond Harbour	Kolkata
Paris of India	Jaipur	Switzerland of India	Kashmir
Manchester of India	Ahmedabad	Rice Bowl	Chhattisgarh
Kashmir of South	Kerala	Fruit Bowl	Himachal Pradesh
Son of Sea	Lakshadweep	Ganga of South	Cauvery
Queen of Mountains	Mussourie	Pitsburg of India	Jamshedpur
Iron City	Jamshedpur	City of Bridges	Srinagar
Hollywood of India	Mumbai	Residence of God	Allahabad
Scotland of East	Meghalaya	A Cross-road (Quadrivial) of National Highways	Kanpur
City of Nababs	Lucknow	Heart of India	Delhi
City of Temples & Ghats	Varanasi	Black River	Sharda
Land of Five Rivers	Punjab	City of Festivals	Madurai
City of Golden Temple	Amritsar	Queen of Deccan	Pune
Garden of India	Bangaluru	Sorrow of Bihar	Kosi River
Spice Garden of India	Kerala		

Major Indian Crops

Crops	Temp(°c)	Water(cm)	States where Produced
Wheat	15°-25°	60-90	Uttar Pradesh, Punjab, Haryana.
Rice	24°-26°	80-200	West Bengal, Uttar Pradesh, Andhra Pradesh, Bihar, Punjab
Maize	18°-21°	50-60	Karnataka, Uttar Pradesh, Maharashtra
Jowar	20°-35°	40-60	Maharashtra, Madhya Pradesh, Karnataka
Soyabean	25°-27°	50-120	Madhya Pradesh
Cotton	20°-30°	80-150	Maharashtra, Gujarat, Karnataka, Madhya Pradesh
Tobacco	20°-25°	75-80	Andhra Pradesh, Madhya Pradesh, Gujarat, Karnataka, Maharashtra, Uttar Pradesh
Tea	24°-30°	100-200	Assam, West Bengal, Kerala, Tamil Nadu, Uttar Pradesh
Ground Nut	15°-25°	60-130	Gujarat, Maharashtra

❒ ❒ ❒

3

Indian Polity

INDIAN CONSTITUTION

- Demand for a Constituent Assembly composed of the people of India officially asserted by the Congress for the first time in 1935.
- The election for Indian Constitution Assembly held in 1946 according to the *Cabinet Mission Plan.*
- The first session of the Assembly was held in New Delhi on December 9, 1946. *Sachidanand Sinha* was elected provisional chairman of the session.
- On December 11, 1946, Dr. Rajendra Prasad was elected as the Permanent Chairman of the Constituent Assembly.
- The Constitution was framed by the Constituent Assembly of India, set-up in December 1946, in accordance with the Cabinet Mission Plan, under the Chairmanship of Sachidanand Sinha, initially.
- The total membership of Constituent Assembly after partition was 299, among them 70 were representatives from the Indian states and others from British India.
- The Chairman of the Drafting Committee was **Dr. BR Ambedkar**, also called the Father of the Constitution.
- The Constituent Assembly took 2 years, 11 months and 18 days to complete the Constitution.
- The Constitution, adopted on 8th November, 1949, contained 395 Articles and Schedules.
- The Constitution was delayed till 26th January because, in 1929, on this day Indian National Congress demanded Poorna Swaraj in Lahore Session under JL Nehru.
- Indian Constitution is a comprehensive document and it is the lengthiest written Constitution in the World.

THE PREAMBLE

- ***The Preamble of the Constitution:*** "We the people of India, having solemnly resolved to Constitute India into a Sovereign, Socialist, Secular Democratic Republic and to secure to all its citizen:

  Justice, Social; economic and political;

  Liberty of thought, expression, belief, faith and worship;

  Equality of status and of opportunity; and to promote among them all;

  Fraternity assuring the dignity of the individual and the unity and integrity of the nation;

  In our Constituent Assembly, this twenty-sixth day of November, 1949, do hereby adopt, enact and give to ourselves this constitution."

Foreign Sources of Indian Constitution

Foreign Sources	*Subject*
Britain	Parliamentary system, collective responsibilities of Cabinet
America	Fundamental right, Independent Judiciary, Judicial review
Canada	Division of powers
Ireland	Directive principles
Germany	Emergency provisions
Russia	Fundamental duties
Australia	Concurrent list

IMPORTANT ARTICLES

PART - I

UNION AND ITS TERRITORIES (ARTICLE 1 - 4)

- The Constitution says, "India, that is Bharat, shall be a Union of States".
- Parliament has the power to create any State, reduce it, change the name of boundaries of any State.

PART - II

CITIZENSHIP (ARTICLE 5 - 11)

- The Constitution provides for a single Citizenship.
- ***Indian Citizenship can be acquire:***
  1. by birth
  2. by descent
  3. by registration
  4. by naturalisation
  5. by incorporation of territory
- ***Indian Citizenship can be lost by:***
  1. renunciation;
  2. termination — it takes place if a citizen of India voluntary acquires the citizenship of another country; and
  3. deprivation — if the Government terminates the citizenship.

PART - III

FUNDAMENTAL RIGHTS (ARTICLE 12 - 35)

- Following fundamental rights are enjoyed by every Indian citizen, irrespective of caste, colour, creed and sex:
  1. ***Right to Equality:*** No special privileges, no distinction on grounds of religion, caste, creed and sex.
  2. ***Right to Freedom:*** The right to freedom of expression and speech, the right to choose one's own profession, the right to reside in any part of the Indian Union.
  3. ***Right to Freedom to Religion:*** Except when it is in the interest of public order, morality, health or other conditions, everybody has the right to profess, practice and propagate his religion freely.
  4. ***Cultural and Educational Rights:*** The Constitution provides that every community can run its own institutions to preserve its own culture and language.
  5. ***Right against Exploitation:*** Traffic in human beings and forced labour and the employment of children under 14 years in factories or mines, are punishable offences.
  6. ***Rights to Constitutional Remedies:*** When a citizen finds that any of his fundamental rights has been encroached upon, he can move the Supreme Court, which has been empowered to safeguard the fundamental rights of a citizen (Article 32).

PART - IV

DIRECTIVE PRINCIPLES OF STATE POLICY (ARTICLE 36 - 51)

- Directive principles are not enforceable through courts. Main aim of Directive principles is to provide social and economic base of a genuine democracy.

Some Important Directive Principles:

- Provisions for adequate means of livelihood for all citizens (Art. 39).
- Right to work (Art. 41).
- Right to human condition of work and maternity relief (Art. 42).
- Right to a living wage and condition of work ensuring decent standard of life of worker (Art. 43).
- Common Civil Code (Art. 44).
- Prohibit consumption of liquor (Art. 47).
- Prevent slaughter of useful cattle (Art. 48).
- Organise Panchayati Raj (Art. 40).
- Separate the judiciary from the executive (Art. 50).
- Protect and maintain places of historic monuments (Art. 49).
- International peace (Art. 51).

PART - IV A

FUNDAMENTAL DUTIES (ARTICLE 51A)

- The fundamental duties for the Indian citizens have been incorporated in the Constitution through the Constitution (42nd) Amendment Act, 1976. These duties are:
  1. to abide by the Constitution and respect its ideals and institutions, the National Flag and the National Anthem;
  2. to cherish and follow the noble deeds which inspired our national struggle for freedom;
  3. to uphold and protect the sovereignty, unity and integrity of India;
  4. to defend the country and render national service when called upon to do so;
  5. to promote harmony and the spirit of common brotherhood amongst all the people transcending religious, regional or sectional diversities and to renounce practices derogatory to the dignity of women;
  6. to value and preserve the rich heritage of our composite culture;
  7. to protect and improve natural environment including forests, lakes, rivers and wildlife, and to have compassion for living creatures;
  8. to develop the scientific temper, humanism and the spirit of inquiry and reform;
  9. to safeguard public property and to abjure violence;
  10. to strive towards excellence in all spheres of individual and collective activity so that the nation constantly rises to higher levels of endeavour and achievement.
  11. who is parent or guardian to provide opportunities for education to his child or, as the case may be, ward between age of six and fourteen years.

PART - V

UNION (ARTICLE 52 - 151)

THE PRESIDENT

- The President is the Constitutional head of the Republic of India. He is more or less the titular head of the executive.
- He is the constitutional head but not the real executive. The real power is vested in the hands of the Council of Ministers.
- President is the first citizen of India.
- ***Qualifications:*** (i) Indian citizen, (ii) age not less than 35 years, (iii) should have qualification for election to Lok Sabha, (iv) should not hold any office of profit, (v) should not be a Member of Parliament or State Legislature.
- ***Election:*** Indirectly elected through Electoral College consisting of elected members of both the Houses of the

Parliament and elected members of the Legislative Assemblies of the States.

- According to the 70th Amendment Act, 1992, the expression 'States' include the National Capital Territory of Delhi and the Union Territory of Puducherry. Members of the Legislative Councils have no right to vote in the Presidential election.
- ***Powers:*** He makes appointments to all the constitutional posts.
- He can address either House of Parliament and dissolve Lok Sabha.
- All Bills passed by Parliament must receive his assent to become an Act.
- He issues ordinances when Parliament is not in session. No Money Bill can be introduced in Lok Sabha without his recommendation.
- He appoints 12 members of special repute in the Rajya Sabha.
- He has the power of *Pardon* to a criminal in special cases.
- The President holds the office for a period of five years. He is eligible for re-election.
- He is also entitled to rent free official residence called Rashtrapati Bhawan.

Vice-President

- ***Article 63*** of the Constitution stipulates a Vice-President for India.
- The Vice-President acts as the ex-officio Chairman of the Council of States (Rajya Sabha).
- He is elected by an electoral college consisting of the members of both Houses of Parliament in accordance with the system of proportional representation by means of the single transferable vote. He must be a citizen of India, not less than 35 years of age, and should be eligible for election as a member of the Council of States.
- Disputes in connection with election of a president or a vice-president are to be a dealt with in accordance with Article-71. Such disputes shall be decided by the Supreme Court.

Council of Ministers

- The Constitution of India provides for a parliament system of government under which the President is only Constitutional ruler and the real power is exercised by the Council of Ministers, headed by the Prime Minister.
- Council of Ministers is composed of all Union Ministers—the Prime Minister, Cabinet Ministers, Ministers of State and Deputy Ministers.
- The Council of Ministers is Collectively responsible to the Lok Sabha.
- The Prime Minister is a link between the President and the Council of Ministers.

Prime Minister

- The Prime Minister is the leader of the majority party in the Parliament.
- He is appointed by the President. Other Ministers are appointed by the president on his advice.
- The Prime Minister is the head of the Government and the head of the Council of Ministers.
- Jawaharlal Nehru was the first Prime Minister and the longest serving so far.

Union Legislature

- The Legislature of the Union, which is called 'Parliament' consists of the President and the two Houses of Parliament known as the Council of states (Rajya Sabha) and the House of the People (Lok Sabha).

RAJYA SABHA

- The Rajya Sabha is the Upper House of the Parliament and it is constituted of representatives from the States or the Constituent units of the Indian Union.
- It is a permanent body, one third of its members retiring after every two years.
- Its maximum strength is 250. Out of these, twelve members are nominated by the President from well-known personalities in the realm of Science, Art, Literature and Social Service. Rest of 238 representatives of the States and Union Territories are elected.
- Currently, the strength of the Rajya Sabha is 245.

LOK SABHA

- The Lok Sabha whose life is five years, is the Lower House of Parliament and comprises of members directly elected by the people.
- The House of the people (Lok Sabha) at present consists, 543 members directly elected from the states and Union Territories. By the 104th Constitutional amendment Act, 2019 the 2 Anglo-Indian reserved seats nominated by President in Lok Sabha are abolished.
- The House of the People shall continue for five years (unless sooner dissolved) from the date of its meeting and no longer and the expiry of the said period of 5 years shall operate as dissolution of the House.

Parliamentary Committees

- There are several Parliamentary Committees to assist the Parliament in its deliberations.
- These are appointed or elected by the respective Houses of Lok Sabha and Rajya Sabha on a motion made or are nominated by their presiding officers.
- Among the Standing Committees, three are financial Committees: (i) Public Account Committee; (ii) Estimate Committee; (iii) Public undertaking Committee.

Speaker of Lok Sabha

- Speaker is elected by the Lok Sabha from among its members.
- The Speaker will have the final power to maintain order within the House of the People and to interpret its rules of procedure.
- A Deputy-Speaker is also elected to officiate in absence of the Speaker.
- *G.V. Mavlankar* was the first Speaker of the Lok Sabha (1952-1956).

Supreme Court

- The Constitution provides for the Supreme Court, which consists of Chief Justice and 33 judges. They are appointed by the President of India.

QUALIFICATION AND TENURE

- Eligibility conditions for a judge of the Supreme Court are that he must be : (i) a citizen of India; (ii) a judge of a high court for a minimum period of 5 years; or (iii) an advocate of a high court for at least ten years or a distinguished jurist.
- Judges hold office till the age of 65.
- They can resign earlier or can be removed by the President on the recommendation of the two Houses of the Parliament by 2/3rd majority of the members present and voting.

Powers

- *Original jurisdiction:* Cases involving Government of India and the states or cases involving the enforcement of Fundamental Rights fall under original jurisdiction.
- *Appellate Jurisdiction:* In cases which are brought to it in the form of appeals against the judgement of the lower courts—It hears appeals in civil and criminal cases.
- *Advisory functions:* the Supreme Court advises the President on the constitutionality of a particular legal matter. However, its advice is not binding on the President.

Other Powers:

1. it is a court of record and can punish for contempt of itself;
2. it can make rules for regulating the practice and procedure of courts with the approval of the President; and
3. it can recommend to the President the removal of chairman and members of the UPSC. Supreme Court enjoys the power of judicial review (right of the court which declares as unconstitutional, the laws passed by the legislature and orders issued by executive) though it is not specifically mentioned in the Constitution.

- The first Chief Justice of India was H.J. Kania (1950-51).

COMPTROLLER AND AUDITOR GENERAL (CAG) (ARTICLE 148-151)

- The Comptroller and Auditor General of India is guardian of the public purse.
- It is his duty to see that not a *paisa* is spent out of consolidated fund of India or of a state without the authority of the appropriate legislature.
- He is appointed by President of India.
- A person with long administrative experience and knowledge of accounts is appointed.
- Holds office for 6 yrs or till 65 yrs of age.
- The President can remove him only on the recommendation of the 2 houses of Parliament (as in case of judge of Supreme Court).
- The CAG submits its reports to the President (in case of accounts relating to the Union Government) or to the State Governors (for State Government Accounts).
- The first CAG of India was *V Narahari Rao* (1948-1954).
- The CAG is not eligible for further office under the Union or State Governments. The expenses of the office of the CAG is charged to the Consolidated Fund of India.

ATTORNEY GENERAL OF INDIA

- The Attorney General of India is the first law officer of the Government of India.
- Though he is not a member of cabinet he has the right to speak in the House of Parliament, but he has no right to vote.
- The Attorney General of India shall be appointed by the President and shall hold office during his pleasure.
- His duty shall be to give advice on such legal matter from time-to-time as may be referred to him by the President.
- To be appointed as Attorney General, a candidate must be qualified to be appointed as a Judge of the Supreme Court.
- The Attorney General can participate in proceedings of the Parliament without the Right to Vote (Article 88).
- The first Attorney General of Independent India was MC Setalvad (1950-1963).

PART - VI

THE STATES (ARTICLE 152 - 237)

The Governor

- The Governor is appointed by the President and holds office during the pleasure of the President.
- Apart from the power to appoint the council of ministers, if the governor finds that the government of state cannot be carried on in accordance with the provisions of the

constitution (Art. 356), he may send his report to the President who may assume to himself the functions of the government of the state. (This is popularly known as 'President's Rule').

- Article 161 gives the Governor the power to grant pardons, reprieves, remission of punishment to persons convicted under the state law.
- Article 171 states that the States where Legislative Councils exists, the Governor can nominate some members from amongst those distinguished in literature, science, arts, cooperative movement and social service.

STATES LEGISLATURE (ARTICLE 168 - 212)

- The state legislature consists of Governor and legislative assembly.
- In some state like *Bihar, Maharashtra, Andhra Pradesh, Karnataka, Uttar Pradesh and Telangana* have a legislative council.
- The membership of the council should not be more than *one-third* of the legislative assembly but not less than 40.
- The legislative assembly of each state shall be composed of members chosen by direct election on the basis of adult suffrage and the number of members shall not be more than 500 or less than 60.
- The assembly of Sikkim, Goa, Puducherry and Mizoram have less than 60 members.

HIGH COURTS (ARTICLE 214-232)

- The High Court stands at the apex of the State Judiciary.
- As per the Constitution, there shall be a High Court in each State. But there may be a common High Court for two or more States and Union Territory, if it is provided by a law of the Parliament. For example, the Chennai High Court has its Jurisdiction over the State of Tamil Nadu and the Union Territory of Puducherry.
- The State Government has no control over it.
- There are 25 High Courts in India.
- The Calcutta High Court, established in 1862, is the oldest High Court in India.

THE PANCHAYATS (ARTICLE 243-243 O)

- Panchayati Raj was introduced in India with a view to associate the people with administration at grass-root level.
- It is a three-tier system as recommended by Balwant Rai Mehta Committee.
- Introduced by the 73rd Amendment Act, 1992 which envisaged a three tier system of local governance.

These are:

1. Gram Panchayat at the village level
2. Panchayat Samiti at the block level
3. Zila Parishad at the district level.

Jurisdiction and Seat of High Courts

Name	Year	Territorial Jurisdiction	Seat
Allahabad	1866	Uttar Pradesh	Prayagraj (Bench at Lucknow)
Andhra Pradesh	2019	Andhra Pradesh	Amaravati
Bombay	1862	Maharashtra, Goa, Dadar and Nagar Haveli and Daman and Diu	Mumbai (Benches at Nagpur, Panaji and Aurangabad)
Calcutta	1862	West Bengal and Andaman & Nicobar	Kolkata (Circuit Benches at Port Blair and Jalpaiguri)
Chhattisgarh	2000	Chhattisgarh	Bilaspur
Delhi	1966	Delhi	Delhi
Guwahati	1948	Assam, Nagaland, Mizoram and Arunachal Pradesh	Guwahati (Benches at Kohima, Aizawl and Itanagar)
Gujarat	1960	Gujarat	Ahmedabad
Himachal Pradesh	1971	Himachal Pradesh	Shimla
Jammu and Kashmir and Ladakh	1928	Jammu & Kashmir, Ladakh	Srinagar and Jammu
Jharkhand	2000	Jharkhand	Ranchi
Karnataka	1884	Karnataka	Bengaluru (Circuit Benches at Dharwar and Gulbarga)
Kerala	1958	Kerala & Lakshadweep	Ernakulam
Madhya Pradesh	1956	Madhya Pradesh	Jabalpur (Benches at Gwalior and Indore)
Madras	1862	Tamil Nadu & Puducherry	Chennai (Bench at Madurai)
Orissa	1948	Odisha	Cuttack
Patna	1916	Bihar	Patna
Punjab and Haryana	1966	Punjab, Haryana and Chandigarh	Chandigarh
Rajasthan	1949	Rajasthan	Jodhpur (Bench at Jaipur)
Sikkim	1975	Sikkim	Gangtok
Uttarakhand	2000	Uttarakhand	Nainital
Tripura	2013	Tripura	Agartala
Meghalaya	2013	Meghalaya	Shillong
Manipur	2013	Manipur	Imphal
Telangana	2019	Telangana	Hyderabad

THE MUNICIPALITIES (ARTICLE 243 P-243 ZG)

- Big cities have municipal corporations headed by the elected Mayor.
- For small towns there are elected boards or councils, in turn, elect their Presidents.
- Introduced by the 74th Amendment Act, 1993 which envisages three types of urban local bodies, namely, municipality (nagar palika), city council (nagar panchayat).
- Municipal governance in India was first introduced in Madras in 1688.

PART - XIII

(ARTICLE 301 - 307)

- In this part from Article 301-307 trade, commerce and intercourse within the territory of India are given.

PART - XIV

(ARTICLE 308 - 323)

- In this part services under the union and the states are given.
- ***Article 312:*** *All India Services* and ***Article 315:*** Public Service Commissions for the Union and for the States.
- The first Public Service Commission was set up in 1926, on the recommendations of the Lee Commission.

UNION PUBLIC SERVICE COMMISSION (UPSC)

- This Commission is responsible for:
  1. recruitment to all civil services and posts, under the Union Government by written examinations, interviews and promotions, and
  2. advising the Government on all matters relating to methods of recruitment, principles to be followed in making promotions and transfers. Its Chairman is appointed by the President.

STAFF SELECTION COMMISSION (SSC)

- The Union Government has constituted a Staff Selection Commission for recruitment to non-technical Class III posts in the central government and in subordinate offices.
- The Administrative Reforms Commission had recommended the setting up of such a Commission.
- The Commission has also been entrusted with the responsibility of making recruitment to Group 'B' services like Assistants' and Stenographers Grade 'C'.
- The Commission has a chairman and two members.

ELECTIONS (ARTICLE 324-329)

- The Constitution provides for an independent election commission to ensure free and fair election to the Parliament, the State legislature and the offices of President and Vice-President.
- Consists of Chief Election Commissioner +2 Election Commissioners. They all enjoy equal powers.
- The Chief Election Commissioner and other Election Commissioners are appointed by the President.
- Election Commissioners are appointed for a term of 5 yrs.
- They are not eligible for re-appointment. Also, they cannot hold any office of profit after their retirement.
- The Election Commission was established on 25th January, 1950 under Article 324 of the Constitution.
- The first Chief Election Commissioner was *Sukumar Sen.*

Functions

- Preparation of electoral rolls and keeping voters list updated.
- Recognition of various political parties and allotment of election symbols.

NITI AAYOG

- The Indian government has replaced Planing Commission with a new institution named **NITI Aayog (National Institution for Transforming India).**
- The Niti Aayog will comprise the following:
  1. Prime Minister of India as the Chairperson.
  2. Governing Council comprising the Chief Ministers of all the States and Lt. Governors of Territories.
  3. Regional Councils will be formed to address specific issues and contingencies impacting more than one state or a region. These will be formed for a specified tenure. The Regional Councils will be convened by the Prime Minister and will comprise of the Chief Ministers of States and Lt. Governors of Territories in the region. These will be chaired by the Chairperson of the NITI Aayog or his nominee.
  4. Experts, specialists and practitioners with relevant domain knowledge as special invitees nominated by the Prime Minister.
- The full-time organizational framework will comprise of, in addition to the Prime Minister as the Chairperson:
  1. Vice-Chairperson : To be appointed by the Prime Minister.
  2. Members : Full-time.
  3. Part-time members : Maximum of 2 from leading universities research organizations and other relevant institutions in an ex-officio capacity. Part time members will be on a rotational basis.
  4. Ex Officio members : Maximum of 4 members of the Council of Ministers to be nominated by the Prime Minister.
  5. Chief Executive Officer : To be appointed by the Prime Minister for a fixed tenure, in the rank of Secretary to the Government of India.
  6. Secretariat as deemed necessary.

FINANCE COMMISSION

- The constitution of the Finance Commission is laid down in Art. 280. The chairman must be a person having experience in public affairs; and the other four members also having wide experience in financial matters.
- It consists of Chairman and 4 other members.
- It shall be the duty of the Finance Commission to advice the President on matters such as the distribution between the Union and States of the net proceeds of taxes that is required to be shared.
- The Finance Commission is not a permanent body. It is dissolved after it has submitted its recommendations.

❒ ❒ ❒

4

Indian Economy

NATIONAL INCOME

- According to the National Income Committee (1949), "A national income estimate measures the volume of commodities and service turned out during a given period counted without duplication". Thus, national income measures the net value of goods and services produced in a country during a year and it also includes net earned foreign income. In other words, a total of national income measures the flow of goods and services in an economy.
- National income is a flow concept not a stock concept.
- In India, National income estimates are related with the financial year (April 1 to 31st March).
- The various concepts of national income are as follows:
  - *(i)* **GNP (Gross National Product):** GNP refers to the money value of total output or production of final goods and services produced by the nationals of a country during a given period of time, generally a year.
  - *(ii)* **NNP (Net National Product):** NNP is obtained by subtracting depreciation value from GNP. NNP can be calculated in two ways: *(a)* at market prices of goods and services and *(b)* at factor cost.
  - *(iii)* **National Income:** When NNP is obtained at factor cost, it is known as National Income. National Income is calculated by subtracting net indirect taxes from NNP at market prices. The obtained value is known as NNP at factor cost or National income.
  - *(iv)* **Personal Income:** Personal income is that income which is actually obtained by nationals. Personal income is obtained by subtracting corporate taxes and payments made for social securities provisions from national income and adding to it govern-ment transfer payments, business transfer payments and net interest paid by the government.

Methods of Measuring National Income

- According to Simon Kuznets, national income of a country is calculated by following mentioned three methods:
  - *(i)* **Product Method:** S. Kuznets gave a new name to this method, *i.e.*, product service method. In this method, net value of final goods and services produced in a country during a year is obtained and the total obtained value is called total final product.
  - *(ii)* **Income Method:** In this method, a total of net incomes earned by working people in different sectors and commercial enterprises is obtained.
  - *(iii)* **Consumption Method:** It is also called expenditure method. Income is either spent on consumption or saved. Hence, national income is the addition of total consumption and total savings.
- In India, a combination of production method and income method is used for measuring estimating national income.
- For measuring national income in India, in 1868, the first attempt was made by *Dada Bhai Nauroji*. He, in his book, *"Poverty and Un-British Rule in India"*, estimated Indian per capita annual income at a level of ₹ 20.
- After independence, the Government of India appointed the National Income Committee in August, 1949, under the Chairmanship of Prof. P.C. Mahalanobies, to compile authoritative estimates of national income.
- Estimation and publishing of National Income data by CSO (Central Statistical Organization) is done every year.
- National income includes the contribution of three sectors—primary sector, secondary sector, Tertiary sector.
- Under Primary Sector—Agriculture, Forest, Fisheries and allied sector are included.
- Under Secondary Sector—Manufacturing, Construction, Electricity, Gas and Water Supply are included.
- Under Teritiary Sector—Trade, Transport, Communication, Banking, Insurance, Real Estate, Community and Personal Services are included.
- The contribution of primary sector in GDP was 55.4% in 1950-1951. But now the share of primary sector in national income has come down. In 2020-21, the contribution of primary sector in GDP was 19.9%.
- The contribution of secondary sector has shown a steady increase from 15% in 1950-51 to 25.8% in 2020-21.
- The contribution of tertiary sector indicated a sharp improvement from 29.6% in 1950-51 to about 54.3% in 2020-21.
- At present estimation of national income is based on the base year of 2011-2012.

POPULATION

Census-2011: Population, Density, Decadal Growth Rate

S.N.	State/UTs	Population 2001	Population 2011	Density 2001	Density 2011	Decadal G. (%) 2001–2011
1.	J&K	10,143,700	1,25,41,302	100	124	23.6
2.	Himachal Pradesh	6,077,900	68,64,602	109	123	12.9
3.	Punjab	24,358,999	2,77,43,338	484	551	13.9
4.	Chandigarh	900,635	10,55,450	7,900	9258	17.2
5.	Uttarakhand	8,489,349	1,00,86,292	159	189	18.8
6.	Haryana	21,144,564	2,53,51,462	478	573	19.9
7.	Delhi	13,850,507	1,67,87,941	9,340	11320	21.2
8.	Rajasthan	56,507,188	6,85,48,437	165	200	21.3
9.	Uttar Pradesh	166,197,921	19,98,12,341	690	829	20.2
10.	Bihar	82,998,509	10,40,99,452	881	1106	25.4
11.	Sikkim	540,851	6,10,577	76	86	12.9
12.	Arunachal Pradesh	1,097,968	13,83,727	13	17	26.0
13.	Nagaland	1,990,036	19,78,502	120	119	–0.6
14.	Manipur	2,293,896	28,55,794	103	128	31.79
15.	Mizoram	888,573	10,97,206	42	52	23.5
16.	Tripura	3,199,203	36,73,917	305	350	14.8
17.	Meghalaya	2,318,822	29,66,889	103	132	27.9
18.	Assam	26,655,528	3,12,05,576	340	398	17.1
19.	West Bengal	80,176,197	9,12,76,115	903	1028	13.8
20.	Jharkhand	26,945,829	3,29,88,134	338	414	22.4
21.	Odisha	36,804,660	4,19,74,218	236	270	14.0
22.	Chhattisgarh	20,833,803	2,55,45,198	154	189	22.6
23.	Madhya Pradesh	60,348,023	7,26,26,809	196	236	20.3
24.	Gujarat	50,671,017	6,04,39,692	258	308	19.3
25.	Daman & Diu	158,204	2,43,247	1,413	2191	53.8
26.	Dadra & N. Haveli	220,490	3,43,709	449	700	55.9
27.	Maharashtra	96,878,627	11,23,74,333	315	365	16.0
28.	Andhra Pradesh	76,210,007	4,93,86,799	277	308	11.0
29.	Karnataka	52,850,562	6,10,95,297	276	319	15.6
30.	Goa	1,347,668	14,58,545	364	394	8.2
31.	Lakshadweep	60,650	64,473	1,895	2149	6.3
32.	Kerala	31,841,374	3,34,06,061	819	860	4.9
33.	Tamil Nadu	62,405,679	7,21,47,030	480	555	15.6
34.	Puducherry	974,345	12,47,953	2,030	2546	28.1
35.	AnJaman & Nicobar Islands	356,152	3,80,581	43	46	6.9
36.	Telangana	—	3,51,93,978	—	307	13.58
	India	**1,028,737,436**	**1,21,08,54,977**	**325**	**382**	**17.7**

AGRICULTURE

- Agriculture is an important sector of the economy. Though the share of agriculture in national income has come down since the inception of planning era in the economy but still it has substantial share in GDP.
- In terms of composition, out of the total share of 14.65 per cent that agriculture and allied sector had in GDP in 2019-20.
- Agriculture in our country provides livelihood to about 49% of the population.
- Gross Capital Formation (GCF) in Agriculture and Allied sector relative to GVA in this sector has been snowing a fluctuating trent from 18.3 per cent in 2011-12 to 16.34 per cent in 2020-21.
- Agriculture provides raw materials to various industries and other agro-based industries. Cotton and Jute textile industries, Sugar, Vanaspati industry etc. are directly dependent on agriculture.
- India's foreign trade is deeply associated with Agriculture Sector. Value of agriculture exports to total exports of the country was 13.8 per cent in 2013. But the share of agriculture has come down in foreign trade at present. Share of agriculture in foreign trade was 11.76 per cent in 2018-19.

Various Crops and their producing states

Crops/Groups of Crops	Producing State (In Descending Order)
I. Foodgrains	
Rice	West Bengal, Uttar Pradesh, Punjab
Wheat	Uttar Pradesh, Madhya Pradesh, Punjab
Maize	Karnataka, Madhya Pradesh, Maharashtra
Total Nutri/ Coarse Cereals	Rajasthan, Karnataka, Maharashtra
Gram	Madhya Pradesh, Maharashtra, Rajasthan
Tur	Maharashtra, Karnataka, Telangana
Total Pulses	Madhya Pradesh, Rajasthan, Maharashtra
Total Food-grains	Uttar Pradesh, Madhya Pradesh, Punjab
II. Oilseeds	
Groundnut	Gujarat, Rajasthan, Tamil Nadu
Rapeseed & Mustard	Rajasthan, Madhya Pradesh, Haryana
Soyabean	Maharashtra, Madhya Pradesh, Rajasthan
Sunflower	Karnataka, Haryana, Odisha
Total Oilseeds	Rajasthan, Maharashtra, Madhya Pradesh
III. Other Cash Crops	
Sugarcane	Uttar Pradesh, Maharashtra, Karnataka
Cotton	Maharashtra, Gujarat, Telangana
Jute & Mesta	West Bengal, Bihar, Assam

Source: Economic Survey 2020-21

ECONOMIC PLANNING

☞ **Five Year Plans in India**

Plans	*Period*	*Investment (₹ Crore)*	*Objectives*
First Plan	April 1, 1951-March 31, 1956	1,960	Priority to agriculture, electricity and irrigation.
Second Plan	April 1, 1956—March 31, 1961	4,672	Development of basic and heavy industries.
Third Plan	April 1, 1961—March 31, 1966	8,577	Long term development of India's economy.
Annual Plan	April 1, 1966—March 31, 1967	2,137	
Annual Plan	April 1, 1967—March 31, 1968	2,205	
Annual Plan	April 1, 1968—March 31, 1969	2,283	
Fourth Plan	April 1, 1969—March 31, 1974	15,779	Enlarge the income of rural population and supply of goods of mass consumption.
Fifth Plan	April 1, 1974—March 31, 1979	39,426	Attain increased self-reliance and employment avenues.
Annual Plan	April 1, 1979—March 31, 1980	12,176	
Sixth Plan	April 1, 1980—March 31, 1985	1,09,292	Removal of unemployment
Seventh Plan	April 1, 1985—March 31, 1990	2,18,730	Food work and productivity were the basic priorities.
Eighth Plan	April, 1992—March 31, 1997	4,95,670	Raising employment
Ninth Plan	April 1, 1997—March 31, 2002	9,41,041	Agriculture and rural development
Tenth Plan	April 1, 2002—March 31, 2007	14,91,610	Growth rate 7.8 percent per annum.
Eleventh Plan	April 1, 2007—March 31, 2012	36,44,718	Literacy, Employment, Rural development & Transport development.
Twelfth Plan	April 1, 2012–March 31, 2017	43,30,000	Longterm development of India's economy.

15-YEAR VISION PLANE

With the end of the Twelfth Plan in March 2017 the era of five year plans came to an end. NITI Aayog has come forward with a draft 15-year vision plan to catapult the country's economy to more than three times as compared to the present day. The new plan is set to replace the centralised five-year plans the country has been following for decades. The new plan is accompanied by shorter sub-plan—a seven-year strategy for 2017-24, and a three-year 'Action Agenda' from 2017-18 to 2019-20. No less than 300 specific action points covering a wide range of sectors points covering a wide range of sectors have been drawn up as part of the 15-year vision.

MONEY AND BANKING

RESERVE BANK OF INDIA

- Reserve Bank of India (RBI) is the central bank of the country.
- Reserve Bank of India was established on April 1, 1935 under Reserve Bank of India Act, 1934 with a authorised capital of ₹ 5 crore.
- The Reserve Bank of India was nationalised on January 1, 1949.
- The general administration and direction of RBI is managed by a Central Board of Directors consisting of 20 members which includes 1 Governor and 4 Deputy Governors.
- The head office of the Reserve Bank of India is in Mumbai.

☞ Establishment Years of Major Financial Institutions in India

Imperial Bank of India	1921
Reserve Bank of India (Nationalisation of RBI took place on January 1, 1949)	April 1, 1935
Industrial Finance Corporation of India (IFCI)	1948
State Bank of India (SBI)	July 1, 1955
Unit Trust of India (UTI)	Feb. 1, 1964
IDBI	July 1964
NABARD	July 12, 1982
SIDBI	1990
EXIM Bank	January 1, 1982
National Housing Bank (NHB)	July 1988
Life Insurance Corporation (LIC)	Sept. 1956
General Insurance Corporation (GIC)	Nov. 1972
Regional Rural Banks (RRBs)	Oct. 2, 1975
Risk Capital and Technology Finance Corporation Ltd.	March 1975
Housing Development Finance Corporation Ltd. (HDFC)	1977

❒ ❒ ❒

5

General Science

IMPORTANT INVENTIONS

Name of Invention	Inventor	Nationality	Year
Aeroplane	Orville & Wilbur Wright	U.S.A.	1903
Ball-Point Pen	John J. Loud	U.S.A.	1888
Barometer	Evangelista Torricelli	Italy	1644
Bicycle	Kirkpatrick Macmillan	Britain	1839-40
Bifocal Lens	Benjamin Franklin	U.S.A.	1780
Car (Petrol)	Karl Benz	Germany	1888
Celluloid	Alexander Parkes	Britain	1861
Cinema	Nicolas & Jean Lumiere	France	1895
Clock (mechanical)	I-Hsing & Liang Ling-Tsan	China	1725
Diesel Engine	Rudolf Diesel	Germany	1895
Dynamo	Hypolite Pixii	France	1832
Electric Lamp	Thomas Alva Edison	U.S.A.	1879
Electric Motor (DC)	Zenobe Gramme	Belgium	1873
Electric Motor (AC)	Nikola Tesla	U.S.A.	1888
Electro-magnet	William Sturgeon	Britain	1824
Electronic Computer	Dr. Alan M. Turing	Britain	1943
Film (moving outlines)	Louis Prince	France	1885
Film (musical sound)	Dr. Le de Forest	U.S.A.	1923
Fountain Pen	Lewis E. Waterman	U.S.A.	1884
Gramophone	Thomas Alva Edison	U.S.A.	1878
Helicopter	Etienne Oehmichen	France	1924
Jet Engine	Sir Frank Whittle	Britain	1937
Laser	Charles H. Townes	U.S.A.	1960
Lift (Mechanical)	Elisha G. Otis	U.S.A.	1852
Locomotive	Richard Trevithick	Britain	1804
Machine Gun	James Puckle	Britain	1718
Microphone	Alexander Graham Bell	U.S.A.	1876
Microscope	Z. Janssen	Netherlands	1590
Motor Cycle	G. Daimler	Germany	1885
Photography (on film)	John Carbutt	U.S.A.	1888
Printing Press	Johann Gutenberg	Germany	c.1455
Razor (safety)	King C. Gillette	U.S.A.	1895
Refrigerator	James Harrison & Alexander Catlin	U.S.A.	1850
Safety Pin	Walter Hunt	U.S.A.	1849
Sewing machine	Barthelemy Thimmonnier	France	1829
Ship (steam)	J.C. Perier	France	1775
Ship (turbine)	Hon. Sir C. Parsons	Britain	1894
Skyscraper	W. Le Baron Jenny	U.S.A.	1882
Slide Rule	William Oughtred	Britain	1621
Steam Engine (condenser)	James Watt	Britain	1765
Steel Production	Henry Bessemer	Britain	1855
Steel (stainless)	Harry Brearley	Britain	1913
Submarine	David Bushnell	U.S.A.	1776

Name of Invention	Inventor	Nationality	Year
Tank	Sir Ernest Swinton	Britain	1914
Telegraph	M. Lammond	France	1787
Telegraph Code	Samuel F.B. Morse	U.S.A.	1837
Telephone (perfected)	Alexander Graham Bell	U.S.A.	1876
Television (mechanical)	John Logie Baird	Britain	1926
Television (electronic)	P.T. Farnsworth	U.S.A.	1927
Thermometer	Galileo Galilei	Italy	1593
Transformer	Michael Faraday	Britain	1831
Transistor	Bardeen, Shockley & Brattain	U.S.A.	1948
Washing Machine (elec.)	Hurley Machine Co.	U.S.A.	1907
Zip-Fastener	W.L. Judson	U.S.A.	1891

IMPORTANT DISCOVERIES

Discovery	Discoverer	Nationality	Year
Aluminium	Hans Christian Oerstedt	Denmark	1827
Atomic number	Henry Moseley	England	1913
Atomic structure of matter	John Dalton	England	1803
Chlorine	C.W. Scheele	Sweden	1774
Electromagnetic induction	Michael Faraday	England	1831
Electromagnetic waves	Heinrich Hertz	Germany	1886
Electromagnetism	Hans Christian Oersted	Denmark	1920
Electron	Sir Joseph Thomson	England	1897
General theory of relativity	Albert Einstein	Switzerland	1915
Hydrogen	Henry Cavendish	England	1766
Law of electric conduction	Georg Ohm	Germany,	1827
Law of electromagnetism	Andre Ampere	France	1826
Law of falling bodies	Galileo	Italy	1590
Laws of gravitation & motion	Isaac Newton	England	1687
Laws of planetary motion	Johannes Kepler	Germany	1609-10
Magnesium	Sir Humphry Davy	England	1808
Neptune (Planet)	Johann Galle	Germany	1846
Neutron	James Chadwick	England	1932
Nickel	Axel Cronstedt	Sweden	1751
Nitrogen	Daniel Rutherford	England	1772
Oxygen	Joseph Priestly; C.W. Scheele	England; Sweden	1772
Ozone	Christian Schonbein	Germany	1839
Pluto (Planet)	Clyde Tombaugh	U.S.A	1930
Plutonium	G.T. Seaborg	U.S.A	1940
Proton	Ernest Rutherford	England	1919
Quantum Theory	Max Planck	Germany	1900
Radioactivity	Antoine Bacquerel	France	1896
Radium	Pierre & Marie Curie	France	1898
Silicon	Jons Berzelius	Sweden	1824
Special theory of relativity	Albert Einstein	Switzerland	1905
Sun as centre of solar system	Copernicus	Poland	1543
Uranium	Martin Klaproth	Germany	1789
Uranus (Planet)	William Herschel	England	1781
X-rays	Wilhelm Roentgen	Germany	1895

GEOGRAPHICAL EXPLORATIONS/DISCOVERIES

Place	Explorer/Discoverer	Nationality	Year
America	Christopher Columbus	Italy	1492
Hawaii Islands (Sandwich Islands)	Captain James Cook	England	1778
Newfoundland	John Cabot	England	1497
New Zealand	Abel Janszoon Tasman	Holland	1642
North Pole	Robert Peary	USA	1909
Sea Route to India (via Cape of Good Hope)	Vasco da Gama	Portugal	1498
South Pole	Roald Amundsen	Norway	1911

SCIENTIFIC INSTRUMENTS

Name of Instrument	*Used for*
Altimeter	measuring altitude
Ammeter	measuring strength of an electric current
Anemometer	measuring the velocity of wind
Audiometer	measuring level of hearing
Barometer	measuring atmospheric pressure
Callipers	measuring the internal and external diameters of tubes
Calorimeter	measuring quantity of heat
Compass	finding out direction
Dynamo	converting mechanical energy into electrical energy
Eudiometer	measuring volume changes during chemical reactions between gases
Galvanometer	detecting and determining the strength of small electric currents
Hydrometer	measuring specific gravity of a liquid
Hygrometer	measuring the humidity in the atmosphere
Lactometer	measuring the purity of milk
Manometer	measuring the gaseous pressure
Micrometer	measuring minute distances, angles, etc.
Microscope	seeing magnified view of very small objects
Photometer	measuring intensity of light from distant stars
Pyrometer	measuring high temperatures
Radar	detecting and finding the presence and location of moving objects like aircraft, missile, etc.
Radiometer	measuring the emission of radiant energy
Rain Gauge	measuring the amount of rainfall
Seismograph	measuring and recording the intensity and origin of earthquake shocks
Sextant	measuring altitude and angular distances between two objects or heavenly bodies
Spectrometer	measuring the refractive indices
Spherometer	measuring the curvature of spherical objects/surface
Sphygmomanometer	measuring blood pressure
Stethoscope	ascertaining the condition of heart and lungs by listening to their function
Stroboscope	viewing objects that are moving rapidly with a periodic motion as if they were at rest
Tachometer	measuring the rate of revolution or angular speed of a revolving shaft
Telescope	viewing magnified images of distant objects
Theodolite	measuring the horizontal and vertical angles
Thermocouple	measuring the temperature inside furnaces and jet engines
Thermometer	measuring human body temperature
Thermostat	regulating constant temperature
Ultrasonoscope	measuring utrasonic sounds
Viscometer	measuring the viscosity of a fluid
Voltmeter	measuring potential difference between two points.

DISEASES AND THE PARTS OF BODY THEY AFFECT

Disease	*Part of body affected*	*Disease*	*Part of body affected*
AIDS	Immune system of body	Jaundice	Liver
Arthritis	Inflammation of joints	Meningitis	Brain or spinal cord
Asthma	Lungs	Pleurisy	Pleura (inflammation of)
Cataract	Eyes	Polio	motor neurons
Conjunctivitis	Eyes	Pneumonia	Lungs
Diabetes	Pancreas	Pyorrhoea	Sockets of teeth
Diphtheria	Throat	Tuberculosis	Lungs
Glaucoma	Eyes	Typhoid	Intestine
Eczema	Skin	Malaria	Spleen
Goitre	Front of the neck (due to enlargement of thyroid gland)	Leukaemia	Blood
Gout	Joints of bone	Rickets	Bones

❒ ❒ ❒

6

Miscellaneous

CAPITAL & CURRENCIES

Country	Capital	Currency
∗ Afghanistan	Kabul	Afghani
∗ Algeria	Algiers	Dinar
∗ Angola	Luanda	New Kwanza
∗ Argentina	Buenos Aires	Peso
∗ Australia	Canberra	Dollar
∗ Austria	Vienna	Euro
∗ Azerbaijan	Baku	Manat
∗ Bahrain	Manama	Dinar
∗ Bangladesh	Dhaka	Taka
∗ Barbados	Bridgetown	Dollar
∗ Belarus	Minsk	Ruble
∗ Belgium	Brussels	Euro
∗ Bhutan	Thimphu	Ngultrum[1]
∗ Bolivia	La paz	Dollar
∗ Brazil	Brasilia	Real
∗ Bulgaria	Sofia	Lev
∗ Canada	Ottawa	Dollar
∗ Chile	Santiago	Peso
∗ China	Beijing	Yuan
∗ Colombia	Bogota	Peso
∗ Croatia	Zagreb	Kuna
∗ Cuba	Havana	Peso
∗ Cyprus	Nicosia	Euro
∗ Czech Republic	Prague	Koruna
∗ Denmark	Copenhagen	Krone
∗ Ecuador	Quito	Sucre
∗ Egypt	Cairo	Pound
∗ Ethiopia	Addis Ababa	Birr
∗ Fiji	Suva	Dollar
∗ Finland	Helsinki	Euro
∗ France	Paris	Euro
∗ Georgia	Tbilisi	Lari
∗ Germany	Berlin	Euro
∗ Ghana	Accra	Cedi
∗ Greece	Athens	Euro
∗ Guyana	George Town	Dollar
∗ Hungary	Budapest	Forint
∗ India	New Delhi	Rupee
∗ Indonesia	Jakarta	Rupiah

Country	Capital	Currency
∗ Iran	Teheran	Rial
∗ Iraq	Baghdad	Dinar
∗ Ireland	Dublin	Euro
∗ Israel	Jerusalem	Shekel
∗ Italy	Rome	Euro
∗ Japan	Tokyo	Yen
∗ Jordan	Amman	Dinar
∗ Kazakhstan	Akmola	Tenge
∗ Kenya	Nairobi	Shilling
∗ Korea (S)	Seoul	Won
∗ Korea (N)	Pyongyang	Won
∗ Kyrgyzstan	Bishkek	Som
∗ Kuwait	Kuwait City	Dinar
∗ Laos	Vientiane	Kip
∗ Lebanon	Beirut	Pound
∗ Liberia	Monrovia	Dollar
∗ Libya	Tripoli	Dinar
∗ Malaysia	Kuala Lumpur	Ringgit
∗ Maldives	Male	Rufiyaa
∗ Mali	Bamako	Franc
∗ Mauritius	Port Louis	Rupee
∗ Mexico	Mexico City	Peso
∗ Mongolia	Ulan Bator	Tugrik
∗ Morocco	Rabat	Dirham
∗ Myanmar (Burma)	Nay Pyi Taw	Kyat
∗ Namibia	Winohoek	Dollar
∗ Nepal	Kathmandu	Rupee
∗ Netherlands	Amsterdam	Euro
∗ New Zealand	Wellington	Dollar
∗ Nigeria	Abuja	Naira
∗ Norway	Oslo	Krone
∗ Oman	Muscat	Rial
∗ Pakistan	Islamabad	Rupee
∗ Panama	Panama City	Balboa
∗ Peru	Lima	New Sole
∗ Philippines	Manila	Peso
∗ Poland	Warsaw	Zloty
∗ Portugal	Lisbon	Euro
∗ Qatar	Doha	Riyal
∗ Russia	Moscow	Ruble

Country	Capital	Currency
✶ Saudi Arabia	Riyadh	Rial
✶ Slovakia	Bratislava	Euro
✶ Spain	Madrid	Euro
✶ Sri Lanka	Colombo	Rupee
✶ Sudan	Khartoum	Dinar
✶ Sweden	Stockholm	Krona
✶ Switzerland	Berne	Swiss Francs
✶ Syria	Damascus	Pound
✶ South Africa	Capetown (Legislative) Pretoria *(Administrative)*	Rand
✶ Tadzhikistan	Dushanbe	Ruble
✶ Taiwan	Taipei	Dollar
✶ Tanzania	Dodoma	Shilling
✶ Thailand	Bangkok	Baht
✶ Tunisia	Tunis	Dinar
✶ Turkiye	Ankara	Lira
✶ Ukraine	Kiev	Hyrvnia
✶ United Arab Emirates	Abu Dhabi	Dirham
✶ U.K.	London	Pound Sterling
✶ U.S.A.	Washington	Dollar
✶ Uruguay	Montevideo	Peso
✶ Uzbekistan	Tashkent	Som
✶ Venezuela	Caracas	Bolivar
✶ Vietnam	Hanoi	Dong
✶ Yemen	Sana'a	Rial
✶ Zimbabwe	Harare	Dollar
✶ Congo (Zaire)	Kinshasa	Zaire
✶ Zambia	Lusaka	Kwacha

GEOGRAPHICAL EXPLORATIONS/DISCOVERIES

Place	Explorer/Discoverer	Nationality	Year
America	Christopher Columbus	Italy	1492
Hawaii Islands (Sandwich Islands)	Captain James Cook	England	1778
Newfoundland	John Cabot	England	1497
New Zealand	Abel Janszoon Tasman	Holland	1642
North Pole	Robert Peary	USA	1909
Sea Route to India (via Cape of Good Hope)	Vasco da Gama	Portugal	1498
South Pole	Roald Amundsen	Norway	1911

NATIONAL MONUMENTS OF SOME FAMOUS COUNTRIES

Monument	Country
Great Wall of China	China
Taj Mahal (Agra)	India
Emperial Palace (Tokyo)	Japan
Opera House (Sydney)	Australia
Eiffel Tower (Paris)	France
Pyramid (Giza)	Egypt
Kinder Disk	Denmark
Leaning Tower of Pisa	Italy
Statue of Liberty (New York)	USA
Kremlin (Moscow)	Russia

INTELLIGENCE AGENCIES OF SOME PROMINENT COUNTRIES

Country	Intelligence Agency
✶ India	*Research & Analysis Wing (RAW), Intelligence Bureau (I.B.), Central Bureau of Investigation (C.B.I.)*
✶ Pakistan	*Inter Service Intelligence (I.S.I.)*
✶ U.S.A.	*Central Intelligence Agency (CIA), Federal Bureau of Investigation (FBI)*
✶ Britain	*Military Intelligence (M.I.)-5 and 6, Special Branch, Ultra, Joint Intelligence Organisation*
✶ Israel	*Mosad*
✶ Egypt	*Mukhabarat*
✶ Japan	*Nicho*
✶ Russia	*K.G.B. (Komitel Gosudarstvennoy Bezopasnosty) (Committee for State Security)*
✶ Canada	*Security Intelligence Service (SIS)*
✶ S. Africa	*Bureau of State Security (BSS)*
✶ Iran	*Sabak*
✶ Iraq	*Al-Mukhabarat*
✶ Australia	*Australian Security and Intelligence Organisation (ASIO)*
✶ France	*S.D.E.C.E.*
✶ Spain	*C.E.S.I.D.*

MAJOR LANGUAGES OF THE WORLD AND THEIR SPEAKERS

Listing the languages spoken by approximately 1% of humankind (those spoken by more than 60,000,000 people), this table enumerates speakers of each tongue as a primary language.

Language	Speakers (millions)
∗ Chinese	1,298.6
∗ Spanish	442.4
∗ English	378.3
∗ Hindi	260
∗ Arabic	315.3
∗ Portuguese	222.7
∗ Bengali	242
∗ Russian	153
∗ Japanese	128
∗ Javanese	84
∗ Lahnda	118
∗ German	76.8
∗ Korean	77.2
∗ French	76.8
∗ Telugu	74
∗ Marathi	71.8
∗ Turkish	71
∗ Tamil	68
∗ Vietnamese	68
∗ Urdu	69.2
∗ Italian	64.8
∗ Malay	60
∗ Persian	61.5

***(Source:** The World Almanac-2019)*

NAME OF PARLIAMENTS OF SOME COUNTRIES

Country	Name of Parliament
Afghanistan	Shora
Argentina	National Congress
Australia	Federal Parliament
Austria	National Assembly
Bangladesh	Jatiya Sansad
India	Lok Sabha and Rajya Sabha
Bhutan	Tshogdu (National Assembly)
Britain	House of Commons and House of Lords
Canada	House of Commons and Senate
China	National People Congress
Denmark	Folketing
Iran	Majlis (Islamic Consultative Assembly)
Israel	Knesset
Japan	Diet
Myanmar	Pyithu Hluttaw (People's Assembly)
Nepal	Rashtriya Panchayat
The Netherlands	States-General
Norway	Storting
Poland	Sejm
Russia	Federal Assembly (Council of the Federation and State Duma
South Africa	National Assembly and Senate
Spain	Cortes Generales
Sweden	Riksdag
Switzerland	Federal Assembly (Nationalrat and Standerat)
North Korea	Supreme People's Assembly
South Korea	National Assembly
U.S.A.	Congress (Senate and House of Representatives)
Ethiopia	Federal Council and House of Representatives
Iceland	Alpingi
Bulgaria	National Assembly
Cuba	National Assembly of People's Power

LARGEST AND SMALLEST COUNTRIES (Top 5)

Largest Country	Largest Country	Smallest Country	Smallest Country
(Area-wise)	(Population-wise)	(Area-wise)	(Population-wise)
Russia	China	Vatican City	Vatican City
Canada	India	Monaco	Nauru
China	USA	Nauru	Tuvalu
United States	Indonesia	Tuvalu	Palau
Brazil	Brazil	San Marino	Monaco

RELIGIONS OF THE WORLD

Religion	Member	Percentage	Religion	Member	Percentage
Christianity	2.4 billion	32.9%	Buddhism	521 million	7%
Islam	1.7 billion	23.6%	Sikhism	25 million	0.3%
Hinduism	1.01 billion	13.7%			

NATIONAL EMBLEMS OF IMPORTANT COUNTRIES

Country	National Emblem	Country	National Emblem
America	Golden Rod	Australia	Kangaroo
Ireland	Shamrock	Italy	White Lily
Israel	Candelabrum	Iran	Rose
Canada	White Lily	Great Britain	Rose
Chile	Candor and Huemul	Germany	Corn Flower
Japan	Chrysanthemum	Zimbabwe	Zimbabwe Bird
Denmark	Beach	Turkiye	Crescent and Star
The Netherlands	Lion	New Zealand	Kiwi, Fern Southern Cross
Norway	Lion	Nepal	Kukri
Pakistan	Crescent	Poland	Eagle
France	Lily	Belgium	Lion
Bangladesh	Water Lily	Mongolia	The Soyombo
Russia	Double headed eagle	Lebanon	Cedar Tree
Sudan	Secretary Bird	Syria	Eagle
India	Lioned Capital		

BOOKS AND AUTHORS

FOREIGN

Book	Author
✶ As You Like It	*William Shakespeare*
✶ A Tale of Two Cities	*Charles Dickens*
✶ Ben Hur	*Lewis Wallace*
✶ Das Kapital	*Karl Marx*
✶ David Copperfield	*Charles Dickens*
✶ Hamlet	*William Shakespeare*
✶ Iliad	*Homer*
✶ Inferno	*A. Dante*
✶ In Memoriam	*Lord Tennyson*
✶ Ivanhoe	*Walter Scott*
✶ Julius Caesar	*William Shakespeare*
✶ Lady Chatterley's Lover	*D.H. Lawrence*
✶ Lajja	*Taslima Nasreen*
✶ Les Miserable	*Victor Hugo*
✶ Leviathan	*Thomas Hobbes*
✶ Lolita	*V. Nobokov*
✶ Lycidas	*John Milton*
✶ Mein Kampf	*Adolf Hitler*
✶ Moor's Last Sigh	*Salman Rushdie*
✶ Mother	*Maxim Gorky*

Book	Author
✶ Mother India	*Katherine Mayo*
✶ Nana	*Emile Zola*
✶ Odyssey	*Homer*
✶ Origin of Species	*Charles Darwin*
✶ Othello	*William Shakespeare*
✶ Paradise Lost	*John Milton*
✶ Paradise Regained	*John Milton*
✶ Path to Power	*Margaret Thatcher*
✶ Pickwick Papers	*Charles Dickens*
✶ Razor's Edge	*Somerset Maugham*
✶ Republic	*Plato*
✶ The Tempest	*William Shakespeare*
✶ Time Machine	*H.G. Wells*
✶ Tom Sawyer	*Mark Twain*
✶ Treasure Island	*R.L. Stevenson*
✶ Twelfth Night	*William Shakespeare*
✶ Unto This Last	*John Ruskin*
✶ Utopia	*Thomas More*
✶ Wealth of Nations	*Adam Smith*
✶ Wonder that was India	*A.L. Basham*

INDIAN

Book	Author
* Ain-i-Akbari	*Abul Fazal*
* Anand Math	*Bankim Chandra Chatterjee*
* Arthashastra	*Kautilya*
* A Suitable Boy	*Vikram Seth*
* Bhagwat Gita	*Ved Vyas*
* Chidambara	*Sumitranandan Pant*
* Devdas	*Sarat Chandra Chatterjee*
* Discovery of India	*Jawaharlal Nehru*
* Ganadevata	*Tarashankar Bandopadhyaya*
* Geet Govind	*Jaya Dev*
* Geetanjali	*R. N. Tagore*
* Glimpses of World History	*Jawaharlal Nehru*
* Godaan	*Prem Chand*
* Gul-e-Nagma	*Firaq Gorakhpuri*
* Harsh Charita	*Bana Bhatta*
* India Divided	*Dr. Rajendra Prasad*
* Justice of Peace ke Aansu	Janardan Prasad Singh
* The Judgement	*Kuldip Nayyar*

Book	Author
* Kadambari	*Bana Bhatta*
* Kagaz Te Kanwas	*Amrita Pritam*
* Kamayani	*Jai Shankar Prasad*
* Kitni Nawon Mein Kitni Bar	*S. H. Vatsyayan*
* Kumar Sambhav	*Kalidas*
* Mahabharata	*Ved Vyas*
* Malgudi Days	*R.K. Narayan*
* Meghdoot	*Kalidas*
* Mritunjaya	*B.K. Bhattacharya*
* Mudrarakshasa	*Vishakhadatta*
* Prison Diary	*Jaya Prakash Narayan*
* Raghuvansha	*Kalidas*
* Rajtarangini	*Kalhana*
* Ramayana	*Balmiki*
* Ramcharit Manas	*Tulsidas*
* Rukh Te Rishi	*Harbhajan Singh*
* Satyarth Prakash	*Swami Dayanand*
* Sur Sagar	*Surdas*
* The Guide	*R.K. Narayan*

IMPORTANT DATES AND DAYS OF THE YEAR

*** JANUARY**

5-11 Road Safety Week
12 National Youth Day
15 Army Day
15-21 Pin Code Week
23 National Day of Patriotism
26 Republic Day
30 Martyr's Day

*** FEBRUARY**

1-14 Oil Conservation Fortnight
14 Valentine's Day

*** MARCH**

4 National Safety Day
8 International Women's Day
15 Consumers' Day
16 Immunisation Day
21 World Forest Day
22 World Day for Water
24 World Meteorological Day
1-7 Preservation of Blindness Week

*** APRIL**

7 World Health Day
7-13 Handloom Week
14-20 Fire Service Week
18 World Heritage Day
22 World Earth Day

*** MAY**

1 May Day
5 National Labour Day
8 World Red Cross Day
11 National Technology Day
15 International Day of the Family
17 World Telecommunication Day
24 Commonwealth Day
31 World No-Tobacco Day

*** JUNE**

5 World Environment Day
21 World Yoga Day
26 International Day against Drug Abuse and Illicit Trafficking

*** JULY**

11 World Population Day

*** AUGUST**

1-7 World Breast feeding Week
10 Sanskrit Divas
15 Independence Day
20 Sadbhavana Divas

*** SEPTEMBER**

1-7 National Nutrition Week
5 Teachers' Day
8 International Literary Day
14 Hindi Diwas

23 World Deaf Day
27 World Tourism Day

∗ OCTOBER

2 ∗ Gandhi Jayanti
∗ International Day of Non Violence
∗ Anti-Leprosy Day
4 World Animal Day
6 World Habitat Day *(Ist Monday)*
8 Indian Air Force Day
14 World Standard Day
15 International Day of Rural Women
16 World Food Day
24 United Nations Day
27 Infantry Day
28 World Thrift Day
31 Anti-Terrorism Day

∗ NOVEMBER

2 All Saints Day
14 Children's Day
15-21 National Cooperative Week
19-25 Quami Ekta Week
20 Child Rights Day
26 Constitution Day

∗ DECEMBER

1 World AIDS Day
3 World Day for the Disabled
4 Naval Day
7 Flag Day
8 SMRC Day
10 Human Rights Day
14 National Energy Conservation Day

INDIAN DEFENCE

- The Supreme Command of the Armed Forces is vested in the hands of the President of the Country.
- The responsibility for national defence, however, rests with the Cabinet. All important questions having a bearing on defence are decided by the Cabinet Committee on Political Affairs, which is presided over by the Prime Minister.
- The Defence Minister is responsible to Parliament for all matters concerning the Defence Services.
- All the administrative and operational control of Armed Forces are exercised by the Ministry of Defence. The three services—Army, Navy and Air Force function through their respective service head-quarters headed by the chief of Staff. The post of Chief of Defence Staff (CDS) was created in 2019.

Indian Army Commands

Command	*HQ Location*
Eastern Command	Kolkata
Western Command	Chandigarh
Northern Command	Udhampur
Southern Command	Pune
Central Command	Lucknow
Training Command	Shimla
South-Western Command	Jaipur

Indian Air Force Commands

Command	*HQ Location*
Western Air Command	New Delhi
Sout-Western Air Command	Gandhinagar
Central Air Command	Prayagraj
Eastern Air Command	Shillong
Southern Air Command	Thiruvananthapuram
Training Command	Bengaluru

Indian Navy Commands

Command	*HQ Location*
Eastern Naval Command	Vishakhapatnam
Western Naval Command	Mumbai
Southern Naval Command	Kochi

Commissioned Ranks in Defence Services

Army	*Navy*	*Air Force*
General	Admiral	Air Chief Marshal
Lieutenant-General	Vice-Admiral	Air Marshal
Major-General	Rear-Admiral	Air Vice-Marshal
Brigadier	Commodor	Air Commodor
Colonel	Captain	Group Captain
Lieutenant-Colonel	Commander	Wing Commander
Major	Lt.Commander	Squadron Leader
Captain	Lieutenant	Flight Lieutenant
Lieutenant	Sub-Lieutenant	Flying Officer

INDIAN CULTURE

☛ Dance

India has a very rich tradition of tribal, folk and classical dances.

☛ Classical Dance

Dance	State	Famous Artists
• Bharat Natyam	Tamil Nadu	Yamini Krishnamurthy, Rukmini Devi Arundale, Swapna Sundari, Sonal Mansingh, Vaijanti Mala, Mrinalini Sarabhai, Chandralekha, Indrani, Ram Gopal, Bal Saraswati
• Kathakali	Kerala	Gopinath, K.K. Nayar, Kunju-Kurup, T.K. Chandu
• Kuchipudi	Andhra Pradesh	Sapna Sundari, Raja Reddy, Radha Reddy, Vedantam Satyanarayan, Vimpanti Chinna Satyam.
• Kathak	North India	Birju Maharaj, Gopi Krishna, Shambhu Maharaj, Sitara Devi, Vishnu Sharma, Durga Lal, Shobhana Narayan
• Odissi	Odisha	Kelucharan Mahapatra, Indrani Rehman, Madhavi Mudgal, Pratima Bedi, Samyukta Panigrahi, Sonal Mansingh, Debudas
• Manipuri	Manipur	Uday Shankar, Bipin Singh, Suryamukhi, Darohra Jhaveri

☛ Famous Folk-Dance

- Andhra Pradesh: *Dandari, Banjara*
- Asom: *Bihu, Keli Gopal, Sataria*
- Bihar: *Chhau, Magahi, Durga dance*
- W. Bengal: *Kirtan, Kalatri, Asweabadh, Brita, Kalidance*
- Chhattisgarh: *Saila, Karama, Bhagoria*
- Gujarat: *Garba, Rasalila, Tippani, Dandia,*
- Haryana: *Damyal, Lahoor*
- Himachal Pradesh: *Dussehra dance, Hikat, Notio*
- Jammu & Kashmir: *Dumhal*
- Jharkhand: *Jhau, Ghumakudia, Jadur, Sarhul, Soharai, Karama, Vaima, Loojhari, Jat-Jatin, Vidayat*
- Karnataka: *Yakshagan, Dolu Kunitha*
- Kerala: *Mohini Attam, Padayuni*
- Madhya Pradesh: *Lota Nritya, Jawara*
- Maharashtra: *Tamasha, Dahi Handi, Gof, Deepak Dindi*
- Manipur: *Dhol Cholam*
- Meghalaya: *Nongakarem*
- Nagaland: *Bamboo dance*
- Odisha: *Chhau, Maya Shabari, Dalachai*
- Punjab: *Gidda, Bhangra, Panihari*
- Rajasthan: *Ghumar, Kathaputali, Tera Tali*
- Tamil Nadu: *Terukalathu, Kabalatam, Kargam, Pulivesham*
- Tripura: *Hazagiri*
- Uttar Pradesh: *Rasalila, Nautanki, Thali, Huraka, Dhurang, Jhumela, Bol.*
- Uttarakhand: *Kajari, Karan*
- Goa: *Dhode Modini*

☛ Musical Instruments and Artists

- **Flute:** Hari Prasad Chaurasia, Panna Lal Ghosh, T.R. Mahalingam, N. Ramani, Vijaya Raghava Rao
- **Tabla:** Allah Rakha, Gudai Maharaj, Latif Khan, Zakir Hussain
- **Violin:** Lalgudi Jayaraman, L. Subramaniam, M.S. Gopal Krishnan, S. Subrahmaniam, V.G. Jog, N. Rajan
- **Shehnai:** Bismilla Khan, Imrat Khan
- **Sarod:** Ali Akbar Khan, Amjad Ali Khan, Alauddin Khan, Saren Rani, Brij Narayan
- **Sitar:** Pandit Ravishankar, Vilayat Khan
- **Santur:** Shiv Kumar Sharma
- **Rudraveena:** Zia Mohiuddin Dagar
- **Pakhawaj:** Govind Rao, Anokhe Lal, Kanthi Maharaj
- **Mridanga:** Palghat R. Raghu, U.S. Burman
- **Harmonium:** Purushottam Walawakar, M. Dhaulpuri
- **Guitar:** Pt. Vishnu Mohan Bhatt, Brij Bhushan Kalra
- **Ghatam:** T.H. Vinayakaram
- **Janjira:** V. Nagarajan
- **Symphony:** Jubin Mehta

WORLD HERITAGE SITES IN INDIA

A World Heritage Site is a place that is listed by UNESCO for its special cultural or physical significance. The list of World Heritage Sites is maintained by the international 'World Heritage Programme', administered by the UNESCO World Heritage Committee. The United Nations Educational, Scientific and Cultural Organization (UNESCO) seeks to encourage the identification, protection and preservation of cultural and natural heritage around the world considered to be of outstanding value to humanity. This is embodied in an international treaty called the Convention concerning the Protection of the World Cultural and Natural Heritage, adopted by UNESCO in 1972. India has 40 world heritage sites that include 32 Cultural properties, 7 Natural properties and 1 mixed site.

Cultural Sites in India

- Agra Fort (1983)
- Ajanta Caves (1983)

- Archaeological Site of Nalanda Mahavihara at Nalanda, Bihar (2016)
- Buddhist Monuments at Sanchi (1989)
- Champaner-Pavagadh Archaeological Park (2004)
- Chhatrapati Shivaji Terminus (formerly Victoria Terminus) (2004)
- Churches and Convents of Goa (1986)
- Elephanta Caves (1987)
- Ellora Caves (1983)
- Fatehpur Sikri (1986)
- Great Living Chola Temples (1987, 2004)
- Group of Monuments at Hampi (1986)
- Group of Monuments at Mahabalipuram (1984)
- Group of Monuments at Pattadakal (1987)
- Hill Forts of Rajasthan (2013)
- Historic City of Ahmedabad (2017)
- Humayun's Tomb, Delhi (1993)
- Jaipur City, Rajasthan (2019)
- Khajuraho Group of Monuments (1986)
- Mountain Railways of India (1999, 2005, 2008)
- Mahabodhi Temple Complex at Bodh Gaya (2002)
- Qutub Minar and its Monuments, Delhi (1993)
- Rani-ki-Vav (the Queen's Stepwell) at Patan, Gujarat (2014)
- Red Fort Complex (2007)
- Rock Shelters of Bhimbetka (2003)
- Sun Temple, Konarak (1984)
- Taj Mahal (1983)
- The Architectural Work of Le Corbusier (2016)
- Victorian Gothic and Art Deco Ensembles of Mumbai (2018)
- The Jantar Mantar, Jaipur (2010)
- Dholavira : a Harappan City (2021)
- Kakatiya Rudreshwara (Ramappa) Temple, Telangana (2021)

Natural Sites in India

- Great Himalayan National Park Conservation Area (2014)
- Kaziranga National Park (1985)
- Keoladeo National Park (1985)
- Manas Wildlife Sanctuary (1985)
- Nanda Devi and Valley of Flowers National Parks (1988, 2005)
- Sundarban National Park (1987)
- Western Ghats (2012)

Mixed Site in India

- Khangchendzonga National Park (2016)

UNITED NATIONS (UN)

- The United Nations (UN) is an association of states which have pledged themselves to maintain international peace and security and cooperate in solving international political, economic, social cultural and humanitarian problems towards achieving this end.
- Trygve Lie of Norway (1946-52) was the first Secretary-General of the UN.
- ***Origin:*** UN Charter was signed by 50 members on June 26, 1945. Poland signed the charter later to become one of the original 51 member-states. It officially came into existence on October 24, 1945.
- ***UN Charter:*** The Charter is the Constitution of the UN and contains its aims and objectives and rules and regulations for its functioning.
- ***Aims and Objectives:*** They are security, welfare and human rights.
- ***Headquarters:*** New York.
- ***Flag:*** The flag is light blue in colour, and emblazoned in white, in its centre is the UN symbol—a polar map of world embraced by twin olive branches open at the top.
- ***Official Languages:*** The official languages of the UN are: English, French, Chinese, Russian, Arabic and Spanish. However, working languages are English and French only.
- ***Present Membership:*** At present 193 countries are members of the UN. South Sudan is the latest entrant to this world organisation.
- ***Main Organs of the UN:*** There are six main organs:
  1. General Assembly
  2. Security Council
  3. Economic and Social Council
  4. Trusteeship Council
  5. International Court of Justice, and
  6. Secretariat.

1. *General Assembly:* It consists of representative of all members of the UN. Each member country has only one vote. It meets once a year and passes UN Budget. It is the main place for discussions and policy making in the UN.

2. *Security Council:* It is the Executive body of the UN and is mainly responsible for maintaining international peace and security. It has 15 members, 5 of which (USA, UK, France, Russia and China) are permanent members. The 10 non-permanent members are elected by General Assembly for two-year term and are not eligible for immediate re-election.
3. *Economic and Social Council:* It has 54 members elected by General Assembly.
4. *Trusteeship Council:* It looks after interest of the people in areas not yet independent and leads them towards self-government.
5. *International Court of Justice:* It has 15 judges, no two of whom may be nationals of the same state. They are elected by General Assembly and Security Council for a term of 9 years. The Court elects its President and Vice-President for a 3-year term.
6. *Secretariat:* It is the Secretariat of the UN and is headed by the Secretary General.

AWARDS AND HONOURS

NATIONAL AWARDS

BHARAT RATANA

- Bharat Ratna is India's highest Civilian Award. It was first awarded in 1954.
- The actual award is designed in the shape of a *peepal* leaf with Bharat Ratna inscribed in Devanagri script in the Sun Figure.
- This is India's highest civilian award. It is given for exceptional work on art, literature, science and recognition of public service of the highest order.
- The emblem, the Sun and the rim are of platinum. The inscriptions are in burnished bronze.
- Government servants are not eligible for it. The table shows the recipients of the award:

Bharat Ratna Award Winners

1.	Dr. S. Radhakrishnan	1954
2.	C. Rajagopalachari	1954
3.	Dr. C.V. Raman	1954
4.	Dr. Bhagwan Das	1955
5.	Dr. M. Visvesvaraya	1955
6.	Jawahar Lal Nehru	1955
7.	Govind Ballabh Pant	1957
8.	Dr. D.K. Karve	1958
9.	Dr. Bidhan Chandra Roy	1961
10.	Purushottam Das Tandon	1961
11.	Dr. Rajendra Prasad	1962
12.	Dr. Zakir Hussain	1963
13.	Dr. Pandurang Vaman Kane	1963
14.	Lal Bahadur Shastri	1966
15.	Indira Gandhi	1971
16.	V.V. Giri	1975
17.	K. Kamraj	1976
18.	Mother Teresa	1980
19.	Acharya Vinoba Bhave	1983
20.	Khan Abdul Ghaffar Khan	1987
21.	M.G. Ramachandran	1988
22.	Dr. B.R. Ambedkar	1990
23.	Dr. Nelson R. Mandela	1990
24.	Rajiv Gandhi	1991
25.	Sardar Vallabhbhai Patel	1991
26.	Morarji R. Desai	1991
27.	Maulana Abul Kalam Azad	1992
28.	Jehangir Ratanji Dadabhai Tata	1992
29.	Satyajit Roy	1992
30.	Shri Gulzari Lal Nanda	1997
31.	Mrs. Aruna Asaf Ali	1997
32.	Dr. A.P.J. Abdul Kalam	1997
33.	M.S. Subbalakshmi	1998
34.	C. Subramaniam	1998
35.	Jaya Prakash Narayan	1999
36.	Prof. Amartya Sen	1999
37.	Pt. Ravi Shankar	1999
38.	Gopinath Bardoloi	1999
39.	Lata Mangeshkar	2001
40.	Bismillah Khan	2001
41.	Bhimsen Joshi	2009
42.	C.N.R. Rao	2014
43.	Sachin Tendulkar	2014
44.	Pt. Madan Mohan Malaviya	2015
45.	Atal Bihari Vajpayee	2015
46.	Pranab Mukherjee	2019
47.	Nanaji Deshmukh	2019
48.	Bhupen Hazarika	2019

REPUBLIC DAY AWARDS

Padma Awards

They fall in line after the Bharat Ratna. They are also discontinued in 1977 along with the Bharat Ratna and award was started again in 1980.

There are three Padma Awards:

- ***Padma Vibhushan:*** This award is given for exceptional and distinguished service in any field, including service rendered by Govt. servants.
- ***Padma Bhushan:*** This award is given for distinguished service of a high order in any field, including service rendered by Govt. servants.
- ***Padma Shri:*** This award is given for distinguished service in any field, including service rendered by Government servants.

Gallantry Awards

- ***Param Vir Chakra:*** The highest award for bravery or some daring and pre-eminent act of valour or self-sacrifice in the presence of the enemy, whether on land, at sea or in the air.
- ***Mahavir Chakra:*** It is the second highest decoration and is awarded for acts of conspicuous gallantry in the presence of the enemy, whether on land, at sea or in the air.
- ***Vir Chakra:*** It is the third in order of awards given for acts of gallantry in the presence of enemy, whether on land, at sea or in the air.
- ***Ashok Chakra:*** This medal is awarded for the most conspicuous bravery or some daring or pre-eminent act of valour or self-sacrifice on land, at sea or in the air but not in the presence of enemy.
- ***Vishishta Sewa Medal:*** It is awarded to personnel of all the three Services in class I, II and III in recognition of distinguished service of the "most exceptional" and "exceptional" and a "high" order respectively. Prefixes Parma and Ati are added before first two categories of medals respectively.
- ***Jeewan Raksha Padak:*** Awarded for meritorious acts or a series of acts of a human nature displayed in saving life from drowning, fire and rescue operations in mines etc.

OTHER NATIONAL AWARDS

SAHITYA AKADEMI AWARDS

- These prizes are awarded annually to the authors of the most outstanding books of literary merit published in each of the 22 languages recognised by the Akademi.
- There are also two awards for Sanskrit and English. The award, in form of a casket containing an inscribed copper plate and a cheque of ₹ 1 lakh is given to the author or his/her heir.

DADA SAHEB PHALKE AWARD

- The award carries a cash prize of ₹ 10 lakh, a Shawl and Swarna Kamal. Mrs Devika Rani Roerich was the first person to receive Dadasaheb Phalke Award in 1969.
- The Award for 2020 has been given to Asha Parekh.
- The award for 2019 has been given to Rajinikanth.

BHARATIYA JNANPITH AWARD

- Instituted in 22nd May, 1961, carries a cash prize of ₹ 11 lakh, a citation and a bronze replica of Vagdevi (Saraswati).
- Instituted by a literary organisation in India.

SARASWATI SAMMAN

- Given for outstanding literary works, value ₹ 15 lakh.

KALINGA PRIZE

- This award is given each year by the UNESCO and founded by former Odisha Chief Minister late Shri Biju Patnaik for popularisation of science.

INTERNATIONAL AWARDS

NOBEL PRIZES

- These Prizes were instituted in 1901 by a Swedish scientist, Dr. Alfred Nobel; the discoverer of Dynamite.
- Six prizes are awarded annually for (*i*) Chemistry, (*ii*) Physics, (*iii*) Medicine, (*iv*) Literature, (*v*) Peace and (*vi*) Economics—started since 1969.
- Five Indians so far have been awarded these Prizes, (*i*) Rabindranath Tagore for literature in 1913 for his work 'Gitanjali', (*ii*) C. V. Raman for Physics in 1930, (*iii*) Mother Teresa for Peace in 1979, (*iv*) Prof. Amartya Sen for Economics in 1998, (*v*) Kailash Satyarthi for Peace in 2014.
- In addition, four non-resident Indians have also been awarded the Nobel Prize. They are: (*i*) Hargobind Khurana for Medicine in 1968, (*ii*) Subramanian Chandrasekhar for Physics in 1983, (*iii*) Venkatraman Ramkrishnan for Chemistry in 2009, (iv) Abhijit Vinayak Banerjee for Economics in 2019.

GANDHI PEACE PRIZE

- The government instituted this ₹ 1 crore prize on the lines of the Nobel Peace Prize in 1995.
- It is the highest Civilian International award by the Govt. of India.

MAN BOOKER INTERNATIONAL AWARD

- The Man Booker International Prize was established in 2005, biannually rewarding an author for a body of work originally written in any language as long as it was widely available in English.
- From 2016, the prize became a translation prize, awarded annually for a single work of fiction, translated into English and published in the UK. Underlining the importance of translation, the £ 50,000 prize is divided equally between the author and the translator.

Highest Honours of Some Countries

Country	Highest Honour
India	Bharat Ratna
Pakistan	Nishan-e-Pakistan
Kuwait	Mubarak-Al-kabir Medal
Saudi Arabia	Shah Abdul Aziz Medal
Argentina	The Order of Sona Martin
Nicaragua	Augusto-Caesar Sandino Order
Vietnam	The Order of the Golden Star
Hungary	The Order of Banner
Britain	Member of British Empire, Victoria Cross
Japan	Order of Moulovenice Sun
Denmark	Order of Diana Brog
France	Legend of Honour
America	Presidential Medal of Freedom
Germany	Pore Lee Merit Iron Cross
The Netherlands	Netherlands Lion

SPORTS

OLYMPICS

- First of all these games were held by the Greeks in 776 B.C. on Mount Olympus in honour of the Greek God Zeus. In this way, the history of Olympic Games is about twenty eight hundred years old. These games continued to be held every four years until 394 A.D. when these games were stopped by a royal order of the emperor of Rome.
- The modern Olympic Games which started in Athens in 1896, are the result of the devotion and dedication of a French educator Baron Pierre de Coubertin and the first Olympic meet in the modern series was held in 1896 in Athens, the Capital of Greece. Since then, they are being held every four years except for breaks during world wars.
- The Olympic flag is white in colour with five coloured rings, each ring symbolic of a continent. Summer as well as Winter Olympics are held in the same year.
- The 2020 Olympic Games was held at Tokyo, Japan in 2021.
- The official Olympic Motto is *Citius, Altius, Swifter, Higher, Stronger*. The Head Office of International Olympic Committee (IOC) is at Lausanne (Switzerland).

COMMONWEALTH GAMES

- The Commonwealth Games are held every four years, in the year in which Asian Games are held. All the Commonwealth Countries (former colonies of Britain) can take part in it.
- The first Commonwealth Games were held in 1930 at Hamilton (Canada).
- There are currently 56 members of the Commonwealth of Nations, and 72 teams participated in the games.
- The 2022 Commonwealth Games, officially known as the XXII Commonwealth Games or Birmingham, 2022, held in Birmingham, England between 28 July to 8 August 2022.

ASIAN GAMES

- After the Second World War, most of the Asian Countries gained independence. On the lines of Olympic Games, Asian Games were planned every four years.
- India hosted the first Asian Games in 1951.

WORLD CUP CRICKET

- The first Cricket World Cup was organised in England in 1975. A separate women's Cricket World Cup has been held every 4 years since 1973.

List of Cricket World Cup

Year	Venue	Winner/Runner
1975	England	*West Indies beat Australia*
1979	England	*West Indies beat England*
1983	England	*India beat West Indies*
1987	India & Pakistan	*Australia beat England*
1992	Australia	*Pakistan beat England*
1996	India, Pakistan & Sri Lanka	*Sri Lanka beat Australia*
1999	England	*Australia beat Pakistan*
2003	South Africa	*Australia beat India*
2007	West Indies	*Australia beat Sri Lanka*
2011	India, Sri Lanka, Bangladesh	*India beat Sri Lanka*
2015	Australia, New Zealand	*Australia beat New Zealand*
2019	England	*England beat New Zealand*

HOCKEY WORLD CUP

- The first Hockey World Cup was organised in Barcelona (Spain) in 1971. Women's Hockey World Cup has been held since 1974.

FOOTBALL WORLD CUP

- The Football World Cup is organised by FIFA (Federation of International Football Association). The World Cup is called 'Jules Rimet Cup' named after the name of FIFA President Jules Rimet. The first Football World Cup was organised in Uruguay in 1930.
- In 1942 and 1946, the Football World Cup was not played due to World War II.
- Brazil is the only nation to have participated in every World Cup so far.

IMPORTANT CUPS & TROPHIES

International

- *American Cup* : Yacht Racing
- *Ashes* : Cricket
- *Davis Cup* : Lawn Tennis
- *Derby* : Horse Race
- *Grand National* : Horse Streple Chase Race
- *Jules Rimet Trophy* : World Soccer Cup
- *King's Cup* : Air Races
- *Merdeka Cup* : Football
- *Swaythling Cup* : Table Tennis (Men)
- *Ryder Cup* : Golf
- *Thomas Cup* : Badminton
- *U. Thant Cup* : Tennis
- *Walker Cup* : Golf
- *Wightman Cup* : Lawn Tennis
- *Rothman's Trophy* : Cricket
- *European Champions Cup* : Football
- *Grand Prix* : Table Tennis
- *Edgbaston Cup* : Lawn Tennis
- *Grand Prix* : Lawn Tennis

National

* *Agha Khan Cup* : Hockey
* *Beighton Cup* : Hockey
* *Bombay Gold Cup* : Hockey
* *C.K. Naydu Trophy* : Cricket
* *Deodhar Trophy* : Cricket
* *Duleep Trophy* : Cricket
* *Durand Cup* : Football
* *Dhyan Chand Trophy* : Hockey
* *Dr. B.C. Roy Trophy* : Football (Junior)
* *Ezra Cup* : Polo
* *Guru Nanak Cup* : Hockey
* *Holkar Trophy* : Bridge
* *Irani Trophy* : Cricket
* *Indira Gold Cup* : Hockey
* *Murugappa Gold Cup* : Hockey
* *Nehru Trophy* : Hockey
* *Nixan Gold Cup* : Football
* *Rani Jhansi Trophy* : Cricket
* *Ranji Trophy* : Cricket
* *Rangaswami Cup* : Hockey
* *Ramanujan Trophy* : Table Tennis
* *Rene Frank Trophy* : Hockey
* *Rohinton Baria Trophy* : Cricket
* *Rovers Cup* : Football
* *Santosh Trophy* : Football
* *Subroto Cup* : Football

SPORTS TERMS

* ***Badminton:*** Mixed doubles; Deuce; Drop; Smash; Let; Foot work; Setting.
* ***Base Ball:*** Pitcher; Put out, Strike; Home; Bunt.
* ***Billiards:*** Cue; Jigger; Pot; Break; In Baulk; In Off; Cannons.
* ***Boxing:*** Upper cut; Round; Punch; Bout; Knock down; Hitting below the belt; Ring.
* ***Bridge:*** Finesse; Dummy; Revoke; Grand Slam; Little Slam; No Trump; Rubber.
* ***Chess:*** Bishop, Gambit; Checkmate; Stalemate.
* ***Cricket:*** L.B.W. (leg before wicket); Creases, Popping-creases; Stumped; Bye; Leg-Bye; Googly; Hattrick; Maiden over; Drive; Bowling; Duck; Follow-on; No ball; Leg Break; Silly point; Cover point; Hit-wicket; Late-cut; Slip; Off-spinner; In-swing.
* ***Football:*** Off Side; Block; Drop-kick; Penalty-kick (or goal kick); Corner-kick; Free-kick; Dribble; Thrown-in; Foul.
* ***Golf:*** Boggy; Foursome; Stymic; Tee; Put; Hole; Niblic; Caddie; Links; The green; Bunker.
* ***Hockey:*** Carried; Short Corner; Bully; Sticks; Off side; Roll in; Striking Circle; Under-cutting; Dribble.
* ***Horse racing:*** Jockey; Punter.
* ***Polo:*** Bunker; Chukker; Mallet.
* ***Tennis:*** Back hand drive; Volley; Smash; Half-volley; Deuce; Service; Let; Grand Slam.

Stadiums and Places Associated with Sports

Name of Stadium	*Sports*	*Place*
Narendra Modi Stadium	Cricket	Ahmedabad
Arun Jaitley Stadium	Cricket	Delhi
Jawaharlal Nehru Stadium	Athletics	Delhi
Shivajee Stadium	Hockey	Delhi
National Stadium	Hockey etc.	Delhi
Ambedkar Stadium	Football	Delhi
Brabourne Stadium	Cricket	Mumbai
Wankhede Stadium	Cricket	Mumbai
National Stadium	Hockey etc.	Mumbai
Eden Garden	Cricket	Kolkata
Green Park Stadium	Cricket	Kanpur
Keenan Stadium	Cricket	Jamshedpur
Nehru (Chepauk) Stadium	Cricket	Chennai
Barabati Stadium	Cricket	Cuttack
Lords, Oval, Leeds	Cricket	Britain
Hedingle Manchester	Cricket	Britain
Black Heath	Rugby Football	London
Henley	Boat race	England
Wimbledon	Lawn Tennis	London
Wembley Stadium	Football	London
White City	Dog-race	England
Aintree	Horse-race	England
Tentbridge	Cricket	England
Patnee Martlake	Boat-race	England
Tibankham	Rugby Football	England
Sandy Lodge	Golf	Scotland
Forest Hill	Tennis	New York
Brooklyn	Baseball	New York
Melbourne	Cricket	Australia

Name of Playing Compound of Different Games

Name of Compound	Related Sports
Court	Lawn Tennis, Badminton, Netball, Hand ball, Volleyball, Squash, Kho-Kho, Kabaddi
Diamond	Baseball
Ring	Boxing, Skating, Wrestling, Circus, Riding display
Course	Golf
Board	Table Tennis
Pool	Swimming
Alley	Bowling
Mat	Judo, Karate II
Arena	Horse Riding
Vellodrum	Cycling
Field	Polo, Football, Hockey
Track	Athletics
Pitch	Cricket, Rugby
Rink	Ice Hockey

7

Multiple Choice Questions

1. Match List-I with List-II and select the correct answer from the codes given below the lists:

List-I	List-II
(*a*) Napoleon Bonaparte	1. 'A history is contemporary history'
(*b*) Jean Jacques Rousseau	2. 'Liberty what crimes are committed in thy name'
(*c*) Croce	3. 'Man is born free but everywhere he is in chains.'
(*d*) Madame Roland	4. 'I am the Child of Revolution'

Codes :

	(*a*)	(*b*)	(*c*)	(*d*)
A.	1	2	3	4
B.	4	3	1	2
C.	3	4	2	1
D.	3	4	1	2

2. Abraham Lincon was elected the President of United States in:
A. 1862 B. 1860
C. 1875 D. 1855

3. Who was known as the 'Prince of Humanists'?
A. Francisco Petrarch B. Dante
C. Boccacio D. Erasmus

4. D-Day is the day when:
A. Germany declared war on Britain
B. US dropped the atom bomb on Hiroshima.
C. Allied Troops landed in Normandy
D. Germany surrendered to the allies

5. Whose teachings inspired the French Revolution?
A. Locke B. Rousseau
C. Hegel D. Plato

6. At a time when empires in Europe were crumbling before the might of Napoleon which one of the following Governor-Generals kept the British flag flying high in India?
A. Warren Hastings B. Lord Cornwallis
C. Lord Wellesley D. Lord Hastings

7. Which one of the following statements regarding Fascism in Italy is *not* true?
A. The Fascists came to power as a result of popular uprising
B. In 1926, all political parties except Mussolini's party were banned
C. The Fascists suppressed the Socialist movement
D. The Fascists were hostile to the Communists

8. The fall of Czar Nicholas-II is known as:
A. Bloody Sunday
B. Bolshevik Revolution
C. February Revolution
D. October Revolution

9. Industrial Revolution took place first in:
A. France B. Germany
C. United Kingdom D. Japan

10. The British Prime Minister at the outbreak of World War II was :
A. Churchill B. Baldwin
C. Attlee D. Chemberlain

11. The 'Great Depression' (1929) economic crisis was met by adopting the policy of
A. Stimulus B. Marshall Plan
C. New Deal D. Open Door

12. The slogan "No taxation without representation" was raised during the:
A. American War of Independence
B. Russian Revolution
C. French Revolution
D. Indian Freedom struggle

13. In the nineteenth century the people of Europe started moving from the villages to the cities due to the impact of :
A. Epidemics
B. War
C. Industrialisation
D. Population explosion in villages

14. The important cause of the Civil War in America was:
A. Abolition of slavery
B. Quest for freedom
C. Industrialisation
D. Rebellion by the native Americans

15. Industrial Revolution could not have come about without:
A. Merchant capitalism
B. The Enclosure Movement
C. The services of the proletariat class
D. An agricultural revolution

16. Consider the following statements :
The French Revolution came about mainly due to the:
1. Extreme poverty of the people
2. Impact of the works of great writers
3. Cruelty of the rulers
4. Impact of impulsive reaction

Which of the above statements are correct?
A. 1, 2 and 4 B. 2 and 3
C. 1, 3 and 4 D. 1, 2, 3 and 4

17. Asia's oldest and largest Buddhist monastery is situated in :
A. Tawang (Arunachal Pardesh)
B. Lhasa (Tibet)
C. Trincomallee (Sri Lanka)
D. Ulan Bator (Mongolia)

18. Who was the main architect of the Russian Revolution?
A. Karl Marx B. Lenin
C. Stalin D. Tolstoy

19. V.I. Lenin is associated with :
A. Russian Revolution of 1917
B. Chinese Revolution of 1949
C. German Revolution
D. French Revolution of 1789

20. Which one of the following statements is *not* correct?
A. Voltaire believed in Natural Religion
B. Rousseau wrote *Social Contract*
C. Montesquieu authored *The Spirit of Laws*
D. Necker believed in 'General Will'

21. 6th April, 1930 is well known in the history of India because this date is associated with...........
A. Dandi March by Mahatma Gandhi
B. Quit India Movement
C. Partition of Bengal
D. Partition of India

22. Which ruler enforced the system of 'Price Control' in India?
A. Mohammad Tughlak B. Razia Begum
C. Alauddin Khilji D. Sher Shah Suri

23. The concept of 'Din-e-Elahi' was founded by which king?
A. Dara Shikoh B. Akbar
C. Sher Shah Suri D. Shahjahan

24. Who are supposed to be the earliest inhabi-tants of India? Where did they come from?
A. Aryans from Central Asia
B. Dravidians from Mediterranean
C. Negroids from Africa
D. Bhils and the Santhals from West Asia

25. The one chief characteristic of temple architecture of the Gupta Age was :
A. Absence of dome
B. Huge size
C. Beautiful carvings
D. absence of a covered courtyard for the gathering of worshippers

26. The Rigveda consists of :
A. 1000 hymns B. 2028 hymns
C. 1028 hymns D. 1038 hymns

27. The central point in Ashoka's dharma was :
A. royalty to kings B. peace and non-violence
C. respect to elders D. religious tolerance

28. The social evil which was conspicuously absent during ancient India was :
A. *Sati*-System B. *Devadasi*-System
C. Polygamy D. *Purdah*-System

29. Which, among the following, can be accepted as a novelty introduced by Mughal emperors to their buildings?
A. Domes B. Minarets
C. Arches D. Attached gardens

30. The first ruler of India who defeated Muhammud of Ghur was :
A. Mularaja II of Gujarat
B. Prithviraja Chauhan of Delhi
C. Jayachand of Kannauj
D. Parmaldeva of Bundelkhand

31. What important event happened in India in 1911?
A. Bengal was partitioned
B. Non-Cooperation movement was launched
C. India's capital was shifted from Calcutta to Delhi
D. Mahatma Gandhi presided over the Congress session

32. The first phase of the Congress Party (1885-1905) was characterized by its efforts to secure:
A. limited independence
B. complete freedom
C. Indianization of services
D. constitutional reforms

33. The Muslim League demanded a separate homeland for the Indian Muslims openly for the first time at its annual session held in Lahore in the year :
A. 1931 A.D. B. 1936 A.D.
C. 1940 A.D. D. 1941 A.D.

34. Under whose governorship did the East India Company secure the Diwani Rights in Bengal, Bihar and Odisha from Emperor Shah Alam?
A. Lord Cornwallis B. Lord William Bentinck
C. Lord Clive D. Lord Wellesley

35. The Simon Commission was generally boycotted by the Indian political parties. What was the reason for this general non-cooperation?
A. the Commission aimed at dividing the people
B. it was an 'all white' Commission
C. it came after the Jallianwala Bagh carnage
D. it was an eye wash

36. Aligarh Muslim University was founded by :
A. Dr. Saifuddin Kitchlu
B. Mohammad Ali Jinnah
C. Sir Syed Ahmed Khan
D. Maulana Mohammad Ali

37. Ibn Batutah was an African traveller visiting India during the time of :
A. Alivardi Khan
B. Ala-ud-din Khalji
C. Iltutmish
D. Mohammad-bin-Tughlaq

38. The battle of Wandiawash was fought in :
A. 1726 B. 1760
C. 1818 D. 1857

39. The abolition of *Sati* by government regulation was at the time of :
A. Warren Hastings B. Lord Wellesley
C. Lord Bentinck D. Lord Ahmerst

40. Pick out the wrong combination :
A. Dilwara Temple : Mt. Abu
B. Pashupati Temple : Kathmandu
C. Padmanabh Temple : Bangalore
D. Minakshi Temple : Madurai

41. Match the following:
(*a*) Chanhudaro (*b*) Kalibangan
(*c*) Lothal (*d*) Surkotada
1. Alleged discovery of the skeleton of horse.
2. Bead making.
3. Traces of a dock and ship on seal.
4. Evidence of ploughing the fields.

The Correct code is :

	(*a*)	(*b*)	(*c*)	(*d*)
A.	2	4	3	1
B.	2	1	3	4
C.	1	2	3	4
D.	2	1	4	3

42. Match the Harappan settlements with the banks of rivers on which they were located :
(*a*) Harappa 1. Ravi
(*b*) Mohenjodaro 2. Indus
(*c*) Ropar 3. Sutlej
(*d*) Kalibangan 4. Ghaggar
(*e*) Lothal 5. Bhogava

Codes :

	(*a*)	(*b*)	(*c*)	(*d*)	(*e*)
A.	1	2	3	4	5
B.	1	2	3	5	4
C.	2	1	3	5	4
D.	2	1	4	3	5

43. The Goddess 'Kannagi' whose many temples were erected during the 'Sangam Age' was the goddess of:
A. Chastity B. Love
C. Prowess D. Wisdom

44. The Jain goal of life is to attain deliverance from the fetters of mudane existence, the way to which lies through three jewels. Which one of the following was not included among the 'three jewels' of Jainism?
A. Right faith B. Right action
C. Right knowledge D. Right conduct

45. The most striking feature of the Ashokan pillar is polish. Name the Ashokan pillar which is considered to be the most graceful of all Ashokan pillars.
A. Sarnath B. Rampurva
C. Laurya-Nandangarh D. Rummindei

46. Which are the correct statements?
1. The land grants, started in Satavahana period, paved the way for feudal developments in India.
2. Silk and spices were the Chief Indian export articles of Indo-Roman trade.
3. The Guptas issued the largest number of gold coins in ancient India.
4. The first memorial of a 'SATI' dated 510 A.D. is found at Eran in Madhya Pradesh.

A. 1 and 2 B. 1, 3, and 4
C. 1 and 4 D. 1, 2, 3 and 4

47. Who among the following patronised the 'Gandhara' (Indo-Greek style) School of Art?
A. Ashoka, the Great
B. Harsha Vardhana
C. Kanishka
D. Chandragupta Vikramaditya

48. The Sultanate of Delhi had five ruling dynasties. The dynasty having longest and shortest period were :
A. Ilbari and Khalji B. Tughlaq and Khalji
C. Tughlaq and Sayyid D. Ilbari and Lodis

49. Which one of the following events took place at the last during reign of Muhammad-bin-Tughlaq?
A. Introduction of token currency
B. Increase of land-revenue in Doab
C. Transfer of Capital from Delhi to Devagiri.
D. Conquest of Khurasan and Iraq

50. The most learned medieval Muslim ruler who was well versed in various branches of learning including astronomy, mathematics and medicine was :
A. Jalaluddin Khilji B. Sikander Lodi
C. Ghiyasuddin Tughlaq D. Muhammad-bin-Tughlaq

51. The 'Sufis' had 12 silsilas. They propounded the idea of Union with God through:
A. Love B. Rituals
C. Fasts D. Prayers

52. Match the following:
(*a*) Peshwa 1. Foreign affairs
(*b*) Panditrao 2. Audit and accounts
(*c*) Amatya 3. Providing grants to scholars
(*d*) Sumant 4. General supervision
5. Military affairs

Select the correct code :

	(a)	(b)	(c)	(d)
A.	2	3	4	5
B.	4	1	2	3
C.	4	3	2	1
D.	3	1	4	2

53. The Regulating Act of 1773 can be regarded as the first measure to :
A. assert the right of British Parliament to legislate for India
B. separate the legislature from the executive
C. separate the judiciary from the executive
D. centralise law-making

54. What was the exact constitutional status of the Indian Republic on 26th January, 1950?
A. A Democratic Republic
B. A Sovereign, Democratic Republic
C. A Sovereign, Secular, Democratic Republic
D. A Sovereign, Socialist, Secular, Democratic Republic

55. When the British obtained the grant of Diwani of Bengal, Bihar and Odisha they acquired the right to:
A. maintain law and order in these territories
B. administer civil justice and collect revenue in these territories
C. collect revenue and establish revenue administration in these territories
D. militarily defend these territories

56. Which of the following were responsible for the growth of nationalism in India during the British rule?
1. Economic exploitation of India.
2. Impact of western education.
3. Role of the Press.
Select the correct answer using the codes given below :
Codes:
A. 1, 2 and 3 B. 1 and 2
C. 2 and 3 D. 1 and 3

57. Which one of the following nationalist leaders has been described as being radical in politics but conservative on social issues?
A. G.K. Gokhale B. B.G. Tilak
C. Lala Lajpat Rai D. Madan Mohan Malviya

58. Provincial Autonomy in British India was envisaged by the :
A. Act of 1909 B. Act of 1919
C. Act of 1935 D. Act of 1947

59. Dyarchy means :
A. double government
B. a government in which the centre is very powerful
C. a government based on division of power between centre and provinces
D. None of the above

60. The Indian National Congress observed 'Independence Day' for the first time on 26th January in :
A. 1920 B. 1925
C. 1930 D. 1947

61. ....is situated near the banks of Sabarmati River
A. Bhavnagar B. Aurangabad
C. Ahmedabad D. Rajkot

62. Sericulture is:
A. science of the various kinds of serum
B. artificial rearing of fish
C. art of silkworm breeding
D. study of various cultures of a community

63. The most abundant constituents of earth's crust are:
A. Igneous rocks B. Sedimentary rocks
C. Metamorphic rocks D. Granite

64. Indian Standard Time is based on:
A. 80°E longitude B. 82½°E longitude
C. 110°E longitude D. 25°E longitude

65. Tides in the oceans are caused by :
A. Gravitational pull of the moon on the earth's surface including sea water
B. Gravitational pull of the sun on the earth's surface only and not on the sea water
C. Gravitational pull of the moon and the sun on the earth's surface including the sea water
D. None of these

66. Nagarjunasagar Project is situated on the river:
A. Tungabhadra B. Cauvery
C. Krishna D. Godavari

67. The difference between the Indian Standard Time and the Greenwich Mean Time is:
A. – 3½ hours B. + 3½ hours
C. – 5½ hours D. + 5½ hours

68. Which of the following dams is not on Narmada river?
A. Indira-Sagar Project
B. Maheshwar Hydel Power Project
C. Jobat Project
D. Koyna Power Project

69. Which of the following statements is **not true** about the availability of water on the earth, the crisis for which is going to increase in the years to come?
A. About 97.5 per cent of the total volume of water available on the earth is salty
B. 80 per cent of the water available to us for use comes in bursts as monsoons
C. About 2.5 per cent of the total water available on the earth is polluted water and cannot be used for human activities
D. Possibility is that some big glaciers will melt in the coming ten-fifteen years and sea level will rise by 3-4 metres all over the earth

70. Which of the following is **not** a cash crop?
A. Jute B. Paddy
C. Cashewnut D. Sugarcane

71. Through which States does Cauvery River flow?
A. Gujarat, M.P., Tamil Nadu
B. Karnataka, Kerala, Tamil Nadu
C. Karnataka, Kerala, Andhra Pradesh
D. M.P., Maharashtra, Tamil Nadu

72. Indian Standard Time is the local time of 82½°E which passes through :
A. Guntur B. Delhi
C. Allahabad D. Kolkata

73. The 17th parallel defines the boundary between:
A. North and South Korea
B. USA and Canada
C. North and South Vietnam
D. China and Russia

74. During the period of south-west monsoon, Tamil Nadu remains dry because:
A. the winds do not reach this area
B. there are no mountains in this area
C. it lies in the rain shadow area
D. the temperature is too high to let the winds cool down

75. Which country does top in producing cocoa?
A. Ivory Coast B. Brazil
C. Ghana D. Nigeria

76. The biggest reserves of thorium are in :
A. India B. China
C. Russia D. U.S.A.

77. The Girnar Hills are situated in which of the following states?
A. Gujarat B. Karnataka
C. Madhya Pradesh D. Maharashtra

78. During December 22nd the sun is vertically over:
A. Tropic of Cancer B. Tropic of Capricorn
C. The Equator D. None of the above

79. Photosphere is described as the :
A. Lower layer of atmosphere
B. Visible surface of the sun from which radiation emanates
C. Wavelength of solar spectrum
D. None of the above

80. Broadly, there are three layers of the earth of the crust, the mantle and the core. The crust forms what percentage of the volume of the earth?
A. 0.5% B. 2.5%
C. 7.5% D. 12.5%

81. The grassland of Argentina is known as :
A. Pampas B. Campos
C. Savanna D. None of the above

82. Different seasons are formed because :
A. Sun is moving around the earth
B. of revolution of the earth around the Sun on its orbit
C. of rotation of the earth around its axis
D. All of the above

83. Eskers and Drumlins are features formed by:
A. underground water B. running water
C. the action of wind D. glacial action

84. Match List-I and List-II and select the correct answer using the codes given below the Lists :

List-I *(Rivers)*	**List-II** *(Towns)*
(*a*) Ghaghara	1. Lucknow
(*b*) Brahmaputra	2. Hoshangabad
(*c*) Narmada	3. Ahmedabad
(*d*) Sabarmati	4. Guwahati
	5. Ayodhya

Codes :

	(*a*)	(*b*)	(*c*)	(*d*)
A.	4	5	1	2
B.	5	4	2	3
C.	5	4	3	1
D.	3	5	2	1

85. Which of the statements as regards the consequences of the movement of the earth is not correct?
A. Revolution of the earth is the cause of the change of seasons.
B. Rotation of the earth is the cause of days and nights.
C. Rotation of the earth causes variation in the duration of days and nights.
D. Rotation of the earth effects the movement of winds and ocean currents.

86. The world is divided into :
A. 12 time zones B. 20 time zones
C. 24 time zones D. 36 time zones

87. The 'Kiel' canal links the :
A. Pacific and Atlantic Oceans
B. Mediterranean Sea and Red Sea
C. Mediterranean Sea and Black Sea
D. North Sea and Baltic Sea

88. Match the following :

List-I	**List-II**
(*a*) Himadri	1. Outer Himalayas
(*b*) Shivalik	2. Inner Himalayas
(*c*) Himanchal	3. Middle Himalayas
(*d*) Sahyadri	4. Western Ghats

Codes :

	(*a*)	(*b*)	(*c*)	(*d*)
A.	1	2	3	4
B.	4	2	3	1
C.	2	1	3	4
D.	1	2	3	4

89. The term 'Regur' refers to:
A. Laterite soils
B. Black Cotton soils
C. Red Soils
D. Deltaic Alluvial Soils

90. Location of sugar industry in India is shifting from north to south because of:
A. cheap labour
B. expanding regional market
C. cheap and abundant supply of power
D. high yield and high sugar content in sugarcane

91. Consider the following statements :
1. Ozone is found mostly in the Stratosphere.
2. Ozone layer lies 55-75 km above the surface of the earth.
3. Ozone absorbs ultraviolet radiation from the Sun.
4. Ozone layer has no significance for life on the earth.

Which of the above statements are correct?
A. 1 and 3 B. 2 and 4
C. 2 and 3 D. 1 and 4

92. Match List-I with List-II and select the correct answer using the codes given below the Lists :

List-I (Crops)	***List-II (Producer)***
(*a*) Banana	1. Brazil
(*b*) Cocoa	2. Ivory Coast
(*c*) Coffee	3. India
(*d*) Tea	4. China

Codes :

	(*a*)	(*b*)	(*c*)	(*d*)
A.	2	3	1	4
B.	3	2	1	4
C.	3	2	4	1
D.	2	3	4	1

93. Darjeeling and Dharamsala would be the right places to visit if one wanted to get a clear view respectively of :
A. Kanchanjunga and Dhauladhar ranges
B. Nandadevi and Dhauladhar ranges
C. Kanchanjunga and Nandadevi ranges
D. Nandadevi and Nanga Parvat

94. Atmosphere exists because:
A. The Gravitational force of the Earth
B. Revolution of the Earth
C. Rotation of the Earth
D. Weight of the gases of atmosphere

95. Victoria lake is located in the continent:
A. Africa B. Asia
C. North America D. South America

96. The famous Lagoon Lake of India is :
A. Dal Lake B. Chilka Lake
C. Pulicat Lake D. Mansarover

97. Where are most of the earth's active volcanoes concentrated?
A. Indian Ocean B. Pacific Ocean
C. Aral Sea D. Atlantic Ocean

98. Through which of the following states does the river Chambal flow?
A. U.P., M.P., Rajasthan B. M.P., Gujarat, U.P.
C. Rajasthan, M.P., Bihar D. Gujarat, M.P., U.P.

99. Which country is called the sugar bowl of the world?
A. Cuba B. India
C. Argentina D. USA

100. The area covered by forest in India is:
A. 46% B. 33%
C. 21.71% D. 23%

101. A closed economy is the one which :
A. does not permit emigration or immigration
B. permits emigration but no immigration
C. engages in no foreign trade
D. engages in no foreign and domestic trade or transit

102. In a developed economy the major share of employment originates in the :
A. primary sector B. tertiary sector
C. secondary sector D. any of the above

103. The Economic and Social Commission for Asia and Pacific (ESCAP) is located at :
A. Bangkok B. Kuala Lumpur
C. Manila D. Singapore

104. Commercial vehicles are not produced by which of the following companies in India?
A. TELCO B. Ashok Leyland
C. DCM Daewoo D. Birla Yamaha

105. In India, the Public Sector is most dominant in:
A. transport
B. steel production
C. commercial banking
D. organised term-lending financial institutions

106. The main argument advanced in favour of small scale and cottage industries in India is that:
A. cost of production is low
B. they require small capital investment
C. they advance the goal of equitable distribution of wealth
D. they generate a large volume of employment

107. The most serious economic problems of India are:
A. Poverty and unemployment
B. Stagnation, not poverty
C. Unemployment, not poverty
D. Underdevelopment, not poverty

108. Which of the following is not one of the three central problems of an economy?
A. What to produce B. How to produce
C. When to produce D. For whom to produce

109. If saving exceeds investment, the national income will:
A. fall B. rise
C. fluctuate D. remain constant

110. In which of the following industries in India are the maximum number of workers employed?
A. Sugar B. Jute
C. Textiles D. Iron and Steel

111. Terrace Cultivation is practiced mostly:
A. in urban areas B. on slopes of mountains
C. on tops of hills D. in undulating tracts

112. Which of the following is a Selective Credit Control method?
A. Bank Rate B. RBI directives
C. Cash Reserve Ratio D. Open market operations

113. Which of the following taxes is not shared by the Central Government with the States?
A. Union excise duties B. Customs duty
C. Income tax D. Estate duty

114. ICICI is the name of a:
A. Financial Institution
B. Chemical Industry
C. Cotton Industry
D. Chamber of Commerce and Industry

115. Structural Unemployment arises due to
A. Deflationary conditions
B. Heavy industry bias
C. Shortage of raw material
D. Inadequate productive capacity

116. Which of the following is the largest single source of the government's earning from tax revenue?
A. Excise duties B. Customs duties
C. Corporation tax D. Income tax

117. The largest public sector bank in India is:
A. Central Bank of India B. Punjab National Bank
C. State Bank of India D. Indian Overseas Bank

118. Which of the following statements best explains the term contraband goods?
A. Goods produced only for exports
B. Goods produced in joint sector only
C. Goods for the trading of which licence is not required
D. Goods that are forbidden, from export, import or even possession, by law

119. Price in the market is fixed by:
A. Stock exchange rates
B. The demand and supply ruling in the market at a particular time
C. The Finance Minister
D. None of the above

120. Devaluation of currency helps to promote:
A. National Income B. Savings
C. Imports at lower cost D. Exports

121. Balanced economic growth can be achieved only if:
A. All the sectors of economy grow at the same rate
B. Population growth is arrested
C. All the inter dependent sectors grow in harmony
D. Basic and heavy industries are assigned highest priority

122. First share market in India was established in:
A. Mumbai B. Delhi
C. Kolkata D. Chennai

123. 'MODVAT' stands for:
A. Ad Valorem tax on output
B. Deduction of cost of inputs from the value of output
C. Reduction in import duties
D. Imposition of tax on professions

124. The headquarters of ILO is at:
A. Washington B. Geneva
C. The Hague D. Manila

125. The term 'devaluation' means:
A. Reducing the value of a currency in terms of another currency
B. Increasing the value of a currency
C. Revising the value of a currency
D. None of the above

126. Per capita net availability of pulses has shown a tendency of:
A. Increase over time
B. Decrease over time
C. Constant over time
D. First increase then decrease

127. National Income is the same as:
A. Net national product at market price
B. Net domestic product at market price
C. Net national product at factor cost
D. Net domestic product at factor cost

128. Which one of the following is not an example of indirect tax?
A. Sales tax B. Excise duty
C. Customs duty D. Expenditure tax

129. The major aim of devaluation is to:
A. encourage imports
B. encourage exports
C. encourage both exports and imports
D. discourage both exports and imports

130. Structural unemployment arises due to:
A. deflationary conditions
B. heavy industry bias
C. shortage of raw materials
D. inadequate productive capacity

131. When was the Family Planning Programme officially started in India?
A. 1950 B. 1952
C. 1956 D. 1962

132. When was the Reserve Bank of India nationalised?
A. 1947 B. 1949
C. 1950 D. 1951

133. Which of the following is *not* a feature of the Indian economy?
A. High rate of population growth
B. Disguised unemployment
C. Lowest rate of adult literacy
D. High rate of exports

134. The 'Relative Deprivation' approach for measuring poverty has been adopted by:
A. developing countries
B. developed countries
C. under-developed countries
D. None of the above

135. One of the main factors that led to rapid expansion of Indian exports is:
A. Imposition of import duties
B. Liberalisation of the economy
C. Recession in other countries
D. Diversification of exports

136. Sustainable economic development means an increase in the rate of growth of real:
A. total and per capita product
B. total and per capita product and level of literacy rate
C. total and per capita product and life expectancy at birth
D. total and per capita product, taking into account the cost of degradation of the quality of environment in this process

137. Functional unemployment occurs when:
A. unemployed have no qualification for job
B. people frequently change their job
C. people were thrown out from job due to recession
D. None of these

138. Which among the following does **not** have a 'free trade zone'?
A. Kandla B. Mumbai
C. Visakhapatnam D. Thiruvanantpuram

139. Sun Belt of USA is important for which one of the following industries?
A. Cotton textile B. Petrochemicals
C. Hi-tech electronics D. Food Processing

140. Commercial banking system in India is
A. unit banking B. branch banking
C. mixed banking D. None of the above

141. Who gives recognition to political parties in India?
A. Parliament
B. President
C. Supreme Court
D. Election Commission

142. The Quorum of the Legislative Council is :
A. one-fourth of its total membership
B. one-third of its membership
C. one-tenth of its membership
D. 25

143. The Indian Constitution is:
A. federal
B. unitary
C. a happy mixture of the federal and unitary
D. federal in normal times and unitary in times of emergency

144. Universal adult franchise implies a right to vote to all:
A. adult residents of the State
B. adult male citizens of the State
C. residents of the State
D. adult citizens of the State

145. When a resolution prefering a charge against the President has been passed by a specified majority in the House, it is sent to the other House for investigation. If, as a result of such an investigation, a resolution is passed through a specified majority by the other House, declaring that the charge has been sustained, the President shall leave his office. The specified special majority must not be less than :
A. two-third of the members present and voting
B. one-third of the members present and voting
C. three-fourth of the members present and voting and two-third of the total membership
D. two-third of the total membership

146. Which one of the following judicial powers of the President of India has been *wrongly* listed?
A. he appoints the Chief Justice and other judges of the Supreme Court
B. he can remove the judges of the Supreme Court on grounds of misconduct
C. he can consult the Supreme Court on any question of law or fact which is of public importance
D. he can grant pardon, reprieves and respites to persons punished under Union Law

147. The Vice-president of India can be removed from his office before the expiry of his term if :
A. the Rajya Sabha passes a resolution by a majority of its members and the Lok Sabha agrees with the resolution
B. if the Supreme Court of India recommends his removal
C. the President so desires
D. None of the above

148. The Chief Justice of a High Court in India is appointed by the :
A. Governor of the State
B. Prime Minister of India
C. Chief Justice of the Supreme Court
D. President of India

149. Which of the following statements is constitu-tionally not true about the passing of the Union Budgets, and Finance Bill in India?
1. Under the law, Finance Bill should be adopted by both the Houses of the Parliament within 45 days of its introduction.
2. If the Finance Bill is not adopted within specified period, the government loses its authority to levy the taxes proposed in the budgets.
3. In the absence of full budget, a vote-on-account gives the power to the government to spend.
4. Government cannot raise revenues without a proper approval of the Finance Bill

A. Only 2 B. Only 3
C. Only 4 D. Only 1, 2 and 3

150. Normally, on whose advice the President's Rule is imposed in a State?
A. Chief Minister
B. Legislative Assembly
C. Governor
D. Chief Justice of High Court

151. Which Article of the Indian Constitution deals with Amendment procedure?
A. Article 368 B. Article 358
C. Article 367 D. All of these

152. Government is the agency through which the will of:
A. the state is expressed
B. the people is expressed
C. the head of the state is expressed
D. the majority is expressed

153. In a unitary system of government :
A. The centre is all powerful
B. The centre is weaker than the states
C. The centre and states stand at par
D. The states and centre are supreme in their respective spheres

154. In Cabinet System of Government the real executive authority rests with :
A. The Council of Ministers
B. The Prime Minister
C. The Constitution
D. The Parliament

155. The Head of the State under a parliamentary government:
A. is an elected representative
B. is a hereditary person
C. is a nominated person
D. may be any one of the above

156. In the event of a ministerial proposal being defeated on the floor of the legislature, under the parliamentary system :
A. the government waits for a general no-confidence motion
B. the minister concerned is taken to task by the Prime Minister
C. the minister is forced to resign
D. the whole Council of Ministers resign

157. The "due process of law" is an essential characteristic of the judicial system of:
A. UK B. France
C. USA D. India

158. Under the Constitution it is :
A. obligatory for the President to accept the advice of the Council of Ministers but is not obliged to follow it
B. obligatory for the President to accept the advice of the Council of Ministers
C. not obligatory for the President to seek or accept the advice of the Council of Ministers
D. obligatory for the President to seek the advice of the Council of Ministers if his own party is in power

159. Which one of the following statements is correct?
A. the Presiding Officer of Rajya Sabha is elected every year
B. the Presiding Officer of Rajya Sabha is elected for a term of two years at a time
C. the Presiding Officer of Rajya Sabha is elected for a term of six years
D. the Vice-President of India is the ex-officio Presiding Officer of Rajya Sabha

160. The introduction of "no confidence" motion in the Lok Sabha requires the support of at least:
A. 50 members B. 70 members
C. 60 members D. 80 members

161. The High Court comes under :
A. State List B. Union List
C. Concurrent List D. None of the above

162. Which one of the following has been wrongly listed as a Fundamental Duty of the Indian citizens?
A. to develop scientific temper, humanism and spirit of inquiry and reform
B. to work for raising the prestige of the country in the international sphere
C. to protect and improve the natural environment
D. to strive towards excellence in all spheres of individual and collective activity

163. Which one of the following is not a Fundamental Duty as outlined in Article 51A of the Constitution?
A. to abide by the Constitution and respect its ideals
B. to defend the country and render national service when called upon to do so
C. to work for the moral upliftment of the weaker sections of society
D. to preserve the rich heritage

164. The main characteristics of the Directive Principles of State Policy given in the Indian Constitution are :
A. not enforceable by any court
B. fundamental in the governance of the country
C. 'Like instruments, instructions, political manifesto and a code of moral precepts which have to guide governors of the country'
D. no law can be passed, which is opposed to these principles

165. Of the following which are true?
A. In a State, the Legislative Council is dominant with regard to non-financial bills and the Legislative Assembly with regard to financial (money) bills
B. Vidhan Parishad can virtually block legisla-tion even if the same is passed by the Vidhan Sabha
C. In case of a tie between the two Houses, the Governor is duty-bound to call a joint session of the two Houses to have the issue settled on a majority verdict
D. If a Bill is twice approved by the Vidhan Sabha, it becomes law even if rejected by the Vidhan Parishad

166. Which one of the following types of emergency can be declared by the President?
A. Emergency due to threat of war and external aggresion
B. Emergency due to break-down of constitu-tional machinery in a State
C. Financial emergency on account of threat to the financial credit of India
D. all the three emergencies

167. The chairman of which of the following parliamentary committees is invariably from the members of ruling party?
A. Committee on public undertakings
B. Public accounts committee
C. Estimates committee
D. Committee on delegated legislation

168. Which of the following is not a formally prescribed device available to the members of parliament?
A. Question hour
B. Zero hour
C. Half-an-hour discussion
D. Short duration discussion

169. Which of the following is not a tool of executive control over public administration?
A. Power of appointment and removal
B. Line agencies
C. Appeal to public opinion
D. Civil services code

170. If the Speaker of the State Legislative Assembly decides to resign, he should submit his resignation to the:
A. Judges of the High Court
B. Deputy Speaker
C. Chief Minister
D. Finance Minister

171. Provision for free legal aid is mentioned in:
A. Fundamental Rights
B. Fundamental Duties
C. No Where
D. Directive principles of State policy

172. India is a Federal State because of:
A. dual judiciary
B. dual citizenship prevalent here
C. share of power between the Centre and the States
D. rigid Constitution

173. Residuary Subjects are those subjects which are:
A. contained in the State list
B. contained in the Union list
C. contained in the Concurrent list
D. not covered by any of the three lists

174. Which of the following writs can be issued, by the Supreme Court, to enforce Fundamental Rights?
A. Writ of Habeas Corpus
B. Writ of Mandamus
C. Writ of Quo Warranto
D. All of these

175. When the offices of both the President and the Vice-President of India are vacant, who will discharge their functions?
A. Prime Minister B. Home Minister
C. Chief Justice of India D. The Speaker

176. The Supreme Court tenders advice to the President of India on a matter of law or fact:
A. on its own
B. only when such advice is sought
C. only if the matter relates to some basic issue
D. only if the issue poses a threat to the unity and integrity of the country

177. Six months shall **not** intervene between two sessions of the Indian Parliament because :
A. it is the customary practice
B. it is the British convention followed in India
C. it is an obligation under the Constitution of India
D. None of the above

178. The States of the Indian Union can be recognised or their boundaries altered by:
A. the Union Parliament by a simple majority in the ordinary process of legislation
B. two-thirds majority of both the Houses of Parliament
C. two-thirds majority of both the Houses of Parliament and the consent of the legisla-tures of concerned States
D. an executive order of the Union government with the consent of the concerned State governments

179. The Basic Feature theory of the Constitution of India was propounded by the Supreme Court in the case of:
A. Minerva Mills Vs. Union of India
B. Golaknath Vs. State of Punjab
C. Maneka Gandhi Vs. Union of India
D. Keshavananda Vs. State of Kerala

180. Which one of the following writs is issued by a court in case of illegal detention of a person?
A. Habeas corpus B. Mandamus
C. Certiorari D. Quo-warranto

181. Name the instrument with the help of which a sailor in a submarine can see the objects on the surface of the sea.
A. Telescope B. Periscope
C. Gycroscope D. Stereoscope

182. 'Hemophillia' is the disease of ....
A. liver B. blood
C. brain D. bones

183. Vitamin A is abundantly found in ....
A. Brinjal B. Tomato
C. Carrot D. Cabbage

184. .... is not soluble in water.
A. Vitamin A B. Vitamin B
C. Vitamin C D. None of these

185. The blood vessels with the smallest diameter are called ....
A. capillaries B. arterioles
C. venules D. lymphatics

186. Out of the following .... has the greatest elasticity.
A. steel B. rubber
C. aluminium D. annealed copper

187. Cooking gas is a mixture of which of the following two gases?
A. Carbon Dioxide and Oxygen
B. Butane and Propane
C. Carbon Monoxide and Carbon Dioxide
D. Methane and Ethylene

188. The substance most commonly used as a food preservative is:
A. sodium carbonate B. tartaric acid
C. acetic acid D. benzoic acid

189. Normally, the substances that fight against diseases in human systems are known as:
A. dioxyribonucleic acids B. carbohydrates
C. enzymes D. antibodies

190. The SI unit of temperature is ....
A. Kelvin B. Celsius
C. Fahrenheit D. None of the above

191. One of the common fungal diseases of man is :
A. plague B. ringworm
C. cholera D. typhoid

192. A clear sky is blue because:
A. red light is scattered more than blue
B. ultraviolet light has been absorbed
C. blue light is scattered more than red
D. blue light has been absorbed

193. Jenner introduced the method of making people immune to :
A. small pox B. rabies
C. cholera D. polio

194. The largest cell in the human body is :
A. Nerve cell B. Live cell
C. Muscle cell D. Kidney cell

195. What is the device that steps up or steps down the voltage?
A. Dynamo B. Conductor
C. Inductor D. Transformer

196. The protein deficiency disease is known as :
A. Kwashiorker B. Cirrhosis
C. Eczema D. Clycoses

197. Iron deficiency causes :
A. rickets B. anaemia
C. cirrhosis D. goitre

198. Blood group of an individual is controlled by :
A. Haemoglobin B. Shape of RBC
C. Shape of WBC D. Genes

199. In a normal man the amount of blood pumped out by the heart per minute is about :
A. 1 litre B. 3 litres
C. 4 litres D. 5 litres

200. Red/green colour blindness in man is known as :
A. Protanopia B. Deutetanopia
C. Both A and B above D. Marfan's syndrome

201. The blue colour of the water in the sea is due to :
A. Reflection of the blue light by the impurities in sea water
B. Reflection of the blue sky by sea water and scattering of blue light by water molecules
C. Absorption of other colours by water molecules
D. None of the above

202. The image formed on the retina of the eye is:
A. upright and real B. larger than the object
C. small and inverted D. enlarged and real

203. Unit of loudness of sound is:
A. bel B. decibel
C. phon D. none of these

204. Oil rises up the wick in a lamp :
A. because oil is volatile
B. due to the capillary action phenomenon
C. due to the surface tension phenomenon
D. because oil is very light

205. The 'stones' formed in human kidney consist mostly of :
A. calcium oxalate
B. sodium acetate
C. magnesium sulphate
D. calcium

206. We hear the sound later, while the light is seen earlier:
A. because light's speed is more than that of sound
B. because lights travel in a straight direction while sound in a zigzag direction
C. because sound's frequency is lower than light
D. All of the above

207. Which part of an eye is transplanted?
A. Cornea B. Retina
C. Iris D. Sciera

208. The Universal donor group of blood is:
A. O B. A
C. B D. AB

209. The green colour of the leaf is due to :
A. Presence of Chloroplast
B. Presence of Chromium
C. Presence of Nicoplast
D. Presence of excess of oxygen

210. Voice of a child is more shrill than that of an elderly person because:
A. the pitch of the child's voice is higher than that of the person
B. the pitch is lower
C. the child is more energetic
D. None of the above

211. Camel uses its hump for :
A. storing water
B. storing fat
C. for balancing the body
D. temperature regulation

212. A man standing in a free falling lift releases a ball from his hand. The ball would be :
A. moving down B. moving up
C. stationary D. moving up and down

213. To change the quality of sound produced by an instrument we need to vary the:
A. pitch B. loudness
C. amplitude D. number of overtonnes

214. The disease caused by Asbestos is:
A. Emphysema B. Paralysis
C. Diarrhoea D. Dysentery

215. Sweetness of a sound depends upon its
A. wavelength
B. frequency
C. amplitude
D. periodicity and regularity

216. Bats can fly in the dark because :
A. they have a better vision in the dark
B. the pupils of their eyes are very big
C. they are guided by ultrasonic waves produced by them
D. any bird can do so

217. Blood is formed in the human adult by the :
A. heart B. spleen
C. kidney D. bone marrow

218. Pencil 'lead' is made up of:
A. graphite B. charcoal
C. lead oxide D. lampblack

219. The deficiency of which one of the following vitamins leads to bleeding of gums and loosening of teeth?
A. Vitamin D B. Vitamin C
C. Vitamin B D. Vitamin A

220. How much blood does a normal person have in his body?
A. 8 litres B. 4 to 5 litres
C. 10 litres D. 2 litres

221. Match List-I with List-II and select the correct answer using the codes given below the Lists :

List-I	***List-II***
(*a*) Visakhadatta	1. Mrichhakatika
(*b*) Shudraka	2. Ritusamhara
(*c*) Kalidasa	3. Kamasutra
(*d*) Vatsyayana	4. Devichandraguptam

Codes :

	(*a*)	(*b*)	(*c*)	(*d*)
A.	1	4	2	3
B.	4	1	3	2
C.	1	4	3	2
D.	4	1	2	3

222. In which one of the following langauges is the *Dalit* writing more conspicuous?
A. Punjabi B. Assamese
C. Marathi D. Odiya

223. The first writer to use Urdu as the medium of poetic expression was:
A. Amir Khusrau B. Mirza Ghalib
C. Bahadur Shah Zafar D. Faiz

224. The religious text of the Zoroastrians is named as:
A. Torah B. The Analects
C. Tripatika D. Zend Avesta

225. Name the music duo which composed music for Raj Kapoor's film 'Bobby'?
A. Laxmikant Pyarelal B. Shankar Jaikishen
C. Kalyanji Anandji D. Nadeem Shravan

226. Raja Harishchandra, an early Indian film, was produced by :
A. D.G. Phalke B. Ashok Kumar
C. Ardeshir Irani D. None of the above

227. All films are certificed by .... before they are publicly exhibited.
A. Films Division
B. National Film Development Corporation (NFDC)
C. Directorate of Advertising and Visual Publicity (DAVP)
D. Central Board of Film Certificate (CBFC)

228. Who among the following was the director of the film 'Taal'?
A. Gulzar B. Shekhar Kapoor
C. Satish Shah D. Subhash Ghai

229. Who amongst the following actresses has played the leading role in the film Elizabeth?
A. Gwyneth Paltrow B. Cate Blanchett
C. Simi Garewal D. Kim Basinger

230. The film 'Train to Pakistan' is based on the novel of the same name, written by:
A. Bhishma Sahani B. Khushwant Singh
C. Amrita Pritam D. Khwaja Ahmed Abbas

231. Which of the following is a folk dance form of Jharkhand?
A. Pali B. Jhumar
C. Nati D. Chhau

232. The first feature film (talkie) to be produced in India was:
A. Hatimtai B. Alam Ara
C. Pundalik D. Raja Harishchandra

233. Who directed the film "Bombay"?
A. Shyam Benegal B. Meera Nair
C. Shekhar Kapoor D. Mani Ratnam

234. Late Iftekhar Ahmad was famous in which of the following fields?
A. Acting B. Singing
C. Music D. Literature

235. Who among the following is the director of the film 'Kaho Na Pyar Hai'?
A. Subhash Ghai B. Shekhar Kapoor
C. Ramesh Sippy D. Rakesh Roshan

236. The character played by Jim Carrey in the movie *Man on Moon* is based on:
A. Andy Kaufman B. Edwin Aldrin
C. John Glenn D. Neil Armstrong

237. A popular Hindi film-based on the famous Sanskrit play *Mrichhakatika*, was titled:
A. Meghadoot B. Amrapali
C. Utsav D. Shakuntala

238. Who composed the song 'Zara Yad Karo Kurbani'?
A. Javed Akhtar
B. Pradeep
C. Nusrat Fateh Ali Khan
D. Raghupati Sahay 'Firaq'

239. Who was the producer of the serial 'Mahabharat'?
A. Shyam Benegal B. B.R. Chopra
C. Ramanand Sagar D. Mani Ratnam

240. Which of the following is a folk dance of Rajasthan?
A. Garba B. Dandya
C. Jhumar D. Kathak

241. 'The Colonel' is the nickname of which Indian Test Cricketer?
A. Colonel C.K. Naidu B. Rahul Dravid
C. Mohinder Amarnath D. Dilip Vengsarkar

242. The term 'Grandmaster' is used in which of these games?
A. Judo B. Chess
C. Bridge D. Karate

243. The term "Derby" is related with which of the following?
A. Polo B. Swimming
C. Racing D. Horse Racing

244. With which game is Geet Sethi associated?
A. Basketball B. Chess
C. Snooker D. Tennis

245. Beighton Cup is related with which of the following?
A. Hockey B. Polo
C. Cricket D. Soccer

246. Match List-I with List-II and select the correct answer using the codes given below the Lists :

List-I	***List-II***
(*a*) Basketball	1. Lob
(*b*) Bridge	2. Revoke
(*c*) Golf	3. Pivot
(*d*) Tennis	4. Bunker

Codes :

	(*a*)	(*b*)	(*c*)	(*d*)
A.	2	3	1	4
B.	2	3	4	1
C.	3	2	1	4
D.	3	2	4	1

247. The head office of the International Cricket Council (ICC) is situated in :
A. Zimbabwe B. Australia
C. South Africa D. UAE

248. Match the following :

List-I	***List-II***
(*a*) Deodhar Trophy	1. Volleyball
(*b*) Durand Cup	2. Football
(*c*) Davis Cup	3. Cricket
	4. Tennis

Codes :

	(*a*)	(*b*)	(*c*)
A.	3	2	4
B.	3	1	4
C.	2	3	1
D.	1	2	4

249. Which of the following is called 'Grand Slam'?
A. Winning the highest number of medals in the Olympic games
B. Winning the men's singles title in Wimbledon Championship
C. Winning the Wimbledon Singles title successively for two years
D. Winning all the four championships Australian, French, Wimblendon and US

250. With which game is the term 'butterfly stroke' associated?
A. Swimming B. Cricket
C. Gliding D. Skiing

251. Who is the first Indian to win the 'International Grand Master' title in Chess?
A. Anupama Abhayankar
B. Bhagyashree Sathe Thipsay
C. Vishwanathan Anand
D. D.V. Prasad

252. The XXII Commonwealth Games were held in 2022 in:
A. Kuala Lumpur B. Bangkok
C. Victoria D. Birmingham

253. The term 'Tee' is associated with which of the following sports?
A. Golf B. Table Tennis
C. Polo D. Judo

254. The famous woman Tennis player who was stabbed during a match, is
A. Steffi Graf B. Monica Seles
C. Mary Pierce D. Martina Navratilova

255. The term 'Baseline' is related to which of the following?
A. Golf B. Hockey
C. Badminton D. Polo

256. In which Indian State did the game of Polo originate?
A. Manipur B. Rajasthan
C. Gujarat D. West Bengal

257. World Environment Day is Celebrated on :
A. June 9 B. June 11
C. June 5 D. June 13

258. Rafael Nadal is the well-known player associated with:
A. Hockey B. Cricket
C. Tennis D. Chess

259. Gagan Narang is the well-known player associated with :
A. Shooting B. Golf
C. Table Tennis D. Chess

260. Eden Garden, a famous Cricket stadium, is located in:
A. Kanpur B. Kolkata
C. Jamshedpur D. Pune

261. Maharaja Ranjit Singh Trophy is associated with :
A. Golf B. Hockey
C. Soccer D. Tennis

262. Neeraj Chopra is a distinguished athlete in which of the following games?
A. Swimming B. Weightlifting
C. Javelin Throw D. Archery

263. Cricket was an Olympic event at which of the following Olympics?
A. London, 1908 B. Amsterdam, 1928
C. Paris, 1900 D. Melbourne, 1956

264. WISPA competitions are associated with :
A. Squash B. Yatching
C. Boxing D. Billiards

265. Ryder Cup is the famous trophy of :
A. Golf B. Chess
C. Boxing D. Polo

266. Davis Cup is associated with the sport of :
A. Cricket B. Football
C. Tennis D. Hockey

267. 'Volley', 'Chop' and 'Drive Spine' are the term associated with :
A. Lawn Tennis B. Badminton
C. Table Tennis D. Golf

268. Lal Bahadur Shastri Stadium is located at :
A. Hyderabad B. Chennai
C. Ahmedabad D. Varanasi

269. The first winner of "Rajiv Khel Ratna Award" (Now Major Dhyanchand Khel Ratna Award) was :
A. Geet Sethi B. Sachin Tendulkar
C. Viswanathan Anand D. Karnam Malleswari

270. 2019 Cricket World Cup was held in :
A. England B. Sri Lanka
C. Bangladesh D. Australia

271. The first team event introduced in 1900 at Paris Olympics was :
A. Hockey B. Football
C. Cricket D. Baseball

272. Which of the following international tennis tournaments is held on grass court?
A. US Open B. French Open
C. Wimbledon D. Australian Open

273. Which cricketer is nicknamed as the pied piper of Punjab?
A. Yuvraj Singh B. Harbhajan Singh
C. Mohinder Amarnath D. Navjot Singh Sidhu

274. 'Merdeka Cup' is associated with ....
A. Golf B. Football
C. Squash D. Hockey

275. The first time athletes marched into the stadium behind their nation's flag in Olympics:
A. at St. Louis 1904 B. at London 1908
C. at Antwerp 1920 D. at Paris 1924

276. The "Dronacharya Award" is associated with:
A. Eminent Surgeons
B. Famous Sports Person
C. Sport Coaches
D. Expert Engineers

277. Which cricketer is nicknamed as 'Jumbo'?
A. Venkatesh Prasad B. Anil Kumble
C. Glenn McGrath D. Shane Warne

278. The first time the Olympic Games were organised by a private company at:
A. Montreal, 1976 B. Los Angeles, 1984
C. Atlanta, 1996 D. Rome, 1960

279. In which Asian Games Cricket was played first?
A. Guangzhou, 2010
B. Doha, 2006
C. Busan, 2002
D. Seoul, 1986

280. The term 'Penalty cick' is used in :
A. Hockey B. Football
C. Baseball D. Golf

281. "Green Revolution" began in India during the year:
A. 1972-73 B. 1977-78
C. 1980-81 D. 1967-68

282. Khmer Rouge is a dictatorial party of :
A. Cambodia B. Indonesia
C. Malaysia D. Thailand

283. Which country is not a member of SAARC?
A. Russia B. Bangladesh
C. Nepal D. Pakistan

284. The headquarters of WTO is located at :
A. Geneva B. Paris
C. The Hague D. Washington

285. The main function of the World Trade Organisation (WTO) is:
A. enforcing of Uruguay Round Agreements
B. facilitating multi-lateral trade relations of member countries and reviewing trade policies
C. administering trade dispute settlement procedures
D. None of the above

286. The Secretary-General of the UNO is appointed by the:
A. General Assembly B. Security Council
C. Trusteeship Council D. World Bank

287. The United Nations officially came into existence in 1945 on :
A. November 24 B. October 14
C. October 24 D. November 14

288. Which one of the following is true of the International Court of Justice?
A. The Judges of the Court are appointed according to the discretion of the Secretary General
B. No two Judges may belong to the same country
C. The Court consists of 20 Judges
D. The statute of the International Court of Justice is not an integral part of the UN Charter

289. Which of the following was not among the six founding countries of the European Community?
A. Belgium B. France
C. Germany D. UK

290. The smallest country in South America is:
A. Ecuador B. Guyana
C. Surinam D. Uruguay

291. In which year "Human Rights Resolution" was adopted by the U.N.?
A. 1945 B. 1946
C. 1947 D. 1948

292. Where is the headquarters of INTERPOL located?
A. Berlin B. California
C. Lyons D. Montreal

293. Parliament of which of the following countries is known as Great People's Khural?
A. Malaysia B. Mongolia
C. Thailand D. Indonesia

294. Numbers of major organs of United Nations are:
A. 3 B. 4
C. 5 D. 6

295. When is the UN Day celebrated?
A. October 24 B. January 24
C. June 24 D. September 24

296. Which one of the following organ of United Nations is known as the 'Policeman of the World'?
A. Security Council
B. International Court of Justice
C. The Secretariat
D. General Assembly

297. The members of the NAFTA include:
A. USA, Canada and Mexico
B. USA, Canada, Mexico and UK
C. USA, UK, Russia and Mexico
D. USA, Canada and Brazil

298. The sits of International Court of Justice is located at:
A. Vienna B. Paris
C. Hague D. New York

299. Which of the following is known as the Constitution of the UN?
A. UN Charter B. UN Assembly
C. UN Security Council D. UN Secretariat

300. The Headquarters of the Amnesty International is located at :
A. New York B. London
C. Geneva D. Addis-Ababa

ANSWERS

1	2	3	4	5	6	7	8	9	10
B	C	D	C	B	C	A	C	C	D
11	12	13	14	15	16	17	18	19	20
C	A	C	A	A	D	A	B	A	D
21	22	23	24	25	26	27	28	29	30
A	C	B	C	D	C	B	D	D	B
31	32	33	34	35	36	37	38	39	40
C	D	C	C	B	C	D	B	C	C
41	42	43	44	45	46	47	48	49	50
A	A	A	B	C	D	C	B	B	D
51	52	53	54	55	56	57	58	59	60
A	C	A	B	B	A	B	C	A	C
61	62	63	64	65	66	67	68	69	70
C	C	B	B	C	C	D	D	D	B
71	72	73	74	75	76	77	78	79	80
B	C	C	C	A	A	A	B	B	A
81	82	83	84	85	86	87	88	89	90
A	B	D	B	C	C	D	C	B	D
91	92	93	94	95	96	97	98	99	100
A	B	A	A	A	B	B	A	A	C
101	102	103	104	105	106	107	108	109	110
C	B	A	D	D	D	A	C	D	C
111	112	113	114	115	116	117	118	119	120
B	B	B	A	D	C	C	D	B	D
121	122	123	124	125	126	127	128	129	130
C	A	A	B	A	D	C	D	B	D
131	132	133	134	135	136	137	138	139	140
B	B	D	A	B	D	B	D	D	C
141	142	143	144	145	146	147	148	149	150
D	C	D	D	D	B	A	D	C	C
151	152	153	154	155	156	157	158	159	160
A	B	A	A	A	D	C	B	D	A
161	162	163	164	165	166	167	168	169	170
B	B	C	B	D	D	C	B	B	B
171	172	173	174	175	176	177	178	179	180
D	C	D	D	C	B	C	A	D	A
181	182	183	184	185	186	187	188	189	190
B	B	C	A	A	A	B	D	D	A
191	192	193	194	195	196	197	198	199	200
B	C	A	A	D	A	B	D	D	A
201	202	203	204	205	206	207	208	209	210
B	B	B	B	A	A	A	A	A	A

211	212	213	214	215	216	217	218	219	220
B	A	A	A	D	C	D	A	B	B
221	**222**	**223**	**224**	**225**	**226**	**227**	**228**	**229**	**230**
D	C	A	D	A	A	D	D	B	B
231	**232**	**233**	**234**	**235**	**236**	**237**	**238**	**239**	**240**
D	B	D	A	D	D	C	B	B	C
241	**242**	**243**	**244**	**245**	**246**	**247**	**248**	**249**	**250**
D	B	D	C	A	D	D	A	D	A
251	**252**	**253**	**254**	**255**	**256**	**257**	**258**	**259**	**260**
C	D	A	B	C	A	C	C	A	B
261	**262**	**263**	**264**	**265**	**266**	**267**	**268**	**269**	**270**
B	C	C	A	A	C	C	A	C	A
271	**272**	**273**	**274**	**275**	**276**	**277**	**278**	**279**	**280**
B	C	A	B	A	C	B	B	A	B
281	**282**	**283**	**284**	**285**	**286**	**287**	**288**	**289**	**290**
D	A	A	A	B	A	C	B	D	C
291	**292**	**293**	**294**	**295**	**296**	**297**	**298**	**299**	**300**
D	C	B	D	A	A	A	C	A	B

❑ ❑ ❑

BIHAR GENERAL KNOWLEDGE

1. Which of the following inscription provide information about the Pala rulers?
   A. Munger copper-plate inscription of Devapala
   B. Bhagalpur copper-plate inscription of Narayanpala
   C. Bangarh copper-plate inscription of Vigrahapala
   D. All of the above

2. The earliest source for the history of Bihar is:
   A. Upanishads B. Atharvaveda
   C. Samaveda D. Aranayaks

3. Which of the following inscriptions belong to the Mauryas?
   A. Lauriya Areraj B. Lauriya Nandangarh
   C. Rampurva D. All of the above

4. Which of the following texts provide information regarding the mahajanpads in Bihar?
   A. Vinay Pitaka B. Anguttaranikaya
   C. Kalpasutra D. Dighanikaya

5. Which aspect has been covered by the Arthashastra of Kautilya?
   A. Political B. Economic
   C. Social D. Religious

6. The Panchobha copper plate inscription belongs to:
   A. Skandagupta B. Chandragupta
   C. Samgramagupta D. Samudragupta

7. The story of which epic has been depicted on the brick wall of a Vishnu temple excavated from Aphsad in Gaya district?
   A. Ramayana
   B. Mahabharata
   C. Srimadbhagvadgita
   D. The story of Nal-Damyanti

8. Who excavated the Nalanda Mahavihara at Baragaon in Nalanda?
   A. Mckenzie B. Wheeler
   C. Spooner D. Cunningham

9. The excavations at Saraitila in Nalanda have yielded:
   A. Buddhist Vihara of Mauryan times
   B. Buddhist Vihara of Pala times
   C. Temples of Gupta period
   D. Buddhist Vihara of Shunga period

10. Which Jaina canon gives an account of Lichhavis of Vaishali?
    A. Bhagvati Sutra B. Kalpsutra
    C. Kathakosa D. Parisisthaparvana

11. The Buddhist canons Digha Nikaya and Vinaya Pitaka gives an account of:
    A. Monarchy of Magadha and republic of Vaishali
    B. Post-Mauryan Bihar
    C. Both A and B
    D. Neither A nor B

12. Which Buddhist text throws light on the political history of Bihar under the Guptas?
    A. Dipavamsha
    B. Mahavamsha
    C. Aryamanjusrimulakalpa
    D. Vinaya Pitaka

13. The Chalcolithic age remains have been found at:
    A. Chechar (Vaishali) B. Chirand (Saran)
    C. Sonpur and Maner D. All of the above

14. The evidences of the first appearance of human beings in Bihar are found at:
    A. Munger and Nalanda
    B. Gaya and Dehri
    C. Chamaparan and Muzaffarpur
    D. None of the above

15. Punch-marked coins which were found in abundance in Bihar were made of:
    A. Gold B. Silver
    C. Lead D. Copper

16. The early stone age site has been excavated at Paisara, located in the district of:
    A. Munger B. Bhagalpur
    C. Patna D. Gaya

17. From which neolithic site the antler bone tools have been unearthed?
    A. Maner B. Barudih
    C. Chechar D. Chirand

18. An ivory female-dancing figure with articulate limbs has been discovered at:
    A. Champa B. Taradih
    C. Maner D. Sonpur

19. An 80-pillared hall belonging to Mauryan period was excavated at:
    A. Kurkihar B. Rampurva
    C. Lauriya Areraj D. Kumrahar

20. Which of the following rulers did not issue a larger number of coins?
    A. Palas B. Guptas
    C. Mauryas D. Senas

21. Which text provides the crucial information about the Aryan expansion in North Bihar?
A. Rigveda B. Upanishads
C. Vayu Purana D. Satapatha Brahmana

22. The Aryans arrived in Bihar during:
A. Later Vedic period B. Rigvedic period
C. Mahajanapada period D. None of these

23. Which factor was responsible for the spread of the Aryans in Bihar as well as eastern India?
A. Extension of agriculture
B. Expansion of dynasties
C. Use of iron
D. Trade development

24. Which text mentions for the first time about the geographical area of Bihar?
A. Rigveda B. Shatapatha Brahmana
C. Vayu Purana D. Samaveda

25. The word Vratya mentioned in Atharvaveda refers to people of:
A. Anga B. Vajjis
C. Videha D. Magadha

26. Which of the following was an important state in the later vedic period in Bihar?
A. Vajji B. Videha
C. Magadha D. Anga

27. Who was the last ruler of Nanda dynasty and was a contemporary of Alexander?
A. Mahapadma Nanda B. Kalashoka
C. Pushyamitra D. Dhana Nanda

28. Which of the following Mahajanapadas was not situated in the region of modern Bihar?
A. Anga B. Vajji
C. Vatsa D. Magadha

29. In which regions of Bihar was the Anga Mahajanapada situated?
A. Bhagalpur and Munger
B. Muzaffarpur and Vaishali
C. Patna and Gaya
D. Hajipur and Siwan

30. The first capital of Magadha Mahajanapada was:
A. Pataliputra B. Girivraja
C. Gaya D. Champa

31. Which of the following ruling clan was not a part of Vajji republic?
A. Lichchavi B. Jnatrika
C. Chedi D. Videha

32. The capital of Lichchavi was:
A. Vaishali B. Kundagrama
C. Mithila D. Champa

33. Which river demarcated the Mahajanapadas of Magadha and Anga?
A. Assi B. Champa
C. Gandak D. Varuna

34. Which of the following Mahajanapadas in Bihar was a union of eight ruling clans?
A. Vajji B. Magadha
C. Anga D. All of the above

35. Patna and Gaya districts of Bihar were part of the Mahajanapada:
A. Anga B. Vajji
C. Asmak D. Magadha

36. The capital of Anga Mahajanapada was:
A. Gaya B. Girivraja
C. Vaishali D. Champa

37. Which of the following rulers permanently made Pataliputra the capital of Magadha?
A. Shisunaga B. Ajatashatru
C. Bimbisara D. Kalashoka

38. The founder of Nanda dynasty was:
A. Dhanananda B. Mahapadma Nanda
C. Munda D. None of the above

39. Bimbisara and Ajatashatru belonged to which dynasty?
A. Haryankas B. Sisungas
C. Nandas D. Brihadarathas

40. The last ruler of Haryanka dynasty was:
A. Udayin B. Anuruddha
C. Mundaka D. Nagadashka

41. Which dynasty established its rule after the fall of Haryanka dynasty?
A. Sisunaga dynasty B. Maurya dynasty
C. Nanda dynasty D. Gupta dynasty

42. Which of the following rulers established his capital at Vaishali?
A. Nagadashka B. Mahapadmananda
C. Shisunaga D. Kalashoka

43. Which ruler made a gift to Buddha of Venuvana (Bamboo-garden) near Rajagriha?
A. Bimbisara B. Ajatashatru
C. Shisunaga D. Udayin

44. Which of the following is considered as the real founder of Magadha dynasty?
A. Bimbisara B. Shisunaga
C. Jarasandha D. Mahapadma

45. Both Gautama Buddha and Mahavira died during the reign of:
A. Bimbisara B. Ajatashatru
C. Kalashoka D. Dhananda

46. Which of the following rulers made Pataliputra the capital of Magadha for the first time?
A. Kalashoka B. Ajatashatru
C. Udayin D. Bimbisara

47. Who among the following was a contemporary of Gautam Buddha?
A. Nagarjuna B. Kanishka
C. Kautilya D. Mahavira

48. The concept of Anuvrata was advocated by:
A. Mahayana Buddhism B. Jainism
C. the Lokayata school D. Hinayana Buddhism

49. With which religion is Kaivalya associated?
A. Buddhism B. Jainism
C. Hinduism D. Sikhism

50. At which place did Gautama meet the five Brahmanas after achieving his enlightenment?
A. Sarnath B. Bodh Gaya
C. Kusinara D. Lumbini

51. Gautama gained enlightenment on the banks of the river:
A. Ganga B. Niranjana
C. Son D. Gandak

52. The famous Buddha disciple Sariputra was born in:
A. Gaya B. Vaishali
C. Patna D. Nalanda

53. The famous Mahabodhi temple was built at Bodh Gaya where:
A. Gautama Buddha was born
B. Gautama Buddha gave his first sermon
C. Gautama Buddha achieved englightenment
D. Gautama Buddha had died

54. The birth place of 12th Jaina Tirthankara was:
A. Champa B. Vaishali
C. Patna D. Gaya

55. Mahavira died at which place?
A. Vaishali B. Videha
C. Pavapuri D. Rajagriha

56. Mahavira's mother Trishala was a princess of:
A. Lichchavi B. Sarnath
C. Anga D. Videha

57. Mahavira's father Siddhartha was related to:
A. Kapilavastu B. Videha
C. Sarnath D. Vajji republic

58. Kundagrama, the birth place of Mahavira is situated in:
A. Patna B. Vaishali
C. Munger D. Champaran

59. The first Buddhist council was held at:
A. Rajagriha B. Vaishali
C. Pataliputra D. Kundalavana

60. The second Buddhist council was held during the reign of:
A. Ashoka B. Kalashoka
C. Kanishka D. Ajatashatru

61. Who was the founder of Ajivika sect?
A. Ajita Keshakambalin B. Makkhali Ghoshala
C. Pakudha Kaccayana D. Purana Kasyapa

62. Who was the founder of the Maurya dynasty?
A. Ashoka B. Chandragupta Maurya
C. Bindusara D. Dasaratha

63. Who helped Chandragupta Maurya in ascending the throne of Magadha?
A. Chanakya B. Seleucus
C. Megasthenes D. Radhagupta

64. The Greek ambassador Megasthenes lived in the court of:
A. Ashoka B. Bindusara
C. Chandragupta Maurya D. Kunala

65. During the reign of which Maurya King a 12-year long drought took place?
A. Ashoka B. Bindusara
C. Samprati D. Chandragupta Maurya

66. Who was the prime minister of Chandragupta Maurya?
A. Chanakya B. Radhagupta
C. Bhadrabahu D. Megasthenes

67. When did Ashoka invade Kalinga?
A. 298 B.C. B. 273 B.C.
C. 261 B.C. D. 232 B.C.

68. The Arthasastra is a treatise on which of the following?
A. Economics
B. Environment
C. Political Philosophy
D. Religion in Administration

69. Which one of the following edicts mentions the personal name of Ashoka?
A. Kalsi B. Rummindei
C. Bhabhru D. Maski

70. Who was the last ruler of Maurya dynasty in Bihar?
A. Brihadratha B. Samprati
C. Salisuka D. Kunala

71. The book written by Megasthenes is:
A. Arthasastra B. Indika
C. Mudrarakshasa D. Rajatarangini

72. Who was the successor of Bindusara?
A. Ashoka B. Tivara
C. Dasaratha D. Pushyamitra

73. Important evidence of the Maurya period has been found at which place?
A. Kumrahar B. Rajgir
C. Champa D. Sasaram

74. Who claimed that the affairs of the city of Pataliputra were conducted by a body consisting of 30 members which was divided into 6 boards of five members each?

A. Fa-hien B. Vishakhadatta
C. Taranath D. Megasthenes

75. The Greek ambassador Deimachus visited Magadha during the reign of:
A. Chandragupta Maurya B. Bindusara
C. Ashoka D. Brihadratha

76. Ptolemy Phillandelphus of Egypt sent Dionysius as his ambassador at the Mauryan court of:
A. Bindusara B. Chandragupta
C. Ashoka D. Dasaratha

77. Who built the famous temple named Gopika Kuha Bhawan in Nagarjuni Hills near Gaya?
A. Dasaratha B. Ashoka
C. Chandragupta D. Bindusara

78. The Mauryan palace excavated at Kumrahar was chiefly made of:
A. bricks B. stones
C. mud D. wood

79. During Ashoka's period there were 5 provinces after the addition of Kalinga. The capital of Kalinga (Prachyapatha) was at:
A. Pataliputra B. Tosali
C. Taxila D. Ujjaini

80. Which of the following edicts of Ashoka was not found in Bihar?
A. Lauriya Areraj B. Rummindei
C. Lauriya Nandangarh D. Rampurwa

81. In which district of Bihar, the edicts of Ashoka have been found?
A. Champaran B. Kaimur
C. Chhapra D. Bhagalpur

82. Which of the following sources mentions about the administration of Pataliputra?
A. Divyavadana B. Arthashastra
C. Indika D. Edicts of Ashoka

83. Which dynasty ruled Magadha after the fall of the Nandas?
A. Shungas B. Guptas
C. Mauryas D. Kushans

84. Megasthenes, who lived in the court of Chandragupta Maurya was the ambassador of:
A. Seleucus B. Alexander
C. Ptolemy D. Antiochus I

85. The central court of the Mauryas was situated at:
A. Pataliputra B. Avanti
C. Vaishali D. Suvarnagiri

86. Ashoka's Dhamma was:
A. a moral code
B. a religious law
C. an administrative system
D. a war code

87. The palace of Chandragupta Maurya was situated at:
A. Rajgriha B. Vaishali
C. Maner D. Kumrahar (Patna)

88. Who among the following had defeated the Hunas?
A. Chandragupta II B. Samudragupta
C. Skandagupta D. Ramagupta

89. Aryabhatta, the great mathematician and astrologer was related to which place?
A. Odantapura B. Pataliputra
C. Vaishali D. Nalanda

90. Gupta period coins have been found from which place?
A. Rajgir B. Vaishali
C. Sasaram D. Munger

91. Which Gupta ruler married Kumaradevi, a Lichchavi princess?
A. Chandragupta I B. Samudragupta
C. Chandragupta II D. Kumaragupta

92. The capital of Guptas was at:
A. Kanauj B. Ujjain
C. Pataliputra D. Allahabad

93. Nalanda University was established by the:
A. Mauryas B. Kushans
C. Palas D. Guptas

94. Nalanda University is famous for:
A. Medicine B. Philosophy
C. Buddhist Philosophy D. Physics

95. For how long did the Chinese pilgrim Fa-Hien stay in Pataliputra?
A. 3 months B. 1 year
C. 3 years D. 14 months

96. The Mahabodhi temple in Bodhgaya was established during the reign of:
A. Mauryas B. Palas
C. Guptas D. Later Guptas

97. The coronation ceremony Chandragupta-I took place at:
A. Prayag B. Banaras
C. Kanauj D. Pataliputra

98. The last ruler of the Later Guptas was:
A. Adityasena B. Jivitagupta II
C. Madhavagupta D. Kumaragupta III

99. In which one of the following inscriptions are Samudragupta's achievements mentioned?
A. Allahabad Pillar Inscription
B. Junagarh Rock Inscription
C. Mehrauli Iron Pillar Inscription
D. Hathigumpha Edict

100. In Sanskrit plays written during the Gupta period women and sudras speak:
A. Sanskrit B. Prakrit
C. Pali D. Sauraseni

101. Which one of the following is not a work of Kalidasa?
A. Ritusamhara B. Meghaduta
C. Kumarasambhava D. Dashakumaracharita

102. In Gupta period, the king's share of product was known as:
A. Bhaga B. Bhoga
C. Kara D. Hiranya

103. The largest grant of villages to temples and brahmanas was given by the ruling dynasty known as:
A. Guptas B. Palas
C. Rashtrakutas D. Pratiharas

104. Which university in Bihar was famous during the reign of Harshavardhan?
A. Vikramashila B. Gaya
C. Patna D. Nalanda

105. Which of the following authors stayed in Bihar and provided first hand information about the attacks of Bakhtiyar Khalji?
A. Minhas-us-Siraj B. Ziauddin Barani
C. Mullah Taqia D. Rizquallah

106. Which of the following books provide an account of land revenue in Bihar?
A. Tabakat-i-Nasiri B. Ain-i-Akbari
C. Akbarnama D. Tarikh-i-Firozshahi

107. The Arabic and Persian inscriptions in Bihar are predominantly found in:
A. Patna B. Sasaram
C. Bihar Sharif D. All of the above

108. Name the author of the book Corpus of Arabic and Persian Inscription of Bihar?
A. Cunningham B. Prof. Qyamuddin
C. Buchanan D. Z.A. Desai

109. The definite proof of minting of coins in Bihar comes from:
A. Tirhut-urf-Tughlaqpur B. Munger
C. Gaya D. Sasaram

110. Narsimhadeva was the king of:
A. Mithila B. Bhojpur
C. Sasaram D. Videha

111. Who founded the independent Karnat dynasty in Mithila?
A. Nanyadeva B. Narsimhadeva
C. Harisimha D. Devapala

112. Who founded the famous Odantapura Vihara?
A. Devapala B. Gopala
C. Rampala D. Narayanpala

113. Who was the last great king of Karnata dynasty?
A. Nanyadeva B. Harisimhadeva
C. Narsimhadeva D. None of the above

114. Who built the Sonapura Vihara in North Bengal?
A. Devapala B. Dharmapala
C. Gopala D. Vigrahapala

115. The Munger Copper Plate inscription belongs to which Pala King?
A. Devapala B. Gopala
C. Mahipala D. Dharmapala

116. The first important victory of Bakhtiyar Khalji in Bihar was:
A. Bihar Sharif (Oddantapuri)
B. Patna
C. Bhagalpur
D. Munger

117. Who destroyed the Nalanda University?
A. Mahmud Ghazni B. Bakhtiyar Khalji
C. Babar D. Muhammad Ghori

118. Who was the first ruler of Delhi Sultanate to invade Bihar?
A. Balban B. Alauddin Khalji
C. Aibak D. Iltutmish

119. At which place was Bakhtiyar Khalji buried?
A. Lakhnauti B. Munger
C. Bihar Sharif D. Rajgir

120. Who established the Turkish rule in Bihar?
A. Aibak B. Bakhtiyar Khalji
C. Iltutmish D. Malik Husam-ud-din

121. Which ruler established a mint-town at Tirhut which was also called Tughlaqabad-urf-Tirhut?
A. Ghiyasuddin Tughlaq
B. Firoz Tughlaq
C. Muhammad-bin-Tughlaq
D. Alauddin Khalji

122. Which Sultan ended the rule of Karnata dynasty?
A. Muhammad-bin-Tughlaq
B. Ghiyasuddin Tughlaq
C. Firoz Shah Tughlaq
D. Muhammad Tughlaq

123. Who defeated the Karnata dynasty ruler Harisimha Deva?
A. Ghiyasuddin Tughlaq B. Iltutmish
C. Firoz Tughlaq D. Alauddin Khalji

124. Which Sultan constructed a fort and a Jama Masjid in Darbhanga?
A. Firoz Tughlaq
B. Iltutumish
C. Ghiyasuddin Tughlaq
D. Muhammad-bin-Tughlaq

125. Which Sultan of Delhi conclusively controlled Bihar?
A. Tughlaqs B. Khaljis
C. Mamluks D. None of the above

126. In the 14th century Firoz helped in establishing the rule of which dynasty?
A. Karnata B. Vainvaar
C. Mitra D. Thakur

127. Who was the founder of Nuhani dynasty in Bihar?
A. Jalal Khan Nuhani B. Darya Khan Nuhani
C. Bahar Khan Nuhani D. Daulat Khan Lodhi

128. Who among the following was placed as the administrator of Bihar by Babar after removing Mahmud Lodhi?
A. Bahar Khan B. Jalal Khan
C. Farid Khan D. Hasan Khan

129. Who was deputed by Sikander Lodhi in 1495-96 as the head of Bihar?
A. Farid Khan B. Hasan Khan
C. Bahar Khan Nuhani D. Darya Khan Nuhani

130. The Sur dynasty was established by:
A. Sher Shah B. Hasan Khan
C. Muhammad Nuhani D. Darya Khan

131. Sher Khan's father Hasan Khan was a Jagirdar of:
A. Patna B. Gaya
C. Sasaram D. Arrah

132. Patna was made a provincial capital of Bihar by:
A. Ibrahim Lodhi B. Hasan Khan
C. Sher Shah D. Azim-us-Shaan

133. Sher Khan was appointed as the caretaker of which ruler of Bihar?
A. Darya Khan B. Jalal Khan
C. Hasan Khan D. Muhammad Nuhani

134. Sher Shah defeated Humayun in which of the following battles?
A. Kanauj or Bilgram B. Chausa
C. Both A and B D. None of the above

135. Who was the last Afghan ruler of Bihar?
A. Ibrahim Shah Sur
B. Ibrahim Lodhi
C. Dawood Khan Qararani
D. Sulaiman Qararani

136. Akbar merged Bihar and Bengal in Mughal empire in:
A. 1550 B. 1575
C. 1572 D. 1576

137. Who was the Governor of Bihar during Akbar's reign?
A. Munim Khan B. Baj Bahadur
C. Daud Khan D. None of the above

138. Who was the first Mughal ruler to be sworn in Patna?
A. Farrukhsiyar B. Bahadur Shah
C. Jahangir D. Shahjahan

139. Which Mughal ruler made his grandson as the Subedar of Bihar?
A. Akbar B. Shahjahan
C. Jahangir D. Aurangzeb

140. Who was the first Mughal Prince to be appointed as the governor of Bihar?
A. Prince Salim B. Prince Azim
C. Prince Parvez D. Prince Khurram

141. Raja Man Singh was appointed the governor of Bihar by:
A. Akbar B. Shah Jahan
C. Jahangir D. Aurangzeb

142. Who built the Shahi Idgah in Patna City?
A. Itiqad Khan B. Shaista Khan
C. Zulfiqar Khan D. Saif Khan

143. Who was the Dewan of Bihar when Prince Azim was the governor of Bihar?
A. Saadat Khan B. Safdarjung
C. Murshid Quli Khan D. Allahawardi Khan

144. Daud Khan was defeated by Akbar in the battle of:
A. Bahadurpur B. Munger
C. Rajmahal D. Chausa

145. The East India Company proclaimed the diwani rights of Bengal, Bihar and Odisha during the reign of:
A. Mir Qasim B. Shah Alam II
C. Farrukhsiyar D. Alivardi Khan

146. Who became the deputy Nawab of Bihar after the Battle of Plassey (1757)?
A. Mir Jafar B. Miran
C. Shujjat Khan D. Tabtabai

147. The first British traveller to visit Bihar was:
A. Bishop Heber B. Peter Mundy
C. John Marshall D. Raulf Fitch

148. Which Nawab of Bengal transferred his capital from Mushidabad to Munger?
A. Mir Jafar B. Siraj-ud-Daulah
C. Mir Qasim D. Alivardi Khan

149. In which year the Dutch established their first factory in Bihar?
A. 1620 B. 1651
C. 1609 D. 1632

150. In which year the Danes established their factory in Patna?
A. 1774 B. 1664
C. 1631 D. 1786

151. The Britishers established their first trading centre in 1620 Bihar at:
A. Munger B. Alamganj (Patna)
C. Purnea D. Champaran

152. Who among the following was the first to oppose the British rule in Bihar?
A. Ali Gauhar B. Haider Ali Khan
C. Kunwar Singh D. Mir Qasim

153. In which year was the Revenue Council of Patna established?
A. 1770 B. 1765
C. 1801 D. 1719

154. In which year did the company remove Dhiraj Narayan and replaced him with Raja Shitab Rai as the Naib Diwan of Bihar?
A. 1801 B. 1767
C. 1791 D. 1765

155. The Golghar in Patna was constructed during the reign of:
A. Warren Hastings B. Lord Hardinge
C. John Shore D. Lord Cornwallis

156. The first English magistrate of Patna was:
A. James Alexander B. Charles Francis Grand
C. Robert Palk D. John Vansittart

157. The battle of Buxar was fought on:
A. October 22, 1764 B. September 23, 1761
C. June 24, 1764 D. June 24, 1761

158. Who was the commander of British army in the battle of Buxar?
A. Clive B. Lord Hastings
C. Hector Munro D. Major Knox

159. Who emerged victorious in the battle of Buxar?
A. Shuja-ud-daulah B. East India Company
C. Shah Alam II D. Mir Qasim

160. Who was appointed as the Naib Diwan of Bihar by Robert Clive?
A. Omichand B. Shitab Rai
C. Raja Durlabh Rai D. Manik Chand

161. Which of the following is not related to Wahabi movement?
A. Syed Ahmad B. Shah Waliullah
C. Vilayat Ali D. Birsa Munda

162. In which year Wahabi movement was started?
A. 1820 B. 1830
C. 1840 D. 1850

163. Which of the following was/were the centres for the Wahabi Movement?
A. Patna B. Sittana
C. Both A and B D. None of these

164. Who led the Kol revolt?
A. Budhu Bhagat B. Sidhu and Kanhu
C. Birsa Munda D. Raja Porhat

165. Who led the Bhumij revolt?
A. Ganga Narayan B. Sidhu and Kanhu
C. Sayed Hasan D. Raja Porhat

166. Who among the following participated in the revolt of Tana Bhagat?
A. Ho tribe B. Munda tribe
C. Santhal tribe D. Oraon tribe

167. The Tana Bhagat movement was essentially a _______ movement.
A. religious B. political
C. social D. natural

168. The occupation of which of the following region led the HO uprising?
A. occupation of Singhbhum
B. occupation of Chhotanagpur
C. occupation of Kalahandi
D. None of the above

169. In which year Kol uprising began?
A. 1832 B. 1831
C. 1833 D. 1834

170. Who among the following was the leader of Ho tribals movement?
A. Raja Parhat B. Sidhu and Kanhu
C. Birsa Munda D. Budhu Bhagat

171. In which year Bhumij revolt started?
A. 1831 B. 1832
C. 1833 D. 1834

172. The term 'ulgulan' means:
A. Rebellion B. Courageous
C. Tribal movement D. Tribal song

173. Santhal uprising was led by:
A. Sidhu and Kanhu B. Birsa Munda
C. Budhu Bhagat D. None of them

174. Kunwar Singh was the King of:
A. Hamirpur B. Dheerpur
C. Jagdishpur D. Rampur

175. The leaders of the revolt of 1857 in Bihar was:
A. Maulvi Ahmadullah B. Tatya Tope
C. Nana Sahib D. Kunwar Singh

176. Who among the following had established an arms and ammunition factory at Jagdishpur?
A. Amar Singh B. Kunwar Singh
C. Pir Ali D. Harkishen Singh

177. Which region in Bihar was unaffected by the revolt of 1857?
1. Danapur 2. Patna
3. Ara 4. Muzaffarpur
5. Munger
Choose from the following options:
A. 4 and 5 B. Only 5
C. Only 4 D. 3, 4 and 5

178. The rulers of which state denied entry to Kunwar Singh in his state?
A. Rewa B. Azamgarh
C. Awadh D. Banda

179. Kunwar Singh fought his last war against which English captain?
A. Douglas B. Lugard
C. Le Grand D. Eyre

180. Who was the leader of Patna uprising in 1857?
A. Jaimangal Singh B. Inayat Ali
C. Vilayat Ali D. Pir Ali

181. Who arrested Amar Singh, the leader of revolt of 1857?
A. Lugard
B. Maharaja Jang Bahadur
C. Maharaja Rai Bahadur
D. Samuels

182. Kunwar Singh tried to meet which of the following leaders in October 1857?
A. Lakshmibai B. Liaqat Ali
C. Tatya Tope D. Begum Hazrat Mahal

183. Pir Ali, the leader of Patna rising was convicted and hanged on:
A. July 7, 1858 B. July 7, 1857
C. August 7, 1857 D. August 7, 1858

184. At which place in Bihar the revolt of 1857 started comprehensively for the first time?
A. Patna B. Munger
C. Muzaffarpur D. Rajgir

185. When did Kunwar Singh die?
A. 10 April, 1858 B. 23 April, 1858
C. 26 April, 1858 D. 20 June, 1858

186. Amar Singh initiated the guerilla war against the British in the hills of:
A. Rajgir B. Ranchi
C. Kaimur D. None of the above

187. The Zamindars of the following places helped the Company during the revolt of 1857?
A. Hathua B. Pandaul
C. Bettiah D. All of the above

188. Kunwar Singh captured which of the following districts on March 25, 1858?
A. Rewa B. Kanpur
C. Azamgarh D. Kalpi

189. Kunwar Singh helped Nana Saheb in the war of:
A. Lucknow B. Kanpur
C. Shahabad D. Jhansi

190. Who had invited Gandhiji in West Champaran district in Bihar?
A. Raj Kumar Shukla B. Mahadeo Desai
C. Rajendra Prasad D. Narhari Parikh

191. Which of the following Government Acts separated Odisha from Bihar province?
A. 1909 Act B. 1919 Act
C. 1935 Act D. 1948 Act

192. In Bihar, resolution for Non-cooperation Movement was passed in 1920 provincial meeting under the leadership of:
A. Rajendra Prasad B. Mazhar-ul-Haq
C. Shah Mohammad D. None of the above

193. In which year the period of Swarajist Movement started in Bihar?
A. 1920 B. 1922
C. 1921 D. 1923

194. The All India Congress Session in 1922, December was held in:
A. Patna B. Gaya
C. Bhagalpur D. Champaran

195. Which of the following movements is called first Civil Disobedience Movement?
A. Champaran B. Bhagalpur
C. Bardoli D. Gaya

196. Patna Yuvak Sangh was formed in:
A. 1929 B. 1926
C. 1928 D. 1927

197. Where was Anushilan Committee Branch established in Bihar?
A. Gaya B. Patna
C. Muzaffarpur D. Munger

198. When the British prince visited Bihar?
A. 1921 B. 1922
C. 1923 D. 1924

199. Who had formed Bihar Provincial Kisan Sabha (BPKS)?
A. Shahjanand Saraswati
B. Mohammad Zubair
C. Sri Krishna Singh
D. Rajendra Prasad

200. Champaran Satyagraha was against:
A. Tinkathiya system B. High rent
C. Outsiders D. Illegal transfer of land

201. When was Bihar Socialist Party established?
A. 1934 B. 1932
C. 1931 D. 1933

202. Who was the leader of Salt Satyagraha in Bihar?
A. Rajendra Prasad B. Jawaharlal Nehru
C. Gandhiji D. Professor Abdul Bari

203. Salt Revolt in Patna had started from which of the following dates?
A. 16th April, 1930 B. 18th April, 1930
C. 4th May, 1930 D. 3rd April, 1930

204. Which of the following physical features form the North-Western Part of Bihar?
A. Someshwar range B. Kaimur Plateau
C. Nawada hills D. Rajgir hills

205. In Bihar, Kaimur series of rocks are found in which district?
A. Bhojpur B. Aurangabad
C. Buxar D. Kaimur

206. Geologically southern plateau of Bihar was formed in the period.
A. Pre-cambrian B. Oligocene
C. Miocene D. Pleistocene

207. Mica deposits are found in which kind of rocks?
A. Dharwar B. Tertiary
C. Vindhyan D. Quaternary

208. The highest place of Bihar is:
A. Santpur B. Kaimur hills
C. Someshwar range D. Barabar hills

209. In which period was Ramnagar Dun formed?
A. Dharwar B. Quaternary
C. Vindhyan D. Tertiary

210. Bihar was maximum areal extent in which of the following natural regions?
A. Terai region of Shiwalik
B. North Gangetic Plan
C. South Gangetic Plan
D. None of the above

211. Chuars found in the Bihar plain are:
A. flooded plain B. levees
C. oxbow lakes D. highlands

212. In which district(s) of Bihar, gneiss, quartzite and schist rocks are found?
A. Munger B. Gaya
C. Sheikhpura D. All of these

213. The capital of the Shungas was at:
A. Sialkot B. Rajagriha
C. Kannauj D. Pataliputra

214. Out of the total geographical area of India, Bihar comprises:
A. 3.76% B. 6.76%
C. 4.02% D. 2.86%

215. The total geographical area of Bihar is:
A. 94,162 sq.km B. 94,163 sq.km
C. 94,164 sq.km D. 94,165 sq.km

216. Bihar forms an international boundary with which country?
A. Bhutan B. Bangladesh
C. Nepal D. China

217. Which district of Bihar has the longest border with Nepal?
A. West Champaran B. Sitamarhi
C. Kishanganj D. East Champaran

218. The highest part of Ramnagar Dun is:
A. Someshwar fort B. Santpur
C. Gridhkut D. Barabar

219. The length of Bihar from east to west is:
A. 483 km B. 362 km
C. 401 km D. 415 km

220. Harha valley which is located in north-western Bihar is also known as:
A. Ramnagar Dun B. Dun Valley
C. Someshwar Range D. None of the above

221. Which of the following ranges form a boundary between India and Nepal?
A. Kaimur Hills B. Ramnagar Dun
C. Someshwar Ranges D. None of the above

222. Gogaville Bird Sanctuary is situated in which district of Bihar?
A. Arwal B. Aurangabad
C. Araria D. Banka

223. Mandar Vidyapeeth is situated in:
A. West Champaran B. Vaishali
C. Darbhanga D. Banka

224. The Indian Oil Refinery is located in which district of Bihar?
A. Begusarai B. Sitamarhi
C. Katihar D. Supaul

225. Ustad Bismillah Khan was a native of:
A. Ara B. Dumraon
C. Darbhanga D. Sasaram

226. Bela Industrial Area is located at:
A. Sitamarhi B. East Champaran
C. Darbhanga D. Purnea

227. Raxaul town is also known as:
A. Gateway to Nepal
B. Gateway to Bangladesh
C. Gateway to Bhutan
D. None of these

228. Vishnupad Temple was rebuilt by:
A. Ahilya Bai Holkar B. Sher Shah
C. Kunwar Singh D. Kameshwar Thakhur

229. Where is Tal soil found in Bihar?
A. In terai region
B. In plains
C. In desert
D. In backwater belt of river Ganga

230. Tal soil extends from Buxar to:
A. Banka B. Gaya
C. Bhagalpur D. Champaran

231. What are the major crops that can be grown of Balthar soil?
A. Rice B. Jowar and Bajra
C. Sugarcane D. Pulses

232. Lowest temperature in Bihar is found in:
A. Gaya B. Buxar
C. Rohtas D. Darbhanga

233. Which type of soil is predominantly found in the plains of Ganga?
A. Residual soil B. Alluvial soil
C. Both A and B D. None of the above

234. In which district of Bihar Balsundari soil is found?
A. Saharsa B. Darbhanga
C. Muzaffarpur D. All of the above

235. The old alluvial soil is found in which of the following districts of Bihar:
A. Nalanda B. Munger
C. Bhagalpur D. All of the above

236. Which district of Bihar records the highest temperature?
A. Aurangabad B. Gaya
C. Saran D. Siwan

237. The Bhagar soil in Bihar is found in:
A. Gaya–Bodhgaya–East Champaran Bhagalpur area
B. Purnea–Saharsa–Darbhanga–Muzaffarpur area
C. Gaya–Nalanda–Bodhgaya–Saharsa area
D. East Champaran–Nalanda–Gaya–Sasaram area

238. The Old alluvial soil in Bihar is found in:
A. Rohtas–Gaya–Patna–Munger–Bhagalpur area
B. Purnea–Saharsa–Darbhanga–Muzaffarpur area
C. Saharsa–Darbhanga–Muzaffarpur–Saran area
D. None of the above

239. In which area of Bihar the concentration of lime in the soil is found:
A. North Bihar plain
B. South Bihar plain
C. North-West Bihar plain
D. South-East Bihar plain

240. Consider the following statements about Norwesters.
(*i*) It is a cyclonic wind
(*ii*) It brings rainfall of about 10 cm in Bihar plain
(*iii*) It is useful for crops like mango, litchi, rice and jute.
(*iv*) It is a hot wind blowing from west.

Which of the above statement/s is/are wrong?
A. (*i*), (*ii*) and (*iii*) B. Only (*iv*)
C. (*i*) and (*iv*) D. (*iii*) and (*iv*)

241. In which of the following districts Khadar soil is found?
A. Bhagalpur and Araria
B. Patna and Nalanda
C. Purnea and Saharsa
D. None of the above

242. What is the older alluvium of Ganga plains called?
A. Bhabhar B. Bangar
C. Khadar D. Balsundari

243. Which district of Bihar gets highest rainfall?
A. Araria B. Kishanganj
C. Gaya D. Aurangabad

244. The local winds loo blowing in Bihar has following wind velocity:
A. 10-16 km/hr B. 10-14 km/hr
C. 8-16 km/hr D. 12-16 km/hr

245. The rainfall during monsoon in Bihar is due to:
A. Eastern monsoon B. South-east monsoon
C. Southern monsoon D. South-west monsoon

246. Which of the following crops is grown in red and yellow soil?
A. Pulses B. Sugarcane
C. Rice D. Wheat

247. Usar soil is found in which district?
A. Saran B. West Champaran
C. Siwan D. Nawada

248. Which of the following Wildlife Sanctuaries has hot springs?
A. Bhimbandh B. Vikramshila
C. Sanjay Gandhi D. Kaimur

249. The tropical seasonal swamp forests (canebrakes) are predominantly found in:
A. Gopalganj B. East Champaran
C. Sitamarhi D. West Champaran

250. A Wildlife safari is being established at which place?.
A. Rajgir B. West Champaran
C. Sasaram D. Jamui

251. Bhimbandh Wildlife Sanctuary is famous for:
A. Tiger B. Elephant
C. Leopard D. Resident Birds

252. Find the wrong match:

	Wildlife Sanctuaries	**District**
A.	Valmiki	West Champaran
B.	Kaimur	Rohtas
C.	Vikramshila	Begusarai
D.	Bhimbandh	Munger

253. In which of the following wild life sanctuaries is Anupam lake situated?
A. Vikramshila B. Valmiki
C. Bhimbandh D. Kaimur

254. The largest wildlife sanctuary in Bihar is:
A. Bhimbandh
B. Valmiki
C. Sanjay Gandhi Udyan
D. Kaimur

255. Area of very dense forest is highest in:
A. West Champaran B. Siwan
C. Nawada D. East Champaran

256. The Vikramshila Gangetic Dolphin Sanctuary is located in:
A. Jamui B. Munger
C. Bhagalpur D. Vaishali

257. Kusheshwar Asthan Bird Sanctuary is located in:
A. Vaishali B. West Champaran
C. Samastipur D. Darbhanga

258. Gautam Buddha Bird Sanctuary is located in:
A. Rohtas B. Gaya
C. Nalanda D. Sasaram

259. Udaypur Vanya Prani Sanctuary is located in:
A. East Champaran B. Munger
C. West Champaran D. Rohtas

260. Baraila Jheel Salim Ali Jubba Sahni Bird Sanctuary is located in:
A. Vaishali B. Sheohar
C. Darbhanga D. Banka

261. The Bihar Government declared the Sanjay Gandhi Jaivik Udyan in Patna as protected forest in which year?
A. 1991 B. 1983
C. 1984 D. 1982

262. Nagi Dam Bird Sanctuary and Nakti Dam Bird Sanctuary are located in which district of Bihar?
A. Begusarai B. Siwan
C. Gaya D. Jamui

263. The Centre of Noise Pollution Control Board has been set up at:
A. Siwan B. Bhagalpur
C. Muzaffarpur D. Patna

264. The main vegetation of Bihar is:
A. Deciduous B. Tropical Evergreen
C. Mixed D. Alpine

265. In which of the following districts the Sal mixed deciduous forests are found?
A. Gaya B. Bhagalpur
C. West Champaran D. East Champaran

266. Which river is also known as Niranjana?
A. Gandak B. Phalgu
C. Sone D. Mahananda

267. Why is Bagmati considered as a dangerous river?
A. Due to its changing course
B. Due to its origin in the Himalayas
C. Due to its tendency to create floods
D. None of the above

268. ______ river emerges from Nampa of Nepal situated at Himalayan ranges.
A. Gandak B. Bagmati
C. Kamla D. Ghaghra

269. The North tributaries of the Ganga river are Gandak, Bagmati, Kosi Kalikosi and _____ .
A. Son B. Karmanasa
C. Punpun D. All of these

270. Durgavati and Chandraprabha are important tributaries of which of the following rivers?
A. Karmanasa B. Punpun
C. Phalgu D. Saryu

271. Which pair of springs of Bihar along with their places is not correctly matched?

	Springs	**Places**
A.	Sita Kund	Rajgir
B.	Rishi Kund	Munger
C.	Surya Kund	Rajgir
D.	Brahma Kund	Rajgir

272. Which river does not originate from Himalayas?
A. Bagmati B. Ganga
C. Kamla Balan D. Son

273. Triveni canal gets water from which river?
A. Son B. Kosi
C. Gandak D. Mayurakshi

274. Which of the following rivers of Bihar is almost dry in summer season?
A. Ganga B. Gandak
C. Punpun D. Kosi

275. Which of the following rivers has second longest length in the Bihar state?
A. Ganga B. Bagmati
C. Mahananda D. Burhi Gandak

276. Which river has the largest catchment area in Bihar?
A. Ganga B. Sone
C. Kiul Harohar D. Kosi

277. In which of the following districts river Ganga enters into Bihar?
A. Gopalganj B. Buxar
C. Rohtas D. Siwan

278. Which river is known as 'Sorrow of Bihar'?
A. Karmanasa B. Kosi
C. Son D. Subarnarekha

279. Which river is the sacred river for Hindus?
A. Punpun B. Phalgu
C. Karmanasa D. Sone

280. Name the bridge constructed over the river Ganga which connects Patna to Hajipur.
A. Mahatma Gandhi Setu
B. Hirakund Setu
C. Gopalganj Bridge
D. None of the above

281. Which river of Bihar does originate from the Someshwar hills and flows parallel to river Gandak?

A. Burhi Gandak B. Gandak
C. Kamla D. Bagmati

282. The deposits of manganese are found in the district(s) of:
A. Rohtas B. Kaimur
C. Darbhanga D. Patna and Gaya

283. Uranium is found in which of the following districts of Bihar?
A. Gaya B. Rohtas
C. Munger D. Banka

284. Gold is found in:
A. Munger B. Jamui
C. Siwan D. Saran

285. The deposits of Monazite are found in which districts of Bihar?
A. Siwan and Saran
B. Patna and Aurangabad
C. Gaya and Munger
D. Banka and Bhagalpur

286. Amjhor is famous for which of the following minerals?
A. Coal B. Pyrite
C. Mica D. Gold

287. Pyrite Phosphate and Chemicals Ltd. is located at:
A. Bihta B. Amjhor
C. Jamui D. Nawada

288. The least populous district of Bihar is:
A. Sheikhpura B. Madhubani
C. Saran D. Gaya

289. According to Census 2011, the child sex ratio of Bihar is:
A. 935 B. 938
C. 918 D. 925

290. Which among the following districts of Bihar has the lowest sex ratio?
A. Vaishali B. Arwal
C. Saran D. Siwan

291. Which among the following districts of Bihar has lowest population density?
A. Arwal B. Madhubani
C. Saran D. Kaimur

292. Which among the following districts of Bihar has the highest population density?
A. Sheohar B. Siwan
C. Saran D. Sitamarhi

293. The most populous district of Bihar is:
A. Patna B. Madhubani
C. Saran D. Gaya

294. As per Census 2011, the literacy rate of Bihar is:
A. 61.8% B. 71.2%
C. 52.5% D. 23.5%

295. As per Census 2011, the population density of Bihar is:
A. 223 B. 153
C. 1106 D. 123

296. According to Census 2011, what is the sex ratio of Bihar?
A. 918 B. 982
C. 972 D. 935

297. Which among the following districts of Bihar has the highest sex ratio?
A. Saran B. Sheohar
C. Madhubani D. Gopalganj

298. Which among the following districts of Bihar has the lowest child population?
A. Vaishali B. Arwal
C. Saran D. Siwan

299. According to Census 2011, the total population of Bihar is:
A. 10,40,99,452 B. 56,58,509
C. 68,70,997 D. 70,68,997

300. Highest production of wheat is recorded in which of the following districts?
A. Siwan B. Rohtas
C. Kaimur D. Muzaffarpur

301. Highest production of potato is recorded in which of the following districts?
A. Nalanda B. Patna
C. Saran D. Katihar

302. Sonaru Fish Seed Farm is being developed at which of the following places?
A. Badh B. Muzaffarpur
C. Gaya D. Fatuha

303. Which districts of Bihar has the highest population of goats?
A. Bhagalpur B. West Champaran
C. Araria D. East Champaran

304. Which district of Bihar is the leading produce of maize?
A. Katihar B. Madhepura
C. Khagaria D. Kaimur

305. The district of Bihar having the highest productivity (kg/hectare) of rice is:
A. Rohtas B. Lakhisarai
C. Sheikhpura D. West Champaran

306. A Fishery Research Centre has been established at which place:
A. Sonepur B. Fatuha
C. Mithapur D. Araria

307. The leading fish producing districts in Bihar are:
A. Kaimur, West Champaran, Madhubani
B. Madhubani, East Champaran, Darbhanga

C. Sitamarhi, Vaishali, Banka
D. Bhagalpur, Supaul, Saharsa

308. Which districts will be benefitted by the Budi Gandak–Noon-via-Ganga link scheme?
A. Samastipur, Begusarai, Khagaria
B. Jamui, Bhagalpur, Banka
C. Jamui, Banka, Lakhisarai
D. Kanpur, Rohtas, Aurangabad

309. The main cereal rops of Bihar are:
A. Groundnut, Coffee, Wheat
B. Sugarane, Tea, Barley
C. Rice, Wheat, Maize
D. None of the above

310. Which of the following district in Bihar is leader in terms of pulses production?
A. Patna B. Aurangabad
C. Nalanda D. Rohtas

311. Which of the following districts of Bihar has highest percentage of net sown area?
A. Siwan B. Gopalganj
C. Buxar D. Bhojpur

312. Which district of Bihar has the largest area under wheat cultivation?
A. East Champaran B. Rohtas
C. Kishanganj D. Siwan

313. Which district of Bihar has the largest area under rice cultivation?
A. Madhubani B. Samastipur
C. East Champaran D. Rohtas

314. Which district of Bihar has the largest area under maize cultivation?
A. Samastipur B. East Champaran
C. Begusarai D. Khagaria

315. Which district of Bihar has recorded highest productivity (kg/hectare) of sugarcane?
A. West Champaran B. Nalanda
C. Jehanabad D. East Champaran

316. Who has described agriculture as the Core Competence of Bihar?
A. APJ Abdul Kalam B. Pranab Mukherjee
C. Atal Behari Vajpayee D. M.S. Swaminathan

317. The marketing of dairy products in Bihar is done by which of the following organization?
A. KVIC B. COMFED
C. BIADA D. PMEGP

318. The medicine industry is situated in which of the following places?
A. Naryanpur B. Rampur
C. Bela D. Fatuha

319. The major implementing agency for Prime Minister Employment Generation Programme (PMEGP) is:
A. SIPB B. KVIC
C. KVI BOARD D. DIC

320. A Food Park is being established at which place?
A. Buxar B. Araria
C. Katihar D. Bettiah

321. In which year the Bihar State Milk Cooperative Federation was established?
A. 1984 B. 1981
C. 1980 D. 1983

322. Mukhyamantri Integrated Handloom Development Scheme was started in year:
A. 2011-12 B. 2012-13
C. 2013-14 D. 2014-15

323. The gun factory in Bihar is situated at which place?
A. Bhagalpur B. Sitamarhi
C. Munger D. Patna

324. In which five year plan was Barauni Oil Refinery in Bihar established?
A. Third B. Second
C. Fifth D. Fourth

325. In which district of Bihar the first Jute Park is being established?
A. Purnea B. Aurangabad
C. Begusarai D. Khagaria

326. At which place is Bihar Institute of Silk and Textiles located?
A. Nabinagar B. Fatuha
C. Bihta D. Nathnagar

327. The yarn produced under Mukhya Mantri Kosi Mulberry Scheme will be marketed under the brand name of:
A. Koshiki B. Mulberry Silk
C. Resham D. Tassar Silk

328. Which institute is the Cluster Monitoring and Technical Assistant (CMTA) for Bhagalpur Mega Handloom Cluster?
A. Rajendra Agriultural University, Pusa
B. NIFT, Patna
C. Bihar Institute for Silk and Textiles, Nathnagar
D. Bihar Agricultural University, Sabour

329. Match the corret pairs:

Cities	Industry
(*a*) Muzaffarpur	1. Tea
(*b*) Purnea	2. Tourism
(*c*) Kishanganj	3. Jute
(*d*) Gaya	4. Leather

Codes:

	(*a*)	(*b*)	(*a*)	(*d*)
A.	1	2	3	4
B.	4	3	2	1
C.	2	3	4	1
D.	4	3	1	2

330. In which of the following district of Bihar Castor Silk Development Project has been approved?
A. Purnea B. Katihar
C. Begusarai D. Kishanganj

331. The Plywood industry in Bihar is located in:
A. Hajipur B. Siwan
C. Muzaffarpur D. Motihari

332. Find out the incorrect pair:
A. Hajipur Plywood
B. Purnea Jute
C. Chakulia Leather
D. Samastipur Paper

333. Which city of Bihar is also known as Silk City?
A. Bhagalpur B. Purnea
C. Banka D. Madhubani

334. In which year was the sugar industry established in Bihar?
A. 1904 B. 1908
C. 1916 D. 1921

335. Which NGO is involved in the Tasar Silk Development at Chakai in Jamui?
A. Pahal B. Pradan
C. Prabandh D. Prarthna

336. The first diamond polishing unit in Bihar is being established at:
A. Patna B. Gaya
C. Muzaffarpur D. Samastipur

337. Mokama in Bihar is famous for:
A. Shoe factory B. Wagon of goods train
C. Brewery D. All of the above

338. The jute industry in Bihar is concentrated in which region:
A. North-western B. North-eastern
C. South-eastern D. Central

339. The Oil Refinery in Barauni was set up with the help of which country?
A. USA B. USSR
C. Britain D. Germany

340. The first radio station in Bihar was established at which place?
A. Muzaffarpur B. Patna
C. Darbhanga D. Sitamarhi

341. Abdul Bari Bridge is on the river Son at:
A. Koilwar B. Sonpur
C. Mokama D. Bhagalpur

342. The BSRTC was established in:
A. 1957 B. 1958
C. 1960 D. 1959

343. Which zone of Indian Railways lies in Bihar with its headquarters at Hajipur?
A. North-East Frontier Railways
B. East Central Zone
C. North-East Zone
D. Central Zone

344. Which two places in Bihar have international airports?
A. Patna and Muzaffarpur
B. Gaya and Bhagalpur
C. Patna and Gaya
D. Patna and Rajgir

345. Which National Highway in Bihar is a part of Golden Quadrangle project?
A. NH2 B. NH 31
C. NH 35 D. NH 38

346. The waterways present in river Ganga between Allahabad and Haldia is:
A. NW 2 B. NW 3
C. NW 1 D. NW 4

347. In which year was Bihar Rural Road Development Agency established?
A. 2004 B. 2003
C. 2002 D. 2001

348. A flying club is situated in which of the following places?
A. Nalanda B. Gaya
C. Patna D. Bhagalpur

349. Jaiprakash Narain International Airport is situated at:
A. Patna B. Nalanda
C. Bhagalpur D. Gaya

350. The capital of the Kanvas was at:
A. Ujjain B. Mathura
C. Pratishthan D. Pataliputra

351. Find the wrong pair:
A. Darbhanga – Nehru Setu
B. Bhagalpur – Vikramshila Setu
C. Mokama – Rajendra Setu
D. Patna – Gandhi Setu

352. In which of the following cities Vayudut service has been started?
A. Muzaffarpur B. Gaya
C. Raxaul D. Patna

353. Kataiya Hydro Power Project is located in which district of Bihar?
A. Supaul B. Katihar
C. Arwal D. Kishanganj

354. The highest installed capacity for power generation in Bihar is from:
A. Hydel Projects
B. Wind Projects
C. Thermal Power Projects
D. Nuclear Power Plants

355. In which district of Bihar an Ultra Mega Plant of 4000 MW capacity is being established?
A. Buxar B. Supaul
C. Katihar D. Banka

356. In which year was Bihar State Electricity Board established?
A. 2000 B. 1958
C. 1936 D. 1948

357. Find the wrong Match:
A. Nirmali Hydel Project Madhubani
B. Tejpura Hydel Projet Arwal
C. Rajpur Hydel Project Supaul
D. Amethi Hydel Projet Rohtas

358. Which of the following schemes have been launched by the central government for expanding the coverage of electricity supply?
A. IPDS B. DDUGJY
C. BRGF D. All of the above

359. Kosi Hydel Power Station is under the administration of:
A. BSHPC B. BREDA
C. BSEB D. None of the above

360. NABARD has identified how many districts in Bihar for promoting and financing women SHGs through positioning an anchor NGO in each identified district?
A. 15 B. 16
C. 17 D. 18

361. Which of the following reasons have been identified by NABARD for the dismal performance of SHGs in Bihar?
A. delays in opening SHG accounts
B. inadequate outreach in many regions
C. non-approval of repeat loans even when the first loans were repaired promptly
D. All of the above

362. Which of the following sectors are convered by RIDF?
A. Agriculture and Related sector
B. Social sectors
C. Rural connectivity
D. All of the above

363. Which district of Bihar has the highest participation of women in employment under MGNREGA?
A. Begusarai B. Darbhanga
C. Supaul D. Saharsa

364. The total number of Zila Parishads in Bihar are:
A. 36 B. 38
C. 41 D. 31

365. The chairperson of Zila Parishad is called:
A. Adhyaksha B. Mukhiya
C. Pramukh D. None of these

366. The Chairperson of Panchayat Samiti is called:
A. Mukhiya B. Adhyaksha
C. Pramukh D. Sarpanch

367. The Chairperson of Gram Panchayat is called:
A. Mukhiya B. Pramukh
C. Adhyaksha D. None of these

368. Bihar Panchayat Strengthening Project is being implemented with the help of:
A. SBI B. IMF
C. ADB D. World Bank

369. Which two cities of Bihar have received administrative approval for the implementation of Heritage City Development and Augmen-tation Yojana (HRIDAY)?
A. Ara and Sasaram B. Patna and Muzaffarpur
C. Gaya and Patna D. Gaya and Bodh Gaya

370. Which agency has been given the task of preparation of Detailed Project Report (DPR) for Patna Metro Rail Project?
A. CPWD B. DMRC
C. RITES Ltd. D. SE Railway

371. In which town of Bihar is Satyagraha Park being developed?
A. Motihari B. Bettiah
C. Ara D. Bhagalpur

372. Buddha Smriti Park is developed in which city of Bihar?
A. Vaishali B. Bhagalpur
C. Hajipur D. Patna

373. In which year was Bihar Urban Infrastructure Development Corporation (BUIDCO) established?
A. 2007 B. 2008
C. 2009 D. 2010

374. UIG and UIDSSMT are the sub-components of which of the following urban development programmes:
A. AMRUT
B. HRIDAY
C. Swachh Bharat Mission
D. Namami Ganga Scheme

375. The Namami Gange Scheme, a Central government programme aiming at the cleaning and rejuvenation of the river Ganga is being implemented in how many towns of Bihar:
A. 31 B. 20
C. 34 D. 35

376. The Support Programme for Urban Reforms (SPUR) is being implemented in 28 largest ULBs in Bihar with the support of:
A. USA B. Russia
C. France D. UK

377. Which three cities in Bihar have qualified to be developed under Phase I of Smart City Mission?
A. Patna, Bhagalpur, Muzaffarpur
B. Bhagalpur, Muzaffarpur, Gaya
C. Bhagalpur, Muzaffarpur, Biharsharif
D. Muzaffarpur, Biharsharif, Patna

378. The year for achieving the goals of Bihar Urban Agenda prepared by the state government is:
A. 2029 B. 2030
C. 2031 D. 2032

379. The first two towns in Bihar where property survey has been completed along with unique house numbering and number plate fixing:
A. Katihar, Banka B. Purnea, Banka
C. Katihar, Purnea D. Bhagalpur, Darbhanga

380. Which are the two mission cities in Bihar under the Urban Infrastructure and Governance (UIG) component of AMRUT?
A. Patna Urban Agglomeration, Bodhgaya
B. Gaya, Bodhgaya
C. Gaya, Jehanabad
D. Patna Urban Agglomeration, Gaya

381. JnNURM, a flagship programme for improving urban infrastructure in mission cities has been replaced by:
A. HRIDAY
B. Namami Gange Scheme
C. Swachh Bharat Mission
D. AMRUT

382. Which are the best three districts in Bihar in terms of availability of health infrastructure?
A. Sheohar, Sheikhpura, Sitamarhi
B. Jamui, Sheikhpura, Nawada
C. Bhagalpur, Banka, Bhojpur
D. Patna, Muzaffarpur, Darbhanga

383. In which district a new medical college Vardhamaan Ayurvigyan Sansthan, has been established?
A. Patna B. Samastipur
C. Bettiah D. Nalanda

384. Which of the following is incorrect?
A. IGIMS Patna
B. Government Medical College Bettiah
C. Narayan Medical college Kishanganj
D. Vardhaman Ayurvigyan Sansthan Nalanda

385. In which of the following districts of Bihar, Indira Gandhi Matritva Sahyog Yojana is operational?
A. East Champaran and West Champaran
B. Banka and Saharsa
C. Vaishali and Sitamarhi
D. Vaishali and Saharsa

386. Which of the following statement/statements is/are true regarding SABLA scheme?
A. It is a 100 per cent centrally sponsored shceme.
B. It is a comprehensive intervention for adolescent girls in the age group of 11-18 years.
C. It has a special focus on out-of-school girls.
D. All of the above

387. Consider the following statements regarding Janani Suraksha Yojana (JSY):
(*i*) It is an intervention for safe motherhood
(*ii*) It operates under National Health Mission
(*iii*) It is aimed at reducing maternal and neo-natal mortality by promoting institutional delivery among the poor women.

Which of the above statements are true regarding JSY?
A. (*i*) and (*ii*) B. (*ii*) and (*iii*)
C. (*i*) and (*iii*) D. All are true

388. Gargi Samhita mentions the attack of Greeks on Pataliputra. This attack took place during the reign of:
A. Vasudeva B. Dhanananda
C. Chandragupta II D. Pushyamitra

389. In which of the following district of Bihar the extent of institution delivery is highest?
A. Samastipur B. Purnea
C. Patna D. East Champaran

390. The bed occupancy rate means that the hospitals admit people with serious illness for their treatment. It reveals the availability of health infrastructure in a state. For Bihar as a whole, the bed occupancy rate is very high. Which of the following districts in Bihar has the highest bed occupancy rate?
A. Patna B. Bhojpur
C. Muzaffarpur D. Gaya

391. According to Manav Vikas Mission the target for Pupil-Teacher Ratio (PTR) in elementary education based on enrolment is:
A. 32 : 1 B. 40 : 1
C. 35 : 1 D. 30 : 1

392. The Mid-Day Meal Scheme (MDMS) covers the children belonging to classes:
A. I to VIII B. VI to VIII
C. I to V D. I to X

393. Bihar Education Project (Council) is the implementing agency for which of the following schemes:
A. Mid-Day Meal Scheme
B. Sarva Shiksha Abhiyan
C. Mission Gunwatta
D. None of the above

394. Pratham, a reputed non-government organization has been conducting learning assessment tests in every state, including Bihar. The results of these tests are presented in Annual Status of Education Report (ASER).

Consider the following results of ASER and identify which of the statement/statements is/are correct.

(*i*) In standard III, the percentage of students with satisfactory reading skills is lower in Bihar than the national average, while for mathematical skills it is nearly the same.

(*ii*) For standard V students, the percentage of students with satisfactory reading skills is same for both Bihar and India, however, for mathematics skills, the figures for Bihar are much higher.

A. Only (*i*) is correct
B. Only (*ii*) is orrect
C. None of them are correct
D. Both (*i*) and (*ii*) are correct

395. A high level committee has been constituted in Bihar under the chairmanship of Chief Secretary for the inclusion of which tribe in the category of scheduled tribe in Bihar.

A. Tharu B. Munda
C. Mal Pahariya D. Oraon

396. The Government of Bihar has decided to appoint Vikas Mitras at the Gram Panchayat and ward level for an effective implementation of various development and welfare schemes for a particular community. Name the community.

A. SC B. ST
C. Minorities D. Mahadalits

397. Which institution has been appointed as the nodal agency for imparting physical training to minority candidates for appearing in the examination of Bihar Police Service Recruitment?

A. Patna University
B. Mazharul Haque Arabi-Persian University
C. Magadha University
D. Tilka Manjhi University

398. The Government of Bihar has introduced reservation for women in panchayati raj institution and urban local bodies. How much reservation is provided?

A. 50 per cent B. 33 per cent
C. 51 per cent D. 75 per cent

399. In which of the following districts of Bihar, the state government operates AASRA, a 50-bedded special residential home for mentally challenged women and girls.

A. Samastipur B. Gaya
C. Siwan D. Patna

400. How much reservation is provided to women in direct recruitment for the posts of constable and in appointing junior inspector in the police force?

A. 33 per cent B. 50 per cent
C. 40 per cent D. 35 per cent

401. The objective of Samajik Punarvas Kosh Yojana which is in operation in all the districts of Bihar is:

A. to provide financial assistance to poor families at the time of marriage of girls who have attained the age of 18
B. to rehabilitate survivors of violene and human trafficking
C. to help mentally challenged women and girls
D. to provide free psychological legal of aid to victims and domestic violence

402. The state government operates speical schools for blind girls and a special school for deaf and dumb girls. These schools are respectively known as:

A. DRISHTI and KOSHISH
B. AASARA and SAHAYATA
C. DRISHTI and AASRA
D. SAHAYATA and KOSHISH

403. The state government has started a special school called KOSHISH, for deaf and dumb girls at:

A. Bettiah B. Motihari
C. Kishanganj D. Supaul

404. Which is the best district in terms of Mid-Day Meal Scheme Coverage?

A. Sitamarhi B. Sheohar
C. East Champaran D. Madhepura

405. Which of the following schemes are associated with drinking water and sanitation in Bihar?

A. Lohiya Swachhatta Yojana
B. Mukhyamantri Chapakal Yojana
C. Mukhyamantri Kshetra Vikas Yojana
D. All of the above

406. The head of state of Bihar, the Governor, is appointed by:

A. the President of India
B. the Chief Justice of India
C. Speaker of Lok Sabha
D. Speaker of Legislative Assembly

407. Governor holds office for a term of:

A. 5 years B. 4 years
C. 6 years D. 7 years

408. All the ministers are administered oath by:

A. Governor B. Chief Ministers
C. Speaker D. Deputy Chairman

409. Who was the first Governor of Bihar?

A. Sir James Sifton
B. Sir Maurice Garnier Hallett
C. Sir Thomas Alexander Stewart
D. Sir Thomas George Rutherford

410. Who appoints the Chief Minister?

A. Governor
B. President
C. Speaker of Legislative Assembly
D. Chairman of Legislative Council

411. After independence of India, who was the first Governor of Bihar?
A. Madhav Srihari Aney B. R.R. Diwakar
C. Jairamdas Daulatram D. Zakir Hussain

412. First Chief Justice of Patna High Court was:
A. Nand Lal Untwalia
B. D.P. Wadhwa
C. Vimal Chand Basak
D. Sir Edward Maynerd Champs Chamier

413. Bihar Public Service Commission (BPSC) is a body created by:
A. The Constitution of India
B. The extra constitutional provision
C. Legal provision
D. Administrative procedure

414. The Bihar Public Service Commission came into existence from:
A. 1st April, 1949 B. 1st April, 1950
C. 2nd April, 1953 D. 2nd April, 1951

415. The Bihar Public Service Commission initially began its functioning for the State of Bihar with its headquarters at:
A. Ranchi B. Patna
C. Gaya D. Muzaffarpur

416. Who was the first chairman of Bihar Public Service Commission?
A. Rajandhari Sinha B. Krishnakant Sahay
C. Bhupender Singh D. None of the above

417. The number of Divisions in Bihar are:
A. 6 B. 7
C. 8 D. 9

418. Gopalganj falls under which division:
A. Saran B. Tirhut
C. Magadha D. Patna

419. The total number of districts in Bihar are:
A. 27 B. 38
C. 37 D. 39

420. The sub-division is headed by SDM or SDO who is:
A. a newly recruited member of IAS
B. a member of state civil service
C. Both A and B
D. None of the above

421. Vaishali falls under which division:
A. Saran B. Tirhut
C. Bhagalpur D. Munger

422. A Panchyat Samiti is a local government body at which level?
A. Block level B. Village level
C. District level D. None of the above

423. What percentage of reservation has been provided to scheduled caste and scheduled tribe population in Panchayat election?
A. 1/2
B. 1/3
C. in proportion to their population
D. 1/5

424. The departments, not included under Panchayat Samiti work is:
A. Agriculture B. Education
C. Transport D. Social welfare

425. A Janpad Panchyat is constituted for each:
A. block B. village
C. district D. locality

426. Who is responsible for his work to the CEO of ZP?
A. BDO B. SDO
C. Sarpanch D. None of these

427. The schemes implemented by PRIs are financed by:
A. Backward Region Grants Fund (BRGF)
B. Grants from the Union Finance Commission
C. Grants from the State Finance Commission
D. All of the above

428. Panchayati Raj System was formalised in 1992 by which amendment to the Indian Constitution?
A. 73rd B. 74th
C. 75th D. 76th

429. Which of the following statement is true about panchayat election qualification:
A. must have 21 years age
B. must be qualified to be a member of legislature
C. Both A and B
D. None of the above

430. Which one of the following parts were added to the Constitution by 73rd Constitutional Amendment Act?
A. IXth B. Xth
C. XIth D. XIIth

431. The Panchayat Samiti is elected for a term of:
A. 5 years B. 3 years
C. 2 years D. 4 years

432. Zila Parishad has:
A. a President
B. a Vice President
C. a Chief Executive Officer
D. All of the above

433. The intermediate level of Panchayat is provided in which of the following state?
A. region with 10 lakh population
B. region with 15 lakh population
C. region with 20 lakh population
D. region with 25 lakh population

434. Bihar Panchayati Raj Act came in which year?
A. 2005 B. 2006
C. 2007 D. 2008

435. States appoints a finance commission to review the working of Panchayats:
A. every 2 year B. every 3 year
C. every 4 year D. every 5 year

436. The reservation for chairperson of Panchayats can be made by:
A. State B. Centre
C. Finance Commission D. Election Commission

437. The member of Block level Panchayat are:
A. ex-officials
B. elected by Gram Sabha
C. elected by Gram Panchayat
D. None of the above

438. The panchayat samiti is elected for a term of 5 years and is headed by:
A. A chairman and a deputy chairman
B. A chairman
C. A sarpanch
D. None of the above

439. How are the members of Zila Panchayat elected?
A. From the district on the basis of Adult Franchise
B. From the district on the basis of selection by the President
C. From the district on the basis of reommendation by the President
D. None of the above

440. Each Janpad Panchayat has a President, a Vice President and a:
A. Development Officer
B. Chief Executive Officer
C. Sarpanch
D. Both B and C

441. Which of the following statements is false about Karma dance?
A. It is performed mainly by tribes
B. It is mainly done at crop sowing and crop harvesting time
C. It is done to please Lord Karma
D. All of the above

442. The God worshipped in Karma dance form is:
A. Lord Rama B. Lord Krishna
C. Lord Indra D. Lord Karma

443. Find the incorrect match:

	Folk theatre	Main theme
A.	Bhakuli-Banka	Rural Life
B.	Domkuchh	Marriage
C.	Jat-Jatin	Child birth
D.	Kirtaniya	Krishna

444. Dhobia dance form is done in which region?
A. Bhojpur B. Gaya
C. Darbhanga D. Katihar

445. Hathiyar and Kalibanga are the two types of _______ dance.
A. Launda B. Chhau
C. Karma D. Kholdin

446. Sama Chakewa is organised in which month?
A. Kartik B. Magh
C. Phagun D. Shravan

447. Which of the following dance theatres has devotional theme?
A. Kirtaniya B. Jat-Jatin
C. Domkuchh D. Bhakuli-Banka

448. In which of the following festivals, Fagua songs are sung?
A. Holi B. Deepawali
C. Shravan D. Teej

449. Vidyapat dance is performed in:
A. Purnia B. Gaya
C. Siwan D. Saran

450. ________ dance is performed by ladies in moonlight in the month of Shravan to Kartik.
A. Jharni B. Jat-Jatin
C. Jogira D. Vidyapati

451. Pawadia dance form is performed on:
A. marriage B. child birth
C. gauna D. harvesting season

452. In which of the following regions, nunachar is sung?
A. Darbhanga B. Katihar
C. Nawada D. Gaya

453. Find the correct match:

	Dance Form	Occasion
A.	Kholdin	Child birth
B.	Karma	Harvesting
C.	Chhau	Holi
D.	Jogira	Marriage

454. Find the incorrect match:

	Dance Form	Occasion
A.	Jogira	Holi
B.	Kariya	Marriage
C.	Jharni	Muharram
D.	Launda	Child birth

455. Lalit Kala Manch is located at which place?
A. Gaya B. Patna
C. Muzaffarpur D. Darbhanga

456. Find the correct statement:
A. Chhau dance form has Veer Rasa and is performed at war time
B. It is perfomed by males only
C. It is basically performed in South Bihar
D. None of the above

457. The Chief markets of Tikuli are:
A. Varanasi B. Patna
C. Kolkata D. All of these

458. Shah Daulat's tomb in Maner is best example of:
A. Mughal style B. Turks
C. Afghan D. None of these

459. Patna Kalam was an offshoot of:
A. Mughal painting B. Afghan painting
C. Pala painting D. None of the above

460. Yaksh and Yakshini statues are the examples of finest sculpture of Mauryan period, which has been obtained from:
A. Patna B. Darbhanga
C. Gaya D. Bihar Sharif

461. The tradition of carpet making in Bihar dates back to:
A. Buddhist and the Mauryan period
B. Mughal period
C. Later Mauryan period
D. Afghan period

462. Sher Shah's tomb of Sasaram was built in which style?
A. Mughal style B. Afghan style
C. Jusks style D. Salve style

463. Manjusha Kala or Angika Art is another Bihari art form, practiced in the:
A. Vaishali region B. Magadh region
C. Anga D. None of the above

464. Madhubani painting depicts:
A. Nature and Hindu religious figures
B. Buddhist life
C. Marriage ceremony
D. None of the above

465. Tikuli works is a form of craft made from:
A. Broken glass B. Weeds
C. Applique D. Zari

466. Nalanda and Kurkihar has got evidence of which period?
A. Pala B. Mauryan
C. Post Mauryan D. None of these

467. Lacquer craft is famous for:
A. Bangles and stools B. Jewellery
C. Paintings D. Zari work

468. Which one is true?
A. Brass and stone statue gained prominence in Pala period
B. Dhiman and his son Vitthalpal had taken main role in its development
C. Both A and B
D. None of the above

469. Which is a very famous centre of wooden toy making?
A. Patna B. Gaya
C. Nawada D. Nalanda

470. Mandar hill features the unique image of which God from the Gupta period, in his man-lion incarnation?
A. Lord Vishnu B. Lord Shiva
C. Lord Ganesha D. None of the above

471. Patna Sahib is related to which of the following Sikh Gurus?
A. Guru Gobind Singh B. Guru Nanak
C. Guru Angad D. None of the above

472. In Saurath, in which month a fair on marriage is held?
A. Jayeshtha-Asharh B. Bhadrapada
C. Magha D. Kartik

473. Find the correct match:

Fair		District
A. Baunsi	-	West Champaran
B. Saurath	-	Begusarai
C. Brahmeshwamath	-	Buxar
D. Simariya	-	Bhagalpur

474. Sonpur fair is held on which day?
A. Navami of Chaitra month
B. Kartik Purnima
C. Tryodashi of Chaitra Shukla
D. None of the above

475. Which one of the following fairs is celebrated by Tharu tribe?
A. Sahodhara B. Simaria
C. Saurath D. Baunsi

476. Singheswar fair is held in which district?
A. Supaul B. Madhepura
C. Katihar D. Purnia

477. Which of the following fairs is celebrated to Rama and Laxman arrival?
A. Buxar fair B. Sitamarhi fair
C. Sonpur fair D. None of these

478. When was Patna book fair held for the first time?
A. 1970 B. 1975
C. 1972 D. 1971

479. What does Mahalaya in Bihar mean?
A. Devpujan B. Govardhan
C. Pitrapaksha D. Ganeshapujan

480. Sitamarhi fair is celebrated for which occasion?
A. Saraswati Pooja B. Krishnashtami
C. Ramnavami D. Chhath

481. 'Jeutia' is celebrated on which day?
A. Ashwin Krishna Paksha Ashtami
B. Ashwin Shukla Paksha Ashtami
C. Kartik Krishna Paksha Ashtami
D. Kartik Shukla Paksha Ashtami

482. In which of the following places Loard Vishnu had taken holy bath?
A. Baunsi B. Simarya
C. Sitamarhi D. None of the above

483. In Chhath festival which God is offered Arghya?
A. Sun B. Vishnu
C. Shiva D. Rama

484. Which festival in Bihar is celebrated as a belief of the awakening of God after 4 months of sleep?
A. Chhath festival B. Govardhan
C. Mahalaya Amavasya D. Devotthan Ekadashi

485. Jeutia festival is celebrated by females for:
A. husband B. son
C. daughter D. none of these

486. Pitrapaksh fair in Gaya is held in which month?
A. Ashwin B. Kartik
C. Magh D. Chaitra

487. Brahmeshwarnath fair is basically:
A. an animal fair B. Jain's fair
C. Hindu's fair D. None of the above

488. Firangiya and Batohiya are written in which of the following languages?
A. Magadhi B. Maithili
C. Bhojpuri D. Angika

489. Which of the following languages is not a part of Munda language family?
A. Angika B. Vajjika
C. Maithili D. None of these

490. Which among the following languages in Bihar is included in the Eighth Schedule of the Indian Constitution by the 92nd Constitutional Amendment Act, 2003.
A. Maithili B. Magadhi
C. Bhojpuri D. Urdu

491. Urdu was granted second language in Bihar in which year?
A. 1980 B. 1985
C. 1984 D. 1989

492. 'Varn Ratnakar' is the first written com-position of which language?
A. Maithili B. Magadhi
C. Bhojpuri D. Angika

493. When was 'The Patna Times' started?
A. 1912 B. 1924
C. 1944 D. 1916

494. Who is the first poet of Magadhi/Magahi?
A. Ishan B. Siyaram
C. Manoranjan Singh D. Nagarjuna

495. Who have researched widely on the dialects of Bihar?
A. V.S. Smith B. George Grierson
C. William Taylor D. Jyon Dren

496. Ambpali was written by whom?
A. Ram Briksha Benipuri B. Vachaspati Mishra
C. Nagarjuna D. Vidyapati

497. Who among the following is not a Magadhi poet?
A. Chaturbhuj Mishra B. Yogeshwar Singh
C. Suresh Dubey D. Dariya Das

498. 'Gautam' Mahakavya was written in Magadhi language by whom?
A. Yamuna Pathak B. Yogeshwar Singh
C. Harihar Pathak D. Sridhar Mishra

499. Who wrote 'Kaikeyi' and 'Rituvansh' in Bhojpuri language?
A. Kapilmuni Pathak B. Ratneshwar Pathak
C. Pt. Kedarnath Mishra D. Suman Sahay

500. 'Bidesiya' is a work of:
A. Bhikhari Thakur B. Kedarnath Mishra
C. Dariya Das D. Dharti Das

501. Which of the following languages is not a part of Aryan family?
A. Maithili B. Magadhi
C. Vajjika D. Bhojpuri

502. Tej Narayan Kushwaha has contributed to which language?
A. Angika B. Magadhi
C. Vajjika D. Maithili

503. Bhim Rao Ambedkar University is situated in which district?
A. Buxar B. Darbhanga
C. Muzaffarpur D. Nawada

504. In which year was Magadha University established?
A. 1976 B. 1903
C. 1962 D. 1980

505. Patna University was established in:
A. 1917 B. 1919
C. 1915 D. 1916

506. Khuda Baksh Oriental Library is situated in:
A. Munger B. Gaya
C. Bhagalpur D. Patna

507. IGIMS, Patna was established in which year?
A. 1984 B. 1990
C. 1980 D. 1983

508. Arabic and Persian Research Institute is situated in:
A. Darbhanga B. West Champaran
C. Patna D. Bhagalpur

509. Jawaharlal Nehru Medical College is situated in:
A. Banka B. Bhagalpur
C. Katihar D. Kishanganj

510. Bhitarwara Asharam related to Gandhiji is situated in which district of Bihar?
A. West Champaran B. Patna
C. East Champaran D. Sitamarhi

511. Gandhiji experimented satyagraha at which place for the first time?

A. Siwan B. Saran
C. East Champaran D. West Champaran

512. At which place the highest Buddhist Stupa in India is located?
A. Nalanda B. Rajgir
C. Vaishali D. Kesariya

513. Ahirauli related to Ahilya is situated in which district of Bihar?
A. Saharsa B. Buxar
C. Darbhanga D. Gopalganj

514. Bodhgaya is religious palace of which religion?
A. Buddhism B. Hinduism
C. Jainism D. Islam

515. Kabar Jheel Bird Santuary is located in which district?
A. Begusarai B. Sitamarhi
C. Jamui D. Banka

516. Matsyagandha Tourism complex is located in which district of Bihar?
A. Supaul B. Saharsa
C. Sitamarhi D. Bhagalpur

517. Goraul Sharif a muslim pilgrimage, is situated in which district:
A. Supaul B. West Champaran
C. Sitamarhi D. Patna

518. Jarasandh's Akhara is situated at which of the following places?
A. Patna B. Rajgir
C. Vaishali D. Bodhgaya

519. Padri Ki Haveli was constructed in which year?
A. 1705 B. 1771
C. 1707 D. 1772

520. The Kundeshwari Devi Temple at Kundghat is situated at which place?
A. Jamui B. Banka
C. Kaimur D. Bhojpur

521. Which of the following tourist sites is located in Nalanda?
A. Vajrasana B. Guneri
C. Venuvana Vihara D. Vikramshila

522. The Vishwa Shanti Stupa is located at which place of Bihar?
A. Hajipur B. Rajgir
C. Bodhgaya D. Maner

523. Which of the following is an incorrect pair?
A. Maniar Math – Gaya
B. Vasokund – Muzaffarpur
C. Mandar Hill – Banka
D. Bisram – Bhojpur

524. Which is the most famous treasure of Patna Museum?
A. Shiva Statue B. Buddha Statue
C. Didarganj Yakshini D. Vishnu Statue

525. The tomb of Yahiya Maneri is situated in:
A. Bettiah B. Gaya
C. Manersharif D. Rajgir

526. Dargah of Makhdum Hazrat Sultan Ahmed Charampose is situated in which district?
A. Bihar Sharif (Nalanda) B. Gopalganj
C. Sitamarhi D. Nawada

527. Who wrote several collections of Hindi poems including 'Umang'?
A. Gopal Singh Nepali B. Naval Kishore Dhawal
C. Ramnarayan Sharma D. Bhikari Thakur

528. Who was the author of Chandrakantha?
A. Devkinandan Khatri
B. Navin Vilochan Sharma
C. Kedarnath Mishra
D. None of the above

529. Veer Kunwar Singh University is in which district?
A. Bhojpur B. Gaya
C. Siwan D. Saran

530. Swami Sahjananda Saraswati had set-up an Ashram at which place?
A. Arrah B. Patna
C. Muzaffarpur D. None of the above

ANSWERS

1	2	3	4	5	6	7	8	9	10
D	B	D	B	A	C	A	D	B	A
11	**12**	**13**	**14**	**15**	**16**	**17**	**18**	**19**	**20**
C	C	D	A	B	A	D	A	D	A
21	**22**	**23**	**24**	**25**	**26**	**27**	**28**	**29**	**30**
D	A	C	B	D	B	D	C	A	B
31	**32**	**33**	**34**	**35**	**36**	**37**	**38**	**39**	**40**
C	A	B	A	D	D	D	B	A	D
41	**42**	**43**	**44**	**45**	**46**	**47**	**48**	**49**	**50**
A	C	A	A	B	C	D	B	B	A

51	**52**	**53**	**54**	**55**	**56**	**57**	**58**	**59**	**60**
B	D	C	A	C	A	D	B	A	B
61	**62**	**63**	**64**	**65**	**66**	**67**	**68**	**69**	**70**
B	B	A	C	D	A	C	C	D	A
71	**72**	**73**	**74**	**75**	**76**	**77**	**78**	**79**	**80**
B	A	A	D	B	A	A	D	B	B
81	**82**	**83**	**84**	**85**	**86**	**87**	**88**	**89**	**90**
A	C	C	A	A	A	D	C	B	B
91	**92**	**93**	**94**	**95**	**96**	**97**	**98**	**99**	**100**
A	C	D	C	C	C	D	B	A	B
101	**102**	**103**	**104**	**105**	**106**	**107**	**108**	**109**	**110**
D	A	A	D	A	B	D	B	A	A
111	**112**	**113**	**114**	**115**	**116**	**117**	**118**	**119**	**120**
A	B	B	B	A	A	B	D	C	B
121	**122**	**123**	**124**	**125**	**126**	**127**	**128**	**129**	**130**
A	B	A	D	A	B	C	B	D	A
131	**132**	**133**	**134**	**135**	**136**	**137**	**138**	**139**	**140**
C	C	B	C	C	D	A	A	D	C
141	**142**	**143**	**144**	**145**	**146**	**147**	**148**	**149**	**150**
A	D	C	C	B	B	D	C	D	A
151	**152**	**153**	**154**	**155**	**156**	**157**	**158**	**159**	**160**
B	A	A	B	D	B	A	C	B	B
161	**162**	**163**	**164**	**165**	**166**	**167**	**168**	**169**	**170**
D	A	C	A	A	D	A	A	B	A
171	**172**	**173**	**174**	**175**	**176**	**177**	**178**	**179**	**180**
B	A	A	C	D	B	B	A	C	D
181	**182**	**183**	**184**	**185**	**186**	**187**	**188**	**189**	**190**
B	C	B	A	C	C	D	C	B	A
191	**192**	**193**	**194**	**195**	**196**	**197**	**198**	**199**	**200**
C	A	D	B	A	D	B	A	A	A
201	**202**	**203**	**204**	**205**	**206**	**207**	**208**	**209**	**210**
A	A	A	A	D	A	A	C	D	B
211	**212**	**213**	**214**	**215**	**216**	**217**	**218**	**219**	**220**
C	A	D	D	B	C	A	B	A	B
221	**222**	**223**	**224**	**225**	**226**	**227**	**228**	**229**	**230**
C	C	D	A	B	C	A	A	D	A
231	**232**	**233**	**234**	**235**	**236**	**237**	**238**	**239**	**240**
B	A	B	D	D	B	B	A	A	B
241	**242**	**243**	**244**	**245**	**246**	**247**	**248**	**249**	**250**
C	C	B	C	D	A	C	A	D	A
251	**252**	**253**	**254**	**255**	**256**	**257**	**258**	**259**	**260**
D	C	D	D	A	C	D	B	C	A
261	**262**	**263**	**264**	**265**	**266**	**267**	**268**	**269**	**270**
B	D	D	A	C	B	A	D	D	A
271	**272**	**273**	**274**	**275**	**276**	**277**	**278**	**279**	**280**
A	D	C	C	B	A	B	B	B	A
281	**282**	**283**	**284**	**285**	**286**	**287**	**288**	**289**	**290**
A	D	A	B	C	B	B	A	A	B
291	**292**	**293**	**294**	**295**	**296**	**297**	**298**	**299**	**300**
D	A	A	A	C	A	D	A	A	B

301	302	303	304	305	306	307	308	309	310
A	D	C	A	B	C	B	A	C	A
311	312	313	314	315	316	317	318	319	320
C	B	A	A	B	A	B	A	D	A
321	322	323	324	325	326	327	328	329	330
D	B	C	A	A	D	A	B	D	C
331	332	333	334	335	336	337	338	339	340
A	C	A	A	B	A	D	B	B	B
341	342	343	344	345	346	347	348	349	350
A	D	B	C	A	C	B	C	A	C
351	352	353	354	355	356	357	358	359	360
A	D	A	C	D	B	B	D	A	B
361	362	363	364	365	366	367	368	369	370
D	D	A	B	A	C	A	D	D	C
371	372	373	374	375	376	377	378	379	380
A	D	C	A	B	D	C	C	C	A
381	382	383	384	385	386	387	388	389	390
D	B	D	C	D	D	D	D	A	C
391	392	393	394	395	396	397	398	399	400
B	A	B	D	A	D	B	A	D	D
401	402	403	404	405	406	407	408	409	410
B	A	B	C	D	A	A	A	B	A
411	412	413	414	415	416	417	418	419	420
C	D	A	A	A	A	D	A	B	C
421	422	423	424	425	426	427	428	429	430
B	A	C	C	A	A	A	A	A	A
431	432	433	434	435	436	437	438	439	440
A	D	C	B	D	A	A	A	A	B
441	442	443	444	445	446	447	448	449	450
D	D	C	A	B	A	A	A	A	B
451	452	453	454	455	456	457	458	459	460
B	A	B	D	A	A	D	A	A	A
461	462	463	464	465	466	467	468	469	470
A	B	C	A	A	A	A	C	A	A
471	472	473	474	475	476	477	478	479	480
A	A	C	B	A	B	A	D	C	C
481	482	483	484	485	486	487	488	489	490
A	A	A	D	B	A	A	C	C	A
491	492	493	494	495	496	497	498	499	500
C	A	B	A	B	A	D	B	C	A
501	502	503	504	505	506	507	508	509	510
C	A	C	C	A	D	D	C	B	A
511	512	513	514	515	516	517	518	519	520
C	D	B	A	A	B	C	B	D	A
521	522	523	524	525	526	527	528	529	530
C	B	A	C	C	A	A	A	A	B